Popular Participation in Social Change

World Anthropology

General Editor

SOL TAX

Patrons

CLAUDE LÉVI-STRAUSS
MARGARET MEAD
LAILA SHUKRY EL HAMAMSY
M. N. SRINIVAS

MOUTON PUBLISHERS · THE HAGUE · PARIS
DISTRIBUTED IN THE USA AND CANADA BY ALDINE, CHICAGO

ʋular Participation in
ɔɔɔɩal Change

Cooperatives, Collectives, and
Nationalized Industry

Editors

JUNE NASH
JORGE DANDLER
NICHOLAS S. HOPKINS

MOUTON PUBLISHERS · THE HAGUE · PARIS
DISTRIBUTED IN THE USA AND CANADA BY ALDINE, CHICAGO

General Editor's Preface

For those who still think of anthropology as a discinpline concerned primarily with small traditional communities and exotic cultures, this book wil be a way station. Few if any of the worldwide group of active anthropologists in its scenario would shy away from problems of the industrialized and economically interrelated world. The present volume, however, deals mainly with grass-roots people as they operate in the larger society. Cooperatives, as the editors point out in their masterful introduction, are communities of a special sort which show how people direct themselves to form, out of the same old human material, new institutions to cope with their changing world.

Like most contemporary sciences, anthropology is a product of the European tradition. Some argue that it is a product of colonialism, with one small and self-interested part of the species dominating the study of the whole. If we are to understand the species, our science needs substantial input from scholars who represent a variety of the world's cultures. It was a deliberate purpose of the IXth International Congress of Anthropological and Ethnological Sciences to provide impetus in this direction. The *World Anthropology* volumes, therefore, offer a first glimpse of a human science in which members from all societies have played an active role. Each of the books is designed to be self-contained; each is an attempt to update its particular sector of scientific knowledge and is written by specialists from all parts of the world. Each volume should be read and reviewed individually as a separate volume on its own given subject. The set as a whole will indicate what changes are in store for anthroplogy as scholars from the developing countries join in studying the species of which we are all a part.

The IXth Congress was planned from the beginning not only to include as many of the scholars from every part of the world as possible, but also with a view toward the eventual publication of the papers in high-quality volumes. At previous Congresses, scholars were invited to bring papers which were then read out loud. They were necessarily limited in length; many were only summarized; there was little time for discussion; and the sparse discussion could only be in one language. The IXth Congress was an experiment aimed at changing this. Papers were written with the intention of exchanging them before the Congress, particularly in extensive pre-Congress sessions; they were not intended to be read aloud at the Congress, that time being devoted to discussions — discussions which were simultaneously and professionally translated into five languages. The method for eliciting the papers was structured to make as representative a sample as was allowed when scholarly creativity — hence self-selection — was critically important. Scholars were asked both to propose papers of their own and to suggest topics for sessions of the Congress which they might edit into volumes. All were then informed of the suggestions and encouraged to rethink their own papers and the topics. The process, therefore, was a continuous one of feedback and exchange and it has continued to be so even after the Congress. The some two thousand papers comprising *World Anthropology* certainly then offer a substantial sample of world anthropology. It has been said that anthropology is at a turning point; if this is so, these volumes will be the historical direction-markers.

As might have been foreseen in the first postcolonial generation, the large majority of the Congress papers (82 percent) are the work of scholars identified with the industrialized world which fathered our traditional discipline and the institution of the Congress itself: Eastern Europe (15 percent); Western Europe (16 percent); North America (47 percent); Japan, South Africa, Australia, and New Zealand (4 percent). Only 18 percent of the papers are from developing areas: Africa (4 percent); Asia-Oceania (9 percent); Latin America (5 percent). Aside from the substantial representation from the U.S.S.R. and the nations of Eastern Europe, a significant difference between this corpus of written material and that of other Congresses is the addition of the large proportion of contributions from Africa, Asia, and Latin America. "Only 18 percent" is two to four times as great a proportion as that of other Congresses; moreover, 18 percent of 2,000 papers is 360 papers, 10 times the number of "Third World" papers presented at previous Congresses. In fact, these 360 papers are more than the total of ALL papers published after the last International Congress of Anthropological and Ethnological Sciences which was held in the United States (Philadelphia, 1956).

The significance of the increase is not simply quantitive. The input of scholars from areas which have until recently been no more than subject matter for anthropology represents both feedback and also long-awaited theoretical contributions from the perspectives of very different cultural, social, and historical traditions. Many who attended the IXth Congress were convinced that anthropology would not be the same in the future. The fact that the next Congress (India, 1978) will be our first in the "Third World" may be symbolic of the change. Meanwhile, sober consideration of the present set of books will show how much, and just where and how, our discipline is being revolutionized.

This book was one of several which profited greatly from a series of international conferences held in Oshkosh, Wisconsin immediately preceding the Congress itself. That conference resulted in several books on economic and political problems — on development, community organization, education, ethnicity, and on social and cultural change in many parts of the world — and the questions they probe relate directly to those examined by the scholars writing for the present volume.

Chicago, Illinois　　　　　　　　　　　　　　　　　　　SOL TAX
March 19, 1976

Preface

In the spring of 1972 the organizers, Professor June Nash of CUNY-City College, Professor Jorge Dandler of Universidad Católica del Perú, and Professor Nicholas S. Hopkins of New York University, met to discuss the special approaches that anthropology has to contribute to understanding the formation and genesis of cooperation and other forms of popular participation in production and distribution. Convinced that there was an important area of comparative research focussed on the understanding of the role these emergent forms have to play in economic development and social mobilization, the organizers sent out a call for papers. This call elicited an almost universally favorable response.

The original call specified five questions, which were to provide the basic format for our discussions. These questions were:

1. What problems are involved in moving from one set of structures (lineages, village councils, petty capitalism, wage labor) to another (cooperatives, collectives, nationalized industry)? Can it be said that one set of structures contains the germs of another, so that evolution is conceivable, or must the old be destroyed before the new can grow?

2. Do cooperatives, collectives, or nationalized industries lead to centralization or can decision making be decentralized in the new framework? How are decisions taken and what is the role of local leaders?

3. Do these new social forms reinforce patterns of internal dominance? What are the behavioral concomitants of dominance and dependency?

4. Do spontaneous movements of industrial and agricultural workers provide for more effective building of new institutions than do movements sponsored by governments or other bureaucratic institutions?

5. What is the dialectic between cooperative and collective ideology and the national goals and program? What are the moral incentives to production?

Our idea was to solicit papers based on European, East European, United States, and Third World experience. Our interest was both in descriptive analysis of experiences from all parts of the world and in applying anthropological insights to the prospective analysis of modes for popular participation. Our hope was to make a contribution both to the anthropological study of cooperatives and similar institutions and to the eventual solution of problems incurred in the building of such new institutions. The necessity for coming to intellectual grips with the problem was driven home once again by the Chilean tragedy, which occurred shortly after our conference in which discussion of the Chilean experience had played such a large part.

THE CONFERENCE

Eventually 29 people from 15 different countries showed up in Oshkosh; 8 others were unable at the last moment to attend. Table 1 breaks these figures down by country for those who attended and those who contributed papers to this collection.

Table 1.   Participants and contributors shown by country

Country	Number present	Number of papers
United States	9	7
Canada	1	1
Mexico	1	1
Colombia	–	1
Peru	1	1
Bolivia	1	1
Chile	1	1
Argentina	–	1
France	2	3
United Kingdom	2	2
Netherlands	1	1
Italy	1	1
Tunisia	3	4
Algeria	1	1
Israel	3	3
India	1	1
Bangladesh	1	1
Totals	29	31

Thus more than two-third of the participants were from outside the United States; almost all of these made the trip here from their home countries to participate. Invited participants from the Soviet Union, Yugoslavia, and the German Democratic Republic were unable to come at the last minute. About half the participants presented papers dealing with their home countries. Eight of the presentations were in French, 2 in

Spanish and 18 in English. One quarter of the participants were women. The conference was also interdisciplinary; in addition to anthropology, the other disciplines that were represented included geography, sociology, social psychology, and economics. Despite all this variety, however, participants in the conference spoke for themselves, not for representatives of a country or discipline.

The entire proceedings were bilingual, with translation between French and English. The Spanish speakers all understood either English or French, so translation from and into Spanish was eliminated to save time, though some preferred to speak in Spanish. The procedure of translating each presentation or comment after it was made was somewhat laborious, but it served to hold the group together. No one seemed to mind and it served to facilitate communication across linguistic and national lines.

We met first in an organizational session on Monday evening, August 27, and decided to use our five main questions as the basis for the organization of five discussion sessions to be held on August 28, 29, and 30. During these sessions each participant in turn took a quarter of an hour or so to present her/his paper after which it was translated and then discussed. Towards the end of our sessions it became apparent that we would not have enough time to complete our work, so we decided to prolong our stay in Oshkosh by 24 hours. This allowed us to stretch the final two sessions over three and then to schedule two sessions of general discussion. During the first of these the whole group gathered to discuss the possibility of working out a general summary framework for our deliberations; during the second, the group was broken down into two, which discussed, respectively, the internal structure of the cooperatives (and similar organizations) and the relationship of cooperatives (and similar structures) to national governments and international systems of domination. The purpose of these final two sessions was first to work out our own ideas in summary fashion after all the presentations spread out over 4 days, and, second, to prepare the presentation which we were scheduled to give in Chicago on September 5.

Several of our participants took part in this presentation. With Jorge Dandler (Bolivia) in the chair, Nicholas S. Hopkins (U.S.) summarized the content of the papers. Then Joan Vincent (U.K.), B. S. Baviskar (India), and Hamid Aït Amara (Algeria) gave brief summaries of their points of view and conclusions from the conference, and June Nash (U.S.) sketched in implications for the future of cooperatives as an institution and for the study of cooperatives. We were joined at this session by Professor Yuri Mgrtumian (U.S.S.R.), who presented a brief summary of collectivization among nomads in the Caucasus.

We combined work with pleasure, inviting scholars from other conference sessions to luncheons and dinners served to us as a group. A luncheon on August 28 initiated our sessions, and on August 30 another joint lunch enabled us to continue our formal discussions informally. On August 29 we gathered for a dinner to which members of the conference on land reform, organized by Bernardo Berdichewsky of the Technical University of Chile, were invited. This was followed by an address by Jacques Chonchol, former Minister of Agriculture under the Allende government in Chile, on "Le context politique de la reforme agraire en Chile." This was followed by a general discussion of the programs for development in rural Chile led by Dr. Berdichewsky. One of our participants, Gael Alderson-Smith, showed us a series of films she had taken in China during the summer of 1971 and provided a commentary to them. The films dealt mostly with life in agricultural collectives in three different areas of China.

The papers in this volume, together with the introduction, are an attempt to provide a published record of our conference. The papers in French and Spanish have been translated into English under the auspices of the Congress and Mouton Publishers; editing of content has been kept to a minimum to preserve the flavor and feeling of our sessions in the Pioneer Inn in Oshkosh and subsequent discussions. It is our profound hope that this collection of papers from different parts of the world and from different points of view will open the door wide to serious anthropological and social science discussion of the human problems raised.

ACKNOWLEDGMENTS

The organizers of the symposium of the IXth I.C.A.E.S. entitled "Cooperatives, collectives, and coparticipation as modes for popular participation in national development," and the editors of this volume, wish to express their gratitude to the many individuals and institutions that made it possible for us to come together in extremely congenial surroundings in the Pioneer Inn in Oshkosh, Wisconsin, from August 27 to September 1, 1973, and who facilitated the publication of the papers in such a short time.

Our thanks must first of all go to the institutions which generously provided financial support. Our principal benefactor was the American Council of Learned Societies which made a grant for travel and conference expenses through the American Anthropological Association. The Board of Directors of the American Anthropological Association favored us with a designation as their officially sponsored session, thus enabling us to receive the grant from the American Council of Learned Societies. Finally, the Ford Foundation through its offices in Dacca and Tunis provided travel funds for three of our participants.

We are very grateful, too, for the excellent support work that was provided in Oshkosh by Professor James Riddell of the University of Wisconsin at Oshkosh and his hardworking and cheerful staff of students and local citizens. The smoothness of our meeting was made possible only by their devotion and imagination in what are often called thankless tasks. We wish to express our appreciation, too, to the many citizens of Oshkosh who welcomed us along with the other participants of the Congress who met at the Pioneer Inn. We remember warmly the boat rides on Lake Winnebago and the invitations to dinners in local homes, as well as the generosity with which much-needed typewriters and photocopy machines were provided for use. We wish especially to thank Mr. Vernon Peroutky of the University of Wisconsin extension services in Oshkosh who arranged for members of local service clubs to drive a number of conference participants on a visit to two local dairy farms.

The organizers/editors would also like to thank the contributors to this volume for being such fine conference fellows in spite of frequent organizational snags. Those who were prepared to rearrange their schedules in order to come from abroad on short notice deserve particular thanks, and we apologize to those who were prevented from attending by poor organization. We feel that a real collectivity developed at the conference thanks to everyone's good humor and real efforts at understanding.

We also owe a debt to those who have preceded us down the path of cooperative studies. Of particular interest are three collections of papers, which were unfortunately not available to us as we were planning the conference. These are Peter Worsley's collection, *Two blades of grass*, based on a conference held at the University of Sussex (England) in 1969, and two collections edited by Carl Gösta Widstrand of the University of Uppsala (Sweden), entitled *Co-operatives and rural development in East Africa* and *African co-operatives and efficiency*. The first was based on a conference held at Uppsala in 1970; the second on one held at Langata, Kenya, in 1971. Dr. Widstrand was present at Oshkosh, attending another session; we were pleased that he was able to attend two of our sessions.

Nash and Hopkins would like to thank Professor Rudi Supek of the University of Zagreb and his fellow organizers for their kind invitation to attend the First International Sociological Conference on Participation and Self-Management, convened in Dubrovnik, Yugoslavia, on December 13–17, 1972. They benefitted immeasurably from the stimulating debates in agreeable circumstances, as well as from the personal contacts established there.

Our sessions at Oshkosh were brightened by several joint sessions held with the conference on agrarian reform organized by Dr. Bernardo Berdichewsky, then of the Technical University of Chile. We are grateful to him and his fellow participants for the added interest and new insights they provided. Ms. Gael Alderson-Smith also added to the conference by showing us several fine films she had made on cooperatives in the People's Republic of China.

As editors we owe a particular debt to Ms. Karen Tkach of Mouton. She consulted with us in Chicago concerning the format of the eventual publication, and she has kept us working away ever since. Her steadiness and cheerfulness have made working with her a pleasure. We are also grateful to the translators, copy editors, and typists who have worked on the papers in this collection; we have not been in direct contact with most of them and so cannot cite them by name. Our thanks also to Ms. Mary Ann Castle for calling the Mauss article to our attention.

Finally, we would like to extend our gratitude and respect to the organizers of the IXth International Congress of Anthropological and Ethnological Sciences, under the inspiration and leadership of Professor Sol Tax of the University of Chicago. His vision contributed immeasurably to making the Congress the truly international and interdisciplinary encounter that it was; his energy and attention to detail guaranteed that it would run as smoothly as any large meeting of academics could hope to run. In addition, we owe a particular debt of thanks to Dr. Tax for helping us find funding for our conference and for arranging *per diem* payments to those of our foreign participants who attended the Chicago phase of the Congress.

During the Congress in Chicago we were ever conscious of the dedicated work being done by the unsung heroes of the support staff, student volunteers, and others, who gave of themselves so freely that others might come together in the best possible circumstances.

JUNE NASH
City College
City University of
New York

JORGE DANDLER
Universidad Católica
del Perú

NICHOLAS S. HOPKINS
New York University

Table of Contents

INTRODUCTION

Anthropological Approaches to the Study of Cooperatives, Collectives, and Self-Management

JUNE NASH and NICHOLAS S. HOPKINS

> The union and the cooperative society are the foundations of the future society generated within the capitalist structure. They are the preserving forces, the guarantees against reaction; they are the powerful and legitimate heirs of capitalism; they are the corporate groups to which one could make the transfer of present property, for reaction would no more dare to dispossess them than the Bourbons would have dared to dispossess the bourgeoisie and the peasants, who had acquired the property of the feudalists. Even now the accomplishments of the action of the unions and cooperatives are splendid. They are the strength and the resistance of socialism; they are the means by which socialism creates. Cooperative economic organizations guarantee the perpetuation of the future society.
>
> MARCEL MAUSS

INTRODUCTION

Cooperatives, collectives, and self-management have been with us for a long time; in their modern form their origin goes back to the late nineteenth century, and in the last generation or two they have emerged or been suggested as the key institutional form for broadening social participation in a range of different historical circumstances. "Cooperatives" have thus had to bear a heavy symbolic load as the future basis for social organization. In addition, as Mauss suggested, they were to contribute to the solution of social and psychological as well as economic problems. The interest that anthropology has for cooperative forms of organization derives from the principle that "anthropology seeks to extend the areas which reason can understand and perhaps to some extent control" (Kluckhohn 1959:251). By studying cooperative forms of organization we learn more about an important type of organization; we also place our studies thoroughly within the path of development that the real societes we study may take. As Hymes (1974:35) remarks, "The opportunity, then, is this: to employ our ethnographic tradition of work, and such ethnological insight as informs it, in the study of the emergence of cultural form in concrete settings and in relation to a world society." Cooperative forms of organization are interesting for anthropology precisely because they are interesting for those who live them; they are relevant to a theoretical anthropology precisely because they are conceived in order to be lived. It is this element of willful control of one's own social forms that makes movements toward cooperative forms of organization an essential part both of the human experience and of anthropology's field of study.

Such an approach could be labeled a "prospectivist anthropology." A prospectivist anthropology should be concerned first of all with a kind of "urgent anthropology" that consists of understanding the social forms into which we may be about to move. It combines a desire for a rational future with "...a focus on a renewed sense of the possibilities of human nature and culture through knowledge of cultural worlds already formed" (Hymes 1974: 14, paraphrasing S. Diamond). Insofar as we want to use our values, knowledge, and techniques in the present to mold the future, we can do so better if we understand the nature of the forms (i.e. cooperatives) towards which we may be moving. Here is a task that anthropology, with its comparative understanding of the entire range of human forms of social and cultural organization, is eminently suited for.

The first step is a thorough and sensitive study of cooperative forms in order to gain a more complete understanding of the structural implications of these forms, and to indicate the pitfalls and promises of different proposals. Such an interest on the part of anthropologists would also ensure that our discipline is truly comparative, not, after all, just a study of exotics, but instead a study of all human societies and experiments.

The second step is the analysis of the social process that brings cooperative forms of organization into being and which they in turn sustain. As the outcome of social movements, they contribute to adaptive change and integration.

There is another reason for trying to understand cooperatives and movements towards cooperatives. Anthropologists do research among peoples who live in this world; our careers are dependent upon theirs; thus we cannot avoid a human intertwining of interests. Our work is going to affect the people among whom we do research; the problem is to ensure that the effects are as positive as we can make them. This can be phrased negatively by saying that we should "protect" these people (through anonymity, self-censorship, and the like); but it can also be phrased positively as a responsibility to carry out research that leads to an increased consciousness on the part of those among whom we do research in the hopes that this increased consciousness will contribute to popular liberation. It is in this perspective that research on cooperatives, collectives, and industrial self-management becomes relevant. Indeed, cooperative forms of organization are as important an option for the industrialized societies of the West as for the agrarian and industrializing societies of the tricontinental Third World. Research can illuminate both the internal structural and processual implications of the various cooperative forms, and also the relationship that exists between the cooperative or collective on the one hand and its environment on the other. Here there are two possible approaches: the relationship between cooperative and environment at a given point in time, and the developmental relationship — in other words, what are the conditions that seem most conducive to the emergence of the cooperative form of social organization? This dialectic between structure and movement will be a major theme in this introduction and throughout the book.

We have organized this overview of cooperative and collective forms in four parts. In the first of these, we summarize the papers presented at the Oshkosh conference according to four roughly developmental categories. In the second part we discuss the structural implications of the case studies of cooperativistic forms with the purpose of developing a model to serve heuristically in the analysis of cooperatives, collectives, and self-management. In the third part, we approach the cooperative, the collective, and self-management from an historical and comparative viewpoint of the social movements of which they have been a part. Finally, we conclude with a brief section setting out our understanding of the importance of studying cooperatives for anthropology, and of the importance of anthropological studies for the future of cooperatives.

THE CONFERENCE

The range of the papers presented at the conference was considerable, although we lay no claim to having covered all typological or geographical cases. The present summary wil classify the papers into four categories: the introduction of cooperatives into peasant societies; the transformation of capitalist agricultural systems into cooperatives; the relationship between sociopolitical movements and a cooperativistic or communalistic ideology; and the problems posed by cooperatives in an industrial or commercial context. These categories represent a progression from societies having relatively little contact with the urbanized, industrialized world to those located fully within that sector, and thus suggest a possible line of argument describing the changes in the potential role for cooperatives according to these different circumstances.

Several of the papers dealt with the problem of the introduction of cooperatives into peasant situations, notably in the case of the African farmers who are in some ways more a lineage society than a peasant society. Raulin for Niger and Roth for Tanzania argued that the traditional society offers useful take-off points for cooperatives, which perceptive local leaders can make use of for development. Gosselin argued that cooperative planners often failed to take the composition of local structures into account, even when they thought they were basing their new cooperatives on traditional structures, with the result that plans often went astray. On the other hand, Vincent showed that the manipulation of the new structures is often for personal political advantage, while Derman for Guinea and Hopkins for Mali, two more avowedly socialist countries, showed that the initial concern there for government-sponsored cooperative systems was not based on respect for local values, but rather was derived from general ideological principles. In Guinea the cooperatives did not "take" at all while in Mali they did so only by changing their nature. Alderson-Smith found something similar in the Peruvian highland village he studied, where the local community resented national efforts to introduce a cooperative structure which they felt threatened their continued existence. This latter case, which might be described as an attempt to marginalize the peasants or to integrate them into the national system in a subordinate position, was also described for Spain by Palerm Viqueira. The deliberate use of traditional institutions of cooperation is seen as an attempt to prevent these communities from entering the national society. On the other hand, Rahim argued for Bangladesh that the centrally sponsored cooperative movement encouraged modernization of agriculture, not least by spreading knowledge of new techniques. Vessuri and Bilbao present a successful case of collectivized agriculture that transformed the organization of crop production in Argentina and reversed the trend toward single-crop, highly capital-intensive exploitation to diversified crops with labor-intensive organization.

There are clearly many factors here, and it is essential to sort them out. Three points might be suggested: (1) There is probably no single set of favorable conditions for the transformation of traditional institutions into more adaptive modern ones. It may depend on similarity between the two poles, or on a favorable political situation in which massive transformation is accepted, or on other factors. Whatever the case, the favorable conditions are bound up in the problem of relations between the state, the community, and the individual. (2) Both traditional and modern institutions are subject to manipulation and exploitation at all levels, either for personal advantage or for systematic oppression. (3) Even if the primary purpose of centrally sponsored cooperatives is control, there may be side effects such as spread of knowledge and politicization.

A second set of cases involved attempts to transform capitalistically organized agriculture — the farms of North Africa and the haciendas of Latin America — into a more equitable and socialist institution. Here the typical solution was to take the former workers and to organize them into a production cooperative or collective (whereas the attempts to organize peasants generally focused around service cooperatives). Three such cases were from Peru. Alberti discussed the transformation of sugar plantations into cooperatives, showing the political conflict that arose between technicians, workers, union leaders, and seasonal workers. Greaves provided some background for this analysis in his study of the shift in worker consciousness from client to workers, while Alderson-Smith complemented his village study with an analysis of a livestock-raising cooperative which repeated some of the problems discussed by Alberti. The emerging gap between a socialized sector where cooperative members are relatively favored and are thus set off against traditional smallholders was discussed for Chile by Chonchol and for Algeria by Aït Amara. Aït Amara described the interesting development in Algeria where workers see themselves as a cooperative of workers renting out their services collectively to the state which owns the land. For Tunisia Makhlouf showed the political opposition that an attempt to extend the cooperative structure beyond the state-owned lands aroused, which led to its abandonment, while Ben Salem discussed the centralization of the decision-making process to the detriment of participatory values. The Schneiders analyzed the case of western Sicily, where the cooperatives, which were unsuccessful, were supposed to form in the smallholder sector: in a sense Sicily seems to have begun similarly to the other cases, and yet it developed differently. Eckstein and Carroll emphasized the necessity to consider the economic point of view; their views were based on the Latin America and particularly on the Mexican cases. A separate but related theme was the transformation of industry into worker-managed enterprises, discussed by Nash for Bolivian tin mines and by Winn for Chilean textiles. The first case proved to be a failure, not because of worker inability, but because of managerial restriction on the role of the workers which was limited to that of a powerless watchdog. The second case study showed the potential for self-management by workers as demonstrated in the textile factory takeover, but the experiment was cut short by the 1973 coup.

The papers here made constant references to problems centering around the division of labor between technicians, workers (both permament and seasonal), national bureaucracies, and politicians. The general tendency seemed to be to localize the decision-making power in the hands of the technicians, often in the capital, with negative effects on the significance of participation among those actually working on the cooperative. The problems of external dependency — balance of payments and international division of labor — also created certain pressures which tended to push the cooperatives away from the ideals of their founders. At a local level, the relations between cooperative members and workers who were not cooperative members (whether they were seen as seasonal workers or as rivals for government favors) arose here in a particularly acute form: Alberti reported, for instance, a strike by seasonal workers against the cooperative, as an instance of this division among the working class.

The third category of cases involved the relationship between social-political movements and a cooperativistic or communalistic ideology. Huizer argued that such an ideology, a larger view, and an analysis of their situation in society, were necessary ingredients in the success of peasang movements. Dandler showed how a popularistic and communal movement in Bolivia could be coopted and absorbed into a national political structure founded on the principle of the division of the spoils, so that a movement leader became a dispenser of patronage. Fals-Borda, Apthorpe, and Inayatullah surveyed a wide range of data from Africa, Asia, and Latin America to conclude that the cooperative movement must be motivated by a radical new ideology if it is to achieve the goals set for it. There were also more particular studies. Greenblatt focused on the problem of changing consciousness as exemplified by the case of China, showing how the Chinese attempted an extensive campaign to modify people's attitudes before the collective movement could succeed. De Weck, a cooperative technician from Peru, offered a lucid insider's view of the relationship between the ideology-bearing technicians and the increasingly aware peasantry. Gagnon analyzed three cases (Senegal, Tunisia, and Cuba) to show that a successful cooperative movement might come to rival the state apparatus in importance, and so invite the state to limit, if not eliminate, the movement in a gesture of self- defense.

The problem that was implicitly raised here was whether the movement was an outgrowth of the ideology, or the ideology a product of the concrete circumstances of the movement; whether consciousness or institutions comes first, and what the dialectical relationship between them is. There was also the problem of whose ideology — that of intellectualized leaders or of peasants — was to be considered. The consensus seemed to be that the growth of an egalitarian communalistic ideology was a necessary preliminary to the successful institution of cooperatives.

Finally, a fourth set of cases focused on the role of cooperatives in a commercial or industrial setting. Sethom described the history of a service cooperative, and Zamiti analyzed a merchants' cooperative, both in Tunisia; both stressed that one of the functions was to drain capital off the center and that this affected inner workings and successes. On the other hand, describing Maharastra, Baviskar argued that the importance of a sugar-processing cooperative for local politics was a guarantee of both its success and its survival as each faction tried to convince supporters that it could best defend cooperative interests, and technicians were hired locally. Describing the Bolivian nationalized tin mines, Nash argued that attempts to establish workers' control gave workers a voice in criticizing the administration but failed to provide an entry into decision-making processes. The failure to maintain a separation of roles between union leadership and participation in worker control led to criticism by workers. Leviatan argued that maintenance of the kibbutz principle of participation and productivity were linked. But here also there were workers who were not cooperative members, as there were in the case of the Israeli transport cooperative described by Bar-Yosef and Rosenman. This transport cooperative, which has a monopoly situation in the country, is highly cooperativistic internally but has a quite complex and somewhat exploitative relationship to its workers, who have called a strike. Brognetti discussed the fate of agricultural cooperatives in France as agriculture becomes increasingly technical and mechanized. She showed that when these cooperatives (originally intended to "marginalize" the peasants) come increasingly to resemble firms, cooperative members see no difference between themselves and other farmers who work directly with firms. This leads some of them to show solidarity with the workers of their cooperatives when they go on strike.

This final set of cooperatives shows much the same kinds of practical and analytic problems as the second category. One new problem here, however, is that of productivity of workers in these situations; what is it that motivates Bolivian miners, Tunisian shopkeepers, French farmers or Israeli factory workers to work productively? Here the value of participation as a defense against alienation and an encouragement in itself was shown by both positive and negative examples. It is also difficult, though not impossible, for participation and local self-government to fend off attempts by the government to establish control over the cooperatives and use them for its own purposes and benefit.

STRUCTURE OF COOPERATIVISTIC FORMS

To talk of a "cooperative" or a "collective" is quite vague; the range of concrete examples can be extensive, as the cases in this collection show. The basic meaning of the word refers to the organization of work; in principle it refers to an organizational structure in which all are equally workers and managers, and so exploitation is absent. Such an organizational structure is, however, more difficult to achieve in practice than to imagine in theory.

Several kinds of organizational forms can be noted. One frequent kind of cooperative is the "service" cooperative, in which producers join together to accomplish more efficiently in common some task than they could do separately, but without necessarily affecting the organization of work within the production unit. As an example, while we were in Wisconsin for the conference, a number of conference participants visited a dairy farm whose owners belonged to a cooperative for artificial insemination. Frequently the impetus for this kind of cooperative is to provide a service more cheaply and with less danger of exploitation than the private, capitalist organization could or would do (Shannon 1945: 329–348). There is a tendency, however, as Gide (1930) pointed out, and as Brognetti's paper in this collection confirms, for such cooperatives to take on the traits of the capitalistic enterprises with which they deal or are in competition. Thus the large American dairy cooperatives are big businesses and act as lobbyists, contributing financially to politicians in a position to influence decisions concerning milk products. Sometimes the tendency goes even further, as Kravitz (1974) points out with reference to recent American experience:

The average farmer is being pushed aside as co-ops invite food firms and conglomerates to form partnerships with the cooperative, invite corporate executives to sit on the cooperative's board of directors, and even invite corporations to join cooperatives.... As a final step cooperative leadership increasingly argues that the vast majority of farmers must be content to assume the role in big co-ops that the vast majority of shareholders assume in big corporations.

The service or marketing cooperatives seem particularly vulnerable to concentration of power in the hands of those in management, who are generally not producers themselves but rather full-time managers (cf. Vincent, Roth, and Ben Salem papers in this collection). This division of labor leads to control.

A more elaborate form is the production cooperative, where people are organized together for work with the product of the labor divided on some equitable basis among the member-workers. Here the workers are much closer to the management, as the work generally takes place on a single farm or in a single factory, and consequently more people tend to be in a position to observe what is going on. Still, here the cooperative is not perceived as a total experience, and many aspects of people's lives may be organized on quite different principles. Family life and recreation fall outside, typically, and, in addition, in many cases cooperative members may have outside economic interests. An interesting case that came up in our discussion was the observation by Aït Amara that in Algerian agriculture there was a tendency for the worker groups on the self-managed farms to view themselves as a cooperative for labor that rented its services out as a unit to the employer, in this case the government (Spiro 1970:55, for a possible analogy in 1920's Palestine). Production cooperatives in North Africa and in Latin America tend to have complicated land-tenure histories; in Tunisia before 1969, for instance, some land was state-owned and some owned by some of the cooperative members, while other members owned no land at all. Yet all the members were organized into a single work unit and all had, in theory, an equal voice in the management of the unit, as well as an equal share in the profits.

A rationalization of this situation leads to a collective, viewed as a more totalizing experience. Not only do people work in common, but they base the rest of their lives on the common work experience; they are held in some sense to be equal owners of the means of production. In this situation, the collective is viewed as an all-purpose cell in the body politic, which itself is generally held to be composed of numerous such cells. As in the case of the cooperative there is likely to be a framework of service and marketing organizations, perhaps organized as cooperatives or as organisms of the state which link the various basic cells together.

Most of the papers in this volume deal with cooperatives in rural areas. It is not by intent that so few instances of cooperative and collective work arrangements in industry or in mining are included here; we feel that the same kinds of consideration of organization, insertion in the society, and so on, apply to all such arrangements regardless of the sector they are in. Cooperatives seem to be particularly common in agriculture; this may be a reflection of the marginal status of many farmers and agricultural workers. It also clearly reflects the fact that much agriculture around the world is organized in units that are too small to take advantage of all the capital improvements that modern agriculture seems to require (tractors and other machines, irrigation, fertilizer, quality control) so that cooperative organization is selected in order to create units large enough to benefit by economies of scale and also large enough to stand up against capitalistic enterprises where they exist. For the same reason, cooperatives are often seen as an advantageous solution for fishermen and miners, who are both in the primary sector, and for certain craftsmen in the secondary sector. The analogy might be extended to the transport cooperative (tertiary sector) described by Bar Yosef and Rosenman.

Thus in one sense or in another all the cases here represent attempts to cope with certain basic problems that are perceived as a result of the development of the capitalist system on a world-wide basis. One of these problems is the division of labor as the process of work becomes ever more complicated, for division of labor leads to specialization of function and of knowledge, and thus to control. Another of these problems is that of the survival of small-scale units (this survival is often considered important because of the social values that such units are believed to maintain) in the face of constant encroachments on the part of large national and multinational corporations. Thus there is an internal problem and an external problem.

The evidence suggests that the cooperative (or collective, or coparticipation scheme) works best, i.e. works most according to the cooperative norms, when there is a maximum flow of information between all the individual members of the cooperative so that not only do they have rights to formal participation in the decision-making, self-governing process, but also they have the knowledge and the skills with which to exercise these rights. Lilia Ben Salem's paper on the decision structure of Tunisian cooperatives is relevant here, as are papers such as Joan Vincent's which show how failure to meet these norms results in a concentration of decision-making power in the hands of a relatively small elite. Another way of phrasing this same situation is in terms of what R. F. Dore called "institutionalized suspicion" (1971:52–57) — the collection and diffusion of knowledge (information) within the cooperative should depend not on the information-gathering skills of individual members, but on regular institutionalized procedures such as the public auditor's report and the rotation of officers. To proclaim the principle that the free flow of information is important for a cooperative might be no more than the polemical statement of an ideologue; however, it is also essential to point out that it indicates a method for anthropological (social science) analysis of the internal structure of a cooperative. Following through on this method is particularly likely to point up the difficulties in the internal structure of a cooperative. In this case the comparison between an ideal-type model of a cooperative and real cases is a definite aid in the analysis and understanding of those real cases.

Another set of internal problems has to do with the attractiveness of the idea (for national ideological reasons, often) that cooperative structures are implicit in the traditional social structure of the area or group in question. The notion here is that certain structures present a natural take-off point for cooperative and collective forms of modernization (as Roth and Raulin suggest in this volume). This notion has been much attacked in recent years. Dore points out that "even if traditional communities are solidary and egalitarian it is difficult for them to take on the formal institutions of modern cooperatives, such as rational auditing and control over managers, without destroying the very bonds of solidarity and mutual trust which are supposed to be their advantage" (1971: 60). And of course, the traditional social structures are often authoritarian, particularly within the family (Gosselin 1970:37). Under such conditions, a community will either reject a cooperative because it threatens its own kind of egalitarianism, or the cooperative will simply reinforce and accentuate the inequalities (between old and young, between men and women, etc.) already present in that community. Thus it is not surprising to hear such a comment as this:

The attempts to superimpose productive and mercantile institutions, such as the cooperative, on the lineage or village community, is bound to fail or to transform the society into an eventual class system. A real concern for development should consider dissolution of those communities and their replacement by newly organized ones (Meillassoux 1972:102).

Many of the studies in this collection implicitly endorse this point of view, which runs counter to the self-serving anthropological wisdom. The focus in Guinea (Derman), Uganda (Vincent), Mali (Hopkins), Peru (Alderson-Smith), Spain (Palerm Viqueira), and Dahomey (Gosselin) is on the difficulties that the traditional social structure caused for the formation of cooperatives. These difficulties took several forms. On the one hand, there was a tendency for the cooperatives to be taken over by local power figures, because that suited the organizers of the cooperative at the center, or because those organizers were impervious to the political processes at the microscopic level. For instance, the structure of dependency within the extended family was often not understood. On the other hand, the traditional structures themselves often turn out not to be so conducive to serving as the foundation for cooperative organization of labor or to marketing as ideologically inclined observers initially argue. Often, too, such important but subtle questions as land tenure, organization of work, and the role of noneconomic activities such as ceremonials are poorly understood. In the developing areas, cooperatives never emerge spontaneously as a reflection of preexisting social patterns; they are always borrowed, if they are not imposed from above. They are thus a product of capitalism, not of spontaneous socialism.

The chief external problem of the cooperative as a social form in a particular society is that other social groups and classes are trying to manipulate the ideologically respectable cooperative form for their own purposes. Cooperatives are frequently encouraged by central governments; their motivations for doing so include the desire to set up a bureaucratic structure through which the central government could increase its control of the countryside, and perhaps at the same time ensure that the excess production of agriculture or mining is drained off for the purposes of the national society centered in the capital. In other cases, the cooperative structure was conceived of as the mechanism through which the rural people could be mobilized against some enemy of the government (merchants, either foreign or domestic) or for a far-reaching program of social change (Rahim). Whatever the ends of the government, or of the segment of the bureaucracy responsible for the cooperatives, the end result was to treat the cooperatives essentially as a political arm of the government. This, of course, is contradictory to principles of their internal structuring which tend to stress autonomy.

Cooperatives can also be politicized in other ways. Gagnon points out that the cooperative structure in some countries (Senegal and Tunisia) became a new and separate power base that threatened to enter into competition with the existing party or other structure. In both these cases, the party and administration hastened to intervene to "tame" the cooperative movement. It is clear how this happens.

Whenever a new bureaucracy is established there is a great fresh supply of patronage jobs, whose holders are beholden to the leader of the cooperative movement; in addition, independent channels of communication and influence not under the inspection of the party and administration are established, and cooperative members at the base may come to feel an involvement with the movement. Baviskar describes how this patronage network of cooperatives in India reinforces the party structure. In still other cases, the politicization of the cooperatives may be the result of purely local factors, a manifestation of parish politics independent of national concerns. Finally, a successful cooperative structure at the local level, as in Mali and to some extent in Peru, Uganda, and Tanzania, becomes an instrument with which the local community can fend off the desires of the national government to interfere.

In contrast to the cases where the government of a developing nation (and all nations are developing in one sense or another) encourages the cooperative movement so as to draw the bulk of the population into the national community (and under its influence), in other cases (Spain, France until a decade ago, Mexico, and Peru) one has the impression that cooperative structures are felt to be suitable for the more marginal sectors of the population. By conceding them a certain degree of autonomy and an aura of modernity, such sectors could be compensated for their very marginality; the cooperative becomes a sop thrown to the marginals. Put another way, the cooperative is assigned the task of easing the integration of these individuals and communities into the national (capitalistic) society; as soon as there are real economic values in these marginal sectors, the cooperatives are then superseded or transformed.

The external problem of cooperative and collective forms is based on the fact that they exist in a politicized environment whose values and principles of operation are likely to be radically different from those held to obtain inside the cooperative. To the extent that the cooperative manages to retain its internal structure, it may be obliged to withdraw from its national society; conversely, its internal structure may be determined more by its political environment than by any adherence to cooperative rules and principles. Thus the internal and the external problems meet and are in dialectical relationship with each other. Numerous are the studies, in this collection and elsewhere, that show how a cooperative structure has been used and modified, if not destroyed, by the contact experience. A political field is set up by the establishment of cooperatives, and there then ensues a political struggle for the control of that field, between the various segments of the national government and the local community.

SOCIAL MOBILIZATION AND COLLECTIVE AND COOPERATIVE ACTION

The political field generated by cooperatives and other forms of collectives and coparticipation contains two contradictory currents: (1) stabilization and reform within the existing structure, and (2) social mobilization for change directed toward a fundamental transformation of society. Organized as a defensive reaction to private capitalist formation, cooperatives often become the institutions that stabilize the private expropriation of profit in production. As cooperatives became identified with reformism and systems of cooptation, the movement inspired by communalistic ideals chose the terms "collective," "coparticipation," or "self-management." Regardless of terminological shifts, the drive toward reform remains in opposition to the drive for structural change and provides the dynamic for continual transformation. In the mobilization of populations in the new nations as well as those countries trying to free themselves of neo-colonial ties, this dynamic can be summarized in two major problems: (1) relating new cooperative forms to traditional social institutions, and (2) breaking from the dependencies implied in world trade. In the first case, the problem is to incorporate disprivileged sectors, given the inequalities in education and preparation inherited from the colonial or neo-colonial past, without losing the mutual aid and solidarity implicit in tribal and communalistic societies. In the second case there is the problem of advancing socialist forms in world trade dominated by multinational corporations.

Reform Movements

The contemporary movements that tend toward stabilization and reform trace their roots to the Owen cooperatives of 1832 and to the Rochdale Pioneers of 1843. Accepting the free market as a base for economic organization, they worked toward limiting the control of capitalist institutions by providing islands of autonomous production and distribution. The Owenite and Rochdale ideals of democracy, voluntary action, autonomy, equity, and mutuality became reified in rules that subscribed to capitalist institutions in England, Europe, and the United States in the twentieth century. These rules and the ideology that supported them are laid out by Bogardus (1964:19 ff.):

DEMOCRACY is assured in that there is open membership to all who wish to join regardless of race or creed.

VOLUNTARY BASE is assured in that each member shall have one vote and there shall be no proxy voting.

AUTONOMY is guaranteed in that capital invested will receive a predetermined and limited rate of interest.

EQUITY is underwritten in that net savings will be distributed to the members on the basis of their patronage of the cooperatives and on trading on a cash basis as well as observing fair market prices.

MUTUALITY was to be achieved by frequent discussion meetings of the members and regular auditing of accounts.

The very rules to achieve these goals limited the cooperative impact: decentralization in the interest of democracy limited the impact cooperatives had on the increasingly centralized business interests with which they competed; the ability of each person to withdraw limited the control over membership in time of stress; autonomy, interpreted as an apolitical stance, inhibited the cooperatives from seeking leverage in the wider society. The individualistic cooperation that Bogardus (1964:10) calls for was to provide "the dynamic field of social relations within which competition may take place." In the course of taming cooperatives, the reformists had transformed them into the same competitive, capitalistic institutions they had initially opposed.

This process of adaptive decline provoked Gide's paradox that the more successful cooperatives are economically, the more likely they are to fail socially (1930:7). Empirical case studies after the thirties reinforced Gide's theory: Lipset's study of agrarian radicalism in Canada in the thirties revealed that, as soon as guaranteed prices for wheat were introduced in Saskatchewan, the cooperatives shifted from a socialist to a conservative ideology (Lipset 1971:xiv). Brognetti's paper in this collection confirms the tendency contemporaneously. Fals-Borda sums up the effect or cooperatives in Latin America as having reinforced existing power structures (1972:136). Guelfat (1966:22) sums up the historical experience of European cooperatives and other "extracapitalistic" forms of collective associations by invoking Franz Oppenheimer's "law of transformation," by which the dominant economy brakes, then arrests, the development of certain enterprises outside the capitalist system and makes them capitalistic. Rosa Luxemburg (1970:69) explains the failure of production cooperatives "which either become pure capitalist enterprises or, if the workers' interests continue to predominate, end by dissolving" on the basis of the exploitation of labor as a condition for the survival of each enterprise. In modern productive enterprises, the trend is toward capital-intensive processes rather than intensification of exploitation through longer hours and speedup, but the net result is contrary to workers' interests in contributing to unemployment. The United Nations Ad Hoc Expert Group (1969:17) accepts this as inevitable, pointing out that "Cooperative production must be competitive and for this purpose cooperatives must be prepared to adopt labour-saving equipment, provided that responsibility was accepted for finding alternative employment for displaced workers."

It is this model of a competitive enterprise geared to promote "social progress and a better standard of living" (United Nations Ad Hoc Expert Group 1969:9) within the capitalist framework that was shipped to underdeveloped countries. India is a case in point. In India, cooperatives organized from above and representative of urban and rural middle class populations began in 1904 and were given legal status in 1912 during the British colonial administration (Goyal 1972:54). Following independence, the government promoted cooperative community organization as the most effective means "for raising the level of productivity, extending improvements in technology and extending employment so as to secure the basic necessities for every member of the community" (Government of India 1962:1). In the early days of independence, the government still relied on experts from England, who took up the "white man's burden" again, this time in the guise of foreign aid rather than colonial maintenance. Campbell, one of these postempire carriers of the Kipling tradition, called these areas of penetration "the undeveloped, ill-educated and poverty-stricken masses in the less fortunate countries," contrasting them to the inhabitants of "highly-developed, well-educated and sophisticated countries" (Campbell 1951:xv). Evoking a picture of the lonely European as a cooperator "filled with ideas, who confronts a mass of apathetic illiterates," he calls for patience and fortitude in stimulating in such unlikely material the desire for objects and creation of discontent (1951: xvi). The ethnocentric bias of the author is matched by the statement by C.F. Strickland in the foreword to Campbell's book: "Since, therefore, the world is, as a result of Western example and education, moving towards Western principles and practices, the qualities in which the non-European is deficient become more valuable." Casselman (1952:8), echoing the ethnocentric views of Campbell with regard to "the non-civilized peoples" whose "social sense is not adequately developed," clearly states the goal of export cooperativism as a means to repair the capitalist system (Casselman 1952:89). Accepting private property as a basis for economic structures, he concludes that the only thing wrong with it is that too few people have it (Casselman 1952:92).

The mood and goals expressed by Campbell and Casselman characterized, sometimes to a lesser degree but with some of the same ethnocentric overtones, the attitude of the United States and other European developers. In Africa, the cooperative movement prior to independence paralleled that of the European countries that controlled the administration and economy of the countries. In East Africa before the end of World War II there were mostly Asian or European cooperatives, with a few developments of native cooperative unions in areas with fewer whites (Migot-Adholla 1970:29). Similarly, the first cooperatives in Tunisia were French and Italian (Sethom, this volume). The kind of European ethnocentrism expressed in British administrative centers in Asia can be seen in Englemann's claim (1968:155) that "the greatest obstacle to cooperative education was the Ugandans themselves. Solidarity, responsibility, and other basic requirements of cooperative work were unknown ideas to most of the people." Oblivious of the significant role of women in many African societies, Englemann (1968: 53) states that cooperatives might be the means to awaken women to their rights by taking Western women as a model.

Mobilization in the New Nations

The effect of these ethnocentric views was to reinforce the defensive barriers of "apathy" and distrust with which the populations of underdeveloped areas defended themselves (cf. Huizer's critique of literature on peasant resistance [1970]). As the independence movements developed in Third World areas, governments turned from foreign experts and advisors to internal agents. We shall summarize some of the cases from countries that, following independence, tried to go beyond the Western reform model they inherited from colonial administrations by addressing ourselves to the first problem area defined above: how do new forms of mobilization relate to existing traditional structures? The second problem area, that of redefining one's position in the world market, is primarily related to countries which have chosen socialist models for change.

Baviskar attacks the first problem area in his analysis of a sugar factory cooperative he studied in India by raising the question as to whether the modern cooperatives, predicated on equality among members and democratic administration, come into conflict with caste. The state government overcame the opposition of lower-caste Mali to the factory cooperative, based on fear that it would lead to domination by the Maratha dominant caste, by setting discriminatory rules of growing for nonmembers. The caste split was overridden by political factions based on multi-caste alliances which cooperated with the objective of gaining power. While the successful economic operation of the cooperative was attributed in part to the dominance of the Maratha clan, some of the social impact of cooperative approaches was minimized by the persistence of traditional groupings. In his contribution to this volume, Baviskar shows how politicians build up a base in the traditional networks of caste, kinship, and village loyalties, but find a means of mediating these conflicting interests in the networks based on distribution of loans, jobs, and patronage exercised through the cooperatives. Cooperatives continue to be successful in the cash-crop areas where the dominant castes operate, while consumer and worker cooperatives have shown poor results. He calls for a political orientation involving less patronage and manipulation and more ideology and programming for redistribution of wealth.

In Africa the issue of the relationship of traditional loyalties to new organizations existed only where the cash economy had not penetrated: marginally productive areas, women's subsistence activities, and tribal retreat areas. Migration, usually by young males, to production centers dominated by Europeans, usually meant a complete break with the traditional past (Migot-Adholla 1970:25).

Following the relaxation of British administration after 1945, cooperatives became centers of political opposition against colonial governments (Migot-Adholla 1970:29). Based on lineages which were also the administrative unit, the new cooperative societies of East Africa expanded beyond the old areas of communal cooperatives. The new cooperatives differed from the old cooperativistic units in that participation was voluntary, motivation was for individual benefit rather than the common good, and relationships were no longer embedded in multiplex organizations (Migot-Adholla 1970:32). Roth shows in his contribution to this collection the effectiveness of this kind of grafting of new organizations on the traditional kinship and communal organizations in Tanzania. The government of Tanzania tried to transform rural society by a strategy of democratic, labor-intensive developments linking modern developmental objectives to traditional communal values of *ujamaa* policy (Cliffe 1970:38).

If we look at cooperatives at one point in time rather than in historical perspective we might conclude, along with Widstrand (1972:236), that they are more a liability than an asset. The rural face-to-face group that lives and works together is too small to form a modern cooperative and proves inflexible in the large unit since it is based on exclusion and because the poor peasant has not challenged the exploitation existing in the traditional system. However, as the Chinese experience shows, the peasants seemed to have to gain a sense of themselves in the postrevolutionary period by entering into collectivistic arrangements after a period of individualistic, small-plot production. Following that, they could hark back to village communalistic forms, rejecting the old dependencies on the dominant groups. Vessuri's and Bilbao's case (in this collection) of the Argentine agricultural collective also reveals how the initially negative effects of traditional institutions can, at a later stage of development, provide positive rewards in communal forms. It is possible that the African experience with cooperative and collective forms of organization will also need to break with the past in order to rediscover the positive elements in the old communalistic order. As Dore points out in his analysis of cooperatives in traditional communities (1971:51), an individualizing phase can serve as an equalizing phase, without which modern forms of cooperatives would be impossible.

Social Mobilization for Change

In reaction to the negative tendencies found in reformist types of cooperatives, socialist action groups turned to collectives and self-management forms for mobilizing political action and expanding the degree of participation of workers in decision making. Tracing their roots to the Paris commune, the Kronstadt communes of the Russian revolution, and those of the Spanish civil war, they called for a holistic approach to change that was denied in the later stages of the cooperative movement. The Paris communes of 1871 persist as a model for such fundamental change. In Marx's terms (Fener 1959:369), it was no less than "the political form at last discovered to work out the economic emancipation of labor." In its few weeks in power, the French working class "broke the physical force elements of the old government" in abolishing conscription and the standing army, they attacked "the spiritual forms of repression" by decreeing the separation of church and state and establishing secular education, and they "undermined the bureaucratic control of the state apparatus" by declaring universal suffrage and wages to government officials equal to those of workers (Fener 1959:366).

The fundamental transformation of societies in the Russian Revolution and more recently in Algeria, Cuba, and Chile led to similar attempts to transform society on all fronts. In Russia, spontaneous participatory forms were shortlived and became the target for attack as planned state intervention took over. As Alderson-Smith points out in his contribution to this collection, too much centralized planning is the antithesis of participation. State farms (*sovkhozes*) were introduced along with the collective farms (*kolkhozes*) that preceded them. After the destruction of the Kulaks as a class in the winter of 1929–1930, the peasants became the expropriated class as the Soviets extracted a share of their produce for the town population of industrial workers, the Red Army, the bureaucracy, and export trade (School of Slavonic Studies 1934:4, 9). State control was assured through the tractor stations which received 20 percent of the total harvest.

Just as the cooperative model was shipped out to the neo-colonial world in the post-World War II period, so the collectivist model was transferred to Eastern European countries within the Soviet orbit. Shanin (1971:263) speculates that because collectivization was the step taken in Russia, it was seen as the necessary condition for socializing production in the rest of Europe. The Polish peasants, however, rejected the model and opted for individual holdings under state-farm distribution agencies after 1956 (Galeski 1971:253). Although 99 percent of the peasants operate on individual farms, there has been little socioeconomic polarization because, as Shanin points out (1971:269), rapid industrialization led to emigration of the poorest, and vertical corporations and state policies have contributed to the leveling of incomes.

The Poznan strikes of 1956 dramatized the Polish industrial workers rejection of centralization. Worker councils were set up to establish work regulations and the organizational structure of the enterprise, but the government retained the right of control over quantity and value of products, wages, and profits. The tripartite membership in the councils of party representative, director of the enterprise, and the shop councils minimized the threat to the government (Clegg 1971:16).

China's experience with collectivization in agriculture shows the potential — indeed necessity — for continual reinterpretation of collective forms to meet changing conditions. As Shillinglaw (1971:138) points out in his analysis of the process, collective ownership in postrevolutionary China was at first predicated on the male-dominated family as the unit of production with mutual aid labor sometimes based on egalitarian and sometimes inequitable exchanges. Land reform abolished the traditional forms of property ownership from 1949–1951 and established individual allotments as the basis for the new egalitarianism, with cooperativized forms of exchanges. In 1955 there was a reorganization of individual shares to collectives; after 1958 there was a rationalization of systems of work, sometimes organized with multi-village communes. These multi-village communes soon broke down to the natural village base, and the government responded in 1960–1961 by recognizing this as the unit for decentralized organization (Shillinglaw 1971:145–6). Even after twenty years of experience, the Cultural Revolution of the later sixties was still a necessary further step to raise the political consciousness and enthusiasm for collective production, asserting *yu banfa*, meaning, "there is a way" (Hinton 1972:91–2).

Among those new nations which followed socialist models for mobilizing popular support following independence was Algeria. While 50 percent of the trade was still with France after independence in 1962, the seizure of farms by those who worked them and the need for mobilizing worker support in the newly nationalized industries provided conditions for generating new forms for widening popular participation. Although influenced by the ideology of socialist countries, especially Yugoslavia, the worker-control councils followed the French model as applied in the Renault factory (Clegg 1971:136). State capitalism which filled the vacuum left by the departed French entrepreneurs had re-created a bureaucratic apparatus which continued to underwrite "the separation between those who actually produce and those who manage" (quoted from the Charter of Algiers in Clegg 1971:125). The limitation of the worker-control councils to day-to-day issues limited the impact that this form of participation could have on national development (cf. Aït Amara, this collection; Ben Salem in this collection makes a similar point in Tunisia). Similarly in some of the cooperative structures of East Africa, the workers in self-management enterprises continued to accept the status hierarchy of the traditional society (Clegg 1971:160). Paradoxically it was the failure of the firms to redistribute profits that caused the workers to lose the sense of socialist goals (Clegg 1971:173). As the case of the worker-control organizations in the nationalized tin mines of Bolivia described by Nash in this volume also shows, the consciousness of class was turning against the state bureaucracy.

Drawing from the African experience with new forms of social participation following independence, it is not enough to restate the truism that new forms do not imply new attitudes or new habits. Rather, we must analyze each case to discover how behavior and consciousness were influenced by the new set of conditions. Both cooperative and collective forms were the framework in which groups privileged in the colonial period were able to find a new niche, but in most cases there were new segments of the indigenous population who found some accommodation within them. Usually their position in political movements gave them the necessary leverage to warrant the cooptation. Since the framework in which that cooptation process operated was determined outside the cooperative or collective, it is not enough to condemn the particular organization and seek new forms as a solution, but rather to seek solutions at a more global level.

A comparative analysis of cooperative and collective forms within a region is instructive in order to sort out which aspects of the success or failure of the particular organization are due to the forms and which are due to the ideology and economy of the wider system. Latin America provides such a comparative dimension because of the wide variety of sources from which cooperatives sprang and the excellent analysis of them by Fals-Borda, Carroll, Eckstein, and others.

While in Europe cooperatives were spontaneously organized in reaction to some of the abuses within the capitalist system, in Latin America they were imposed from outside (Fals-Borda 1972:135). Church, state, United States AID, and other agencies competed with each other to establish cooperatives. Paternalism, familistic loyalties, reinforced by *compadrazgo*, or fictive kinship ties based on godparenthood, were often reinforced in the context of cooperatives imposed from above (Fals-Borda 1972; Hermitte and Heran 1970; Carroll 1971:213). When, as in the case of La Carlota and Mesitas cooperatives in Colombia, the *campesinos* seized control of the cooperative and operated it, it was more dynamic. However, as soon as such leaders in the cooperatives began to raise the political consciousness of the members, they were no longer given the special privileges accorded them because of the affiliation with the church (Fals-Borda 1972:53, 59).

As a consequence of the authoritarianism which persisted within the cooperatives, not so much because of the apathy attributed to members but because any attempt to deviate from control was undercut, cooperatives in Latin America were converted into mechanisms of adjustment for the given social order. Although they gave lip service to Rochdale principles, the control by privileged groups served to defuse social protest rather than diffuse it to a wider group. Ultimate control was mediated through the market system and the systems of credit, distribution, and taxation controlled by the dominant business interests.

In Mexico, as in Asian and African countries, successful cooperatives judged by economic criteria served to reinforce wealth differences. This is particularly true in areas where irrigation projects and other large capital outlays were involved, as Baviskar indicated for India (1971) and Carroll and Eckstein point out in this collection. Economies of scale diminish after a certain point, maximally 500 hectares as Carroll and Eckstein's data indicate. When a large state agency such as the Banco Nacionál de Credito in Mexico becomes the promoter of credit and technical inputs, there is generally a shift to individual accounts on the part of the receivers (Carroll 1971:206). In such circumstances the small operators do not find any advantage in turning to such agencies for help since the cost in bribes to secure a fair assessment of their crop weights and the time involved in taking the crop to the receiving centers take a larger percentage of their total crop than is worthwhile to the individual (Nash 1970).

Summing up the structural factors limiting the effectiveness of cooperatives, Fals-Borda (1972) points to (1) vested interests in unjust patterns of exploitation and trade due to caste and class, (2) excessive control by central political and religious authority, and (3) inadequate attention to education for the new responsibilities. Cooperatives as an export product already accommodated to the United States or European business interests, served to reinforce a local power base rather than stimulate structural change. Where they did try to realize the potential for radical social change, they threatened the power structure that proceeded to cut off their resources.

Experience with self-management and coparticipation in industry has been relatively limited in Latin America. However, the Yugoslav model has excited considerable interest in Peru and worker-control councils were an integral part of the revolutionary demands of labor in Bolivia in the fifties and, until the recent coup, in Chile. The "industrial community" model introduced in Peru has had little more impact than the cooptive "profit-sharing" plans of United States firms, and worker-control schemes have been the first victims of military regimes in both Bolivia and Chile. The experience indicates, however, the ability and initiative of workers to enter into decision making, and their demise can be directly attributed to political manipulation outside of enterprise. Self-management programs are more vulnerable to macro-economic systems since they are involved more directly in the productive processes of major enterprises and do not have the opportunity that some cooperatives have had to insulate themselves from the wider economy. Selser (1970) summarizes some of the Latin American experiences and Nash and Winn describe case studies in this collection.

The future of participatory forms of production and distribution depends on the social mobilization of people not only for the revolutionary stage but for sustained involvement in the day-to-day decision-making of enterprises. The potential for sustained mobilization depends on action movements outside of the immediate enterprises in which cooperative and coparticipatory forms find expression. For this reason, we have felt it important to include discussions on the social movement in which such forms are generated, in the contributions made here by Jacques Chonchol, Jorge Dandler, and Gerrit Huizer.

In Chile, Chonchol shows how the agrarian reform law and the opening up of trade union movements during the Christian Democratic government of Frei's presidency set the stage for a greater entry of workers and peasants into political and social processes. The victory of Allende at the polls in 1970 did not solve the problems raised in the Frei period as mass action came into conflict with vested interests, but rather raised the conflict to a higher level in which broader scope was given to the level of participation of the masses. He points to three kinds of contradictions that emerged in the Allende period: (1) disequilibrium between demand and production as higher wage levels for workers made possible a greater entry into the consumers market, (2) conflict between different sectors of the peasantry, and (3) confrontation between the peasants and the bureaucrats. All of these contradictions were aggravated by the pressure put on the economy by outside interests, especially those coming from United States business. Caught in the dependency relations of maintaining a position in the world economy, the Chilean road to socialism was cut short before internal contradictions could be solved.

Dandler reveals another aspect of the central problem that Chonchol comes to grips with, namely that the internal structure of the enterprises and institutions of a society remain intact even after a major social change. In Bolivia, after the revolution of 1952, the agrarian *sindicatos* were the major social and political innovation in the countryside. In the counterrevolutionary movements that came to the fore after 1960 especially, the *sindicatos* became coopted in a political patronage network in which vertical political clienteles fell under a regional peasant leader loyal to political figures in the national scene. The countervailing tendencies of mobilization and stabilization, constantly at odds in periods of rapid social change, were settled in favor of a stabilizing or cooptive model as national interests braked the social mobilization set into action in the early days of the revolution.

The experience gained by peasants in the struggle to obtain land stands in good stead as they organize cooperatives to exploit the new resources. What set these struggles going in Bolivia, Indonesia, and Japan seems be, in Huizer's analysis, pressure from economic power holders for increasing land holding so that the balance was shaken, or, in the case of "revolutions of rising expectations," the elite's "resistance to change" promotes the escalation of peasant demands.

Using the conflict model approach suggested by Huizer we can assess some of the future pathways for the participatory forms of production and distribution. The kinds of contradictions that we have seen emerge in the cases mentioned — the marginalization and unemployment of workers when the cooperative follows the modernizing dictum of capital-intensive rather than labor-intensive systems of production, the failure to support the democratizing goals by not providing the educational infrastructure to maintain and increase responsibilties of workers-partici-pants, the conflict between technicians and workers when the preexisting inequalities in wage and prestige are reinforced in contradiction to egali-tarian ideologies — all of these point to the new areas where conflict is bound to occur and where solutions will point to the emergent structural forms. The success and future of cooperatives, collectives, and co-participation depend on the depth and continuity of social mobilization against the many forces that threaten these emerging institutions.

ANTHROPOLOGY AND THE STUDY OF COOPERATIVES, COLLECTIVES, AND COPARTICIPATION

So far the attempt has been to sketch in some of the parameters of the problems that arise in the study of cooperative forms of social-economic organization. The effort has been twofold: on the one hand to develop an ideal-type model of a cooperative for the heuristic purpose of sug-gesting problem areas to be covered in the study of cooperatives by anthropological methods in the field, and on the other hand to spell out some of the practical problems that face cooperatives and the social movements that give rise to and sustain them. These two procedures are basically, then, complementary aspects of the same reality. The view of cooperatives that has been presented is considerably more complicated than the question that most anthropologists found appropriate to ask of the institution: how does it derive from the preexisting social struc-tures? Instead of taking the cooperative as an emanation from some other social pattern, the cooperative is made the principal subject of study. Indeed, this is most appropriate in circumstances where there are or have been attempts to generalize cooperative structures as the dominant social pattern in a society (Israel, Tunisia, Chile), and it is also relevant in areas where cooperatives play an important role locally. Only when cooperatives are studied in themselves will anthropologists (and other social scientists) begin to understand them better. If this conference and this volume contribute to this they will have fulfilled their minimal purpose.

The study of cooperatives is clearly an important contribution to the understanding of the processes of development. Too often anthropological research on economic development has focused on entrepreneurial activity and the development of market-oriented, capital-based firms with the assumption that they would replace collective forms. If we can study the firm or the factory, then we can study the cooperative, coparticipation, and self-management, both to understand how they work and to clarify the reasons why they do not always work as well as the ideal type suggests.

High expectations of the revolutionary role of the cooperativistic forms of organization have often led analysts of particular instances to conclude that success was at best partial, or, indeed, that cooperatives had effects opposite to those intended. Surveying the literature on rural American cooperatives in the late nineteenth century, the historian Shannon (1945:409) remarked, "That the zeal for cooperation far outdistanced the results is revealed in part by the voluminous literature on the subject"; yet his own analysis suggests that later developments among American farmers were only possible because of the trials and errors of this period. That cooperatives do not "work" as well as they are "supposed" to is clearly neither a reason for ignoring them in anthropology (after all, the same judgment could be made of most lineages), nor one for misjudging the useful role they can play in long-run economic development.

The study of cooperatives is important not only for the understanding of development, but also for promoting development itself. We should not underestimate the impact that our research can have on development. By explaining and legitimizing the cooperative, social science can help create an atmosphere where such institutions are more likely to emerge successfully. Chonchol makes a similar point when he states that the concern of the Alliance for Progress, the F.A.O., and other U.N. organizations for agrarian reform contributed in Chile to a favorable atmosphere for the enactment of the agrarian reform laws under the Frei regime.

The anthropological contribution to the study of cooperatives and similiar institutions is manifold. (1) Anthropologists can contribute to the understanding of the inner workings of the cooperative at the local level by focusing on the actual patterns of cooperation and leadership that seem to work either to foster the cooperative or to hinder it. (2) Through our comparative knowledge of the total range of human behavior, it is possible to suggest various alternatives, and to reflect on the implications of real and imagined situations. Cooperatives may have as part of their ideological baggage the goal of creating a new psychological type (a "new man," the "new woman," or "new person" being all too often left aside), but none would work if it required such a new personality to exist as a precondition for the cooperative. (3) The relationship between ideology and action (culture and behavior) in social movements, which often define as their goal the development of cooperative forms, is another area of concern to cooperatives, which are often the goal of a social movement and on which anthropological experience and expertise can shed some light.

But cooperatives and cooperative movements have much to teach the anthropologists as well. They draw anthropology into the study of contemporary and emerging institutions which have a vitality and a forward-looking quality that makes them an essential addition to the total range of human behavior which it is anthropology's task to study. The study of cooperatives and cooperative movements is something that can be done now (and should be, if this is the proper sense to give to "urgent" anthropology), and that could result in a remodeling of the intellectual structure of anthropology. Without abandoning the tools that have brought us thus far, we can apply them to a whole new range of phenomena which will oblige us to rethink our methods of analysis and our notions of the nature of anthropology as a discipline.

Our discussions brought home that cooperatives, collectives, and similar institutions are TOTAL institutions whose analysis requires many disciplines and points of view. Here is a role for a prospective anthropology which would utilize the comparative approach of anthropology to the total range of human variability to (1) analyze the social movements that give rise to the need for new forms of participation; (2) evaluate the social consequences of projected new forms of social relations whether proposed from "below" or from "above," keeping in mind the distinction between what is theoretically imaginable and what is concretely possible; (3) study the emergent forms of social organization such as cooperatives, collectives, and coparticipation in management, both to understand them better and to bolster them by injecting them into main areas of social science concern; (4) on the basis of the comparative knowledge of anthropology, suggest possible new directions in which human social and cultural evolution might be guided; and (5) ensure in this process of research and evaluation that our major effort is towards a dialogue with people, affecting their consciousness, rather than with governments of any kind. We look forward to a future cooperative effort which hopefully would include participation of Chinese and representatives of other countries experimenting in communal ventures to broaden our understanding of the phenomena and widen our comparative base.

To review possible methods of approach for cooperatives is to review anthropological methodology, for the cooperative, being a community, is a total institution. This is why the study of cooperatives as social and cultural forms, only just beginning, promises to be so rich both in its subject matter and in its implications for an understanding of the directions in which human society, given awareness, is moving and can move.

REFERENCES

BAVISKAR, B. S.
   1971   "Cooperatives and caste in Maharashtra: a case study," in *Two blades of grass*. Edited by Peter Worsley, 275–292. Manchester: University of Manchester Press.
BOGARDUS, EMORY S.
   1964   *Principles of cooperation*. Chicago: The Coop League of the U.S.A.
CAMPBELL, W. G. H.
   1951   *Practical cooperation in Asia and Africa*. Cambridge: W. Heffer and Sons.
CARROLL, THOMAS F.
   1971   "Peasant cooperation in Latin America," in *Two blades of grass*. Edited by Peter Worsley, 199–219. Manchester: University of Manchester Press.
CASSELMAN, PAUL H.
   1952   *The cooperative movement and some of its problems*. New York: Philosophic Library.
CLEGG, IAN
   1971   *Workers' self-management in Algeria*. New York: Monthly Review Press.
CLIFFE, LIONEL
   1970   "Traditional Ujamaa and modern producer co-operatives in Tanzania," in *Co-operatives and rural development in East Africa*. Edited by C. G. Widstrand. New York: Africana.
DORE, RONALD F.
   1971   "Modern cooperatives in traditional communities," in *Two blades of grass*. Edited by Peter Worsley, 43–60. Manchester: University of Manchester Press.
ENGELMANN, KONRAD
   1968   *Building cooperative movements in developing countries: the sociological and psychological aspects*. New York: Frederick A. Praeger.
FALS-BORDA, ORLANDO
   1972   *El reformismo por dentro en America Latina*, Mexico City: Siglo XXI.
FENER, LEWIS *editor*
   1959   *Excerpts from "The civil war in France," by Karl Marx*. New York: Doubleday Anchor.
GALESKI, BOGUSLAW
   1971   "Types of collective farms in Poland," in *Two blades of grass*. Edited by Peter Worsley, 253–261. Manchester: University of Manchester Press.

GEERTZ, CLIFFORD
1963   *Peddlers and princes.* Chicago: University of Chicago Press.

GIDE, CHARLES
1930   *Communist and cooperative colonies.* Translated by Ernest F. Dow. London: G. G. Harrupt.

GOSSELIN, GABRIEL
1970   *Développement et tradition dans les sociétés rurales Africaines.* Geneva: International Labor Office.

GOVERNMENT OF INDIA
1962   *Cooperation in India.* Delhi: Ministry of Community Development and Cooperation.

GOYAL, S. K.
1972   *Consumers' cooperative movement in India.* Delhi: Meenakshi, Prakashan.

GUELFAT, ISAAC
1966   *La coopération devant la science économique.* Paris: Tiers-Monde Collection, Presses Universitaires de France.

HERMITTE, ESTHER, CARLOS HERAN
1970   Patronazgo o cooperativísmo? Obstaculos a la modificaciòn del sistema de interacción social en una comunidad del noroeste Argentina. *Revista Latinoamericana de Sociologia* 70 (20):293–317.

HINTON, WILLIAM
1972   *Turning point in China: an essay on the cultural revolution.* New York: Modern Reader.

HOPKINS, NICHOLAS S.
1969   "Leadership and consensus in two Malian cooperatives," in *The anthropology of development in sub-Saharan Africa.* Edited by D. Brokensha and Marian Pearsall, 64–69. Society for Applied Anthropology, Monograph 10. Lexington, Ky.: Society for Applied Anthropology.

HUIZER, GERRIT
1970   "Resistance to change" and radical peasant mobilization: Foster and Erasmus reconsidered. *Human Organization* 29:303–322.

HYMES, DELL
1974   "The use of anthropology: critical, political, personal," in *Reinventing anthropology.* Edited by Dell Hymes, 3–82. New York: Vintage.

KLUCKHOHN, CLYDE
1959   "Common humanity and diverse cultures," in *The human meaning of the social sciences.* Edited by D. Lerner, 245–284. New York: Meridian Books.

KRAVITZ, LINDA
1974   *Who's minding the co-op?* Washington, D.C.: Agribusiness Accountability Project.

LIPSET, SEYMOUR MARTIN
1971   *Agrarian socialism.* Berkeley: University of California Press.

LUXEMBURG, ROSA
1970   *Rosa Luxemburg speaks.* Edited and with an introduction by Mary-Alice Waters. New York: Pathfinder Press.

MAUSS, MARCEL
   1899   "L'action socialiste." *Le Mouvement Socialiste* (October 15): 449–462.
          Paris.
MEILLASSOUX, CLAUDE
   1972   From reproduction to production: a Marxist approach to economic
          anthropology. *Economy and Society* 1:93–105.
MIGOT-ADHOLLA, S. E.
   1970   "Traditional society and cooperatives," in *Co-operatives and rural
          development in East Africa*. Edited by C. G. Widstrand, 17–37.
          New York: Africana.
NASH, JUNE
   1970   *In the eyes of the ancestors; belief and behavior in a Maya community*.
          New Haven: Yale University Press.
PUSIC, EUGENE
   1972   "Participation and the multidimensional development of complexity,"
          in *Reports, First International Conference on Management*, 174–199.
          Zagreb.
SCHOOL OF SLAVONIC STUDIES
   1934   *Collectivized agriculture in the Soviet Union*. School of Slavonic and
          East European Studies of the University of London, Monograph 2.
SELSER, JORGE
   1970   *Participación de los trabajadores en la gestión economíca*. Buenos
          Aires: Ediciónes Libera.
SHANIN, TEODOR
   1971   "Cooperation and collectivization: the case of Eastern Europe,"
          in *Two blades of grass*. Edited by Peter Worsley, 263–274. Manchester:
          University of Manchester Press.
SHANNON, FRED A.
   1945   *The farmer's last frontier: agriculture, 1860–1897*. New York: Holt,
          Rinehart and Winston.
SHILLINGLAW, GEOFFREY
   1971   "Traditional rural cooperatives and social structure: the communist
          Chinese collectivization of agriculture," in *Two blades of grass*.
          Edited by Peter Worsley, 137–157. Manchester: University of Man-
          chester Press.
SPIRO, MELFORD
   1970   *Kibbutz: venture in utopia* (augmented edition). New York: Schocken.
UNITED NATIONS AD HOC EXPERT GROUP
   1969   *Nature and role of industrial cooperatives in industrial development*.
          United Nations Ad Hoc Expert Group Meeting on Industrial
          Cooperatives. Vienna.
WIDSTRAND, CARL GOSTA, *editor*
   1970   *Cooperatives and rural development in East Africa*. New York:
          Africana.
   1972   *African cooperatives and efficiency*. New York: Africana.
WORSLEY, PETER, *editor*
   1971   *Two blades of grass*. Manchester: University of Manchester Press.

The Introduction of Cooperatives into Peasant Societies

Organized Cooperation and Spontaneous Cooperation in Africa (Niger Republic)

HENRI RAULIN

Our title demands an immediate explanation, for the gist of the demonstration that follows is contained in it. The geographical precision of the title indicates that we are more concerned here with particular facts and with deductions of a concrete nature than with *a priori* general theoretical conclusions. The observations and reflections thus stimulated are only valid for a single part of Africa. Although they refer to a single time period which carries the official name of "independence," it is difficult to extrapolate from them since the ecological and social contexts of the different countries of West Africa are far from similar. While the countries of the Sahel area are quite close to one another, nothing is less comparable than the economies of Niger and the Ivory Coast. The focus of this paper is directed at the contrast between organized and spontaneous cooperation, although it is quite evident that this single phenomenon cannot be isolated from the greater problem that includes among other things the economic and technical aspects of the process of agricultural development. Since this development is currently only being undertaken within the framework of aid to underdeveloped countries by overdeveloped or well-off ones, these countries impose their own plans and projects, carried out by Europeans or by Africans educated in European schools, which amounts to the same thing. These experts, quite competent as far as problems of agricultural hydraulics, agronomy, or economy are concerned, seem to lose some of their effectiveness when they are called upon to handle a project in which the indigenous human element might play a part — as is generally the case.

Both technical systems and the organization of work in these development programs are imposed from above, with no attention being given to the preexisting frameworks. Cooperation aiming at strictly technical and material goals is organized between individuals considered to be autonomous and independent. The land and the people of Africa appear to be no more than an empty page on which new concepts, machines, and products are imprinted. Without really insisting on the validity of macroeconomics, one can note that the former two of these items must necessarily be imported as well, and that at least a portion of the latter must be exported. Here, a problem arises with respect to the relationship between the world economy and the local economy. It would be a fiction to pretend that these two converge, but in the present state of relations between under- and overdeveloped countries, this facet is being questioned. A review of the whole concept of development must soon be carried out, stressing its ultimate goals. Currently, only increases in the level of exports are being considered. In fact, looking back on the last ten years, one can note that volume has been more the focus than value; since these two are in inverse relation, such a fact necessarily implies an end to the process. It will then remain for us to find new forms of development: will the increase in production remain the only goal? Since basic needs must be satisfied, a population increase requires a production increase. But what then? It would be very risky for Africans to try to attach their economy too closely to world markets. They cannot ignore the refusal of the European Community to lift agricultural protectionism to allow entry of off-season products. September 1972 was a real eye-opener for them.

Without bringing in notions of hedonism here, since the concept of happiness is too subjective, it is nonetheless possible to note that Africa cannot count exclusively upon an improvement in its economic level to be fully satisfied. At the very time that developed countries are questioning the value of the consumer society, some Africans are also becoming aware of the values of their society. They are beginning to abandon some of the ideas borrowed during the long period of contact with the Europeans. This new position was evident at a conference in Lomé, Togo, in July, 1972, where the conventional educational system — i.e. copied after the French model — was first challenged. It is within the context of affirmation of the specific nature of Africa, then, that we must analyze spontaneous forms of cooperation which experts in development, particularly those dealing with human potential, have neglected or even failed to recognize. As failure of the educational system can lead to its adjustment to the real needs of Africa, so failures in plans for development are an extremely valuable starting point for the new orientation of agricultural production systems. In terms of classical theories, we can refer to Durkheim for the contrast between the mechanical solidarity of individuals and the organic solidarity of rural and archaic societies; this contrast will be seen to correspond to that between organized and spontaneous cooperation. This latter term has been preferred to that of "traditional," whose connotations include permanence or even immobility. Actually, however, tradition is capable of evolution, adaptation, and even innovation within the framework of the values and concepts of African societies. It is in this sense that it can be called spontaneous. It is endowed with a kind of social dynamism that has been emphasized on numerous occasions by anthropologists. The form of cooperation which we are analyzing here differs from that which is characteristic of family groups: we note only that the impact of the monetary economy, by disintegrating the family unit, has allowed other social forms to develop. These forms existed within the society's repertory of forms, but in the former economic circumstances, where the relations of production corresponded closely to those of the family, there was nothing to stimulate their growth. These social forms were complementary to the family groups, and had a different range. Upon the family structures, then, another structure was superimposed.

Most of the populations of West Africa have a well-defined age grading system. If we take initiation as a necessary condition for the existence of age grades, we shall have to conclude that age grading is unknown in Niger, except among the Gourma of the extreme western part of the country. Without attempting to account for the disappearance of initiation ceremonies and age grades, we can nonetheless point out that relatively informal groups exist even here. "Samari," a widespread young men's organization, is based on traditions which have much in common. The boys and the girls form separate groups bound together by common residence and by affective ties. The notion of age is emphasized, since they themselves name their groups *Wadi Wada* among the Djerma Sonrai, or *Wari* among the Hausa, both terms signifying "equal in age." The boys who are members of these associations form subgroups based on age divisions around five years apart. This distinction is an absolute necessity in an organization that ranges from boys of 12 years to men of 25 or 30 years of age. Boys can ask for admission into a group as soon as they have the physical ability to participate in agricultural work with the other members of the group, and they will then not leave the system until they marry (among the Hausa), their first son is named (among the Fulani of Say), or they have a son old enough to take part himself (Sonrai).

Most of these organizations of the traditional type require either an entrance fee on the order of 200 CFA francs (Fulani of Say), or fixed dues to be paid periodically, or some other monetary contribution according to individual circumstances and to the eventual needs of the group.

The most obvious goal of these groups is the periodical organization of meals among the young people, but the more essential function is to aid members who marry, through offering gifts of all sorts.

The young members of the group are determined to stress these ceremonial practices, but this must not lead us to lose sight of the means employed to procure the money needed to carry them out. Generally, money is derived from sales of part of the harvest brought in by each member from his own small field assigned to him by the head of his family. These fields are farmed collectively in turn by a small group of young people. This system of labor mirrors that used by the extended family, in which all the men work together on the same field rather than work separately in different places. This system has a general diffusion throughout all preindustrial societies, both in those of medieval Europe and in those of present-day Africa: it allows satisfying returns for difficult or painstaking work. Once cooperative links have been established through the "Samari" they are maintained. Among the heads of families "equal in age" who have belonged to them, they play a very basic role in the formation of networks of mutual aid and solidarity. And they do so far more clearly than do neighborhood or kinship ties.

Network members seek mutual trust above all, for the system can only work to the extent that it is based on absolute reciprocity, inasmuch as each member must repay the work from which he has benefited. Every mutual aid network includes as well an aspect of social security: the members must work without thought of return on behalf of any member who is absent or ill. Other rules set out the material aid which members of the network owe each other, especially in the domain of foodstuffs. Any member may obtain from another whatever he lacks at the moment, whether it be millet, condiments, oil, etc. If the person approached for the particular items has them at the time, he cannot refuse to give them away; he knows, however, that the loan may not be returned to him very soon, and that he will be unable to claim its repayment. It is not a debt — either a long-term one or a short-term one — but rather a permanent, interest-free loan. Reimbursement cannot be demanded as a condition without the lender's being covered with shame. In fact, in order to liquidate these loans, people must wait until they themselves have need of such services. When this veritable network of indebtedness functions simultaneously, i.e. such that all members are both debtors and creditors, it constitutes a powerful factor of social cohesion.

A mutual help network generally includes from ten to twenty members, an optimum number with regard to ease of meeting and the best returns from the work done. Nevertheless, networks can also be found that include fewer than ten people, and some individuals may belong to two different small-sized networks.

The activity of these networks is not limited to the two weedings of the fields of millet and sorghum that make up the largest part of farm work. It extends as well to land-clearing and to harvest work. While there is no *gàyyaa* for seeding, the system is used in building huts and shelters in the fields. The various stages of this work are treated separately: work with wood or with straw, for earthen walls, for fences made from grass or dirt.

A particular type of joint activity grew up spontaneously when onion-growing expanded. It concerned the gardening jobs carried out in the dry season, which require a minimum infrastructure that is nonetheless difficult for a single person to manage. It is necessary to dig a well, not too deep a one if the land were chosen properly; the area must be enclosed by a millet-stalk fence to keep out the cattle that always wander freely in this particular season. Generally, five or six members of a network combine their efforts to perform the task, to prepare the beds and the tiny canals permitting proper irrigation of the plants. Sowing, replanting, and maintenance of the planted areas are all carried out separately on the different beds allotted to each. As with all systems of joint labor, the harvest is strictly personal. The only permanent collective obligation consists in using calebashes to draw water by turns during the growing period of two or three months.

Is it possible to escape the framework of the system and to use this form of community in the perspective of a modernization of agrarian techniques? To what extent might it be possible to depend upon such a trend as this to expand, for example, the use of animal-drawn plows that in certain circumstances contributes to technical progress? Mutual aid group members are experienced in making choices between what can and must be done by the group as a whole and what should be done by individuals.

One could certainly have trusted them to find and apply the most judicious technical and juridical procedures for the use of animal-drawn plows (Unités de culture attelée = U.C.A.). Instead, the U.C.A. were pushed on some village chiefs who did not know how to make the best use of oxen or tools. Many others were handed over to the privileged local representatives of commercial capitalism (dealers trading cattle to coastal markets and organizers of caravans to oases on the edge of the Sahara). These men have been able to take advantage of material bought on credit and at reduced prices thanks to a subsidy. They monopolize plows and draft animals in a region. In their hands is also concentrated an important part of the money given farmers by the "Compagnie Française pour le Développement des Textiles" [C.F.D.T. or "French Textile Development Company"] as advances against the cotton harvest.

This process demonstrates that the African economy, as long as it is advised, and therefore directed, by experts whose outlook is shaped by the European capitalist experience, can only be a bad copy of our own. It will have all of the disadvantages of varnishing a specific local reality with imported structures.

Even admitting that the distribution of the U.C.A. to the mutual aid networks might not have been fully satisfactory, it would not have been as clear a failure as the attempts to spread animal-drawn plows to a great number of villages. At any rate, this effort would have been rich in lessons for future experiments. It is also just as interesting to try to understand the difficulties met or the failures of a superimposed organizational framework when the reality of the existing social structures has been ignored.

In south-central Niger, the existing landholding pattern has been respected, but the high degree to which landholdings are fragmented means that it is necessary to look to pooling or reallocation of land. These measures have been necessary in order to carry out parasite eradication programs which can only be done over a wide area.

To achieve this Mutual Progress Groups (G.M.P. = Groupements Mutualistes de Progrès) have been created, grouping together the farmers of neighboring parcels of land, whether these users are proprietors or nonproprietary users.

The heterogeneity in the make-up of these G.M.P., from the point of view of economics, and to a certain extent of ethnicity, has presented some problems. In the larger villages, one can find entire wards, each populated by a group having a different origin. Smaller villages have a "stranger" ward. In almost all of the cases in which a G.M.P. has grouped elements of different origins, difficulties have arisen. In the face of such facts, it does not seem that there could be any ready-made solution to the problem. It would be necessary to conciliate the interests of people who have not always had any ties between them, for the village lands are not contiguous units and inheritance by daughters often leads to strangers farming land quite close to a village. Moreover, the ability of different people to spend money for the care of their fields is not always the same, and some people, not knowing that such an operation is profitable in the long run, refuse to take part. In such cases the majority rules, and the person who disagrees must submit to a new type of servitude, to the collectivity. The type of modern farming proposed in the G.M.P. format in fact includes twelve operations, eight of which are obligatory (removal and burning of old cotton plants, preparation of the soil, field layout, joint sowing in lines to a density of 40 × 80, hoeing and splitting into two different plants three weeks after sowing, the first chemical treatment 45 days after sprouting, subsequent treatments according to the development of parasites, and a minimum of three weedings), and four optional (plowing, use of mineral fertilizer, threshing, and crop rotation). It will be noticed that traditional agrarian techniques are compatible with the methods of plow farming, which might make it easier to set up these groups. It is difficult to predict what their cohesiveness and duration will be, considering that they are adapted exclusively to the cultivation of cotton. On the other hand, it may be possible to hope that individual advantages will prevail over personal conflicts and thus to foresee their disappearance in favor of G.M.P.'s whose members would have been brought together by a system of spontaneous solidarity, i.e. they would all belong to the same mutual aid network. In either case, a solution can only be sought through a partial or complete reorganization of village lands — partial in the sense that those few members of the G.M.P. not in agreement with the others would agree to land exchanges; complete in the sense of working towards the emergence of G.M.P.'s corresponding to the mutual aid networks. It seems that experimentation remains quite possible and easily attainable in some cases; notably in the redistribution of lands in development zones. Rather than improvising as, for example, when the (preliminary) distribution of land is done, with each farmer being invited to take over certain delimited plots, it might perhaps be wise to ask the interested parties what they would think of a distribution made as a function of current relationships of functional solidarity.

One case of total failure is that of a development project in the Niger river valley, near Tillabéri, which occurred despite a prior anthropological study. The sort of technical improvement adopted was that of irrigation from a pumping station, the water then passing through canals to reach the fields. The area concerned passed under national jurisdiction and was then redistributed according to the number of workers in each family economic unit. *A priori*, there did not appear to be any major impediments to the success of this project, either from the point of view of the newly introduced techniques (animal-drawn plows and double cropping, i.e. farming both in the rainy season and in the dry winter season) or from the point of view of the human environment which was to be the object of this change. Two points had been particularly well studied in research on human factors: on the one hand, detailed maps were made of the existing plots so that the landholdings of the various families could be taken into account in the redistribution process; and on the other hand, a plan was elaborated for the organization of the youth into a "samari," which had become partly a money-making enterprise, so that the young people would develop a sense of work and of management of their own affairs while working in the general interest as well.

We can only observe here that these suggestions have not been taken into consideration. The lands were redistributed just as if they had been virgin soil belonging to no one. This supposedly egalitarian division dispossessed some farmers, most of whose fields were on the terrace part of the valley. They were then obliged to look elsewhere, quite far from the village, for fields where they could cultivate millet for their families. On the other hand, others benefited from the redistribution. Although it created ferment of resentment and internal disagreement, this redistribution was not in itself the direct cause of the failure of the development project. At the different stages of this project, and even during its worst phase, reports were made which were quite revealing but which failed to clarify the main contradiction: the distribution of land was carried out in terms of the number of workers in a family economic unit, i.e. essentially the head of the family and his unmarried sons, assuming thus that the latter would work for their father. What might have been true in the context of a subsistence economy was no longer true in a market economy, i.e. as soon as the product of labor becomes commercialized. The young men participated in farm tasks aimed at producing food, but they did not want to be unpaid farm workers on a farm which henceforth has as its principal goal a monetary profit benefiting only the head of the family. This explains the greater and greater disillusionment of the young men, which ultimately expresses itself in their disinterest in anything but paid labor.

This contradiction is quite well perceived by the heads of farms, who know that they will be unable to count on their sons and who are obliged to hire laborers in order to cope with peak periods. But this problem is not too significant for them: the one that they have felt to be their major difficulty was that of the fees demanded from them or held back from the total amount of the sale of cotton, and which came to around a third — indeed, sometimes even a half — of the total. The five headings under which these fees came (farming aid, fertilizer, water, insecticides, administration) were certainly costly and were likely to become even more so each year as the subsidy was scheduled to decrease by 5 percent each year. No one was prepared to accept this system, and the points of view of the government and the farmers were no longer reconcilable.

These facts — technical successes ending in partial or complete failures — demonstrate the inadequacy of the knowledge of the men directly involved, even when a prior study of the social organization had been carried out. The lack of agreement between experts and anthropologists stands out clearly: the picture of the society under study can certainly be unsettling for someone who only knows the mechanisms of his own society. Knowledge of urban societies is hardly a sound basis for understanding Western rural behavior, let alone for acquiring a clear idea of attitudes and responses in African rural societies. Economists such as Gunnar Myrdal have gone beyond the simplistic schemas of Eurocentric theories, but their message has not yet sunk in: those Africans who remain the closest to their original culture are still assimilated to a Western *homo economicus*, even though their attitudes do not derive from the same logic.

A society's pattern of values is the expression of its internal structure, and this cannot always be discerned from the visible expression of social relationships. The analysis of the internal structure of a society is all the more delicate and complex when that society is in transition. Certain individual behavioral reactions, those related to the laws of the market system, may then appear to be comparable to those of Western man. Even then one discovers that Western man's behavior is differentiated according to his origin and training. The rural world has, to a certain extent, remained apart from any changes in mentality. Peasants, after having first considered technical progress to be an end in itself, are much more aware than other people of the poverty in human relationships that seems to be determined by it. Why should we not consider this as a warning concerning these exotic peoples whose life presents certain positive factors? We are acquainted with the wealth and diversity of their social relationships, the equilibrium between generations, sexual attitudes free of obsessive aspects. May this picture encourage development experts to modify imported schemas, to temper their desire to introduce the market economy and individual profit which have here as elsewhere contributed to the depersonalization of societies which had a certain style in life. The entire problem of the development of Third World countries must be rethought.

Traditional Social Structure and the Development of a Marketing Cooperative in Tanzania

WARREN J. ROTH

The data for this paper were gathered in the course of fieldwork among the Sukuma people of Tanzania (then Tanganyika) from July 1961 to September 1962. This fourteen-month period included the gaining of independence by Tanzania on December 9, 1961, and the initial stages of movement toward the economic structure and certain ideals which have come to be known as African Socialism. As a popularly based system of development, African Socialism is realized only where grass-root-type organizations are formed and allowed to grow. This paper is concerned with one such organization, a cotton-marketing cooperative. After a brief account of the formation and growth of the cooperative, the paper will examine the relationship between this modern economic organization and the traditional culture of the Sukuma people.

THE COTTON-MARKETING COOPERATIVE

Cotton was being grown in Tanganyika at least as early as 1885. Because of problems of transportation, the first areas of cultivation were near the coast, but by 1925 the center of production had moved from the eastern part of the country to Lake Province, well inland and just south of Lake Victoria. Lake Province was the home of the Sukuma people, the largest single ethnic group in Tanganyika and the second largest ethnic group in East Africa.

In 1925, while Tanganyika was under British rule, cotton production for the entire country had reached 17,500 bales. World War II increased the demand for raw materials from Africa and, by 1945, Lake Province alone was producing over 31,000 bales. The real impetus to growth in production came as a result of the organization and growth of the cotton-marketing cooperative. At the time of this study, statistics from the Lint and Seed Marketing Board for 1960 showed that Lake Province produced 155,568 bales of ginned cotton. This dramatic increase of production represented more than a reaction to coming independence on the part of the people of Tanganyika. It can be related directly to the efforts of a small group of young Sukuma men, led by a veteran of World War II, Paul Bomani, who encouraged traditionally oriented Sukuma farmers to help themselves. The British colonial administration did not aid the organization and development of the cooperative; in fact, the organizers were often hindered by agents of the government which feared the political ramifications of the growing organization.

The situation for Sukuma cotton growers in the late 1940's was one of exploitation. They were, in most cases, illiterate, economically unsophisticated, and unorganized. They were producing a crop which in its raw state was almost completely useless to them and which as individuals they could not store. They had no means of transportation except their own backs and those of other family members. Their disadvantageous position was worsened by a system, maintained by law, which favored the processors by granting each a monopoly in his own area as

...the 1949 legislation, crystallizing current custom, contained provisions restricting the purchase of cotton to agents of ginners, each ginnery being empowered to purchase all cotton within a defined area; and movements of cotton between areas were prohibited (Gorst 1959:171).

This monopoly was theoretically an efficient way for a processor to handle a difficult marketing problem. The ginnery was a large capital investment and the crop produced by Sukuma farmers was as unpredictable as prices on the world market. The processor, therefore, had some legal protection against uncertainty, but he was also indirectly helping in the establishment of the cooperative which would eventually put him out of business.

Cotton marketing in the years before the cooperative was an ordeal for the grower because it turned out to be a contest between himself and the buyer. The buyer, representing a ginner, was paid a flat rate of 1.60 shillings for each one hundred pounds of seed cotton purchased. Since the price to be paid to the grower was fixed by government regulation and payment was always in cash, the buyer could keep whatever he could make by deception or short weights. Some buyers would handle as much as a million pounds of seed cotton during a good season and the potential for illegal income was great. When farmers complained, the buyer would either ignore them or he would penalize them and others seeking to sell by closing down his operation until the following day. This forced the complainer and others to stay overnight, usually in the open, because of the distance and difficulty involved in making the trip home. Needless to say, social pressure weighed heavily on complainers.

In 1947, Paul Bomani got a job in Mwanza, the largest town in Sukumaland, and came into contact with the problems of the cotton growers among his people. He found that a traditional young-men's society, Basumba, had begun setting up independent scales and telling the farmers what they should be paid before they went to the buyers. Bomani spread the word about work of the Basumba and in a short time ten villages sent representatives to meet with him and explore the possibility of forming an organization to safeguard their interests. There followed a battle of wits in which the buyers tried to counter each measure used to keep them honest. Bomani quickly realized that nothing significant could be accomplished until the crucial step of buying the cotton came under the control of the growers themselves. This realization led Bomani and a small group of Sukuma to tour the cotton-marketing cooperatives already operating in Uganda. With this background, they returned to their own people and began to organize a cooperative.

In early 1952, Bomani and his followers began holding organizational meetings. The first was a failure, but at Nassa, a small town where Bomani was well known, the young men of the Basumba society assembled a crowd of over two hundred people who listened with interest as Bomani appealed to their ethnic pride as well as their economic needs. The speaker made a point of the fact that the ginners were not Sukuma and that they were getting rich while the growers were exploited and remained poor. The result of this meeting was the establishment of the first society of the new cooperative.

The success at Nassa, a chiefdom center, demonstrated to the organizers that further meetings should be scheduled at other chiefdom centers. Besides being the residences of the highest traditional authority among the Sukuma, these centers were also the foci of decision making and the seats of justice. In at least two subsequent meetings, the local chiefs joined the new cooperative and thus helped to sway those who were hesitant.

In a little less than two months of almost daily meetings, Bomani and his organizers were able to call a general meeting of thirty newly founded cooperative societies or, as they were first called, "branches." These branches represented thirty of the most populous chiefdoms and the most important cotton-growing areas of the forty-seven chiefdoms of the

Sukuma. The economic power of these first thirty groups was tested when a levy of one shilling was placed on each member to finance further organizational operations. Within two months, 30,000 shillings had been raised and the cooperative, calling itself the Lake Province Growers Association, was functioning with its own truck and duplicating machine.

The development of the organization was evident in its growth statistics. In April 1953, a year after the first successful meeting, there were thirty-eight societies which were purchasing 13.2 percent of the cotton produced by Sukuma farmers. The following year, the number of societies had risen to sixty-five and these were purchasing 32.5 percent of the cotton crop. By the end of 1959, the cooperative boasted 324 societies and had attained its original goal — 100 percent purchase of cotton produced by Sukuma growers.

Most of this growth came about despite opposition from local colonial government officials. At one point after the Nassa meeting, Bomani was being watched and was restricted to travel only within the District of Mwanza. In a number of instances, the British officials sided with the processors when disputes arose between ginners and the cooperative. The attainment of the goal of complete monopoly by the cooperative within seven years suggests that cultural factors in this case might be examined with profit.

CULTURAL FACTORS

Two cultural factors which played a role in the organization and growth of the cotton cooperative have already been mentioned. The Basumba society is, for traditional Sukuma youths, the first contact with communal work such as housebuilding or cultivating. Basumba membership was mandatory for all young men at about age fifteen (Juma 1960:27). It provided the Sukuma teenager with experience and appreciation of cooperative work. Each village had a group of Basumba who were available to help when there was need. The young man lived at home but was summoned by the head of the group, a person elected by the village, when there was work to be done. Failure to show up meant a fine. Work, however, was rewarded with a feast, food, and beer. It was therefore perfectly natural for the cotton cooperative organizers to call upon the Basumba for help in their work of organization. It can also be assumed that Bomani did not have to stress the value of cooperation in getting a job done. All of his hearers had already put in their time of service and many had probably called upon the Basumba to help them in cultivating their cotton land.

The other factor already mentioned was the holding of meetings at chiefdom centers. Although the role of the Sukuma *ntemi* had been altered by the British and he had been forced into the colonial category of "chief," the *ntemi* was still an important person in Sukuma society in the 1950's. He still received a great deal of respect and his judgment was sought by the people in many matters. Some of the chiefs still maintained their claims to supernatural power. Therefore, an organizational meeting held in a chiefdom center would have at least an implicit presumption of the *ntemi's* sanction. Where a chief gave the cotton cooperative open support, a great deal of the organizers' work was already done.

Structural elements in traditional Sukuma culture seem to provide the most fertile field of exploration in explaining the success of the cotton-marketing cooperative. The Sukuma, as a people, have built a society with a strong emphasis on voluntary associations. Some of these voluntary associations had members scattered over large parts of Sukumaland. Although called "dance societies" because of their most obvious but secondary function, they were primarily cooperative work groups. As with the Basumba, these voluntary associations would get together and do cultivating or housebuilding for their members. Food and beer were expected by those who worked but these voluntary associations never asked a fee for such work from members. Membership was obtained by the payment of a simple entrance fee.

The internal organization of these dance societies was a hierarchical one. There was a leader who in some societies was called *"ntemi."* There was also a second-in-command and a group of men acting as a council for the leader. Since the voluntary associations extended beyond the borders of chiefdoms, the leaders of these groups were looked upon as men of power and of considerable prestige. Partly because of the status of dance society leaders, new groups formed from time to time as individual members became alienated from an established society.

In almost every respect, the cotton cooperative fitted the pattern of a traditional Sukuma organization. The cooperative of members took different forms but had essentially the same effect whether the activity was cultivating fields or marketing their produce. The theme of the early organizational meetings was one of working together by selling cotton only to the cooperative society. In fact, the traditional fine used in the Basumba and some of the dance societies was employed against members of the cotton cooperative who gave in to the temptation to sell outside of the cooperative before it had attained a monopoly. Such a member had to pay the cooperative society twice what he had received. The society's buying stations even became places at which the traditional dances were held. It may be argued that this had nothing to do with the similarity of the cotton cooperatives and the dance societies, but it was a fact at the time of this study.

The most impressive similarity between the cotton cooperative and the traditional dance societies was the authority structure. Each cooperative society had a chairman and a vice-chairman and a committee which acted as councilors and helpers for the chairman. As the cotton cooperative spread throughout Sukumaland and as it grew in economic importance, the chairman and other officers of each society received respect which they could only have expected if they had held positions of authority in a dance society. Sukuma society did not have any recognized path of upward mobility except within the traditional dance societies. The cotton cooperative opened the way for a great many men, especially young men, to move up without going outside of a traditional type of structure.

The growth of the cotton cooperative was also aided by another element of Sukuma culture — ostracism as a method of social control. After the first thirty societies had been formed, growth took place not only by the addition of new societies, but by the increase of membership in existing societies. Some Sukuma farmers showed reluctance to join the new organization and continued to sell to the representatives of the ginners who became more and more generous as the cooperative grew. As cooperative members gained strength in an area, they threatened to declare the holdouts *mbisi*, which meant that their behavior was to be considered as detrimental to the whole community (Cory 1953:113). A person so declared was cut off from others in the village and surrounding area. No one would speak to him or visit him and villagers would even refuse to help in time of illness or fire in his house. There is no evidence of how effective this method was but is was definitely used when membership was the prime object of the cooperative.

The leaders of the cooperative society used a traditional means of communication in the early days of organization. The dance societies provided recreation for their members by holding song competitions. Each society in a competition was led by a specialist in composing songs and improvising dances. This man was called a *ningi* and he was expected to make up lyrics to fit well-known melodies. The object of the competition was for one group to draw around itself the majority of the spectators. This group would win and share the prize which had been put up by the competition's sponsor. During his performance, the *ningi* would often make up songs on topics of current interest to the people. In a number of cases, the organizers of the cooperative were able to persuade *ningi* to sing about the cooperative, its advantages, and the importance of total participation. Once again, although there is no way to judge just how effective this method of communication was, it probably had some impact because the Sukuma considered the song competitions a kind of oral newspaper. People would come from great distances to hear famous *ningi* and would go away singing the songs they had heard. A clever song could be expected to spread far beyond the group which heard it sung originally.

As a final consideration, there is an aspect of Sukuma culture which may possibly be the most important factor in the rapid and complete acceptance of the cotton cooperative by the Sukuma people. The theme of equality and the mechanisms for maintaining it are suggested in many different ways in Sukuma behavior. Except for chiefs, their families, and the men who have high-status positions in the dance societies, there is a widespread desire among the Sukuma to keep everyone on the same social and economic level. Traditional dress is notable for its drab similarity and houses are in no way an indicator of the wealth of their owners. Food is stored in such a way that those outside the family get no chance to estimate the amount. Cattle, the real criterion of wealth, are put out in trust with friends who live at a distance so that herds will not look too large. When a man is suspected of having a special source of wealth, relatives and friends will seek hospitality until the newly rich is reduced to the level of those around him. Cases came to light in the course of the study indicating that destruction of property and the burning of fields took place simply because the owner seemed wealthier than his neighbors.

If equality maintenance is the proper interpretation of this evidence, the cooperative provided the perfect vehicle for the acquisition of wealth without fear. Each member paid the same entrance fee, the price paid for cotton was fixed before the selling season opened, and all members shared equally in the benefits of dividends distributed as second payments. Moreover, payments for cotton were made in public so that suspicion about secret amassing of wealth could be dispelled.

An interesting part of a speech by Paul Bomani in 1962 suggested that equality maintenance was still operating. Bomani, then a minister in the Tanzanian government, exhorted the Sukuma "to pick all the crop" of cotton. Since prices paid to the farmers were set, there seemed to be no economic reason to let cotton rot in the fields. It was theorized that some growers left the cotton in the fields rather than sell it and be looked upon as more wealthy than others. It would hardly be worth the effort for a farmer to bring in a big crop only to have his wealth drained by demands for hospitality and requests for loans.

CONCLUSION

At the time of this study, the cotton-marketing cooperative was a visible reality all over the 19,000 square miles inhabited by the Sukuma. Over 360 buying stations with their metal storage buildings dotted the landscape. The cooperative was a case of popular participation in the development of both an ethnic group and a nation. At the same time, it represented an innovation introduced to and accepted by a group of people who had not been noted for their willingness to change. The Sukuma were proud of their success in a self-help project they considered completely their own. They were eager to talk about the cooperative and especially proud when they heard that others were using their cooperative as a model to be copied.

In a very real sense, however, the Sukuma people were only acceptors of an innovation brought to them by men who were intercultural in their experience and outlook. Paul Bomani and, to a somewhat lesser extent, those who organized with him, were active innovators who saw a problem, discovered a solution in another society, and finally worked to introduce the new idea to their own people. Their innovation, the cooperative, fit well into Sukuma patterns of organizational structure and behavior. Further, the innovators were able to use many customs to their advantage, but the compatability between the cooperative and traditional Sukuma culture was only a condition, a situational *sine qua non* which aided in their success. Without such intercultural individuals, the cooperative might not have come into being at all, or at least the Sukuma would have remained an exploited people for many more years.

Grass-roots success in economic development always involves more than simple conformity between traditional social structure and innovation. If there can be said to be a key to such success, it must be the combination of cultural compatability and informed, active, innovative work. The intercultural individual knows his own culture and has a feeling for what might be accepted by his people at a particular time and in a given set of circumstances. He also knows how to modify what he learns from other peoples to fit the culture of his own people. No outsider, regardless of ability or training, can think or react as a Sukuma. The true agent of diffusion is the person who passes the knowledge of one people through the filter of his own cultural background.

REFERENCES

CORY, HANS
  1953   *Sukuma law and custom.* London: Oxford University Press.
GORST, SHEILA
  1959   *Co-operative organization in tropical countries: a study of co-operative development in nonself-governing territories under United Kingdom administration, 1945–1955.* Oxford: Blackwell.
JUMA, WAZIRI
  1960   The Sukuma societies of young men and young women. *Tanganyika Notes and Records* 54:27–29.

Traditional Collectivism and Modern Associations: The Example of Southern Dahomey

GABRIEL GOSSELIN

In 1961 the government of Dahomey (West Africa) established a National Society for Rural Development (Société Nationale de Développement Rural or SONADER). Palm oil and palmetto almonds are Dahomey's chief exports. Research to improve the exploitation of the palm groves which cover the south of Dahomey is one of the essential objectives in the development of the country. In order to do this, SONADER has set up rural development zones, which amounts to a kind of agrarian reform without the name, and farming cooperatives to which the peasants who benefit from the redistribution of the land must belong.

About 900,000 inhabitants are divided among the villages of southern Dahomey, where the population density is seventy-five people per square kilometer in the rural areas. The region is administratively divided into three districts — southeast, south, and southwest — in which live 400,000, 214,000, and 290,000 rural inhabitants respectively. The densities of the rural parts of these districts average (in the same order) eighty-five, sixty-seven, and seventy-six inhabitants per square kilometer. The principal rural populations of the southern region are the Nago in the southeast, the Fon in the south, and the Adja in the southwest. These three groups comprise respectively 155,000, 287,000, and 123,000 people. (The Fon are also found in central Dahomey.)

Palm oil and palmetto almonds represent 70 percent of the value of Dahomean exports, a figure which appears all the more important when one considers the fact that in 1962, for example, only 15,000 tons were exported from a total production of about 50,000 tons.

DIVISION OF LABOR AND TRANSFORMATION OF THE TRADITIONAL COLLECTIVE STRUCTURES

It is men especially who perform agricultural tasks. The women rarely take part: it is frowned upon, and they are not obliged to do such work. Women's activities are very specialized and vary according to the season. They have expanded significantly with the development of the market economy. In parctice, all the women are traders, and trading is exclusively a feminine concern. This division between the productive work of the men on the one hand and the processing and trading by the women on the other assures a great deal of independence to the latter in all areas. This division of labor does not mean, however, that men have no monetary income. On the contrary, they often sell maize, and more important, they own the palm trees. All the income from the palm grove is reserved for the men. They also employ one another as salaried workers. But the women have a monopoly of all the local trade. Now, nothing is free in the villages; everything is bought, even between husband and wife.

The distinction between masculine and feminine sources of income is inherited from a tradition which ties each individual to his paternal lineage. This exclusiveness has permitted the formation of a feminine economy which is not subject to the vicissitudes of the husband's farming.

The women, oriented toward speculation and credit, are frequently the creditors of a household, and their financial advances are guaranteed by the future delivery of the crops which their husbands will harvest (Tardits, et al. 1956:12).

Men are obliged to assume irregular, but heavy, expenditures. They are responsible for the basic support of their wives and children. They must assume all costs of farming (notably labor), pay taxes for the whole family, and meet the expenses of recreation and rituals (especially funerals). In masculine budgets, however, the rhythm of income does not correspond to that of expenditures. Of course, their resources could often be increased if new, unworked areas were brought under cultivation, but a lack of cash to pay for the manpower which their own families can no longer sufficiently provide creates a vicious circle tending to reduce the cultivated areas.

When they are unable or unwilling to pawn their land (see Gosselin 1970) or to ask their wives for a cash advance, these peasants try to balance their budgets by hiring themselves out as temporary laborers, or by participating in *tontines*, the very widespread rotating credit associations of southern Dahomey. This type of solidarity, as a defense against the development of the monetary sector and the new expenses which beset the economically isolated individual, is also practiced among women.

The *tontines* are constituted, through individual initiative, by a group of adherents who are committed to periodically depositing a predetermined assessment. The total sum gathered at each collection is then given in rotation to each participant. Participation is voluntary and independent of any familial or residential consideration. Each village includes a great number of such associations, which thus attract considerable funds. Their chief aim is periodically to place sums of money which they could not have amassed through individual savings in the hands of individual peasants; this permits the peasants to meet expenses which are otherwise incompatible with the fragmentation of their income.

The division of activities between men and women limits polygamy, because the head of a family can hardly support more than two spouses and their children. It likewise limits the conflicts between wives, or between husband and wife; each one has a separate budget. But the total amount of productive work is similarly diminished: in the majority of African societies, the women in fact contribute a good share of the agricultural work. In southern Dahomey, the woman is economically indispensable, but her activity is parasitical. The multiplication of transactions is as deplorable as the loss of time.

The number of traders being equal to that of buyers, one can consider that the system is statistically reduced to the following arrangement: the husband sells his crop to his wife, who in turn sells him household food while deducting a profit which constitutes her personal budget (Hurault and Vallet 1963:45).

In southern Dahomey, the woman thus plays the role of a usurious dealer who also assumes the role of a local, but foreign, merchant.

Land tenure in the regions of Abomey and Ouidah differs from land tenure in Porto-Novo and Ouémé. Abomey and Ouidah are characterized by a persistent joint possession, in which ownership is vested in a patrilineage. Corresponding with this form of land tenure is an equally well-preserved, and more hierarchical organization of work, where the most characteristic form is the *donkpé*, the association for collective work grouping all the young men of the village.

This institution antedates the royal dynasty of Abomey, which, however, modified it through manipulation. Under the Abomey kings, the *donkpé* did not work exclusively for the king, but only the king had the right to mobilize all the *donkpé* of the country. The king was known as the "father of the *donkpé*," and a chief of all the *donkpé*, named by the king, lived in his capital.

The *donkpé* is a hierarchical organization. At the top level is the *donkpégan*, assisted by three dignities who second him in funeral ceremonies and in the direction of work. In theory, there is one *donkpégan* per village; the office is hereditary, but each nomination must be formally approved by the king. The *donkpégan* was solemnly enthroned by the *Migan*, the prime minister. His authority is absolute over all men of working age. They cannot refuse to go when called to work, under penalty of fine and at the risk of relinquishing normal funeral ceremonies. In addition, each group of men greater than five automatically falls under the *donkpégan*'s authority. Every man, every collectivity can use the *donkpé*'s work especially for hoeing, the construction of walls, the assembly of roofing. He addresses himself to the *donkpégan* to whom he gives a gift while explaining the task to be performed. The man then sets the day and has the responsibility of providing the food for the workers. He owes nothing else. Moreover if he is poor or sick, very old and alone, the *donkpé* does not demand payment. It thus resembles, in certain cases, a mutual aid society (Mercier 1952:89–90).

In using the *donkpé*, the king theoretically exercised a right which any individual possessed. In reality, it was a way for him to have at his disposal considerable manpower for public works, out of proportion with that available to an ordinary man.

Today, the *donkpé* at work is still a familiar sight of village life. However, the young men are no longer as submissive to the *donkpégan* as in former days. They can escape from his request by emigrating far from their villages, in town, or by hiring themselves out as workers. Mutual aid in work tends to be done by more restricted groups, whose organization is less "official" and less standardized.

The *donkpé* was instituted as we have seen, prior to its use by a conquering, unifying, and organizing dynasty. But it was used and reinterpreted in such a way that today it remains the vestige of a time when everything was or could be submitted to the control of a single man, when the control of the king over the country was complete.

In the other regions of southern Dahomey, the organization of the work has always been more flexible, more decentralized, and more egalitarian; in this context, it is better to speak of mutual aid societies rather than associations for collective work.

At about the age of fifteen years, young men of the same village were organized into an *adjolou*, to which they continued to belong and which aged with them. Only men belonged to this kind of society as it was limited to agricultural work. Each *adjolou* worked by rotation in the fields of its members. This system permitted the peasant farmer to accomplish large tasks without spending money. Juxtaposed without being coordinated or organized hierarchically, these institutions fell within the pattern of most societies in Lower Dahomey.

Their role and their organization evolved with the breaking up of property, and generally speaking, with the crisis of lineage and of relationships within the familial group: by affirming his right to land, the individual renounces henceforth the benefit of the solidarity of a group which he no longer wants to profit from his own work.

That is why the new forms of the *adjolou* are nothing more than teams of men from two or three households. The former system was adapted to an economy wherein several heads of extended families controlled the direction of the work. It lacks flexibility when it comes to responding to the simultaneous needs of several hundred independent landowners.

In order to augment the mutual aid teams — and often even to replace them — the farmers call upon wage labor. In fact, only the cost of the laborers limits their use and necessitates the continuity of the traditional mutual aid.

This simultaneous use of a traditional form and a modern form of the organization of work, neither of which responds fully to the demands of exploitation, masks the present inadaptability of the social structure to the modern economy (Tardits, et al. 1956:47).

This growth of wage labor is an extremely important phenomenon. Two or three decades — a generation — ago the villages included, apart from a few artisans, only one category of rural folk: extended families jointly working their collective property. Today a great economic and social differentiation has taken place.

The full-time laborers are men whose land may have been lost as a consequence, for example, of a mortgage or a trial, or adults belonging to large families who may no longer be satisfied by the rewards, partly in kind, derived from working increasingly crowded family lands (Tardits, et al. 1956:40).

Temporary workers are recruited among landowners who work borrowed lands and users of mortgaged land.

What is essential in the growth of agricultural wage labor is this necessity for members of extended-family operations and the users of borrowed or mortgaged land to find a complementary source of revenue; that of their own farm is not sufficient. The situation of the landowners is not very good either, as many of them control insufficient family manpower — despite an often small acreage — and do not have enough money to pay laborers. Sometimes forced to rent out their own labor, they can scarcely think of increasing their domain, their manpower, or their revenue.

The troubles of a large part of the palm groves are thus connected to discrepancies between the property structure (size of properties), the social structure (size of families), and the economic structure (level of monetary revenue). Because of the archaic techniques of exploitation, of the division of labor which bars half of the active population from agriculture, and the inability of old forms of solidarity to adapt, only wage labor currently brings to the economy of Lower Dahomey the flexibility necessary for its evolution, for its very survival. The situation remains paradoxical — under-exploitation of the land or the palm groves and the feeble cash revenue, lack of manpower and underemployment of women, cash needs in agriculture and profitable parasitism of the activities of processing and of commercialization. The equilibrium between large properties and large families no longer exists, and nothing has yet replaced it.

It would be inexact, however, to consider wage labor as established in the villages and rapidly developing. It is more a question of tendencies which are still curbed and sometimes reinterpreted by old habits and values. The work contract usually lasts only a day or two, from 6 A.M. until 1 P.M.; the rest of the time is given over to the personal work of the wage earners. Then again, it is very often the same individuals who are in turn employers and employees, to the point that one can see there the evolution, into a monetary system, of the former system of mutual aid. Another tendency confirms this analogy: rather than engaging ten men for ten days, the one who leases the land will prefer to engage fifty men for two days, in order to increase the rivalry and the festival character which characterized the former days of collective work. Very few live only from their wages; the system of pawning and of borrowing allows each one to find land, provided that he changes field each year — this is judged preferable to wage labor. Also, few live only from the work of others without working the land themselves. However, it is a matter of prestige to be able to hire salaried workers, and those who habitually work as laborers have less prestige.

PRODUCTION COOPERATIVES: SOCIAL CATEGORIES AND TRADITION

The Integration of the Different Social Categories into the Cooperatives

The agrarian reform of SONADER does not intervene to destroy or change traditional joint possession. It intervenes in order to remedy the inconveniences of the disruption which has already upset the old property structures. In the same way, the "obligatory" cooperatives do not oppose traditional structures of "collectivist" work, nor are they grafted on to them. They are organized in a rural community where these structures are already decomposing and on the way to being replaced by agricultural wage labor. All the institutions which used to permit a grouping of efforts and the accomplishment of great works of public interest are in fact corroded by the development of "individualism." "The organizing capacity of the contemporary Dahomean farmers is no more than a slight fraction of that of the preceding generations" (Hurault and Vallet 1963:49).

The cooperatives of SONADER are, above all, cooperatives for the communal farming of the "reconstituted" palm groves. But on lands officially regrouped within a rural development sector or zone, the different categories of peasants profit unequally from the creation of an infrastructure and thus have more or less interest in rationalizing the exploitation of the palm groves to the maximum.

1. The OWNER-OPERATORS are the most involved and the most concerned. They are also the very large majority. They collect a 3 percent interest on the value of their land and rebates proportionate to their work time.

2. The SONS OR NEPHEWS of the men in the first category, dependent family members who are limited in number, do not collect either rent on the land or rebates; they profit only from the enrichment of the head of their family and only insofar as he shares it with them.

There exists, however, an ambiguity in the regulations which do not indicate whether the rebates of the owner-operators are proportionate to their personal work time or to the total work of the various members of their families. In the first case, the work of the sons and the nephews would receive no recompense. Such a solution would be profoundly unjust. It would be inefficient besides, because it would not incite the young men to work and would make the heads of families totally indifferent to the work of their dependents. In these conditions, the family would be quickly reduced to its head alone.

Instead one must accept the second situation in which the head of the family profits from the work of his dependents. Just and effective in the framework of the traditional values and solidarities, such a situation will appear more and more unjust to the young, in the context of an economy based on individual stimulation and responsibility within which the reflexes of protection and solidarity on the part of the head of the family risk being stifled. It will appear especially maladapted to the collective economy which the SONADER wants to implement insofar as this experiment is intended to develop new solidarities and more rational behavior. It finally risks discouraging the interest of the younger generation who will, however, be indispensable in a few years when the cooperatives will be truly self-managed. There is a strong chance that the dependent family members will feel more and more intensely their economic and social dependence, even if, objectively, they gain by the enrichment of the heads of their families. For their part, the latter cannot avoid being tempted to use their dependents to increase their wealth through the cooperative. The generation conflicts are thus likely to become increasingly severe.

This movement is all the more predictable because another rule forbids members of the immediate family of the landowners to join the cooperative as workers. This is being done to limit the disintegration — already very advanced — of the families and to preserve their economic and social integrity. In fact, it only leads to imprisoning the young, in the new cooperative structure, within the same traditional dependence relationship. This rule — the rebates going only to the heads of the families, and the prohibition on young dependents joining as workers — can only increase the conflicts. It is thus contradictory to the goal which it is supposed to favor.

Ousted from all direct participation in the cooperatives as being immediate relatives of landowners, practically excluded from the financial benefits which they received as traditional dependents, how can the young hope to participate in the movement? They do not have the means to lease land. Their only outlet is to borrow a parcel of land so that they may be considered as independent workers. Yet, they must find something to borrow. If not, the only thing left is to emigrate. For this social category, statistically a minority but important for the future, the perspectives for integration are therefore gloomy.

Their natural tendency already is to flee their villages. For them to remain and participate in cooperative development, they must be able to belong as workers. It is difficult to envisage a means which will compel the heads of families to hand over to them the rebates corresponding to their work; and they cannot draw them directly, because they are not shareholders. Even if juggling the accounts permitted it, what would they live on while waiting for the cooperative to have profits to share out?

3. The position of the FARMERS OF PAWNED LAND is not very clear either. If the pawn is considered a sale, then the pawnee can join as an owner-operator. This is a fair but unlikely solution, for there is likely to be pressure to retain at least the old property structures and family properties (in other words, the traditional landowners). In order to achieve this, however, a second solution would be more willingly accepted: the pawnee can belong only as a worker, and the pawner is considered as a nonfarming landowner.

But the attempt to reconcile the requirements of the property system with the rules of modern cooperative organization can only be a mask for a choice which cannot be acknowledged, or for an illusion. It is in fact the pawner who then profits from the cooperative at the expense of the pawnee; he receives from the pawnee the monetary value of his parcel of land, according to the old rules, and he receives from the cooperative a rent, according to the new rules. On the other hand, the pawnee has paid twice — once to the pawner for the land he farms, and once to the cooperative for his share as a member — because he will have to work 200 days to have even the right to a share as a worker. There again, one must therefore choose between the preservation of old property laws and the change which the introduction of land into the monetary system represents; in other words, one must choose between the traditional landowners who become incapable of exploiting their land and the pawnees, even if they are "capitalists," who develop the land. This option is confirmed as even more urgent inasmuch as pawning is a very widespread practice.

4. The situation of the FARMERS OF BORROWED LAND, who are few in number, is more distinct. They are considered by the cooperatives as non-landowning workers. In this way, a "full-share" participation, which they cannot hope to obtain in the traditional system, is offered to them after 200 days of work. Therefore, they have everything to gain from a cooperative action and nothing to lose — because they have paid nothing to the lender and because their position is precarious.

5. The NONFARMING LANDOWNERS are, for the most part, elderly people who can no longer work. The rent, which is limited to 1.5 percent and which the cooperative gives to them (as interest on their shares as members), permits them to live. Their position seems to be unambiguous.

However, the status of the existing cooperatives in fact excludes them from management. Logical from a perspective of rationalizing farming and stimulating development, such a measure almost certainly appears discriminatory to the interested parties — according to the traditional system to which they most often refer. In the traditional system, age and power are in fact synonymous, and an elderly and influential man may not work with his hands. Here again, it is necessary to make a choice. It is very significant to observe that it has been resolved, by the majority of the members of cooperatives, in a sense unfavorable to tradition.

The existence of nonfarming landowners implies the existence of NONLANDOWNING FARMERS. They may be sons or nephews; their situation then risks appearing to them even more unjust than if the head of the family himself worked. They can also be pledgees or borrowers. They can even be full-time or part-time laborers.

6.   In the cooperatives, the PART-TIME LABORERS have the status corresponding to their principal activity: farming landowner, dependent family member, pawnee, or borrower.

7.   The situation of the FULL-TIME WORKERS is much more instructive. To men lacking land and prestige in the traditional context, the cooperative movement offers a totally new possibility of gaining a place in their society; they have only to work 200 days. Insofar as wage earning is an important tendency in the evolution of southern Dahomey, it is a matter of great significance and important implications. Here the "revolutionary" vocation of the cooperation is manifested in the strict sense; it goes against the stream and is proposed as a complete alternative to the traditional socioeconomic system, slowly being integrated into an exchange economy.

By refusing to the nonworkers, be they landowners or elderly men, management rights in the cooperatives, and by offering to the workers, be they laborers lacking all prestige, the right to this same control, the cooperative movement of the SONADER is opposed both to the traditional rules and to the logic of the market economy. That which tradition has proved incapable of doing — preventing wage labor — the cooperative movement can succeed in doing. That which the market economy has proved incapable of doing — rationalizing exploitations and their administration — the cooperative movement can again succeed in doing.

Cooperative legislation and regulations were first intended for the owner-operators, who are the most numerous. The nonfarming landowners and the full-time laborers are marginal categories, diametrically opposed, and few in number. But particularly for these reasons the analysis of their position within the cooperative reveals the underlying tendencies of the program of action undertaken by the SONADER. In order to be consistent, and to attain the goal which it seeks, this organization must, however, remove the remaining ambiguities concerning the cooperative status of the intermediary categories, for they are also important. The dependent family members represent the future of the movement, and they must be able to join it as workers. The farmers of pawned lands are numerous, and this practice is revealed as one tending toward sales. The pawns must be transformed into real sales, and the real pawnees must be made to participate as owner-operators.

When the palm groves reach their productive stage, when the movement becomes self-managed, the SONADER's joint-farming cooperatives will compensate their members with rebates proportionate not to production but to the time spent at work. If one considers that the acreage is remunerated by the interest paid on the membership shares of the landowners, and that the rebates must be based on the quantity of work furnished, one thus avoids paying the landowners twice — once for their land and once for the production of that land, which is necessarily related to the amount of land. In this way one encourages the work of nonlandowners, who will be able to have membership shares and rebates commensurate with their work and to earn — as the landowners do — interest on their shares. This solution therefore encourages all to work and tends to equalize the situations of the landowners and of the workers; on this point again, only the cooperative movement can hope to act with neither hypocrisy nor lies.

This action, however, has its limitations, and the situations of the different social categories will never be altogether the same. The landowners, in fact, can also acquire shares through their work. Small landowners who work a great deal will therefore be able to "overtake" lazy large landowners; and dedicated nonlandowners will be able to obtain a position analogous to that of certain landowners. Given equal work, however, the large landowners will remain richer than the small landowners, who will remain richer than the nonlandowners. Each one, certainly, will have the same "weight" in the joint management — one man equals one vote. But one cannot base the existence of the cooperatives totally on the principle "to each according to his work"; the existence and the importance of property rights will always play a role in some way unless property rights are suppressed, which is not contemplated.

The cooperatives of the SONADER therefore encourage work and tend to equalize the situations of the landowners and the workers, but they do not suppress the differences related to the right of property itself.

The Role of Women in Development

All the social categories analyzed thus far are composed only of men. Women are excluded from rights to land; agriculture is the task of men; the revenue from the palm groves is monopolized by men. Women apply themselves to the activities of processing and trade.

In the traditional society as transformed by a market economy, the economic function of the women, although parasitic in large part, is indispensable (given the division of labor between the sexes). But in a cooperative economy — even one limited to the palm grove — their role becomes much less necessary. For here they no longer carry out the processing and commercialization of the products of the palm grove, and the cash income earned by the men permits the men to limit the role of their spouses even in the production of food crops. Even if specialists in the processing and commercialization of food crops do not emerge, the men no longer resort to borrowing money from their wives. The old division of work has been transformed.

Dispossessed in large part of her habitual "fief," what role can a woman have in development? The SONADER has not foreseen anything on this subject. Let us only say here that three directions are possible. First, the creation of cooperatives of transformation or — especially — of commercialization can be instigated and entrusted to the women. The "cooperative sector" is thus extended, and the division of work between the sexes is reestablished on another level. Second, the women can be included in the male farm cooperatives which will probably be very difficult. In order to do this, some strong habits of organization would have to be broken, some basic property rights of women would have to be recognized, female work in the palm grove would have to be accepted by all. The obstacles seem insurmountable. Or, the last solution, women can be left outside the cooperative economy; in other words, the situation is allowed to develop. By doing this, one is deprived of the work and the skill of half of the active population, and we run the risk of a "proletarianization," or a revolt, of the women.

It is interesting to compare here the situation of the women of the Dahomean palm groves with the women of the palm groves of Adioukrou in the Ivory Coast. There, the traditional collective structures have been preserved in large part and subsist alongside an "individualistic" and monetary economic sector. The great dry-season harvest keeps its character of a collective operation divided among the different age-grades and between the sexes. The processing operations are also done collectively, and the profits are not divided; they are added to the joint property of the clan (here matrilineal), administered like public funds by its chief. During the rest of the year and for other activities, the members of the village work for themselves and sell for themselves. The woman transports, processes, and sells, but the man receives the money and pays his spouse like a wage earner.

The monetary sector has therefore profoundly penetrated this society, which, nonetheless, keeps some solid collective structures. The palm tree has been there as long as in Dahomey and is as badly cared for. But, while in Dahomey the palm tree assumes more and more importance and this increasing interest entails a development in the exchange economy, in the Ivory Coast it formerly had a great value which it has slowly lost; coffee and cacao are now producing a much greater profit, and the old palm oil trade has not been replaced by a modern commerce. The collective structures formerly associated with the palm tree could be maintained because the palm tree is losing ground. If it had gained ground as in Dahomey, the whole economy of Adioukrou would be "individualistic" and money oriented.

Whatever may be the case, from a similar division of labor between sexes one observes two divergent evolutions: integrated into the collective organization or paid by her husband, the Adioukrou woman remains dependent. The Dahomean woman, in contrast, has acquired a great autonomy, rejects the collective constraints, and organizes processing and commercialization for her own profit. She is carried, one could say, by the general movement, while the Adioukrou woman is held back in her emancipation by the economic regression.

This comparison points out well that traditions do not foster development. On the contrary, development breaks the old collective structures (Dahomey). These structures are maintained only if development is at a standstill (Adioukrou).

Traditional Collectivism and Production Cooperation

Such an interpretation is contrary to that proposed by some German authors, especially Trappe and Seibel. Seibel in fact analyzes the *donkpé* as a "traditional cooperative." After having written "…there are quite a few elements in the social structure of traditional society and its culture which are favorable to a cooperative organization in its modern sense," he adds: "there are even in traditional Africa many organizations which can be called traditional cooperatives or pre-cooperatives or pre-forms of cooperatives… they are cooperatives not in the modern legal sense, but in their sociological structure… and this alone is of importance (Seibel 1966:1).

The author bases his remarks on a conference of African cooperative movements held in Tanzania in 1962, which was attended by the representatives of about ten English-speaking countries. This reunion, writes Seibel, had arrived at this conclusion: "The social structure of traditional African society is most favorable to the implantation of cooperatives, and there are certain socio-economic elements in traditional society which reveal a cooperative character" (Seibel 1966:1). After having emphasized that these traditional structures include communal and individual elements, he gives certain examples of "precooperatives," including the *donkpé*.

He admits in conclusion, however, that "the push to modernization usually came from outside, e.g. from the government, and not from the cooperative itself." Despite that, he thinks that it is possible to transform the traditional forms of cooperation into modern forms by "modernizing" the methods of production, the products, or the organization. "It is quite sure that the fact of the existence of traditional cooperatives creates basically a positive attitude to the foundation of modern cooperatives and a readiness to the participation in its activities, supposing an economic aim is given" (Seibel 1966:18).

This interpretation does not seem to be at all evident to us. To recognize that old habits and structures must have an economic goal and an innovative impulse imposed or proposed from the outside is already to admit that these traditions cannot "evolve" of themselves. But one must go further.

We have analyzed the decline of the forms of mutual aid and the growth of wage labor. In all of southern Dahomey, properties and families are splitting up, and the traditional solidarities are under strain. We have especially seen that the cooperative movement emerging from the SONADER was obliged to oppose both the old collective structures and the laissez faire policy of the market economy. If this experience has some chances of success — and we believe that it has — it is precisely because it refuses to "return to the traditional origins" without, however, ceasing to present itself as an alternative to the degradation of these collective structures by the market economy. And it is insofar as it hesitates about the choices which are imposed upon it that it runs the risk of laying itself open to some fatal ambiguities. If we compare it to some other experiments in development, we see in fact that it has owed its chances for success to a traditional milieu long encroached upon by colonial capitalism, and to men already sensitized to the monetary economy.

Not only is it impossible, thus, for traditions to evolve from themselves, but they are also opposed to any evolution. To recognize that the traditions cannot lead to development by themselves is to recognize already that they block development. This is so because to instigate or direct movement "from the outside" is to control, limit, extend, or to regiment tradition in such a way that tradition serves a cause and utilizes means which it would not have chosen by itself. To recognize that one must "go outside tradition" ever so little is to admit that tradition is an iron collar. To recognize that one must ever so little "use it" is to admit that in itself it is useless and harmful. As soon as one admits the necessity of intervening in the functioning of traditional institutions or in their "natural" evolution, one changes the meaning of these institutions, and one imposes a new logic. Even if one can still use old habits, reflexes, knowhow, and mechanisms, they no longer enable one to master the situation.

Such is the case with the *donkpé*. Formerly, before the conquest of the country by the Abomey dynasty, the *donkpé* was an institution of mutual aid. Used by the new royalty, it was reinterpreted; it became a means of requisitioning manpower, an institution serving hierarchies. Those peasants who fled the Abomey region to settle in the south certainly saw it that way. Obligatory work groups in the service of powerful men, the *donkpé* were therefore no longer "democratic" tools at the time of colonization, which, though it suppressed the power of the ruler of Abomey, did not erase the memories and the suspicious reactions of the peasants. In the regions of Abomey and Ouidah, the *donkpé* retains, moreover, its character of *corvée* in the service of large landowners and the important families.

In independent Dahomey, the SONADER undertakes an "obligatory" reorganization of lands, in certain places, but it does not force the peasants to work on these reorganized lands. On the contrary, in the case of the refusal of the landowners it calls upon the voluntary labor of nonlandowning workers. Therefore it is not undertaking any action "in line with" the *donkpé*; the work in the farm cooperatives is not work for the chiefs; cooperative work is not donated work.

In regard to the forms of mutual aid of the *adjolou* type, it has been seen that they cannot be used in property and social structures which have been broken and dispersed; they are breaking up because they too have been reduced to work of minor importance. The problem of the utilization of the traditional structures poses itself only if these structures are extant.

The cooperative movement must therefore invent new solidarities. If it seeks to use the typical "reflexes" of the *donkpé* or of the *adjolou*, it will doubtless perceive that these "reflexes" are closely related to particular situations and structures and that it can be dangerous to resurrect ghosts. Even though it has started out well, the movement can still deviate toward, and be swallowed up by, ambiguity and compromise a situation which will not be a loss for some such as the local chiefs, the big landowners, and other urban speculators.

REFERENCES

GOSSELIN, G.
  1970 *Développement et tradition dans les sociétés rurales africaines.* Geneva: International Labor Organization.
HURAULT, J., J. VALLET
  1963 *Mission d'étude des structures agraires dans le Sud-Dahomey.* Paris: Institut Géographique National.

MERCIER, P.
1952 *Le travail en Afrique noire*. Paris: Présence Africaine.
SEIBEL, D.
1966 "Cooperatives in traditional Africa and their relevance for a modern cooperative movement." Unpublished manuscript.
TARDITS, C., *et al.*
1956 *Société paysanne et problèmes fonciers de la palmeraie dahoméenne*. Paris: L'Homme d'Outre Mer.
TRAPPE, P.
1966 *Entwicklungsfunktion des Genossenschaftswesens am Beispiel ost-afrikanischer Stämme*. Berlin: Luchterhand.

Rural Competition and the Cooperative Monopoly: A Ugandan Case Study

JOAN VINCENT

The Gondo cotton-marketing cooperative was officially recognized in October 1956 and served three northern Teso (Uganda) parishes. Until 1968 it coexisted alongside an Asian-owned ginnery which both bought and processed cotton. In 1966-67, 87 percent of the population of Gondo parish sold its cotton to the Asian ginnery. Gondo parish has had a markedly polyethnic population since 1912 and the membership of the voluntary cooperative marketing association included members of ten ethnic groups, both sexes, both political parties, and all religious denominations. Its membership was, however, predominantly of wealthier, older farmers and thus age and social class differences were reflected in its composition. Moreover, the advantages of membership served to reinforce these cleavages. Its leadership was of poorly educated men. Competition in the parish at large was largely cohortative among "Big Men" and occurred within the cooperative arena and in competition for agricultural labor.

After 1968 the cooperative society had a monopoly in cotton buying. Officials from Ngora in southern Teso, men with more advanced education, were sent in to run it; membership became *de facto* obligatory; ethnicity was politicized, the management expressing hostility against non-Iteso as well as against non-UPC (Uganda Peoples Congress) parishioners.

Economic arguments against monopoly abound; this case study ex-

My fieldwork in Teso District was carried out as a research fellow at the East African Institute of Social Research from 1966 to 1967 and financed by a grant from the Ministry of Overseas Development, London. Enquiries into the Teso Cooperative Union, as well as into the primary society, were first made at the request of Dr. E. A. Brett. I would like to thank Dr. Brett, M. Crawford Young, Raymond Apthorpe, and Colin Leys for keeping me abreast in the field of cooperative studies in Eastern Africa.

plores some of the political and social side-effects of monopoly in one
rural area that had previously known economic competition.

GONDO TOWNSHIP AND PARISH

Before placing the development of the Gondo Farmers Cooperative
Society within the context of rural economic and political competition, it
is necessary to look at the social composition of Gondo Township and the
parish in which it lies.

Gondo Township was established at the eastern end of Lake Kyoga by
the Uganda Protectorate government in 1912. It was intended as a major
port for cotton and cattle export from the eastern region and for the import of men and material to open up the territory to economic development. Within a few years, two cotton ginneries had been built in Gondo
— both, at that time, European owned. The township's population in
1912 consisted of eight Europeans, ten Asians, and over 5,000 Africans;
but, as the commercial prosperity of the port increased, the relative numbers of European and Asian shopkeepers, ginnery employees, officials of
government, port, railway, post and telegraph, and commercial entrepreneurs also increased, while that of the African population (many of
whom had been recruited as laborers in the construction phase of the
township) declined. By 1929, when the railway reached Soroti, the administrative center of Teso District, Gondo had become a backwater and
the district had been opened up for expansion through its three southern
counties.

By 1966 the population of Gondo had shrunk to 819, of whom seven
were Asians and none European. There was only one ginnery, Asian-
owned. Its employees might be placed in at least ten distinct ethnic categories, but 20.5 percent of them were permanent residents of Gondo
parish. The commerce of Gondo centered around eight small shops and,
seasonally, around the ginnery gates where itinerant traders from the
neighboring countryside sold their wares. Commercial fishing had developed since 1912 and, by 1966, provided an important source of income,
mostly for Kenyi and Luo fishing teams. Cattle were highly valued by the
Teso and other parishioners for social reasons, but few entered the local
market. Agriculture consisted primarily of subsistence cultivation, the
staple being millet. Although cotton had been introduced into Teso as
early as 1908, the acreage devoted to it in 1966 was small, no peasant
growing more than two acres. There was no systematic diversification or
large-scale marketing of minor crops. Marketing facilities were poor. A

government marketplace had burned down in 1956 and had never been rebuilt; a weekly market held in the open on the outskirts of Gondo was sparsely attended. All cotton was sold either to the Gondo Farmers Cooperative Society (formed in 1956) or to the Asian-owned Gondo ginnery; the price was set by the government and was thus identical at both places. Cotton sold at both places was processed at the ginnery.

The Gondo Farmers Cooperative Society served what are today the three parishes of Ogera, Gondo, and Ogelak. This study is concerned primarily with Gondo parish, although comparative data are drawn upon where this is useful. Intensive fieldwork inquiries were carried out in Gondo between 1966–67; a short return visit in 1970 permitted the comparison of conditions then with those prevailing at the earlier period. It is hoped that this analysis may be placed alongside the results of what *The Times Literary Supplement's* review of Chayanov's "Theory of Peasant Economy" called "aggregism" (1968:1422) and what Widstrand termed "single operationalism":

As always when we try to discuss complicated but probably real concepts like justice, love or cooperation, there is a risk to yield to "aggregism" — the attempt to avoid small-scale field studies by confining analysis and policy to the manipulation of big aggregates — or "single operationalism" — love is a warm puppy, cooperatives are good for you, etc. (1970:11).

Our research was directed towards finding out just whom cooperatives are good for in one Ugandan parish.

PHASES IN THE DEVELOPMENT OF THE COOPERATIVE MOVEMENT

The relationship between the cooperative movement and the government of Uganda has always been a somewhat ambiguous one. The cooperative movement began in Uganda, as in other British East African territories, as a protest against the large role of Asian entrepreneurs in the marketing and processing industries and, as such, as a protest against the prevailing regime.

In Teso District in eastern Uganda, the movement was sparked by organizers from the Federation of Uganda African Farmers. Rural discontent, expressed largely by small shopkeepers, traders, and the more ambitious farmers, was provided with a vehicle of protest. The Teso administration moved in quickly to suppress the indigenous movement, countering with a bureaucratically organized Cooperative Department. This provided for more economically viable marketing societies, as it could be informally supported by the infrastructure of the administration and the Teso local government — but it was, from the point of view of the aspiring entrepreneurs, politically bankrupt. During this period (which in Teso we may date from 1956 to 1963) government policy was directed "as much, if not more, towards the control of the cooperative movement, than towards the stimulation of societies" (Apthorpe 1972: 151). In his annual report of 1953 the District Commissioner had regretted the delay in the appointment of a Cooperative Officer, because in the interim the Federation of Uganda Farmers had organized "quasi-political marketing groups" throughout the district. But by 1954 he was able to report that thirty-four of the existing forty-two cooperative societies had been brought under the aegis of the Iteso Cooperative Union (Teso District Archives n.d.a).

During the first years of independence when the reins were formally in the hands of the Democratic Party (DP), there was no marked change in cooperative policy. With the assumption of power by the UPC, however, and even more after the "Move to the Left" of 1966, the relationship between the Cooperative Movement and the ruling Party became increasingly involuted. Several former cooperative officials occupied prominent positions in the Obote government (Brett 1970: 13) and, by 1968, cooperatives had been given complete control over the processing of both coffee and cotton. The ultimate ideological expression of the UPC goals to re-educate the citizenry "towards co-operation in the management of economic institutions, and away from individual and private enrichment" came in "The Common Man's Charter" in 1969 (Uganda Government 1969: 18).

Although the formation of a society in Gondo in 1956 was comparatively late in Uganda's cooperative history (the first society of major importance having been formed in Buganda in 1923), it was well within the mainstream of the cooperative movement's struggle for the cotton marketing and processing industry. There were 401 primary societies in the agricultural sector and five unions representing 36,620 farmers in 1951; by 1967 half a million farmers were enrolled in 1,920 primary societies which belonged to thirty-one producers' unions (Kasfir 1970: 178). The Gondo Farmers Cooperative Society was, however, unique in that it was the last in Uganda to have to face the marketing competition of an Asian-owned ginnery within the parish.

Cooperative enthusiasm in Gondo was sparked by a visit of Ignatius Muzazi to Serere Township in 1955,[1] and, in its first phase, the society

---

[1] Accounts of the Muzazi movement may be found in Shepherd (1955) and Stonehouse (1960).

was most certainly an institutional protest against Asian predominance in commerce. Very quickly, however, political criticism was subverted and within a year the Gondo society was registered, allocated a number, inspected, controlled, and sanctioned by the Cooperative Department. Those founding members who had seen in the movement a vehicle for political mobilization turned their energies elsewhere; in the case of Gondo's leaders, to UPC party activity (Vincent 1970). When, after independence, government policy urged the development of Uganda's agriculture through the cooperative movement, the local society again became the institution of a "moral community" — this time not one with racially negative overtones (the African "we" against the Asian "they") — but a moral community of government supporters, of political activists in a period of postpartum political apathy. Finally, with the acquisition of the Gondo ginnery by the Iteso Cooperative Union and its monopoly over cotton marketing, the local society ultimately became that "mainly economic institution" that it is perceived to be elsewhere in East Africa (Migot-Adholla 1970), wholly government sponsored, relying for economic survival on compulsory membership and, in the eyes of the peasant farmer, part and parcel of government itself.

Distinctions between government, administration, and agricultural marketing have always been fine in Teso. Cotton had been introduced by the colonial government backed by the coercive acts of local chiefs. Later, bylaws of the District Council regulated seed distribution, the acreages sown, spraying, spacing, uprooting, and burning. Marketing zones and the annual cotton price were decided in Entebbe. Those who broke the regulations were subject to beatings, fines, or imprisonment. Only once in Teso's history was the peasant's potential power of withholding his crop from the market used against the administration, and only at the instigation of a "renegade" county chief (Vincent f.c.). Throughout its development the cooperative society was organizationally (if not structurally and ideologically) as much a part of Teso District administration as the hierarchy of village, parish, subcounty, and county chiefs. This was most forcibly seen in Gondo in June 1966 when, after a series of abortive attempts to collect sufficient members, the only special general meeting that could be assembled came together under the auspices not only of the cooperative officials but also of the parish and subcounty chief (Soroti Cooperative Records n.d.a).

Perhaps it was not then a very marked change in the affairs of Teso when the cooperative movement came to be viewed as an economic arm of government, or more specifically of "the UPC, the ruling party," as one respondent after another described it in 1967. Yet there was a very marked change in the cooperative affairs of Gondo parish after the mono-poly of 1968. Until that time the Cooperative Society, like all other forms of national penetration into the parish, was mediated by local men and assimilated, as it were, into the existing, constantly changing, patterns of rural life. After 1968, however, the bounds of the arena were enlarged, as we shall see, and new representatives of an alien political class[2] took over the cooperative affairs of the parish. They came from Ngora county in southern Teso. They were salaried officials and, by and large, they looked on the lesser-educated parish leaders as inferiors. The cooperative monop-oly had pradoxical implications both for the well-being of the Gondo peasants and for national ideology in 1968.

Introduced as a means of organizing the interests of African cotton growers against the commercial interests of Liverpool and Bombay, the cooperative movement became, after independence, an ideological vehicle for the expression of party sentiments about the welfare of the peasant farmer and the creation of national unity and, in the later part of Obote's period in office, it was also a grassroots organization to counter the emer-gence of class in a socialist state. By 1970 the Cooperative Union, as it had developed in Teso District, was more a motor of *embourgeoisement* than a driving force in Obote's move to the left.

Before considering this further, it is necessary to present in some detail the working of the Gondo Farmers Cooperative Society, both as an economic institution and as a political arena before 1968, in order to de-scribe how competition worked itself out in the context of the local econo-my and grassroots politics. The social and political effects of that situation will then be compared with the effects of monopoly.

THE COOPERATIVE SOCIETY AS AN ECONOMIC INSTITUTION

A comparison must be made at the outset between the economic costs of selling cotton to the Gondo ginnery and to the Cooperative Society. An

---

[2]   See First (1970: 10): "African development has been held to ransom by the emergence of a new, privileged, African class. It grows through politics, under party systems, under military governments, from the ranks of business and from the corporate elites that run the state, the army and the civil service.... National styles, territorial distinctions, and even divergent policy commitments blur into the continent-wide style of the newly rich. They are obsessed with property and personal performance in countries where all but a tiny fringe own hardly more than a hoe, a plastic bucket, an ironware cooking pot or two, and perhaps a bicycle."

underlying assumption is made by many that each grower will want to maximize profits and that, "all things being equal," he may do so. In the following section, this assumption will be questioned.

The distance of a grower's homestead from either ginnery or cooperative store would appear a likely factor in his consideration of where to sell his crop. The cooperative store was situated at the northern end of Ogera parish in 1966, about four miles away from the ginnery which lay at the heart of Gondo Township. The homesteads in two of Gondo's six wards (Aojabule and Agologolo) were indisputably closer to the cooperative society than to the ginnery. Kabola ward, lying along the shore of Lake Kyoga to the north of Agologolo, lay midway between ginnery and store. Another ward, Adiding, lay to the east of the ginnery but entirely within the township's two-mile radius; the township ward enveloped the ginnery and the westerly ward of Opucet lay on the other side of it.

Thus for the cotton growers of the two southern wards it was clearly closer to transport their cotton to the cooperative; for those of one ward the matter was debatable, but for the remaining three wards the ginnery was certainly closer. In the light of these considerations, figures showing the distribution of cooperative members by ward in Gondo parish (Table 1) take on some significance. It will be seen that in the two

Table 1. Cooperative Society members by ward (Gondo parish)

Ward	Number of		
	Household heads	Cooperative members	Percentage
Aojabule	20	9	45
Agologolo	29	5	17.2
Kabola	35	3	8.5
Adiding	28	4	14.3
Township	103	11	10.7
Opucet	63	6	9.5

closest wards 45 and 17.2 percent of the peasants sold their cotton to the cooperative store; in the marginal ward only 8.5 percent of the peasants were members of the society; and in the three wards closest to the ginnery 11.5 percent (on average) belonged to the Cooperative Society and, in many cases, actually transported their cotton past the gates of the ginnery to take it to the store.

The Gondo Farmers Cooperative Society, as we have seen, draws its membership from three parishes. The homesteads of Ogera parish as a whole are nearer to the cooperative store and over half of the Society's membership is made up of Ogera farmers. Ogelak parish lies on the western side of Gondo and is farthest from the Cooperative Society. Only one farmer in nineteen in Ogelak belonged to the cooperative in 1960, in spite of a store having been set up at certain periods in Ogelak to facilitate their membership. Correspondingly, Ogelak parish accounted for only 8.5 percent of the Society's members. (These population figures refer to adult males, and it is assumed that all residents grow some cotton). It is in Gondo parish, lying between Ogera and Ogelak, that factors other than distance and proximity can most readily be perceived.

The question of proximity is, of course, clearly related to the matter of transport. For the cotton grower who sold to the ginnery, distance was no economic cost, since the ginnery trucks were sent out to make door-to-door collections. This had been the practice for several decades and a large part of the work of the parish chief and the ward headmen had consisted of seeing that the paths linking the dispersed homesteads were kept cleared. Growers who needed cash in a hurry carried loads of cotton to the ginnery on the backs of bicycles, but this was rare and had, in the past, been discouraged by the administration, as the cotton might be damaged in transit. Members of the Cooperative Society, on the other hand, were responsible for carrying their crop to the cooperative store themselves, and the bicycle was the sole form of transport used. There were no wheeled trucks, private cars, or any other four-wheeled forms of conveyance in the parish.[3]

Transport difficulties affected the cooperative member in another way. After purchase by the officials, cotton was kept at the cooperative store until it could be taken to the ginnery, where it was passed to Patel for processing and for seed extraction. (Gondo lay in a segregated zone in which all cotton grown had, by statute, to be sent only to that one ginnery.) For this, trucks were required and these had to be hired from Patel who owned the only fleet in the area. The Cooperative Secretary-Manager charged that Patel often kept him waiting three days for the trucks and, during that time, the cooperative could not buy cotton from the growers because its storage sheds were full. Many members became dissatisfied and sold their cotton directly to the ginnery in spite of the fact that they might be fined for doing so. As Patel, the ginnery owner, explained, his trucks were naturally fully engaged in his own cotton collection at that time; to let the cooperative hire them at all was a magnanimous concession on his part and, he might have added, not a matter of good business, as the Society

---

[3]   This is not strictly accurate. An Asian mechanic living permanently at the ginnery had a car, although it was up on blocks during 1966–67. There were 128 bicycles in Gondo in 1966. Only on four occasions was I asked to carry cotton in my Renault Roho — an indication of the overall adequacy of the ginnery's collection service.

was, after all, his only competitor. Taken as a whole, then, as far as transporting the crop was concerned, it was in the economic interest of growers to sell to the ginnery rather than to the society.

There were also less obvious advantages. The bundles of cotton were collected from the doorsteps and transported, along with their owners, to the ginnery, which was located close by the main shopping area of the three parishes. Cash was always paid, although sellers might have to wait in turn for their cotton to be weighed and bought. This provided an opportunity for sociability and conviviality.

It should, perhaps, be noted in passing that selling cotton to the ginnery was apparently not related to employment possibilities there. Ginnery employment (mostly as porters) was economically valued in Gondo, and a core of residents of all ethnic groups had made it a regular occupation over several generations. Most men at some time in their lives sought wage employment. There appeared to be no discrimination against cooperative members (or their sons) and several of the more skilled jobs at the ginnery during the season were held by cooperative committee members, Similarly, two full-time ginnery employees were members of the Cooperative Society.

The disadvantages of selling to the ginnery were seen by the farmer to be that the Asians cheated over weighing and that the ultimate profit went into non-African hands. Evidence on the first score is contradictory. One of the present cooperative committee members, formerly a village chief whose responsibility it had been to stand by the scales to ensure that Africans were not cheated, openly declared that he had accepted bribes to set aside his duty. He was proud that there was no such cheating at the cooperative. The respondents to the Brett/Young inquiry into the cooperative movement in Uganda had less confidence than this committee member. "Cooperative members differed widely as to the honesty of cooperatives, but tended to regard the cooperatives as more honest than Asian or African private traders.... In Teso, 56.2% thought coops were honest only some of the time, and a further 22.6% thought they were never honest" (Young 1971). These figures would not appear to reflect warm endorsement. In Gondo, moreover, one Asian buyer, Valji, was looked upon as a go-between by many residents selling cotton to the ginnery, whereas the Ogera men who were cooperative officials were virtually unknown to them. Valji lives permanently in Gondo, pays very little tax (an indication of his poverty), and speaks fluent Ateso. In response to a questionnaire, many respondents gave Valji's presence at the ginnery as the reason for preferring to sell their cotton there rather than to the African-run cooperative (Vincent 1971:182).

Today, paradoxically, if the weighing at the ginnery is honest, the man who sells his cotton there may be at a disadvantage because, in the past, the weighing at the cooperative store appears frequently to have been inaccurate and the balance was in the grower's favor.[4] At the ginnery, where receipts were written in Gujerati, he could not cheat the buyer; at the cooperative store he could and did alter the receipts, according to the secretary-manager, and so could claim more cash than was actually due.

At this point it would be useful to look more closely at the organization of the Gondo Farmers Cooperative Society as a working institution, as any consideration of the economic advantages and disadvantages of selling cotton to it rather than to the ginnery must take into account, first, a distinction between the ideal and the actual working of the society and, secondly, the fact that the advantages of cooperative membership must be viewed from at least two stances — that of the cooperative committee and that of the ordinary members. In a sense, their interests were opposed, because the economic benefits of the latter were predicated upon the ideal working of the society, while the interests of the former were advanced by its malfunction.

THE COOPERATIVE SOCIETY AS A POLITICAL ARENA

The structure of cooperatives in Uganda — and Gondo fits into this framework exactly — has been concisely outlined by Brett (1970:3):

The primary cooperative unit is the Cooperative Society which contains on average 240 farmers and is responsible for buying their produce after harvest. Each society is administered by a committee elected at an Annual General Meeting; the larger societies employ Secretary-Managers on a full-time basis; the majority, however, are run by the committee members themselves. Each society owns a produce store, a scale and the receipt books, stationery, etc. required to buy produce and keep records. Since the societies are small and exist in well-established communities the members know each other and especially the members of their committee; procedures and records are relatively simple so that they can be undertaken by people with no more than primary education and some instruction from the Cooperative Department.

Primary societies are, in turn, organized into Cooperative Unions.... These Unions are responsible for the produce bought by the societies... and for providing the societies with credit required to pay growers for their produce (crop finance) and may also provide them with other services if they wish to do so. Unions tend to coincide with districts, the major unit of local administration. They are managed by Executive Committees elected at Annual General Meet-

---

[4] Discrepancies in the cash book summaries were frequently accounted for in this way (Soroti Cooperative Records n.d.a.). The scales were checked annually.

ings attended by delegates from all the constituent societies. Day to day management is in the hands of permanent officials controlled by a Secretary-Manager directly responsible to the Committee.

The efficiency of the Gondo society within this cooperative structure has been discussed elsewhere (Vincent 1970; see also Brett 1970; Leys 1971) and we are here concerned more with the internal organization of the farmers' society as an institution subject to all the stresses and strains of interpersonal relations in a fairly close-knit, multiplex, rural situation where, as Brett observes, all the members are known to each other, among them especially the members of the committee.

By 1966 the Gondo society was demonstrably an exclusive organization and, if it be assumed that those joining it believed that they gained something by doing so, it must also be queried whether they believed that even more was to be gained by keeping others out. The bylaws of the society addressed themselves to the economic and social benefits accruing to membership. Copies should have been made available to every new member at a very small charge within two months of his joining, but whether this was, in fact, so was not clear.[5] The object of the society was to:

...promote the economic interests of its members and more particularly
(a) to encourage improved methods of agriculture and to supply expert advice
(b) to increase the quantity and improve the quality of members' crops by better land utilization and better farming
(c) to market and process the agricultural produce of members cooperatively
(d) to purchase the agricultural and building requirements of members cooperatively
(e) to encourage members to save money through accepting their deposits
(f) to make loans to members for productive purposes on the security of their agricultural produce
(g) to do such other things as may be necessary for the attainment of these objectives
(h) to encourage in members a spirit and practice of thrift, mutual help and self-help (Soroti Cooperative Records n.d.b).

We need not dwell long on these aspirations, since few became realities in Gondo. The cotton crop was marketed cooperatively and the acquisition of the processing unit (to wit, the local ginnery) was an incentive before the committee members for many years. A few simple agricultural implements (hoes and sprays) were sold to members at cost, but the most needed asset, expert advice, never materialized. A great many loans were made — discriminately and not in accord with the Union regulations, as will be

---

[5] This was one of the many issues on which the evidence is contradictory. The cash accounts of the Society record income from the sale of bylaws, but this only reflects sales to sixty members. Many members interviewed did not know of their existence.

seen. The educational goals did not seem to be actively pursued and no vast improvement in the agriculture of members, as compared with other farmers in the parish, was apparent. The actual marketing of cotton — the society's prime activity in 1966 — was, as we have seen, less efficient than that of the ginnery.

The most important aspect of the Cooperative Society, in the eyes of its members, was that cash could be obtained through it, although the nature of the society and the obligations entailed were not well understood. Nevertheless, it was in respect to access to cash loans, bonuses, and the Credit Scheme that a "self-help" axiom was most manifest. Any spirit of "mutual help" was less in evidence and, indeed, data from Gondo support the general conclusion that cooperatives are used to entrench the already advantageous positions of local notables yet further. Cooperatives have served more to reinforce the local political and economic power structure than to reform it (Apthorpe 1972:152). There was a clear divide between the committee members and large farmers, on the one hand, and the ordinary members of the society, on the other. Full membership required the purchase of a share which cost twenty shillings in addition to a membership fee of two shillings; no member was allowed to hold more than three shares. These were quite considerable sums in an economy where an average farmer's income from cotton was 600 shillings and a ginnery porter's was eighty shillings a month in a six-month season and where a graduated income tax ranging from sixty to 200 shillings a year might be abstracted from a man's earnings. Annually in the parish, between five and fifteen young men were sent to prison for failure to pay taxes.

In 1966, after the Cooperative Society had been in existence for ten years, only 13 percent of the farmers of Gondo parish sold their cotton to it. In gross terms, this membership was not markedly dissimilar to the composition of the parish. It included members of ten ethnic categories, both sexes, both political parties, and all religious denominations. Nor did clanship or kinship provide the basis for exclusion or for factionalism.[6] What was reflected in the society's membership were Big Men, their dependents, and their peers — a representative stratum of Gondo's cohortative politics (Vincent 1971:63).

From its regulations it might appear that any resident of the three

---

[6]   The ethnic categories represented were Iteso (T), Bakenyi (K), Ipagero or Bachopi (P), Banyoro (N), Basoga (S), Luo (J), Acholi (A), Kumam (Kum), Karamojong (Kar), and Banyankole or Bahima (H). Religious denominations included Christian Protestant and Catholic, Muslim, and "pagan." Apart from the Balokole sect, no evangelical movements were represented in this part of Teso (cf. Long 1968). These facts take on significance in the light of the factionalism found in local cooperative societies in Buganda, Acholi, Bugisu, Bunyoro, and Kigezi (Brett and Young 1969).

parishes over eighteen years of age and able to afford twenty-two shillings might join the society, provided that he was judged to be "a farmer of good character" (Soroti Cooperative Records n.d.b). It was this last clause, presumably, that permitted one farmer to seek the exclusion of another at an annual general meeting in 1956. Farming practices and achievements were remarkably uniform throughout the parish and only a discussion of character provided a platform on which exclusion could be openly urged. There was, unfortunately, no full record of this incident or of others like it and local memories proved short. Committee members insisted that anybody could join the society who wished to do so.

Ideally, the society should have been engaged in building up as large a membership as possible — such was certainly a measure of success in the eyes of Union officials — but, in reality, two major considerations operated against this. First, open membership might threaten the entire geronto-cratic order on which social life was patterned in the parish. Second, it would inevitably have brought with it numerous demands for shares in the finite cash benefits that the union was relaying to the local society.

The basis of the Cooperative Society's exclusiveness was, then, age and social class differentiation in its overall structure and factionalism within it. Of the thirty-eight Gondo members of the society in 1966, twenty-six were over forty-five years of age, and eleven over sixty. All were heads of their respective *atutben* or residential clusters. Of the twenty-two individuals denoted as "Big Men" by a representative sample of Gondo residents (Vincent 1971:278), sixteen were members of the Cooperative Society. The absence of the others could in nearly every case be accounted for in terms of the known hostilities in the parish, accepting that the society was indeed monopolized and controlled by its founders and earliest members, a matter to be demonstrated shortly.[7] The ephemerality of power-holding in a peasant society like Gondo was also clearly reflected in the cooperative membership year by year. A full processual analysis cannot be made here but, simply to take up two careers discussed in *African elite* (Vincent 1971),

---

[7] The four cases of Emenu (T402), Ekwaru (T104), Elamu (T601), and Okello (T201) were all discussed in *African elite* (Vincent 1971:224; 225–227; 212, 241; 148, 215 respectively). In this and the notes that follow the same pseudonyms and identifications are used for Gondo parishioners. The first letter of the identifying code indicates ethnicity (as above), the number that follows indicates the ward in which the individual lives. These are identified as follows:

101–120 Aojabule
201–229 Agologolo
301–335 Kabola
401–428 Adiding
501–563 Opucet
601–6103 Township

a farmer whose economic position became marginal in 1966, after the loss of two wives, dropped his membership in the society although he had been one of the largest cotton producers in his ward. Similarly, the waning influence of the *emorimor*, who coordinated the work of all the ward headmen, became crystallized in his resignation from the Society in 1967.[8]

Of those Society members who do not fall into the category of elder, and who cannot possibly be considered Big Men or influentials, a handful were women or young men who might be looked upon as a potential support group for a Big Man — his "moral core," in Bailey's terms (1969) — when issues were put to a vote. Few of these supporters were dependent kinsmen, however, although a number of eldest sons were members concurrently with their fathers. By and large, Gondo fathers and sons infrequently stood in a supportive relationship to each other. Where hostility between them was known, only the father was a member of the society. One such support group within the cooperative surrounded the late and powerful Obiero, a farmer with considerable land in Ogera and Aojabule. This had at its core one of his wives, his eldest son, and his Karamojong herdsman (Vincent 1971: Ka 120) who was also a cultivator. Odico (1971: T 606), the Gondo tailor who helped found the Society in 1955, was similarly supported by one of his wives and a stepson (1971: T 605), likely to be his heir. In Gondo, domestic clusters operated as joint-farming enterprises, sharing land, plow, and implements. As it was in the interest of each joint enterprise to diversify marketing opportunities, a member of the cooperative not especially interested in attaining political office within it would be more likely to have his wife or son sell some of his cotton at the ginnery at times when he needed immediate cash, and so would not actively encourage their joining the cooperative society. Nevertheless, the sponsoring of admission to the society contained within it an element of that patronage that spun alliance threads throughout the parish as a whole.

A final category of cooperative member that must be placed alongside the gerontocrats and their supporters is that of entrepreneurs whose income came as much, if not more, from trade or wage employment as from farming.[9] Their intricate ties with others in the parish and the various paths by which they could attain political power and prestige cannot be discussed here, but, given the nature of the local leadership of the cooperative in 1966, its national ideology and its goals, membership might clear-

[8]   These were Ogola (T 203) and Ocen (T 532). See Vincent (1971: 198, 237–8). The political career of Anyapo (T 109) is also important in this context and will be analyzed elsewhere.
[9]   The Gondo residents who fell into this category were N 638, K 319, T 626, J 691, A 669, S 658, S 426, and K 319.

ly be looked upon more as insurance than as investment. This cannot be evaluated very concretely. First, it will be remarked that many of these small shopkeepers, traders, and wage earners were non-Iteso Gondo residents. Membership in the Cooperative Society might be thought of as insurance, if the Gondo cooperative (as was the case with others elsewhere) were considered to be UPC-dominated at a time when the UPC in Teso District was chauvinistically urging not merely Africanization but "Itesoization." Secondly, cooperative membership might serve as insurance for shopkeepers and traders, not only in the face of the society's goal to extend its activities in the field of minor crop marketing, but also in terms of the general antipathy of the cooperative movement towards trade in general — not so much against class and capital as against caste and commerce, as Apthorpe put it (1970:228). The intricate interweaving of affinal and economic relations between members of different ethnic groups which existed in Gondo parish, mechanisms having grown up over time so that all parishioners were known to each other as "whole persons," did not — except in the case of the Iteso and Kenyi — extend into the neighboring parishes. Members of the society from these parishes might well have looked upon the non-Iteso Gondo residents as aliens and foreigners. While the Gondo entrepreneurs insured against future risk, the Gondo Big Men gained present supporters.

It may be suggested, then, that the cotton-marketing cooperative was more valued as a political than as an economic institution. This contention may be assessed by comparing plow ownership and society membership in Gondo parish. The ownership of a plow gives control of a commanding resource in the community where only one man in six possesses one, and also reflects an economic initiative that is out of the general run. Time is a crucial factor in the preparation of land for planting in Teso and it is in the economic interest of any ambitious farmer to obtain his own plow. Sharing it also gives him an incremental advantage in many noneconomic transactions as well. The fact that only fourteen of the thirty-eight plow owners in Gondo belonged to the Cooperative Society would appear to support the suggestion that membership was not seen as a necessary economic asset. The fact that all Gondo cotton was ultimately processed at the ginnery made membership in the Cooperative Society more of a political gesture than a source of income.

At this point we clearly need to look more closely at the committee responsible for running the affairs of the Cooperative Society and at the advantages accruing to positions of leadership within it. In the course of its ten-year history, thirty individuals have, at various times, sat on the ten man committee (Table 2). Throughout, the reins of power have, by and

Table 2.   Gondo farmers cooperative society committee members, 1956–1966

	1956	1957	1958	1959	1960	1961	1962	1963	1964	1965	1966
Aringo (Ogera)	**	*	*								
Obirai (Ogelak)	**	**	**	*		*	*				
Eledu (Ogera)	*	**	**	**	**						
Odico (Gondo)	*	*	*			**	**	**	**	*	*
Obiero (Ogera)	*	*	*	*	*	*	**	**	**	**	**
Anyapo (Gondo)	**	**	**	**	**	**	**				
Ekau (Gondo/Ogelak)	*	*	*	*							
Okimoi (Ogera)	*	*					*	*	*		
Aringa (Gondo)	*	*	*								
Eyeru (Ogera)	*	*									
Oceunna (Ogera)					**	**	**				
Ocaalo (Gondo)			*	*		*	**	**	**		
Okello (Ogera)					*	*	*	Secretary-Manager			
Oddi (Ogera)				*			*	*	*		*
Apuda (Ogelak)				*		*		*	*		
Adingo (Ogera)				*	*	*					
Edumu (N.K.)					*	*	*				
Eliedu (Ogelak)					*	*					
Angala (Ogelak)					*	*					
Ocaet (N.K.)			*								
Odeke (Ogera)								*	*		* Secretary-Manager
Ocen (Gondo)								*	*		
Okello (Ogelak)								*	*	*	
Odongo (N.K.)								*	*		
Ogot (Gondo)										**	**
Ederu (Ogera)										*	*
Otieno (Gondo)											**
Ekiau (Ogelak										*	*
Adeu (N.K.)										*	
Ocala (Ogera)											*

** Chairman; ** Vice-Chairman; ** Treasurer; * Committee Member; N.K. Not Known

large, been in the hands of four men: Isaya Obiero and Eledu, an exvillage chief and ex-District Councillor from Ogera; Musa Obirai, an exvillage chief and ex-County Councillor from Ogelak; and Odico, the little tailor of Gondo. All four were among the founders of the society in 1955 and each in turn has held the two highest offices — those of chairman and vice-chairman — of the society. Faithfully serving them as treasurers have been, from among their peers, Anyapo, the catechist, and Ocaalo, both Big Men from Gondo; and, as the society's secretaries, three comparatively well-educated young men from Ogera parish.

The control of the charter members was clear throughout, but the rising stars of Oceunna, Ocaalo, and Oddi were to be seen after 1959, and after 1965 a drastic revamping of the committee took place. These three phases I have elsewhere characterized as those of the spiralist, the patriarch, and the common man, respectively, each related to the fortunes of the Cooperative Society and its organizational needs in the light of bank debts, credit schemes, and union demands (Vincent 1970). During all these phases, however, the composition of the committe reflected clearly the great social divide within the rural society. With the exception of the three secretaries, all the committee members (like that of the cooperative in general) were over forty-five, established household heads with one or more wives and growing sons, and educated only to the primary level. Most importantly of all — and this is what distinguishes them from the ordinary society member — all but two had once held official positions in the local government or administrative systems. All had once been parish, subcounty, county, or even district councillor; or they had been ward headman, village or parish chief, road headman, teacher, dispenser, agricultural assistant, subcounty clerk, member of the Teso Parents and Elders Association, and so on. None had risen high in the echelon in which he served but all had, as it were, reinvested their gains from office-holding in the local arena to which they had "retired" and their election to the committee of the Cooperative Society set the seal on their endeavors.[10]

Oceunna, the Muslim builder from Ogera who held the vice-chairmanship from 1959–1961, was an interesting exception to this pattern. His migration to Kaberamaido in 1961 disrupted a mode of succession to office which had consolidated power in the hands of the society's founders. Another interesting exception was that of Ogot, the Luo shopkeeper from Gondo who was elected chairman during a financial crisis in May 1965, when a drastic revision of the committee leadership was undertaken. Structurally outside the factionalism of the community, as he was an immigrant from Kenya, Ogot's election might be interpreted in the light of Simmel's thesis on the role of the "stranger" in society, more able to make decisions impartially and to carry out duties bureaucratically.

At that point in the society's history, bureaucratic impartiality was

[10] This phenomenon of a lowly official returning to become a Big Man in his natal parish is discussed elsewhere (Vincent 1971:54). It must be observed that not one of the 1966 officials of the three parishes belonged to the cooperative.

certainly needed, for the stratagems of successive commitees had, over the years, greatly deflected the distribution of the spoils. There were several ways in which this had occurred. It has already been noted that loans were made to members in excess of the regulation value, i.e. "2/3 of the crop average or ten times the member's share whichever is the less" (Soroti Cooperative Records n.d.a). Several malpractices occurred. For example, in October 1963, fifty shillings were given to a farmer who should have received one and six, and a quick review of the figures showed a general tendency for round sums of between fifty and 500 shillings to be paid out regardless of the size of crop. The records could not be very profitably used by the researcher because, as the Cooperative Assistant himself noted, there had been a "lot of 'crossings' so that members should get more than they were entitled to."

The profits that did accrue from such record keeping were quite widely distributed, although it was clear that the larger sums were loaned only to influential men. Many of these were, of course, among the producers of the largest cotton crops, as one would expect from the politics of agriculture (Vincent 1971 : 187–208). But, even so, loans were disproportionate and ordinary members with crops not much smaller received far less; also, fictitious names were used in the loans register. Thus, when applications for loans were checked at random in May 1964, for example, it was found that a Y. Otim had been given 200 shillings although no such person was listed in the produce ledger as having sold his crop to the society in the 1963–64 season.

The record of the Gondo cooperative, like that of many in East Africa, was one of unpaid debts, although an effort was made to hold the committee members responsible. They were themselves among the chief offenders and it was rare to find a committee member not receiving a loan for a second year in spite of the fact that he had not repaid the first. Besides these sources of personal profit, committee members were able to claim expenses of various kinds, and almost certainly received kickbacks from patronage. The cooperative store required an inordinate amount of repair compared with other buildings in Gondo prior to the emigration of the aforementioned Vice-chairman Oceunna, and the recorded wages paid to porters and night watchmen might have been expected to start an inflationary spiral. Privileges also attached themselves to committee office. Whereas the ordinary member was often obliged to wait several weeks for payment for his crop because the local society had exhausted its supply of ready cash, it was rare to find the name of a committee member on the listings of the society's creditors. A list of forty-nine members who were owed the total sum of 1,431 shillings in June

1967, for example, was made up entirely of ineffective young Ogera farmers.

That committee members quarreled a great deal among themselves was clear from the record. "There is disagreement between the members of the committee and as a result no cotton has been sold yet," was the notation for December 1957, a month after the cotton-selling season had begun. "The members of the society are quite keen but the leadership is lacking. Each member of the committee seeks for personal benefit," observed the Cooperative Assistant in 1962 (Soroti Cooperative Records n.d.a). Quarrels between Odico and Anyapo led to the latter's fall from grace in May 1961, and disputes among committee members were sufficiently open and significant to appear in the society's records for October 1957, December 1957, May 1961, and February 1963.

Protests were recorded against the manipulation of the society by its committee. Thus an anonymous member from Gondo asserted that the election of Okello as secretary-manager in 1963 was against the wishes of the voting majority who had wanted Oiko. The not inconsiderable salary of a hundred shillings per month was at stake in this issue, apart from questions of competence and honesty. Okello was dismissed from this post in 1965 after ledger frauds were revealed; charges were brought against him which were later dropped.

As the financial gains to be had from the Cooperative Society grew, so did the visible gap between the committee and the ordinary members. Between 1957 and 1965 debts had been allowed to accrue, but after March 1965 when the society was warned that it could not participate in a credit scheme unless its outstanding debt of 6,675 shillings on a bank loan of 20,000 shillings were paid, a drastic step was taken. Two members were appointed to a newly formed subcommittee for loan collection: one was Ogot of Gondo Township, the other Apuda of Ogelak. The action of committee members in March 1965 was reminiscent of that of parish chiefs who banded together touring the parishes to harass tax defaulters. On the twenty-second, the committee went to debtors' houses, individually and as a group, but returned with no money. The following day they returned with a confiscated bicycle. As it happened, their failure was ameliorated by the intervention of the Union, which paid the immediate debt to the bank, but one wonders whether Ogot's election to the chairmanship at the next annual general meeting was due to his value to the Big Men in this unpopular role of taskmaster. After this, more formal action was taken against debtors. Committee members might still go around singly to harass debtors, but the parish chief also cooperated in "chasing them up." Bicycles and granaries could be confiscated. Ten bicycles had been seized, according to the Secretary-Manager, in 1967. One man, at first willing to "pawn" his granary of millet in this way, later changed his mind and paid the cash he owed instead. Although the threat of court action was held over the heads of debtors, it was never brought. Even Okello, the Secretary-Manager who profited so handsomely from his service to the committee, got off scot-free.[11]

COMPETITION IN GONDO

Competition in Gondo in 1966 generally bore the features of cohortative politics with agricultural entrepreneurs competing for land and labor as political facilities. Given the controlled price of cotton, the restrictions on its buying and selling, and the small return from its cultivation, cotton was not, in itself, important coin in the political realm. Instead the politics of agriculture revolved around the cultivation of millet which, accompanied by the prestation and sale of millet beer, became the visible manifestation of a man's control over a work force, and so provided for successful entry into the parochial political system (Vincent 1971:187–208).

When one asks, then, why the cotton ginnery continued to do so well for so long in Gondo, the final explanation can only lie in the outside interests that maintained cotton cultivation as the mainstay of the Teso economy and reinforced the quality of its production with administrative and local government sanctions. The interests of alien experts were protected and prolonged for the sake of the national econmy. As cotton was the crop of the paternalistic administration, it occured to few Gondo parishioners (apart from those who had been out and about in the world) that they would do better with other crops. For the politically ambitious parishioner, cotton-growing was a small part of his operations. The Cooperative Society was, therefore, less important as a means of improving agricultural production than as a means of access to cash that could be invested in nonagricultural enterprises. It was political office in the local society that was valued — and jealously guarded by the Big Men and elders — for its contacts with the power structures beyond the parish, its potential political clout, and its kickbacks. The same would have been true of any other voluntary association that was given administrative blessing

---

[11]   Brett notes that it was difficult for the Cooperative Department "to persuade the police to take committees to court because of the complexity of the issues and the difficulties of producing an effective case. Thus despite very large and growing evidence of embezzlement at the society level up to 1967, very few cases were ever taken up and fewer individuals punished" (1970:16).

at the grassroots level. In Gondo, where no such other voluntary associations existed, the Cooperative Society became the cockpit of political ambitions.

At a structural level, the Cooperative Society served to restrict economic competition to the dominant stratum of peasant society. Women, the poor, and the young were restricted, in effect, to interactions only in the more conflict-laden, asymmetrical situations, such as those between husband and wife, father and son, parish chief and parishioner, landowner and sponsored immigrant, employer and porter, ginnery management and labor, permanent landowner and transient herdsman. Conflict in these relations had three possible outcomes: recourse to the law; retreat from the political situation; and open violence (Vincent 1971:212). The last two were most commonly resorted to.

While the local political ring was held in this manner by the Big Men and elders, the Cooperative Society was used not to improve the lot of the depressed strata but to express ideological opposition to an alien institution, the Asian-owned ginnery, first as a preliminary to the reshuffling of power that was expected after independence and then, more realistically, as a prelude to obtaining jobs of petty management or labor-brokerage within it. Given the processing regulations of the segregated zone, the Cooperative Society was never truly in economic competition with the ginnery. Nevertheless the ginnery provided a means of expressing dissent for the poorer peasant farmers. Every sale of cotton to the ginnery was, in essence, a gesture of disrespect and sometimes even defiance to those who hoped to use the local society as a launching platform. Outside support alone, in the form of credit schemes and government-negotiated bank loans, kept the cooperative society in existence. Thus, ironically, schemes intended to bring about change and development in the rural sector served to reinforce the backwater status quo — and conservative farming. It becomes clear, then, for whom the Farmers Cooperative Society in Gondo was good.

THE COOPERATIVE SOCIETY AS AN ENCAPSULATED INSTITUTION

It is finally necessary, in our consideration of the local Cooperative Society within the total context of rural social and economic competition and the changes it underwent between 1956 and 1970, to view it as an encapsulated institution. Not only parochial issues (such as those discussed in the two previous sections) but also district-wide and national issues became crystallized in the affairs of the society. District-wide issues were frequently couched in the political idiom of ethnicity, i.e. as rivalry between Kumam, Kenyi, and Iteso or between Ngoratok and Iseera, the southern and northern Iteso. National issues, as we have already seen, were once couched in the idiom of race — i.e. Africans *vis-á-vis* Asians — but, by 1967, were more frequently put in terms of party political issues.

The issue that concerns us here is the cleavage between the Ngoratok of the three southern counties of Teso (Ngora, Kumi, and Bukedea, south of Lake Bisina) and the Iseera of the northern and western counties (among them Serere, in which Gondo, Ogera, and Ogelak lie), for it is necessary to see the Gondo monopoly of 1968 in relation to this old issue of Teso political history.

Broadly conceived of as dialect groups or divisions (Gulliver and Gulliver 1953; Lawrance 1957), hostilities between Iseera and Ngoratok had only become politically important with the greater centralization of economic advantage in the cauldron of the Teso District Council. This ideological expression of sectional interest in terms of Ngoratok and Iseera reflected the greater success of the three southern counties in the race for schools, missions, hospitals, progressive farmers, administrative appointments, and almost every other visible aspect of Teso's economic development under colonial rule. Flagrant hostility had brought about the temporary dismissal of the District Council by the Protectorate Government in 1958.

There were no manifestations of this factionalism in Gondo parish in 1966, although foreshadowings of it had begun to appear in neighboring Ogera and Kaberamaido. Migrants from the southern counties were few and far between in Gondo, and none held positions of authority or power. Within the Cooperative Society, as we have seen, the only salaried officials were both Ogera men; membership was polyethnic and the question of Teso north and south had simply not arisen in its ten-year history. By 1970, however, a year after the Gondo ginnery had been acquired by the Teso Cooperative Union, the dominating presence of Ngoratok cooperative officials in the parish was most apparent. They lived in the large stone houses that had once housed Asian and European ginnery owners; they had cars; their wealth and education were clearly visible. They formed a small cohesive elite of "new men."

To what extent this change in the local situation reflected the outcome of a political struggle within the Teso Cooperative Union I am unable to say. Looking back, one sees indications that this may have been the case; on the other hand, the Gondo ginnery, because of its importance in the segregated zone, would presumably require the best management available and it may well be that, given the educational history of Ngora county, such management would more likely be found among Ngoratok. In 1957, in his report to the District Commissioner, the Cooperative Officer commented upon the political stresses in the District Council and what he described as "the factional rivalry between Ngoratok and northern and western dialect groups of Iseera, Kumama [*sic*] and Usuku." These were now apparent within the cooperative movement which displayed tendencies to split three ways into Ngoratok, Iseera and Iseera-Kumam interests and, he reported, "there were symptoms of desire for at least three cooperative unions based on these three factional-geographical interests" (Teso District Archives n.d.b). Until the political history of the Teso Cooperative Union is written, I can only report the visible new "social divide" that appeared in Gondo in 1970 following the cooperative monopoly.

One of the results of the new monopoly of the Cooperative Society by Ngoratok officials appears to have been a purge of non-Iteso employees at the ginnery. Hostility has also been voiced against former Democratic Party supporters and none now serves on the committee. While at one level this may be understood in terms of political segmentary theory, at another it appears as the victory cry of a cooperative movement that has brought down the last bastion of non-African participation in the cotton industry. In any case, the Gondo Cooperative Society would seem to have become, since 1968, an even more effective instrument, perpetuating and deepening the exploitation of the peasantry. No longer is there merely the parochial exploitation of commonors by Big Men, themselves subject in the end to the leveling mechanisms built into a rural system of competition. The exploitation is now that of a political class of urban-centered bureaucrats and politicians. This is the difference between competition and conflict. Competition occurs when a struggle is played out according to known and observed rules in a familiar arena, where today's loser may become tomorrow's winner and where there are sufficient countervailing forces at work so that the "winner" can never truly "take all" for very long. Conflict is likely to occur where there is no equality of chance among the combatants, where the odds are not even, the rules not agreed upon, and the victory may be final and complete. Where there is no longer recourse to a competitive arena, violence and bloodshed are likely to ensue (Bierstedt 1950; Bailey 1969).

CONCLUSION: MONOPOLY IN GONDO

Concluding a review of the problems of cooperative development in Uganda, Brett makes this observation:

...in the worst cases the cooperative can serve as a means of taxing the masses for the benefit of the elite... the cooperative itself will stagnate and provide very little direct impetus for change, the elite will benefit and the masses will be confirmed and maintained in their present poverty. To the extent that the process continues, cleavage in the political sector will increase and various forms of violence will ultimately become possible (1970:51).

He also notes that, as the cooperative is so closely identified with the government, such a situation is likely to lead to generalized political discontent directed against the existing political authorities.

Yet there is an even greater reason for anxiety over the 1968 cooperative monopoly in Gondo. It is yet to be officially recognized in Uganda that cotton has long been one of the least rewarding cash crops for the peasant farmer. Young (1971:141) has described cotton as one of "the lumbering oxen that draw Uganda's chariot of development." Yet, as far as Teso District is concerned, that particular lumbering ox has been stuck in the Teso mud for almost five decades. The marketing of cotton as a cash crop has brought the Gondo farmer no economic advancement since 1924. Profit has not led him to increase his acreage, grow cotton more intensively, weed more thoroughly, pick more timely. The nature of land tenure, soil erosion, poor marketing facilities; a lack of investment capital for sprays, carts, weeders; banking conservatism and rural insecurity — all contribute to this.

Those who have profited in Gondo are those who have invested their efforts in cattle trading, fishing, cash crops other than cotton, and, above all, education for their children. The range of goods stocked in the shops — which themselves are few and far between in Teso — is little different from that of 1924. Any cash that is made from cotton and which is surplus to the bare necessities of life, goes for taxes, licences, and, more rarely, school fees. Cotton as a cash crop for the peasant does little more than take care of that part of his divided world that relates to the surplus or rent demanded of him by the urbanized political class of his country (cf. Wolf 1966). Cotton is the farmer's rent to government to be left alone. Cattle provide a social and religious asset in the local arena; millet a social and political asset — but cotton is singularly a crop of governmental penetration, and one that is superimposed upon, not incorporated into, the Gondo agricultural cycle.

Although from the point of view of the economist, policymaker, and agriculturalist, the cotton-marketing cooperative must be evaluated as an economic institution, to the peasant farmer its side effects are often more important. This might not be the case, of course, if the profits from marketing Uganda's cotton in the world markets had been relayed down to the rural areas. Then gains might well be seen in the form of household water supplies, paved roads, electricity, mobile banking facilities, a more extensive police force. These are all means of saving (in time, labor, and finances) that would permit the farmer an equally rational allocation of his efforts to what he is currently indulging in — a five-hour working day in a nonexpansive farming regimen — because there is no more to be gained from more effort within the rural infrastructure or peasant farming in Gondo today. The entrepreneur turns to fishing, a sewing machine, a road gang, even to employment as an *ayah*, in an attempt to break the vicious circle of rural neglect.

Before 1968, when the Gondo marketing cooperative was an inefficiently run voluntary association, it could do no great harm — although it did serve, as we have seen, to consolidate wealth in the hands of an established local elite. But when, after 1968, it became more highly politicized, supercharging the parish with district and national tensions, the enhanced powers of its officials became more ominous. Even more will this be the case if the cooperative movement is to be given the greater marketing monopolies advocated by its supporters in government, especially if Apthorpe is right in his judgment that any "historically complex social organization with spiritual as well as practical ramifications that have become ends in themselves" (like the Catholic Church or the cooperative movement) tend to defy rational evaluation (Apthorpe 1970:209). So much rhetoric and ideology have been invested in the struggle for a cooperative monopoly in the cotton industry that this has become the issue, rather than economic efficiency or social justice. One is reminded of the story of the distinguished Africanist who, asked what the concept of "penetration" and "participation" in rural development really meant, suggested that it was the peasants who really knew because it was they who got exploited. "It may not be RURAL livelihood that rural social participation promotes" (Apthorpe 1972:155) in East Africa, any more than it is in Latin America, where the maintenance of a "backward sector" sustains the wealthy few (cf. Frank 1967; Petras 1968).

REFERENCES

APTHORPE, RAYMOND
    1970   "Some problems of evaluation," in *Co-operatives and rural development in East Africa*. Edited by Carl Gosta Widstrand, 209–229. Uppsala: The Scandinavian Institute of African Studies.
    1972   Co-operatives in rural Africa. *Journal of Administration Overseas* 11: 150–161.

BAILEY, F. G.
1969   *Stratagems and spoils*. New York: Schocken.

BIERSTEDT, ROBERT
1950   An analysis of social power. *American Sociological Review* 15:730–738.

BRETT, E. A.
1970   "Problems of cooperative development in Uganda." Report to the United Nations Research Institute for Social Development, Geneva. Unpublished manuscript.

BRETT, E. A., M. CRAWFORD YOUNG
1969   "Survey of Uganda Farmers." Unpublished manuscript.

FIRST, RUTH
1970   *The barrel of a gun*. London: Penguin.

FRANK, A. G.
1967   Sociology of development and the underdevelopment of sociology. *Catalyst* 3:20–73.

GULLIVER, PAMELA, P. H. GULLIVER
1953   *The Central Nilo-Hamites*. London: International African Institute.

KASFIR, NELSON
1970   "Organizational analysis and Ugandan co-operative unions," in *Cooperatives and rural development in East Africa*. Edited by Carl Gosta Widstrand, 178–208. Uppsala: The Scandinavian Institute of African Studies.

LAWRANCE, J.
1957   *The Iteso*. London: Oxford University Press.

LEYS, COLIN
1971   "Political perspectives," in *Development in a divided world*. Edited by Dudley Seers and Leonard Joy. London: Penguin.

LONG, NORMAN
1968   *Social change and the individual*. Manchester: Manchester University Press.

MIGOT-ADHOLLA, S. E.
1970   "Traditional society and co-operatives," in *Co-operatives and rural development in East Africa*. Edited by Carl Gosta Widstrand, 17–37. Uppsala: The Scandinavian Institute of African Studies.

PETRAS, J.
1968   U.S. Latin American studies: a critical assessment. *Science and Society* 32:146–168.

SHEPHERD, G. W.
1955   *They wait in darkness*. New York: J. Day.

SOROTI COOPERATIVE RECORDS
n.d. a   Reports of the Cooperative Assistant on the Gondo Farmers Cooperative Society, 1956–1967. SCR 1326/x.
n.d. b   Bylaws of the Gondo Farmers Cooperative Society. SCR 1326/y.

STONEHOUSE, JOHN
1960   *Prohibited immigrant*. London: Bodley Head.

TESO DISTRICT ARCHIVES
n.d. a   Annual reports of the District Commissioner, Teso District. TDA ADM 14/1953, 1954.
n.d. b   A collation of reports from members of the District Team for use in

the Annual Report of the District Commissioner, Teso District, 1957. TDA ADM. 14/57A.

The Times Literary Supplement
  1968   "Back to grass roots." *The Times Literary Supplement* December 19: 1421–1423.

UGANDA GOVERNMENT
  1969   *The common man's charter.* Kampala: Consolidated Printers.

VINCENT, JOAN
  1970   Local cooperatives and parochial politics in Uganda: problems of organisation, representation and communication. *Journal of Commonwealth Political Studies* 8:3–17.
  1971   *African elite: the Big Men of a small town.* New York: Columbia University Press.
  f.c.   "Teso society in transformation: the political development of Teso District (1896–1934) and its contemporary significance," in *Political and administrative penetration in East Africa.* Edited by James Coleman, Lionel Cliffe and Martin Doornbos. London: Oxford University Press.

WIDSTRAND, CARL GOSTA
  1970   "Introduction," in *Co-operatives and rural development in East Africa.* Edited by Carl Gosta Widstrand, 11–16. Uppsala: The Scandinavian Institute of African Studies.

WOLF, ERIC
  1966   *Peasants.* Englewood Cliffs, New Jersey: Prentice-Hall.

YOUNG, M. CRAWFORD
  1971   "Agricultural policy in Uganda: capability and choice," in *The state of the nations: constraints on development in independent Africa.* Edited by Michael F. Lofchie, 141–164. Berkeley: University of California Press.

Participatory Decision Making and Modern Cooperatives in Mali: Notes Towards a Prospective Anthropology

NICHOLAS S. HOPKINS

It may well be that the decade of the 1970's will mark a return to the stolidity of the 1950's after the ferment, more or less revolutionary, of the 1960's, when the coming of independence in Africa and elsewhere overthrew the established forces in many countries and left the field open for new social and political arrangements. Now that most of these countries have been independent for a decade or more, the outlines of the new establishments are increasingly firm, and the trend now, as in the 1950's, is change with order: one finds urban and national elites organizing the rest of society in accordance with their own concepts and interests. This tendency was not absent in the initial periods of revolutionary nation building, of course, but could not be taken for granted because of a still fluid balance of powers and optimistic hopes for expansion.

One of the lessons to be drawn from the experiences of recent years in the development of these societies is that, whatever the hopes and justifications of the various programs were, they have tended to benefit mostly a relatively small class of people – either bureaucrats or those with enough private capital to benefit from development – at the expense of the rest of the people. The replacement of traditional forms of society by new ones under independent regimes has usually led to an increase in political and economic differentiation. Sometimes this has been by design, sometimes by ignorance of the various new forms of society and their implications.

The fieldwork described here was supported by the National Institute of Mental Health in 1964–1965. The article was written away from familiar libraries and so lacks some elements of the scholarly apparatus.

Here, precisely, is a role for anthropology. By studying and writing about the human problems involved in the emerging social and cultural forms and by suggesting the implications of anthropological research for future forms of society, anthropologists can fulfill at least part of their responsibility to those whom they study. In this way they can contribute to an increased awareness among those who are the actors of this drama, without losing themselves in facile denunciations or taking over the responsibility for recommending or initiating programs themselves. The responsibility of the social scientist is not only to the governments and other centralized authorities that are interested in realizing various programs, but also to the people who will be living under such forms. Increased consciousness enables the people to exert informed and deliberate control over the social and cultural forms that characterize their environments.

The responsibility of anthropology goes beyond this. Anthropology is the study of human society from a broadly comparative point of view, and it can be eclectic in its search for an understanding of the realities it is confronted with. Anthropology has long ceased to be merely descriptive and has developed analytical frameworks for understanding social and cultural processes across the entire range of the human experience. Now it is time to turn these accumulated analytical skills to cooperatives as well as clans, to socialism as well as totemism.[1]

In studying the newly emerging social forms the responsibility of the anthropologist is twofold: to look behind the rhetoric, propaganda, and other pronouncements from above in order to analyze the structure and functioning of existing institutions, and to bring their comparative understanding of the wide range of human possibilities to bear on the structural implications and human realities of the various projects that have been set up by governments, local communities, and ideologues. This approach might be called "prospective anthropology," and it is a prime direction in which the anthropology of the future ought to move.

A prospective anthropology would recognize the inventiveness and the creativeness of ordinary people as well as of intellectuals and planners. Among the possible approaches of a prospective anthropology would be the analysis of the structural principles of proposed emergent social forms (usually formulated legalistically), the analysis of traditional and neotraditional forms of society to suggest lines of possible development, and the study of experiments in social organization which represent pos-

---

[1] While the approach is basically the same, it is conceivable that an anthropologist would be committed to cooperatives or socialism in a way unlikely for clans or totemism.

sible new lines of development and social change. New forms of society are imaginable and their understanding may be facilitated by comparison with known human solutions.

Prospective anthropology draws inspiration from the major lines of social interpretation which have guided other anthropological studies, notably the directions indicated by the trio of Marx, Weber, and Durkheim; in so doing it would undoubtedly serve to renew some of the tenets of these approaches. Remaining close to the aspirations and inspirations of ordinary people in their attempts to improve and control the circumstances of their lives, prospective anthropology would thus unite a concern with emergent forms of social organization on the one hand with the full gamut of anthropological experience and theory on the other.

The cooperative is one of the new social forms that has often been cited as an important new direction for society. Because it offers a way of organizing human relations on a scale wide enough to take advantage of technological advances without falling under the domination of banks, landowners, capitalists, and state enterprises, it has been seen as an essential element in a noncapitalist path of development (Desroches 1963). To some it offers the advantage of local control, to others the advantage of equality and freedom from domination, and to still others a way of mobilizing people in processes of national development. Cooperatives can take many forms, including consumers' cooperatives, service cooperatives for farmers and others, merchandising cooperatives, credit cooperatives, producers' cooperatives tending ultimately to take the form of collective production systems, and others. Though its forms vary widely, a broad, however vague, definition might be that a cooperative is an institutionalized social form tending to assure local control of economic matters in a context of equality among its members.

Some of the problems that are frequently mentioned in the analysis of cooperatives include (1) the relationship to central authority, (2) the reconciliation of competency and equality, (3) the passage from prior social forms to a cooperative structure, (4) the maintenance of a cooperative in a context organized around other principles, (5) the tendency for cooperatives to become reinterpreted according to local ideas and interests, and (6) the inadequate analysis of the human implications of the cooperative structure itself. These are all problems on which anthropology can shed some light and perhaps by so doing suggest possibilities for improvement. In this paper these topics will provide the structure for the analysis of Malian village cooperatives.

First, while traditional patterns of the organization of work frequently stress the inequality and individuality of workers, cooperative structures imply that everyone is equal and in some sense interchangeable. This formal equality, however, runs into difficulties raised by the division of labor. Such difficulties are particularly salient when status differences inside the cooperative are a reflection of the status differences that members have brought with them, such as age, sex, education, family position, social rank, or involvement with other organizations such as parties or bureaucracies. Thus the first problem that any cooperative must face is the contradiction between the formal equality of its members and the structural inequality based on the differentiation of the tasks that members must perform. The greater the complexity of the task that a cooperative must accomplish, particularly if it is an all-embracing production cooperative, the more difficult it will be to resolve this problem.

Second, there is the problem of knowledge and communication, for on these depends participation in decision making and thus ultimately power. If all are to be equal in the cooperative, then all must have equal access to information, and thus there must be ways of assuring the diffusion of that information equally among the members of the cooperative. Some cooperatives are small enough for face-to-face methods to be effective, but they might well be too small for efficient use of modern technology. In other cases the principle of rotation could be used to ensure equality of information, but here, too, complexity may require more specialization than is compatible with rotation. There are also problems of personality, inclination, personal drive, and so on: not everyone picks the same information out of the air. Yet if these problems are not overcome, a bureaucratic elite can control the cooperative by controlling the information concerning its operation, arranging affairs in such a way that no one can question the "experts." There is a particular danger of this when cooperatives are administered from a central point.

Third, there are the problems relative to the social context in which a cooperative operates. Some theorists have suggested that the way to build socialism is to start with such aspects of life as one can control, set an example, and build from there; but others, more recently, have worried that a pure form of the cooperative cannot be expected if the environment is organized according to quite different principles. For instance, an environment organized around patron-client type personal relations will be likely to encourage the formation of similar kinds of relationships within the cooperative. By the same token it seems difficult to reconcile bureaucratically organized support structures (agricultural agencies providing technical assistance) with effective egalitarianism within the cooperative. The problem of the environment is equally present in a cooperative enclosed within a capitalist system and in one encouraged by a Jacobin Third-World government characterized by a centrally controlled bureaucracy.

In Mali during the period from the granting of internal autonomy in 1958 to the military coup of 1968, the intellectuals who played such an influential role in policy making were keenly interested in establishing cooperative structures to replace the previously existing combination of patriarchal family structures and a mercantilism in which African merchants were playing an increasing role (Badian 1964). Their scheme was to pass through the stages of cooperativization, of commercialization of produce, and of purchase of consumer goods to cooperative production. Economic and political factors, mostly extraneous to the cooperatives per se, led to the military coup of 1968 before more than a small part of this scheme could be carried out (Jones 1969; Hopkins 1972:221–224).

The development of socialism and cooperatives in rural Mali has attracted the attention of a number of scholars. Jones (1970) worked in a Niger valley village not far from Bamako, in the same area where Leynaud (1966) did research. Jones described the economic structure of the village while Leynaud was interested in the mobilization of youth for development. Ernst (1971) carried out research in a Niger valley village downstream from Bamako, where he was particularly interested in the development of new forms of productive relations.

The situation that I knew best was an Association of Village Cooperatives (AVC) grouping nine village cooperatives (Groupements Ruraux de Production et de Secours Mutuel or GRPSM), centered around the village of Benduguba, twelve kilometers east of Kita in western Mali. This is Maninka country (Hopkins 1971). In 1965, when this study was carried out, the cooperatives were used essentially to replace the old mercantile network, under political attack.[2] They acted as primary collection points for the peanuts and other agricultural products which peasants wished to sell to the government (the monopoly buyer), and they distributed a certain range of government monopoly staple goods, such as suger, salt, tea, matches, kerosene, cloth, and so on. All the farmers in these villages were considered to be members of their village GRPSM and of the AVC, and the AVC's weighing station and store were the focal points of a considerable amount of activity. Much of this activity, however, consisted of individual acts of purchasing or selling and thus in no

---

[2] Meillassoux (1970:106-107) and Diop (1971:230) interpret the struggle between bureaucrats and merchants for political supremacy in Mali as essentially a class struggle; socialism as a policy favored the interests of the bureaucrats.

way corresponded to any cooperative or solidarity spirit. Schemes to involve the village cooperatives in productive activity, working notably
through the collective field that each village was required to have, did not
advance very far before the coup d'état of November 1968.

As I have analyzed this cooperative already (Hopkins 1969a:65-67;
Hopkins 1969b), my purpose here will be to comment on the structures
and on the lessons that anthropology might derive from this experiment.
I will deal first of all with the division of labor and the problems of the
reconciliation of competency and equality, then with the implications of
equality of knowledge for decision making, and finally with the relationship between the internal structure and social organization of the cooperative and those of the institutional environment. In making this last
point I will stress particularly the implications of the role of participatory decision making, for this is one of the key features of the Malian
cooperative experience.

There was relatively little division of labor in the cooperative because
there were only a few specialized roles (weigher, storekeeper, intermediaries with the government bureaucracy in Kita), and the occupants of these
roles were treated essentially as employees of the whole cooperative (of
which they were also members). Because cooperative members were called
on to do so few things, none of them tasks implying any division of labor,
the device of making such specialized roles as there were employee roles
served the function of reasserting the equality of all the members of the
cooperative. Doubtless the fact that these men kept the accounts and dealt
with the central government institutions in Kita gave them a greater role
in the affairs of the cooperative, but at the annual meeting that I attended
in 1965, once these few officials had made their reports they played no
greater part in the discussion that followed than anyone else. Further,
the members were not without recourse against their specialists, as is
illustrated by the discharge of a set of leaders who had proved incapable
of running the affairs of the cooperative without losing money.

Even this specialization of tasks left some leaders ill at ease. One village
leader told me in 1970 that he had been physically ill all during the cooperative period but when his job with the cooperatives disappeared after
1968 his health improved markedly. He attributed the illness to the strain
of being caught in the middle, in a role where he could satisfy neither
his fellow villagers nor the representatives of the central government.

The reconciliation of equality and competence did not present any
formidable problems because this was a buying-selling cooperative which
associated independent farmers in their relations with economic organizations outside and beyond the family, and not a work or production

cooperative. The intention of the government to extend the cooperatives to production would, however, probably have raised problems of a much more difficult sort. The traditional methods of agricultural production here, as generally in Mali, are carried out within a patriarchal family structure which places considerable power in the role of head of household (*lutigi*) who has the right of stewardship over the lands farmed by the family and over the labor of his younger brothers and sons who have not left the household (Hopkins 1971). The *lutigi*, whose power was based on his control of spiritual factors as well as on his knowledge of techniques (Meillassoux 1960), was able to mobilize collective labor on certain fields, the *furuba*, from whose output the bulk of the family's food was drawn and which served to finance the marriage of the community's members.

The system was not monolithic, however, and women often farmed their own fields of vegetables, rice, or maize from which they contributed to the household and covered certain personal expenses, while ambitious non-*lutigi* took advantage of their free time to farm fields of their own, known as *dionforo*. The output of the *dionforo* went for their personal needs, including the accumulation of enough capital to branch off on their own, while the work of the same men on the *furuba* was the cllective property of the household. Households under this system could be quite large, although all degrees of effective solidarity were found. In the zone surrounding Kita, the average household for tax purposes (somewhat larger than the productive unit average) was around thirty individuals, or from three to ten adult males.

The tools of Maninka agriculture are simple and available to everyone, but land as a means of production is both more important and more complex. Maninka agriculture around Kita is a form of shifting cultivation in which a field may be farmed for ten or twelve years, and then allowed to lie fallow for a generation. The ultimate owner of the land in the traditional conception was the village as a community, represented by a chief whose title, *dugutigi*, implied his special role in dealing with earth and its supernatural inhabitants.[3] Families and individuals have use rights in land, based on the act of clearing away the bush from it, and they retain a preemptory right over land they have once used for as long as people remember it. If someone wants to farm land known to have been farmed by another, he must ask permission, and this permission may only be refused if the last user intends to use the plot in that year.

---

[3]   Similar to the earth priests found among many other West African savanna peoples.

The Kita area is not one of land pressure; on the contrary it is in many ways a frontier area with population spreading north, east, and west, and most villages have at their disposal adequate land for all their members. Benduguba, for instance, was settled around 1900 by farmers from the foot of Kita mountain as part of a still continuing process of expansion into empty territory. Its land is on the edge of a zone of river-blindness infection in which permanent settlement is impossible but where there are rich and fertile soils. In every generation there are some who take the risk of farming these lands, all too frequently paying the price of blindness for their momentary prosperity. Generally speaking, around Kita anyone unable to find suitable land within the village finds it easy to move on somewhere else, not too far away; pressure on the land must be understood within this wider regional context rather than simply within the village itself.

A shift from the household to the village as the productive unit would have entailed a massive reorganization of the system. Such a shift would have to be accompanied by a modernization of agriculture in the direction of mechanized and scientific farming in order to become more than a paper transformation. The same people doing the same work would see no reason to organize it differently. Technological changes would lead to the replacement of the elderly leaders by younger men skilled in accounting, handling machinery, and dealing with bureaucracies.

Skills would be less evenly distributed in the population, and variation would be a function of education rather than age. There would also be a more complex division of labor. For this reason the egalitarian youth association, oriented towards work-as-fiesta (Leynaud 1966), would not be adaptive. Not only would the *lu* have to be broken up into its constituent parts (Ernest 1971), but measures would have to be taken to ensure that family values did not reassert themselves at that level, the most effective measures being precisely the modernization of agriculture and the change in the mode of production (Kostic 1972). A shift in this direction has, of course, many implications for the future of central control to which I will return below.

The Benduguba cooperative, like others in Mali, was essentially an association of men active in farming, the effective leaders of their households. It did not touch the productive structures of the village. Indeed, it would not be too much to suggest that it misunderstood them fundamentally, for it glossed over the difference between individual and household memberships, paid no attention whatsoever to the productive role of women, and was not in the least prepared to cope with the political problem of its tranformation into a cooperative of production.

This "failure" was, perhaps, an intended result from the point of view of the villagers. As I have pointed out in my original analysis, this cooperative succeeded at the village level because it was "naturalized": it was made a village institution, part of village defenses against intrusion from Kita or from the central government. This occurred because the cooperative could be made to "fit" into already existing village structures. In these terms the AVC assembly of 1965 that I observed was simply a village meeting extended to a group of nine villages; as in village meetings the senile, the young, and the women did not take part, and decisions were reached by a form of "sense-of-the-meeting." This decision-making process tends to reinforce the dominant role of the mature (but not yet senile) men. Giving a larger role to a cooperative in this situation might lead to a consolidation of the power of the mature men, as Gosselin observed among the Bisa of Upper Volta.

The process of decision making itself, however, allows all those present to have their say and is thus participatory as far as the group assembled is concerned. I have analyzed these Maninka patterns of collective decision making as follows (see Hopkins 1972:168): everyone present has the right to speak up, and the decision is not considered to have been made until there is no more vocal opposition. All those present are engaged by the decision, for their silence implies acceptance. Decisions made in this way are occasionally subject to question. Strong opponents, sensing which way the consensus is going to go, may simply avoid the meeting in order to allow themselves freedom of action afterwards; and there is no system of enforcement to assure that those who assent at a meeting in fact carry out the desicion, For this reason decisions that require everyone to act on them are the hardest ones to realize, for people must not only agree but also follow through on them. Still, the legitimacy of any decision depends on how it was made, and the chances that people will follow through on a decision improve immeasurably if they feel it is legitimate.

There is both a value and a danger in this kind of decision making. The value is that it guarantees the acceptability of the decisions made, for the assent derives from participation; the danger is that people rarely make innovative decisions in this way, except under great pressure, for it is hard to move consensus away from trodden paths. This was especially clear in Benduguba where one of the functions of the AVC in the minds of the members was precisely to protect the villages from outside interference. Villagers were proud of their ability to manage their own affairs[4]

---

[4]   In 1965 the villages around Kita raced to see which one would complete its tax payments first. The village council was in charge of collecting taxes and did so publicly for the most part.

and keen to continue doing so. Attempts by the central government to bring about changes in village ways and structures were resented, independent of their merit, as attempts to supersede village autonomy.

The Malian government had instituted the AVC by presenting the villages with a *fait accompli*: the old mercantile structures were simply abolished and this was the only alternative open to the villagers. But they were left alone, on the whole, to run their AVCs and cooperatives as they saw fit. Insofar as cooperative affairs were village affairs it became essential to disguise them from the government in order to lessen the impact of government on them — one of the oldest adages among the Maninka is that if knowledge is power, then ignorance is impotence. The less government knows the less it can interfere, and the less it can affect local patterns of society and culture.

Despite the dangers that it may reinforce traditional structures by eliminating certain categories of the population from the decision-making process and that it may tend to make conformist and conservative decisions because of the necessity for consensus, there remains much that is valuable in participatory decision making. It is interesting to analyze some of the requirements of such a system. First of all, it is obvious that it assumes agreement on the identity and goal of the body making the decision, and that it supposes a willingness to reach a decision — to compromise if necessary, to accept being overruled by a majority, and so on. It also requires an institutionalized procedure for allowing such participation: in the case of Benduguba, this was the annual AVC general assembly; for other, busier cooperatives, an annual meeting might be a formality permitting little real control, and a meeting of any kind might not be the best solution for a large cooperative.

In order for people to participate equally and fully, they must have equal access to information, for without this there will be a tendency for monopoly of information to lead to control of decision. For the opinions of all to be equal all must be equally informed. This seems to have been possible in the Benduguba AVC because the information involved was relatively simple in nature and comprehensible to all. Much of the necessary information was information about each other, about the history of the village and the kinship and alliance relations found there, and about the general economic situation, such as the size of the crop. The affairs of the cooperative, while handled by a few, were accessible to all. The skill possessed by the leaders that distinguished them from the mass was literacy but once the information was presented orally it was easily grasped. Information about how the government wanted the cooperatives to develop and information about the future context of the cooperatives was possessed by no one. Lacking this information the decisions of the AVC were limited to short-term, management-type decisions, such as whom to pay how much salary.

In summary, the conditions of successful participatory decision making in the Benduguba AVC were the acceptance of the established boundaries as relevant ones for talking together, willingness to come to a decision, the presence of a proper means — the general assembly — and a relatively equal diffusion of information on which decisions could be based. This participatory framework for making decisions relative to the life of the cooperative acted as a shield or buffer between the hierarchical structures of the national bureaucracies on the one hand and the hierarchical structure of the Maninka households on the other.

This is another indication that the participatory, egalitarian elements present in the cooperative itself could work only as long as the cooperative had to deal with affairs marginal to the village on the one hand and to the bureaucracies on the other. The affairs were marginal to the village because they involved commercialization and did not affect the productive base; they were marginal to the state because it was not in a position to intervene in the affairs of each individual village. Between these two systems the cooperative acted as a link; it was a union of producing enterprises where each was equal and it was possible to ignore the hierarchy on either side.

The paradox of local control of a cooperative is thus that it may be conservative in its foundations and its effect and act to block progressive changes from whatever source. At the same time, radical governments may become too impatient of local reluctance and develop schemes to bypass consent and oblige villagers (and others) to follow common patterns laid down in the center; such a threat to village integrity stimulates a corresponding response, and whatever progressive tendencies there may be in the village will be overcome by the need for village defense. This paradox of popular government brings to mind the dilemma of those addicted to formulating broad plans of social transformation in the name of the people; how does one react when people do not like the plan that has been prepared for their benefit? Does one force them to swallow it on the grounds that they will realize it is in their interests? Should one attempt to persuade the people, or switch to a different scheme that they will accept? By maintaining their integrity, the villagers of the Benduguba AVC were retaining their power to judge the innovations that might be thrust upon them.

This defensive reaction on the part of the villagers suggests that the problems of "direct" passage from traditional social structures to modern socialist ones is more complicated than a simple comparison of traits and structures of the two to see if transition is conceivable. Comparison is an essential first step, but the task of the anthropologist must also be to illuminate the dynamics and dialectics of the passage from one set of social institutions to another. There is a tendency in the literature to consider the passage in terms of the distance between the original state and the desired result (generally either entrepreneurial peasant capitalism or some form of cooperatives or collectives under the aegis of a central-ized bureaucracy), rather than in terms of the detailed mapping out of the path. Starting from the causes in which we know the beginning and point the forces for change, and can analyze what happened, we should try to extrapolate to the dynamic cases of the present.

Ideally the results of anthropological reflections on the possible future paths and present states of different societies should be made available to members of the societies in question. This is the only way to avoid being intellectual cannibals. Yet we know we are talking about local communi-ties, not nations, and so it is no longer adequate to talk about depositing copies of the thesis in the National Library, and so on. I do not know what the answer to this is (and do not claim more virtue than another, MY thesis being in the National Library), but it is clear that anthropology should be a dialogue between the researcher and the people who are the subjects of his research, not just between the researcher and the intellec-tual elite of the country of his research. Recently it has been made clear that ethnocide in more or less extreme versions is not the unique attribute of nations having conquered faraway territories but can take place, like most accidents, at home.

Certainly, this essay based on material collected with different ends in view, will not be entirely persuasive of the necessity or feasibility of a prospective anthropology. But perhaps it will at least serve to open a dialogue and enable us to put some of our ideas in order. Whether in this form or another, anthropology and anthropologists should accept a responsibility concerning the welfare of the people to whom they owe their research opportunities and who are generally among the damned of the earth.

REFERENCES

BADIAN, SEYDOU
   1964   *Les dirigeants africains face à leur peuple*. Paris: Maspéro.

DESROCHES, HENRI
1963   *Planification et volontariat dans les développements coopératifs.* Paris and The Hague: Mouton.

DIOP, MAJHEMOUT
1971   *Histoire des classes sociales dans l'Afrique de l'Ouest. I. le Mali.* Paris: Maspéro.

ERNST, KLAUS
1971   "La communauté traditionelle et le progrès social en Afrique occidentale," in *Sociologie de l'impérialisme.* Edited by Anouar Abdel-Malek, 339–63. Paris: Editions Anthropos.

HOPKINS, NICHOLAS S.
1969a "Leadership and consensus in two Malian cooperatives," in *The anthropology of development in sub-Saharan Africa.* Edited by D. Brokensha and M. Pearsall, 64–69. Society for Applied Anthropology Monograph 10. Lexington, Ky.: Society for Applied Anthropology.
1969b Socialism and social change in rural Mali. *Journal of Modern African Studies* 7:457–467.
1971   "Maninka social organization," in *Papers on the Manding.* Edited by C. T. Hodge, 99–128. African series, volume three. Bloomington: Indiana University Publications.
1972   *Popular government in an African town: Kita, Mali.* Chicago: University of Chicago Press.

JONES, WILLIAM I.
1969   The Keita decade: economics of the coup. *Africa Report* (March-April): 23–26, 51–53.
1970   The food economy of Ba Dugu Djoliba, Mali," in *African food production systems.* Edited by P. F. M. McLoughlin, 265–306. Baltimore: The John Hopkins University Press.

KOSTIC, CVETKO
1972   "Forms of the family and land ownership in Yugoslav rural areas," in *The Yugoslav village.* Edited by Vlado Puljiz, 189–199. Zagreb: Department of Rural Sociology.

LEYNAUD, EMILE
1966   Fraternités d'âge et sociétés de culture dans la haute vallée du Niger. *Cahiers d'Etudes Africaines* 6:41–68.

MEILLASSOUX, CLAUDE
1960   Essai d'interprétation du phénomène économique dans les sociétés traditionnelles d'autosubsistance. *Cahiers d'Etudes Africaines* 1(4): 38–67.
1970   A class analysis of the bureaucratic process in Mali. *Journal of Development Studies* 6:97–110.

Peasant Response to Cooperativization Under Agrarian Reform in the Communities of the Peruvian Sierra

GAVIN ALDERSON-SMITH

[One of] the goals of the Peasant Communities [is]... to revive the traditional norms and values compatible with national development.

Statute of peasant communities, Article 8d

The problem then, to be found in the economic structure of the land can be put in the following dilemma: either we continue along the route laid down by the Colonial economic system, i.e: the hoarding of the land of the State and the *Comunidad* for the benefit of the great latifundia – colonized or *yanaconized*, or simply capitalist with its enslaving economic system; or, in contrast, we give free rein to the *ayllus'* communal aspirations to preserve their lands, directing them toward the twofold task firstly of modernizing the institutions they possess today in order to rationalize production and, secondly of giving a new ideological content to our agrarian masses.

CASTRO POZO,
Del ayllu *al cooperativismo socialista*

The Peruvian government has made clear its desire to revive dormant traditions in the peasant communities. In recent articles, both Giorgio Alberti (1973) and Norman Long (Long and Winder 1973) have emphasized that the new statute will not so much overthrow the existing power relationships in the peasant communities as simply emphasize existing elements in the local political process. While Alberti stresses the lines of dominance tying the communities to the larger power structure of the area, Long focuses on the various institutions within the village through which power may be exercised. I agree with their conclusions on this point, and in this paper I shall amplify their analysis to include a larger historical and political perspective. I shall also comment on the role that the anthropologist can play in the process of agrarian reform of the kind exemplified by the Peruvian experience.

THE LEGISLATIVE AND IDEOLOGICAL BACKGROUND

Until the arrival of the present regime, legislation concerning peasant communities during this century reflected the paternalism of the Right and/or the idealism of the Left. Because the one element that could really make any difference to the *comunero*'s situation — namely, the land — was consistently missing, the laws either remained dead letters or actually backfired.

At least in law (despite the actual physical devastation of the communities), it would seem that the communal ownership of land, rooted in the pre-Inca *ayllu*, was respected during the Colonial Period in Peru. But contemporary liberalism led Bolivar in two decrees — on April 8, 1824, and on July 4, 1825 — to order the breaking up of community lands into private lots.

The 1919 constitution was the first attempt to return legal recognition to the communities, but it was the constitution of 1933 that recognized the legality of the *personero* as the official representative of the community and ordered the formal inscription of the communities under the *Consejos Departmentales*, which had been set up in 1873. It was hoped that, through reference to a proper list of the estimated 5,000 communities, something might be learned about their needs. But the legislation again remained largely ineffective until the *Decreto Supremo* of 1938 created the *Dirección de Asuntos Indígenas* (DAI) to look after all affairs relating to the communities. This, in effect, set the formal pattern for the legal make-up of what were then called "indigenous communities."

To receive official recognition the communities were required:
1. to accredit the number of years that the community had existed (which proved in the majority of cases to be impossible);
2. to present a map and communal titles to lands; and
3. to record the population by age and sex; the agricultural, livestock, and industrial capital that they possessed; and their schools and school attendance.

The law also set up the rules for election of communal officials (to be approved by the DAI) and forbade the sale or rental of communal lands.

If the law was designed to improve indigenous conditions, it was bound to fail without any simultaneous land reform. Besides marginal benefits that might have been gained through the extremely weak office of indigenous affairs, the communities could hardly have seen much advantage in registration. In the 1940 census, only 1,472 communities, of an estimated 4,623, had so inscribed.

Given the central topic of this paper, I can only suggest here that the (possibly unintentional) result of this law was to place the communities in a political and economic vacuum. While local elections were subject to departmental approval, the peasant economy in the communities was supposed to function on an island of cooperation in a sea of capitalist competition. In effect, the concept of the *comunidad indígena* as a backwater of Peruvian society was given legal trappings.

It will be important to bear in mind this outline of legislation during the earlier part of this century when we look at rural reactions to present legislation. Both the concepts behind the 1970 legislation and the rural reactions to it are closely tied to this earlier experience.

The peasants themselves could see the 1933 law in whatever terms they thought suitable, and although there was no land reform, in the case that I know best, those terms were land. For this reason it is most likely that the first communities to register as such were those engaged in land disputes. In my own experience, however, because the new law was not rigidly upheld, particularly *vis-à-vis* large and established *predios*, and because the *comuneros* in many cases had limited legal experience, there is no reason to suppose that the law encouraged any more land *revindicación* than already existed.

During the period of this legislation by the established government, there existed in Peru an extremely vocal group of socialist writers. If the actions of the legislators reflected a belief that the protection of the traditional community was vital as a way of making the peasants PERIPHERAL to national development problems, the ideology of the left saw these traditional communities as a CENTRAL solution to national development. While the basic emphasis of the government today may be different, the idea that the principles of socialism lie dormant to be tapped still remains.[1]

I have already suggested this heritage in the opening quotation by

---

[1]   Article 2 of the statute of 1970 reads in part: "The Peasant Community is a grouping of families... who are tied by common social and cultural roots, by communal work and by mutual aid."

Castro Pozo, the founder of the Peruvian Socialist party. From Manuel Gonzalez Prada to Luis Valcarcel and José Carlos Mariátegui there was a consistent desire to form a national brand of socialism around the principles of the Indian community. Two quotations will illustrate the tenor of these sentiments. In 1928 Mariátegui wrote:

The Indian never felt less free than when he felt alone.

For this reason, in the Indian villages where families are gathered, among whom connections of patrimony and communal work have been extinguished, there still exist, robust and tenacious, the habits of cooperation and solidarity which are the empirical expression of a communist spirit. The *comunidad* corresponds to this spirit. It is its organism. When expropriation and repartition began to dissolve the *comunidad*, indigenous socialism always provided the means to reconstruct and maintain it (1970:83).[2]

And eight years later Haya de la Torre (1961) wrote:

The 400-year-old fight of the *comunidad* against the latifundio and the decadence of the latter, historically prove that the Inca *comunidad* constitutes the basis for the restoration of a national economy. The reorganization of our unhinged economy, the great agricultural cooperative that will be Peru, can only be established on the base of the marvelous economic organization of the Incas, modernized with all the advantages of modern technology and protected by the State not only from the *latifundistas* but also from the (large) producers.

This, then, is a very quick sketch of the background to the new Statute of Peasant Communities, which took effect in 1970. In turning now to the contemporary rural response to these laws, I want to emphasize that these historical antecedents should be kept in mind.

THE SETTING: LIMITS AND LIMITATIONS

There are limitations both to a general study of peasant response to the agrarian reforms being carried out in Peru and to a more locally specific study. The variations in local conditions from one end of the Peruvian sierra to another reduce the value of all but the vaguest general statements. In any case, my own financial resources have made such a study impossible. A narrower study can illustrate the actual effect of reform policy and is

---

[2] I do not wish to simplify Mariátegui's argument here. His note (1970: 78) qualifies his position somewhat. Moreover, statements such as these should be seen in terms of the writer's purposes at hand. Nonetheless, having made this point, I do not think that it detracts from the view that the present legislation finds a base in these writings. (The slogan of the *Reforma Agraria* is taken from Mariátegui's 1927 statement, "Lucha por LA TIERRA PARA LOS QUE LA TRABAJAN, although the last part of the sentence is missing: "exproplandola sin indemnización."

far better suited to an examination of the actual PROCESS of response. Certain general statements can be made, and these may be further enhanced by comparisons with studies of other areas, but while I shall attempt to draw some broad conclusions at the end of this paper, I must caution that I have just finished my fieldwork and therefore have made only a preliminary analysis of my findings.

My research was done (January 1972 to August 1973) in the high *puna* (about 13,000 feet) that lies to the west and south of the Mantaro Valley, in that part of the Department of Junin which borders on the Departments of Huancavelica and Lima (Figure 1.) While many villages in this area rely on some agriculture for household consumption, the

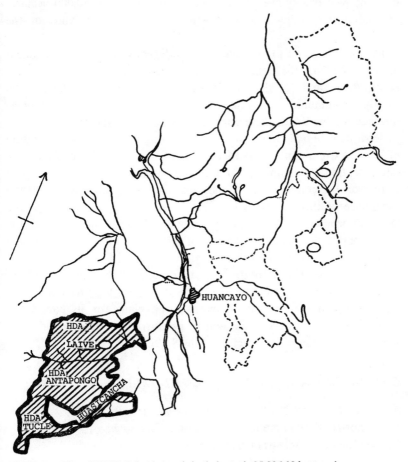

Figure 1.   Map of SAIS *Cahuide* (total shaded area is 85,826.02 hectares)

(Note: The shaded area indicates the Margen Derecha of the SAIS. The unshaded area cutting it virtually in two is the communal land of the village.)

major occupation is raising livestock — sheep, cattle, and in the higher areas, llamas. Two distinct types of economic unit characterize the area: the large livestock cooperative and the small peasant community. The cooperative is the Margen Derecha section of the larger *Sociedad Agrícola de Interés Social* (SAIS) *Cahuide*, which extends over a total area of 685 square miles (of which the Margen Derecha occupies 275). Surrounding this cooperative are roughly fifteen peasant communities.

All but one of these communities not only function as independent economic units, but also as members of the cooperative. I shall describe below the nature of this "membership." The one exception is a community that, as a result of extensive land *revindicaciónes* (invasions) over the past twenty-five years, has accumulated about 30,000 hectares of communal grazing land that extend deep into the lands of the SAIS.

Thus I should like to examine here (1) the early effects of government attempts to turn the communities themselves into efficient economic cooperatives, and (2) the way in which the large SAIS relates to its member communities. It must be understood that besides acting as members of the SAIS, these communities are also expected to function as separate economic units and are thus entirely affected by the Statute of Peasant Communities. By focusing the first part of this paper on the one exceptional community, I hope both to illustrate the effects of this statute on the communities of the area and to suggest that the actual experience of this exception in effect constitutes an alternative to the land "reform" initiated by the government through the SAIS. In the second part, I shall examine the role of this larger cooperative from the viewpoint of the member communities.

In both cases I shall begin with an outline of the relevant reform program. In the first case, this means specifically the legal restrictions on membership in the peasant community and plans for its conversion into a more efficient economic unit of production. In the second case, it means an outline of the structure of the SAIS.

COMUNEROS AND EMPRESAS COMUNALES

According to Article 23 of the new law, a *comunero* must:
1. be born in the community or be the son of a *comunero*;
2. be head of a family or in his majority;
3. have stable residence in the community;
4. be basically a worker in farming;
5. not be an owner of landed property in or outside the community;

6. not have a major source of income outside the community; and
7. not belong to another community.

A man may acquire the status of *comunero* through assimilation (presumably an ex-*comunero* may do likewise) by:
1. being accepted by the majority of votes in the General Assembly of the community;
2. being a worker in farming; and
3. having formed a permanent home with a member of the community.

As I noted above, the promulgation of such laws is less important than their administration, and it is in this area that the new laws are more significant than their predecessors. The government agency *Sistema Nacional de Movilización Social* (SINAMOS), one of whose branches administers these laws, is able to offer a considerable number of benefits to complying communities, and an extensive propaganda program has accompanied application of the laws. Nonetheless, in all the communities with which I have had any experience, the *comuneros* consider that each aspect of the law is applicable only if approved by the General Assembly of the community (which existed before the new laws). Thus, for example, three years after the enactment of the law restricting residence to the physical area of the community itself, many communities refuse to accept the validity of this legislation.

The laws themselves must be seen in the context of a diffusion program designed to encourage the communities to rationalize their economic administrations along cooperative lines. It is suggested that the statute itself provides the basis for successful economic development. For example, for cooperatives within the community itself to acquire recognition (and hence to receive aid from the state), they must fulfill specific criteria, among which are the requirements that at least 50 percent of all *comuneros* must be members and that there may be no disproportionate holdings on the part of some members within the cooperative.

It is envisaged that in a community (like those discussed here) that is to all intents and purposes identical in membership to the *municipalidad*, the importance of the positions of mayor and governor will give way almost entirely to the officers of the community, which itself will take on a more specific meaning, as an *empresa comunal* [communal firm].[3] Those parts of the statute that call for the farming and administration of communal lands as single units, rather than as individually farmed family plots, have so far had little effect, but the SINAMOS field staff has

[3] According to members of the regional and zonal offices of SINAMOS in Huancayo and Huancavelica, in June 1973.

outlined a series of steps for this transition to the *empresa comunal* and are already attempting to implement them.[4]

THE PEASANT RESPONSE

Background Information

The anomalous community contains 308 *comuneros* and about 1,500 residents in total. Every *comunero* has a small amount of agricultural land, ranging from half an acre to about fifteen hectares, to which he has no legal title but which he regards as his own and which is passed down by inheritance. This land varies considerably in quality, but with few exceptions it is used to produce food for family consumption only. Some 30,000 hectares are owned by the community and used for livestock grazing. Although in principle this land is undivided communal property, *comuneros* build their own *estancias*[5] on it and pay a fee to the community for each head of livestock grazed. Because inventory taking is impossible, given the mountainous and extensive area of the land, collection of rents in proportion to pasture use becomes a matter of guesswork and depends on the diligence of the president of the community. For the same reasons, it is not easy to estimate differences in ownership (and hence wealth), but this varies from 5 to 500 head of sheep.

Besides these two major local resources, residents of the community may migrate for one to five months of the year. In some cases this may involve some kind of street-selling in Huancayo, the provincial capital, or working with a relative who has a more permanent business there. But in the majority of cases this temporary migration is directed toward Lima, where the villagers sell strawberries during the season, which

---

[4]   The *empresa comunal* will be considerably more sophisticated than the present *comunidad campesina* and, in those cases where members of neighboring communities hold land in each other's territory (through marriage, for example), may embrace two or three communities. This reflects the problem that is anticipated in persuading peasants to relinquish rights to the use of land not specifically in their own community. In some areas — in a valley, for example — where two or three communities are close together, the interrelationship of land use is so thorough that members of one community may in fact farm more land in their land in their neighbor's territory.
  The stages in the formation of the *empresa comunal* are: (1) assessing each situation; (2) internal arrangement – members must vote acceptance of the new structure; (3) land inventory; (4) consolidation of property; (5) restructuring; and (6) formation of the *empresa comunal*.
[5]   Although in a strict sense the word *estancia* in Peru means a small hut and accompanying corral, its meaning varies according to context. It may thus be extended to refer to the area of the communal pasture that a man considers his own pasturing zone.

runs from late November to March and thus happens to suit well the agricultural cycle in the village. Here, too, residence in the city and the acquisition of fruit for selling depend on contacts with sons of the village.

Of course the lure of the city, especially for young people, is great,[6] and often a two-month migration extends to five months and then a year. The migrant may return for a while and then go off to Lima for two, four, or six years. At least 300 migrants who have left since 1945 have not yet returned, and they, of course, provide the city contacts for today's villagers.

It may be true that virtually all *comuneros* voice concern about the advancement of the village and see it in terms of adapting to outside forces, of which the new laws are a part, but this is of no help in the problem at hand. Experience has shown the peasant that both at the communal level (in the case of the land invasions) and at the individual level, any relations with another party are better when dealing from a position of strength. This belief may offset a belief in the prospect of accruing benefits from conformity to government plans.

I shall illustrate how this is articulated by examining the crisis caused by the failure of the first officeholders under the new community statute aftereffects leading up to new elections. This period runs from January to December 1972. I shall concentrate, for the sake of clarity, on the roles of key actors. This method is used by Bailey (1964, 1971) and Van Velsen (1967) and to some extent is embraced by Victor Turner's term "the social drama" (1957). The dangers of such an approach are: (1) what appears to be purely descriptive is inevitably highly selective, particularly in a paper of this length, and (2) it is not always easy for the reader to decide which are the ideas of the writer and which are those of the actors (see Moerman 1969). I have tried, in the latter case, to confine descriptions of personalities to adjectives used by local residents and have otherwise tried to show which views are my own and are not necessarily shared by the actors.[7] The advantage of the approach is

---

[6]   After six months of research among the villagers resident in Lima, initial findings reveal that purely economic variables are not sufficient to explain migration (see Gavin Alderson-Smith i.p.).

[7]   Peter Lloyd (1973) adds: "My criticism of these approaches is that in focussing so intently upon the minutiae of personal interaction... one so easily loses sight of... the relative position of individuals in their total society, the structure of that society." This is the chicken and the egg problem with regard to process and structure. It also relates to the kind of explanation that the social scientist is seeking. In any event, it can be solved, in a larger study, by locating the process being described and the actors involved in the larger society, always bearing in mind the dynamic effect that these processes have on the greater structure. Structure remains, nonetheless, an abstract tool having no

that it allows the reader, to a small extent, to draw his own conclusions from the events described.

I usually interviewed a number of actors prior to events such as general assemblies, elections, etc., and then taped the events themselves and eventually interviewed people afterward. By talking to others in the pueblo besides central actors, I was able to gain some insight into what they felt a central actor would do and then what they thought his acts really signified. I tried to add to this by holding group sessions after events, and less formal information was gathered in bars and on street corners. I was further helped by a research assistant, Don Pedro Caño, an anthropology student at the Universidad del Centro in Huancayo and a son of the pueblo. He was often able to obtain personal opinions that were not otherwise available to me.[8]

The Dismissal of the Authorities

In January 1972, the important village positions and the people who held them were:

1. *Alcalde*: Fernando. He had about 30 sheep and less than an acre of land but made most of this living from his trade as a mason in the community. He had learned the trade in Huancayo but had long since ceased to migrate there. He was best known for frequenting one or another of the local drinking spots. He was forty-three years old.

2. *Gobernador*: Lucio. His property extended to 5 horses, 58 sheep, 4 cattle, and 1.5 hectares of land. He had, he told me, taken his position in rivalry with his brother-in-law, Primitivo, who had been fired from the job by the community for being too officious. Lucio was forty-one years old.

3. *Presidente del consejo, administración, de la comunidad*: the articulate Victor. He moved freely between Huancayo and the village, quickly took up and dropped various enterprises in his travels, and was presently selling plastic articles on the Huancayo-Huancavelica train when out of the village. His freshly painted house and flamboyant air reflected his own view that he was a man "on the make." He had more than 150 sheep, 6 cattle, and 1.5 hectares of land. He was thirty-seven years old.

1. *Presidente del consejo, vigilancia, de la comunidad*: Silvestre. Until

---

greater reality than that prescribed by the purpose at hand (on the part of the social scientist or anyone else).

[8]   At later stages in fieldwork I considerably modified this method, with particular reference to the writings of Alfred Schutz and Maurice Natanson.

his tenure, he had gone to Lima each year to sell fruit with his brother, who lived there permanently. Besides 2 hectares of land, he had more than 70 head of sheep and one of the two gasoline-run mills in the pueblo, which he shared with his brother in Lima. He was forty-three years old.

5. *Presidente de la pre-cooperativa* (which had existed precariously since 1968 and had 82 members, who held as shares 3 to 20 sheep): Fagustino. He was the crusty old owner of 200 head of sheep. He had never migrated and was fifty-nine years old.

6. *Secretario de la pre-cooperativa*: Arcadio. He had more than 500 head of sheep and was thirty-seven years old.

Soon after I arrived in the village, impeachment proceedings were started against the two presidents of the community. They — Victor in particular, as Silvestre was described as merely a puppet — were accused of persuading the community to buy a tractor that had proven virtually useless on the steep inclines of the area (and in fact had toppled over and killed the driver, a local man), and then renting the tractor in Huancayo and stealing the proceeds; of selling community-owned sheep and again pocketing some of the proceeds; and of being absolutist and antirevolutionary leaders.

Victor and Silvestre retaliated in a handbill accusing specific ringleaders of being wolves in sheep's clothing. These included the exgovernor's brother; a graduate of an agricultural school who had returned to live in the village; and Artico, a man who held no office but was well known in the community for his respect for old customs and institutions. No notably powerful or well-off opponents were named, but occasionally their close relatives were mentioned, as in the case of the exgovernor's brother. At least two other commonly despised people were included. Their motive was said to be to sow discord in the community. Victor and Silvestre also tried to unearth a rival scandal involving the local primary school principal, but with little success. The handbill, in fact, was not printed or even distributed in the village itself; instead it was passed around among the residents' clubs in Huancayo, La Oroya, and Lima, inviting them to come to the next General Assembly.

Nevertheless, Victor and Silvestre managed to accumulate virtually no support whatever at the assembly. Instead they had to sit and be publicly chastized by almost everyone present. The meeting went on from 10:00 A.M. to 10:00 P.M., with two hours for lunch (which was provided at Victor's expense for all outside vistors who had managed to come). Victor and Silvestre were also accused of lacking respect for the community; not really being proper members of the pueblo (*gloss*: village, people) because they really lived outside (in fact this charge applied no more to them than to many others present); and maladministering the pre-cooperative (they were not in charge of it anyway).

They were defended in an impressive speech by a Huancayo resident who, I was told, had once been the provincial secretary for the *Alianza Popular Revolucionario de América* (APRA). During the entire day, he was the only person, including all speakers from the floor, who spoke in Wanka (the local Quechua dialect). He made no concrete remarks but appealed for unity and consideration by the villagers of the public reputation of the pueblo. Here he noted that a foreign anthropologist had come to study the community because of its great fame abroad. Victor himself varied from being silently insulted and personally hurt to making stinging replies, which included the suggestion that the small owners in the pre-cooperative were being manipulated by the rich and that they should watch out.

With the exception of two or three wealthy *comuneros*, among them Arcadio, the secretary of the pre-cooperative, the community appeared in full force. Victor's handbill, on the other hand, had only managed to produce five residents of Huancayo and none from Lima. A number of older *comuneros* and some women *comuneras* did not come, nor did one or two of Victor and Silvestre's close friends.

Almost entirely as a result of the efforts of the well-dressed, Wanka-speaking Huancayo resident, the villagers were persuaded to limit themselves to a vote of censure. The "residents" (sons of the village living elsewhere are termed, rather confusingly, *residentes*) left early the next morning. By midday I had already heard that the villagers were unhappy with the decision and that the following Sunday a meeting was to be called, without the presence of any "residents," in which the two officials were definitely to be removed. The following weekend this was done.

Because Victor and Silvestre had been the first officers elected under the new statute, the ensuing period was important for establishing how these events reflected, and in turn determined, the local response to the law.

The mayor was not prepared to shoulder suddenly the entire administration of the municipality and the community; he frequently emphasized that his duties did not embrace such a wide area. Nonetheless, attendance at *faenas* [work parties] of the municipality fell off and the biggest fiesta threatened to be a flop, To avoid having all this linked to his name, the mayor resigned. This left only the governor, who had taken office to satisfy family rivalries. Thus the field was open for others to enter the arena, but an air of confusion and caution prevailed and there was no rush to run for the vacated positions. Before discussing the reasons for this, however, I must comment on the fate of Victor.[9]

Victor

The accusation of corruption was a well-tried method of removing unpopular officials from office, I was told by a number of *comuneros*. But I had considerable trouble finding any deeper explanation of Victor's unpopularity beyond this misdemeanor. Some young *comuneros* who were anxious to have the community quickly accept the new statute (which they saw as a crucial step to advancement) told me that Victor had been a victim of circumstance and that he, and most of the community, did not understand the new laws. But they did not amplify this. Nonetheless, at no time did anyone ever question Victor's ability as a leader.

I then asked what the expresidents had tried but failed to do while in office. It became clear that they had made early attempts to apply the new law but had not managed to get sufficient support from the community. Emphasizing that the pre-cooperative, ineffective though it was, held the key to cooperative development in the village, they attempted to mobilize the small owner-members to remove the wealthy administration of the cooperative and to enact a leveling law to equalize holdings in the cooperative.

Many small owner-members openly agreed that the control of the cooperative by the rich was wrong, but they seemed to feel that the success of the rich in livestock raising acted as some kind of guarantee for the cooperative. Meanwhile, a number of wealthy members of the cooperative resigned while they could, and they took with them some poorer relatives. The result was that the membership dropped from 127 members to 82. As SINAMOS had already made clear that the acceptance of the pre-cooperative as an official cooperative depended on its representation of at least 50 percent of the *comuneros*, Victor suggested that sanctions be brought against nonmembers by increasing their payment per head for grazing privately owned animals on the communal lands. In so doing, he lost the support of another sector of the poorer *comuneros*

---

[9] An analysis of the role played by various people involved in these political events should be considerably more exhaustive than I can offer here. I shall therefore concentrate only on those elements that I consider relevant to a view of the effects of the new Statute of Peasant Communities.

who were not members of the pre-cooperative. This explained the accusation that he was guilty of maladministering the cooperative.

Furthermore, Victor was known to favor some attempt to return communal agricultural land to the administration of the community officials, removing it from individual families. Many people to whom I spoke felt that this was motivated by a desire for greater personal power on his part. His attempt to disband the traditional institution of the *varayoc*,[10] which had no formal recognition from any government department, confirmed beliefs that he was bent on concentrating power in his person. This was reflected in the accusations that he had no respect for the community and was an absolutist ruler.

Of course, no one argued that Victor and Silvestre should be removed because of too much diligence in applying the law. On the contrary, many felt that they were misapplying the law and acting against its spirit, which was to preserve, rather than destroy, the community. Others argued more specifically that they actually broke the new law by spending too much time outside the community.

That Victor and Silvestre directed their defense, in the form of handbills, toward the migrants outside the community indicates that they expected support in that area. Indeed, as holders of moderate numbers of livestock in the pueblo and also as ambitious villagers, they themselves depended upon the money that they gained through migration. While the fact that few of the migrants returned for the assembly reflects the feeling that Victor was already a lost cause, it is significant that they nevertheless did send one of their most articulate representatives to defend him.

Victor was one of the middle-income peasants who, in varying degrees, used their ties to migrate out during the year. He himself felt that he could draw on support from poorer peasants who did likewise, and by attempting to mobilize them to modify the cooperative, he hoped to increase his support. He was a flamboyant and articulate speaker. Many told me that they considered him the brightest man in the village, and they usually added that this also explained why he was a thief. This is well reflected in the word *vivo*, which literally means "lively" but can also mean "sharp," which (as in English) may have the connotation of

---

[10]   The institution of *varayoc* or *campo de vara* appears to be a Spanish adaptation of an Inca system. Although at one time the *alcalde de vara* and his men probably controlled the community, today membership is largely restricted to those with little schooling (though not necessarily complete illiterates), and their task is guarding animals and crops from damage by forces of man or nature (foxes, frost, hail, etc.). They show respect to both the Christian god and Wamani, the god of the hills.

being sly: "A man like Victor, with one eye closed he can tell people like us that bread is meat, and we believe him."

Being an articulate speaker, however, may be rather more of a mixed blessing in a rural society than it is in our own. For one thing, many members of the opposition cannot be attacked in open speech and similarly are themselves unlikely to attack that way. Nevertheless, if Victor had just been fighting a simple battle against wealthy influences in the pueblo, he might have had more success. But nobody saw the event in such simple terms. Generally speaking, he was up against two elements of opposition, represented by two people whose positions are hard to describe precisely because they were both reluctant to articulate them.

Arcadio

Victor himself told me that although he had to attack people like the brother of the exgovernor Primitivo, it was Primitivo himself and other wealthy villagers, among them Arcadio, the secretary of the pre-cooperative, who were really to blame. Yet neither Primitivo nor Arcadio even came to the assembly. Although their names were never actually mentioned, various *comuneros* often referred to them by implication as powerful people who were controlling the cooperative and using more than their share of the communal grazing land. Much later, when I was working in Lima, thse same people were picked out by the Lima residents as the greatest enemies of the community.

Of course they, too, had their backers. Just as Victor seemed to be a good leader because of his charm and worldliness, so Arcadio seemed to be leadership material because his own wealth was proof of his ability. *Astucia* [cunning] is a word used frequently in the pueblo and it applies to both men. It makes them good leaders, just as it makes them suspected thieves.

It is, I think, essentially for this reason that people like Arcadio, with his 500 head of sheep, are seen both as a source of community ills and as a source of community leadership. I shall not argue the apparent contradiction of these statements here except to say that the social scientist is often mistaken in assuming that it is imperative for people in the social world to resolve the inherent inconsistencies of such thinking (see Schutz 1964).

As I have said, although his relatives and friends were there, Arcadio never came to the impeachment ceremony. He thus avoided the necessity of defending himself in the event that Victor should decide to attack him directly. He also, whether intentionally or not, removed his person from the entire breakdown of the community administration. He later reemphasized this disinterest in the formal community as defined by the statutes by pointedly avoiding the new elections for an assembly some four months later.

Throughout the subsequent eight months, he never spoke at any open assemblies except to reply to specific questions about the cooperative. But in any small group conversation, he would emphasize fairness, hard work, and individual responsibility. The last he would sometimes illustrate by contrasting it to the idle fields and empty, rotting houses of the absent "residents" in the cities. When he talked about expansion of the cooperative, Arcadio (unlike Victor) spoke, not about increased membership, but rather about an increased reserve of communal pasture for cooperative sheep, which could be acquired if absent "residents" gave up their animals. He once said to me, "Expand the cooperative lands and the membership will soon follow."

The contrast with Victor is striking. Arcadio confessed that his one experience of migration had been one too many. He distrusted slickness (*mañoso*) or political jargon of any sort, and yet he was in many ways far more political than Victor. Although he never openly sought office, he never missed a chance, in informal conversations, to express confidently his ideas for the future and to show the steps that would be involved.

Victor saw in the community the spirit of cooperativism and some sort of equality as a means of entering the modern world. Moreover, he associated the modernity of the community with the modernity of the villagers residing in the cities, who had traditionally taken a large role in village affairs, paying for the roofing on the girls' school, making the football field, etc. For him, the community was a dynamic network, finding its strength in the two lives of pueblo and town.

Arcadio, on the other hand, wished to embrace precisely that part of the new law that broke this connection. The community for him was a physical entity located in the village itself. It cannot have gone unnoticed to the local *comuneros* that Arcadio's future was far more dependent upon the economic success of the pueblo than was Victor's, whose income derived largely from outside. Arcadio, as an acknowledged authority on livestock raising, was also able to appeal to a very concrete common cause within the pueblo, as opposed to abstract expressions of need for unity. Furthermore, he did not discuss the new statute unless called upon to do so. His emphasis on individual hard work as the source of success was suitable to his economic position but led him to deemphasize the government or the government statute as a crucial step to success.

Although Arcadio's later success was probably an unintentional result of his policy of not speaking out, I think his accomplishments may
have had a great deal to do with the fact that, by never publicly articulating his feelings that the community must operate alone, he was able
to avoid the confrontation between public and private morality that this
implied for each *comunero*. Many *comuneros* who were forced to migrate during part of the year may have felt that, in an ideal world, only
local residents should have rights to community property. They may even
have entertained the possiblity that the release of the land of the "residents" would allow them to terminate their migration. But in the meantime, the individual *comunero* was dependent on one or another of his
relatives. Many *comuneros* told me that they favored restricting *comunero*
status to local residents, but that they felt that THEIR relatives should be
exceptions for some very good reason or other.

I have purposely avoided talking about "factions," "political groupings," and the like. While the nature of the interaction process following
Victor's dismissal is of course important, I have tried to show that the
relationship between Victor and Arcadio was never made clear. Arcadio
was always a hidden force and could afford to remain so. The nature of
the election process as understood in the village made this quite possible.
I am in no position to describe the process in the days prior to the present regime, but the suppression of political parties by the government
meant that if at one time party allegiances had channeled local groupings under like circumstances, there was now no similar institution to
replace them. At election time three lists were put together by the General
Assembly, and between then and the elections themselves, open cam-
paigning was discouraged. I shall not discuss at length the implications
of this except to say that one result was that the process we are examining
never acquired the clear lines that are associated with the term FACTION.
Someone like Arcadio was led to imply that what he WAS, rather than
what he SAID, was important. And this meant that the numerous inherent contradictions in his position never had to be confronted.

Artico

A third view was represented by Artico. Similarly slow to take the stage,
Artico did in fact speak — slowly and deliberately — at meetings and was
one of the people openly attacked by Victor. It was he who, without
actually attacking Victor, expressed profound hurt at the threat to the
institution of the *varayoc*; he also confessed that he knew very little about

the new statute. But he was immediately elected as head of the inter-mediate *Junta de Notables* after the mayor had resigned and the harvest had not been brought in. When I once expressed surprise at his being so obvious a choice, a *comunero* told me, "He understands the community and we understand him."

Older than the other two, Artico had been in the administrations of many other leaders but, having never actually led one himself, he was always free from accusations of ambition or association with the one or two mistakes that every leader seemed to have made at one time or another. I think that any support that he might have gained represented disillu-sionment stemming from the uncertainty and complexity of the new statute — a feeling held particularly by those old enough to remember the ineffectiveness of the previous law. The very lack of any consistent plan, coupled with Artico's frequent lauding of the old values, made him an attractive figure for those distrustful of their ability to outfox another leader like Victor.

Events Following the Dismissal

To return briefly to the situation itself, the removal of Victor and Sil-vestre led to a long battle which involved the SINAMOS authorities. Victor denounced attempts to vote in a new president as being illegal and refused to accept his own removal. He went to Huancayo and re-ported the events to the regional office there. New elections were held, however, although candidates on two of the three lists declared their reluctance to run. One of these two lists actually won, but SINAMOS, apparently upset to find that the first officers to fill positions under the new statute had been sacked, sent an official to the village to cancel the elections and persuade the villagers to reinstate the old officials, at least until December, the proper time for new elections. Unfortunately for this official, there were no city residents around this time to support him, and he was quickly shouted down. His compromise — to set up a temporary ruling group rather than permanent officers — was accepted, however, and Artico and Primitivo, among others, were elected to it.

Faenas fell off dratically, nevertheless, and the biggest fiesta of the year was a generally acknowledged flop. A feeling of anxiety pervaded the village, especially when any advances in the neighboring SAIS cooperative were announced in the local papers. In an attempt to offset this, Primitivo quickly reasserted the officiousness and strictness for which he had been noted in the days of his governorship, so that when he later ran for mayor, his chances were very small.

As the time for the new elections approached, it became very clear that although many people saw the present vacuum as a good opportunity for taking political office, there was surprising lack of interest in the positions of *presidente de la administración* and *presidente de vigilancia* of the community. The wealthiest agriculturalist in the community rejected a request to run by jokingly suggesting his wife for the position. To his complete surprise, he found her name on one of the lists. She won and is now the first woman president (*vigilancia*) in the history of the community.

The position of governor in the village has had a disproportionate importance compared with that position in neighboring pueblos, because the villagers physically threw the police out in 1959 and turned the obstructive police post into a constructive secondary school. The police have not been seen since. While the position of governor has little effect on village policy, it is important in terms of power in the village; it is therefore not surprising that some people were anxious to run for that position. Far more surprising was that the hitherto minor position (at least in this pueblo) of *alcalde* suddenly became Arcadio's target.

This, I think, is extremely important in terms of the new laws and the possibility of their applicability in the forming of cooperatives. The experience of Victor's downfall, his own loudly articulated belief that the new position was impossible to run, and the uncertainty that is felt about future government plans have all made the position of president (administration) particularly unattractive. Whereas the traditional position of *personero*, which this new office replaces, involved simply representing the *comuneros'* interests, the new position — at least while the government is anxiously trying to implement a cooperative policy — creates a dilemma for the president: he must represent both the interests of the *comuneros vis-à-vis* the outside and the interests of the government *vis-à-vis* his own *comuneros*. If pressure is brought to bear on the president to implement various government plans, as the *comuneros* expect, his viability will be further reduced.

Moreover, if plans for the future of the communities remain uncertain, the president's position will weaken progressively, while the *alcalde*, free from such ties, can consolidate his position. Arcadio, who eventually won the elections for *alcalde*, has been extending his influence into community activities. His achievements so far in the municipal sector — the reconstruction of the approach road, the building of a bullring, the opening of a new weekly market, the purchase of a public-address system — make the *comuneros* only too willing that he continue to do so.

Conclusions

This paper is clearly preliminary, and facts about the backgrounds of the individuals involved and their relationships to the rest of the community are highly selective. Nor do I suggest that there are not many other ways to approach the question of peasant response. However, I have purposely described in some detail the events themselves, as I saw them, in order to give a specific example of the response produced by the new statute. Because of the nature of this approach, it is not possible to prove any hypotheses or cite any variables. Instead, I can confine myself to suggesting some interpretations.

I think that this approach makes clear the importance, when designing any program of imposed structural change (such as new cooperative laws), of recognizing that the general concerns of a group as a whole can be seen only in the context of the daily concerns of its members. These daily concerns are constantly acting to modify the general ones.[11]

Furthermore, peasants, like everyone else, would far prefer to enter into any relationship, whether with some other economic party or with a government agency, from a position of strength. What they consider such a position to be will obviously vary considerably. But in the case under discussion, there was a feeling of powerlessness after the dismissal of Victor, and this was perceived as a direct result of the new statute. It had a great deal to do with Arcadio's subsequent success, because he did not threaten the existing structure within the pueblo and was ambivalent about relations outside it. While the poor peasant is as anxious as anyone else to see a more equal sharing of wealth, he must deal not only with the powerful in his pueblo, but also with the "broad and alien" world outside it. He may prefer the evil he knows at home to the threat of powerlessness in face of an evil he does not know coming from outside.

I think that in this pueblo, the individual peasant was quite confident of his ability to manipulate to his advantage numerous well-established relationships. The introduction of new structures, on the other hand, means two things: (1) the resulting powerlessness that he may feel from his lack of skill in manipulating them may lead to his complete rejection of these structures and (2) if they are "accepted," he will inevitably manipulate those structures.

But rather than talk of the manipulation of "structures" — a rather

---

[11]   The effects of the daily concerns of individuals on group action should be a topic of particular importance in any study of revolutionary consciousness. The Chinese programs of *su ku hue* [speak bitterness] would seem to reflect an awareness of this dynamic (see Gael Alderson-Smith: i.p.).

dubious concept anayway — I would prefer to talk of the manipulation of people. I do not necessarily mean the manipulation of followers by leaders, because so-called followers may in fact attempt to reduce the possibilities of being so manipulated. In the absence of complete trust — something reserved for saints — a potential leader's success may depend upon the degree to which people perceive that his own individual interests are closely tied to those of the group as a whole, particularly if individual advantage is seen in close association with group maintenance. Because the people of this particular pueblo felt that anyone bright enough to be a good leader was too bright to be trusted, Arcadio represented a better bet than did Victor, who received a large portion of his income from outside.[12]

But here I must mention a point that was emphasized time and again by events and talks in the community. There is a considerable literature on the inability of peasants to find leaders. There is also an abundant literature on their inability to act collectively. It is often concluded that there is a conflict between individual success and communal action. My own experience is that it was precisely because of confidence in their own individual ability and intelligence that the people of this community were capable of acting together.[13] It is entirely conceivable that the honest leader, like the honest politician, is a contradiction in terms, and a long history of turncoats cannot have left peasants entirely unaware of this phenomenon. Conversations with members of this community revealed time and again that honesty had its place, but that is was not expected in positions of leadership. Frequently a leader might fall from office amid accusations of cheating, only to be voted back again two years later. It would be absurd to suggest that this was just the result of bad memory. Rather, *comuneros* had very high faith in their own abilities to catch a leader once his latent dishonesty became too manifest. I believe that there was an acknowledged feeling in this community that anyone who thinks that living in this world depends upon trust relationships is a fool. Therefore economic programs that hope to appeal to some traditional sense of "community" will fail unless they can convincingly answer the question: "Unity for what?"

But if the Peruvian government appears to have overemphasized the traditions of communalism in this sense, they may have underesti-

[12] I tried to make clear above that the community was by no means in agreement on specific community goals. This point acts to qualify my statement here. Clearly, over and above being a "community man," Arcadio had his own "class" interests, which influenced his choice of the correct community goals.
[13] I am not in any sense talking about "achievement" in the sense stressed by McClelland (1961).

mated it in another sense. It is quite possible that the peasant's concept of *comunidad* does not carry with it the sense of physical location that he associates with *el pueblo*. I myself have never heard a peasant refer to the *comunidad* as a physical spot represented by the limits of the communally owned land. A number of villagers have argued to me that "*comunidad*" has to do less with residence than with feeling.[14] If this is indeed a prevailing view, then peasants may look for some other logic behind the government's desire to cut off those *comuneros* who do not happen to be on a particular physical spot.

SINAMOS has so far been particularly anxious to apply the article of the law referring to residence, and I have asked a number of *comuneros* why they thought this was so. One man, although he agreed with me that he and his fellow villagers might gain at least some pasture and agricultural land, said that this gain did not make the action just. This man, who in fact had voted for Arcadio, said that cutting the community in two in this way would kill it, "like a chicken without a head." When I asked him why, then, the government had passed such a law, he said, "That's why," and walked off. For him the reason for the law was precisely to threaten, rather than to aid, the peasant. Later, he and I joked that before you can eat a chicken, you have to kill it.

Although the present government has succeeded in considerably reducing suspicion, a number of peasants, like this one, continue to argue that the specific purpose of the new law is to cut off the peasants from the leadership in the cities. They suggest that the communities will be so weakened as a result that the government will be able to exploit them endlessly. They further emphasize this point by adding that people like Victor will ultimately leave the village for good and, under the new statute, will thus cut off all connections with the community. If this is so, then one of the aims of the statue — to reduce migration — will actually have the reverse effect. And if a vigorous program of local industries is not set up immediately, enterprising *comuneros* will move their capital from the communities into the towns.[15]

The final point I must make is that the above description of events makes clear that the statute as presently applied has done nothing to

[14]   On the nearby Laive production unit of the SAIS, I have similarly been told by workers (who, incidentally, are often not *comuneros*) that the more impersonally run SAIS lacks the sense of "*comunidad*" that was felt on the old hacienda (see below: "The Workers").

[15]   Where the peasant community does not embrace the entire municipality, as in the the case of Matahuasi (studied by Long [Long and Winder 1973]), those wealthy residents who are NOT *comuneros* are not forced to migrate and have no restrictions on their ability to exploit the poorer *comuneros*.

reduce existing stratification. It has only reordered the rules of the game. It may be that the poor peasant's reluctance to throw off ties with the out-migrants is related to his belief that the second part of the statute, limiting the wealth of groups WITHIN the community, will not be enforced. Where the permanent outside "residents" may have acted as a balance against power groups within the community, the new law will give people like Arcadio no opposition. Moreover, that same poor peasant will be no happier with the application of this second part of the law if it means simply the replacement of guidance from other wealthy *comuneros* by guidance from well-paid government *técnicos*.

I conclude with a quotation from Bujra's article (1973:150):

Any government which places great ideological stress on national unity to the extent of repressing opposition, in fact encourages factionalism at local levels. Instead of creating a consensus of public opinion disposed toward the tasks of development, it may find itself saddled with a local "circulation of elites" (to use Pareto's phrase) which is far from being motivated toward such ends.

THE *SOCIEDAD AGRÍCOLA DE INTERÉS SOCIAL* (SAIS)

So far I have dealt with peasant response to the initial attempts to make the *comunidades campesinas* into economic units along cooperative lines. In addition to this program, however, many communities will be increasingly affected by their relationship to some of the more extensive cooperatives that the government is setting up. Owing to the wide diversity of types of farm production in Peru, these cooperatives vary considerably in nature. On the coast, large sugar and cotton complexes, characterized by both stable wage earners and casual laborers, have been converted into cooperatives. In some areas of the highlands, agricultural farms using varying amounts of intensive labor have also been expropriated. Across these diverse types of cooperatives, attempts are being made to form larger integral units called PIAR (*Proyecto Integral de Asentamiento Rural*) and PID (*Plan Integral de Desarrollo*), of which the best functional example is the PID de los Valles Santa, Lacramarca, Nepena, on the coast about ten miles north of Chimbote (see CRYRZA/DESCO Report).

The government was also faced with the complex situation created by the expropriation of the extensive livestock haciendas of the *altiplano*, where landlord exploitation of labor was accompanied by a long history of the usurping of peasant community lands, which had led, in retaliation, to land invasions throughout Peru in the first half of the 1960's. Starting from a base provided by the French example, the military government began to set up very extensive cooperatives called *Sociedades Agrícolas de Interés Social* (SAIS), the first of which was created in 1970 from lands formerly belonging to Cerro de Pasco Corporation. It was called SAIS Tupac Amaru. I shall now examine one of these cooperatives. Those that are devoted almost entirely to livestock ranching (as is the one I shall discuss) are of particular interest because of the continuous dilemma between the desire for the participation of the largest possible number of peasants and the knowledge that meat and wool ranching requires a very small labor force.

Because we are talking here, not about one small community of 300 families, but about twenty-eight such communities as well as former hacienda employees, I shall abandon the strictly ethnographic approach used above in favor of a more general examination of the SAIS. There are inevitable pitfalls in an analysis of peasant response over such a large area, and my skepticism about the value of attitudinal questionnaires combines with the practical impossibility of my making any such studies. For attitudinal information I shall therefore rely on conversations I had in a number of communities on the Margen Derecha of the SAIS and at the main production unit in the former hacienda of Laive-Ingahuasi.

After the creation of SAIS Tupac Amaru, the government was left with an assortment of haciendas lying on the high ground surrounding the Mantaro Valley.[16] A number of these were held by the livestock combine Sociedad Ganadera del Centro — these haciendas were expropriated in bulk. Besides these, on the right bank of the Mantaro, the haciendas of Tucle-Rio de la Virgen were finally handed over to the SAIS by the *Reforma Agraria* on June 2, 1972.

It was decided that the entire area on both sides of the valley would have to be formed into one large economic unit, and while the specifics of this could be worked out, a special committee (Central Sierra) was set up to administer it from April, 1970, to March, 1971.

What faced the government was a set of seven former hacienda properties extending over an area of 269,155 hectares (685 square miles), which in the case of the Margen Derecha (85,862 hectares or 275 square miles) shared common borders and were surrounded by peasant communities. Although sons of these communities may in fact have worked on the haciendas, if they did so they also took up residence there, so that apart from casual labor at harvest or shearing time, the communities

[16] The Mantaro Valley itself, the second largest of the inter-Andean valleys in Peru, is made up of small and medium-sized agricultural holdings, which have so far not been the objects of agrarian reform.

as units did not have any function within the daily running of the haciendas (but see below: "The Communities") at the time of the expropriations. But, as I have already stated, in the early sixties there had been growing tension between the haciendas and the communities that surrounded them. This varied from a general increase in *pasadero* animals (animals owned by *comuneros* and illegally grazed on hacienda land) to occupancy of the land by peasants, often misleadingly referred to as "invasions." Thus there was both the growing pressure by the communities for the *revindicación* of their rightful lands and the question of what to do with the laborers on the haciendas, who also claimed the right to their own means of production.

In an AGRICULTURAL cooperative, the size of the work force may make the distribution of shares among workers a reasonable practice and still allow for the efficient operation of the unit. In contrast, on this LIVESTOCK cooperative, a meager 535 employees representing only 500 families were surrounded by sixty-five peasant communities that petitioned to be members of the cooperative. Moverover, from the beginning it was felt that efficiency could be maintained only by preserving the integrity of the haciendas as units, while not creating a group of privileged rural workers, as would have resulted from distribution to only the former hacienda employees. Indeed, the government declared its intention of making the improvement of economic conditions in the entire area the goal of every cooperative.

A study was therefore made of the sixty-five postulant communities. They were rated according to coefficients that were based largely on the needs of the community in terms of land already available to the *comuneros* and the reasonableness of their claims to the former hacienda lands. Eventually, twenty-six postulants were admitted, and two more were later added, bringing the total number of dependents from the member communities to 15,300, compared with the 2,450 workers and dependents living on the former haciendas themselves.

The workers on the former haciendas were formed into the *Cooperativa Servicios Alta Sierra Ltda.*, a unit that would act as, among other things, their representational institution. In the General Assembly of the SAIS this unit would have two votes. Each of the twenty-eight communities would also have two votes, for a total of fifty-eight. On April 20, 1970, the *Reforma Agraria* sold the land and equipment to the newly formed SAIS Cahuide, at a cost of 237,707,535 soles ($5,528,082) to be paid over the next twenty-five years (the first five payments of interest to be considerably less than the remaining twenty).

In effect, then, the 3,500 *comuneros* in the twenty-eight communities are nonworking shareholders represented by fifty-six votes, while the 535 working shareholders, including technical staff, etc., are represented by a total of two votes. From the beginning, it seems, the government has envisioned two separate groups having very different relations to the SAIS. But these groups have in common the dilemma resulting from the government's desire to separate the economic and production goals of the SAIS from the political ones. This is made particularly difficult because of the kinds of decisions that will have to be made in supposed isolation from one another. Economic goals must be reached in a free market environment, where supplies of fertilizer, fodder, and equipment are bought on the open market while produce is sold on a controlled market. The political goals are seen in conjunction with the Statute of Peasant Communities, which is geared toward the leveling of economic status among the peasantry and the general improvement of conditions in the communities.

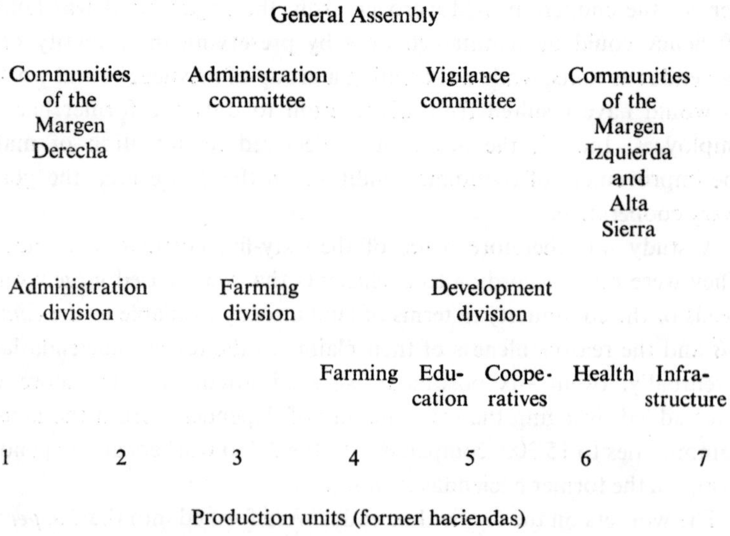

General Assembly

Communities of the Margen Derecha	Administration committee	Vigilance committee	Communities of the Margen Izquierda and Alta Sierra

Administration division	Farming division		Development division			
	Farming	Edu-cation	Coope-ratives	Health	Infra-structure	

1	2	3	4	5	6	7

Production units (former haciendas)

Figure 2. The organizational structure of the SAIS

The structure of the SAIS recognizes three distinct functions: administration, production, and social activities. Participation in the form of a General Assembly of elected representatives takes place at the administrative level. There are two ordinary meetings per year for this, and other decisions can be made by the twelve-member *consejos* of administration and vigilance. At the production level, the SAIS employs a manager and a series of specialists who also have a vote through their membership in Alta Sierra; they also are able to make extensive daily decisions concerning sales, purchases, etc. In addition, the Development Division has the special task of allotting funds for the needs of the various communities, quite apart from the distribution of profits at the end of the year. This is designed to fulfill social needs by concentrating on the greater needs of those communities lagging behind the others. For this purpose the division is allotted a stipulated amount, before the declaration of net profits (see Figure 2).

THE PEASANT RESPONSE

I would suggest that IF THE OPERATION OF THE SAIS WERE TO FOLLOW THE LINES PROPOSED BY THE GOVERNMENT, the effect would be to depoliticize the peasant members. (1) By giving, at least nominally, the land to the communities, the government has managed to deprive them of a form of political initiative represented by the land invasions, despite their obvious disadvantages. (2) On the other hand, by discouraging the formation of a workers' syndicate while at the same time forming a vertical representational unit from administration down to worker (Alta Sierra), which nominally has a voice in the running of the cooperative, the government has created a source of potential conflict between two subgroups WITHIN the SAIS. This obscures the greater conflicts confronting the peasants generally OUTSIDE it.

I do not mean to imply by the first point that all government accessions to demands from the base will necessarily depoliticize that base, but in this particular case, the communities remain alienated from the property that they are told is rightfully theirs by the encumbrance of a heavy debt to the former owners. This will severely limit the ability of the cooperative to provide capital for the development of labor-absorbing projects in the communities themselves. This means that, WERE THE PRINCIPLES OF THE SAIS TO WORK, the communities would have their attention diverted from the question of their position in the overall structure of a society that continues to exploit the countryside in favor of industrial development; instead their attention would be directed entirely toward their status as nonproductive profit-seekers in a large enterprise.

The rationale for the kind of "autogestion" that the government has chosen for the SAIS may indeed have been to deactivate the rural fuse while keeping food supplies moving into the cities, where fresh capital —

now released from the countryside — could breed an industrial middle class. But the Indian peasant, at least in this area of Peru, has become enmeshed so deeply in the political process that probably no government — military or otherwise — will succeed in making him again irrelevant to the national political process. It follows, then, that if the SAIS as presently constituted is a depoliticizing force, the peasantry that was already sufficiently conscious of its position in the economic structure of the country would seek solutions denying this government rationale for the SAIS. The COMMUNITIES would cease payments of the expropriation debt, which encourages industry, not in their own area, where it is most needed, but rather in Lima, where the former *hacendados* reside. The WORKERS would form a union. Moreover, these separate subgroups would perceive the unity of their interests in terms of the greater society, over and above their differences within the SAIS.

Indeed, the workers have, as of this date, formed a union, and the communities have openly discussed the possibility of not paying off the expropriation debt. Furthermore, certain economic issues in the area have drawn the *comuneros* and the workers together as peasants against outsiders, as was the case in the community discussed above.

I shall now turn to the process that has led to this position.

The Workers

Generally, the daily lives of the workers in the various production units have been affected more than have those of the *comuneros*. Because one of the major aims of the special committeee, Sierra Central, and later the SAIS management, was to rationalize the running of the former haciendas, their initial changes only accelerated a trend that the owners themselves had tried to begin. Martinez Alier (1972a) has shown, through the examination of the record of a number of haciendas in the Sierra Central, that is was generally the *hacendados* who sought to extend the cash relationship with their employees, and not the other way around. They were not entirely successful in their endeavor.

The production units that interest us here — Laive, Antapongo, and Tucle — employ roughly three categories of labor: technicians, *operarios* (workers at the production unit buildings themselves — carpenters, milk processors, etc.), and pastors (shepherds who live in small huts made of piled stones and covered with straw roofs). Most of my discussion here concerns the last of these three.

The relations of peonage varied considerably from one area to another throughout Peru. In the case of the three haciendas on the Margen Derecha[17] of what is now the SAIS, the encroachment of the haciendas onto communal land had the twofold effect of providing more land for livestock and, by reducing the land of the communities, making them more dependent for their livelihood on the hacienda. The surrounding villages provided communal work forces for the haciendas at times of harvest and shearing as well as for specific projects like the building of a road. Individual members of the communities might also work on the hacienda. Because the communal land was reduced to the area closest to the village, which was generally (with the single exception of the community of Cachi) used for agricultural production, the only ways of maintaining livestock were either to use hacienda pastures illegally (*pasadero*) or to offer labor to the hacienda in return for the right to graze animals on its lands. Although in theory the number of animals permitted per worker was fairly restricted,[18] in fact, because of the wild nature of the landscape, pastors on the hacienda were able to increase their stock above these limits.

Although the turnover of pastors may have been rapid, nonetheless certain people in the village did tend to build closer relations with the hacienda than did others. They became known by the administrator or mayordomo, and it was in the interests of the hacienda to employ people it knew. The pastor's ability to keep *huacchas* [his own animals] on the hacienda gave him an economic position in the community that was comparable to that of the migrants. And if the hacienda on which he was working bordered on his own community, the pastor's position was improved by his ability to take a greater role in village affairs than could migrants. Moveover, through the system of *michipas* [animals belonging to other villagers that the pastor grazed in return for certain economic favors], he was able to extend his influence further. Another dimension that written contracts found in the old haciendas do not reveal was that the actual contractor could, if he wished, leave the task of pastor to his wife and family for much of the time, while he took up some political role in the village. Indeed, the nature of the job of shepherding made

---

[17] Documentary material used here is from the records of Hacienda Tucle, now collected in Lima under the auspices of the *Reforma Agraria* and the *Universidad Nacional Mayor de San Marcos*. I am grateful to Sr. Humberto Rodriguez, Sta. Madalengoitia, and Sr. Juan Martinez for ordering and indexing these materials.

[18] Two examples of pastor contracts (1953: Folio 10): i. For 1 year plus Sundays; S/.85.00 per month (S/.200 in advance) plus *huacchas*: 7 cattle, 2 horses, 2 donkeys. More animals will be considered *michipas*.

ii. For 1 year plus Sundays; S/.60 per month (S/.50 in advance); *huacchas*: 8 cattle, 60 sheep, 3 horses, 3 donkeys.

it impossible for a man without family to perform his job very well through the extensive hours. Finally, although the hacienda discouraged it — for obvious reasons — the pastor could always let his *chusco* ewes go among the finely bred rams of the hacienda, with subsequent improvements to his own stock. For all these reasons, then, despite many of the hardships involved, the position of pastor could be turned to advantage.

Nonetheless, this tended to be the case only for those who became familiar with the job. Those who took on rather more infrequent jobs were less able to establish relations in the community that would allow them to pasture *michipas*, and anyway the low status of their job would not allow them to pasture sufficient animals to make this possible. Meanwhile, the hacienda was trying to reduce the turnover of its pastors. This meant that during the 1950's, a few men became more or less permanent pastors (see below). The location of their families on the hacienda further reduced contact with the village. But although the pastors often had a rather tenuous connection with the community (the ambiguity of their position was emphasized when their community invaded hacienda land), they have not always, or even recently, been entirely isolated from influence in the community.

A pastor who had provided a sheep for a village fiesta at the expense of hacienda stock rather than his own, or a pastor who had driven off a few animals to be sold illegally to one of the numerous *negociantes* around, might have found it convenient to disappear and find work on another hacienda or in the neighboring mine of Cercapuquio. In an attempt to prevent this, the *hacendados* drew their major source of labor from the communities that were closest to their land, and the three haciendas agreed that they should not accept a pastor who had held a previous appointment on a neighboring hacienda without a clear letter of release. Attempts to make a similar arrangement with the mine, however, seem to have failed.

But, in addition to the uncooperative mine, there were other places to work besides the haciendas. The administrators attempted to increase their hold on employees by reducing their number of *huacchas* (which in any case were using pasture that could be grazed far more profitably by the better animals of the hacienda) and by increasing the wage payment that could take the form of advances to be paid off by subsequent labor (in other words, promoting a debt relationship). It seems, however, that the pastors were not at all willing to reduce their *huaccha* animals in this way (see Martinez Alier 1972a, 1972b).

There were, of course, other ways of tying employees to their work, albeit somewhat less direct ones. I shall not go into these extensively. Other writers have dealt with the institutions of fiesta and *compadrazgo*. In addition, the *hacendado* often helped a worker through some family crisis of health or money, provided strategic hand-outs of free milk and butter, etc. These conditions, moreover, tended to lead to complex and tacit systems of bargaining, not between employees as a group and their employers, but between individuals and the *hacendado*, administrator, and mayordomo, all of whom were reasonably permanent figures whose personalities could be ascertained over time.

The importance of these kinds of ties in dissipating or preventing class cohesion can easily be overemphasized, however. Writers have tended to focus on the *hacendado's* ability to give, rather than the pastor's ability to politely but firmly demand. The records of Hacienda Tucle (1950–1953: Folio 10, contracts), for example, reveal that one pastor was frequently employed less for his faithfulness to the hacienda than for his latent ability to mobilize a large number of peasants should he feel so inclined. Hacienda policy wavered between employing this man (and giving him considerable responsibilities) and having him carted off to prison as a provocateur.

This, then, was the situation in 1966 when the Belaunde government began to consider a land reform that would eventually affect these haciendas. The *hacendados*, meanwhile, frequently stated that they were only interested in production and that politics, particularly in the form of workers' unions, should be kept out of the running of the haciendas.

From its initiation, the SAIS has shown a similar sentiment. Until quite recently, its major preoccupation with respect to labor since the formation of the special committee has been to rationalize relations along a cash basis. Although the PERCENTAGE of *huaccha* animals to total stock given in the *Memoria anual* (1973) shows only a change from 11.32 percent in 1972 to 10.27 percent in 1973 — a difference that would simply suggest a steady number of *huacchas* while the total stock increased — new ways of calculating this percentage obscure a 22 percent drop in the ACTUAL number of *huacchas*. Also, while the old practice had been that the pastor kept his animals on his *estancia* near those of the hacienda, on the Laive Production Unit today, the *huacchas* are kept entirely separate and are shepherded by two pastors who do nothing else. Other employees are no longer permitted any *huaccha* animals.

Pastors have now been cast into three categories according to their efficiency. Their wages are $1.05, $1.00, and $0.95, depending on their category, and they can have a maximum of sixty *huacchas* (a cash scale gives them up to $5.80 per month if they have no animals at all). As in the past, these salaries involve the work, not of one man, but of his entire family. Besides his wages, of course, the pastor gets other benefits, but every pastor to whom I have spoken argues that these do not compare with what was available from a "good" landlord, and no doubt in their final few years, landlords felt far greater pressure to be "good" in this way than they did formerly. Pastors compare the special rate they get on the purchase of meat at $0.28 per kilo (which accounts for less than 10 percent of total sales of sheep by unit) with the old *hacendado* practice of giving away animals. Moreover, the present managers, unlike the previous administrators, cannot give fiestas.

All this should come as no surprise. Old rules-of-thumb have had to be replaced by new rules that are applicable equally throughout the SAIS and are operated by the administrative staff with a relatively high turnover which has replaced the old, and often more permanent, administrators. But it has meant that the feeling of flexibility that the individual peasant felt under the old system has disappeared, leading him to look for new ways of manipulating the system. Whatever else may be said of the old administrator, he and the pastors (like Arcadio and his constituents above) were committed to the same institution — in this case, the hacienda. The new *técnicos*, however, are less permanent and seek a mobility far less tied to the future of the SAIS.

But by far the most frequently heard specific complaint concerns the rigid system of fines that the SAIS has instituted for the loss of sheep. According to the pastors, nowhere was a rule-of-thumb more evident in the old days than on this point. If a pastor had a good record, he could be fairly sure that the *hacendado* would turn a blind eye to the occasional unexplained loss of an animal or two. Certainly, there is very little evidence in the records of Hacienda Tucle of punishments being regularly meted out for this crime. In the SAIS, however, the loss of a full-grown ram brings down a fine of $18.60 and an ewe, $8.15. This, of course, can reduce a man's monthly wage to zero and, at its worst, can even put him in debt to the SAIS. It is hard to say exactly what constitutes a finable loss (usually an animal whose carcass cannot be found), but of the 6,600 animals lost in the fiscal year 1973, 48.6 percent were lost through accidents or the rapacity of the local foxes.

This, then, represents the picture of the daily problems facing the pastor. As I have said, in light of the new situation, he is likely to look for new channels to express his needs. These have supposedly been provided for him in the form of the Alta Sierra, but in fact the Alta Sierra places the pastor in an almost unrelievedly bad position. In the few years immediately preceding the *Reforma Agraria* of this government, very little was done for the benefit of the hacienda employee at the level of national policy, but neither was the wind entirely in the favor of the land-lord. In a particularly bad situation, it was possible for employees to shift the almost immovable bureaucracy of the *Reforma Agraria* to protect them over some specific grievance. Today it is unlikely that any government forces, such as SINAMOS or *Reforma Agraria,* can be so mobilized. SINAMOS, after all, is telling the workers that they ARE the SAIS, and the *Reforma Agraria* created it. Nor are there any legiti-mate political parties to be mobilized against it. Supposedly, all grievances should be channeled through the Alta Sierra, through which the workers have two votes in a General Assembly of fifty-eight which, under normal circumstances, would meet in ordinary sessions just twice a year.

A further handicap is found in the structure of the SAIS, which sepa-rates the supposedly social grievances of the workers (which are to be channeled through the Development Division) from the more general economic questions of the running of the SAIS (which come under the *Agropecuaria* [Farming Division]). If the very fundamental policy decisions of the SAIS are truly to be in the hands of its members, it is hard to see how these two functions can be separated.

Moreover, the experience of this SAIS should act as a caution against those who stress education as the source of the success of cooperatives. In the first year of operation of the SAIS, both *comuneros* and pastors informed me that they felt that the government was really running the SAIS. In addition to the suspicion felt toward the *técnicos,* who gave most of the daily orders and, at least in the early stages of the SAIS, tended to dominate the meetings, many informants felt that the educational programs directed toward delegates acted to confuse their loyalties. A number of senior delegates — those on the Administration Committee — were referred to as SINAMOS puppets. Here the dilemma of loyalties that we saw above in the case of the president of the community is repeated.

For these reasons, the first steps to form some organization besides the SAIS General Assembly or the Alta Sierra were made, not by the communities, but by the workers. In a meeting of the Alta Sierra held late in 1972, it was voted that 30 percent of the annual funds should be put aside to form a workers' defense committee, and on January 6, 1973, the workers' syndicate was officially formed.

The Communities

In addition to the pastors, whose positions enabled them to maintain animals on hacienda land, others in the community were able to keep a minimal number of animals on that part of the community lands not usurped by the hacienda and unsuitable for agricultural use. Although the situation varied considerably from one community to another — Cachi had 532 hectares of communal pasture, while Llamapsillon had 0.09 and Chicche had none — through animal reproduction alone, the pressure on this land steadily increased. The solution, besides a land invasion, was to pasture animals on the hacienda illegally. The degree to which this could be done without recriminations depended to a great extent on the nature of the hacienda land bordering the community. If the land was relatively flat, trespassing animals could be seen from some distance, and peasants — who often did not have horses and anyway could not move their sheep as fast as a *caporal* could reach them by horse — were easily caught. If, on the other hand, the land was made up of chasms, steep and rocky hillsides, caves, and boulders, the encroaching peasant could often get away without being seen, and even if he were seen, catching him on horseback was a slow and often dangerous business.

If animals were caught, they were driven off to a corral at the hacienda compound especially devoted to *pasadero* animals. To recover them, the owner had to work on the hacienda for a certain number of days, that number depending on the number of animals caught. Attempts to levy fines on owners, even in recent years, were unsuccessful. The number of animals actually caught in the process related as much to the hacienda's yearly cycle as it did to the community's. When labor was needed for building a pigsty, *caporals* would be told to be especially diligent in rounding up *pasaderos*. On the other hand, *comuneros* could afford to be considerably more aggressive when their crops were not demanding much of their time and they could therefore easily work on the hacienda. Because the hacienda was tied more closely to a livestock cycle and anyway used communal work forces for any harvesting to be done, there was not necessarily too much conflict over this tacit arrangement for the allotment of labor. It would have been an unwise administrator who decided to put up a pigsty at the height of the potato harvest.

The communities as units provided work forces for specific tasks, for which they received a lump payment and the provision of cocaine leaves and cigarettes.[19] Although this was a cash arrangement, it was considered an obligation of the community which the *hacendado* could expect them to fulfill. From the point of view of the community authorities, the

---

[19]   Contract between Hacienda Tucle and the community of Huasicancha: for three days of harvesting barley, employing the whole village (men and women), payment was 800 soles when the job was done, with coca and *raciones* provided.

flexibility lay in the *comuneros'* ability either to work reasonably hard and turn up in force, or to confuse and muddle the whole work process and arrive on the job at half strength, rather than in an ability to refuse outright to work for the price. In the last years of the haciendas, these work forces were noted for their boredom in comparison with community *faenas*, where a band played from 7:00 A.M. to 4:00 P.M., where *chicha* was drunk in quantity, and where rest periods involved an entertaining ritual, with ennobling speeches and discussion of *varayoc* business.

In the SAIS today, the communities are still expected to contribute work forces, though less for harvest than for the construction of irrigation canals, sheep dips, and roads. There is no direct payment for this, but at the end of the year, the amount of profit distributed to each member community is calculated against the record of the year's contribution to these work parties. The degree to which this is a satisfactory arrangement for the communities varies considerably and depends in large part on the extent to which the task in question can be seen as directly beneficial to the community. Nonetheless, while there is much talk at the administrative level of getting the communities involved as much as possible in SAIS work, in terms of efficiency the trend must be away from this practice because, if anything, the SAIS is already overemploying permanent staff. Furthermore, in view of the kind of payment made for this work, it is unlikely that the communities would ever regard it as a satisfactory substitute for the development of work-absorbing projects in their own villages.

The SAIS can promise a great deal, but so far it has produced very little. Historically, however, peasants have found that a bird in the hand is worth at least ten in the bush, and they are more responsive to the trends they discern than to the promises that are made. Nowhere is this clearer than in the question of *pasadero* animals. Attempts to cut down on the number of *huacchas* for the pastors have been accompanied by similar attempts to reduce the number of *pasaderos* for the communities. But both the pastors and the communities feel that these animals represent the only direct profit they receive from land that they are told is theirs. The *comuneros* to whom I have spoken seem particularly irate at attempts to add a new moral dimension to the violation of trespassing laws. They refuse to accept that the illegal pasturing of animals, once a way of life, has now become a moral offense. The institution of fines in place of work duties has so irritated some communities that in May 1972, the possibility of invading SAIS land was discussed in my presence; it was finally decided to see what happened over the next few years. An intermediary solution was reached later in the year when the General

Assembly decided to rent small areas of pasture to communities, like Chicche, that had none.

The SAIS goal of generally improving conditions in the entire area depends, of course, on the amount of capital it will be able to find for this purpose. So far, the Development Divison, far from stimulating local industry, has been able only to repair roads and buildings. Its lack of funds leads it to concentrate on the far less expensive task of easing in the new Statute of Peasant Communities through educational programs. But this will hardly be met with enthusiasm in view of what is expected of the division, particularly because of the implied threat that noncompliance may lead to the reduction of benefits from the division.

This applies especially to attempts to reduce stratification in the communities, because if the division cannot provide alternative work possibilities in the communities themselves, this will inevitably lead to emigration. The community of Cachi, for example, has succeeded in putting a ceiling on the number of animals permitted to each *comunero*, but those thus forced to reduce their stock have so far found that the Development Division can give them little help in relocating capital of such relatively small amounts. There is no seed capital available to them. As one of the primary tasks of the SAIS and of the Statute of Peasant Communities is to reduce migration, this problem piovides a major contradiction. It would seem that SAIS Cahuide, like SAIS Tupac Amaru before it, is contemplating a project of jungle colonization as a possible solution, but the cost of developing the jungle is considerably higher than the cost of local development, not to mention the social upheaval involved, the resulting destruction of the Peruvian *selva*, and the poor history of such projects in the past.

The major problem is that even if the SAIS delegates could at least come to some agreement with the government over goals for the SAIS, it is unlikely that there will be any accord over the matter of the debt; and because this represents the crucial hindrance to any local development, it has become the central issue for the communities and the one that draws them into an alliance with the workers on the SAIS. The argument runs as follows: From April, 1971, to March, 1972, the installment of the debt to be paid to the government was S/.3,683,399.80. Of a gross profit of S/.12,464,668.00, the amount of profits distributed to the communities was S/.2,168,414.60. The communities argue that although each *comunero* receives an average of S.532.00 ($12.35) per year, or S/.44.00 per month, paid in the form of some community project or other, he is in effect paying out S/.904.00 ($21.00) per year in debts. If distributed profits were to increase at a rate of 10 percent per annum, by 1977 he would be getting 857 soles ($20.00), but by then the per annum debt payments will be S/.10, 949,997.85, or 2,688 soles ($62.50) per head.

Thus the grievances that the member communities feel toward the SAIS serve to draw them into a crude alliance with the workers. Both groups feel threatened by the apparent rigidity of the structure and rules governing the new cooperative. The dissipation of profits, moreover, means that both SINAMOS and the Development Division — supposedly agencies to improve the social conditions of the peasantry — are first experienced as constrainers, rather than expanders, of the peasant's horizons. Past experience makes it difficult for peasants to accept constraints on the basis of promises that in the past have remained so much hot air.

Apart from historical experience, present hindrances would seem to confirm peasant skepticism. The concentration of capital and organizational resources into one visual project that might belie this peasant cynicism has never been forthcoming. On the contrary, the construction of an irrigation canal that would enrich an extensive piece of land surrounding the Laive Production Unit has been plagued with bureaucratic hesitancy. Similarly, the communities have long been aware of the availability of electricity from a hydroelectric plant built by a local and soon-to-be-exhausted mine, but government reluctance to deal firmly with the mine owners, who have long exploited the cheap local labor of the peasantry, and the limitation of capital for the construction of a supply net make this simply another unfulfilled possibility. Nor is it correct to lay the blame on the lack of peasant initiative. In the case of the hydroelectric plant, it was peasant initiative that suggested the possibility and made frequent, expensive trips to the national capital to press for action, and it was the bureaucracy that did not respond.

Conclusions

A number of social scientists familar with the highland SAISs have remarked on the contradictions between technicians, workers, and communities.[20] I have tried to show here that these contradictions exhibit far more clearly the theoretical structure of the SAIS than the actual conflict of interests facing these groups. In many cases, the rationality of the SAIS has produced differentiations where no such lines actually existed. Nonetheless, it would be a mistake to see the present unity of interests in terms of the formation of a permanent class consciousness.

[20] I am referring here to informal conversations. But see the *Memoria anual* (1973) for an example.

The way in which the community I described in the first section of this paper was drawn together to tackle the specific question of land invasion illustrates that specific experiences of struggle alone are not sufficient to create a lasting sense of unity. In fact, a similar set of specific experiences are acting to unite member communities and workers for the moment.

These events have served to connect two grievances in the eyes of the peasants under one heading of government opposition to their best interests. These two grievances are seen as the opposition to the formation of a workers' union and evidence of government unwillingness to give economic protection to the peasants, as exemplified by the payment of the expropriation debt.

On January 6, 1973, in a meeting of the General Assembly of the SAIS, the formation of the Workers' Defense Committee was announced. Initial SINAMOS truculence over this event immediately changed the focus of the union from grievances within the SAIS to more general issues. SINAMOS officials in Huancayo expressed the view that the workers were being encouraged by the technicians and a number of university students working in the area, and that the motive of these agitators was to sow discord within the SAIS by setting the workers against the communities. In the field, officials suggested to *comuneros* that the union was fundamentally against the concept of the SAIS. At one point, SINAMOS openly stated that these workers were in the pay of the former *hacendados*. This gave the workers the opportunity to reply openly that, on the contrary, by opposing the union, SINAMOS was acting like the former *hacendados*.

As this confrontation progressed, displeasure with the government in general arose among the communities of the Mantaro Valley, which also included many of the member communities on the *Margen Izquierda* of the SAIS. This resulted from the fixing of prices on wholesale potatoes by *Empresa Publica de Servicios Agropecuarios* (EPSA). Because many of the larger producers managed to slip through control points to sell potatoes at illegal prices in Lima, the small producer was hardest hit. Some seventy communities called a meeting in Huancayo, at which the workers' union stated its support for their cause.[21]

This support of the communities by the workers was later matched by community support for the workers when pressure grew on the union.

[21]   A number of SINAMOS officials remarked to me that it was a shame that the peasants did not seem to know the difference between EPSA and SINAMOS. My own experience, however, was that peasants did so distinguish, but they could not understand why SINAMOS was not offering them more support, if it really meant to aid the hitherto exploited. And in view of this reluctance, they could do no more than lump the two agencies under the common heading of government.

At one time, police were sent to Acopalca, the center of the *Margen Izquierda*, but were quickly withdrawn, and some of the union leaders were threatened with a trip to the jungle prison colony of Sepa. But when the *Consejo Administración* of the SAIS suggested in a meeting that they should vote to censure the union, a number of delegates from the communities threatened to resign and take their communities with them. Meanwhile, a majority of the union members rejected a government compromise suggesting that the union seek affiliation with the government-sponsored Confederation of Revolutionary Workers of Peru (CRTP).

The extent to which the present situation is the result of outside provocateurs, as SINAMOS officials in Huancayo suggested to me, is not a point for discussion here. My interest is in the peasant response to the cooperative program. I am suggesting that any such program, claiming to be "revolutionary," must demonstrate at least some willingness to reapportion wealth, and that the system of expropriation demonstrates to peasants no such willingness. Insofar as the bonds issued to former owners are transferable into investment in approved industries, the peasant is being asked to bear the burden of a form of industrial development that in no way contributes to development in the expropriated areas. This particular economic fact cannot easily be obscured by the elaborate creation of an SAIS or a PIAR, or by a program of rural education and propaganda. If it requires the presence of so-called agitators to make this clear to peasants — and in this instance, I doubt that it did — then the government would be better advised to reexamine the policy, rather than to attempt to remove the "agitators."

"AUTOGESTION" AND THE SOCIAL SCIENCES

I have discussed in this article, first, the response of one peasant community that was not a member of any larger cooperative system to the new Statue of Peasant Communities, and second, the response of workers and member communities to the formation of a large cooperative. I have used a rather microscopic and descriptive approach to the study of the smaller unit and a far more general approach to the much larger SAIS. I have tried to show that these two cases have points in common because both units tend to respond to newly imposed structures in terms of their perceptions of how they can best strengthen their individual positions with respect to the greater society. At times this may mean emphasizing a distinction between the peasantry in general and some other group;

at other times differentiation within the peasantry itself may be emphasized. This depends upon how the problem at hand is perceived and is
unlikely to take the form of a more permanent class consciousness
without the presence of some agent that allows the individual to convert
isolated experiences into larger concepts. In most cases, such an agent
would be a political party.

I hasten to add that I do not think that this is a particularly helpful
or even observant statement. Had a similar microscopic study been done
on a community that WAS a member of the SAIS, and had it then been
placed in the general context given here, we would have had a much
better idea of how these people conceive of the SAIS. Only with such an
"interpretive" approach to social science can we really understand behavior. I think that the anthropologist is particularly well equipped to
make such a microstudy and thus add an important dimension to the
macrostudies of the other social sciences.

Small-scale "interpretive" studies will take on particular significance
if we are to take seriously such phrases as "autogestion," "worker participation," and "self-management," because it will become important
to understand how participants reach decisions rather than how they
"respond" to plans. I think, too, that the examples I have presented above
make clear that, irrespective of government plans to the contrary,
people are often prepared to take the business of participation very
seriously. One SINAMOS official, in conversation with me, referred —
hopefully, I think — to "planned participation." It seems to me that the
contradiction in this expression reveals a fundamental problem for government, which will by no means be solved by education as a way of
persuading people to PARTICIPATE as planned. The two examples I have
given here reveal the kind of contradictions a government will face when
it attempts to tie the politics of participation to rigid development plans
and goals that were not made by the people supposed to contribute to
their fulfillment.

The military regime in Peru has consistently voiced its rejection of
both the capitalist and the communist roads to development. The two
above examples tend to indicate that, in very broad terms, the government holds a consensus model of society, while the peasants, through
long experience, hold a conflict model. The former leads to a tendency
to seek palliative compromises, while the latter admits of the possibility
of dynamic solutions in the heat of experience. A useful political contribution would be for the social sciences to study how the cumulative
empirical experiences of development and planning, as felt by the base,
could be converted into a dynamic contribution to the solution of problems.

In such a view of development, government plans become no more than hypotheses to be verified or modified through confrontation with the experience of the base. If critics would argue that this, in reality, is always happening in development, then I would emphasize that government plans should be presented with the open declaration that they should function in this way. Capacitation programs, to which SINAMOS is presently attracted, would have to take on an entirely different design in such a system, so that the government would be presented, not as the source of all solutions, but only as the catalyst for a series of "problem relationships" between government and base.

The kind of peasant response that I have presented in this paper would then be, not simply a nuisance to be overcome, but an essential part of the duality that contributes to real dynamic development. Solutions do not answer questions so much as they raise new ones, and the acceptance of these new questions as problems to be solved is evidence of a proper dynamic relationship between government and people toward further development.

A social science that could contribute to such a process would cease to convert people into objects by emphasizing the rules and structures that supposedly dominate their lives; rather it would seek a way in which it might contribute to this dangerous relationship between government and man. Instead of asking, What are the rules by which men live?, we would ask, Why do men think there are rules at all? and, What is it that makes men follow the rules of their society?

REFERENCES

ADAMS, R. H.
  1959   *A community in the Andes*. Seattle: University of Washington Press.
ALBERTI, GIORGIO
  1973   Unpublished manuscript.
ALDERSON-SMITH, GAEL
  i.p.   *China comunal: la historia, la teoría, y la practica*. Lima: Mosca Azul.
ALDERSON-SMITH, GAVIN
  i.p.   In *Anthropological perspectives on Latin American urbanization*. Edited by Cornelius and Trueblood. Latin American Urban Research 4.
BAILEY, F. G.
  1964   "Two villages in Orissa (India)," in *Closed systems and open minds*. Edited by M. Gluckman. London: Oliver and Boyd.
  1969   *Stratagems and spoils*. Oxford: Blackwell.
BAILEY, F. G., *editor*
  1971   *Gifts and poison*. Oxford: Blackwell.

BUJRA, J. M.
1973   The dynamics of political action: a new look at factionalism. *American Anthropologist* 75 (1).

CASTRO POZO, H.
1972   *Del ayllu al cooperativismo socialista.* Lima: Edición Juan Mejia Baja. (Originally published 1936.)

CRYRZA/DESCO
1972   *P.I.D. de los Valles Santa, Lacramarca, Nepeña,* four volumes. Lima: May.

HACIENDA TUCLE
1950–1953   Records.

HAYA DE LA TORRE, V. R.
1961   *El plan de acción.* Lima: Edición Pueblo.

LLOYD, P. C.
1973   "Social anthropology and the Third World slums." Paper presented at the meeting of the Association of Social Anthropologists, Oxford, July 1973.

LONG, N., D. WINDER
1973   "An analysis of the policy and social consequences of peasant community reform in a smallholder zone of central Peru." Paper presented at the meeting of the Association of Social Anthropologists, Oxford, July 1973.

MC CLELLAND, D. C.
1961   *The achieving society.* Princeton: Van Nostrand.

MARIÁTEGUI, J. C.
1970   *Siete ensayos de interpretación de la relidad Peruana.* Lima: Amauta. (Originally published 1928.)

MARTINEZ ALIER, J.
1972a   "Los huacchilleros en las haciendas de la Sierra Central del Peru desde 1930: algunas hipótesis preliminares." Paper presented at the Segundo Simposio sobre Historia Económica de América Latina, Rome, September 1972.
1972b   "Relations of production in Andean haciendas: Peru." Paper presented at the Symposium on Landlord and Peasant in Latin America and the Caribbean, Cambridge, December 1972.

Memoria anual
1973   *Memoria anual* 6, 1 April 1972–31 March 1973. Sociedad Agrícola de Interés Social "Cahuide," Huancayo, Peru. Lima: Cencira.

MOERMAN, M.
1969   In *Cognitive anthropology.* Edited by, S. A. Tyler. New York: Holt, Rinehart and Winston.

NATANSON, M.
1970   *The journeying self.* New York: Addison-Wesley.

SCHUTZ, A.
1962   *Collected papers,* volume one. The Hague: Martinus Nijhoff.
1964   *Collected papers,* volume two. The Hague: Martinus Nijhoff.

TURNER, V. W.
1957   *Schism and continuity.* Oxford: Oxford University Press.

VAN VELSEN, J.
1967 "The extended case method and situational analysis," in *The craft of social anthropology*. Edited by A. L. Epstein. New York: Barnes and Noble.

Change in the Traditional Forms of Agrarian Collectivism in Spain: Theoretical and Methodological Considerations

JUAN-VICENTE PALERM VIQUEIRA

I. Collectivism as a subject of discussion and speculation among politicians and those studying society (anthropologists, historians, sociologists, economists, etc.) surely antedates the oldest formal principles of their respective disciplines. Indeed it could probably be traced to the very origin of the forming of social hierarchies. It is certainly closely linked with the origin and development of utopian thought. Under the heading of collectivism we include forms of distribution involving sharing of work, the means of production, the profits obtained through the production of goods (agricultural as well as industrial), and the power derived from all of this. It is a subject which has arisen persistently over the course of history. It has done so particularly during periods of crisis, instability, and transformation (radical or moderate) of the socioeconomic and political structures of nations.

Within the contemporary historical process of Western society, especially within those nations whose socioeconomic system started with the Industrial Revolution, collectivism has played a prominent role in the formation of ideological systems and in the working out of supporting programs. This has almost always been within a highly conflicting context. At the present time collectivism in those countries which are barely starting their industrialization process (imitating or trying to follow a similar pattern within different historical circumstances) appears to exist within a different context. The latter is less conflicting and radical and is apparently an indispensable part of the programs or plans for change and national development proposed by the groups in power.

Although it is not my intention to study the variations or modifications of a semantic or practical nature which this term has undergone in different ideological contexts and historical occasions, or to examine the causes which gave rise to these variations, one must question the meaning of collectivization of agriculture, or even the cooperative movement, within the framework of programs of change in developing countries. Does it imply sharing of work, the means of production, subsequent profits, and the power derived therefrom? Or should we define it, instead, as a means of balancing agricultural and industrial production, qualitatively and quantitively — collectivization of the organization, mass-production, and specialization of the labor force and the goods produced? To use the language of the program designers, does it imply adopting the so-called "rational" socioeconomic forms against the "irrational" ones, with the latter including all those which do not fit into the circumstances, needs, and immediate interests of the State or dominant group?

In other words, is it the intention of socioeconomic development programs in the agrarian sector to offer greater and better distribution of power, wealth, and decision-making authority or self-determination, thus consequently providing more equable forms? Or is it to subordinate the rural population and production even more within structures that are already asymmetrical in themselves? That is, through the destruction or weakening of local forms and institutions of power and their replacement by other centralized ones belonging to the state, will these new forms serve to reinforce relationships of control and dependency and to establish direct systems of tutelage?

At this point we cannot reply with certainty to the question we have raised. However, we assume that there must be a great variety of cases. Some, on the one hand, are in accordance with the real intentions behind each particular program proposed by the dominant group, with its degree of authority and effective potential for exercising it. Others, on the other hand, accord with the capacity and possibilities for resistance and negotiation on the part of the rural social sector.

Nevertheless, we must declare in advance our mistrust and skepticism with regard to the real intentions of the groups in power in proposing and supporting these changes or the means of achieving them. We base our mistrust, first, on a long and significant record with a negative balance concerning relationships which have always characterized State interference with the peasantry; second, on the growing gap which has been observed for some time between developed and developing countries; and finally, on the growing internal disparity of the countries in question — between the rich minorities who control the economy and the masses, who in practice are without resources and who are increasingly plunged into poverty.

In this sense we are frankly disturbed by the results which some specialists obtain when carefully and critically analyzing this situation. Take, for example, the results recently published in Mexico in a small book entitled *The beneficiaries of regional development* (Barkin 1972). It seems to be proven here that the effects resulting from a development policy have been diametrically opposed to those originally claimed. One is led to be suspicious not of the failure of planning, but of the excessive brilliance of its designers.

All of the above shows that the intentions declared in national development plans, particularly those affecting the agrarian sector, are impossible today, or at least seriously disputed. What appears to emerge from all this discussion is that State intervention in the rural sector, through its national development plans, consists of a compulsory transmission of local power to state institutions. It seeks an affirmation of political power and compliance with interests alien to those of the rural population, rather than acting to benefit them.

Only in the best of cases (among which we might possibly regard Spain) is this loss of local sources of power compensated for by the introduction of technological modernization combined with accessibility to credit and the opportunity for the rural population to migrate to developing urban centers. However, this situation appears to be offered only by those countries whose demographic growth does not nullify or dilute development efforts. In the majority of cases it appears that this condition is not met and the compensations do not materialize, or else they are realized on such a reduced scale that the desired results do not emerge.

We could conclude by saying that, in the case of the developed countries, collectivism or ideologies which on specific historical occasions advocated collectivist forms played a dialectic role in opposition to the dominant groups. In the case of developing countries, collectivism tends to be converted into just one more of the instruments of power used by the dominant groups to facilitate exploitation while at the same time minimizing risks of popular uprisings. Undoubtedly there is political manipulation of the concept and the charismatic content which inspired the popular movements and ideologists of the past.

This is the basis or critical perspective on which we think that many of the cases should be discussed, where collectivism or collectivist forms are introduced within plans for change or national development proposed by the groups in power. The results obtained by this critical vision will immediately justify or invalidate our apparent initial subjectivism. Adhering strictly to our initial position, we will consider that at the present time collectivism or other similar forms, except on rare occasions, cannot be regarded or assessed as legitimate means of popular participation in national development; indeed, their net effect is to eliminate local control and self-management.

Independently of the historical variability mentioned above concerning the content and utilization of the term in question, there is another level of contradiction which merits brief consideration. This second level, furthermore, falls more directly within the analytical possibilities of the traditional methods of anthropology. We are referring to the inevitable contradiction which must occur in situations of confrontation between collectivist forms proposed by the State and existing collectivist forms which have long operated in the rural environment. Particularly relevant are those situations where one may observe how the State scorns local forms and instead of using and strengthening them and allowing them great vitality, it breaks them up and replaces them with others which can be manipulated more easily. In these cases the conflict or dialectic between the group in power and the rural population must prove to be more obvious and it must likewise prove to be more difficult to hide or disguise the true intentions of centralization — grabbing power and political and economic control of the population and rural production.

II.   Within the limitation of the problems which we outlined in the previous pages, we will consider Spain as presenting a combination of circumstances which makes her an exceptionally interesting case, one deserving greater attention by the social sciences. We shall explain below in outline form some of the reasons or circumstances which induce us to consider Spain in this way.

In the first place, Spain is a country which seems to be located midway between the two blocks formed by the developed, industrialized countries and the developing countries, without belonging entirely to either but at the same time sharing features of both. Although Spain had industrial origins similar to those which existed in most of the rest of Europe, her development was hampered and held back by a series of internal circumstances. Thus, until very recently she has been a nation whose economy was fundamentally based on agriculture.

Furthermore, in spite of the fact that Spain may also be regarded as a developing country (her whole economic, social, and political apparatus operates with regard to and is obsessed by a development course), she still cannot be identified fully with the countries constituting this second block, often called the Third World. This is surely closely linked to her low index of demographic growth, in comparison with Third World countries. It is also linked to her geographic proximity to European industrial centers, which absorb a considerable part of her active population which has moved from the country and to her present political stability, which attracts and guarantees substantial amounts of foreign capital in the form of investments for industrial development. Other special factors, such as her natural, cultural, and economic resources, serve as attractions for the development of a large-scale tourist industry.

It could be said that Spain is a nation which, within a special conjuncture, has been able to hitch on to the train of socioeconomic progress of the industrialized countries while carrying along a combination of sociopolitical forms which are more characteristic of developing countries.

In the second place, with regard to conflict and divergency between the centralizing power of the State and local forms, Spain presents a combination of problems which is almost ideal for its study. This is due, on the one hand, to her well-known internal diversity in social, cultural, ecological, and economic terms; and, on the other, to the existence at the present time of an authoritarian political system unprecedented in her history and with the effective potential to exercise power practically without any obstacles. Of course the conflict between the centralist tendencies and the regions is not the result of the power exercised by the present regime; on the contrary, it has historical antecedents which may be traced continuously through the last five centuries, specifically from the Castilian hegemony, in the wealth of historical documents contained in regional and national archives.

Finally, the Spanish case becomes particularly interesting when we observe the number of existing traditional forms of agrarian collectivism in her rural boundaries. These spontaneous developments provide the social scientist with many possibilities for studying the dialectic between the collectivist forms proposed by the State and the "spontaneous" forms which operate in the country.

Another source of knowledge about cooperatives and collectives is the large amount of documentary information concerning such forms which was gathered around the end of the last century with methods comparable, if not identical, to those of modern ethnography. These documents permit synchronic and diachronic analysis within a period of time representative of the change from a characteristically preindustrial stage to one of intense industrialization during which the national society in general and agriculture in particular were transformed. Of particular value are the works and information gathered by Joaquín Costa and his collaborators on agrarian collectivism, common law, and other sociological and political questions of the rural Spanish environment (Costa 1898, 1902) which we have consulted in our study of agrarian collectivism. We organized our excursions to the country and located the principal areas of study through a methodical system of reinspection of the communities or regions studied by him.

In our present work we shall offer in a preliminary, provisional, and incomplete manner some of the results which we have obtained in the course of this survey on the basis of the critical focus explained above.

III.   We have endeavored to organize the information gathered within a few broad interpretative statistical charts and have sought to avoid an excessively realistic treatment of particular concrete cases. This we did by choosing to accept (although only by way of demonstrating) the ideal of "levels of sociocultural integration" proposed by Julian Steward as an operational concept for the study of processes of adopting higher cultures in complex societies (Steward 1951). Independently of the fact that we do not believe that the interpretative device which Steward suggested at that time may be applied directly to the Spanish cases of adopting higher cultures (and even considering that the latter should be reexamined for some of the specific cases to which he applied it), we have found that the concept of sociocultural levels in itself constitutes a good methodological instrument of work.

In applying the concept of levels of sociocultural integration to a typology of Spanish rural communities which we had already worked out (Palerm Viqueira 1972), five basic and operational levels for studying conflicts which occur in processes of adopting higher cultures or in national integration almost automatically emerged. We are provisionally going to apply these levels in order to present in synthesis form the information we have gathered concerning agrarian collectivism or other forms of local organization and its conflict with the State or national society.

The five sociocultural levels which emerged from the typology of communities are based on the criterion of the degree of complexity or social cohesion of the communities or groups considered. In this way one may think in terms of a sociocultural continuum which starts with systems of simple cohesion, based fundamentally on the family or multi-family groups, and culminates with more complex systems based on an ethnic identity or on a national culture. Within this continuum we have selected the following basic levels as significant points: the family, community, association, social class, and ethnic group. We believe that each of the levels has different and special forms and intensities of manifesting its relations or conflicts with the national society in the integration process. This also applies to the State's methods of reacting to them. By way of example we may consider rapidly the following real situations as representative of the sociocultural levels suggested.

a.   The Galician society constitutes a good example of the first sociocultural level, the family or multi-family group, as well as its special process of integration. A frequent case of the family group is that of two families which form the nuclei of different generations, with unmarried relations living together. Practically the whole of rural Galician society operates at this level of sociocultural organization, with other more complex forms of stable social cohesion being exceptional. In general terms, a large part of the north and northwest of the Peninsula is socially formed in this manner.

Given the fact that the family is the basic nucleus around which practically all socioeconomic activities develop, combined with the fact that social forms or bonds which might link relationships with other family nuclei of the community in a more concrete and lasting way are few in number, relations with state institutions take a personal form (individual-institutional). These tend to be amorphous, or at least unpredictable, and render any attempt at overall action based on the community useless before one starts. The staff of state organizations often have to establish on their own behalf a broad network of personal relationships in order to be able to discharge their functions with a minimum of efficiency.

Furthermore, the community seems to suffer from a lack of organizing capacity to coordinate a joint action or attitude with regard to state institutions and their regulations. The State faces a mass of rural population which is so diluted, fragmented, and inconsistent that it finds it difficult to consolidate its intervention over it, and therefore feels that it must create and superimpose its own institutions and mount training and "education" campaigns. The peasants respond to the latter with a strong dose of indifference and "passiveness." At the same time an agricultural system of subsistence exists which is sufficiently efficient to impede or weaken possible external economic pressures.

We give warning in advance that we do not share the ideas of the Banfields (1958) (at least we do not believe that their "predictive hypothesis" can be applied to the case we are now discussing). However, solely for the provisional purpose of facilitating communication we could, with much caution, speak of a "familism" or a generalized "amoral society" which both impedes local organization and joint action and obstructs the application of administrative, economic, and political measures adopted by the State.

Nevertheless, in using the term "amoral familism" we do not wish it to be understood that suprafamily forms of organization do not exist or cannot arise in specific situations, or that they lack the capacity for this. In fact, we have been profoundly surprised to see how and with what care members of a community have met, studied, discussed, analyzed, and settled relatively complex problems which directly involved over fifty different family groups. We are referring to the operation of mutual cattle-protection societies in Galicia, to which we hope to be able to devote our attention on another occasion. These sporadic manifestations of perfect social coordination and solidarity (which always occur with a minimum of formality or "ritual" and which break up once their mission has been accomplished) have made us suspect on more than one occasion that the Galician peasant, far from lacking organizing ability, has found a weapon of resistance in his apparent disorganization, anarchism, and excessive individualism. We cannot resist the temptation to compare this behavior with that of the "pygmies" described by Turnbull, where behind an apparent social disorganization perfectly coordinated activities spontaneously occur, such as large-scale hunting, the distribution of catches, "beating," etc.

In general terms, this first family sociocultural level coincides with Type 1 described in our typology of Spanish rural communities (Palerm Viqueira 1972:82).

b.   The second sociocultural level, which we have called "community," is composed of a quite wide range of rural communities which on first sight may seem to be very different from one another. Nevertheless, they have specific local forms of sharing by the people of work, means of production (land and implements), the profits obtained, and the power which permits their joint consideration. Some of these forms have developed in a parallel manner or in combination with the development of modern capitalist forms, for example, the production, marketing, and consumers' cooperatives. Others have deeper historical antecedents and occur particularly as neighborhood community forms of land tenancy in common and with methods for internal distribution of work and productivity.

Although the two types are culturally and historically different, we shall consider that both reveal processes for the adopting of different cultures or integration and relations with the national society which are structurally identical.

The type which we will discuss in more detail is that which has been defined on other occasions as the "corporate community." The studies of Arguedas (1968) in Zamora, and Kenny (1966) and Freeman (1970) in Soria, are representative cases of this sociocultural level. Susan Tax Freeman (1968) even came to consider it an "Iberian structural type," and

Dias (1948, 1953) has devoted special attention to it in Portugal. It is very possible, furthermore, that the emergence and development of modern cooperative forms may be the result of a process of development and integration of the forms which we have previously considered as more traditional.

At this community sociocultural level, interaction between the community and the State or its institutions adopts its own characteristics and perhaps much more specific ones. Although the systems of local social organization are much more effective, permanent, and binding than those of the previous level, they are nevertheless more vulnerable and susceptible to alteration through action exerted over them by the State or a dominant group. Furthermore, they lack sufficient strength to offer serious resistance or opposition, since these communities are practically detached socially, economically, and politically from other nearby rural centers. Each of them constitutes a kind of autonomous world, which is enclosed and antagonistic with regard to the outside world.

If, in addition, we consider its economic dependence (its production of specialized goods for a national market), it may be appreciated that perhaps it constitutes the most favorable sociocultural level for exercising interference and change. This is because the system offers in advance the institutional or structural basis on which the state apparatus can operate and it lacks a social cohesion which is sufficiently broad, territorially and demographically, to constitute a grave threat of popular uprisings.

Thus we should not be surprised by the historical fact that there have necessarily been communities or areas corresponding to this second sociocultural level which have suffered more directly and intensely from the impact of the decisions and policy of the groups in power. Two sociohistorical instances are illustrative of what we have stated above. First, the effects in comparative terms with the other levels of the application of the laws on disentailment promulgated during the past century and, second, the intensity of the change resulting from the present-day national development policy.

Types 2, 5, and 6 suggested in our typology (Palerm Viqueira 1972:84–85) may be included within this second sociocultural level.

c.   Some representative situations of the "association" (*mancomunidad*) sociocultural level and its processes of integration are the so-called irrigation communities. These may be found in practice in the basins of all the important Spanish fluvial systems which were submitted to irrigation in times prior to the present-day national hydraulic policy. Those found along the eastern littoral are particularly representative. This third sociocultural level presents systems of organization and social cohesion broader and more complex than the two discussed previously. The systems of social cohesion operate with regard to requirements for the distribution of hydraulic resources and the maintenance of irrigation systems. Consequently, they integrate a considerable number of communities within a sociopolitical unit which we call association.

Many of these associations have developed their own deliberative, legislative, legal, and administrative systems and institutions, such as the well-known water tribunals in the Valencian region. Situations of contact, interference, and interaction, therefore, present specific characteristics. Facing the sociocultural levels which we discussed earlier (the family and community), we now have a case where the systems of social organization are completely institutionalized and supported by considerable popular solidarity. If we add to this the importance or economic potential of associations as producers of highly specialized agricultural goods for a national and international market which produces foreign exchange and shares in the balancing or stabilizing of the national balance of payments, we become aware of its potential for negotiation and resistance with regard to the leaders of the State. Furthermore, the very existence of local institutionalized organizations obliges national institutions to establish contact at an institutional level.

Nevertheless, precisely owing to the institutionalization of the systems of local organization, the institutions and the whole sociopolitical and economic system prove to be extremely vulnerable in a confrontation with an authoritarian state apparatus. Control over local institutions and over hydraulic resources undoubtedly implies total control over the economy and society of the association.

In general terms, the associational sociocultural level coincides with Type 4 as set forth in our typology (Palerm Viqueira 1972:84).

d.   The areas of large landed estates, for their part, are characteristic of the fourth sociocultural level proposed, which we have called "class." A clear social segmentation emerges in them which takes the characteristic forms of a dual system of antagonistic but interdependent or symbiotic classes: landowners and salaried workers.

While the first group usually forms a regional or national oligarchy, the second (salaried workers or day laborers) organizes locally into work crews, frequently formed by big families, which are contracted en bloc to carry out specific agricultural tasks which require large contingents of cheap manpower for certain periods of the year: the harvesting of grapes, olives, sugar, general harvesting, etc.

But the degree of social cohesion of the salaried workers is not limited to mere work crews which basically fulfill work requirements imposed by the large landed estate systems. As a consequence of the wide geographic mobility of these groups and their frequent and recurring contact and interrelationships with other groups which share the same problems, they tend to organize themselves into relatively complex entities of a trade union type and to become incorporated or integrated within political parties. The development and apogee of anarchism in Andalucía during the past century and the anarchical trade unionism during the first part of the present century are processes characteristic of the sociocultural level to which we are referring.

These forms of organization (trade unions, political parties, or even militant ideologies) must also be regarded as specific means of agrarian social cohesion. Their relations with the national society and the State constitute, perhaps, the type of rural conflict situation which has been best studied up to now. This is possibly due to its identification with situations of conflict produced in modern industrial centers. Nevertheless, their closeness is probably not as near as might appear at first. It is evident that the conflict situation between antagonistic classes in the country has been useful for and has facilitated the introduction or spread of ideological systems originating in urban industrial centers. So it has also been useful for students who have adapted examples explaining urban industrial conflict to rural situations. A more thorough analysis of the problems and dynamism of the rural sector would surely give us results which are contradictory, or at least divergent, from those which we are used to obtaining by means of the urban-industrial example.

In any case, it is clear that this sociocultural level, whether or not it is related to urban sociopolitical and ideological systems, acquires an important potential for acting as a pressure group as well as a propellent force, or recipient, of radical programs of change. Nevertheless, owing basically to their radical positions which require substantial changes in the whole sociopolitical and economic structure of national society, they do not have any alternative within an authoritarian system other than rebellion. And the State's only alternative is to react by means of repression and the breaking up of the organizing systems.

This sociocultural level coincides with the general features we used to describe Type 3 of our typology of rural communities (Palerm Viqueira 1972:83–84).

e.   The last sociocultural level which we have regarded as relevant to our outline is what we might call the "ethnic group." Social cohesion in this case is not motivated by requirements of an economic order as in the previous levels, but is established through cultural identification. The cultural group which is defined as such seeks to select, work out, disseminate, and preserve an aggregate of cultural elements, characteristics, or features (history, language, tradtions, etc.) to strengthen and preserve its personality or ethnic identity with regard to other national cultural groups or the idea of national character. The system minimizes internal differences of a socioeconomic nature and exaggerates exceptional features of a cultural nature which are similar for the whole population. The Catalan case is a good example for Spain.

In fact, the ethnic group may be defined as a sociocultural system parallel to the national system but subordinate through systems of power within and through the second. It is by nature antagonistic to and competitive with the national system and consequently expands and acquires vitality through conflict itself.

This sociocultural level, surely, includes both rural and urban populations. Nevertheless, rural problems acquire special importance since a large part of agrarian sociocultural resources are considered as a preserve for the most legitimate traditions or characteristics of the ethnic group. Any attempt to alter or transform agrarian socioeconomic and cultural systems is regarded as a direct threat against the whole ethnic group. Its processes of adopting higher cultures and integration turn out to be enormously complex, since they are in large part the result of subordinating one culture to another which defines itself as a national culture.

Before concluding, it is perhaps appropriate to warn that we do not consider each of the basic sociocultural levels proposed in our outline as autonomous closed systems. This would lead us to commit the same errors made by the majority of studies being carried out concerning the peasantry. That is to say, we do not intend to select a specific level for a community or sociocultural group in particular and use it to analyze and explain its process of adopting a higher culture or national integration in a one-dimensional manner. The outline of sociocultural levels which we are presenting constitutes an interacting and multidimensional system.

It seems that when Steward (1951) formulated his levels of sociocultural integration, he was referring to the sociocultural conditions of the New World at a specific historical period: that of Spanish contact and domination. In this regard Steward conceived his levels as a way of grouping indigenous societies by means of ecological-cultural criteria and evolutionary levels. His levels coincide with or approach a division of cultural areas. Each of the levels proposed would then endeavor to diagnose and explain independent types of integration processes. As this situation of isolation and autonomy of the indigenous groups was to a large extent real, he was able to construct an operative system of independent and closed levels of sociocultural integration, as well as to regard each situation as a one-dimensional process. It therefore proves to be a methodological focus which is suitable for studying the expansionist process of contact and Spanish domination over the New World. Nevertheless, we believe that a multidimensional and interacting concept of levels should be introduced into Steward's system. In this way the latter would be more effective in helping us to understand and explain the processes and dynamics of change at the most complex levels of contact and domination. We are referring to the level which Steward called "state" or, specifically, contact with the most developed American civilizations, i.e. the Inca State and the Mesoamerican cultures.

For areas, situations, and historical periods other than those of Spanish cultural contact with the New World, the idea of levels, as conceived by Steward in his time, proves to be unsatisfactory. Specifically this is the case of Spain and her internal processes of national integration. It is not possible (and it would be absurd to do so) to conceive of communities, areas, or sociocultural groups within the Peninsula with the same degree of isolation and autonomy as that enjoyed by a large part of the indigenous American cultures at the moment of contact.

All the Spanish sociocultural groups have participated, with greater or lesser intensity, in a common historical process for thousands of years. The internal diversities should not be explained by means of ecological-cultural criteria and independent evolution alone, but also as the product of their relations with the national society or other dominant groups in different historical periods. We are not observing (as some people occasionally seem to think) a process of contact and integration which is in its initial stages, but one moment of a very old and enormously complex historical process. Within this process the expansion of capitalist socioeconomic forms in the rural environment is only a recent chapter.

Therefore, all Spanish rural communities, areas, or sociocultural groups participate and operate, to a greater or lesser degree, within various levels or even all the levels described. It is clear that we will regard one of them as the one which best contributes to an understanding and explanation of the dynamics of a specific community. But this, more than anything, is a requirement of methodological order. From the beginning one must reject or mistrust the one-dimensional idea that a group or specific community is always and solely going to operate within the level which at first sight seems the most significant and which we use to classify the community. A community may just as easily operate simultaneously at different levels, without this implying a contradiction. Or else it may pass from one level to another according to the circumstances of the case. Our experience has been that of observing how a group of peasants changes or alters its level in situations of contact with the national society or the State. It always selects the one which offers the best opportunities for defending its interests or achieving concrete ends. Equally the State, for its part, tries to place the contact relationship at the level most suitable for it. In fact, it seems to us that the determination of the level within which a problem is going to arise is one of the first moments of opposition of local and national interests and constitutes one of the first moments of conflict. If a community, which initially seems to be located and is understood as being within, for example, the "community" level, sees in a situation of conflict of interests with the State better opportunities at another level (i.e. class or ethnic group) for attaining its goals with regard to overall national sociopolitical situations, it will try to adopt it. The State for its part will do the same.

Thus, the student interested in processes of integration and conflict must have a good degree of conceptual and methodological elasticity to be able to obtain the best results possible from his observation. To insist on seeing a situation of conflict at a single level not only may involve the risk of falsifying the description of the conflict, but also may mean that the observer will never manage to understand what is occurring.

IV.   Returning to the subject which concerns us (agrarian collectivism and national development), we clearly believe that its study should be approached by means of the two conceptual instruments which we have proposed throughout our work: a critical conceptual basis of national development and an operational methodology such as we believe the idea of levels to be. Although we have already had the opportunity of working with them in rural areas, studying processes of integration and national development in Spain, we will not at this time be able to present the information obtained. We hope to be able to do so in the near future, in order to support all that we have said throughout this work. Meanwhile, we shall limit ourselves to reporting briefly on the regions and problems in the process of being studied.

Of the five levels of sociocultural integration suggested previously, we have only been able to tackle three with sufficient intensity in field-work situations: (1) the family level in Galicia (Bergondo, La Coruña), through the study of agricultural subsistence systems and suprafamily forms of organization (mutual cattle protection societies) in their confrontation with the State's development plans for this region and with the monopolies of the milk industries; (2) the community level in Castile (Valdelaguña, Burgos), through the study of systems of land tenancy in common and the migration of cattle as opposed to present-day state forestry development policy, which raises a serious situation of conflict of interests with regard to land use; and (3) the class level, through the study in Andalucía (Santisteban del Puerto, Jaen) of the large landed estate systems, the cultivation of olives, and the production of olive oil in relation to the conflict of interests between the land-owning national oligarchy and the oil "cooperatives" on the one hand and salaried workers and political parties on the other hand.

We have planned to start a new stage of our investigations by studying the irrigation systems and citrus fruit production in Valencia ("The Valencian Orchard") to include the association level. We plan to compare it with the results obtained in another period of fieldwork in Extremadura (Badajoz) in order to study the hydraulic systems built there recently by the State. With these four projects in progress we will be able to cover satisfactorily almost all the levels proposed in our outline. The ethnic group level will be covered in the near future through studies which are being carried out by a group of Catalan anthropologists with whom we are establishing close collaboration and an exchange of ideas. Thus we hope that we shall soon be able to offer you the results obtained from our fieldwork and our theoretical and methodological points of view.

Once our investigations are concluded, we hope to be able to establish a combination of conclusions concerning the possessors of power in Spain and to show how the agrarian cooperative forms proposed by the State are far from constituting means of popular participation in national development. We shall try to do this by showing how the State not only does not intend to permit greater distribution of power and wealth, but how it is seeking to destroy local forms of power, replacing them with national institutions and through a progressive proletarianization of the peasantry. In our evidence we shall place special emphasis on situations of conflict between the State's "cooperative" forms in its national development plans and the traditional forms of agrarian collectivism still in existence.

REFERENCES

ARGUEDAS, JOSE MARÍA
1968 *Las comunidades de España y del Perú*. Lima.
BANFIELD, EDWARD C., L. F. BANFIELD
1958 *The moral basis of a backward society*. New York: Free Press.
BARKIN, DAVID
1972 *Los beneficiarios del desarrollo regional*. Mexico.
COSTA, JOAQUÍN
1898 *Colectivismo agrario en España*. Madrid.
1902 *Derecho consuetudinario y economía popular de España*. Barcelona.
DIAS, A. J.
1948 *Vilarinho de Furna, una aldea comunitaria*. Porto.
1953 *Rio de Onor, comunitarismo agro-pastoril*. Porto.
FREEMAN, SUSAN TAX
1968 Corporate village organization in the Sierra Ministra: an Iberian structural type. *Man* 3:377–84.
1970 *Neighbors: the social contract in a Castilian hamlet*. Chicago: University of Chicago Press.
KENNY, MICHAEL
1966 *A Spanish tapestry*. New York.
PALERM VIQUEIRA, JUAN-VICENTE
1972 *Notas para una típología de comunidades rurales españolas*. Madrid.
STEWARD, JULIAN H.
1951 *Levels of sociocultural integration: an operational concept*. Albuquerque.

Cooperatives and Agricultural Development in Bangladesh

S. A. RAHIM

THE TRADITIONAL COOPERATIVE MOVEMENT: 1904–1960

The cooperative movement in Bengal began in the first decade of the twentieth century as a program for supporting agricultural administration. The Indian Famine Commission of 1901 recommended formation of credit cooperative associations and agricultural banks. A committee appointed by the Governor General of India formulated the necessary policies, principles, and legislation; on this basis the Cooperative Societies Act of 1904 laid the foundation of the cooperative movement. The movement was to be initiated, guided, and administered by government officials. The organization was to be along the lines of the European mutual credit association, emphasizing distribution of agricultural credit.

At the top of the cooperative organization in Bengal was the provincial cooperative department, headed by a registrar, which promoted, administered, and evaluated the program. A provincial cooperative bank operated as the apex agency for the central banks. The central banks acted as agents of the department of cooperatives in organizing and supervising primary societies and in operating the credit program. At the village level, primary cooperative societies of groups of farmers who needed agricultural credit constituted the base of the cooperative system. This sytem of cooperative organization continued to operate in Bengal until 1947, when it was replaced by a modified system of multipurpose union cooperatives that was adopted by the government of East Pakistan.

During the first twenty years, the growth of cooperatives in Bengal was encouraging. By 1925 there were more than 10,000 societies, with more than 400,000 members and about 62,000,000 rupees working capital

(Niyogi 1940). The government had confidence in the movement. Its progress was considered comparable to the progress of the cooperative movement in Western countries. But serious problems began to appear, first as isolated events and soon as regular, common, widespread occurrences. In 1930 the registrar noted with concern the declining trend of membership and the poor quality of management in the primary societies. By 1935 the percentage of overdue loans had reached about 80 percent; the percentage of A and B class (excellent and good) societies was only about 2 percent. In 1945 the Rowland Committee found the cooperative movement in a very poor state and compared it to a corpse.

In 1947 the government of East Pakistan decided to "revitalize" the cooperative movement. The old credit societies were abandoned and a new structure was introduced at the rural level. In order to make the primary cooperatives viable business organizations, a larger unit was established — the multipurpose cooperative at the "union" level — covering ten to twelve villages. The multipurpose union cooperatives were to have limited liability and were to conduct input, supply, and marketing operations in addition to credit. But these reform measures failed to improve the situation significantly. As before, some improvements were noticed initially, but the old problems soon began to reappear. An evaluation report written in 1955 termed the efforts of the department of cooperatives as essentially useless. The Credit Enquiry Commission of the government of Pakistan noted in 1959 that the cooperative movement had become more or less stagnant at the primary level.

In the fifties the cooperative movement was overshadowed by a new community development program – the Village Industrial and Agricultural Development (V-AID) program. This program attempted to remove development activities from the local governments and cooperatives. A new department was created and a special cadre of development officers was recruited. The program was expanded very rapidly. Naturally, it created a great deal of interdepartmental conflict and rivalry. By the end of the decade, the program failed because of its own weakness and hostile treatment from other government departments. After the failure of the V-AID program, interest in cooperatives was renewed. The Rural Development Academy at Comilla, originally an institute for training V-AID officers, initiated the modern cooperative movement in what is now Bangladesh.

PROBLEMS OF THE TRADITIONAL
COOPERATIVE MOVEMENT

Attempts had been made to identify and analyze the problems of the cooperative movement by the department of cooperatives and by other bodies appointed by the government. The most common problems noted in the official evaluation reports were:

1. Indiscriminate recruitment of membership without consideration of credit worthiness, cooperative attitude, etc.
2. Indiscriminate distribution of loans resulting in overfinancing or underfinancing of individual members.
3. Lack of supervision of utilization of loans by the members.
4. Absence of a program for regular savings deposits by the members.
5. Poor management by the officeholders and their unwillingness to take action against defaulting members.
6. Poor and ineffective audits and inspections.
7. Lack of participation by the general body of membership.

The failure of cooperatives was mainly attributed to the following causes: (1) low level of efficiency in business management, (2) members' ignorance of cooperative principles and practices, and (3) lack of adequate qualified staff in the department of cooperatives.

The official evaluations were concerned with the business efficiency of the cooperatives rather than with their effectiveness in promoting technological innovations and mobilizing human resources for agricultural development. The Royal Commission on Agriculture noted that for agricultural development to reach every villager, the people must be organized to help themselves and their local organizations must be grouped into larger unions. The commission suggested that the cooperatives would be appropriate organizations for reaching the masses with the teachings of outside experts. However, it appears that the department of cooperatives had a much narrower view – it was primarily interested in developing an efficient credit cooperative organization. Moreover, the department was concerned with building a cooperative system from the top, under the patronage of the government bureaucracy. The cooperative system was designed to assist the administration in its endeavor to control activities at the lowest possible level. It was not much concerned with organizing the peasants into motivated groups of participants in the processes of agricultural modernization.

THE COOPERATIVE MOVEMENT FROM 1960 ONWARD

The East Pakistan Academy for Village Development (now the Bangladesh Academy for Rural Development [BARD])[1] pioneered the modern cooperative movement in what is now Bangladesh with a pilot project entitled "A New Co-operative System for Comilla Thana" in 1959–1960 (Raper 1970). The Comilla cooperatives are organized into an essentially two-tier system of multipurpose cooperatives, with the primary cooperative society at the village level and the *thana* central cooperative association (TCCA), a federation of primary societies, at the *thana* level.

The functional scope of the cooperatives is open, but so far, their activities have been generally confined to organizing the peasants into motivated groups; encouraging capital accumulation through savings deposits; supplying agricultural information, modern inputs, and credit to individual cultivators; and organizing joint use of such indivisible items as power pumps for irrigation and tractors. No attempt has been made to cooperativize or collectivize ownership of means of production at the primary cooperative level. The cooperatives deal primarily with peasants who own land and implements. Sharecroppers and landless laborers are usually not included in the cooperatives.

The primary cooperative is managed by an elected managing committee which includes a chairman and a manager of the society. A "model farmer" takes care of agricultural extension. The TCCA is managed by a committee chosen by an electoral college composed of representatives from the primary societies. The executive functions of the TCCA are conducted by an appointed director and a few supporting officials paid by the government.

The TCCA acts as an agent of change. It organizes weekly training/discussion classes for the managers and model farmers, supplies credit and modern agricultural input, and generally assists the village cooperatives in planning, implementing programs, and maintaining accounts and records. At the village level, the cooperative organizes weekly meetings, where the manager and model farmer act as teacher and information agent. Corresponding to the two-tier organization is a two-step communication system that operates quite effectively. The TCCA also plays an important role as a credit agency. It receives savings deposits

---

[1] The Academy for Village Development started functioning in May 1959. From 1960 to 1965, its faculty consisted of ten social scientists headed by an experienced scholar-administrator.

collected by the cooperatives from the members and distributes loans to the members through the village cooperatives.

The cooperative pilot project in Comilla Thana[2] made rapid progress under the constant guidance of the Academy for Village Development. By June 1970, 301 village cooperatives with a total membership of 11,151 persons were organized. These societies accumulated Taka 974,849 as savings deposits and Taka 961,987 as share values. The cumulative value of loans issued by the TCCA from 1960 to 1970 was Taka 13.2 million, of which Taka 8.6 million or 65 percent was realized during the same period. The cooperatives irrigated more than 11,000 acres, most of which were under improved varieties of rice in the dry season of 1969–1970. A research study conducted by BARD (Rahim 1972) showed that the cooperative members in Comilla were able to increase per acre production of rice by 98 percent in a period of six years (1963–1964 to 1969–1970), as against only a 12 percent increase by similar farmers in a neighboring *thana*. The increased production was primarily due to collective adoption of technological innovations by the cooperative members.

To test the viability of the Comilla cooperative system, the pilot project was expanded to include three additional *thanas* of other districts in 1963. The program was expanded to seven *thanas* of Comilla District in 1965 and to the remaining thirteen *thanas* of Comilla District in 1968. In 1969–1970 the national Integrated Rural Development Programme (IRDP) was prepared. Its objective was to cover the whole country with Comilla-type cooperatives. A variation of the Comilla model showed good results in Rangunia Thana of Chittagong District. It showed some practical means of self-financing and self-management of the TCCA rather than dependence on government grants.

In 1970 and 1971 a number of important events took place in what is now Bangladesh: a devastating cyclone that killed thousands of people and destroyed houses, crops, and livestock; a general election that produced an unprecedented victory for the Awami League; a massive non-cooperation movement against the military government of Pakistan; brutal genocide by the Pakistani army; and finally, the war of liberation and the birth of Bangladesh. All these events left their imprints on the

---

[2] Comilla Kotwali Thana: area 107 square miles; population in 1961 200,000; population density over 2,000 persons per square mile; approximately 30,000 farms; average farm size 1.7 acres; 97 percent of farms under 7.5 acres; 73 percent illiteracy at fifteen years of age. A *thana* is the lowest administrative unit. There are 413 *thanas* in Bangladesh.

cooperative movement. Cooperative members suffered material losses and some members were killed.

After independence, great expectations were aroused. The impact was most clearly reflected in a sharp fall in savings deposits and repayment of loans. Some farmers could not afford to save or to repay loans; many farmers thought that the government would write off old debts as it had abolished land revenue up to twenty-five *bighas* of land. The habitually willful defaulters exploited the uncertain situation by defaulting and encouraging others to default. However, the government took action by repeatedly announcing that cooperatives would be a major instrument of economic development in the new socialist state. The old loans would not be written off. Cooperative laws and acts would be revised to make them consistent with the new objectives of the state.

As a first step toward democratization and reduction of bureaucratic control, the government abolished the system of nomination of members in the managing committee of cooperatives. The Bangladesh Academy for Rural Development organized a seminar on cooperative farming in April 1972, only three months after liberation (Rahim, ed. 1972). In this seminar, national and international groups of scholars examined the problems and prospects of cooperative farming in Bangladesh. In a message to the participants, the prime minister expressed his government's desire "to build up a net-work of co-operatives in the country with a view to augment agricultural production and safeguard the interests of the cultivators from all sort of exploitations." The cooperative farming seminar stimulated a new line of action in the field. In a number of places, experimental joint farming and collective farming schemes were undertaken on local initiatives.

In early 1972, the new cooperative system (IRDP) was operating in only thirty-three of 413 *thanas* in Bangladesh. There were 4,600 village cooperative societies with 114,000 members. The previous system of multipurpose union cooperatives was also in operation, with 62 central banks and 4,100 multipurpose union cooperatives. The department of cooperatives also registered about 25,000 groups of farmers operating low-lift irrigation pumps as cooperatives. These were *ad hoc* cooperatives to be replaced by the new cooperatives under IRDP. In total, more than 1,000,000 peasants (over 10 percent of the peasant population) in Bangladesh were associated with one kind of cooperative or another.

In the first Annual Development Plan (ADP 1972–1973) of Bangladesh, Taka 18,000,000 was allocated to IRDP for expansion of the new cooperative system in an additional fifty *thanas*. In the same plan, Taka 10,000,000 was allocated to various other cooperative programs, mainly the old cooperatives operated by the department of cooperatives. Thus it appears that the government of Bangladesh was eager to promote the new cooperative movement but did not want to abolish the old system by any radical measure.

A REVIEW OF THE NEW COOPERATIVE SYSTEM

In 1963 a research survey (Farouk and Rahim 1967) was conducted to assess the impact of cooperatives on the subsistence agriculture of Comilla and to compare it with a "control area" in the neighboring *thana* of Chandina, which had no cooperative program. This study concluded that the Comilla farmers show

...signs of healthy modern farming through their savings pattern, crop patterns and response to scientific methods. Given the time, training and adequate non-farm income they are likely to do well in future; the growth rate would be larger, if we can reduce the effects of natural calamities and if the prices of farm products increase. The study probably indicates that smallness of the farm size is not a bar to modernization and that there are powerful factors hindering this transition, like market, natural calamities and lack of social overheads (roads, irrigation net-work etc.) which are beyond the power of the individual farmer.

In 1969–1970, a similar study was conducted on the same group of farmers (Rahim 1972). When the economic and production statuses of individual farmers in 1963 were compared with those statuses in 1969, it was found that the rates of increase in agricultural production, marketable surplus, income, and assets formation on the farms of cooperative members in Comilla were substantial and were much higher than corresponding rates of increase on similar farms in the control area. However, the extent of productive capital formation (land under cultivation, livestock, tools, etc.) was negligible. The Comilla farmers added more household goods and more gold or silver ornaments to their assets than did the farmers of the control area; their current cash farm expenditures and current liabilities were also much higher. The contributions of cooperative members to capital formation in the form of shares and savings constituted only a small fraction of the total capital investment of the TCCA.

The impact of cooperatives on the village power structure and the pattern of leadership was analyzed in a series of case studies (Rahim 1970; Hoq 1970). It was found that the cooperative intensified the contradiction between the traditional feudal leadership and the emerging petit bourgeois leadership, and strengthened the position of the emerging pattern of leadership. In another study (Rahim 1968), the degree of leader contact with agencies outside the village was found to be strongly correlated with adoption of technological innovations by the cooperative group. An oligarchic form of power structure in a village cooperative was found to be correlated with early adoption of technological innovations by the cooperative.

The impact of new cooperatives has been analyzed in a number of other studies, but no comprehensive evaluation of the new cooperative system has been made by any governmental or nongovernmental agency. A number of partial evaluations, however, have been made. In 1966 and again in 1970, the government appointed evaluation teams to examine the effectiveness of the new type of cooperative. Both teams based their evaluations on studies of official reports, interviews with officials, and a few field visits. The teams found that the program had succeeded in motivating a large number of farmers, in organizing them into effective groups, and in raising agricultural production. But it was too early to assess the financial soundness of the cooperatives.

From December 1970 to January 1971, Dr. Akhtar Hammed Khan, the founder of the Comilla project, made a tour of twenty *thanas* in Comilla District and wrote his impressions of the drainage, roads, irrigation, and cooperative programs (Khan 1971). He noted that the cooperative program suffered from delay in the release of funds because of bureaucratic red tape and the antipathy of the governor of East Pakistan. In his analysis most of the twenty TCCAs in Comilla Thana rated high in the discipline of savings deposits and loan repayments. But some influential, powerful, and well-informed people were trying to capture the cooperatives and destroy them by willful default in loan repayment.

In evaluating farmer participation, Dr. Khan calculated the percentage of those with small and medium-sized farms who had joined the cooperatives. He found that about 22 percent of the farmers in seven *thanas* where the program started in 1965 and about 10 percent of the farmers in thirteen *thanas* where the program started in 1968 had joined the cooperatives. In the seven *thanas*, 70 percent of the villages were covered by the cooperatives, and in the thirteen *thanas*, 46 percent of the villages were covered. Dr. Khan attributed the generally low level of participation to the hard nature of the program, which demanded discipline and sacrifice on the part of individual members. The cooperatives attracted the innovative farmers and proved to be effective instruments of agricultural extension. However, Dr. Khan observed that the objective of self-management of cooperatives had not been fully realized. Creation of responsible leadership and firmer member loyalty remained the most crucial concerns. He thought that an intensive educational and training program was urgently needed.

In May 1972, the Bangladesh Academy for Rural Development invited numerous representatives from the village cooperatives and some nonmembers from the same villages in Comilla Thana to a seminar to discuss their problems and recommend future courses of action (Hussain 1972). This group felt that the farmers needed their own organization in order to modernize agriculture and increase production. The Comilla cooperative system was a suitable organization. The basic principles of this system did not need to be changed, but measures had to be taken to implement properly those principles. The cooperatives should be opened to all, the small as well as the large farmers, who believed in the ideals and principles of cooperation.

The seminar provided opportunities for self-criticism and debate on various issues by the leaders and ordinary members of the village cooperatives and by the nonmembers. The ordinary members and nonmembers were highly critical of the authoritarian management in the primary cooperative societies. They said that the rich peasants dominated the managing committees. These rich members did not pay much attention to the interests of poor peasants, and they took more loans and defaulted more often than did the ordinary members. Some managers of cooperatives failed to give proper accounts of financial transactions. Managers and model farmers did not serve as teachers and demonstrators of improved agricultural practices. The weekly meetings were concerned mostly with matters relating to credit, and the members did not find the meetings attractive enough to promote regular attendance.

The most recent assessment of the new cooperatives is a tentative report (1973) by René Dumont, a well-known specialist in rural development. Professor Dumont spent two weeks in January, 1973, visiting Comilla Thana and two other *thanas* in northern Bangladesh. He observed that even the best cooperative societies had not been able to make proper use of local resources, particularly labor. Efficient management of innovations introduced from outside was lacking. Most of the investments came from the government, very little from the peasants themselves. Many people were unemployed or underemployed, and much work remained to be done. The new cooperative system had tried "to build a rural society with some kind of KULAK DOMINATION instead of the traditional landlord-cum-money-lender domination." Professor Dumont also observed that the loans were used to build houses, to buy land, and to meet various other consumption needs. The level of participation was low, and a bureaucratic attitude was noticeable. Professor Dumont finally concluded that "all the basic principles of Comilla experience must be revised now, especially because the Integrated Rural Development Programme is extending Comilla experience throughout the country."

The new cooperative system developed at Comilla was one component of a more comprehensive institutional framework. The Bangladesh Academy for Rural Development initiated other experiments to revitalize the local government and government bureaucracy at the *thana* level. The idea was to build a strong center of rural development at this level. Accordingly, the Thana Training and Development Centre was introduced. Simultaneously, the Rural Works Programme was launched to build a physical infrastructure of village roads, drainage and irrigation channels, embankments, etc., through highly labor-intensive projects. The Thana Irrigation Programme was initiated to provide power irrigation facilities to groups of farmers.

These pilot projects were adopted by the government as national programs and were implemented throughout the country. Thus, the cooperative program was part of a comprehensive program of rural development. But it was built within the general framework of a capitalist economic system. The cooperative program was designed to save the peasants from highly exploitative feudal moneylending and trading practices, to replace the traditional agricultural technology with a modern technology, and to develop the individual farms into more productive and efficient enterprises. It attracted the more innovative farmers and depended on them for successful operation. Probably for this reason the village cooperative societies could not develop broad bases. The average size of the membership in a society remained low, including only one-fourth to one-third of the total population of cultivators in the village. In many cases the cooperatives were formed around kinship groups and existing village factions. This grouping was necessary to ensure group solidarity and cohesiveness as there was no strong ideological bond for ensuring solidarity in larger groups.

FUTURE PROSPECTS

The political and administrative leaders of Bangladesh have recently indicated that the cooperative movement should be strengthened and reoriented toward establishing a socialist economic order in Bangladesh. There is a growing awareness that the cooperative movement in isolation cannot make any significant contribution toward agricultural development and modernization of the peasant society. It must be linked with an overall socialist policy and with programs of technological and institutional change. Specific measures of land reform and administrative reform are necessary for a successful cooperative movement aimed at increased production and equitable distribution of income in the agricultural sector. The traditional concept of the cooperative as a business enterprise for supplying only agricultural credit and other inputs needs to be changed. The cooperative organization must be viewed as a basic institution through which the productive forces should be directed toward socially desirable objectives. The cooperative movement must grow from the grass-roots level as a strong, viable organization. The old tradition of government bureaucratic control over management of cooperatives must be replaced by a democratic tradition. The government should formulate policies ensuring that the cooperatives receive all necessary guidance and assistance from the state but remain free to operate as democratic institutions within the broad framework of national objectives and strategies of development.

Today, Bangladesh is faced with an acute shortage of food grains. The immediate task before the government is to launch programs for self-sufficiency in production of food grains within the next five years. But this cannot be done without active participation by millions of small farmers and landless cultivators. The cooperative movement must consider this concrete situation and must support the self-sufficiency program. The planning commission of Bangladesh is currently formulating institutional policies and programs that would meet both the immediate and the long-term needs.

It is expected that the institutional policies and programs in the first five-year plan will be directed toward building an effective rural organizational infrastructure for agricultural and rural development. The major components in the institutional framework will be (1) local government bodies at union, *thana*, and district levels, and (2) cooperatives at village and *thana* levels. New cooperatives under the Integrated Rural Development Programme will be expanded into those *thanas* where the agricultural development program (particularly the food-grain self-sufficiency program) will be concentrated. By the end of the five-year period of the plan, about 40,000 village cooperatives having about 2,500,000 members will be organized. Necessary steps will be taken to ensure that the small farmers and landless cultivators join the cooperatives at the village level and that their leaders are proportionally represented in the managing committees of the cooperatives.

The cooperatives will play important roles in joint planning of the agricultural operations, in distribution of agricultural inputs and credit, in management of irrigation pumps and tubewells, in agricultural extension, and in processing and marketing of agricultural produce. The cooperative program will be directed by a national board which will have an adequate number of representatives from the cooperatives. The government will provide necessary financial and technical assistance to the cooperatives (TCCAs), but only for a short period, so that the movement can grow strongly during the initial years but will not become dependent on government assistance in the future.

REFERENCES

DUMONT, RENÉ
  1973   "A self-reliant rural development policy for the poor peasantry of Sonar Bangladesh." Dacca: Ford Foundation. (Mimeograph.)
FAROUK, A., S. A. RAHIM
  1967   *Modernising subsistence agriculture.* Dacca: Bureau of Economic Research, University of Dacca.
HOQ, ANWARUL
  1970   "Co-operation under extreme traditionalism and unfavourable physical conditions," in *Co-operatives and planned change in Asian rural communities.* Edited by Inayatullah. Geneva: UNRISD.
HUSSAIN, ZAKIR, *editor*
  1972   *Proceedings of Comilla agricultural cooperative seminar.* Comilla: Bangladesh Academy for Rural Development. (In Bengali.)
KHAN, A. H.
  1971   *Tour of twenty thanas.* Comilla: Bangladesh Academy for Rural Development.
NIYOGI, J. P.
  1940   *The co-operative movement in Bengal.* London: Macmillan.
RAHIM. S. A.
  1968   "Diffusion of innovations in a development system: a study of collective adoption of innovations by village co-operatives in Pakistan." Unpublished doctoral dissertation, Michigan State University, East Lansing, Michigan.
  1970   "Introducing technological change through co-operation in Nabinagar," in *Co-operatives and planned change in Asian rural communities.* Edited by Inayatullah. Geneva: United Nations Research Institute for Social Development.
  1972   "Rural co-operatives and economic development of subsistence agriculture." Comilla: Bangladesh Academy for Rural Development. (Mimeograph).
RAHIM, S. A., *editor*
  1972   *Co-operative farming.* Comilla: Bangladesh Academy for Rural Development.
RAPER, ARTHUR F.
  1970   *Rural development in action.* Ithaca: Cornell University Press.

*The Transformation of
Capitalist Agricultural
Systems into Cooperatives*

The Patron-Proletarian Nexus

THOMAS C. GREAVES

I. In the Viceroyalty of Peru during much of the colonial period the *obraje* [wardship; see below] was a widespread form of rural economic enterprise. Silva Santisteban documents vividly the conditions of forced labor and misery:

Stripped to the waist, the Indians were tormented by the cold and the pain of long periods in the same position. Many of the workers labored seated on the ground or a log. In some of the *obrajes*, such as Porcón in Cajamarca, they were chained to prevent their escape. In others, the dark corners of the hovel served as a latrine; poorly circulating air made ghastly the work situation of these miserable people. The body parasites completed the odious situation of these unfortunates (1964:54).

With a labor supply generated by the compulsory *mita* system, the *obraje* was an economic institution that went beyond slavery, the taskmasters were immune even from the responsibilities of ownership.

Though *obraje*-like units may yet exist in remote parts of the Andes (Silva Santisteban 1964:162), I mention them here only as an extreme example of a more general category, the unit of economic production. Whether one is dealing with a collective, a cooperative, a nationalized factory, or an *obraje*, these units of production are always internally stratified. Decision making and the authority to obtain compliance are concentrated in the hands of a few. Those few may be temporary, elected representatives (as in a collective), or permanent, self-appointed masters with the backing of total power (as in the *obraje*), or anywhere in between, the internal division of labor and power is a constant.

What this means is that the question of worker PARTICIPATION, as that word is used in this symposium, turns first on the relationships between managers and the managed in the production unit. In a cooperative we are talking about officers and members; in a nationalized factory we are talking about administrators and workers; in a corporation, about management and labor. The premise of this paper is that to understand the quality of worker participation, we must turn to the interactive nexus between the workers and those who direct them. The quality of worker participation in the national polity must be regarded as secondary to the quality of his participation at the job site. This paper, then, is concerned with the social nexus in the productive unit, where the work gets done.

II.   At this point I would like to make three comments on the framework I have adopted. First, the approach taken here is to analyze this nexus in terms of (1) the characteristics of the component groups within the nexus and (2) their expectations of each other. Marx, of course, took the same approach when he analyzed the firm. There were proletarians and bourgeois capitalists, each with their own interests.

Second, the approach is essentially a dyadic one, in which the entire productive unit is described as having only two groups (e.g. management and labor, officers and members, administrators and workers). This will be a very crude model for any real situation because there are always additional groups — the white-collar bureaucracy, factions among workers, political cliques, etc. — and so without being individualized the model's descriptive and predictive capability for a PARTICULAR productive unit is limited. Nevertheless, a dyadic model is a good place to begin.

The third comment is that a description of this nexus need not implicitly presume that the nexus is a stable one. If it is the case that the component groups share contrasting views of each other's capabilities and motives, the nexus may be unstable and, like radioactive compounds, contain the seeds of its own metamorphosis. Returning to Marx, you will recall that once the industrial revolution was underway, Marx asserted that the relationships between management and labor were destabilized: capitalists became more avaricious, more impersonal, triggering a proletarianization of their workers. Thus, when analysing the nexus between groups in a productive unit, whether it is stable or unstable is a major question.

Clientage

Some examples of the sort of interactional nexus I am describing should be helpful here. The most widely described nexus in the anthropological literature is the patron-client bond, or clientage. To be sure, clientage exists in many other contexts, but there are numerous examples of its occurence in units of production. The hacienda is a prominent example (cf. Tannenbaum 1966:77–94), in its classic form a "baseless triangle" of many clientage bonds with one or very few patrons (Cotler 1969; Whyte 1970:21). The "vertical dyadic contract" put forth by Foster (1967:212 ff) and the observations made by Silverman on brokers (1965) detail the inner dynamics of the bond.

Slavery

An interactional nexus which seems quite different from the patron-client bond is slavery. A recent symposium given for the African Studies Association[1] demonstrated that cross-culturally slavery takes on many forms, but that in Anglo-American slavery the institution was basically founded on the legal definition of personal property. Unlike the client who may, at some cost, elect to terminate his bond with a patron, a slave has no such option short of committing theft by running away. The emotional correlates of being a slave are severe: during slavery times in the United States, a Negro woman who had escaped to Canada is recorded as having remarked, "I feel lighter, the dread is gone. It's a great heaviness on a person's mind to be a slave" (quoted in Stampp 1970:68). But the point here is less consequential. Slavery based on a property concept is another social matrix in which economic production can go forth.

Wardship

Besides clientage and slavery, wardship can be identified as another social matrix in which production activities can take place. The *obrajes* were a case of this, as were all the Andean industries employing Indians during the colonial period. The Indians were wards of the crown, entrusted to designated colonials to be worked in return for the supposed burdens of watching out for their welfare. As we know, the *obraje*, the *chorillo*, the *obrajuelo*, and the *trapiche* of those times made a mockery of Hispanic standards of wardship, but it can be said that wardship sets up different ground rules from those of clientage or slavery.

[1] Symposium on the forms of African slavery; I. Kopytoff, chairman; African Studies Association 1972 Annual Meeting, Philadelphia.

Proletarian contract

Probably the list could grow to many more, but one more example of a nexus is sufficient. Mintz (1953, 1956), Miller (1965, 1967), Nash (1970), and many others have written about unionized wage workers in plantations and mines. These authors have called them proletarians because of their total reliance on what wages will bring, their competitive stance toward employers, their comparatively narrow range of expected employer obligations, and their identification with fellow workers within or beyond their acquaintance as confreres in a social class. Without going into greater detail, it is easily seen that these proletarians are interlocked with employers in a very different sort of nexus than any of the other three I have mentioned.

The recitation of these four sorts of nexus — clientage, slavery, wardship, and contract — has had only the purpose of defining by illustration what is meant by the "social nexus in a productive unit" and some of the variance which a "shot-gun" typology will turn up. Having set forth a working definition, I want to look more closely now at two sorts of nexus, clientage and contract, and to couch them within some data I gathered several years ago.

III.   There is a small valley on the north coast of Peru near Trujillo which is home to about eight thousand people and, until recently, five rather traditional, medium-sized agricultural estates. These have been discussed elsewhere as "coastal haciendas" (e.g. Greaves 1968) and feature, among other things, land being worked under two forms of tenure, sharecropping and direct cultivation with field hands. The owner of such an estate is a single individual, commonly living on the estate and exemplifying an elevated social position as an *hacendado*.

Sharecropping is a thoroughly integrated and entrenched system of tenure on these estates. It is not just an economic and property system, but also very much a social one with generally strong, personalized, dyadic bonds of clientage between the *hacendado* and each of the sharecroppers. A sharecropper will address the *hacendado* as "*don*," go hatless in the *hacendado*'s presence, but also share a drink with him at *fiesta* time and may even find him among the drop-in guests at his mother's birthday celebration. As long as the sharecropper remains in the *hacendado's* good graces, he can count on emergency and fiscal assistance in times of need and be fairly secure that he can sharecrop on the estate for the rest of his life and pass the privilege to his sons. Should he fall out of favor, however, life can suddenly become difficult and his tenure short. Still, the rules by which one gains or looses favor are governed by a consensual morality, so ordinarily life is not capricious. The *hacendado*'s relationship with his wage workers — rural proletarians — is more complex. Unraveling it will lead us to the main point of this paper. What makes the nexus between *hacendado* and wage worker critical is that an *hacendado* and his workers do not understand the nature of their interrelationship and operate on quite different assumptions. This began to dawn on me on Christmas Day, 1966. From my field notes:

For weeks there was great speculation on how much the Christmas bonus payments would be for 1966. The eventual announcement that five days' wages would be distributed to each worker was met with disappointment. There had been persuasive speculation that the bonus might be twice to three times that amount. Don Vicente [a pseudonym] viewed the bonus as a gesture of personal magnanimity, and distributed the bonus money himself to each worker. Not one worker thanked him, and the *hacendado* busied himself with grimly handing out the money and checking off the names on a list. When I mentioned to him that no one thanked him, he said bitterly, "Of course not. They never thank me for such a gesture."

When I mentioned the same pattern to the workers they exclaimed that no gratitude was due the *hacendado*. It was a right they had been seeking to formalize in a bargaining contract for the last two years.

This incident found a number of parallels; the *hacendado* was interpreting the behavior of the workers as that of ungrateful clients while the workers viewed him as an erratic employer who would not take them seriously. The *hacendado* regarded both his sharecroppers and his wage workers as clients and his paternalism he took to be both his duty and an expression of Christian charity. Faced with shrill demands and denunciations from his union, he concluded that his workers were ungrateful and misled, and he continued to view himself as a beleaguered, unappreciated *patrón*. On the whole, only the sharecroppers seemed to reciprocate his actions with proper behavior.

But, while the *hacendado* continued to behave toward sharecropper and worker in the same clientage framework, the unionized workers were progressively narrowing their definition of his role (cf. Greaves 1975). Their bargaining instruments were concerned with wages and working conditions; if the agreement was not complied with, the *hacendado* was denounced to state labor authorities. To the *hacendado*, this was an incredible breach of etiquette, straining his patience and forgiveness.

These haciendas thus illustrate two interactional nexus within the same production unit. These are diagrammed in Figures 1 and 2. With the sharecroppers the *hacendado* maintains a patron-client relationship with consensus at both ends; with the wage workers, the *hacendado* operates in a clientage framework while the workers cast it as a capitalist-proletarian relationship. *This gives rise to the anomalous situation of the patron-proletarian nexus.*

View of hacendado		View of sharecroppers	
Patron	extant bond	Patron	(Static relationship)
(clientage)	(clientage)	Clients Clients	

Figure 1.   The *hacendado*–sharecropper nexus

View of hacendado	View of sharecroppers	
Patron	extant bond Management	
(clientage)	(contract)	(Further steps in the process of proletarianization)
Clients	Proletarians	

Figure 2.   The *hacendado*–proletarian nexus

IV.   On the face of it, a patron-proletarian nexus seems unstable. Sooner or later, one would expect, the *hacendado* would awaken to the fact that his workers had completely and irrevocably renounced a client role to him, and he would adopt the capitalist, contractual relationship with them. One assumes that this will happen eventually, but what is surprising about these haciendas is that, despite being embroiled in labor disputes on an almost daily basis with their estates perilously close to insolvency, *hacendados* could continue to interpret the nexus as clientage. Why the persistence?

The Peru data suggest three important factors inducing the *hacendado* to carry on as a *patrón*. First, the hacienda is not just a business but an institution of enormous symbolic investment. On the Peruvian coast a great deal of this is wrapped up in the term *chalán*, which signifies the *hacendado* on horseback, riding in ritual garb, the epitome of the *patrón*. If the *hacendado* accepts this view of himself, and invests much of his self-esteem in the elegant performance of that role, then it is hard to relinquish even if the wage workers are obstreperous.

Second, the patron-client relationship has a ready-made rationale for clients who do not act like clients. They are foolish, child-like, misled, and prodigal. Time and patience will bring most of them back into line, sheepish about their past misdeeds and dutifully grateful. Given a strong liking for the *chalán* self-image, this rationale holds up under extended overuse.

Third, since *hacendados* maintain a collegial, often familial association with each other, sustained by extensive intervisiting on fiesta occasions, their mutual difficulties are grist for the long-winded commiseration they carry on with one another. Too, these visits provide an effective medium for renewing dedication to the *chalán* and associated *hacendado* traditions because it is at these gatherings that the narrative and display behaviors linked to the *chalán* take place (cf. Greaves 1968:55–61). These three factors certainly cannot sustain the clientage approach indefinitely in the face of aggressive proletarian assaults, but they can account for considerable lag.

V. The most important question to be raised in this paper concerns this matter of lag. We have examined what factors underlie the *hacendado*'s reluctance to abandon a clientage definition of the nexus; we must be equally interested in why wage earners move increasingly toward proletarianization. Why are they not influenced by the *hacendado*'s insistence on being a *patrón*, and resume their role as dutiful clients?

Apart from the general implausibility of such a development, the specifics of this fieldwork suggest some of the reasons. One is that just as the *hacendado* has an interpretive framework which reinterprets proletarian behavior as aberrant clientage, so the workers have a framework in which the *hacendado*'s response to them is recast to that of avaricious employer. For example, when the union raises a dispute, the *hacendado* reacts by suspending the housing repair program. He sees it as a punishment. Meanwhile, the suspension of the house repairs only drives the workers to recognize their vulnerability and to seek wage in-increases so that each worker can afford to fix his own roof. The more services the *hacendado* withdraws, the more the workers seek to contractually guarantee them. In a phrase, the more vigorously the *patrón* seeks to preserve a clientage framework, the more his workers recognize their mutual interest and the more proletarianized they become. Back in 1936, Gregory Bateson called this schismogenesis (1936:175 ff.).

When unions are established, this process is probably further accelerated because of the interaction between *hacendado* and worker being increasingly channeled through union officials. On the haciendas studied, the *hacendados* knew few of their wage workers by name. An *hacendado* once startled me by asking me, on the basis of my research, to tell him what his workers were like and to describe how they lived. With the union being the contact point between a worker and the *hacendado*, an individual worker will find his immediate, personalized claims on the *hacendado* growing cold; his sense of security shifts more and more to what the union can guarantee for him.

Let us now return to the concept of nexus. Not only do the types of nexus vary (depending on the component groups and their perceptions of one another), but some are unstable. The patron-proletarian nexus is one of those; it contains the schismogenic seeds of its own transformation. The strenuous efforts of a *patrón* to bring his clients back into line drive them still further into a proletarian mold. The nexus is dynamic.

VI.   Before concluding, I would like to take note of an implication of these observations for Marxist theory regarding the process by which proletarian consciousness is spawned. Marx assigned to workers a passive role in the early stages of proletarianization. Their alienation and class consciousness grows in response to changes in the work environment introduced by capitalists in their efforts to rationalize the production process. Marx writes:

[The worker] does not fulfill himself in his work but denies himself, has a feeling of misery rather than well-being, does not develop freely his mental and physical energies but is physically exhausted and mentally debased. The worker therefore feels himself at home only during his leisure time, whereas at work he feels homeless (1961:98).

Capitalists made these changes, Marx asserted, because of the growing perception of their economic and class interest. They depersonalized their bonds with workers, repudiated a morality of obligations to them, and converted human effort to a mere cost of production.

The work environment deteriorated, Marx reasoned, and labor was increasingly exploited for capitalist profit. As a RESPONSE, labor recognized its common misery and a class consciousness as proletarians gradually crystallized. In a nutshell, changes on the part of employers brought about changes in labor.

The Peruvian data suggest that, at least for them, a very different sequence occurs. The dyadic, schismogenic process is one where the *hacendado* seeks to conserve the status quo, even though his efforts unwittingly contribute to his workers' proletarianization. The Marxist theory is severely off the mark. This does not mean that the patron-proletarian nexus and the way its instability is worked out are the only routes by which proletarian consciousness emerges, but it does signal clearly that empirical tests of these critical aspects of Marxian theory are overdue.

VII. This symposium is concerned with cooperatives, collectives, and nationalized industry. I am aware that I have not spoken directly about any of these, but there are three implications which, I submit, are of value. First, the unit of study, whether it is a collective, a cooperative, or a nationalized industry, is the unit of production and its nexus of interaction. If we are to seriously examine the quality of labor's participation in such a unit, then the nexus of interaction is the point at which the pluses and minuses of participation are added up.

Second, this research emphasizes the importance of determining whether or not a given nexus is stable or unstable. Certainly national planners would not be advised to predicate a new social and economic order on a unit of production in which the interactional nexus was unstable, unless the end product and the process by which it emerges are part of the plan itself.

And third, this symposium might profitably pose the following questions: what sort of nexus obtains in a collective, a cooperative, or a newly nationalized industrial plant? Is it a desirable one? And is it a stable one? If not, where will it lead?

REFERENCES

BATESON, GREGORY
  1936 *Naven*. Stanford: Stanford University Press.
COTLER, JULIO
  1969 "Actuales pautos de cambio en la sociedad rural del Perú," in *Dominación y cambios en el Perú rural*. Edited by Jose Matos Mar et al., 60–69. Lima: Instituto de Estudios Peruanos.
FOSTER, GEORGE
  1967 *Tzintzuntzan; Mexican peasants in a changing world*. Boston: Little, Brown.
GREAVES, THOMAS
  1968 "The dying Chalán; case studies of change on four haciendas of the Peruvian coast." Unpublished Ph.D. dissertation, Department of Anthropology, Cornell University.
  1972 Pursuing cultural pluralism in the Andes. *Plural Societes* (Summer): 33–49.
  1975 "The Andean rural proletarians," in *Ideology and social change in Latin America*, volume one. Edited by June Nash and Juan Corradi. (Photocopy reprint 1975.)

MARX, KARL
1961   "Economic and philosophical manuscripts," in *Marx's concept of man*. Compiled by Erich Fromm. New York: Ungar.

MILLER, SOLOMON
1965   Proletarianization of Indian peasants in northern Peru. *Transactions of the New York Academy of Sciences*, second series, 27: 782–789.
1967   "Hacienda to plantation in northern Peru: the proletarianization of a tenant farmer society," in *Contemporary change in traditional societies*, volume three. Edited by J. Steward. Urbana: University of Illinois Press.

MINTZ, SIDNEY
1953   The folk-urban continuum and the rural proletarian community. *American Journal of Sociology* 59 (2): 136–143.
1956   "Cañamelar: the subculture of a rural sugar plantation proletariat," in *The people of Puerto Rico*. Edited by J. Steward. Urbana: University of Illinois Press.

NASH, JUNE
1970   Mitos y costumbres en las miñas nacionalizadas de Bolivia. *Estudios Andinos* 1(3): 69–82.

SILVA SANTISTEBAN, FERNANDO
1964   *Los obrajes en el virreinato del Perú*. Lima: Museo Nacional de Historia.

SILVERMAN, SYDEL
1965   Patronage and community-nation relationships in central Italy. *Ethnology* 4(2).

STAMPP, KENNETH
1970   "Between two cultures," in *Slavery and its aftermath*. Edited by P. Rose. Chicago: Aldine-Atherton.

TANNENBAUM, FRANK
1966   *Ten keys to Latin America*. New York: Vintage Books.

WHYTE, WILLIAM
1970   El mito del campesino pasivo: la dinámica de cambio in el Perú rural. *Estudios Andinos* 1(1): 3–27.

Persistence and Change in Structure and Values in the Sugar Plantations of Northern Peru

GIORGIO ALBERTI

On June 24, 1969, the Revolutionary Government of the Peruvian Armed Forces, which had come to power six months earlier, issued a far-reaching agrarian reform law. It was designed to alter the Peruvian land tenure system, based on latifundia and minifundia, and transform it into a new agrarian structure, where associative forms of land exploitation would be of considerable importance. To date, the most important accomplishment in the implementation of the law has been the expropriation of the sugar plantations in northern Peru and their transformation into Agrarian Production Cooperatives. There are now twelve such cooperatives, occupying approximately 350,000 hectares, which employ nearly 25,000 workers.

My purpose is to describe briefly the process of formation of the sugar cooperatives and to examine the extent to which they are providing the structural arrangements necessary for workers' participation in the planning, management, and organization of production and in the benefits which are derived therefrom.

In order to grasp the magnitude of the government action in expropriating the exsugar haciendas, mention should be made of the key role they played in the economic and political development of the country. Since the beginning of the century, when new technology was introduced in sugar production, foreign capital was invested, and international demand and prices for sugar increased, a process of land consolidation and large-scale sugar production was started in the northern valleys of Chicama

This paper is based largely on a previous Spanish article entitled "La Reforma Agraria en las Haciendas Azucareras del Perú" by Giorgio Alberti and Julio Cotler, Instituto de Estudios Peruanos, December 1972.

first, and Lambayeque and Paramonga later; this was to have far-reaching social and political consequences. In fact, the capitalistic expansion and consolidation of sugar production took place at the expense of small and medium producers resulting in their displacement and proletarization.

The dislocation brought about by these changes in the production system affected not only the traditional rural structure but also the urban centers of those regions. As the haciendas increased in size they began to compete with, and later displace, the old cities in furnishing services and commodities to the valley populations. This economic and social uprooting had profound political consequences. Out of this context of intense capitalist expansion, proletarization, and downfall of traditionally dominant groups emerged Peru's most important mass-based political movement, the Alianza Popular Revolutionario Americana (APRA) party (Klaren 1970). From the beginning, APRA and the unionization efforts of the sugar workers, which had started in the first decades of the century, were intimately tied together, forming what is popularly known in Peru as the Solid North of the Apristas. As we shall see, the unions played a prominent role during the formation of the cooperatives and the first years of their functioning.

In addition to the intense political mobilization favored by the sugar haciendas, they were also important in that they provided the economic base for their owners to enter into the political arena and become prominent members of Peruvian oligarchy, which was to hold power until the overthrow of Belaunde's regime.

In view of these considerations, the government expropriation and immediate intervention on the sugar plantations two days after the agrarian reform law was passed, reveal the political intention of destroying the economic foundation of the traditional oligarchy and weakening the Aprista union bases, which were concentrated mainly on the sugar plantations. The aim was to erode the party's ability to mobilize the masses on a nationwide basis.

While the owners apparently did not represent any major obstacle in the process of carrying out the reform, the unions displayed significant influence in spite of, and perhaps because of, the government efforts to marginalize them (see below).

The new socioeconomic organization which was to replace the expropriated haciendas was the production cooperative, where (1) the integrity of the structure of production would be guaranteed, (2) the continuity of technical administration and management would be assured, and (3) workers would participate in management, ownership, and earnings as stated in the reform law.

STATE INTERVENTION AND ADMINISTRATION

After intervening in the haciendas militarily, the government named a comptroller for each enterprise; his main task was to assume control of all financial operations, including the power to freeze accounts and deposits held by the plantations in banks in Lima, Trujillo, and Chiclayo. These inital moments of implementation witnessed a contrasting scene: on the one hand, the workers, employees, and technicians were passively waiting to find out what was going to happen, while on the other, the bureaucrats of the NOARRS (Nationa Office of Agrarian Reform and Rural Settlement) in Lima, which was responsible for the execution of the law, were feverishly engaged in designing a new model of socioeconomic organization for the former plantations.

On August 18, 1969, the Agrarian Reform Supervisory Committee was formed, specifically to act as the sole agency of control and coordination of the sugar enterprises. Its main task was to supervise, study, and resolve problems of administration, marketing, and credit in order to maintain the financial solvency and productivity of the sugar haciendas.

During the initial stages, this supervisory committee assigned a state administrator to each enterprise, who was a member of the technical staff of the same or one of the other plantations. He had broad powers over the organization of production and in the area of social and labor matters, while the financial control, investment planning, marketing, and industrialization remained in the hands of the supervisory committee itself. In most cases, the state administrator concentrated his efforts on social and political matters, delegating a great part of the administrative and productive responsibility to technicians, who thereby assumed a position of special importance. They were the ones who managed the enterprises during this stage, while the workers and the unions looked on. On some plantations, due to the "social sensitivity" of the state administrators, workers received some collective social benefits, such as street cleaning, improvement of parks and garden areas, painting of houses and schools, construction of public meeting places, etc. But in all cases, worker participation was minimal and at most consisted in the carrying out of duties specified by others. Indeed, it was the administrator who, with the help of the *técnicos*, decided what was needed and also assigned the tasks to the service division of the enterprise or to private contractors.

ESTABLISHMENT OF PRECOOPERATIVES

During the period of state administration, committees for the organization of cooperatives were formed on each of the plantations under the auspices of the National Office of Cooperative Planning and Promotion (ONDECOOP), which also recruited dozens of university students to be sent into the area. They were assigned (1) to carry out studies and research that would facilitate the preliminary tasks of forming cooperatives; (2) to further the orientation and training of state officials, on the one hand, and of technicians and *campesinos* on the other; (3) to cooperate with and stimulate the organizing committees; and (4) to advise in the electoral process that would designate the directive bodies of the cooperatives.

The attitude of many ONDECOOP officials was very favorable to active popular participation in the transformation process. They attempted to promote new forms of organizations and to stimulate the formation of a new leadership which would displace the Aprista Union on one side and the technical bureaucracy on the other. This attempt produced a conflictive situation because, while the displacement of the union was in accordance with government objectives, the removal of the *técnicos* went against it. The result was that ONDECOOP found itself attacked from all sides: by the Union leaders who wanted to maintain the legality of workers' institutions as well as by the technical bureaucracy who felt threatened in their new positions of control. The government bureaucracy and state administrators, in order to avoid the very real possibility of a fall in production, exercised a veto power on the plans and programs of ONDECOOP, thus limiting its effectiveness.

THE SPECIAL ADMINISTRATIVE COMMITTEES

While the reorganization was in progress and workers were attending orientation classes to learn about the characteristics of the new organizational structures, special administrative committees were created in each of the sugar enterprises (December 1969 to February 1970), which took over in part the functions of the supervisory committee and of the state administrators. These committees were made up of two representatives from the Department of Agriculture; two from state banks (Banco de Fomento Agropecuario and Banco Industrial); one from the National Office of Agrarian Reform; and two representatives of labor, one elected by the employees and the other by the field workers. Each committee appointed a general manager whose functions were (1) to plan, organize, direct, and control the enterprise's operations; (2) to hire and dismiss personnel; (3) to prepare a proposal for an efficient administrative structure for the enterprise; and (4) to represent the committee before the national executive secretary of the Supervisory Committee. In practice, the general manager maintained internal control over the functioning of the complex, while the Supervisory Committee maintained financial and economic control over the sugar industry on a national scale.

Open conflict first broke out during the functioning of the special administrative committees, where employees and workers had the opportunity of being represented in management. Because this representation meant little or no change in the management of the enterprises, the workers, with union support, questioned the legitimacy of the newly established structure of control, accusing its representatvies of betraying their own interests and demanding more direct participation in the tranformation of the enterprises.

As the legal establishment of the cooperatives neared, conflicts between workers and *técnicos* became more frequent. The problem of income distribution and differential benefits received by the two groups, which were the same as before the reform, were the precipitating factors of this conflict.

THE SYSTEM OF MANAGEMENT CONTROL OF AGRARIAN REFORM

In the face of this conflictive situation, the government decided, in March 1970, to create the System of Management Control of Agrarian Reform (Sistema de Conducción de la Reforma Agraria), in order to coordinate the programs of the various specialized state agencies and to centralize the control and implementation of the agrarian reform law. This system was under the direction of a Central Command, presided over by the Chief of the Army Intelligence Service, and was integrated by three command stations located in each of the provinces where the more important sugar complexes are found. The commands were staffed by military officials and delegates of the various national agencies concerned with agrarian reform. The command in turn was represented by a military officer in each of the complexes, forming an apparatus that arbitrated interinstitutional conflicts and maintained labor peace by attempting to resolve the workers' immediate demands. At the same time the System of Management Control supervised the coordination of activities related to the changeover from haciendas to cooperatives.

While workers were receiving orientation classes on basic principles of cooperativism, democratic management, and equality, the government issued in November 1969 the Bylaws of Agrarian Cooperatives, and later in May 1970, a decree on election procedures. Both legal statements revealed a technocratic approach and an antiunion and antiparty politics orientation in the implementation of agrarian reform in the sugar plantations.

The election of delegates to the cooperative assembly was to be carried out on the basis of a roster containing a list of all members of the cooperative according to the following occupational categories: group A, field workers; group B, agro-industrial plant workers; group C, white-collar and service employees; group D, technicians and administrative staff (Article 33 of the Decree on Election Procedures for the Agrarian Production Cooperatives). Twenty-five percent of the assembly of delegates would come from each of these four occupational groups. This procedure implies a considerable overrepresentation of *técnicos*, given the fact that their number is proportionally much smaller than that of workers. Nearly all of the *técnicos* of any given enterprise would have to be elected in order to fill their 25 percent of the assembly seats.

As to the anti-union and antiparty politics orientation of these regulations, article 37 of the same decree on election procedures states that cooperative members who had occupied leadership positions in unions or political parties during the last three years could not aspire to candidacy. Considering that all members of the cooperative management bodies — the administration and supervisory councils — must come from the assembly of delegates, these regulations virtually excluded union leaders from positions of leadership. According to the same legal procedures, the assembly delegates were to be elected jointly by the cooperative members and the government, in proportion to the amount of the loans allocated by the latter to make the expropriation possible.

This brief examination of the new formal structure of the cooperative reveals a fundamental fact, namely, that workers were represented by a few of their counterparts in the management bodies of the enterprise but that there was no legal mechanism which assured their participation at the various levels of administration and decision making in the daily performance of work activities.

THE ELECTIONS FOR THE COOPERATIVE

Once the preliminaries had been completed and the statutes for the future cooperatives and labor regulations had been written, ONDECOOP called elections for June in Tumán, Cayaltí, and Laredo, and for October in Paramonga, Cartavio, and Casagrande. Following the prescriptions of the election bylaws, the participation of the state in the selection of the delegates to the general assembly was overwhelming, appointing in one ex-hacienda as many as 82 percent of the delegates (Table 1).

Table 1. Composition of delegates to the cooperatives' assemblies

	Delegates elected by the workers	Percent	Delegates named by the government	Percent	Total
Tumán	22	18	98	82	120
Cayaltí	98	82	22	18	120
Laredo	44	37	76	63	120
Paramonga	32	27	88	73	120
Cartavio	55	46	65	54	120
Casagrande	24	20	96	80	120
Total	275	38 percent	445	62 percent	720

Source: Ramón Saldivar (1971:Table 14).

It seems that the selection of the appointees was done by the military coordinator of the System of Management Control in each enterprise with the collaboration of the technical staff which had firsthand knowledge of "its" men. The criteria employed for the appointment of the delegates were (1) good conduct, (2) good working records, (3) not having presented complaints to management in previous years, and (4) not having actively participated in union activities and politics.

In order to cover the 25 percent of the total of the members of the assembly of delegates which the bylaws specified, all the *técnicos* of certain enterprises had to be appointed, due to their reduced number, while workers had generally a very low representation (Table 2). Once the assembly of delegates was elected, it appointed the administrative and supervisory councils as well as the various specialized committees. These activities were controlled and organized by ONDECOOP. Nevertheless, because of the contradiction between restricted representation and limited participation of workers in the election process of delegates, and the cooperativist rhetoric propagated by ONDECOOP, a feeling of deception and frustration developed among the workers which resulted in a general lack of interest in the cooperatives. This was particularly manifested at the public ceremonies that legally established the first three cooperatives on June 24, 1970. In spite of the fact that high-level government officials were present, public interest was minimal and the ceremony was little more than a formality. In certain cases, Tumán for one, some disturbances took place.

In the following months, the first manifestations of open conflict broke

Table 2. Workers by occupational category and their representation in the delegates assembly (DA)

Occupational category	Casagrande				Tumán			Cayaltí		
	Number of workers	Percent of total	Percent of representation in each category in DA		Number of workers	Percent of total	Percent of representation in each category in DA	Number of workers	Percent of total	Percent of representation in each category in DA
A	2158	49	1		869	40	3	2165	86	3
B	1320	30	2		689	31	4			
C	841	19	4		603	28	5	316	13	9
D	89	2	34		20	1	100*	23	1	100*
	4408	100			2181	100		2504	100	

* In these cases the total number of *técnicos* could not fill the thirty seats in the DA

Source: Compiled from existing information in SINAMOS (1972) and Márquez Peirano and Sánchez Fernández Baca (1972).

out. It was the beginning of the process of polarization between the workers, backed by their unions, and the *técnicos*, who had become the new power elite and continued to enjoy special privileges. The growing conflict took the form of strikes and noncompliance with orders given by the new administrators, in spite of the control execised by the state within the executive organisms of the complexes, and of sanctions imposed on these acts, considered by the government as sabotage of agrarian reform.

On October 3, 1970, the last agrarian production cooperatives were legally established on the principal exsugar plantations. As this cycle ended, which theoretically should have led to the formation of "communitary" and "solidary" organizations, as proposed by official ideology, it paradoxically marked the initiation of a new cycle of social conflicts in which the workers and technocrats took sides as opposing protagonists.

CONFLICT AND CHANGE IN THE SUGAR COOPERATIVES

The situation was ripe for the outbreak of open conflict. In effect, during 1971, bureaucratic control had crystallized, making the workers and their organizations totally marginal in the decision-making process in the operation of the cooperatives. In order to compensate for this situation,

ONDECOOP sponsored the formation of "study groups" through its National Center for Cooperative Education. Group members were to be recruited from all labor categories and were to include the largest number of workers possible, so that a mechanism might be created through which the cooperative members could channel their problems and suggestions. The groups were to be directed by a moderator who would come from the assembly of delegates. Grievances and suggestions would be sent to the education department of the cooperative, which would refer them to a permanent group of advisors for distribution to the appropriate speialized committee. Each one of these was in charge of proposing solutions to the administrative committee, which would submit them to the general manager or to the general assembly of delegates for approval. Thus, according to the regulations, the routine channeling of "problems" and suggestions required some sixty steps.

An evaluative study of the functioning of these study groups demonstrated their inefficiency (ONDECOOP 1971).

The study groups failed as a result of their high degree of bureaucratization, and also because they met with a great deal of resistance at different levels within the cooperatives. The technicians, and in some cases the military coordinators, considered them to be "small unions"; on the other hand, the union leaders considered the study groups to be a direct threat to their positions and therefore opposed them. Thus the failure of the study groups left the technicians in direct confrontation with the workers, in the absence of any mechanism for mediation. In this situation, the unions, which had been gathering more and more strength in opposition to bureaucratic control, precipitated a conflict escalation which lasted through all of 1971. Strikes and work stoppages took place in Pomalca, Pucala, Tumán, and Paramonga. Workers demanded the reestablishment of union rights, the rehiring of workers fired by the cooperatives, the rectification of work categories and salary scales set by consulting firms, increased profit-sharing, publication of technicians' salaries, etc.

In June of the same year, workers at Pucala initiated a strike that ended in the jailing of union leaders who were subjected to military justice and condemned to six months in prison for "sabotage." In July, at Cayaltí, there was a strike to demand broader social benefits as well as the rehiring of the union leaders fired by the cooperative. In Pomalca disturbances took place in August. In that same month a mass demonstration was held by the workers at Tumán to protest irregularities attributable to the manager, which resulted in his dismissal by the administrative council. The following month witnessed a strike at Cartavio where the workers demanded salary increases and the reinstatement of union dues and leaves of absences.

In December at Pomalca the workers organized a strike to increase the margin of cooperative dividends to be distributed and asked for the resignation of the majority of the technicians and of the president of the administrative council.

The conflict reached its climax in January 1972, when in most enterprises, particularly in those clustered in the area of Chiclayo — Tumán, Cayaltí, Pomalca, and Pucala — the rebellion against the administration and the technicians reached the point where the latter were in some cases in danger of being lynched.

The government, as well as the press, attributed these conflicts to the agitation of the "counterrevolutionaries" of the "far left." Consequently, according to this definition of the situation, the government entered Tumán with military forces in January 1972, jailing close to fifty union leaders from various sugar enterprises and thereby bestowing on the cooperative problem a national political dimension.

Nevertheless, it seems that the System of Consulting and Fiscalization of the Agrarian Cooperatives (SAF-CAP) — the agency that had replaced the System of Management Control of Agrarian Reform in March 1971 — and the even more recent National System of Support and Social Mobilization (SINAMOS), reevaluated the situation on the basis of first-hand information and successfully pressured the government at high levels to stop its repressive activities. Consequently the government charged SINAMOS with the guardianship of the cooperatives and scheduled general elections for April 16, after significantly modifying the election procedures and freeing the jailed union leaders.

The most important articles of the new election procedures stipulated that any member of the cooperative could announce his candidacy for office (thereby removing the impediment to which political and union leaders had been subjected); that the proportion of obligatory representation from the four occupational categories be rescinded and the state's right to appoint a majority of the members of the general assembly of delegates be annulled; and lastly, it provided for the direct election of the general assembly of delegates as well as of the administrative and supervisory councils.

The elections resulted in an overwhelming victory for the union leaders and for the groups that had been opposed to the administrative control of the *técnicos*. And so it was that in some cases union leaders, set free the day before elections, were voted into the most important cooperative offices.

In this way, the stage of agrarian reform which was characterized by the institutionalization of divisions and opposition between the technocratic apparatus and the workers came to an end. This reorganization of the cooperatives initiated a new stage in which the state attempted to bring about a better integration and conciliation between *técnicos* and workers and a more positive articulation with the sugar industry.

The first year of cooperative functioning after free and democratic elections for the appointment of workers to the delegates assembly and management bodies seems to have brought relative social peace back to the sugar complexes. A new trend is emerging characterized by a tacit pact between technicians and union leaders now incorporated into the cooperative management structures. Corollaries to this pact are the weakening of union activities and the separation between the new bureaucratic control and the mass of workers.

CONTINUITY AND CHANGE IN THE SUGAR ENTERPRISES

An examination of the stages of implementation of the law and of the first years of cooperative functioning suggests that the Peruvian government has realized the economic objectives proposed by the reform, while it has failed to achieve the social aims of the law.

In fact, production and productivity have not fallen and in many cases have increased. In 1970, for example, total production was 794,922 tons as compared to 650,102 in 1969. In Pomalca production went from 1,087 quintals in 1970 to 1,896 in 1971 (Horton 1973). This has been achieved by the bureaucratization and rationalization of the sugar industry, particularly with the centralized administration carried out first by the Agrarian Reform Supervisory Committee and later turned over to CECOAAP (a service cooperative for the sugar industry). The centralization of the purchase of materials, credit, distribution, marketing, planning, industrialization, and investment paved the way for the formation of an integrated sector of the economy. A sugar producers committee had existed before the reform, but it mainly concerned itself with marketing because of the quota system, both domestic and in the United States.

The same government orientation and action that brought about the administrative bureaucratization of the companies was also responsible for the persistence of social stratification. In effect, the government's aim to maintain the production and productivity levels achieved in the period preceding the reform required that the technical management teams remain intact and that the group privileges that they had enjoyed before the reform be maintained.

This stratification was based in the first place on income differences among the various occupational categories within the cooperatives. The salaries that corresponded to the highest level on the pay scale at Pucala in 1972, for example, was thirty-two times that of the lowest level; this same comparison yields a ratio of 25 to 1 at Pomalca and of 15 to 1 at Tumán (SINAMOS 1972). These figures do not take into account differences in fringe benefits such as foodstuffs, living quarters, hospitalization, schooling, and bonuses.

The distribution of yearly profits does not reduce the income differentiation as these benefits are equal for all members of the cooperative and do not take salary differences into consideration. Moreover, the stratification is reinforced by residential segregation and by the notable variations in the quality of housing and public services provided for the different groups according to their occupational status.

There is, however, an important difference in comparison with the situation before the reform. Internal stratification is now based on FUNCTIONAL terms, while before it was determined by CLASS criteria. Where stratification still functions along class lines is in the relationship between the cooperatives, as labor employees, and the seasonal sugarcane cutters. These are contracted for in the same manner as they were by the plantation. This system keeps production costs down, since the mass of unorganized contract labor earns less and does not have access to the social rights and benefits awarded to cooperative members. Thus a member of the cooperative in the lowest occupational category receives, taking into account salary, privileges, and social benefits, four times that earned by a laborer under contract to the cooperative on a seasonal basis: 8,200 and 1,900 soles a month respectively (SINAMOS 1972).

Seasonal workers are hired by a contractor acting as a private employer. This impedes unionization, thereby "marginalizing" them as a group. These workers make up a large proportion of the sugar industry labor force: 14 percent at Pucala, 25 percent at Tumán and Pomalca, and 30 percent at Cayaltí (SINAMOS 1972). There seems be to a generalized opposition to the incorporation of this group into the cooperatives as it would signify an increase in production costs and in the number of people entitled to benefits from the cooperative earnings.

A corollary to the persistence of internal stratification has been the technocratic control of the production, organization and daily work activities. The *técnicos* seemed to be conscious of the dangers involved in the gap which is being created between technocratic management and the workers. But, paradoxically, they tend to argue that the problem is due to "lack of communication." In this respect one *técnico* stated that "one of the biggest problems that we have to [solve] is the communication between the cooperative structure and the workers. But we are going to solve that with the purchase of sixty loudspeakers [sic] so that all workers can hear the opinions of their delegates in the assembly." This anecdote reflects the vertical structure of social relationships within the cooperatives.

Another important element which seems to be continuing from the past is the tendency to increase mechanization and reduce the number of permanent workers. In this respect, a clear division is drawn between those who are members of the cooperatives and those who are not. An incident which occurred recently in Pucala gives a clear indication of this. A short strike of sugarcane cutters was broken by the members who went out into the fields, did the job themselves, and then advertised their feat as an example of "cooperative consciousness."

While the above considerations point to continuities in structure and values, one should not derive from them the erroneous conclusion that the only significant change has been the removal of the *hacendados*. This in itself is a fundamental fact which has in principle altered the internal distribution of power. In fact, we are facing here a basic contradiction. While the technical staff still maintains all its power during the normal functioning of the production process, under conditions of crisis, such as those determined by the previous legal restrictions to appointment in the delegates assembly, the workers can resort to collective action for political purposes.

On a different level, other important changes have occurred, such as a rise in the absolute and relative income of workers, an increase in expenditures on social services, and, of course, workers' participation in management, through their representatives, ownership, and earnings.

The future of the sugar cooperatives as a viable mode of popular participation in the development process depends on (1) the redefinition of the membership criteria in the direction of full membership on the basis of work alone; (2) the integration between workers' representation in management and workers' participation in decision making in the production process; and (3) a government policy oriented toward redistribution on a national scale.

REFERENCES

HORTON, DOUGLAS
    1973   "Haciendas and cooperatives: a preliminary study of latifundist agriculture and agrarian reform in northern Peru." Unpublished manuscript.

KLAREN, PETER
1970   *La formación de las haciendas azucareras y los origines del APRA*. Perú
Problema 5. Lima. Instituto de Estudios Peruanos.

MARQUEZ PEIRANO, JUANA, DORIS SÁNCHEZ FERNÁNDEZ BACA
1972   "Exploración de la participación de los trabajadores en la Cooperativa
Agraria de Producción Casa Grande Ltda." Unpublished thesis for
the diploma Asistente Social 32. Lima: UNMSM.

ONDECOOP
1971   Segundo seminario de evaluación del proyecto de Capacitación-Or-
ganización. Lima.

SALDIVAR, RAMÓN
1971   Elementos para un enfoque general de la Reforma Agraria Peruana.
Cuadernos Agrarios 1 (August):25.

SINAMOS
1972   Datos relacionados sobre la estructura socio-económica del Departamento de Lambayeque.

United Workers Ltd., Campo de Herrera, Tucumán: The First Cooperative for Agricultural Work in Argentina, Five Years After Its Creation

HEBE M. C. VESSURI and SANTIAGO BILBAO

The purpose of this paper is to use a specific experiment as a means of analyzing ideological aspects inherent in a process of social change. We are referring to the organization of rural workers in cooperatives for work and production. Despite the fact that our case is special, we believe that our arguments may be relevant to other experiments in the collective organization of production. It is, therefore, only a preliminary exploration of the ideological background of this type of productive form.

First, we consider the structural situation and combination of events which led to the initiation of the cooperative, examining the central role played by the National Institute for Agricultural Technology (INTA) and the novelty of the experiment for this institution, given its past scope of work. Second, we describe the cooperative's organization in outline form, emphasizing those points regarding the machinery for governing and administration which we consider useful for discussing the subject of basic interest to us. Third, we develop aspects of the cooperative's general and particular orientation, both in terms of the technical problems involved as well as the ideological program of the donor technical team. This includes discussion of the principal changes which occurred in the course of the experiment in relation to the responses and actions of the associated members. Finally, the summing-up centers on a consideration of regional occupational problems and their relation to governmental policy in the field of agrarian reform and the cooperative movement.

Agricultural workers' cooperatives represent a new experiment in many aspects of the overall agricultural panorama not only on the regional level but throughout the country. First of all, the agricultural programs initiated after 1967 institutionalized a new form of land tenure in the collective.

The principal form of agricultural tenure in Argentina's history, starting with the expansion which took place in the second half of the last century was based on individual operation and every prior colonization plan has been effected in this manner. While it is true that forms of collective tenure appeared in the pre-Spanish and colonial period, and some of these do in fact remain in some isolated and very special regions, nevertheless the predominant form is individual tenancy of landed property. Another novel aspect of the program in Argentina was the granting of land to members of the social sector of agricultural workers, who previously had had only marginal access to it. Furthermore, the land which these workers acquire, far from being of marginal quality as in other well-known experiments, is of good quality and is situated in one of the most fertile regions, benefiting from the best infrastructure in Argentina. Finally, it is almost the only successful experiment (economic, technical, and social) of a designed program of agrarian transformation. Those which have been carried out or are in progress using other systems have not had the expected results, or else their cost to the State has been so high that in practice they cannot be repeated. The novelty of this experiment and its success have awakened both interest and disbelief which have made it a controversial matter. These cooperatives and the appearance of the Agrarian Leagues of the Northwest mark two transcendent events in the search for solutions to the country's agricultural problems.

THE ORIGINS OF THE COOPERATIVE

As in so many other Latin American examples, the United Workers Cooperative Ltd. (*La Cooperativa Trabajadores Unidos Ltda.*), located in Campo Herrera, Famaillá Department, Tucumán Province, was not the result of a spontaneous decision by its workers, nor was it imposed by the government. It emerged from a difficult combination of political and economic events and was promoted and initiated from outside the local community. The people had three alternatives: either to join the cooperative, to remain unemployed, or to leave, because the sugarworks previously employing them as agricultural workers had dismissed them in mass.

The most binding factor influencing them was the force and enterprise of a group of informed men from outside the community. The latter had secured the government's minimum support to get this social experiment underway. The loyalty and trust inspired by this technical team, and especially the strong personality of the project director, resulted in a high degree of local participation.

All this occurred within a context of acute social and economic problems affecting the well-being of rural society and the stability of society as a whole. Although it started off within a framework of misery and unemployment, its importance for the technical group was that in its first stage it was truly a technical-social "experiment" where a number of things could be proven. First, the lands of the sugar plantation, if well worked, would yield high profits. In order to work the whole area with a large number of unskilled workers, the technological requirements were so great that is was impossible to subdivide the land into multiple plots. A collective educational process could be carried out more effectively under a cooperative system than by a capital stock company. For these reasons the community development, long proclaimed from above but difficult to realize in practice, could be achieved.

We shall first briefly describe the critical political conditions under which the cooperative arose. This will assist in understanding the characteristics it adopted in its subsequent organization and development.

The Crisis of 1966[1]

The sugar crisis of 1966 recapitulated the cyclical crises of national sugar activity. First, it was a result of stock accumulation resulting from overproduction. Starting in 1958, the sugar industry experienced a gradual and constant increase in its installed manufacturing capacity. In turn, the varieties of cane grown until then were replaced by others with a higher yield of sugar. This resulted in a noticeable increase in sugar yield per hectare. As a corollary of this increased production, the price for the supply declined in the face of an extremely inelastic demand. The economic vulnerability of many enterprises prevented them from absorbing the heavy loss. In some cases, paying of their debts with sugar contributed to an even further reduction of prices.

The high international prices of sugar in 1963/64, produced an expansionist euphoria based on confidence that the situation would continue for many years. This interfered not only with the concept but with the process of production regulation (which had been praised by official institutions such as INTA).

Within this economic framework, social conflicts in the province at times appeared chaotic, especially from the beginning of 1965 to the end

---

[1] The material in this section is a resumé of Chapter VIII of the work by Dominguez and Hervás (1970).

of 1966. Along with the lowering of the price of sugar, which was caused largely because of the capital overhead of many factories and their inability to limit production, there were delays to suppliers and workers of sugar mills and independent sugarcane sellers. Restrictions on output meant that many mills were forced to close.

The normal unemployment in sugar activities in the summer months was swollen by contingents coming from the closed factories. This occurred in August 1966, when the government agents decided to intervene in eight sugar mills, planning to close and dismantle or transform them at a later date. Their intervention evoked protest on the one hand from the independent cane producers, who were trying to collect adequate amounts from industry and who declared that it was impossible to absorb the salary increses which had been ordered to the benefit of agricultural workers. In their turn the sugar mills in which the government had not intervened had to fulfill refinancing agreements for debt entered into with the State. This involved the accommodating of administrative and technical structures to make it possible for them to meet the minimum efficiency required for the reduction of costs and indemnifications. The process contributed to an increase in unemployment.

The result was a considerable increase in social tension, with street demonstrations, occupation of factories, protests, "public disorders," the taking of hostages, etc.

Case Analysis of a Sugar Mill

The case of the Bella Vista Sugar Mill, one of those in which the State intervened, illustrates aspects of this process. It was forced to continue operating, and it initiated a new policy of staff reduction at the beginning of 1967 in response to agreements with the government, discharging some 350 permanent workers, mainly from rural areas. In the face of this situation, which was in opposition to the objectives of social pacification pursued by the government, the company offered to give away up to 2,000 of the 10,000 hectares of land it owned. The intention was to give it to the unemployed workers and thus palliate the impact of unemployment. In addition, the handing over was one of the clauses of the agreement for the sugar mill to receive authorization to reopen.

The initiative was favorably received by the provincial and national governments. Advice was obtained from the appropriate official institutions, including the Famaillá Regional Agricultural Experimental Station of INTA.

THE CENTRAL ROLE OF THE INTA

The technicians in the organization undertook at once to locate the legal antecedents, plans, and maps of lands; they then proceeded to study the technical, agronomical, economic, and human aspects during the months of April and May 1967. The lands offered bordered on those of INTA, thus ensuring general knowledge of the region on the part of the technicians and the possibility of accurate advice. The property included about 1,500 hectares of sugarcane, and the remaining 500 included woods, pasturegrounds, roads, drains, and villages.

The average age of the population to be incorporated into the experiment was forty-six. With almost twenty years of experience in organized trade-union activity, they were hostile to or at best little inclined and scarcely prone to change. The single-crop cultivation of cane in the sugarplantation area involves specialization of activity which results in a working force that is unskilled and inefficient in any other work.

Weighing the local factors involved and the regional economic conditions, INTA's recommendation (which was later implemented) was that the holding should not be parcelled out because it would automatically have produced a structure with very small farms (5.7 hectares per person). It recommended that the land should be worked as a single unit, under an integral cooperative system. The objectives sought would be: (1) to contribute to the diversification of the Tucumán cane area by introducing new agricultural products and by training those associated with the new jobs involved in their cultivation as an alternative to single-crop cultivation of cane; (2) to establish an efficient and competitive enterprise, continually expanding and developing, based on its members' work and managed by modern, low-cost administration, capable of forming capital through its own resources, supplied with the necessary technical infrastructure; and prepared if necessary to be guided to different agricultural activities; (3) to provide employment to its associated labor force not less than 230-240 days a year in its first stage (normally sugarcane activity brings a maximum of 120 days of work per year to permanent workers); (4) to be capable of ensuring an annual income to its members not less than that of an industrial worker, also in the first stage; (5) to be the economic instrument for producing assets and means of payment sufficient to finance development (social, community, and individual) of the people affected by the sugar crisis; (6) to help make the migration of young people unnecessary; and (7) to serve as a pilot scheme for studying the most suitable forms for solving problems of a similar nature in other zones of the province or the country, where *minifundia* conditions, marginal growth, or underdevelopment afflict rural inhabitants (Dominguez and Hervás 1970:141–142).

Promotion of the Project

The workers' trade union and the sugar mill had agreed to carry out a purchase transaction for the lands independent of indemnization for the workers. The latter was a question subject to labor legislation and would be received equally by workers regardless of whether or not they participated in the purchase of the property.

The promotional activity for the recruiting of candidates took place in an atmosphere of general confusion and anxiety. There was distrust of, and in some cases hostility toward, the project, all the more so because it was assisted by a government institution (and the government appeared to be the party responsible for the situation). In addition there was pressure on the part of certain trade-union sectors which generated resistance.

Confusion concerning the significance and manner of operation of the cooperative system was general. Where it had existed, even in its early stages, the system often had represented a setback since it was the product of unsuccessful attempts at consumer cooperatives.

About 140 candidates registered, and the cooperative was formed on this basis, without selection of any kind, with 119 founder members.

Payment for the land was to be made in six annual installments, ending in 1974. This was in accordance with the plan for payment of the mortgage credit granted to the cooperative by the Bank of Tucumán Province (which in fact, did not pay anything, since there was a transfer of mortgage). It should be noted that the bank plan did not meet the specifications of a development transaction. If the project turned out to be viable it was because of the low price for which the lands and other assets were acquired, since the interest payments and amortization period were a very onerous charge in the first years.

The problem of the sugar mill's unemployed affected the permanent staff, who were of middle and advanced age. In recent years the Tucumán sugar mills had ceased taking on permanent staff and young people could only be accepted for employment as transient workers. The sequel to that state of affairs was the emigration of those people who were in the most productive age groups. As to education, 18 percent were illiterate, and if one adds to this figure those who only received education up to the third grade, the figure reaches 84 percent who were functionally illiterate.

Only two of the members had previously had experience in supervising work in the field. The rest were sugarcane dayworkers, farm workers, ox cart drivers, etc.; two had done some work involving gardening and the driving of tractors. The universal lack of training was very important for uniformity of action. This was proven when, after the cooperative was set up, there was no room for some of the unemployed people who had been engaged in work of an administrative type on the plantations since the cooperative was not able to absorb many such employees. During the first sugar season the only possibility for work was in cutting cane. Four persons refused to join the society for this reason.

General skill for cane jobs and the high degree of adaptation to the milieu which the members exhibited were positive factors.

Antecedents for INTA's Extension Work and the Novelty of the Experiment within this Institution

In spite of the fact that there are other organizations which engage in agricultural extension activities on a limited scale, it can be asserted that the setting up of INTA in 1956 marked the beginning of agricultural expansion in Argentina (Fienup, Brannon, and Fender 1972:272–288).

Although the overall objective of INTA's extension service is to contribute to the TOTAL development of the agricultural sector (including the rural family and community life), it has tended as an organization to concentrate its attention on strictly technological aspects of production. Community action took place in Rural Home Clubs for home owners and Young People's 4-A Clubs, which follow the model of the 4-H Clubs of the United States of America. This does not mean that one should underestimate the importance of having the technical infrastructure created in INTA. Very few public organizations have been created in recent decades to promote changes in the country which have achieved the importance and successes obtained by INTA.

But problems which were less pressing during the period of formation and consolidation of the Institute began to emerge more strongly with the passage of time. They derive basically from the absence of an active agricultural policy designed to promote an explicit and coherent agricultural development. This has meant that relationships with state organizations and departments, as well as the producers themselves, were not characterized by the greatest efficacy and efficiency possible (see Oszlak, Sábato, and Roulet 1971:47–95).

Furthermore, INTA's activity has been influenced to a certain degree by the type of training and models followed by the technicians who had been trained in developed countries and later attempted to apply those techniques in an altogether different context.

In addition, as Oszlak, Sábato, and Roulet (1971: 174–179) point out:

Neither research nor extension program carried out were based, in general, on situation studies of their regions of influence containing any sociological, economic or agronomic analysis, or any analysis of land distribution by size, type of tenancy, etc. And where such studies have been carried out, it is difficult to submit them for periodic revision and updating. There is a predominance of the "biological" approach in the work, and great demands are imposed on technicians responsible for carrying out the situation studies. These factors reduce the significance of the economic appraisal of the action carried out and the examination of the sociological conditions constituting the true parameters of this action. Neither is any systematic basic accumulation of information nor projection of its results carried out.

Finally, efforts have been concentrated on the medium and large producer, with a strong tendency to overlook the small producer, it being a highly controversial issue whether it is one of INTA's concerns to cater to the interests of the agricultural worker. The Campo de Herrera experiment was initiated to overcome this problem as well as the first two: the adoption of foreign techniques and lack of overall situation studies.

INTA has contributed constant advice to this experiment involving (in relative terms) a considerable effort in human resources. This very fact has been an object of criticism of the validity of the experiment since it has been repeatedly pointed out that if such advice had not existed, success would not have been achieved. However, it is precisely this systematic devotion and full attention to a large group of problems which embraces a significant mass of rural population that has been one of its most important contributions. Without such an input, there could be no advances on firm ground and no basic structural change.

Management of the Cooperative

As in any cooperative, management functions at two levels. General features, such as the most important decisions, are adopted by the general meeting of members. Subordinate decisions, such as routine or urgent ones, etc., originate from a Board of Directors. According to the statutes, the latter is composed of seven titular members elected directly by the members. However, it is interesting to observe the active participation of the substitute board members and trustees at Board meetings, which brings together a group of eleven persons in charge of decision making. The administration of the cooperative is under its responsibility. From the beginning the Board set a high standard of appointments to the Administration. In general each sector contributed its best people.

The technical team placed stress from the beginning on comanagement with the Board and, in particular, with those in charge in the field. They did this because it appeared to be the most viable form of influencing the members. INTA was the party which took the fundamental decisions in that comanagement. The central idea was, and is, to abandon distinct categories progressively as their own leaders were being trained to discharge their duties efficiently.

But given that comanagement and the fact that in the first stage a large part of the authority delegated to the Board came from the donor group (INTA), one was conscious of the following risks: that both the leaders and the other members would consider that they had changed bosses and would continue with the old attitude of "dependency relationship"; that the leaders would gradually tend to hand over responsibility for certain measures to the donor team in order to avoid personal conflicts; that little by little both parties would accept the permanent influence of the latter, with the instituting of a paternalism which in the last instance would be equally frustrating.

However much the donor group was aware of those risks, there was a basic contradiction. This lay in the impossibility of running economic risks which, although they might be highly educational as experiences of errors, would lead irreparably to the failure of the cooperative. Thus INTA did not agree knowingly to run the risk of failure. It took charge (in quite formal comanagement) of the technical and economic planning. This, in fact, involved making fundamental decisions, to the detriment of the development of a basic leadership. But it could hardly have acted otherwise in the first years of the enterprise. The maximum working capacity had been related to aspects of production and efficiency.

Even today the crop planning and production schedules are worked out by a leader in the field — an engineer or agronomist who is not a member — after prior discussion with the manager and the Board of Directors. This is true even though there is already a leader in the field who has arisen from among the members themselves.

Administration of the Cooperative

The managerial task of the Board is carried out through the Administration made up of a manager (a nonmember public accountant) who, like the leader in the field, is contracted by the cooperative and two administrative employees (one being a member). The management is an essential part of an enterprise of this type. At the beginning, due to a lack of resources such tasks were carried out with INTA's advice. Both the organizing of the bookkeeping and the marketing or purchase structure are run by the Administration, supervised by the Board.

Decisions with respect to production are under the charge of the Board of Management, which transmits them to the leader in the field and the latter to the supervisory staff, made up of three representatives.[2] However, the process may also be reversed. Technical counseling operates at the three levels. The critical points of this productive organization devolve on the management-field leader-representative sequence.

The Technical Problem

The operating plan had to promote the rapid capitalization of the cooperative in order to provide more employment to members, as far as it was able, distributed throughout the year.

The central problem was to ensure work for the whole year. Although sugarcane gives full employment from mid-June to mid-December (six months), it was necessary to find other activities based on crops covering the supply of labor from 15 December to 15 June.

The original plan (see Dominguez and Hervás 1970:164ff.) underwent some modifications. These occurred not so much in the area sown with cane, which was covered in a normal manner in accordance with assigned stages, but with respect to other crops. The plan for the year 1967/68 was divided under the following headings and areas.

Year 1967/68:
1,100 hectares of sugar cane
  300 hectares of maize for consumption
  100 hectares of maize for sowing
   10 hectares of sweet potatoes

The following variation was anticipated in the original production plan for the 1971/72 cycle.

---

[2]   Although the representative's function is similar to that of the overseer in the sugar mill or the private sugarcane farm, the name has been changed in the cooperative to emphasize the aspect of responsibility to the cooperative and not that of control against the workers' interest.

Year 1971/72:
659 hectares of sugar cane
600 hectares of maize for consumption
100 hectares of maize for sowing
200 hectares of wheat
200 hectares of sweet potatoes

But in fact the category of sweet potatoes was abandoned and grains encountered obstacles of a technical nature in addition to noneconomic returns. In place of sweet potatoes, tobacco was introduced, which employs all of the community's manpower from December to March. Thus the figures for the 1971/72 agricultural cycle were the following.

Year 1971/72:
750 hectares of sugar cane
400 hectares of maize for consumption
300 hectares of wheat
 20 hectares of tobacco

Only two production factors could be counted on: land and manpower. There was no capital or entrepreneurial organization. The lack of economic resources of the agricultural workers who were to be the probable new members was slightly compensated for by the fact that there were 70,000 furrows of cane. However, in the beginning the cane ready for harvesting was unmarketable since it had no definitive quota.[3] Finally, the sugarcane which had been planted was a credit factor enabling operation in the first year when it was sold. However, in the second year the cooperative had to face a difficult financial crisis. This occurred when the Bella Vista Sugar Mill did not pay for the cane which the cooperative had sold to the mill in compliance with a clause of the bill of sale for the lands. The value of that cane fluctuated around the sum of 150,000 dollars.

Local Leaders

A fundamental problem of workers' cooperatives is the development of leaders at a local level. When considering local leaders it is neccesary to take into account the specific conditions of the community from which they emerge and the social relationships in which they are involved.

The leaders to whom we refer include all positions of responsibility in the cooperative from the Chairman to the members of the Board of Man-

---

[3] The sugar quota is an authorization granted by an administrative act by the State to sell a specified amount of the stated sugar production. This measure emerged based on the 1966 overproduction crisis, and was intended to regulate sugar production.

agement and the field representatives. It is necessary to distinguish them from the external counselors, although the permanent contact of the latter with the former and the influence they exert over them make them keys to the success of the cooperative experiment.

In Campo de Herrera the position of the Chairman of the cooperative was decisive from the first. The Chairman unites executive powers and those of a representative nature and the authority which confers status on him both within and outside the community. As the local person who symbolizes the cooperative to the outside world, he has the most frequent contacts with people both outside and within the cooperative.

The two Chairmen they have had in Campo de Herrera were about 45 years old. The average age of other members in positions of responsibility is 46. This figure correlates with the average age of cooperative members which, as we saw, was quite high from the very beginning. But it is precisely that "oldness" of the founding population which brings about a quite radical change in the age composition of members within a short time. As older members retire, their shares pass to their young children, who become the new members. The age pyramid of the population exhibits a marked narrowing precisely at the most productive ages. This is a simple consequence of the emigration caused by the recession in the market for sugar labor. This is a process which occurred prior to the creation of the cooperative which, furthermore, has managed to keep the emigratory movement within its area of influence. Old people and young people remained in the field and it is the latter who will rapidly take over the positions of responsibility in the cooperative. This is different from what appears to occur in the cooperative movement of other countries of the Latin American area. Here one has observed a lack of enthusiasm on the part of young people, who show little interest in the cooperative phenomenon. But in Campo de Herrera young people are proving that they are interested in taking over leadership from the hands of the mature elements in the community (Fals Borda 1971:83). This phenomenon of replacement which has generation aspects does not occur without some minor conflicts. However, there has been no observable reaction against the thrust of the young people on the part of older members. This fact is reflected in the influence which certain young elements are acquiring in meetings and on the Board. The present Vice-Chairman of the cooperative is 25 years old.

The educational level of the leaders is low. They have all been born in the zone, unlike the advisors, who come from outside. This involves them in networks of kinship, friendship, and coparenthood relationship with different elements of the neighborhood, with the concomitant difficulties and advantages. Enmities of a personal nature, difficulties with relatives, or accusations of favoritism are inevitable problems in an environment of primary relationships such as exists in a rural neighborhood.

The phenomenon of self-perpetuation in positions has not arisen, because change is provided for every three years, and, starting from 31 March 1973, annually. However, it is true that one can speak of a certain nucleus of leaders representing about 30 percent of the members who retain the various positions of responsibility and who pass on from one position to another, over a less aware mass of members. The exception arises, as we have indicated, among some young members who provide new leadership.

The question of leadership strongly merits detailed analysis since the success or failure of the cooperative in the long run will depend on how it succeeds in improving its position. The initial impulse of the cooperative was due to the presence of the project's creator, the Regional Director of INTA, who was the key to the cementing and consolidation of the factors involved. However, in the long run that influence has to be replaced by a firm and aware leadership which will spread the positions of responsibility downwards as broadly as possible.

Until the present chairman, the cooperative has not had a strong leader.[4] In fact, we may assert that there was no leadership and those functions devolved *de facto* on the donor team from INTA, with the local leaders acting merely as transmitters of their directives and decisions. The apprenticeship work of the leaders, although it was important, was not translated into what we understand as real leadership. Only with the present Chairman has the cooperative found its first leader and key man.

Predictably, given the lack of initiative in taking leadership in the community, this man behaves unusually for his environment and presents a mass of contradictory aspects. However, his role in the cooperative is basically a positive contribution. He is 44 years old, married, with children, and left school when he was in the third grade. He had worked as an agricultural laborer in Bella Vista Sugar Mill since 1942 and in periods of recession in sugar activity he went to the maize harvesting in Santa Fe Province and Buenos Aires. His Creole appearance likens him to the rest of his companions, just like his cultural origin. In many senses he is the epitome of local culture, reflecting the basic features of the members of his community: alert, somewhat roguish, arrogant, with obvious insecurities in the face of circumstances where actions or experiences occur of

---

4 Although the chairmanship of the cooperative has been changed since these lines were written at the beginning of 1973, what has been said with regard to that leader has not lost its validity.

which he knows he is ignorant; he is "macho"[5] in order to assert his authority and dignity.

However, he differs from his neighbors in some fundamental aspects. He has a greater awareness of problems than the majority of the people, which is manifested in his love for reading and information and correct receptivity to the mass media. His reflexive genius and powers of observation permit him to visualize work plans and grasp problems when they are raised, both by advisors and by members. His inclination towards innovation and ability to learn enable him to act effectively in the administration of the tobacco crop, something new in the region. His talent for discharging the role of leader and his devotion to the cooperative are, in short, a deviation from normal role behavior in the community.

The man's apprenticeship process was painful, but unlike other members who had previously held positions of responsibility, he managed to overcome many of the traditional inhibitions of the agricultural worker who was ignorant of the turns and complexities of industrial life, commercial relationships, and links with official organizations.

His strong personality allowed him to exercise a marked influence over his equals. His manner with outside people is dignified and formal. He is remarkably articulate in situations in which the Creole would normally feel inhibited. Although he is somewhat authoritarian with members, he is the person who makes them participate in meetings and who raises and discusses problems until their conclusion.

Although his ability and activity make him the natural leader of his group, he is the target of remarks by his equals, such as "The time will come when you'll find yourself back in the muddy furrows," thus reflecting the transitory nature of his change of status and the ultimate control of members in safeguarding a basic egalitarianism. This is interesting, since it has been observed that one of the intrinsic problems of a leader is that with the passage of time his positive features tend to become negative ones. His success generates a felling of self-satisfaction which tends to make him more remote from his neighbors. His motivations, which may originally have been characterized as altruistic, may be transformed into others which are at times contradictory, such as self-promotion, egotism, and material and moral personal ambitions. This is the time when leaders must be replaced, this being ensured by the machinery for control of leaders within the very system of the cooperative. In other words, leadership as a concept is important and irreplaceable as a catalytic agent for social change and must be encouraged at any cost; but leaders must be kept

---

[5] This word is now accepted in English; it means "assertively masculine."

within proper bounds by those who elected them, while seeking to achieve a dynamic development of this dialectic of forces.

THE IDEOLOGICAL PLAN: CHANGES ON THE SPOT

Considering the above circumstances, it is interesting to analyze the relationship established from the beginning between conceptions concerning this new enterprise existing among the donor group and how they were received by the recipient group. As it has been seen, the latter did not have, nor could it have had, with its limited experience, any precise understanding of the "why" and "how" of the situation it was facing.

Until the time when the recipient group also began to give opinions or interpretations or to prepare norms for the cooperative, only the technical donor group was able and sought to give the experiment an orientation which in its judgment was the correct one.

The question arises, from what central concepts did the donor group proceed, having decided at all costs to advance a project which was regarded as viable and even excellent for solving the economic and social problems which were facing Tucumán? And what were the thoughts of a recipient group which was disoriented and still had not recovered from the blow which meant the loss of a stability and position which had been hard to come by and which provoked the feeling of having been abandoned by the once powerful trade-union organization?

The basic idea was that the cooperative was to be an efficient enterprise which could compete within the context in which it had to function; and as to internal matters, it was to be a fairer distributor of the wealth generated. Implicit in this concept was the aim of lower production cost. Among other things this made the existence of a "businesslike" mentality among members absolutely necessary, for it is through this that the objectives could be more easily and rapidly attained: greater productivity to compete with the outside world and greater wealthy to distribute to the community. In order to achieve this, the following principles were laid down:

a. To open to members the possibility of being "owners" of things.

b. To eradicate pressure devices of a trade-union nature.

c. To avoid deliberation of decisions of an "assembly" nature which would delay or complicate progress and to concentrate power in the Board of Management assumed to be more rapid in its operation and capable of being trained by the donor group.

d. To ensure that information deemed necessary for the members would be spontaneoulsy channeled through the Board of Management.

e.   To ensure that its voluntary nature and "repeated" verbal preaching would lead to awareness on the part of the mass of members.

f.   To emphasize that the only goal worth achieving was associated with a "modern" attitude and that the cultural and social relationships of the land worker contained values that were basically negative or obsolete for the success of the project.

Now let us see how these concepts were received and/or reformed by the recipient group.

The concept of "owner" embraced (for the donor group) certain characteristics close to those of the "middle" agricultural proprietor which were originally manifested in these positive aspects:

a.   Responsibility and care of things.

b.   Complete personal involvement not limited to a work "timetable."

c.   An ability to face difficulties, particularly those of beginning an operation, and to control finances, and save as much income as possible.

As will be seen, these characteristics, which have been accepted as positive, did not take into consideration the large number of individualist and niggardly attitudes with which they were accompanied.

For his part, for the land worker and in particular in this case for the land worker of the cooperative, to be an "owner" meant and continues to mean:

a.   Not to work on jobs requiring great physical effort.

b.   To live on the work of others.

c.   Grudging the worker the improvement in his working conditions.

d.   To be authoritarian and, above all, to have the "right to give orders."

e.   To have unlimited enjoyment of all one's rights.

f.   To be an opponent of everything reminding one of a trade union.

This contradiction in the image of an owner in each group began to be reflected in the behavior of the members, formulated in the following terms:

a.   How could the workers work if they were "owners"?

b.   At the beginning, with the increase in the necessary capitalization and investment of the cooperative, the following dichotomy was formulated: "rich cooperative-poor (owners) members," therefore the cooperative was the owner before whom demands of a trade-union nature had to be raised.

c.   From his outlook, the member considered that everyone had a right to give orders which in practice was restricted to the Board of Management, and even more to those in charge of production (the technical group and three members who were designated as representatives). This along with point b. above, increased the member's disillusionment and displeasure, for he had imagined a role for himself which reality did not allow.

This contradictory situation began to be resolved when the cooperative members began to discuss and analyze critically what "owner" and "worker" meant both for the donor and recipient groups and through a cooperative organization which overcomes that dichotomy. Thus there emerged the role of the cooperative member who now was neither the classic owner nor the classic worker.

It should be noted that the pressure tactics of a trade-union nature which some wished to avoid were considered by the members as the only ones possible for making demands and gaining victories. We must bear in mind that the members felt a "personal" repudiation of the trade union, but not for the trade-union system, as a method for making demands. However, when they tried to apply it, they realized that the matters they raised went against themselves, Without a trade union and without being able to apply trade-union methods (which were the only ones they knew), displeasure and impotence increased in the face of a Board of Directors which, as we have already seen, thought of itself as an "owner."

But with the increasing of deliberations and decisions at the level of an Assembly or an expanded Board of Management, that tendency began to slacken. This was facilitated by a parallel development of the new social role of the cooperative.

Five years after this experiment started, we can assert that the fact of having reserved decisions to the Board of Management during the first years permitted greater speed and efficiency in technical and administrative matters. In fact, this was absolutely necessary, considering the context. However, this served to cut the leadership off from the members. With the failure to bring information down to the members as had been expected, the leadership became visualized as the "owners." Two important control devices emerged from that state of affairs: the nonreelection of leading board members and the increase of gossip as a means for social control. This, on the one hand, fulfilled a significant role, while on the other it accentuated tensions.

This situation was also overcome when, after the initial accumulation, the enterprise began to distribute more earnings and services. There was also a gradual passing on of important decisions to the meeting of members, with a systematized and nonspontaneous supply of information to members.

These facts which we have touched on briefly in our analysis occurred simultaneously, thereby opening a path which permitted greater information, training, and participation of the members. They paved the way for the taking up of social and cultural pursuits by the workers, thus permitting greater creativity. Finally, the critical analysis of the events and contradictions of daily life proved to be more valuable as a factor for creating awareness than "repeated preaching" and voluntary action.

In this give-and-take arrangement, the donor group began to reform its initial concepts in the light of events and interaction with the recipient group, in particular through perception of the fact that the "modern" and "businesslike" stereotypes (as used in the context) contained serious shortcomings and negative aspects which acted against what they were seeking. It implied that this road was leading members to aspirations of consumption and ostentation, to an increase of personnel "prominent" within the community, and to the consequent turning away from the family solidarity which had existed toward an emphasis on the individual.

Thus a new demand arose: the search for a new standard where positive aspects were brought together, principally at the community level. The present situation presents the following contradictory aspects:

a.   The laws in force in the national society are based on an extreme individualistic concept.

b.   Social life in the sugar plantations and in a large part of the cooperatives rests on the internal solidarity of the domestic group.

c.   The aspirations of a strong, more aware group are directed toward a solidarity of a community type as a whole (leveling of income, responsibilities, and access to the organs of leadership).

The following is an attempt to define the present trend:

a.   An increase in participation and deliberations of an assembly nature.

b.   Greater confidence in the machinery of the cooperative and the relationships of work and activity generated by this.

c.   Critical analysis and self-criticism between donors and recipients, overcoming the dichotomy and rejecting any preaching of a voluntary philosophy.

d.   An abandonment of the search for an individualistic businesslike mentality in favor of the crystallization of a community businesslike attitude where the result is measured by the cooperative's produce and not in the sum total of the individual results of the members.

CONCLUSION

The subject of agrarian reform or substitutes for the agrarian reform necessary for Argentina has been discussed increasingly in intellectual and political circles. But recent governments have been slow in taking important measures with regard to the land tenure structure. Only "plans for agrarian transformation" have been drawn up, with very limited effects and generally directed towards consolidating the established system. This is because the celebrated "transformation" was reduced to the granting of contract extensions to tenants against the owner's refusal to sell.[6] In general we may speak of little awareness of the agrarian situation, even in the most radical circles, whose proposals or speeches do not usually go beyond declaratory statements of proposals for the transfer of formulas which have been successful in other areas.

Nevertheless, we may start from two indisputable facts. On the one hand, Argentine agriculture has been stagnant for the last thirty years:

...the true backwardness of agriculture may be seen by comparing its growth indices with those of other sectors. If agricultural production had grown like the rest of the economy since the decade of the 1930's, it would now be double what it actually is; if it had increased in the same proportion as the population, it would be 50% greater. In fact, it hardly exceeds that of the period 1940–1945 (Barraclough and Collarte 1971:113).

On the other hand, the limited growth of employment and the fact that the available manpower is not utilized in the agricultural sector serve to cut the economy's growth power. Thus, it is interesting for us to reflect briefly on the relevance which the type of agricultural enterprise we have analyzed here may have in a process of global change.

Unlike other Latin American agrarian reforms which form part of "a national process of revolutionary transformations, directed by an aggressive array of new social forces and based on the modification of power relationships and institutional norms of 'traditional society,'" it would appear advantageous in the case of Argentina, considering the specific national context, to change the tenure structure in the direction of an agrarian sector, comprised of peasants, rural proletarians, and holders of medium-sized farms. This sector would act as a pressure group playing a role in national society and asserting its claims. In this sense a CONVENTIONAL type of agrarian reform (in Antonio García's terminology) would appear to be more feasible. This would form part of operations negotiated between old and new social forces, but not, as that author indicates, "without changing the institutional rules of the 'traditional society' and approaching reform as an isolated and sectorial question" (García 1970:

[6] These plans start in 1957 with Decree 9991/1957; Law 14,451, Law 16,883 and Law 17,253 of 1967. For a detailed synthesis of the legislative antecedents see Prunetto (1972).

31–32). It would instead be by promoting structural changes from the very moment that those groups, organized as classes, progress to more advanced forms of social organization and point the way to an opening process for an integrated society on the national level. This would incorporate the peasant and rural proletarian masses into the national society's system of aspirations and values.

In these conditions the development of cooperative labor programs which incorporate, train, and organize rural workers, peasants, and small producers (who up to now have been marginal) as pressure groups on the revolutionary vanguards would have decisive importance in the sum total of catalyzing factors of the change required.

The problems to be resolved in a cooperative program are many. We have only referred to some in relation to the very concrete case of a Tucumán work cooperative. One of the most important is not so much to attain the support and participation of the marginal sectors, but to train the technical and administrative cadres necessary to carry the program forward. This will have to be done within the very development of the process, in order to obtain efficient teams in the constructon of a new mentality. As Ribeiro correctly stated: "The agronomists and veterinarians who are graduating today were intended to serve landholders with large estates or to exercise technical-bureaucratic functions as representatives of landholding interests. As such they are not prepared to destroy the old plantation structure nor to create the new agrarian economy, based on cooperatives and communities where the main problem is to employ all the manpower, raise the standard of living of the peasants and facilitate their participation in all spheres of national life" (Ribeiro 1973:6–7). This observation with respect to agronomists does not isolate them as the only professional people open to criticism, nor does it define them as untrained for anything new. However, one does admit the high economic, social, and psychological price their participation in anything new would demand. On the other hand, it could be said that in general terms agronomists are among those professional people who have always been employed in some kind of food production. But the changes of which we speak affect professionals in every field.

In the previous pages we have seen how even with the "best personal intentions of service and social solidarity" ideological contradictions have arisen and are arising at every level. The most important ones are those which embrace the level of technicians, since in this stage their actions have the greatest multiplier effect. It is necessary to emphasize that it is precisely those contradictions which permit one to transcend them through the creative application of what is known to the solution of concrete problems emerging from the urgency of daily life and from things which are historically critical, through investigations formulated with originality, and through the forecast of the results or effects of different forms of action.

The INTA team started with correct premises in contrast to other programs which failed in this respect. It adopted a dynamic perspective, learned much by working and participating personally in the problems of the community, reformulating on the spot its own theories and strategies. The result appears to be a noteworthy course of action for the development of this type of enterprise in our underdeveloped regions.

REFERENCES

BARRACLOUGH, SOLON, JUAN CARLOS COLLARTE
1971   *El hombre y la tierra en América Latina* [Man and land in Latin America]. Santiago de Chile.

DOMINGUEZ, J. A., A. HERVÁS
1970   *Cooperativas agropecuarias de trabajo; una alternativa de solución para el problema Tucumáno* [Agricultural workers' cooperatives; an alternative solution to the Tucumán problem). INTA. Famaillá: EERA.

FALS BORDA, O.
1971   *Cooperatives and rural development in Latin America; an analytic report.* Geneva: United Nations Research Institute for Social Development.

FIENUP, D. F., R. H. BRANNON, F. A. FENDER
1972   *El desarrollo agropecuario Argentino y sus perspectivas* [Argentine agricultural development and its perspectives]. Buenos Aires: Di Tella Institute.

GARCÍA, A.
1970   *Dinámica de las reformas agrarias en la América Latina* [The dynamics of the agrarian reforms in Latin America]. Bogotá.

OSZLAK, O., J. F. SÁBATO, J. E. ROULET
1971   *Determinación de objetivos y asignación de recursos en INTA* [Determination of objectives and assignment of resources in the National Institute for Agricultural Technology]. Buenos Aires: Center for Research in Public Administration, Di Tella Institute.

PRUNETTO, CARLOS A.
1972   *"Tenencia de la tierra en el agro Argentino* [Land tenancy in Argentine agriculture]." Conference report prepared by the Argentine Agrarian Federation at the Institute for Economic and Financial Research of the General Economic Confederation, 13 July.

RIBEIRO, DARCY
1973   "The revolutionary university." A chapter of *La nueva Universidad* reproduced in the Sunday supplement of *La Opinión*, 25 March. Buenos Aires.
i.p.   *La nueva universidad* [The new university]. Buenos Aires: Ciencia Nueva.

Peasant Cooperation in Land-Reform Programs: Some Latin American Experiences

SHLOMO ECKSTEIN and THOMAS F. CARROLL

One of the key issues in the implementation of land-reform programs is finding an adequate postreform model of property–management systems. Clearly, such systems should be based on the equitable and socially more satisfactory tenure arrangements inherent in land reforms, and at the same time should meet expectations of higher production and economic efficiency. The degree to which land reforms have been successful in improving peasant income and welfare and in raising output has often depended not so much on the land redistribution process itself, as on the organizational models chosen.

Fundamental, and hence by their very nature drastic, land reforms have amply demonstrated their capability for creating a more open, permeable rural system in which former inequities in power and status are narrowed. However, such gains can be severely limited and rapidly eroded if the new ways in which the reallocated land holdings and farm production are organized do not insure a more effective use of resources, developed technological possibilities, and, therefore, provide the basis for sustained income growth. In other words, destroying the old feudal sys-

The substantial collaboration of Anna Lehel and Douglas Horton is gratefully acknowledged. This paper is an attempt to identify the main issues related to group farming and joint services in agriculture that are emerging from a broader comparative study of land reform in Latin America being carried out by the authors. The study focuses on the experiences of five countries which have undertaken large-scale land reforms: Bolivia, Chile, Mexico, Peru, and Venezuela.

Shlomo Eckstein is Professor of Economics at Bar Ilan University in Israel. Thomas Carroll is a staff member of the Inter-American Development Bank in Washington, D.C. They have drawn liberally on their previous work in this field. The views expressed in this paper are those of the authors and do not necessarily reflect the position of the institutions with which they are associated.

tem is not enough; new and better land systems must be invented and put into effective use.

Basically, there are three types of postreform organizational models: (1) owner-operated family units, (2) centrally managed state enterprises, and (3) cooperative or collective farms. The first two represent the ideological prototypes of liberal capitalism and statist socialism, respectively; the third, while being paid lip service by both, remains essentially a utopian vision of the "participatory society."

The cooperative model of rural property–management systems has lately gained popularity in Latin America.[1] Rural cooperatives, whether they stress group farming or joint services, are increasingly looked upon as "solutions" to the postreform organizational problem and ways to "optimize" equity and productivity objectives. Cooperativization or collectivization has become an attractive ideological postion, appropriate to growing "Third-World" consciousness.

Cooperative farming is supposed to offer the following advantages: (1) an institutional framework for modernizing agriculture and integrating the peasant into the national society and economy; (2) a scale of operation which is large enough for efficient production under a variety of circumstances; (3) active social participation and community improvement through joint pursuit of group, rather than individual, objectives; (4) mobilization of idle and latent resources; (5) building upon existing forms of traditional peasant cooperation; and (6) assuring a wide distribution of benefits from economic gains. In short, "cooperatives, as ideally conceived, cannot be described as anything but noble" (Lele 1972).

However, the great enthusiasm of social philosophers and theoreticians for rural development through collective endeavor is severely dampened by the skepticism of field workers and public officials, whose practical experiences lead them to question the operational viability of cooperative systems. Rural cooperatives have functioned well and attained important achievements in Israel and some countries in Western Europe; but they failed, on the whole, to show significant results in less-developed countries. In spite of the vigorous support of international agencies (especially the U.N. family), the record of successes is discouragingly poor and stands in no proportion to the magnitude of the change cooperatives had been expected to bring about over the last three decades.

---

[1] A recent expression of this Latin American interest in participatory models is the collection of papers presented at the Expert Consultation on Development of Agrarian Structure in Latin America, held in Berlin in November 1973, sponsored by FAO and by the German Foundation for Developing Countries.

The present paper presents evidence from Latin American experience which sheds light on the potential viability of cooperative farming systems. Among others, it deals with the following issues: (1) the actual economic and social advantages of joint action in farming; (2) the main practical problems encountered in implementation; (3) the sensitivity of participatory systems to some of their basic components, and the interaction among these; (4) the dependence of such systems upon social, economic, and political conditions and changes that occur outside the system. It will be attempted to offer some explanations for the great gap between theoretical expectations and empirical realizations and to derive some operationally meaningful lessons for future programs.

Before proceeding, it should be useful to clarify the meaning of a number of concepts used in this paper. The term "peasant" is broadly interpreted to include both small farmers and farm workers; no distinction is drawn between independent cultivators and estate laborers. Hence, when the term "peasant group" is used in conjunction with land-reform programs, this may refer to a group of smallholders, or of ex-laborers of ex-estates, or a combination of the two. The term "peasant cooperative," as used herein, includes all types of enterprises which are owned and operated by groups of peasants (often with the assistance of hired specialists or government agencies).

Following these definitions, this paper is concerned with all types of joint action on the part of peasants, in farming (collective operation of part or all of their land) or in joint provision of services (such as credit, supply of inputs, marketing, and processing). The specific form of such joint action varies greatly between countries and over time and includes loosely organized peasant groups and associations, pre- or para-cooperatives, cooperatives proper, and similar units, such as *ejido*-societies (Mexico), and *asentamientos* (Chile, Venezuela); both "base-level" and "second-level" institutions (e.g. federations and central cooperatives) are considered.

There are numerous typologies of peasant cooperatives and cooperative-like institutions (Schiller 1968). One of the simplest and most widely used typologies separates peasant cooperatives under two major headings: (1) Production-Oriented Cooperatives: in which productive resources (especially land) are held and operated collectively; (2) Service-Oriented Cooperatives: in which members continue to farm individually, and the joint features are in the input/output matrix (e.g. credit, marketing, and processing). In many cases, however, the differences between these two broad types may be more ideological or philosophical than real. As an illustration, group decisions made by a strong marketing cooperative may influence the production and investment decisions of individual members in important ways.

RETURNS TO SCALE

Arguments for group action in agriculture generally hinge on the issue of "return to scale." Proponents of group action usually argue that strong economies of scale characterize agricultural production, and that social and political advantages of collective effort complement the technical advantages of large-scale production. Arguments against group systems, especially in farming proper, are generally based on the assumption of diseconomies of scale and stress some of the social and political disadvantages of collective effort. What is the balance? Let us begin with the economic aspects.

The Importance of Economies of Scale

Until recently the existence of economies of scale in farming was almost taken for granted, at least up to sizes of about 50 hectares of cropland,[2] based on advantages related to better use of land, capital, and human resources.[3]

For farms below this limit, as size increased, production costs per unit of output were believed to fall. Beyond the range of some 50–100 hectares (depending on the type of activity and technology), average production costs were assumed to stabilize at a minimum level. At much larger scales, average costs were assumed to rise as managerial difficulties began to outweigh any possible technical advantages of large-scale production.

These notions were based primarily on agricultural production theory developed in the United States and tested on private farming enterprises

---

[2]   The size limits cited are, of course, quite arbitrary (depending on type and quality of soil, crop and livestock patterns, irrigation, etc.), but are included to specify a "relevant range," since any discussion of economies of scale "in general" is quite meaningless. An alternative, and important, measure of size of production unit is the number of man-years employed on the farm.

[3]   Better land use here implies crop diversification and rotation, land conservation and preparation, improved water use, large-scale and continuous tillage, plant protection and control, etc. "Capital" is both physical (agricultural machinery and equipment, installations, irrigation facilities, etc.) and financial (credit). Better use of human resources implies division of labor and specialization in production and extension service, etc.

(and technologies) used there. The historic trend observed in developed countries, of a constant rise in the average size of farms on the one hand, but of very few "giants" comparable to the industrial or service sectors on the other, served to further support the theory.[4]

In the postwar period, when development economists began to focus attention on agriculture in the less developed countries, a main concern was with the inability of very small farms to attain productivity levels comparable to those of medium- or large-sized units. Hence it was concluded that, unless beneficiaries could be organized in cooperative or collective production units capable of retaining the main economies of large-scale production, a subdivision of large farms into small family units within a land reform scheme involved a trade-off between equity and efficiency. It followed that if peasants could not be organized, or if their new organizations failed to function well, the land reform's improvement in distributional equity would be accompanied by a reduction of agricultural production and marketings of agricultural products.

Recently this view has been challenged, both with respect to its theoretical validity and its policy implications (Dorner 1972). The conclusion of a symposium on land reform held recently at the World Bank was that there are few economies of scale in agriculture; small farmers can be as productive as, or more productive than, large farmers (Dovring 1973).

Don Kanel has provided a theoretical rationale for the high relative productivity of small farmers (Kanel 1967). Numerous recent empirical studies indicate that a strong inverse relation exists between size of farm and productivity per unit of land (Dayal and Elliot 1966; Dorner and Kanel 1971).

Technically, this is attributed to the fact that most of the new technology inputs, such as seeds, fertilizers, and insecticides, are infinitely divisible. Agricultural machinery, once considered the main "scale factor," seems to be a less important determinant of productivity than are the above-cited factors. Necessary machinery can be used on more than one small farm; not all farmers need to own a full complement of tillage equipment and other machines. Moreover, the inclusion of farm machinery in the optimum technology package for less-developed countries is now being questioned, in view of growing concern with employment problems and rural-urban migration.

These findings suggest that old fears about land reform may be unfounded or at least exaggerated. But if this is so, are there important economic advantages of group action in conjunction with land-reform

---

[4] Again, it should be noted that the size measure employed here is area, not employment. The majority of all farms in the United States are small in terms of employment.

programs? Let us first examine farming proper, then services, and finally the whole picture.

Returns to Scale in Farming Proper

In industry, large operational units are generally far more productive than small units[5] for two main reasons: (1) modern industrial machinery is in general large-scale and indivisible; for example, small paper mills, auto body factories, and steel mills are inefficient and cannot compete profitably with large production units; (2) within large industrial plants, specialization of men and machinery increases productivity and decreases unit costs markedly. At very large scales of operation managerial problems offset the technical advantages of machine use and specialization and effectively limit the size of industrial plants.

In agriculture, the machinery used is smaller than in industry, since it must be mobile. Seasonality makes it impossible for agricultural laborers to become specialized in one or a few tasks and discourages the development of highly specialized machines (Brewster 1950). Moreover, since agricultural work is not highly standardized or machine-paced, managerial problems are far more severe in agriculture than in industry. In agriculture, the intensity and quality of work is highly variable, and independent small farmers generally work harder and better than hired workers.[6]

Another important issue is the nature of costs considered in the productivity calculations. Where the labor input is measured in terms of wage-cost, large-scale capital-intensive production may be more profitable. But where labor finds little alternative employment (as in most less-developed countries) and has a very low social opportunity cost, small-scale production, which employs abundant labor and economizes machine use, is far cheaper on social account.[7] Since small farmers maximize family incomes in kind and cash, and large farmers maximize profits and/or social status, the input mix and production patterns on small

[5]   In other words, industrial production functions are characterized by economies of scale over a substantial range of plant sizes.

[6]   As Juan Martinez-Alier has noted, peasant producers are likely to outproduce wage laborers for two main reasons: (1) they will work more hours or days per year, until the marginal product of labor approaches zero in cases of unemployment; (2) the quality of peasant labor will be higher (what Martinez-Alier terms the "piece-rate effect") (Martinez-Alier 1971).

[7]   This point, and the related point that in most less-developed countries the rural labor force will continue to grow for years to come, regardless of development policies and trends, have been made by Dovring (1964).

farms are likely to be more in accord with social accounting than is the case on large farms.

But even though small farmers are likely to be more efficient and productive than large farmers, three crucial problems remain: First, small farmers in less-developed countries have very little land and have poor access to complementary inputs and services; hence, though they may be productive they remain poor. Second, where the government seeks to raise agricultural production markedly and swiftly through changes in technology, problems in delivery systems (credit, marketing, etc.) and scarcities of personnel and material resources may limit the government's ability to deal effectively with innumerable smallholders. Third, where land reform affects centrally managed estates with heavy equipment and large installations, and where workers have little experience with independent farming, a subdivision of the prereform production unit may result in severe economic dislocations.

In conclusion, returns to scale in farming proper may be of little significance under relatively unsophisticated technological conditions (e.g. primitive subsistence farming) and if growth expectations are modest and gradual, but become extremely important when the reform deals with already highly capital-intensive estates or when greatly accelerated production in the postreform period is desired. In this latter case, joint use of resources (mainly land, water, and equipment) may not merely facilitate the change, but make the change possible.

Several examples illustrate this point:

1. The introduction of vineyards and livestock into the Laguna *ejidos* in Mexico was made possible by the formation of collective groups for this purpose (Eckstein 1966).

2. In the 1960's, the Peruvian government initiated a program on the arid North Coast to substitute the intensive cultivation of fruit trees for subsistence-level corn cultivation. The fruit trees required irrigation and new cultivation methods. The farmers required credit and technical assistance in order to purchase and use the trees and other new inputs, and they needed adequate marketing channels in order to make the change successful. The irrigation system, based on tube wells, lent itself to cooperative rather than to individual use. Economies of scale existed for the government in the supply of inputs, technical assistance, credit, and marketing. Thus production cooperatives were established to facilitate the desired changes in crop and technology (Hatch, personal communication).

3. The sugar estates in Peru present another recent example. Splitting them up into individual holdings was not feasible, since these were

agro-industrial complexes with agricultural workers making up only one-third of the total labor force. In this case, the only realistic alternatives were to manage the whole as a state farm, to separate the industrial facilities from the agricultural operations (along the lines of the Mexican sugar plantations) or, as occurred, to transform the entire estates, intact, into production cooperatives (Horton 1973, 1974).

Returns to Scale in Delivery Systems

Returns to scale become even more crucial when delivery and marketing systems are also taken into account. The difficulty of small farmers in obtaining credit at reasonable terms, adequate technical assistance, improved inputs, and marketing outlets is well known, as are the diverse solutions offered in the form of service cooperatives and specialized public agencies. Credit and marketing are the spheres where rural cooperatives have been most effective and successful in more highly developed countries. It is, therefore, often thought that these types of single-purpose service cooperatives serve as models for the less-developed world.

However, in most poor countries rigid social structures and severe, widespread poverty limit the possible impact of marginal changes or of "single" lines of developmental activity, which leave most of the system intact. Often, one or a few village merchants or landlords provide credit and other services to each peasant and purchase his crop. Under these circumstances a single-purpose approach is doomed to failure: public credit handed out through a cooperative is difficult to recover where members market through the village merchant to whom they also are in debt; a marketing cooperative can often not compete with local buyers who finance production and pay cash for the product. For example, cooperatives established in the Bolivian Yungas have had difficulties competing with the traditional middlemen who provided liberal credit terms, marketed the produce at the most profitable times, and extended a "floating debt" to farmers to allow for crop-price fluctuations. After land reform, only those cooperatives that offered a complementary package of services thrived; all the rest failed (Barnes de Marschall 1970).

In Peru's coastal department of Lambayeque, land-reform beneficiaries were forced to turn to local merchant-money lenders when they wanted to double-crop, since the Agricultural Development Bank's policy was to lend for only one crop each year (Horton 1973).

Large landowners and other entrepreneurs generally fill every gap left in the postreform, supporting institutional system and competing on favorable terms for the needed services. If these businessmen perform useful services (and often they do), there may be no need to replace them; in other words, improving existing marketing organizations might prove easier than building new institutions. In Peru, for example, a severe problem facing many producers who have benefited from the land-reform program is the inadequate governmental marketing systems for rice, seed potatoes, and fertilizers (Horton 1974). In Chile, the Allende government's attempt to create an official market system and to control prices was unsuccessful and led to a proliferation of black market activities (Barraclough 1972).

But, more often, existing local business interests impede major structural and technological changes, and in these cases fundamental institutional innovations are called for. In general, such innovations are effective only when carried out on a broad front, tackling a whole range of related problems — providing technical assistance, credit, and inputs, assuring marketing outlets, changing crop and livestock patterns and farming techniques, etc. — simultaneously. In such far-reaching programs, economies of scale are extremely important, and some form of group action on the part of peasants provides one possible means of attaining these economies.[8]

Returning to the example of the livestock *ejidos* in Mexico, they have been successful in large part because the official *ejido* credit bank also provided the necessary technical assistance, helped organize the peasant groups, conducted training courses, and assured the supply of inputs and the marketing of milk. The whole operation would not have been possible if the bank had had to deal individually with each of the peasant producers (Centro de Investigaciones Agrarias 1970). This illustrates an important fact: in many rural development projects absence of trained manpower, not capital, is the factor which effectively limits the scope and effectiveness of the program. And scarce trained manpower can be most effectively used when these projects deal with groups, not individual peasants. It is not really a matter of cost reduction, but of making it possible to reach a large number of peasants with a given, small number of qualified technicians and extension workers. In northern Peru, the absence of qualified personnel in the Ministry of Agriculture led to

[8] Organization of peasants is only part of the solution to the scale problem. For both economic and political reasons, the government must carry out land-reform and related rural development programs on a large scale at the national level. This is only feasible where some form of peasant organization reduces the number of clients to a manageable number.

the failure of nearly all the cooperatives set up under the Belaunde government's *"Plan Costa"* in the 1960's. Extension agents were to teach cooperative members about new fertilizers and irrigation systems; but there were too few trained agents, and many peasants received no assistance at all. As a result, they overfertilized and underwatered, thereby losing their crop, their credit, and the government's support (Hatch, personal communication).

It must be noted that the scale advantage of operating through groups may be somewhat offset by the fact that dealing with incipient, struggling groups requires more talent and motivation than providing services directly to individual peasants. Regardless of their management skills, administrative personnel recruited from the staffs of feudal haciendas may lack the ability or desire to work effectively with peasant organizations.

MANAGEMENT AND PEASANT PARTICIPATION

As noted above, the fact that certain diseconomies of scale set in at some stage in postreform production processes is in large part explained by the management constraint. As a production unit grows bigger, the growing difficulties and costs of managing, administering, and controlling it outweigh the technical advantages of large-scale production, which result from indivisibilities and the advantages of specialization. In agriculture, this critical stage sets in at a much smaller scale of operations than in industry or services, due to the peculiar nature of production processes, technology, and managerial problems in agriculture.

A cooperative venture has to cope not only with the management problem *per se* but with the additional problems associated with "democratic management" (Barriga 1973). If peasant participation in management were not an explicit reform goal, a state farm could provide an optimum solution to the distribution-efficiency dilemma. In most Latin American countries, however, policymakers seek three major goals, often very hard to reach simultaneously: distributive equity, efficiency, and peasant participation.

Efficiency Versus Participation

In far-reaching land reform programs, success or failure depends in large part upon achieving a workable mix or balance between, on one hand, "internal" and "external" sources of management and, on the other hand, between central and decentralized sources of developmental services.

As concluded in the preceding section, economies of scale, and hence group action, become particularly significant when the aim is to bring about fundamental and rapid structural and technological changes. In all Latin American land reforms, short-run management problems have been serious, as peasant participation cannot be quickly incorporated into management without considerable risks.

The role of "outside" groups, institutions, and individuals is crucial for motivating peasants to form cooperatives and quasi-cooperative institutions. While in some cases this function has been accomplished by foreign promoters or by specialized nongovernmental institutions, most of the responsibility for promotion and assistance falls on national governments (Horton 1974). However, until very recently, governments have not been set up to provide adequate services for peasant groups. As a heritage of pre-land-reform conditions, their staffs have been urban-oriented and generally ill-prepared to play an effective role in rural cooperative organization and assistance.

When governments have become involved with cooperatives or cooperative-type institutions, paternalistic relationships have frequently reappeared in which dependence, control, and continued reliance on outside resources prevent local initiative, self-management, and effective organization.

In Peru, Ministry of Agriculture officials and technicians from the ex-haciendas now have a dominating role in the management of the cooperatives, and a frequent complaint among Peruvian peasants is that the Ministry of Agriculture promotes cooperatives in order to provide its officials and their friends with jobs (Horton 1974).

A relatively small Catholic Church agency in Chile, Instituto de Promoción Agraria (INPROA), has shown flexibility in the promotion and support of four cooperatives on ex-estates of the Church. At one cooperative they replaced an efficient but paternalistic administrator with a former estate worker who turned out to be a good manager with a spirit of cooperativism (Thiesenhusen 1966).

Of course, not all nonofficial agencies are better than government ones in this respect. The problems INPROA faced in establishing cooperatives, with both individual and collective farming, attest to the difficulties inherent in this process for any type of organization (Thiesenhusen 1966). In Peru, a private agency known as DESCO has had several problems establishing and consolidating a central cooperative on the north-central coast. The Peruvian government delegated responsibility for establishing the central cooperative to DESCO, but government agencies, such as the Agricultural Development Bank and the National Land Reform Training Center, have not provided DESCO with the necessary collaboration and support. Consequently, credit and training materials have been inadequate, and member cooperatives[9] are increasingly skeptical of the potential benefits of second-level cooperation. In its first year the central cooperative was effectively managed by DESCO employees, and at the end of this period there seemed to be little member interest in taking over responsibility for either managing or financing the central cooperative's operations (Horton 1974).

"Letting Go"

After land reform, the starting point is usually a quasi-state-farm, with the government's land-reform agency in charge. The desired end goal is a cooperative managed by its members, receiving technical assistance from the government, second-level cooperatives, financial and service organizations, and from private agencies. The problem is how and how fast to get from the necessary starting point to the end goal.

Timing of the changes can be crucial: premature liberation may leave the peasants helplessly facing technical, economic, and personnel problems they are as yet unable to cope with; groups may become overly protected by a bureaucracy that does not want to let loose and hence stifles all local initiative; and there are also cases which achieve neither central control nor local initiative, and get the worst of both worlds (Barraclough 1972).

The case of the sugar cooperatives in Peru illustrates another point: peasant pressure sped up a process that from an "objective-technical" point of view might preferably have matured more slowly. The workers of several of these reform cooperatives went on strike to protest the decision-making power and high salaries of the technicians; in one, they expelled several highly trained specialists, only to call one back later when they realized his value (Horton 1973).

The Optimum Mix

In practice, management problems present themselves at different levels.

[9] By law, the six production cooperatives in the Santa River Valley, in which the central cooperative is located, must be affiliated with it.

Perhaps the most crucial is in production planning: who decides what will be grown, when and how, and what investments are to be made? Is it the financing agency, the national or agricultural planning office, the government-appointed technical advisor, the technician hired by the group, the local leaders, or the general assembly? The classic formula in which a local committee prepares a production and investment plan (advised by a governmental technical advisor) and submits it to the general assembly for approval looks good on paper, but in reality decision-making power is much more concentrated. Moreover, it is not easy to distinguish between decisions affecting profit and income distribution, generally made by the members, and technical operating decisions, entrusted to specialists. Decisions regarding investment versus consumption and short-run versus long-run investments are two examples of overlapping terrain.

Once the long-term or yearly plans have been adopted, a whole series of managerial and administrative functions still remain to be fulfilled, involving both decision making and execution. In most production cooperatives, purely technical decisions[10] are left in the hands of the enterprise's specialized personnel or governmental advisors; routine administrative chores[11] are carried out by members or hired personnel. But in addition, there is a wide range of tasks carrying varying degrees of responsibility which may be performed by hired technicians, public officials, or workers' representatives. For example, in some cases creditworthiness is determined by a local peasant committee, which may create friction and strife; in others by a bank agency, which may take from the credit cooperative much of its power. In some cases a public agency markets the products of numerous cooperatives; in others the group's representative, who might be more (or less) trusted but less (or more) capable than the agent, handles this function.

There are no simple models or "best" solutions. What has worked well in some cases and phases of development has failed completely under different circumstances.[12] It requires a great deal of flexibility to arrive at an efficient and workable division of responsibilities and functions among the local leadership, the professional staff, and public agencies at the local, regional, and national levels. Any given situation involves trade-offs of the following nature: (1) paternalism versus neglect; (2) economic and technical efficiency versus democratic decision making; (3) managerial efficiency versus participation in management; (4) work

---

[10] Such as determining adequate dosages of fertilizer or insecticides.
[11] Such as registration and bookkeeping.
[12] Often at a different period of the same group's development.

discipline versus internal strife; (5) effective versus popular leadership; and (6) excessive control versus corruption.

Even when an acceptable pattern is arrived at, further considerations must be kept in mind. First, the initial division of functions and responsibilities will not remain acceptable for long; flexibility and adjustment to changing conditions are essential. Second, a well-structured flow of information between public agencies and local management, and between management and the membership, is necessary to encourage constructive participation and to avoid distrust. In the latter respect, simple accounting procedures, easily understood by all peasants, are essential.

In general, more groups seem to fail because they are prematurely left on their own than because of excessive paternalism; more succumb to corruption than to excessive controls; more stagnate because of inadequate technical advice than because of inadequate peasant response to good advice.

SOCIAL PROBLEMS

Any form of joint venture in which groups of farmers must continuously interact with each other and with the "outside world" is bound to create more friction and conflict than individual farming and operation. As cooperative enterprises become more comprehensive and integrated, the economic and technical advantages of group action become more significant, but so do the managerial difficulties and social problems.

Evidence indicates that in agricultural cooperatives the social problems of large-scale production may, in fact, outweigh the technical economies of scale. Thus, many groups collapse or fail in spite of their apparent economic merits. To what extent social difficulties are inherent in peasant societies is of great importance; if they are inevitable, the role which joint action can play in land reform and other rural development programs is very limited.[13]

For purposes of our discussion here, social problems are separated into the following four categories:
1. conflicts between the economic interest of individual members and the group;
2. intragroup friction, and subsequent factionalism and division;
3. the individualism of peasants; and
4. delinquency and corruption.

[13] The following draws heavily on Carroll (1969, 1973).

Personal Versus Group Economic Interest

There are many instances in Latin America in which peasant groups have collapsed because their members did not perceive their own interests to be those of the group. Although potentially all members should benefit from the economic prosperity of the group, members often attempt to shirk "a little" in their contribution to cooperative effort, apparently in the belief that their own laxity will not jeopardize the performance of the enterprise.[14]

Examples are numerous: members of a collective farming unit who waste "a little" time during work or do not work as hard as they could; members of a marketing cooperative who sell part of their produce to outsiders when outside prices are higher than prices paid by the cooperative; members who delay "a bit" in the repayment of loans to a credit union. It is important to note that we are not referring here to very serious cases of delinquency. The point is that even a few minor lapses in self-discipline are enough to demoralize other members and cause the ultimate disintegration of the whole group; it is not sufficient that "on the average" members are responsible and well disciplined.

In private enterprises, workers' deviations from enterprise rules are generally sanctioned with formal penalties or rewards. But if cooperatives adopt such strict systems of formal sanctions, they tend to lose member support. Hence, peasant groups must rely to a large extent on informal social sanctions, group conscience, collective motivation, community norms, and the like. The case studies reviewed indicate that without these informal sanctions, a voluntary association cannot survive for very long. On the other hand, it seems clear that these alone are in most cases not enough to ensure high levels of member performance (Barnes de Marschall 1970; Mathiason and Shearer 1967; Williams and Thiller 1973). Some sort of formal reward or penalty must be incorporated into the system.[15] Also, provisions should exist for dismissal of members from the group for specified reasons and for withdrawal from the group by dissatisfied members.

Internal conflicts are of much greater significance in joint production

---

[14] In this respect the cooperative is unstable, in much the same way as the classical example of the cartel in micro-economic theory. Each member of the cooperative, like the cartel, benefits from its existence but is motivated to "cheat a little." But if all members cheat, the cooperative, like the cartel, will disintegrate.

[15] The degree to which formal sanctions are necessary varies according to the subjective values and weights attached by different peasant groups to the social elements just mentioned.

groups than in groups formed solely for the provision of services. A comparision of two groups in Bolivia indicated that the one responsible only for construction of community building and roads received greater enthusiasm than the other, which also included joint agricultural production (Barnes de Marschall 1970). In Peru, land reform efforts to transform all haciendas into joint production cooperatives have met such sharp resistance in areas of former individual cattle grazing and cultivation (*colonato*)[16] that in many cases the government has had to relinquish its plans. In other cases, where the government insisted on joint production, cooperative members have opposed the hiring of managers and often sabotaged cooperative activities (Horton 1973).

Cohesion Versus Creative Factionalism

In the case of Mexico's collective *ejidos* there has been a tendency for the original units to subdivide, so that now it is difficult to find one original group intact.[17] In most cases subdivision was primarily the result of internal conflicts, but often it was aggravated by outside political forces. Often members left groups in which corruption and poor administration were prevalent. Occasionally, ambitious members seceded from the original group and set up new groups in order to gain leadership positions. Finally, a change from river-based irrigation to a system based on tube wells reduced the technical advantages of large-scale cultivation, making subdivision more feasible.[18]

How much internal cohesion is required for survival and consolidation of the group, and how much factionalism may be tolerated? It seems clear that formation of peasant groups requires a minimum degree of similarity of their members' interests, and that survival of the group requires sufficient cohesion to allow for reasonably effective decision making and the avoidance of persistent quarrels and disruptions. In the case of collective land use, group cohesion is even more crucial than in credit, marketing, or other service groups. Cohesion may be achieved by

[16] Under the *colono* system, which was prevalent in the Peruvian highlands prior to the land reform, hacienda residents worked part-time for the central management, and the remainder of their time tilling their own parcels of hacienda land and tending their own livestock.

[17] An extreme example, the *ejido* Nueva Italian, went through 3 stages of subdivision: first, it divided itself into 5 component *ejidos*; later each of these subdivided into still smaller units; and finally they disintegrated into individual parcels (Eckstein 1966).

[18] Nevertheless, subdivision probably would not have occurred if there had been no internal strife or political problems in the *ejidos* (Eckstein 1966).

limiting membership to kinsmen, or by selecting membership from peasants who are already strongly committed to the joint venture. A mechanism to permit secession by dissenters seems necessary for the maintenance of unity.

In general, small associations seem more efficient and durable than larger ones. As noted above, in many cases large groups splinter into smaller ones. In Cotoca, at one of the Bolivian Andean Indian Program bases, all settlers were originally required to belong to the cooperative. The association proved much too heterogeneous and soon failed. However, a minority of the original cooperative members voluntarily agreed to continue joint livestock operations, and their group prospered (ILO 1961). The Quechechueca collective in Mexico survived many disruptions by eliminating dissenting groups until membership was sufficiently homogeneous for effective functioning (Eckstein 1966).

In a number of exceptionally successful cases, cohesive traits have been associated with minority or deviant groups, such as ethnically distinct immigrants, religious sects, or revolutionary political parties. More often than not, groups which have proven successful over a period of years are exclusive or "elitist" — set off from the rest of society by choice or necessity. For almost twenty years, amidst constant official hostility, the communist enclave of Viota in Cundinamarca, Colombia, managed its own affairs (which included communal production and marketing) on coffee estates that were occupied in the 1930's (Hirschman 1963). In the Choapa Valley of northern Chile a similar enclave of a left-wing group formed an effective local government and network of land-use collectives, which laid the groundwork for production cooperatives by fighting for labor and occupancy rights. In Mexico, most of the surviving collective *ejidos* have a membership bound together by radical ideological ties (Huizer 1968). In Peru, the agricultural production cooperatives in which members participate most actively and which appear most likely to survive the test of time are operated by minority indigenous groups in the highlands (Horton 1974).

Almost as important as homogeneity of belief is uniformity of status. Great differences in the economic and social status of group members are damaging to the cooperative spirit and group cohesion. While such heterogeneous associations may continue to operate, they frequently fail under the domination of the high-status members, or become transformed into state-managed farms.[19]

[19]   In this respect, it will be important to observe the future course of Peru's immense cooperatives, in which a few technicians receive incomes several times higher than the incomes of most members.

Another aspect of cohesive behavior which seems favorable to cooperative organization is common hostility towards rival interests. An example of this is the Zacatepec sugar area in Mexico (Schwartz 1962). In this area an atmosphere of distrust, suspicion, and corruption prevailed because of troubled relations between the management of the government-controlled sugar mill and the farmers who sold cane to the mill. On the initiative of one of the village leaders, who refused to become part of a system of financial collusion with the mill management, the peasants established a society for the common exploitation of a mineral water spring located on their lands and waged a successful legal battle to maintain their rights to this resource.

Several commentators have emphasized the importance of a certain amount of heterogeneity or factionalism in a healthy cooperative movement. For example, Vellard (1963) has pointed out that in Venezuela there is less resistance to cooperatives in heterogeneous communities of recent settlement than in more unified traditional communities. He feels that this has occurred because uprooting has broken traditional ties and has given rise to a more experimental and open mentality among the peasants. Cohen (1966) reminds us that some very cohesive communities may indeed reject outside assistance and be hostile toward such essential services to modern cooperatives as bookkeeping.

The problem of cohesion has a territorial or geographic dimension which can be posed in the following way: successful cooperation demands a free association of like-minded individuals which can best be accomplished through the establishment of selective or exclusive groupings but the social structures of rural villages and haciendas are generally composed of many heterogeneous family units with divergent interests and resources whose mobility, and therefore choice, is extremely restricted. Thus the settlement pattern itself limits the possibility of free association. If all or most residents of an area are to benefit from cooperation, all-inclusive types of associations or compulsory groupings of villagers or landholders are needed. One possible solution lies in the use of multiple associations — some of which, by geographic necessity, would have to be all-inclusive (*ejidos, asentamientos, sindicatos,* production cooperatives), while others could be more selective or limited in scope (e.g. credit associations, commodity marketing associations). The Mexican experience illustrates a certain amount of successful adaptation to this problem: membership is available to farmers in a number of overlapping associations, some of which are specialized and exclusive, others being more general and inclusive (Landsberger and Hewitt 1967).

In Peru, although to date most effort has gone into the establishment of production cooperatives, the Velasco government's regional planning units (Proyectos Integrales de Asentamiento Rural – PIARS) provide for the creation of several other types of peasant enterprises (Horton 1974).

Individualism of Peasants

The individualism of peasants is commonly emphasized as an obstacle to cooperative organization. It is argued that once the static passivity of a peasant community is broken by outside stimuli, economic progress results from the actions of individual entrepreneurs rather than by organized peasants; rampant individualism precludes effective cooperation. Erasmus, who is one of the main proponents of this view, believes that the "individual egotist" is the principal source of development. Erasmus is extremely critical of public efforts which promote egalitarian cooperation (in contrast to commercialism) and which, in his view, result in "dependent peasants," institutionalization of paternalism, and the throttling of individual initiative:

True natural leaders spring up very readily in communities not dominated by social welfare administrations, although ... they are often resented by the latter. The able farmer who improves his lot through his own skill and initiative is a thorn in the side of the government technician who seeks dependents — not independent "egotists". The "egotists", however, appear everywhere in an environment made fertile for their managerial abilities and entrepreneurial creativity through social overhead, capital developments ... such projects as roads, irrigation and public power (Erasmus 1969).

The social environment of rewards and sanctions in which these observed motivations are formed is of crucial importance. If the development model is laissez-faire capitalism, with the social system offering little reward for collective or cooperative leadership as a source of personal gratification, it is to be expected that individualistic economic behavior will predominate. But in Latin America, rampant individualism has led to slow overall development, extreme concentration of income, and widespread rural poverty and deprivation. From the point of view of Latin American rural development strategy, the dilemma is precisely one of channeling the emerging energies and initiatives of community leaders and members toward joint, rather than individual, action so that the majority of rural people can benefit from both personal initiative and skills and public programs.

Recently, in a study of a Mexican village, Fromm and Maccoby have

identified several types of peasant character, one of which is the entrepreneurial, aggressive type (termed "productive-exploitative" character
by the authors). Is it possible to harness this type into honest leadership?
Fromm and Maccoby answer in the affirmative:

Given a new set of conditions, the traditional peasant character can to a considerable extent undergo changes, and traditional peasant behaviour can change
from antagonism and selfishness to cooperation. The main problem is to find
those new conditions which in a systematic way are able to bring about these
changes. And this is only achieved by an organization of social life that is
conducive to an increase in the productive elements of the character structure
(Fromm and Maccoby 1970).

Delinquency and Corruption

Corruption is an extremely widespread and debilitating phenomenon in
Latin American rural organizations. Clearly, cooperatives of even the
most rudimentary types cannot survive without a substantial degree of
honesty in their leadership. Where corruption is endemic, even large-
scale land reforms can do little more than "democratize graft."[20]

The stronger the ideological commitment of an organization's leaders,
the less likely is economic corruption. Thus, corruption should be of
least importance in radical peasant movements (Landsberger and
Hewitt 1967). But apart from such commitment, the most effective
remedy for corruption appears to be the creation of mechanisms whereby
local officials, as well as their regional and national representatives, are
paid by the membership and are accountable to the peasantry rather than
to upper levels of the hierarchy. However, in most situations where
cooperatives become established as a result of policies designed at the
national level (not grass-roots movements), it is difficult to make administrators more responsible to the peasantry than to higher officials. This
problem is particularly acute in so-called "forced-decision cooperatives,"
in which a certain degree of coerciveness and strong initial control is
necessary (Dobyns 1967).[21]

Problems of delinquency arise quite frequently in credit cooperatives

[20]   In other words, open up the possibility of peasant participation in bribes and misuse
of resources, previously enjoyed by privileged groups (Senior 1958).
[21]   Irrigation associations, in which competent joint water management is crucial, and
many land-reform projects involving the reorganization of complex commercial units,
are examples of such "forced-decision" organizations. Credit societies also seem to
require strong outside intervention and control in their formative years, even in more
highly developed countries.

(Carroll 1973; Williams and Thiller 1973). Often this is due to inappropriate lending procedures or repayment mechanisms. In some cases, group members feel that credit is a well-deserved gift. Quite often, they use production loans for consumption purposes. In cases where little or no group solidarity exists, the sudden imposition of group responsibility for loans may have a negative effect on the farmer's willingness to receive credit or to be part of an organization in which he becomes liable for the default of others. Recent evidence from Peru's reformed coastal estates indicates that peasants resent such responsibility, conceived as a hindrance to each individual's progress (Horton 1973). In such cases, credit should probably be extended through cooperatives on an individual basis until greater solidarity exists.

Groups in which credit recipients are carefully screened tend to have fewer defaults than those in which no prior selection is made. The INDAP program in Chile suffered because credit was given too easily and without guidelines for the use of loans (Nisbet 1973).

Although there is no single, optimal solution, certain measures have been generally successful. Corruption can be checked considerably by making loans in kind and collecting payments at marketing points. The little evidence available indicates that group credit schemes provide less scope for corruption than individually managed credit programs. One sociological interpretation holds that modern forms of cooperation are based on "institutionalized suspicion," since they have built-in checks and balances.[22] However, in practice the best checks seem to be those which are based on a degree of existing trust. Hence, management is likely to be most honest where cooperative institutions are built on the foundation of already existing social structures, with internalized sanctions against corruption.

POLITICAL FACTORS

The Special Relation Between Land Reform and Cooperatives

Without land reform, rural cooperatives are not likely to prosper, no significant rural cooperative movement is likely to develop, and cooperativism cannot be expected to become an important vehicle for the improvement of peasant welfare. This is true for two fundamental reasons: first, cooperatives threaten established rural economic interests which

[22] Such as auditing, periodic reelection of officers, etc.

only land reform can eliminate; second, agrarian systems characterized by domination and dependency relationships and great disparities in income levels and status do not provide the egalitarian prerequisites for effective cooperation. Whenever cooperatives are established in areas of traditional, latifundist-dominated agrarian structure, neither those associations in which only smallholders participate nor those which include both large and small farmers are likely to function satisfactorily.

These problems are most serious where tenure-related social stratification is very rigid. But it seems clear that in most situations, without land reform cooperatives cannot become a force for structural reform (Fals Borda 1971; García 1968); the best that can be expected is adaptation to the existing social structure and some protection of cooperative members from the more onerous forms of exploitation.

While land reform is a necessary precondition for the development of a viable cooperative movement, the existence of land reform by no means guarantees that cooperation will flower, as the Bolivian experience demonstrates.

Ideology

Ideological commitment on the part of the government seems to be essential for the success of a massive rural cooperativization program. Except for relatively brief periods, such as the Cárdenas administration in Mexico, the Frei and Allende administrations in Chile, and the current Velasco government in Peru, such commitment has been rare in Latin America. Only in countries which have implemented massive land-reform programs have peasant cooperatives enjoyed institutional legitimacy, but even in these cases there has not been a sufficiently strong and sustained ideological commitment to transcend short-term partisan political struggles and ensure the consolidation of a viable cooperative sector. In Mexico, after Cárdenas, the government withdrew support from the collective *ejidos*. The Bolivian government never actively supported the production cooperatives formed in the early years of the revolution, and most of these failed after a very short period. In Venezuela, peasant groups remain isolated and, in general, weak. In Chile, after the overthrow of Allende, most *asentamientos* seem to be disintegrating. The Peruvian reform is too recent to allow historical analysis, although to date the military government's agricultural programs have been characterized more by their pragmatism than by their ideological component.

Political Participation and Power Struggle

Cooperatives and supporters of rural cooperative development, bent on improving the economic and social position of the peasantry, sooner or later become involved in political struggles with nonpeasant interests. Hence, the potential for militant opposition to rural cooperative movements is great, and the legitimacy of such movements becomes an important issue.

Some commentators believe that rebelliousness of cooperative founders is an essential ingredient in the initiation of an effective movement, and that rebellious ideology can be an important complement to, or even a substitute for, traditional solidarity based on common social and economic interests (Dobyns 1967). Rebelliousness directed against political elites, social cliques, and economic monopolies may explain the success of many radical peasant groups in Latin America. Active opposition to the status quo may also be an important focus for rallying smaller peasant groups into larger movements which, in turn, can be mobilized against the establishment. The questions of when and how such a minority rebellion can strengthen a cooperative movement and how, in the process, it can acquire enough legitimacy to survive without being "captured" or coopted, are important.

Thus, as long as outside threats unite peasants, and some mechanism for building up and extending allegiances exists, conflictive situations may stimulate the growth and consolidation of cooperative movements. In some cases, however, peasant rebellion may be directed against government planners and other officials who impose programs upon the peasantry. Reconciliation of long-range developmental plans with peasants' demands is a common problem for governments attempting to promote cooperatives, especially where land use is involved (Ronfeldt 1973; Horton 1974). The key question is: What congruence can be achieved between the interests of the peasants and those of other power holders? In this respect the relationship between cooperatives and peasant associations is crucial.

Cooperatives and Peasant Organizations

Peasant associations which are essentially political pressure groups can be effectively supported by cooperatives which have economic bases but lack political linkages and support. This complementarity has not often been exploited by cooperative promoters or peasant political leaders. In such countries as Bolivia and Venezuela, for example, where strong peasant associations emerged through agrarian reforms, little was done to take advantage of this opportunity to strengthen simultaneously and cumulatively the political and economic position of peasants (Powell 1971; Heath 1969).

In Chile, the Allende government could not unite the various peasant groups into a single movement (Barraclough 1972). In Peru, cooperativization has been promoted by the Velasco government without widespread peasant support, and the lack of real grass-roots support for, and identification with, the cooperative program seems likely to jeopardize the long-term viability of the new production cooperatives (Horton 1974).[23]

The nonpolitization of rural cooperatives in the Western world has been overstated. In Israel, cooperative institutions are strongly integrated into the political and partisan structure of the country. Almost every cooperative "belongs" to some party and is patronized by it, requiring political homogeneity within each group. This may foster social homogeneity, reduce internal strife, and assure some kind of objective treatment on the part of public agencies (depending on the specific political structure of the country). But it also increases the risk that political developments at the national level will run all the way down to the smallest local group, as attested by the painful history of several kibbutzim.[24]

The foregoing suggests that, sporadic successes notwithstanding, large-scale rural cooperative movements must await the emergence of strong, ideologically committed peasant unions, usually in the aftermath of agrarian reforms (Huizer 1972). Only through such a link-up to the national political system can cooperatives obtain essential external support. Cooperatives can, in turn, provide peasant associations with the economic base necessary for their own survival and independence. On the other hand, in the absence of a strong ideological commitment, which transcends partisan politics, the suggested symbiosis between cooperatives and peasant associations entails considerable dangers. If the essential external support depends mainly on established party loyalty, a shift of power to other parties may result in the withdrawal of such support from the cooperatives, as occurred in Venezuela, Mexico, and Bolivia.

[23] This also implies that the land reform program has not earned strong peasant support for the government.
[24] This has also been observed in Mexico and Chile.

The Importance of a Cooperative Sector

The survival and prosperity of individual cooperatives are often strictly limited by inadequate infrastructure and poor integration into the broader economic system. In very few countries have effective regional associations fulfilled these functions. Exceptions are the Brazilian and Colombian regional coffee cooperatives and the national marketing boards assisting Carmenpampa in Bolivia. The lack of "second-level" structures has been regarded by experts as a serious obstacle to the expansion of the cooperative movement in Chile (Barraclough 1972), in Mexico (Durán 1967), and in Colombia (Velez and Feder 1961). In Mexico, it seems clear that official resistance to the development of a strong cooperative sector in the Laguna region was due in part to the fear that second-level federations could turn into powerful political organizations (Eckstein 1966).

Economic linkages to wholesale outlets and/or processing plants is of great importance. Without effective two-way arrangements with such central facilities, local cooperation in marketing has very strict limitations. Once working arrangements between local groups and marketing or processing centers have been established, a crucial determinant of the continued, effective, and democratic functioning of the cooperative system is the degree of member control over the operation of central facilities. Excessive dependence of individual cooperatives upon higher-level decision-making centers undermines peasant identification with, and support for, their cooperatives and precipitates corruption, abuses of power, and bureaucratization of the cooperative movement. In this respect, the advantages of pluralistic, regional and national associations instead of monolithic, politically controlled confederations are substantial.

In recent years in Latin America, the most ambitious attempt to establish a viable cooperative sector is that of Peru. The Velasco government's land-reform and rural cooperativization programs envision the integration of base-level collective production units (cooperatives and quasi cooperatives) into a broad cooperative sector with both regional and specialized central cooperatives. Regional central cooperatives are to provide marketing, credit, planning, heavy machinery, and other services to peasant groups in their area. Certain types of groups, such as coffee, tea, sugar, and wool producers, are to become affiliated with specialized central cooperatives.

To date, the government's land-reform activities have been concentrated on the expropriation of estates and the formation of new base-level production units; only a few central cooperatives have been formed. But the experiences of those central cooperatives which have been established indicate that peasant groups and their leaders often oppose the formation of higher-level groups because they threaten the independence of the already existing base-level units. To date most regional central cooperatives are subsidized by the state, and peasant groups do not seem willing to support them economically.

Specialized central cooperatives, which perform more essential services for their members,[25] have encountered fewer problems in this respect. Whether or not the Peruvian approach, which is characterized by non-politization of the peasantry and a high degree of government control, can lead to the development of a viable cooperative sector remains to be seen (Horton 1974).

FINAL REMARKS

We have treated the merits and problems of economic group action among peasants under the classic headings of economic, managerial, social, and political features. Such groups have both advantages and disadvantages in each of these areas. Economies of scale become significant especially when major structural and technological changes are envisaged. But social problems and managerial difficulties increase with scale and complexity of joint undertakings and tend to offset the strictly technical or "engineering" advantages of large-scale production. Because of the scarcity of trained manpower, operating through groups might be the only way to reach large numbers of farmers and help over-come the peasants' own managerial shortcomings, particularly in the early postreform period. Political participation is crucial, since it provides upward linkages needed to make the whole program work in favor of the peasantry. But more often than not the goals of political groups, even those formed initially by peasants, become diverted from the advancement of peasant welfare to other objectives which conflict with this.

What is the final outcome of this multidimensional problem in which so many factors pull in so many directions? If we could assume constancy and additivity of all factors, we could simply "add them all up" and determine the optimum size and form of peasant groups. But for several reasons, it is impossible to arrive at universally valid answers.

Certain agricultural activities are more sensitive to scale than others.

[25] Such as the exportation of agricultural commodities and importation of specialized machinery.

Certain groups of peasants oppose any pooling of land, no matter how great the possible economic gain; others can be induced by strong economic rewards. The political atmosphere might be appropriate for group action, or entirely hostile to it. In specific cases, the merits of group action depend on which of the opposing forces dominates the picture at that particular point in time. The feasibility of group action also depends on how peasants themselves perceive and evaluate the final balance and on their previous experiences. All these factors change over time. Hence the types of peasant groups which were optimal yesterday need not be optimal today or tomorrow as the result of changing economic, social, and political conditions.

In many cases land which was originally pooled in new settlement areas or in land reform projects was later parceled out among group members as they learned how to farm independently and accumulated the resources necessary to do so. Less often, changes in economic, social, and/or political conditions have induced the spontaneous pooling or re-pooling of resources.[26] Flexibility in tenure and group arrangements is essential if the cooperative system is to survive and play a dynamic role in rural development.

Interaction of Variables

The numerous factors which influence the performance of peasant groups are not simply additive but interactive. Economies of scale depend upon the use of "lumpy" machinery and technical processes and upon specialization. But enhancing the strictly technical aspects of production through expansion of the scale of operation and minute specialization can create serious managerial problems and social frictions. Where technical advantages are considerable, they may outweigh the social problems or produce the necessary motivation to solve them. However, if peasant farmers (particularly subsistence farmers) are collectivized with little or no gain in production or income, social difficulties may prove insurmountable, since peasants have no good reason to struggle in overcoming them. Both the well-documented experience of Mexican collective *ejidos* and the recent experience of Peru's production cooperatives bear this out (Eckstein 1966; Horton 1974).

Most of the factors we are considering should not be considered exogenously "given," but endogenous to the system and affected by its planning, implementation, and performance. Adequate economic and

[26] All three processes have been observed in Moshav in Israel. In Latin America, disintegration of collective production units has been more common.

social infrastructure is as much a part of the group system as are the base-level peasant groups. The choice of production patterns and technology needs to be made in conjunction with the organizational possibilities, and not as something given independently by agronomists or economists. Measures should also be taken to mitigate, to the extent possible, the social problems associated with cooperatives: careful microplanning, training programs, an efficient extension service, simple accounting techniques, and rigorous auditing procedures with clear delegation of responsibilities are all needed. These, of course, require broad public and political support. All these measures increase the likelihood of success for new peasant groups; their absence will definitely undermine the position of peasant groups.

Vulnerability of the System

This brings us to a final consideration. Cooperative systems are highly vulnerable to economic difficulties, even if these are transitory in nature. In contrast to the classic production function in economic theory, where marginal changes in inputs result in marginal changes in output, we are faced with a volatile, "all or nothing" type of function; a small error in management or technical advice, relatively minor cases of member dishonesty, or short-term climatic problems can make the difference between success and failure. One bad year, due to any cause, can destroy the work of many good years and cause irreparable damage to group cohesion, especially during the critical first few years of group consolidation. Hence, in cooperative systems, much more than in systems based on individual farming and servicing, it is necessary to insure against external contingencies (weather, plagues, price collapse), deficiencies in delivery and marketing systems, and delinquency on the part of leaders and functionaries. Reliance on "self-adjusting mechanisms," which tend to solve these problems in the longer run in the systems based on individual farming, cannot be relied upon to the same extent where groups are involved.

Conclusion

There seems to be a significant reciprocal relationship between land reform and peasant cooperation, which so far has not been clearly recognized in the development literature. Without land-reform and other substantial programs which transform the basic socioeconomic structure of rural life, rural cooperatives are not likely to survive or to grow into a significant movement. On the other hand, without adequate postreform cooperative models of resource and social organization, land redistribution is not likely to have a lasting effect on the production and welfare of peasants. Thus, land reform and peasant cooperatives are functionally linked and together provide an institutional framework within which the multiple goals of rural development (growth, justice, participation) can be achieved.

Land-reform and peasant cooperative programs are by no means easy approaches to rural development problems. They are complex and difficult ventures which can have a significant impact on agricultural growth and peasant welfare only when backed with power and commitment on the part of the national government and by political mobilization of the peasantry.

However, experience has shown that what is often referred to as "inherent" social disadvantages of rural cooperative systems may be overestimated. All postreform rural systems appear to offer some scope for group action, especially in the provision of services. Joint land use, while desirable in many situations for technical or economic reasons, is more difficult to achieve. Using a judicious mix of group farming and service cooperatives is better than adherence to a single, ideologically rigid model. Participatory forms of peasant enterprise and supporting service systems can be designed which are viable in the postreform context. However, implementing such systems requires not only a strong and sustained commitment on the part of the government, but also flexibility and local adaptation to existing conditions — qualities in especially short supply, so far, on the Latin American policy scene. Nevertheless, the potential developmental advantages of participatory systems are so great, and the long-term disadvantages of the more easily available alternatives are so substantial, that the "noble experiment," however difficult, is eminently worth trying.

REFERENCES

BARNES DE MARSCHALL, K.
  1970 *Revolution and land reform in the Bolivian Yungas* (revised edition). La Paz: SNRA, Sección de Investigaciones.
BARRACLOUGH, S., *coordinator*
  1972 *Diagnóstico de la Reforma Agraria Chilena (Noviembre 1970-Junio 1972)*. Proyecto "Reforma Agraria y Desarrollo Rural" (PNUD-FAO),

Instituto de Capacitación e Investigación en Reforma Agraria, Santiago de Chile.

BARRIGA, C.

1973   *Management in cooperative farming.* Land Tenure Center Research Paper 54. Madison: University of Wisconsin.

BREWSTER, J.

1950   The machine process in agriculture and industry. *Journal of Farm Economics* 32:69–81.

CARROLL, T. F.

1969   "Peasant cooperation in Latin America," in *A review of rural cooperation in developing areas.* Edited by Orlando Fals Borda and Inayatullah, 1–94. Geneva: United Nations Research Institute for Social Development (UNRISD). (Also appears in 1971 *Two blades of grass: rural cooperatives in agricultural modernization.* Edited by Peter Worsley, 199–249. Manchester: Manchester University Press.)

1973   "Group credit for small farmers," in *A.I.D. spring review of small farmer credit: analytical papers,* volume nineteen. Washington, D.C.

CENTRO DE INVESTIGACIONES AGRARIAS

1970   *Estructura agraria y desarrollo agrícola en Mexico,* three volumes. Mexico, D.F.: Centro de Investigaciones Agrarias and Comité Interamericano de Desarrollo Agrícola.

COHEN, P.

1966   "Traditional societies and modern cooperatives." Paper prepared for the Sixth World Congress of Sociology, Evian.

DAYAL, R., C. ELLIOT

1966   *Land tenure, land concentration and agricultural output.* Geneva: United Nations Research Institute for Social Development (UNRISD).

DOBYNS, H.

1967   "Sociological and anthropological approaches to engineering successful economic organizations." Paper presented at the Agricultural Development Council Seminar at the University of Kentucky, April 1967.

DORNER, P., *editor*

1972   *Land reform and economic development.* Harmondsworth: Penguin.

DORNER, P., D. KANEL

1971   "The economic case for land reform," in *Land reform in Latin America: issues and cases.* Edited by Peter Dorner. Land Tenure Center, Land Economics Monographs 3. Madison: University of Wisconsin.

DOVRING, F.

1964   "The share of agriculture in a growing population," in *Agriculture in economic development.* Edited by C.K. Eicher and L. Witt. New York: McGraw-Hill.

1973   "Land reform: ends and means." Unpublished manuscript submitted to the World Bank Seminar on Land Reform.

DURÁN, M. A.

1967   *El agrarismo Mexicano.* Mexico, D.F.: Siglo XXI.

ECKSTEIN, S.

1966   *El ejido colectivo en Mexico.* Mexico, D.F.: Fondo de Cultura Económica.

ERASMUS, C.
1969 "Agrarian reform: a comparative study of Venezuela, Bolivia, and Mexico," in *Land reform and social revolution in Bolivia*. Edited by Dwight B. Heath, Charles Erasmus, and Hans Buechler. New York: Praeger.

FALS BORDA, O.
1971 *Cooperatives and rural development in Latin America*. Geneva: United Nations Research Institute for Social Development (UNRISD).

FROMM, E., M. MACCOBY
1970 *Social character in a Mexican village*. Englewood Cliffs, New Jersey: Prentice-Hall.

GARCÍA, A.
1968 "Cooperativas y financiamiento agrícola en Aconcaqua." Mimeographed manuscript, ICIRA, Departamento de Cooperativas y Credit, Santiago.

HEATH, D., C. ERASMUS, H. BUECHLER, *editors*
1969 *Land Reform and social revolution in Bolivia*, New York: Praeger.

HIRSCHMAN, A. O.
1963 *Journeys toward progress*. New York: Twentieth Century Fund.

HORTON, D.
1973 *Haciendas and cooperatives: a preliminary study of latifundist agriculture and agrarian reform in northern Peru*. Land Tenure Center Research Paper 53. Madison: University of Wisconsin.
1974 "*Land reform and reform enterprises in Peru: IBRD-LTC report*." Mimeographed manuscript. Land Tenure Center. Madison: University of Wisconsin.

HUIZER, G.
1968 "The role of peasant organizations in the process of agrarian reform in Mexico." Mimeographed manuscript. Washington, D.C.: Comité Interamericano de Desarrollo Agrícola.
1972 *The revolutionary potential of peasants in Latin America*. Lexington, Massachusetts: Heath-Lexington Books.

INTERNATIONAL LABOUR OFFICE (ILO)
1961 "Informe al Director Generale sobre las posibilidades de organización cooperativa entre las comunidades indígenas." Mimeographed manuscript, Geneva.

KANEL, D.
1967 Size of farm and agricultural development. *Indian Journal of Agricultural Economics* 22:26–44.

LANDSBERGER, H., C. HEWITT
1967 "Preliminary report on a case study of Mexican peasant associations." Mimeographed manuscript. Ithaca, New York: Cornell University.

LELE, U. J.
1972 "The role of credit and marketing in agricultural development." Paper presented at the International Economic Association Conference on The Place of Agriculture in the Development of Under-Developed Countries, Bad-Godesberg, Germany. Mimeographed Manuscript. Washington, D.C.: World Bank.

MARTINEZ-ALIER, J.
1971   *Labourers and landowners in southern Spain.* St. Antony's Publications 4. London: George Allen and Unwin.

MATHIASON, J. R., E. SHEARER
1967   *Caicara de Maturin: case study of an agrarian reform settlement in Venezuela.* Inter-American Committee for Agricultural Development. Research papers on Land Tenure and Agrarian Reform 1. Washington D.C.: Pan-American Union.

NISBET, C. T.
1973   "Instituto de desarrollo agropecuario (INDAP)," in *A.I.D spring review of small farmer credit: small farmer credit in South America,* volume three. Washington, D.C.

POWELL, J.
1971   *Political mobilization of the Venezuelan peasant.* Cambridge, Massachusetts: Harvard University Press.

RONFELDT, D.
1973   *Atencingo: the politics of agrarian struggle in a Mexican ejido.* Stanford, California: Stanford University Press.

SCHILLER, O. M.
1968   *Cooperation and integration in agricultural production.* London: Asia Publishing House.

SCHWARTZ, L.
1962   "Morality, conflict and violence in a Mexican mestizo village." Unpublished Ph.D. dissertation, Indiana University, Bloomington, Ind.

SENIOR, C.
1958   *Land reform and democracy.* Gainesville, Florida: University of Florida Press.

THIESENHUSEN, W.
1966   *Chile's experiments in agrarian reform,* Land Economics Monograph 1. Madison: University of Wisconsin.

VELEZ, E., E. FEDER
1961   "The lagging growth of the cooperative movement in Colombia: a preliminary survey of its development and obstacles." Mimeographed manuscript. Ministerio de Agricultura, Servicio Técnico Agrícola Colombiano Americano, Bogotá.

VELLARD, J.
1963   *Civilisation des Andes.* Paris: NRF.

WILLIAMS, S., J. A. THILLER
1973   *Credit systems for small-scale farmers: case histories from Mexico.* Studies in Latin American Business 14. Graduate School of Business, University of Texas at Austin.

The Algerian Model of Agrarian Reorganization

HAMID AÏT AMARA

Despite the vicissitudes of a ten-year-old self-management experience, the Algerian government has chosen to skip the stage of individual distribution of farmland in favor of an extension of the collective sector as part of a radical reform of property relations in agriculture. The government has thus indicated the fundamental importance that it attaches to the rapid modernization of agrarian structures.

However, in contrast to many countries which have collectivized agriculture by gradually integrating individually owned land, collectivization in Algeria has developed only through the collective cultivation of lands belonging to the State.

The first phase in the creation of a collectivized production sector in agriculture came immediately after independence when the state recovered the land occupied by the colonial farms (2,300,000 hectares or 28 percent of the arable land).

Ten years later, the dispositions of the law enacting an agrarian revolution[1] and applied during 1972 are the continuation of this path. The goal was to reorganize the structures of agricultural production on the basis of collective farming and to continue the movement towards the progressive integration of the immense rural proletariat into the modern sector of the economy and the society. The small and middle peasantry, given the new conditions under which the right of property would be exercised, were not involved here. They could join the established cooperative structures[2] or they could continue to coexist with them.

---

[1] The Agrarian Revolution Law applies to Algerian-owned private property, which until then had not been affected by the nationalization measures of 1963.

[2] Charter of the Agrarian Revolution: "The Agrarian Revolution will limit the

AN ORIENTATION FAVORING THE EXTENSION OF THE COLLECTIVE SECTOR

Apart from the lands which were nationalized as part of a program to limit large estates, individual private property was not affected by the extension of the collective sector. Instead, the land needed for the establishment of cooperatives was taken from the National Agrarian Revolution Land Bank, which was established by statute on 8 November 1971. It includes communal land, land from the domains of the Wilayas (the principal administrative subdivision of Algeria) and of the State, and finally lands nationalized according to the terms[3] of the agrarian revolution law which defines the new conditions under which the property right would be exercised.

Access to the ownership of land is based on the single criterion of direct personal labor. The Statute stipulates in this respect that:

The property right exercised on any presently or potentially farmed land by any owner known not to work that land is abolished (article 28).

This is further defined:

Direct and personal cultivation of the land by a given owner consists in the facts of working alone or with the help of his relations in the direct line, of calling agriculture his profession and of living primarily from the product of this activity.

The establishment of a direct relationship between property and work leads by the same token to the use of nationalization to limit the superfluous fields of the large estates. Thus:

The area of agricultural estates is limited to the amount that can be worked by the owner and his family, and that can guarantee him an adequate income (article 2).[4]

The use of wage labor is thus restricted; we read that:

---

working of the land to three well defined modes: self-management which is already a concrete reality of our socialism, cooperatives which constitute a democratic framework of association for poor peasants, and private farming organized in conformity with the requirements of national development."

[3]   Maximum areas for the least productive land have been fixed by the decree of 17 July 1973 at 5 hectares for irrigated land and 110 hectares for dry farming land.

[4]   Article 65: "The area of an individual farm is limited so that the minimum income of an average family living entirely from its product should be the equivalent... of three times the income of the family of a worker on a self-managed agricultural estate working 250 days a year" (one workday = 10 Algerian dinars).

Any farmer who directly and personally farms agricultural land can only hire wage labor on a seasonal basis (article 95).

The lands which have been handed over to the National Agrarian Revolution Land Bank as a result of nationalization, which was total for absentee landowners and partial for large-estate owners, remain State property. They may be subdivided into family farms, with a right of perpetual use but not ownership, but only under the condition that the recipients must form or join a cooperative.

The land distributed in the Agrarian Revolution program is to be farmed in common or in a collective form within the structures of precooperative groups or of agricultural cooperatives created by the recipients of the land themselves.

Individual farming is allowed

...only as long as the economic and social conditions of their common or collective use for farming are not met (article 112).

Depending on the quality of the land, its equipment and improvement, and the investments needed for its development, the Government retains the right to initiate various individual and collective forms of work: either individual farms, development groups, communal-farming cooperatives, or production cooperatives.

The acceptance of a "grantee title" obliges the recipient to join one of the above-mentioned cooperative forms.

The recipients of land from the National Agrarian Revolution Land Bank are thus not allowed to choose the cooperative form that suits them best. If they do not want to abandon their share in the division of lands they must agree to join one of the cooperatives established by the State.

The criterion of technical efficiency, of the modernization of the structures of production, thus took precedence over any other consideration by favoring collective forms of work over the distribution of land to individuals. Thus during the first phase of the "Agrarian Revolution" (1972–1973), the emphasis was above all on the establishment of cooperatives of production. Of 700,000 hectares given out to 50,000 landless peasants, barely 10 percent of the total was allocated to individuals. The rest was transferred collectively. It is estimated that when all the agrarian reform provisions have been carried out, the State will have distributed a total of 1,500,000 hectares to about 110,000 families.

The sector of collective production will then include 2,300,000 hectares under self-management and 1,500,000 in cooperatives, for a total of 3,800,000 hectares, just over half the 7,000,000 hectares of cultivated land. About one-fifth of all peasant families will be integrated into collectivized agriculture.

It should be noted, however, that the stress placed on collective forms of labor takes into account the very advanced state of the process of proletarianization of the peasantry. This proletarianization determines the agrarian reform movement, for peasant aspirations do not lead them to demand individual ownership of farm land.

AN OPTION ON BEHALF OF THE PROLETARIANIZED PEASANTRY

The "Agrarian Revolution" recruits its supporters principally among the agricultural workers, the most destitute section of the rural population and also the one most likely to participate in collective forms of land use as job security and economic progress are effective stimulants for them.

In the first stage, the other categories affected by the division of farm-land,[5] the sharecroppers and renters, doubtless more attached to the principle of individual work, usually abandoned the rights that were theoretically theirs. Thus, only one-quarter of the grantees settled on cooperative land by 1 July 1973 were the former users of this land, despite the priority that the law granted them. Most of the sharecroppers and renters thus preferred to desist in favor of the agricultural workers.

This apparent disenchantment of the previous users underlines the real ambivalence of a whole section of the nonproletarianized peasantry towards Agrarian Reform and the collective forms of work which it initiated. This disenchantment could also reflect the pressures brought to bear by the rural petty bourgeoisie opposed to Agrarian Reform in order to limit and contain the requests for land grants and to discourage peasants from joining the production cooperatives.

The political stakes led the government to give particular emphasis to the economic and social progress of the beneficiaries of the reform, at the risk of satisfying only a relatively small number of the landless peasants. The areas attributed to each worker in the cooperatives are, in fact, calculated with respect to a minimum income threshold regardless of the amount of land available or the number of candidates.

[5]   Article 120 of the Statute enacting the Agrarian Revolution reads: "The grantees are chosen from the following categories of persons, by order of priority: 1) agricultural workers already hired to work on the lands which are the object of the nationalization measures set up by the present Statute, whether they are wage earners or are tenant farmers, sharecroppers, khammès (sharecroppers receiving one-fifth of the crop), or overseers who share in the product of the harvests according to contracts of any sort whatsoever."

Each cooperative member must receive an annual income equal to 3,000 Algerian dinars (U.S. $600) together with all the social benefits heretofore restricted to urban and self-management workers: family allowances, social security, and old age retirement. Furthermore the cooperative members must be rehoused in new "agricultural villages" furnished with all the sociocultural facilities necessary for a full development of social life. A construction program aiming at 1,000 villages was begun in 1972; it augurs massive transformations in the living conditions of that part of the peasantry benefiting from Agrarian Reform.

The need for the enthusiastic support of the workers for collective forms of production did not lead only to the significant material advantages accorded to cooperative members. The new collective enterprises are, in principle, completely decentralized, while State supervision only retains a general nature which allows the State no prerogatives in their operations. By opting for a decentralized system of management and for cooperative autonomy, the State showed it was aware of the experience of the self-managed sector.

THE SELF-MANAGEMENT EXPERIENCE

The creation of self-managed agricultural enterprises based on the large capitalist estates inherited from the colonial period was accompanied by a strong tendency towards the centralization of the management of the estates to the advantage of the technical-administrative apparatus of the State. This centralization was paralleled by a concentration of landholdings and of productive capital in large-scale enterprises. The 22,000 colonial farms were divided into 2,000 self-managed enterprises with an average area of 1,200 hectares and an average work force of 82 workers.

Above and beyond the difficulties in the operation of the enterprise due to the complexity of the large production units which were set up, self-management proved to be unable to destroy the former patterns of work relations inherited from the colonial farms and to transform into facts the rights newly conferred on each worker by the self-management system. The retention of the old schema of work organization, an imitation of the Western model with its allocation of tasks and remuneration schedules, did much to threaten the principles of solidarity of interests and the cohesion of the community of those who work together.

State intervention in the assignment of jobs and the distribution of the social product led to the reappearance of the prior work hierarchies which favored the functions of control and supervision while reducing the role of the actual workers in the execution of particular jobs.

The vast majority of the workers thus found that their status as unskilled agricultural laborers, without any responsibility for production, had been reaffirmed.

This division of labor, which was paralleled by a distribution of salaries favoring those who performed supervisory and management tasks in the production process, led to the emergence of conflicts within the workers' collectives, for the aspirations of some of them had been frustrated.

Thus it was possible to observe the emergence of oppositions. The conflicts which broke out divided the labor communities over the question of the role of hierarchical authoritative structures which give rise to material and social advantages.

The overall pattern of the system of delegates which had been created to guarantee worker participation in management was thus distorted. The elections were sometimes used by certain groups to take over the elective posts and to allow their own members to benefit from a more favorable distribution of jobs and incomes.

From this there resulted problems in the organization of the labor communities and in the operation of the apparatus of management, to the detriment of the general interest.

For these reasons the orientation of this second phase of the "Agrarian Revolution" is towards giving a new dimension to collectivist enterprises and towards a total decentralization of their management. The cooperative members must be able to exercise their autonomy fully without any State intervention. The lessons of the self-management experiences show that the commitment of the workers and their responsibility are the fundamental factors which determine the success or the failure of the present process of change.

The new cooperatives are thus smaller, about 260 hectares, and include fewer members, 19 on the average. Thus one hopes to encourage the birth of a group consciousness and the development of relations between the workers based on trust, and thus to facilitate worker control and the equitable distribution of the social product.

In contrast to the model and to the notions which guided self-management, collectivization is being pursued according to an orientation which allows the workers to govern the process of production themselves. The importance attached to the economic advance of the workers and to their support for the "Agrarian Revolution," as well as the political stakes, attest to the desire of the State to create the most favorable conditions for the success of the cooperatives and to avoid the development of any relationship subordinating the workers to the administrative apparatus.

Centralization and Decentralization of Decision Making in an Experiment in Agricultural Cooperation in Tunisia

LILIA BEN SALEM

While doing research on an experiment in agricultural cooperation in a region of Tunisia, formerly dominated by a colonial structure, we realized that we must ask ourselves to define the role of the cooperative in regional, social and economic development. We were particularly interested in the staffing of the agricultural production units of the region. How could one wanting change reconcile the fundamental democratic principles of cooperative management with the measures that have to be taken in order to transform a traditional type of soil cultivation to a modern type, and how to do this with a population that is unprepared for this kind of disruption in its ways of acting and reacting?

Other studies will recount the history of the Tunisian cooperative movement (see Makhlouf, this volume). We will briefly recall here that the first agricultural production cooperatives were usually based upon a core of state-owned land, formerly the estates of French and other settlers, nationalized by the Tunisian government after the country's independence. Land belonging to small or very small farmers was added to this. The members of the cooperative thus formed were, on one hand, the former permanent laborers of the colonists who had continued to live off the land temporarily managed by the government and, on the other hand, the small rural proprietors who were accepted into the production units along with their land. When in 1969 the project for the division of all of Tunisia's land into production units was challenged, and the principle of establishing cooperatives composed only of members who joined of their own free will was proclaimed, the small landowners withdrew from the production units. Thus, since 1970, the production units have been made up only of the former state lands, and the members are almost exclusively former laborers of the colonists; a few owners of very small plots rejoined the cooperatives, finding when they withdrew in late 1969 that they could not subsist outside of them. Those micro-landowners (there are very few of them), whose land could not be attached to the production unit because it was too small or too far away from the core, have today a position almost identical with that of the former estate workers.

But it is important to note that, whatever the evolution of the terri-torial and human content of the production unit has been, the staffing system, at least in its principles, has remained the same. The fundamental problem of our research project is the relationship between a policy of development and change and a democratic management system; this problem has remained the same.

The choice of a cooperative system is initially the result of a desire for economic growth, but not for growth at any cost. It must take into consideration the social structures of a population sapped by colonial exploitation and underdevelopment. In agriculture the progressive nationalization of the colonized land and the excessive fragmentation of the land posed a problem. A growth policy implies an orientation toward a modern type of agriculture; this can be conceived of only within a framework of technically advanced and profitable farms directed by especially competent people. It is under this condition that agriculture will be able to attain the goals that have been assigned to it by Tunisian economic policy. These goals were clearly stated in the *Perspectives décennales de développement* (République Tunisienne 1962–1971): the agricultural production must come as close to its maximum potential as possible; diversification of production; increase in yield so as to lower the cost per hectare; decrease of expenses for the purchase of intermediary goods and the sale of produce; the improvement of the standard of living of salaried agricultural workers and of small landowners; and the partici-pation of the agricultural sector in the creation and development of the production of goods and services in other sectors, notably in the industri-al sector.

Thus it is important that the formerly colonized land, which is now managed by the state and is almost always among the best of the country, does not decrease its production. This land should serve as a model for all Tunisian agriculture. It is essential in this perspective that the Tunisian government has refused to agree to a division and distribution of this land to small farmers. The fragmentation of the farmland into minute units has already been a subject of great concern; one cannot at present risk lowering the production yield of land cultivated up until now by modern methods by distributing small lots to landless peasants; this would inevitably lead to a subsistence economy. The Tunisian government also has refused to put the fertile lands on the market because doing so would inevitably contribute to the increase of social differences which, since the departure of the colonists, exist only in an embryonic form in the countryside. The decision to rent the land to Tunisian farmers was only a temporary solution; it may have been an experiment, but more than anything else it was intended to insure a decrease in the number of lots managed by the agricultural services, for at that time these services did not have enough competent personnel. But this experiment was scarcely conclusive.

Two things happened then: on the one hand, a speculation trend began with the corollary appearance of entrepreneurs who rented land though they had never been farmers before;[1] on the other hand, the deterioration of the land (which had begun to occur under the colonists who foresaw that they would soon be forced out) continued under the "absentee landlords," who took a short-term view and made only the minimal reinvestment into the land.

The second problem which arises is that of excessive parcelling out of the land (Makhlouf 1968: 17–53);[2] this is a corollary of the problem of a large peasant population that lives in an increasingly marginal subsistence economy and is forced in almost every case to rent or sell their poor fields and to join the flood to the cities. Not being able to adapt normally to an urban economy, these migrants adapt only by augmenting the number of small, parasitic shops.

To preserve the integrity of the lands nationalized after the agrarian decolonization and to draw into the modern sector a peasantry that would be unable to arrive there on its own, there is one solution: the formation of large combinations of land and people. This could be the way to achieve the fundamental goals of the political and economic decision-making centers of Tunisia as they have been formulated since the birth of the party which led the country to decolonization, and, in particular, since independence; these goals include an accelerated economic development and the promotion of human dignity.[3]

---

[1] This phenomenon arose in the regions situated close to the Algerian border when the colonists, leaving the region, themselves rented their land to Tunisian nationals (Attia 1966:31–58).

[2] Concerning the Governorate of Jendouba, consult République Tunisienne (1961–1962).

[3] Cf. Article I of the Law 63-19 of May 27, 1963, concerning cooperation in the agricultural sector: "Agricultural cooperation's function is the utilization in common of all technical and economic means by farmers to aid agricultural production and to

It is only in large farm units that one can make optimal use of the machines necessary for modern agriculture and can establish a crop rotation more complex than the two-year rotations used by the traditional sector and by the colonists who did not care about innovations and long-term perspectives. Only in large units is it possible to diversify production, introduce new crop varieties, manage the livestock in a rational manner, and also give the farmers the financial means and the technical knowledge to improve land when it has been damaged by multiple ploughings, by fallowing, and by the partial destruction of its topsoil.[4]

However, the constitution of large units requires the existence of a strict program of improvement. We have shown what measures must be taken to achieve this solution. It is a question of adopting an agricultural development policy rather than the simple preparation of land holding arrangements conducive to change. And this implies a certain centralization of decision making. At what levels?

In the initial stage, it was important to decide what land would become part of these holdings. It was highly improbable that this decision would emerge spontaneously from the peasants concerned. They were not sufficiently prepared to make such a choice, either by their culture in the anthropological sense of the word, or by the little education made available to them by the Party.

---

increase the value of the products of their farms"; Article 5 of this same Law: "The agricultural production cooperative of the northern part of the country is a company whose object is the constitution of a viable production unit, with predominating rotation of areas, permitting the grouping of land and people in order that they should farm them collectively according to the norms and techniques advised by the Plan National de Développe," and Article I of the Law 67-4 of January 19, 1967 on the *Statut Général de la Coopération:* "Cooperation is a way of development whose objectives are (by the creation of economic enterprises obeying the cooperatives' principles as they were defined by Article 2 which will follow) the renovation of structures, the modernization of techniques, the increase of production and promotion of human dignity."

[4]   The need to carry out the modernization process of Tunisian agriculture in large estate units appears in most of the study reports and speeches published or given since independence. In particular see the economic motions of the *Congrès du Néo-Destour;* the *Perspectives Décennales de Développement* 1962–1971; the *Pré-Plan Triennal* 1962–1964 and the *Plan Quadriennal* 1965–1968; the speeches of President Bourguiba, as well as the speech given on October 19, 1956, by the head of the government while he was distributing land to former resisters:

"...the future owner must belong to a cooperative which will give him the opportunity to work the land as it should be worked, to use modern machines and an ensemble of work tools which are beyond the pocketbook of the individual.

Thus the land will BELONG to him but the modern patterns of labor and production will be in common."

The considerations which influenced the regrouping of the holdings were more of a technical than of a human nature. In fact, it was the technical services of the Ministry of Agriculture which, on the basis of profitability studies, determined both the size of the new units to be created and the number of lots to be integrated into a single unit, especially for the first units, organized around the colonial estates which were called *noyau de terres domaniales* [core of state land.]

Technical studies of the peasant population that lived off the land integrated into the production unit also determined the size of the human group that was to be attached to any given land holding. But at this point the limitations imposed by the human factor were felt: in most cases a problem of overpopulation had to be faced; the transition from traditional agriculture, based on manual labor and animal traction, to agriculture using mechanical means brought into sharp focus the problem of having so large a potential work force.

Because of this the studies made a distinction between active members of the cooperative who work in the new production units and passive members whose land is integrated into the land area, but who do not personally participate in the cooperative work, either because they are physically incapable of doing so, or because they have other sources of income. This is also the reason why the technical services decided that, in most cases, only the head of the family could be considered a member of the cooperative; other members of a family had to find work somewhere else or be content to fill the salaried jobs of the production unit, i.e. perform seasonal work. These measures, however, were not able to prevent many cooperatives from admitting far more people than they really needed to carry out their work on a permanent basis.

The study also had to establish a long-term work plan to be adopted by the production unit. Thus decisions were made from the beginning on how much land was to be sown with wheat, what rotation system was to be used, which trees were to be planted, what the composition of the livestock was to be, etc. A calendar of the work to be done and an investment program were also established at this level. The projected probable profits were taken into consideration when it came to determining the number of families that the unit could decently provide for after the land would be in full production.

It is quite true that the plans established by the studies were later readjusted and even modified according to the results of actual practice. But such decisions are generally made by the technical departments; only opinions and suggestions are offered by the production units, and these come primarily from reports of the technical managers on the spot.

That is why the same layout of agricultural work is common to most of the production units in northern Tunisia.

The role of the unit director, especially in the beginning, consisted mostly of recording the daily achievements of the unit, for he was the technical supervisor, and of making sure the work calendar established by the technical services was followed.

The freedom of the production unit to direct its own daily management is also limited by decisions, made either on a management of all-unit level or on a governmental level, but affecting the day-to-day management of the cooperative. Thus, for example, in addition to the law that applies to agricultural cooperatives and, in particular, provides for a certain division of the profits at the end of the year, it often happens that the sovereign role of the General Assembly is reduced to a simple formality because of the decisions, made on the political or administrative level, concerning, for example, the money to be advanced to the members for each working day. The General Assembly does not really have an opportunity to modify this sum. Similarly, their freedom to make decisions concerning the purchase or sale of agricultural products and/or livestock, the renting of agricultural machines, the undertaking of social works, etc. is very limited.

Necessity dictates that part of the land capital be administered by the cooperative system because if there is to be economic development in the country, it is necessary to control the various steps of the production process, which are almost totally different from what they were before. This implies, as we have already seen, a compulsory centralization of decision making, essentially at the conception level where studies and agricultural plans are made, and at the control level it is most important to have periodic checkups of the farm as it carries out its work.

But then, why create a cooperative system, which theoretically means that the power belongs to the basic unit, which for many reasons, has come together of its own will to manage its own goods?

The decision to create a cooperative system was based on the desire to form large groups which would not, as a consequence, ruin the small landowners and benefit a new bourgeoisie, nor cause a general takeover of part of the Tunisian land capital by the government. The cooperative system, in the Tunisian perspective, is first of all an economic system; but it is also a social system. The objective is to create viable economic enterprises[5] which can benefit from competent technical and economic

[5]   This is a major concern of the Tunisian authorities in terms of economic development; see the speech given by President Bourguiba at the *Congrès National de la*

guidance, while allowing the farmer to feel that he has retained the status of landowner, that he owns a small piece of land, and has a right to make decisions about it.

We will not dwell on the first point, apart from noting that in the Tunisian production units, although the integrated land is not differentiated from the rest as far as working it is concerned, the small landowner, who has been admitted into the cooperative along with his land, still has the legal ownership of this land. When in 1969, the small landowners left the cooperatives, they reclaimed the right to use their land individually. After a period of five years, the state land was to be considered as the share in land for those who did not have any land in the beginning (i.e. the colonists' laborers) or as supplementary land for those who joined the cooperatives with a parcel too small to feed a family. Once the small landowners withdrew from the cooperatives, the core of state land remained the property of the members who had not withdrawn from the unit, i.e. those who joined the unit on the basis of a share in state land only.

Cooperation essentially means "work in common." It implies collaboration between the different members of the unit who live in a cooperative. But the term collaboration must be understood here in the strongest meaning of the word, i.e. that there not only is community in the place of work, as there is in an enterprise of the capitalistic type, but collaboration at all levels and in particular at the management level. These principles of participation are stressed in the legal texts which govern cooperation in Tunisia, as in all cooperative systems: the principle of voluntary membership, i.e. one should not be obliged to join a production unit; and the fundamental role of the General Assembly of the cooperative, which meets periodically to make the important decisions concerning the functioning of the cooperative and to elect its representatives, the administrators of the unit who, during their terms of office, must make sure that the decisions of the

---

Coopération on May 25, 1962: "...we absolutely must exploit each square inch of our land rationally. Individual liberty cannot justify bad exploitation and mediocre production because the most important thing is public interest. In cases of bad faith the government has the right to expropriate or even to suppress the ownership rights...."

"We prefer the intermediate solution, consisting of the creation of cooperatives, to expropriation. Thanks to the resources of modern techniques and to a rational organization, an area of 500 hectares has a much higher production yield than 100 isolated lots of five hectares each...."

"If ownership rights and individual liberty were to constitute obstacles to cooperation, and later on, to the increase of the agricultural yield, the government would have the right to expropriate. But our preference goes to cooperatives, formed by farmers of their own free will, and in which work in common is not compulsory."

General Assembly are observed and that the unit is being well managed.[6]

The choice of the cooperative unit as the unit of development corresponds to a notion underlying *néo-Destourienne* [neo-constitutionalist] thought as expressed in the speeches of Tunisian officials, particularly President Bourguiba, ever since independence, in the motions of the Party Congresses and other national organizations, and in many articles and editorials in the party newspapers. This is the notion of the necessity of the total involvement of the human being in development processes whose objectives are to promote the individual, considered as an integral part of the national collectivity. At the cooperative level, the responsibility of each one of its members is necessary inasmuch as the essential power of decision making belongs to the assembly of cooperative members. One of the fundamental themes of Destourian socialism[7] is precisely that a democracy should be as total as possible; the power of decision making must belong to as many citizens as possible. This is shown in the text published in a report of the Party titled *Les facteurs d'expansion du système coopératif en Tunisie* [Expansion factors of the cooperative system in Tunisia]:

The Tunisian type of socialism, adapted to the economic and social realities of the country, was planned to answer the needs of a constant evolution of our population; this evolution must go hand in hand with the turnover of decision-making power to the grass-roots.

...the ideal toward which we want to go is that the four million Tunisian men and women hold the power of decision making, insuring in this way that Tunisia will have a true economic, social and political democracy....

[6] See Article 33 of the Law of 63–19 of May 27, 1963: "The regular General Assembly must, after the moral and financial report of the Administrative Council and the reports by the commissioners of accounts: examine, approve or rectify the figures; give or refuse the discharge to the administrators; proceed to name the administrators and the commissioners of accounts; verify the variation of the social capital during the exercise; deliberate on any other question on the agenda."

See especially Article 13 of the statute of the northern cooperative of production (decree of August 8, 1965). "The General Assembly regularly constituted represents all the members; its decisions are binding on all, even for those absent and those who disagree. The General Assembly is constituted of all of the members.

The General Assembly has the MAXIMUM RIGHTS concerning the management of the cooperative."

[7] Up until 1964, the party in power, founded in 1934 by a schism from the Destour caused by the youth of the party, led by the president of today, Habib Bourguiba, was called the *Parti Libéral Constitutionnel* or *Néo-Destour* (*Destour* 'constitution'). The party congress which took place at Bizerte from October 19 to 23, 1964, decided to call the party, because of its policies, the *Parti Socialiste Destourien* (the term *Destourien* guaranteeing the continuity of a party that had known how to convert from a party struggling against colonialism to a party in power engaged in another struggle, against underdevelopment).

All texts on the Tunisian cooperative system, as well as on the rules of the cooperatives, emphasize the role to be played by the members of the cooperative in their own units. The booklets published to explain cooperatives to the members also elaborate this point: for example, the *Guide du coopérateur agricole* (agricultural cooperative members' guide) published by the *Union nationale de la Coopération* [National Cooperative Union] after its creation in early 1969, asks: "Who runs the cooperative?" The answer: "The responsibility for management inside the production unit belongs to each and every one of the members of the cooperative." It is also this aspect which is found in the booklet written in simple everyday words with many pictures by the *Centre d'Etudes et de Développement des Entreprises Coopératives* [Center for the Study and Development of Cooperative Enterprises] for the members belonging to the agricultural production units.

Thus we have basically a doctrine which implies an almost utopian decentralization of decision making, while the option in favor of the cooperative system corresponds to a desire for change at the level of the society and not at the individual level.

We have seen that the complete change in the agrarian system, in particular the transformation from subsistence agriculture to market-oriented agriculture, with all the technical transformation that that implies, necessitated not only a well-trained and well-informed staff but also a policy of agricultural development that is inseparable from a certain centralization of decision making.[8]

At this point in our analysis, it is important that we should ask ourselves:

1. To what degree did those who proposed and started the cooperative development in agriculture (the Party leaders as well as the cooperative and technical staff) take into consideration this contradiction at the very heart of the Tunisian cooperative system?

2. Why, in spite of all the efforts put forth at all levels to promote cooperative development, did so many misunderstandings remain, so

---

[8] When we speak of centralization of decision making, we essentially emphasize the fact that it does not belong to the cooperative; the supervisory organisms of the cooperatives, at least in the early days, were very numerous (services of the Ministry of Agriculture Regional Union of Cooperatives); from 1967, the Control Bureau of Northern Production Units; the governors and their delegates (Ben Salem 1971); so that it is correct to speak of a "dispersion of responsibilities and of decisions" (Chérel 1971); but we think that there is centralization nevertheless, inasmuch as it is, in fact, the administration and the state who make all the major decisions. Besides, in general, we have, for example, the same type of organization (agronomic or financial) in all of the production units in the north.

that after four, six, or even eight years of life inside the production units, most of the members left the units in 1969, when the law of September 29, 1969,[9] allowed the members who had come from the private sector to choose whether to remain members or to leave the unit with the land they had brought with them when they had joined.

We have seen that the need felt by the political and economic officials to maintain the large units inherited from the colonial system and to facilitate the transfer of as much land and as many people as possible from the traditional sector to the modern sector implied the formation of large aggregates of land and people.

The choice of the cooperative method corresponded to the desire not to impose such a total reversal on the peasants without making sure that they felt involved in the struggle against underdevelopment for they were to be the first to benefit from these changes. It was very important that "the farmers should feel that they were participating and not to feel that the state had organized them and in so doing had transformed them into a subproletariat." (Dumont and Mazoyer 1969:35).

However, it would have been highly unrealistic to believe that the initiative would come from the farmers who were not sufficiently trained or informed to discover by themselves a way to better their lives. The models of success that they had seen up until then were directly linked to the possession of large private estates.

It was not easy for them to visualize a betterment of their lives in the large groupings composed in the beginning of people as poor as themselves. And of course, as in all peasant milieux, there is the strong tie

---

[9]   The law of September 22, 1969, did nothing more than reaffirm the principle of voluntary membership, already stipulated in the texts of earlier laws. (See Article 2 of Law 67-4 of January 19, 1967.) According to this text it was out of the question for former cooperative members to withdraw from the cooperatives with their piece of land:

Article 8: "...the land owners ... who do not wish to join the UCPA can sell their land and their adjoining production means, to one or more cooperative members, or to the UCPA, or if their land constitutes a viable exploitation, trade it...."

Actually, in the early days the choice was left up to the farmers (included in production units in 1969) to adopt private or cooperative methods of working their land:

"As to the four million five hundred thousand hectares integrated in the cooperative system in 1969, the farmers can either stay in the cooperative or withdraw...."

All the cooperative production units constituted by decree, before the speech given on January 24, 1969, by President Bourguiba, are maintained and benefit from the government's solicitude" (Ladgham, speech in Bèjà, September 24, 1969).

But, thanks to a true movement of the people, the choice was left up to all the cooper‐ative members integrated in the production units with their land to stay in the unit or to withdraw from it. Thus, at the end of 1970 the only ones to remain in the cooperatives were the former laborers of the State Land Office.

between a farmer and his small plot of land which has been handed down to him through the generations by his family; its integration into a large area can only be conceived of as a dispossession, an alienation.

The Tunisian government, once it had adopted the unit of production as the means of development of agriculture, could have had a vast publicity campaign showing the farmers the benefits of forming groups, and then could have waited for the people to join, acting only as a spectator in this stage of the formation of units, supplying only financial and technical help. But the procedure would have taken much too much time and the work to be done seemed too urgent.[10]

The decision was to form areas according to the farms corresponding to the results of the purely technical land tenure studies. It is quite true that before the units were formed information campaigns had explained the advantages of the new structure to the farmers concerned; but if these campaigns succeeded it was only in changing the minds of those who were the most set against them, and they did not arouse any enthusiasm whatsoever.

The political and technical officials of the cooperative system knew that the transition from private farming to collective farming could not be made overnight. And it was much less important to stimulate great enthusiasm than it was to get everyone, more or less freely, to give it a try;[11] the essential educational process would take place in the unit itself.

[10]　"...a most serious problem ... is posed, i.e. the opposition existing between the two characteristics that the cooperative in an underdeveloped country must assume: it should be voluntary and quick. To be voluntary it would have to be slow and to be quick it would have to be compulsory.

But time is one of the primary considerations of the underdeveloped countries; it is most difficult for them to accept that, if the solution to their problem is the cooperative system, they would have to wait until the year 2000 before the system would really be functioning properly. The true problem is right there, because if one wants to avoid the delay by accelerating the evolution artificially, the results might be false achievements, skeletons without flesh....

On the other hand, cooperative expansion left up to the initiative of the people would be very risky also; it might drag on for generations, and remain blocked at secondary activities" (Zouaoui 1968).

It is the same problem that other countries (such as Egypt) have had in their experiment in cooperative development:

"This problem is the *dirigisme* [planning] in itself because of the desire to go as fast as possible, because it is impossible to wait until all of the population is ready, so that in the distant future it can participate in perfect cooperation.

However, one should not go too fast, because if the government substitutes for the cooperative members, if it takes over as far as to make decisions in their place, the cooperatives will not be able to form men, to form citizens" (Hashish 1967).

[11]　This is even more difficult because the integrated cooperative members were mostly elderly people; according to a poll carried out in the Governorat de Béjà, 50 percent of the members were over fifty years of age (Alouane 1970).

Of course, when the production units were being formed, and when the plans of actions to be undertaken in each group were being formulated, decisions came from outside the cooperative. But in the minds of those who started the cooperative system the role of the cooperative officials was to be truly that of the "reporters on change" (Duvignaud 1964:8), "the *agents provocateurs* of progress" (Balandier in INCIDI 1964) because as the Secretary General of the Detourian Socialist Party put it in one of the staff conferences "the units are an excellent school of democracy" (Ladgham 1969a). Of course, the cooperatives were supervised in the early stages; but in the conception of the cooperative movement, not only was this supervision to be oriented from the very beginning towards helping the farmers learn the cooperative way of life, but it was also understood from the very beginning that it was to be only temporary: the cooperative counselors were trained more to be stimulators than managers. The role they were to play in relation to the members is often compared to the one that a foreign technical assistant has in an underdeveloped country whose own technical managers are being trained. The following principles were formulated (Zouaoui 1968):

1. Plan and organize the cooperatives so that their functioning can be followed and understood by as many of the members as possible, and so that they can be run by representatives chosen by the members themselves.

2. Plan them so that the members of the committees, the administrators, and the secretaries get and/or have the training which allows them to carry out their functions competently and judiciously and to carry out their obligations honestly.

Of course in order for the supervision to gradually disappear, a major effort was made from the very beginning to make the concepts of cooperative organization and of business management available to the cooperative members, and to make them aware of the requirements of large-scale mechanized agriculture.

The education of the members, whether in meetings, in simple discussions with the officials of the cooperative system, or simply in the discovery of a new way of life in what one might call an organization, had many effects on the attitudes and behavior of the small farmers. These were manifested more on the level of comprehension and expression of individual as well as collective needs than on the participation level: the General Assemblies that we attended showed us that the discussion had little to do with technical or agronomic questions or with management problems, and even less with the bookkeeping of the enterprise.

The questions that came up most often concerned the standard of living; many social cases, more often than not of a personal nature, were brought to the attention of the Assembly.

Actually decision making, in spite of the desire expressed by those responsible, in spite of real efforts to educate the cooperative members, remains very centralized. It seems that because the desire for economic efficiency was fundamental from the beginning, the official staff, instead of progressively disappearing, has tended to remain and to claim as its own a series of prerogatives which should belong exclusively to the members.

To the first question we asked, we might answer that those who started the cooperative system were quite aware, from the very beginning, of the contradiction between their conception of a very centralized power of decision making and a cooperative system. They thought that they could overcome this, little by little, by giving the members an education and then permitting them to take over more and more responsibilities; but here we get to our second problem: there are so many misunderstandings in such a system that there is a danger that its rigor (and the centralization of decision making that this rigor implies) will persist.

Let us consider the role of the General Assemblies once more. Why is it that the texts regulating cooperatives say that they are sovereign when, in fact, their role is a very limited one? The reasons usually given (i.e. that the standard of living of the members is too low for them to have any preoccupation other than their everyday life,[12] or that their education is too rudimentary) are insufficient.[13] One must also consider the margin

---

[12] During the inquiries we carried out in 1969 in the production units in Jendouba, the advances paid to members amounted to 350 millimes (400 to 500 millimes for those who had particular skills) per workday, which was insufficient if one considers the number of days worked by each person during the year, and the number of dependents most members have. With the reduction of the size of the cooperative farms to the state core, the advances increased up to 550 millimes, which is a little over a dollar, and the division of profits became both more regular and more substantial; but one must note that the needs to be satisfied have also increased.

[13] Most of the Tunisian cooperative members are illiterate or have had very little schooling. In a study made in two cooperatives of Medjex-El Bab, Alouane found that 62 percent of the members were completely illiterate, 26 percent had had a little schooling, usually religious schooling through the *kouttab*, only 6 percent had attended a primary school and 6 percent had attended a secondary school, but all had dropped out soon after they had entered. We too, in our study of the members of the Administrative Councils of the agricultural production units of the Governorate of Jendouba, found that the majority of them (61.5 percent) had attended the *kouttab* not very frequently, where they had been given only a few notions of reading and writing; 20 percent had attended primary schools for some time; 5.4 percent had gone further than primary school; the rest were illiterate. And these were officials chosen most often

of action that remains the exclusive right of the members and their representatives. The staff of the cooperatives, trained by the technical services of the Ministry of Agriculture or by the Cooperative Unions, only carry out decisions made on the regional level or even on the national level. The directors of the production units and the agricultural instructors and the "director-agents" who later replaced them, were, and often still are, simply intermediary officials whose job is to carry out plans formulated by studies which are readjusted each year by the regional technical services of the Ministry of Agriculture and to report the maximum amount of information about the everyday life of the cooperative, taking the pulse, so to speak, of the enterprise (Ben Salem 1971).[14]

Let us take the problem of the assignment of the workdays to members as an example. Once the plan has been established and adopted, even the number of workdays is forecast with only a small margin of fluctuation. One would think that this kind of decision could be left to the judgment of the members and their representatives, the members of the Administrative Council, aided by the director of the unit (whose role changes depending on the "quality of the men") who attends the daily meetings held at the end of the day by this Council.

But if one wants to delve a bit deeper into this problem, one realizes that this question was, and had to be, the stumbling block of the discussion. It is important to note that the number of active members in almost every production unit is greater than the number that the technical study foresaw, and that this happened because the political authority, while trying to answer the human problems, added a human burden too heavy for the production unit. Besides, the number of members forecast by the technical study had been calculated on the basis of the income the unit would have once all of the potentialities of the farm were developed, and not on the basis of the availability of jobs (Chérel 1971).

If the members could have realized how having a positive budget

---

because of their ability to accomplish certain administrative formalities, rather than because they were true representatives of all of the members (Ben Salem 1971).

[14] It seems that the cooperative, the members of the Administrative Council, and the director today have a larger responsibility. The work plan, which had long been a subject of discussion at the regional level, is becoming a dialogue between the director and the Administrative Council, as is the question of borrowing for investment; the director is now the principal person responsible for stock division, for the daily organization of the farm, and for the utilization of all of the production factors. Since 1971, the director has been tied by contract to the cooperative; he is named in accord with the Administrative Council of the unit and receives a share of the profits of the enterprise. But even today, this is but an experiment which must be extended, according to the number of personnel available and the results of the experiment, to all of the production units.

balance at the end of the year would be advantageous to them, they would have established a calendar taking these factors into consideration. But when we conducted our study in 1969 very few members were able to see their budget balance; very rarely had the profits been distributed, and the director did not know how to go about explaining the notion of productivity of work and its relation to the results at the end of the year to the members. The only profits made from the unit by the members consisted in the advance payments calculated from the number of workdays spent working the cooperative's land. Thus, when at an early stage the decision to make work assignments was made by the members and their representatives, the "category wages" absorbed a large portion of the cooperative's budget. The central administration had to step in and the employment norms had to be established by the Bureau of Agricultural Studies for each farming operation; and then an annual and monthly forecast for employment was imposed on each cooperative unit of production. Thus the role of the Administrative Council and of the director consists only in establishing as close a balance as possible between the number of workdays forecast and the number of workdays really worked. When the forecast is overshot, the additional daily wages cannot be paid to the members. There are other consequences which one can easily imagine, but they are doubtless less damaging in interpersonal relations than those of the first method.

Another example is the participation of the members in the solution of the financial problems of the cooperative. According to the principles regulating cooperatives, the members are exclusively repsonsible for the financial management of the enterprise. And besides, they are the first and the only ones who have to suffer the consequences of any mistakes that might be made. But it is the Regional Union of Cooperatives and then the Local Unions which have had, ever since their creation in 1970, the role of supervising the financial management of the cooperatives. Their job was to do the bookkeeping of the units, which paid them to do so; they were to make sure, through the director of the cooperative, that the financial operations conformed with those forecast, as well as to authorize the president of the cooperative and its director to make particular purchases in the cooperative's name. They also were in charge of establishing the annual balance sheet for submission to the General Assembly. Here, also, there was a big misunderstanding inasmuch as the members assumed a responsibility that neither their training nor their knowledge prepared them for. Furthermore, the experience they could have acquired during daily discussions with the cooperative officials was limited by the small amount of training the officials themselves had

had. The director was only capable of recording the operations and of overseeing the execution of an often very detailed plan, but he did not understand the procedure of financial management of the unit well enough to be an instructor in this field. So the balance sheet at the end of the year was usually approved although the members were not able to understand even generally what was going on.[15] In most cases, there was no discussion except about general results, but the discussion collapsed when explanations were called for. The persistence of the mystery of bookkeeping suggests that it might continue forever and serve to stabilize an administration which was intended to be only temporary. Decision making and control of this fundamental area of management of the cooperative could not be turned over to members who were incapable of understanding its different aspects; but the education given to them in this field is so insufficient that it will be a very long time before they will be capable of such necessary understanding. To be complete, one must mention that in a case of a deficit in a unit, the Regional Union of Cooperatives simply would not submit the results of the enterprise to the approval of the members and would postpone convening the General Assembly.

We could add other examples but have here only considered two as symptomatic of the situation. To conclude, we shall emphasize the fact that in the example that we have just considered concerning the Tunisian experiment in an agricultural cooperative system, particularly in the northwestern part of the country that previously was dominated by large colonial enterprises, economic and social development alone was the original, basic goal. Cooperatives were considered to be the best way to achieve this goal, inasmuch as a cooperative system corresponded to the fundamental principles of the Party, which had fought for independence and was in power at that time. The partial retreat from the cooperative system corresponds to the realization that it has, in part, failed to achieve its goals. With this in view, all the effort was put into the "modernization," in both the agronomic and the management areas, of the farming enterprises thus constituted.

In spite of the realization, at all levels, of the temporary character of the management of the cooperatives by the administration and in spite of the prolonged effort of the technical and political officials in this

---

[15] "Even more so because the bookkeeping has to agree with the procedures laid down by the Secrétariat d'Etat aux Plans et Finances, a decision motivated by the establishment of a rational organization and the normalization of the administrative, financial and bookkeeping documents" (circular of the *Direction de la Coopération du SEPF* of December 13, 1964). Although these procedures are very explicit, they are rather complicated and therefore do not circulate widely (Charnoy 1966).

field,[16] the contradictions between the principles of democratic management and the control of an administration which, although belonging to
the cooperative organization, is an expression of the administrative
hierarchy, still exist in the very heart of the Tunisian cooperative system,
at least in the agricultural field. This situation persists in a cooperative
structure which, for the time being, mainly involves people who used
to work for colonists and after that, for the State Land Office. They
were in the cooperative along with small landowners who withdrew from
it while they themselves were unable to do so; as a consequence, these
people more than ever consider themselves to be laborers rather than
members of the cooperative, even though they might receive a slight
bonus at the end of the year. Their participation is no doubt becoming
greater and greater; the discussions in the Assemblies are more animated
and the members participate much more; the director is more the expression of a choice made by the members, who can always refuse to
renew the contract they made with him; but the cooperative remains
linked to the developmental policy put forth by the technical services of
the administration, which impose an identical program on all production
units in the northern part of the country.

REFERENCES

ALOUANE, YOUSSEF
    1970   "Coopération et développement." Thèse de Doctorat de 3ème cycle.
           Parix. Mimeographed manuscript.
ATTIA, HABIB
    1966   L'évolution des structures agraires en Tunisie depuis 1962. *Revue
           Tunisienne de Sciences Sociales* 7:31–58.
BEN SALEM, LILIA
    1971   L'encadrement des unités de production agricoles. *Revue Tunisienne
           de Sciences Sociales* 26:115–162.
BOURGUIBA, HABIB
    1956   Discours du 19 Octobre 1956. *L'Action*, July 10, 1970.

[16]   There were a great many information meetings and training campaigns, especially
during 1969, which were to correspond to the entrance into the cooperative system of
all of the farmers, including all of those who knew how to work their land with modern
methods and all of those who had definite information about the management and
bookkeeping of a farm. It is most probable that if this reform had been completely
carried out, the attitude of the administration would have come to change, and that
the transition from supervision (less close than stultifying) to cooperative autonomy
would have taken place; but the leadership would have no doubt changed hands,
going from the hands of the administration to those of a minority of farmers who are
up-to-date in agricultural techniques and know-how.

1962 De la coopération. Discours du 25 mai 1962. *Publication du Secrétariat d'Etat aux Affaires Culturelles et à l'Information.* Tunis.

CHARNOY, GEORGES

1966 "L'évolution du mouvement coopératif agricole en Tunisie depuis l'indépendance. "Thèse de Doctorat de 3ème cycle. Montpellier. Mimeographed manuscript.

CHÉREL, JEAN

1964, 1971 Les unités de production du nord tunisien. *Revue Tiers Monde* av. juin 1964 et av. juin 1971. 46:303–350.

DUMONT, R., M. MAZOYER

1969 *Développement et socialisme.* Paris: Editions du Seuil.

DUVIGNAUD, JEAN

1964 Le problème des cadres en pays de développement. Colloque organisé par le C.E.R.E.S. *Revue Tunisienne de Sciences Sociales* 1.

HASHISH, ADEL

1967 Aspects du mouvement coopératif en R.A.U. (Égypte). *Revue des Études Coopératives* 149:207–230.

INCIDI

1964 *Problèmes des cadres dans les pays tropicaux et subtropicaux.* Compte-rendu de la 32ème session de l'INCIDI, 1960.

LADGHAM, BAHI

1969a Discours prononcé devant la Conférence des Cadres du Sahel à Mahdia. *L'Action*, February 18, 1969.

1969b Discours prononcé à Béjà. *L'Action*, September 24, 1969.

MAKHLOUF, AZZEDDINE

1968 La modernisation de l'agriculture en Tunisie. *Revue Tunisienne de Sciences Sociales* 15:17–53.

RÉPUBLIQUE TUNISIENNE

1961–1962 Secrétariat d'État au Plan et aux Finances, Services des Enquêtes Statistiques. Structure agraire du Gouvernorat de Souk El Arba 1961–1962. Mimeographed manuscript.

1962–1971 Secrétariat d'état au Plan et aux Finances. *Perspectives Décennales de Développement.*

1967 Loi 67–4 du 19 Janvier 1967, portant statut général de la coopération. *Journal Officiel de la République Tunisienne.*

UNION NATIONALE DE LA COOPÉRATION

1969a *Guide du coopérateur agricole.*

1969b Centre d'Études et de Développement des Entreprises Coopératives. *L'unité coopérative de production agricole* (in Arabic).

ZOUAOUI, ALI

1968 "Les normes et les valeurs de l'entreprise coopérative constituent-elles un accélérateur de développement?" Conférence faite à l'occasion de la Semaine de la Coopération organisée par l'École Nationale de la Coopération. *L'Action*, June 5, 1968. Tunis.

Economic Dependency and the Failure of Cooperatives in Western Sicily

JANE SCHNEIDER and PETER SCHNEIDER

Once the breadbasket of the Roman Empire and later a principal wheat supplier to the booming cities of Renaissance Italy, western Sicily lost its hegemony in wheat in the nineteenth century. Factors in this decline were the steamship, which eased transport of bulk commodities over long distances, and the appearance of mechanically produced American wheat in European markets after the Civil War. In spite of the collapse of a market, the traditional wheat-producing large estates, or *latifundia*, continued to exist, supported by a protective tariff on wheat and by a rapidly expanding population that enlarged the domestic market. Both the tariff and population growth led also to serious pressures on the land and Sicilian peasants experienced severe displacement as landlords rushed to expand their holdings. Unemployed and underemployed, peasants formed leagues which occupied large estates and attempted to organize farm labor strikes. In the 1890's the leagues were suppressed by government troops and by mafia-type henchmen of the large landholders. Following this suppression, thousands of peasants sought relief in the American labor market. In the twentieth century, with the support of emigration remittances from abroad, western Sicilians — many who had stayed behind and some who had returned from America — were gradually able to nibble away at the domain of the large estates. In the first two decades of this century, for example, various political and politico-religious forces transformed some of the old peasant leagues into cooperative associations. Although these associations rarely purchased land, they forced large landholders to rent portions of *latifundia* directly to them, rather than to *gabellotti* — the parasitic intermediaries who rented whole estates to profit by dividing them for sublet to the peasants. Over fifty cooperatives rented some 47,000 hectares of land (Scrofani 1962:253). In the early 1920's, proto-fascist and veterans' associations supported some of these cooperatives, while others were supported by the Socialist Party. The movement was subsequently stifled by fascism. Even at its height, however, cultivation was not organized collectively. The cooperatives paid collective rents, but then allocated small plots to individual members (Scrofani 1962:253).

After World War II, a similar array of communist, socialist, and Catholic cooperatives attempted to rent or purchase portions of *latifundia* by occupying or threatening to occupy land. In the immediate postwar period with the communists in the government, the Gullo Law (after the communist minister of agriculture at that time) recognized and legitimated the occupations. It provided for the collective cultivation and marketing of crops by peasant cooperatives, but very few of the latter (around 10 percent in all of southern Italy and Sicily) took advantage of the law. The Communist Party, in fact, quickly abandoned collectivization as a goal for southern peasants (Tarrow 1967:222-24, 365). In any event, at the local level land occupations met with increasing resistance as peasants were violently suppressed by police action and by local bandits and mafiosi. In the late 1940's and early 1950's, numerous trade union and cooperative leaders, as well as left-wing politicians, were intimidated and murdered in western Sicily (Pantaleone 1962:239–246). As had occurred at the end of the nineteenth century, repression was followed by migration, but this time to northern Europe rather than North America. Again, emigration remittances paved the way for individual acquisitions of land. In other words, cash income from emigration to some degree accomplished what peasant organizations could not do — redistribute land to the peasants. Meanwhile, peasant unrest had moved the national government to institute welfaristic land reform programs in southern Italy and Sicily. These programs empowered land reform agencies to appropriate estates over 200 hectares and estates which were poorly cultivated or left to pasturage for division and assignment to peasants. At the same time, the land reform laws recognized the legitimacy of peasant cooperatives and were supposed to encourage their formation with both technical and organizational assistance.

During the land reform period of the 1950's, the number and size of *latifundia* decreased in western Sicily. Apart from holdings that were actually appropriated and redistributed to peasants, many landlords sought to circumvent the reform by donating the least arable mountainous land to the land reform agencies, or by nominally dividing the land among their heirs. Many cooperatives were formed, most of them under the direct sponsorship of the land reform program. But the cooperatives were short-lived, victims of undercapitalization and corruption. Indeed, the "land reform" transformed the cooperative into little more than a roster of members who would qualify as individuals for small allotments of land and/or other services (credit, a discount on fertilizer, etc.); but they did nothing cooperatively. Like the rental cooperatives of the 1920's, the land reform cooperatives did not organize collective production or marketing, but instead subdivided their (rented or purchased) land for allocation to individual members who combined their allotted fragments with an already disparate set of economic activities (J. Schneider 1969). But, unlike the early rental cooperatives, the reform groups had no peasant leaders. In the 1920's and immediately after the war, cooperatives were relatively independent peasant organizations, although often supported by various political parties. Now membership in a cooperative was obligatory for those who wanted land under the reform and the cooperatives were directed by land reform officials who made no real effort to form viable peasant collectives (Tarrow 1967:351). The *quid pro quo* for membership in the cooperative was loyalty to the Christian Democratic Party (or some local faction of it), for the Christian Democrats controlled the land reform agencies (Bernabei 1972). A few cooperatives attempted to organize marketing, but it was precisely in this area that clientalism and corruption took the heaviest toll. Leaders, technicians, and lawyers favored (or were accused of favoring) friendly merchants with an entire cooperative's output, on terms which were unfavorable to the members. The result was that cooperatives often ended in bankruptcy (Bernabei 1972:102).

By the 1960's, the cooperative movement had all but disappeared in western Sicily and today very few of the landholding and rental cooperatives remain. Many associations are still formed as legal cooperatives but they do not rent or purchase land, let alone promote collective production or marketing. They are formed only to exploit generous government subsidies for the purchase of agricultural machinery — tractors, farm implements, and reaping and threshing combines. The machinery is so ill-suited to the rocky, mountainous terrain and scattered small holdings of the western Sicilian interior that it is subject to frequent breakdowns and is generally inefficient. The use of such mechanical devices does offset the shortage of low-cost labor (lost to emigration), but machine technology here does nothing to increase the productivity of the land. The machines can be profitable for their owners because up to 70 percent of the purchase price is paid by the government, so membership in a "machine cooperative" (no fewer than nine persons, rarely more than twenty) is a speculative venture, attractive to artisans, merchants, and professionals, as well as peasants. Although these associations appear viable for the moment, their net effect is to perpetuate mountain wheat. At the same time, the Italian government and the EEC (European Economic Community) bolster wheat through price supports and subsidies in order to retard rural underemployment and displacement.

When we speak of the failure of cooperatives in western Sicily, we mean additionally their failure to transform agriculture from an extensively cultivated and nonexportable crop – wheat – to such labor-intensive and exportable crops as wine, wine grapes, citrus fruits, and vegetables. Many experts believe that only through such specialized agriculture can the underdeveloped west of Sicily begin to accumulate the capital it needs to spur the regional economy (Lorenzoni 1910: 105; Scrofani 1962:225). Because they are labor intensive, these crops would retard the drain of manpower to Western Europe until such time as it could be employed in local industries. It seems clear that wheat grown by a mechanized technology on the great plains of the world will forever out-distance Sicily's mountain wheat in world markets, even if this wheat is cultivated with machinery. Sicily's hard wheat was once an essential ingredient in bread and pasta. Today, however, chemical additives to soft wheat make it adequate for the purpose (although the product is inferior).

The first cooperatives, in the early twentieth century, concentrated on hard wheat as they sought to intensify its cultivation in order to reduce the cost of production. Large estates once cultivated extensively or left to pasturage were now cropped by peasants who could put more into the land, especially with the aid of emigration remittances. Equipped with mules, plows, and chemical fertilizers, and encouraged by the cooperative associations, peasants planted new strains of wheat and began to include in the rotation cycle forage crops such as fava beans and clover which added nutrients to the soil. The cooperatives, by distributing fertilizer, made these crops possible. Where land had once lain fallow for two or more years following each harvest, it was now continuously cultivated for two or three years (Lorenzoni 1910:133–45; Scrofani 1962:253–256). But the crop was still wheat. Cooperatives rarely succeeded in promoting new crops and the majority never tried. The same has been true in the period since World War II. Limited expansion of orchards or vineyards is the product of individual initiative and not in any way tied to the collective resolution of social problems. Since 1965 vineyards have spread in the coastal and lowland zones of western Sicily, but the most successful operations are owned by a few "gentlemen farmers," some of whom employ Tunisian migrant workers at harvest time. Sicilian labor continues to leave the island.

How are we to analyze the failure of cooperatives to contribute to the transformation of agriculture in Sicily? The most common answer to such a question points to the alleged poverty of Sicilian culture. Sicilians find it difficult to organize collectively for the good of the community. This is often attributed (by insiders and outsiders alike) to a culturally conditioned rivalry and lack of mutual trust, and the reluctance of west Sicilians to invest capital, time, and affect for long-term gain. While such assets are frequently pooled for specific entrepreneurial ventures, the resulting coalitions are unstable and motivated by the prospect of immediate rewards. Entrenched clientalistic structures crosscut social class boundaries, inhibiting class action, leading to corruption and a lack of faith in nominal leaders. Clientalistic structures also contribute to repression of the sort organized by bandits and mafiosi. Many believe that disputes over land boundaries, access to water and passage rights, and disputed inheritances have persistently weakened the solidarity of the cooperatives at the base; while the officers of these associations are often thought to be corrupt, incompetent, or both. In one case studied by Bernabei, members of a cooperative publicly expressed doubts about the honesty of their leaders. In their desire to avoid suspicion, the latter refused to keep written records so as to deny that they had kept false records (Bernabei 1972: 101). In other cases, leaders have been known to abscond with the cooperative's funds, all the while protected by powerful politicians. Thus, an apparent inability to form corporate organizations, a preference for short-term speculative ventures, and rampant clientalism are wedded in the minds of many to the failure of agrarian cooperatives.

We do not wish to minimize the reality of these phenomena; but we suggest that this reality, like the failure of cooperatives itself, is a dependent and not an independent variable. It only describes the way in which the cooperative movement broke down. To really account for the failure of western Sicilian peasant cooperatives, one must examine Sicily's long-standing colonial relationship to Italy and the outside world. Leaders of some of the early cooperatives in the first decade of the twentieth century realized very well that the viability of a true cooperative movement would depend on large-scale, state-run public works to overcome the disastrous effects of centuries of colonial exploitation. Throughout the present century, this theme has persisted in the public expressions of those who care, or profess to care, about the transformation of Sicilian agriculture through hydraulic works, reforestation to halt the erosion of the land and support irrigation, access roads, and (more recently) rural electrification. The failure of the state to build such an infrastructure must be understood in terms of the problems encountered by northern Italy in its own economic development. The consequence is that western Sicily has been unable to produce commodities which are capable of finding stable or expanding markets. This is why the cooperatives had to fail.

Western Sicily, like many underdeveloped regions, suffers from double jeopardy in its relationship to the outside world. It is a backward, dependent region in a dependent society. For centuries a colony or semicolony of various foreign powers, it continued in a subordinate status after the unification of Italy. After unification, the new Italian state became a gatekeeper between Sicily and the rest of the world — not in the interests of Sicily, of course, but in the interests of north Italian industrial development. As we will argue below, north Italian development itself occurred in a semicolonial context which led to several reversals of direction. These reversals were critical for Sicily. In periods when north Italian capitalists sought aid and investments from already established industrial powers such as France and England, national policy supported free trade and encouraged the production of luxury crops for export. Wheat deficits were met by imports from foreign sources which produced wheat more efficiently. In periods when protectionist interests, such as steel and textiles, controlled the national government, the reverse obtained; Italy sought self-sufficiency in wheat and assumed a hostile stance toward outside industrial powers. In so doing it provoked a collapse of the luxury crop market. The result for Sicily of Italian tariff policy was a structured inability to accumulate capital from international trade and the artificial perpetuation of a noncompetitive mode of wheat production. We will review the reversals in national trade policy in the period from unification to the present, and draw some conclusions about their effect on the cooperative movement.

PHASE I: THE LIBERAL ECONOMIC POLICIES OF CAVOUR AND THE PIEDMONTESE MODERATES

The Italian *Risorgimento* of 1860 was largely the work of moderate and elite, rather than radical and popular, social forces. Its leadership, epitomized by Cavour, came from a class of gentlemen farmers in northern Italy. These men, in Gramsci's estimation, organized a royal conquest of Italy by the northern state of Piedmont rather than a "national movement from the bottom" (1949:621). True, Piedmont was modern; it had a liberal constitution, an effective regional bureaucracy along French lines, and, most important for those days, a firm commitment to enlightened progress via free trade and competition. But it excluded from the governing coalition the nationalist and popular action party of Mazzini, as well as the thousands of south Italian peasants (Gramsci 1949:620). In other words, although Italy was unified in 1860, an Italian nation had yet to be created or — as was said at the time — Cavour and the Piedmontese moderates created Italy, but not Italians.

The decade and a half of moderate leadership which followed the *Risorgimento* ensured that Sicily and southern Italy would be agricultural, not industrial, regions of Italy, for the Piedmontese made every effort to create a national market, eliminating at a stroke all tariff barriers throughout the peninsula and islands and subjecting several hundred small industries in less-developed regions like Sicily to competing north Italian manufactures (Mack Smith 1959: 49–50; Rochefort 1961:224–226). In agriculture these less-developed regions encountered no obstacles to the expansion of "luxury" crops at the expense of pastures and wheat, but neither was this expansion encouraged. Funds for land reclamation and irrigation works were earmarked almost exclusively for the rich, alluvial plains and foothills of the Po Valley in northern Italy. Moderate policies on Sicily paid lip service to the necessity of breaking up the *latifundia* and intensifying agriculture. But their programs went no further than to nationalize and repartition ecclesiastical estates. These lands still covered about a tenth of the island's surface area (Romeo 1959:35–36), but the parcels which were sold at auction — each approximately fifty hectares — went almost exclusively to rentiers and gentry-type landowners who continued to crop them in wheat. The state, meanwhile, banked the proceeds from the sales, thus increasing the resources available for north Italian economic development (Mack Smith 1959: 87–88).

PHASE II: AN ERA OF PROTECTIONISM

Had their policies borne fruit, the moderates might have eventually won over the supporters of the Mazzinian action party. Ironically, though, north Italian growth was blocked by shortages of some key natural resource — timber and coal — and above all by the dominance of the rest of Europe. Such industrial and commercial centers as Florence, Milan, and Genoa, which in the sixteenth century had dominated much of Europe, were now far behind. Nineteenth-century Italy, relative to France and England, was a poor and still primarily agricultural country. Cavour was a liberal, an advocate of free trade, and unwilling to cut ties with the international marketplace. No doubt he realized that to do so would invite military intervention from the north. He and his advisors were Anglophiles, afraid of revolutionary France and the ghost of Robespierre. Moreover, they depended heavily upon foreign capital in the unification of Italy. Some of this capital was English; most of it came from a non-revolutionary France. French capital built the railroads which knitted the new Italy together. French financiers owned 20 percent of Italy's national debt and 80 percent of its foreign debt. French capital also contributed to a number of private enterprises in Italy (Cameron 1961: 284–302; Romeo 1959: 30).

The Moderate scheme was a compromise with development. By concentrating on agriculture it maintained the imbalance between "rich nations and poor nations." By depending upon English and French assistance, it further reinforced Italy's dependence *vis-à-vis* the North Atlantic. Most important, it left Italy vulnerable to a great depression which began in the North Atlantic in the early 1870's. This depression undermined the stability of the Moderate government in Italy. In the south and Sicily its effects were compounded by the appearance of American wheat. In the parliamentary elections of 1874 to 1876, rentiers, or *gabellotti*, and the new gentry-type landowners in the south and Sicily voted the Cavourian Moderates out of power and replaced them with a center-left government in which the heirs of Mazzini's Party of Action had a larger voice. According to Mack Smith, south Italian and Sicilian votes were decisive in this shift (1959:107). A Sicilian lawyer and nationalist, Francesco Crispi, became minister of the interior, the most powerful national position after prime minister.

Between 1876 and 1887, little happened. The Piedmontese, Depretis, managed a series of governments through a process which became known as *transformismo* — a process of cooptation in which conflicting interests were transformed through grants of patronage into more or less willing supporters of the government. No clear-cut scheme for protection or free trade characterized this phase. Both alternatives were risky but, as the government treaded water doing nothing, certain conditions deteriorated of their own accord. In particular, the price of soft wheat fell after 1880 from thirty to twenty-two *lire* per *quintale*, while the price of hard wheat, twenty-four *lire* a *quintale* in 1880, fell to thirteen *lire* in 1887 (Cipolla 1965:584). That year (1887) the Sicilian, Crispi, left the ministry of the interior to become prime minister and an articulate policy of protectionism was forged. Italy would become an industrial nation equal to France if not England. Crispi would work for north Italian heavy industrial interests whose greatest need was for political support for what they were about to do. His experience as interior minister, hence patron of prefects throughout Italy, and his homegrown roots in Sicily made him an ideal person to mobilize parliamentary majorities for iron and steel. He became, in effect, the engineer of an alliance between northern industrial and southern agrarian interests. The alliance had nothing to do with agricultural exports. Instead, its *quid pro quo* was a protective tariff on wheat which, as we shall see, reversed earlier efforts to intensify agriculture in western Sicily.

In marked contrast to Cavour, Crispi was a militant protectionist and militantly anti-French. His program became, in fact, a rallying point for all the politicians and businessmen who had resented the intervention of foreign capital during the Cavourian decade (see Cameron 1961). Under Crispi, French capital was withdrawn from Italy, although to some extent German capital replaced it. Crispi's radical conservatism, rampant nationalism, German sympathies, and the fact that he was later canonized by Italian fascists have rendered him and his era anathema to liberal historians, domestic and foreign. This in turn makes it difficult to assess the real meaning of the period. In addition to wheat, the commodities most heavily protected against foreign imports were cotton textiles, iron, and steel. The costs of protection were borne by consumers and one can question the extent to which methods of production were actually improved. In the case of wheat, north Italian, German, and other East European investors spurred a transformation of the milling process in Sicily and the south. The water-driven mills of the countryside were replaced by steam, then gas and electric-powered mills in the towns (see Ciaccio 1900: 94). The crop, however, was cultivated much as before – on large estates in rotation with pastoralism. According to the economic historian Alexander Gerschenkron, protection in general bred inefficiency and corruption. Credit was over-extended through low-interest loans to industry subsidized by government. Bank scandals were the inevitable result. Gerschenkron argues that the economy developed more rapidly in the early 1900's after a series of scandals brought down the Crispians and their tariff policy (Gerschenkron 1955). It is possible, however, that this judgment is unfair; for, given the hegemony of France in late nineteenth century Italy, the free trade alternative was not attractive either. Italy as a whole was (and still is) something of a dependency in the developed world. Furthermore, the industrial growth recorded by Gerschenkron for the first decade or so of the twentieth century might very well have been a consequence of the preceding, protectionist era. We need to know more about the relationship between the two phases.

At any event, the Crispian era, and therefore industrial development in northern Italy, was an unequivocal disaster for the latifundist regions of the south and Sicily. Protectionism necessitated abrogation of a commercial treaty with France which, in 1887, provoked a trade war. The French not only withdrew capital from Italy but also closed their markets to Italian imports. This was a severe blow to the wine and citrus fruit industries so recently built up in the south. Many growers and financiers, most of modest means, went bankrupt. French capitalists meanwhile restocked French vineyards, earlier destroyed by the phylloxera epidemic, with a plant developed in California and invested heavily in Algerian vineyards as well. The phylloxera then came to Italy to deal a final and virtually unresisted blow to wine production there. Between 1833 and 1880 to 1885, the area of land in vineyards had doubled in Sicily, largely as a consequence of changes in land tenure and the pull of French demand. Between 1885 and 1903, almost all the gain was lost as hectares in vineyards declined from over 320,000 to 176,000. In the same period the extension in grain increased from 663,000 to almost 800,000 hectares — a gain of about 20 percent (Scrofani 1962:235). Fruit and vegetable growers, while less severely hit, were unable to mobilize the capital necessary to improve irrigation and remain competitive with California producers. Citrus orchards did not disappear in Sicily and in fact expanded again after 1900; but the island, and especially its western region, failed to become the major producer it might have been.

PHASE III. THE DRAMA REPEATED — "LEARN FOREIGN TONGUES..."

We have explained in such detail the shift in orientation *vis-à-vis* Europe which dominated Italian politics of the late nineteenth century in order to demonstrate a fundamental lack of autonomy in both Sicily and Italy. Important changes in Sicilian agriculture were more or less dictated by changes in national policy, which in turn reflected the difficult position of northern Italian industry. The same problems reappeared in the twentieth century. For much of the decade and a half which preceded World War I, Italy prospered under Giolitti. Industries other than steel and textiles also came to the fore and helped to define the national interest. The Giolittian government liberalized trade with France and England and, once again, Italy and Sicily found export markets for their luxury crops. Meanwhile, the protective tariff on wheat was reduced. By and large, however, the industries lagged behind their counterparts elsewhere. Not only did they fail to find export markets, but they were also vulnerable to foreign competition at home. Their market losses were reflected in the relationship between labor and capital. The Giolittian years in Italy were thus marked by an increasingly severe struggle between nascent trade unions and the owning classes which culminated in the "red week" of factory occupations at the close of World War I.

In other words, a restored economic liberalism had no more resolved Italy's crisis of underdevelopment than had the program of the Cavourian moderates. Unemployment was severe and in danger of becoming more so in the north, while south Italians were migrating by the hundreds of thousands to America's labor markets. Italy's industries could not absorb these displaced rural masses, and labor-intensive vineyards and orchards south of Rome could not expand fast enough to make a difference. Deprived of investment capital by the preceding Crispian phase, and by government disinterest, their growth was halting. In many parts of western Sicily, the reduced tariff on wheat simply led landowners and rentiers to put more land in pasturage, which required very little labor (Lorenzoni 1910:128-132; Morici 1940: 11). As northern industrial workers occupied factories in the aftermath of World War I, southern peasants, organized in cooperatives and bolstered by emigration remittances, occupied land. Their natural target was the vast *latifundia*, cultivated extensively in wheat in rotation with pastoralism, or perhaps not cultivated at all.

The movements toward the occupation of land were not revolutionary, perhaps because, as Gramsci insisted, revolution required an alliance of northern industrial and southern agrarian masses. Except in the north, land occupations were detached from the mainstream of left-wing radicalism in Italy. In the south they aimed at an expansion of peasant small holdings. The consequences for northern Italy are well known. In its moment of failure, the northern labor movement lay wide open and vulnerable to the angry repression of all who had suffered from it – that is, factory owners and ordinary citizens who felt themselves victims, or potential victims, of labor's claim to scarce resources. By mobilizing these repressive elements, a new elite consolidated the base for fascism.

Italian fascists brought Italy back to protectionism. Like Crispi, only with more support, they assumed a hostile stance toward the outside world, especially France and England. The government favored heavy industries such as iron and steel and attempted to acquire colonial territory in Africa (as had Crispi). It cut off domestic as well as foreign emigration as it sought to build up the Italian population and labor force. Most important, it declared that Italy would be self-sufficient in wheat.

An essential cornerstone of fascist development was this self-sufficiency. Again, southern Italy and Sicily were encouraged — forced, in fact — to reestablish their ancient specialization in cereals. And again, they were given little opportunity to accumulate capital from foreign trade. When Italy was open to the outside world, as under Cavour and Giolitti, it imported wheat and exported wine, fruits, olives, vegetables, and raw silk. When it became committed to development from within, as under Crispi and the fascists, these export crops were sacrificed to wheat. The latifundist technology was subsidized, but little was done by way of transforming that technology. Only lip service was paid to land reform, reforestation, and public works projects. Protective tariffs and state subsidies encouraged the *latifondisti* to bring marginal lands into production, but both animal husbandry and the cultivation of export crops suffered in the process (Mack Smith 1968: 516–518).

So postwar western Sicily was, if anything, overspecialized in the inefficient production of hard wheat, a product which lost still more in world markets as chemists of the more advanced countries developed additives that would make the cheaper soft wheat sufficiently malleable for bread and pasta production. Sicilian citrus fruit growers could not meet the competition of Spain and Israel, and other exportable agricultural commodities were at a similar disadvantage (Mack Smith 1968: 517–518). Italy was no longer pursuing a policy of autonomy and protectionism, but the southern cultivators were in no position to take advantage of the new opportunities for foreign trade. At the end of World War II, when Premier DeGasperi was asked, "What can the unemployed peasants of the south do?" he is said to have responded, "Learn foreign tongues."

PHASE IV: THE POSTWAR PERIOD: LIBERALISM RESTORED

Postwar Italy entered the sphere of influence of its former enemies, especially the United States. This helped to restore to prominence those industrial interests favorable to free trade, and those policies which would make Italy a "vital if junior component" in the Western imperialist system (Salvati 1973:3). Much as in the Giolittian era, Italy's new-found harmony with the West was reflected in an economic boom. As in that era too, the boom spent itself rather quickly without appreciably altering either the employment picture or the long-range growth potential. By 1963 it was over; and since that time, labor unrest and inflation have mounted throughout the peninsula, while thousands of migrants have poured from the south into Common Market countries such as Switzerland, France, and West Germany. Migration from southern to northern Italy, while significant in the immediate postwar period, was always equalled or surpassed by rates of migration outside of the country, which increased proportionately as time went on (Renda 1963:139).

In the "boom years" between the late 1940's and early 1960's, a Christian Democratic government established the *Cassa per il Mezzogiorno* [Fund for the South], a variety of agrarian reform programs, and a special "reparations fund" for Sicily. The primary purpose of all of these was to defuse tensions generated by capital-intensive industrial growth. Although they redistributed land, the programs only subsidized but did not transform the antiquated agrarian production. A form of welfaristic investment, they appear increasingly parasitic as today the economy continues to sag under the weight of inflation (Franklin 1969: 174).

It is not inconceivable that Italy will again rearrange her foreign policy in yet another shift from free trade to protectionism. Challenges to the center-left (now the centrist) governing coalition have grown in frequency and seriousness since the late sixties and few observers feel sanguine about the chances of a liberal regime to surmount increased unemployment and intensified class struggle. It is in this climate of uncertainty that agrarian reform in the future must be viewed.

SUMMARY

No cooperatives, however left-wing their leadership and ideology, have sought to collectivize the land in western Sicily. The great majority of cooperatives today were formed not to own, rent, or cultivate land collectively but simply to purchase agricultural machinery with government subsidies available to legal "cooperatives." Cooperatives have, in general, supported the cultivation of wheat to the exclusion of other potentially more profitable commodities, encouraged in this by government price supports and subsidies. The cooperatives have made virtually no contribution to the transformation of agriculture. In western Sicily the occasional large holdings which are irrigated and intensively cultivated to produce luxury crops efficiently are for the most part owned and operated by wealthy individual entrepreneurs. A great many cooperatives have followed the tradition set by their predecessors of going bankrupt. Indeed many west Sicilians assume that cooperative attempts will fail. They are prone to blame this failure on the duplicity of cooperative officers and the inability of the rank and file members to trust each other and sacrifice short-term individual gains for the long-term collective benefit. We have argued that this analysis is not incorrect, but incomplete. We suggest that impossible situations select for and magnify so-called characterological defects which have accompanied the failure of the west Sicilian cooperative movement; but the cooperatives had to fail, because no amount of internal rationalization and reorganization could have provided them with the infrastructure necessary to develop crops for which there would be reliable, and long-range, markets. Such an infrastructure depended upon a level of state intervention which the Italian state, with its own uncertain and shifting relationship to international capitalist markets, has been unprepared to make.

REFERENCES

BERNABEI, LYNNE ANN
  1972   "Why are peasants so unorganized?" Unpublished thesis, Radcliffe College, Cambridge, Massachusetts.
CAMERON, RONDO E.
  1961   *France and the economic development of Europe*. Princeton: Princeton University Press.
CIACCIO, CAN. MARIO
  1900   *Sciacca: notizie storiche e documenti*, volume one. Sciacca: Tipografia Bodoniana.
CIPOLLA, CARLO M.
  1965   "Four centuries of Italian demographic development," in *Population in history*. Edited by D. V. Glass and D. E. C. Eversley, 570–587. London: Edward Arnold.
FRANKLIN, S. H.
  1969   *The European peasantry*. London: Methuen.
GERSCHENKRON, ALEXANDER
  1955   Notes on the rate of industrial growth in Italy, 1881–1913. *Journal of Economic History* 25:360–376.
GRAMSCI, ANTONIO
  1949   *Il risorgimento*. Turin: Einaudi.
LORENZONI, G.
  1910   *Inchiesta parlamentare sulle condizioni dei contadini nelle provincie meridionali e nella Sicilia*, volume six: *Sicilia*. Rome: Giovanni Bertero.
MACK SMITH, DENIS
  1959   *Italy: a modern history*. Ann Arbor: University of Michigan Press.
  1968   *A history of Sicily: modern Sicily after 1713*. London: Chatto and Windus.
MORICI, FRANCESCO
  1940   *Aspette e risultati technicieconomici di imprese pastorali siciliane*. INEA Studie Monografie (Serie Prima) 2.

PANTALEONE, MICHELE
   1962   *Mafia e politica.* Turin: Einaudi.
RENDA, FRANCESCO
   1963   *L'emigrazione in Sicilia.* Palermo: Sicilia al Laboro.
ROCHEFORT, RENÉE
   1961   *Le travail en Sicile: étude de géographie sociale.* Paris: Presses Universitaires de France.
ROMEO, ROSARIO
   1959   *Risorgimento e capitalismo.* Bari: Laterza.
SALVATI, MICHELE
   1973   Impasse for Italian capitalism. *New Left Review* 76:3–33.
SCHNEIDER, JANE
   1969   Family patrimonies and economic behavior in western Sicily. *Anthropological Quarterly* 42:109–130.
SCROFANI, SERAFINO
   1962   *Sicilia: utilizzazione del suolo.* Palermo: E.S.A.
TARROW, SIDNEY G.
   1967   *Peasant communism in southern Italy.* New Haven: Yale University Press.

Movements, Ideology, and Cooperatives

The Strategy of Peasant Mobilization: Some Cases from Latin America and Southeast Asia

GERRIT HUIZER

INTRODUCTION

It is surprising that among development workers, as well as scholars concerned with rural societies, the image of peasants as apathetic, fatalistic, and "resistant to change" continues to prevail. This is in spite of the fact that during the last few decades the peasants in several countries have participated actively in such revolutionary or liberation struggles of worldwide import as the Russian and Chinese revolutions and the anticolonial wars in Algeria and Indochina (Wolf 1969).

Even politically aware persons of Marxist orientation in many countries seem — in spite of the obvious — to be hesitant or reluctant to see in an effort to patiently organize and mobilize the peasant masses a means of gaining power and transforming their society.[1] Up to the end of the last century, however, practically all peasant rebellions failed dismally, and proof that peasants can be organized effectively for radical social transformation is, historically, relatively recent.

In practically all cases, the growth of such peasant movements was a reaction to the introduction or extension of some form of colonialism. The large majority of rural dwellers came to be economically exploited by a relatively small elite, either local or foreign, generally concentrated in the cities or the smaller provincial capitals. In Latin America, the Spanish conquerors established the system of *haciendas* [large estates] from the sixteenth century onward. Lands which were formerly mainly

---

[1] Probably this is partly due to the doubts expressed by Marx about the revolutionary potential, based on experience with small landholding peasants supporting Louis Bonaparte in France in 1848.

communal property of *comunidades* [indigenous communities] were taken away and given to the members of the colonial elite. After the liberation from Spain at the beginning of the nineteenth century, this process of usurpation of indigenous community land was accelerated. While under Spanish colonial rule there was some protection of the remaining *comunidades*, in the second half of the nineteenth century the new elites, descendants of the colonial rulers, introduced private property as the only possible system of landholding that enabled them to take over community lands in an aggressive way.

Protest movements against these activities by the Indian population were bloodily repressed, but resistance flared up time and again. Some movements became so well organized and widespread that they had nationwide impact and brought the land-reform issue — redistribution of large estates — strongly to the fore. Among such movements were the unsuccesful revolt by Zarate Willka and a great part of the Bolivian peasantry in 1899 and the peasant guerillas led by Emiliano Zapata in Mexico (1910–1919), which will be described below.

In most rural areas in Latin America, where peasants vainly tried to defend their traditional rights and possessions, a permanent state of potential violence resulted. The anthropologist Holmberg, who studied a typical area in Peru, called this situation the "culture of repression." It appears that the peasants' proverbial apathy, laziness, and unwillingness to change is not an inherent characteristic, but clearly a result of the "culture of repression" under which they live. Whenever there is a real chance to alter fundamentally the repressive conditions imposed upon them, they will do so with all the energy they have.

When speaking of repression, it should be noted that in several Asian countries the contrast between wealthy landlords and peasants is much less obvious than in Latin America. Except for the Philippines, in most of Asia there are few typically large landholders, but there are many small landlords who may own plots of five to twenty hectares and let that land be cultivated by a considerable number of tenants or sharecroppers. Furthermore, there is a large number of middle-income farmers who work part of their plots (a few hectares mostly) and lease the rest to tenants or sharecroppers. In addition to the large percentage of small owner-farmers, there are in most Southeast Asian countries many peasants whose plot is too small to maintain their families, and who, for that reason, either have to rent additional land from others or work part-time as agricultural laborers. Then there are those tenants who own no land at all but have a certain security through rented land. At the bottom of the hierarchy are the landless agricultural laborers.

Looking at the prevailing rural social structure in Asia from the bottom up reveals that it is not too different from that in Latin America: being exploited by a large, wealthy landowner or by a rich or middle-income farmer is basically the same. Sometimes exploitation by small landowners is worse than by mighty and powerful ones. This makes it understandable that peasant rebellion has been as endemic — at times — in Asia as it has in Latin America.

The most striking precondition for the occurrence of peasant movements is the change in the rural status quo in ways that create acute frustration among the peasantry. The development of peasant organizations has, without exception, been a reaction to inequalities, either in land tenure or the social structure, and particularly to the growth of such inequalities. It was generally a deterioration of a more or less stable, not too unbearable situation for the peasants that initiated some kind of protest movement — either spontaneous and violent, or well organized and channeled.

In both continents certain, generally economic, developments have taken place within the traditional system which have undermined its stability and brought some awareness of the need for change to the peasants. In many instances, landlords have themselves broken the status quo by altering the prevailing system. They have tried to extend their estates or plots at the expense of small landholders, and they have tried to evict tenants in order to start cultivating new cash crops for expanding world markets — actions that introduced or extended the plantation system in some countries.

Particularly if such changes were brought about in a rapid way and without consideration for the rights (traditonal or legal) of the peasants involved, the need for protest and revolt could easily arise. Several of the peasant revolts that took place in Bantam, Java, in the nineteenth century, and the communist-led rebellion in Sumatra in 1926, were directly related to such changes — changes introduced by the elite. In the Philippines, peasants had experienced deteriorating living conditions, particularly after the Spanish colonial regime was replaced by the American system following a largely agrarian revolt in 1898. Not only did the American regime maintain the *caciques* [local landlords and chiefs], but the spread of democratic ideals and, subsequently, some degree of education, made the peasants recognize that their living conditions were intolerable. The introduction of commercial plantation agriculture, particularly in central Luzon (Pampanga and Nueva Ecija), was accompanied by a concentration of land into increasingly larger holdings. Rents went up from 38 to 60 percent between 1903 and 1946. Land grabbing by large owners from adjacent small owners added to the discontent and led to protest movements in several areas, such as the Colorum movement in 1923 in Mindanao; the Tangulan movement in 1931 in central Luzon; and the Sakdal movement in 1935. The latter became a political organization which was dispersed after a violent uprising.

In order to gain a deeper insight into the conditions under which peasant organizations arise, develop, and, in some cases, become more or less effective revolutionary movements, a number of concrete examples in various parts of the world must be described and analyzed. Some outstanding peasant movements, which caused more or less radical changes in the areas where they took place, were the peasant-guerrilla movement headed by Emiliano Zapata in the state of Morelos in Mexico (1910–1919); the peasant syndicates in the area of Ucureña, Cochabamba Valley, Bolivia (1936–1953); the peasant federation headed by Hugo Blanco in the Convención Valley, Peru (1955–1963); the peasant leagues headed by Juliao in northeastern Brazil (1955–1969); the Huk movement in central Luzon, Philippines, headed by Luis Taruc (1938–1952); the tenant unions in Japan (1919–1938); and the Indonesian Peasant Front (*Barisan Tani Indonesia*, BTI), which developed in Java between 1953 and 1956. Because they are less well known, the three movements in Asia will be described in more detail than the Latin American ones.[2]

THE PEASANT GUERRILLAS IN MEXICO (1910–1919)

In the Mexican Revolution, which started in 1910, the peasantry played a crucial role. This should be seen as a reaction to the usurpations of communal lands by large *haciendas*. This took place in the second half of the nineteenth century. Many indigenous communities tried in vain to retain or recover the communal lands from which they had been displaced under new legislation favorable to private property. The *haciendas* had expanded considerably, at the expense of the communities. As a result, in 1910 the peasantry was ready to answer the call to armed revolution.

One of the most outstanding peasant leaders was Emiliano Zapata, the son of a small farmer who had lost his land because of despoliation by the local *hacienda*. It has been said that Emiliano Zapata, when still a child, tried to console his weeping father, saying: "I will take it back when I grow up." At the age of thirty he was elected president of the com-

---

[2]   For ample descriptions of peasant movements in Latin America, see Huizer 1972a; Landsberger 1969; and Stavenhagen 1970.

mittee of his village, Anenequilco in the State of Morelos, which was attempting recovery of the lost lands. This took place shortly after Zapata had returned from a period of forced military service and work with a *hacendado* in Mexico, work imposed on him as a kind of punishment for his rebellious attitude. During this period, Zapata gained experience and insight that served him later as a peasant leader.

Because of his able leadership, three other villages with similar problems formed a committee. These villages, led by Zapata, hired a lawyer to defend their rights in the court against the claims of the large *haciendas*. After legal means proved ineffective, the peasants took the law into their own hands and joined the revolutionary guerrilla movement begun in 1910.

The insurrection was supported in the hope that the revolutionary forces, once they were in power, would do justice to the peasant cause as had been promised. But when the new president gave only lip service to the agrarian reform question, Zapata formulated his own *Plan de Ayala* in November 1911. This plan demanded radical land-reform measures. In accordance with this program, Zapata distributed land to the peasants in the areas that fell under the control of his guerrilla troops. In 1915, President Carranza, to weaken the cause of the peasant guerrilla forces that practically controlled Mexico City, published a decree (January 6, 1915) incorporating the main points of Zapata's program. This is generally considered to be the formal starting point of the Mexican land-reform movement. No effective execution was given to the new decree, so the guerrilla groups led by Zapata withdrew from the capital but kept military control of large areas in and around the state of Morelos. In those regions, a land distribution program was executed. Help was given by a group of agricultural engineering students from the National Agricultural University.

Thanks partly to this continuous organized peasant pressure in various parts of the country, the ideas of the *Plan de Ayala* were integrated into the Mexican Constitution (Article 27) in 1917. In spite of this official acceptance, however, effective distribution of lands took place only in those areas where the peasants were well organized or armed. Arms were needed because the opposition of the landlords to agrarian reform took violent forms. The landowners in many areas formed the so-called "white guards," bands of gunmen who defended the landowners' interests. They did this by intimidating or terrorizing the peasants who had organized the agrarian committees to petition for land. In the meantime, Zapata resisted many attempts to frighten or to bribe him. In 1919, he was assassinated by a man who had pretended to be his ally, but who was actually in league with the government and the landlords.

BOLIVIA: THE PEASANT SYNDICATES IN COCHABAMBA

In Bolivia, scattered peasant revolts had occurred as a reaction to the abuses of the prevailing system of servitude. The Chaco War against Paraguay (1933–1935) accelerated the disintegration of the traditional system. Thousands of Indian soldiers for the first time left the *haciendas* and entered the outside world. Bolivia's defeat left many frustrations and much political bitterness.

In the aftermath of the war, peasant unrest increased in many areas of Bolivia. In 1936, a rural syndicate was formed in Ucureña, in the temper‑ ate, fertile Cochabamba Valley, one of the most prosperous agricultural regions in Bolivia. In this area, the Santa Clara monastery had leased some of its land to large local landholders, and the lease included the right to the labor of the resident peasants. The peasants, in turn, decided to organize a union to rent the land themselves from the Santa Clara monastery and thus avoid the onerous obligation of working for the landholders. Their efforts met with strong opposition from various local landowners who saw in them a direct threat to their traditional rule. It was ultimately the landholders who bought the land from the monastery and evicted the peasant families who had been living and working there for years, destroying their homes and forcing them to leave the area or to revert to serfdom. A young radical peasant leader, José Rojas, whose father had been dispossessed in this fashion, had to escape to Argentina, where he worked as a laborer and acquired a political education. He re‑ turned secretly to Bolivia a few years later and became the undisputed leader of the revived peasant movement in Ucureña.

In the 1952 revolution, a middle-class government, which depended partly on peasant support, came to power in Bolivia. This government, headed by Paz Estenssoro, had to speed up the promulgation of radical land-reform legislation when the peasant syndicates in the Cochabamba area, headed by José Rojas, began taking over the estates by force and creating a movement that threatened to spread all over the country.

In the years following the revolution of 1952 and the radical peasant actions of that period, most of the large estates in Bolivia were taken over by the peasant syndicates in a legal, orderly way as part of the official land-reform program. The peasants took or received arms to defend the new situation against the landed elites' efforts to turn the clock back. The fact that the majority of the Bolivian peasants now work their own land and that the *hacienda* system has been abolished explains why movements, such as the one created by Ernesto Guevara, found little response among the Bolivian peasantry.

PERU: THE PEASANT FEDERATION OF *LA CONVENCIÓN*

In Peru, one of the most important peasant organizations was the federation of peasant unions headed by Hugo Blanco in the Convención Valley in the Cuzco area. The *arrendires* [peasants of the valley] had to render services and a certain number of days of unpaid agricultural work for the landlord in return for a plot of virgin land. When the virgin land was cleared and started to give the *arrendires* a reasonable yield, the landlords increased their demands. The local federation of unions of *arrendires* and their *allegados* (subtenants) was soon strong enough to respond to the challenge of the landlords. The intransigence, and at times abusiveness, of the latter made it easy for radical leadership to propagate, through the federation, action in favor of land reform.

The most effective method was the strike, consisting of a refusal by the *arrendires* to do any work for the landowners while continuing to cultivate their own plots. Their idea was that they had paid for their plots during the years they had worked without pay for the landowners. The peasants also organized local self-defense groups in order to be able to prevent the landowners or the police force (generally known to work with the landowners) from dislodging them from the plots they were working. Various acts of violence from both sides occurred. When the movement became so strong that many landowners left the area, the government promulgated a land-reform decree (Decree Number 14444 of March 28, 1963). This decree was especially designed to bring the conflict in the area to an end. The producers' cooperatives which were later formed in the area, with the assistance of the land-reform agency, appeared to enjoy a good start because of the organizing experience obtained by the peasants in the unions of the prereform period.

BRAZIL: THE PEASANT LEAGUES OF THE NORTHEAST

In Brazil, the *Ligas Camponesas* [Peasant Leagues] were created in the northeast from 1955 on. This movement was started by local peasants in the Galileia estate. They formed an association to raise money to enable them to buy from the landlord the estate on which they worked. This was considered undesirable and the landlord tried to throw the peasants off the land. They called upon a lawyer, Francisco Juliao, who sympathized with them and was willing to defend them in the courts.

It was Juliao's idea to extend this local initiative to the state of Pernambuco and the whole northeast of Brazil. The Peasant Leagues were thus created. Once the movement had gained strength and become more radical, as a reaction to the opposition of the landlords, other groups were created. Some were established by the Church to counterbalance the influence of the leagues. The peasants of the area — both the leagues and other groups — became increasingly convinced of the need for radical reform. A program of *concientizaçao* [making people aware of their needs] by encouraging them in literacy, a method used by Paolo Freire, helped in this. It was probably the growing strength of the whole movement, in which the leagues, the Church, and other groups participated, that caused such fear among the ruling class that the army intervened and organized the *coup d'état* of April 1964. After that the leagues, as well as the other groups, were repressed.

PHILIPPINES: THE HUK MOVEMENT

In one of the most troubled agricultural regions of central Luzon, Pampanga, not far from Manila, the foundations for the Huk movement were laid by Pedro Abad Santos, a Socialist Party leader and lawyer who was also a wealthy landlord in the area. In 1930, he created *Aguman Ding Maldong Talapagobra* (AMT) [The League of the Poor Laborers], which gained strength in the Pampanga area by organizing strikes and protest demonstrations. One of the important collaborators, who helped Abad Santos to spread his movement, was Luis Taruc, son of a peasant who had had some education. Such collaborators visited the villages, organized meetings, and explained the purpose of the organization. Taruc (1953: 37–38) described his own trial-and-error approach as follows:

... I first sounded out the people about their problems and grievances, and then spoke to them in their own terms. Instead of carrying out a frontal assault on the ramparts of capital, I attacked a case of usury here, an eviction there, the low crop rate elsewhere. These were things which our organization could fight, and around which the people could win small, but enormously encouraging victories.

I had to prove to the people that our organization and its leaders were of them and close to them. I sat down with them in their homes, shared their simple food, helped with the household chores. I walked in the mud with them, helped them catch fish, crabs and shell fish, worked with them in the fields. It was not hard for me, nor was it new to me. I was merely rejoining my own people. In their turn, the people would go out of their way to feed and to accommodate the AMT leader.

Within three months I had organized my whole area.

The peasant organizations generally used nonviolent methods — demonstrations, sit-down strikes — to let everyone be arrested and go together to jail. Dramatic stage presentations and similar cultural activities were used to teach the peasants about the labor struggle and to turn the strikes into public manifestations. By 1938, the AMT had 70,000 members who participated to some extent in the organization (Taruc 1953: 38–45).

In 1938, the AMT joined with the illegally existing communist peasant movement, KPMP. As a reaction to the Japanese occupation, the combined peasant organizations created on March 29, 1942, the Hukbalahap (*Hukbo ng Bayan Laban sa Hapon*) [Peoples' Army against the Japanese]. The aims of the Hukbalahap movement were expulsion of the Japanese, cooperation with the allied armies, apprehension and punishment of traitors and collaborators with the Japanese, complete independence for the Philippines, and the establishment of a democratic government with land reform, national industrialization, and guarantees for a minimum standard of living.

From 1942, when the armed struggle against the Japanese was initiated, many peasants carried arms and formed squadrons of approximately a hundred men each. The armed units operated in the areas around the homes of their members.

The Huk movement rallied many people and became so strong that it controlled whole areas of central Luzon where the Japanese could not enter. In those areas, *de facto* political control and local government was in the hands of the resistance forces which had their base in the peasantry. The property of many collaborationist landlords was taken over by the Huks, in areas controlled by them, and harvests were no longer handed over. Landlords who supported the Huk movement could remain on their land, but had to be content with a fixed rent. In some provinces, Huk leaders were elected as governors in December 1944.

Although the efforts of the Huks considerably facilitated the American Army's liberation of the Philippines, relations between the Huks and the Americans were never good. There was fear that the Huks would radically change the social order in the Phiippines if they got the chance.

A popular front formed between Huks and other groups could not win the 1946 presidential elections, but elected representatives were not even allowed to occupy their seats in the National Chamber. The new president, Roxas, a protégé of the United States Army, started a campaign to persecute the Huks. This was done so cruelly that in many areas, as a reaction to the repression, the Huks won increasing support from the peasant population and gained effective control of large parts of central Luzon. When this became threatening, a new policy, with the advice of United States' technicians, was initiated by the Magsaysay government, i.e.

to win over the peasants by reformist measures while using military force in a sophisticated way. It was particularly through inner divisions that the Huk movement finally became so weakened that the government campaign became more or less succesful. Luis Taruc surrendered and was imprisoned in 1954. Constant flare-ups of Huk or related movements have, however, continued until the present time.

JAPAN: THE TENANT-UNIONS BETWEEN TWO WORLD WARS

In Japan the first World War brought about many changes, mainly favorable to the landlords. Land prices went up and landowners had many opportunities for profitable speculation, while small farmers lost their lands through indebtedness, partly as a result of inflationary tendencies. Absentee landlordism increased, and tenant farmers were forced to pay higher rents in kind. This reached such extremes that tenants had insufficient rice for their own survival. The result was the last and largest spontaneous peasant revolt, the Rice Riots of 1918, that spread to more than thirty prefectures and lasted forty-two days.

On the other hand, rapidly increasing industrialization during these years gave greater employment opportunities, causing an influx of the rural population to industrial areas. The bargaining position of urban labor and of the peasantry improved somewhat through the formation of labor unions and the occurrence of strikes. Thus, one effect of industrialization was an improvement in the tenants' bargaining position. Because of the relative labor shortage, they were able to threaten the landlords with noncultivation of the land if they did not get a reduction in rent.

The influence of people who had worked in industry was strongly felt after the war when industry passed through a severe crisis. Many workers were dismissed and returned to their already overcrowded villages. Tension increased rapidly because the backward conditions in which tenants generally lived were more acutely felt by those who returned. The organizing experience they had gained in industry was soon applied to bargaining for better conditions.

The first formally organized tenant unions grew up in the areas around the new industrial centers, particularly Nagoya. The first local tenant organizations were reported around 1916 in the prefectures of Aichi, Gifu, and Mie, soon to be followed by those of Osaka, Hyogo, and Okayama, and a few years later in several prefectures of Kyushu, where there were many former industrial workers from the city of Fukuoka

(Totten 1960: 194; 204; Dore 1959: 69).[3] Local unions grew more or less spontaneously around rent disputes, and generally at the *buraku* [hamlet] level. Workers who had been dismissed because of union activities and who had to return to their villages were particularly influential in these activities. Several of them became effective peasant organization leaders.

The need for an organization at the national and prefectural levels was increasingly felt, but did not materialize until 1922. The increasing acceptance of Christian, democratic, and socialist ideas by Japanese intellectuals and the spread of these ideas in many circles helped to prepare the ground. Thus a group of intellectuals, pressmen, a missionary, and a labor leader took the initiative in creating the *Nihon Nomin Kumiai* (abbreviated: *Nichinō*) [Japanese Peasant Union].

By 1926 the *Nichinō* claimed a dues-paying membership of about 68,000 peasants. Its principal aim was still to reduce rents, but it also had such political aims as legislation protecting the tenants and the rather vague objective of "socialization of the land." After universal suffrage was introduced in Japan in 1925 and the number of voters rose from three million to fourteen million, *Nichinō* became politically more influential. *Nichinō* leaders circulated a request to the twenty-eight labor federations, with more than 1,000 members, to unite in a Workers' and Peasants' Party. Increasing involvement in political and ideological issues caused many consecutive splits and mergers among peasant organizations and political parties, difficult to unravel. One divisive point was whether to include all peasants and small landowners, or only tenants. Another was between those who saw the tenants' struggle against the landlords as a class struggle directed at overall social change and those who were more in favor of compromise and the achievement of concrete benefits.

It was observed that:

These differences were primarily differences between leaders. Which national organization any particular local tenant union was federated with depended more on personal connections with particular leaders than on ideological attachment to one doctrine rather than another. And, indeed, in their practical activities the various federations differed little from each other. Their chief function was to assist tenants engaged in disputes, to encourage the formation of local tenant unions in districts hitherto unorganized, and to direct and coordinate the formulation of tenants' demands (Dore 1959: 77).

Whatever occurred at the national level, the main function of tenant unions was at the local level, in rent disputes with landlords. Many of these disputes had been taken up by *buraku* unions before the national

[3] Information supplied by K. Aoki, a former peasant organization leader (see Huizer 1971).

organization existed, but the struggle at the local level was made more effective through the national union and its officials.

In the campaign to spread the movement, those *buraku*s were chosen in which the most severe and acute problems existed. Great obstacles had to be overcome. Very large landowners were helped by police repression; smaller landowners used their traditional paternalistic control to exert pressure on tenants against joining a union. Kin relationships, refreshments, favors, and threats to force people to pay their debts were also brought to bear. These obstacles could only be overcome by the immediate organization of a union. In the *buraku*s, *org* [potential activists] had to be sought, and a meeting organized with their help. Once a meeting was held, it was essential to continue it until a union had been effectively created by the election of a president, vice-president, and treasurer, and the payment of dues. Some such meetings lasted a day and a night, or even two days.

As peasant unions spread throughout the country and became better organized, the character of their demands changed. Initially, demands were mostly for postponement or reduction of rent payments in cases of a bad harvest and an emergency; later, demands for a permanent rent reduction of 30 percent were increasingly heard.

Landlords more often tried to evict peasants when they began to organize unions. The fact that more and more disputes were brought to the courts (rather than solved through negotiation), which generally ruled in favor of the landlords, made the peasant organizations more aware of the need for political action at the national level. Radical views on the need for drastic social structural change in order to improve the life of the peasants found increasingly positive response. The (leftist) Workers' and Peasants' Party, on the whole supported by the *Nichinó* (both undergoing parallel splits and mergers), won considerable influence during the 1928 elections for the Diet.

The government, alarmed by the rising tide of radicalism in the peasant and labor movement, ordered nationwide arrests of movement leaders in the so-called 3–15 event (March 15, 1928). Most of the top leaders at national and some prefectural levels were imprisoned, a serious blow to the *Nichinó*. Some, such as national leader Tokuda, remained in jail until after World War II.

Despite mounting difficulties, local action continued, showing how strongly the needs and demands of the tenants were felt. In September 1931, the Manchuria incident took place: an explosion engineered by the army near Mukden was used as a pretext for the occupation of Manchuria. This action considerably augmented the authoritarian tendency of the

Japanese government and the influence of the army. A period of serious repression had begun.

This shows how serious the land tenure situation was, and makes it understandable that the efforts to propose reform legislation were on many occasions undertaken by the more enlightened politicians, albeit in vain. It prepared the way before and during World War II for the land reform, finally carried out in 1946, which was relatively radical as a result of the revived peasant pressure (Dore 1959:69).

THE INDONESIAN PEASANT FRONT: BTI

One of the most spectacular peasant organizations in Asia was the *Barisan Tani Indonesia* (BTI) [Indonesian Peasant Front], created and directed by the Communist Party. In 1953, Aidit became secretary-general of the PKI (Indonesian Communist Party). From that time on, the communists tried to come to a "united front" policy and to build up a mass organization, particularly among the peasants.

The strategy followed by the Communist Party workers and the BTI activists was developed by Aidit. In the first place, survivals of "feudalism" in Indonesia were denounced. The need to organize peasants, taking as a point of departure their most strongly felt demands and grievances, was emphasized. It was suggested that local organizations be created around such demands, varying for each particular village or area (Hindley 1964: 63, 161). In each area or community, party cadres were instructed to identify their most acute problems in meetings with the peasants. In order to achieve an appropriate relationship between the cadres and the village population, the policy of "Three Togethers" was followed. Activists were to "live together, eat together, and work together" with the peasants. They were also to help them in the solution of all kinds of practical day-to-day problems regarding rent payment, legalization of titles, etc.

"Small but successful" actions were seen by the PKI and BTI cadres as the best way to mobilize the peasantry. It was emphasized, however, that these "small but successful" actions should be accompanied by stimulating among the peasants an awareness that the basic solution to their problems would come only with the end of landlord exploitation and that this could be achieved through organized struggle. Actions that would directly affect the relationship with the landowners were not to be undertaken, however, until the organization at the local level had gained enough strength. Then the demands for joined land-rent agreements, or for lowered interest rates on loans, or lowered land rents, could be brought up.

The surprising thing about the spread and development of BTI and its activities in Java was that it came about in a society still dominated by tradition and respect for established leadership. However, the first signs of a decline could be noted. To undermine systematically the hold of the traditional wealthy leaders over their villages and bring the people to the point where they would oppose that leadership on such crucial issues as land tenure, was a big step in a tradition-bound society.

It would be an exaggeration to say that there was a clear-cut introduction of class struggle, but there were certain elements of application of the conflict model. Taking up examples of existing, but hidden, grievances against those in power, people were made aware that the harmony in their villages was disappearing or did not exist. Various abuses, such as usury, became more obvious under the modernization process. An awareness of exploitation was bound to increase and the BTI took up these issues as a means of organizing the peasants as an interest group.

In addition to the existence of strongly felt grievances, mainly related to a deteriorating land-tenure situation, strong new leadership was needed to rally the people against the traditional elite. Identification with the fate of the poor peasants was the initial step in gaining the loyalty and admiration of the people.

Loyalty to charismatic and particularly able or courageous leaders became, in many cases, a factor which rallied the Javanese peasants to a struggle for improvement and change. Such leaders could then also take over the "father" role that landlords and wealthy farmers traditionally played among the peasants in their villages.

Once traditional patronage was undermined and new leaders enjoyed enough prestige, it was possible to compete successfully with old leaders in elections for *lurahs* [village heads], and for even higher positions in local government. In several areas, particularly in central Java, BTI or PKI leaders were thus gradually taking over official positions from the established elite.

In spite of many difficulties characteristic of organizational efforts in the highly traditional rural areas, the BTI was the most impressive of all the communist-oriented mass organizations in the country. At the end of 1953 it had a membership of several hundred thousand; by September, 1964, it claimed 8.5 million members. The growing strength of the communist and communist-oriented mass organizations provoked a strong response from the army. A PKI Party Congress to be held in 1959 was first forbidden by the army, but was later allowed, thanks to the support of President Sukarno.

The 1959 elections, which could have given the Communist Party a majority, or the most influential position among other parties, were not held. Presidential rule, "guided democracy," was initiated, and President Sukarno tried to keep a balance between the army, the Communist Party, and other forces, checking one force with the other. The BTI bargaining position and mass organization was, however, strong enough to be able to successfully take up the land-reform issue at the national level and to obtain the promulgation of a land-reform law in 1960.

However, as a reaction to the slow and defective implementation of this land reform, and the determination of which surplus lands were to be expropriated, the BTI and PKI (Communist Party) stepped up their activities and became more militant, endangering the more or less harmonious collaboration which had existed at the national level between them and the various other political currents.

In order to exert pressure for the speed-up of the reform program, Aidit endorsed and encouraged in his 1963 report the so-called *Gerakan Aksi Sefihak* [unilateral action movement] of the peasants. It is difficult to assess whether the "unilateral action movement" was instigated by the BTI or PKI leadership or was a spontaneous reaction of the peasants themselves to such doubtful practices as eviction by landowners.

While the landowners tried through "unilateral actions" to avoid the land distribution, or the peasants' claim to their new rights, the "unilateral actions" of the peasants were directed towards the initiation and acceleration of the land distribution process. The primary tactic used by the peasants was occupation of the lands to which landless peasants were entitled by law. By occupying certain plots of land, the peasants involved tried to indicate which lands were to be distributed.

The frequency and impact of the "unilateral actions" are difficult to estimate. The fact that President Sukarno in August, 1964, more or less endorsed the movement, and that during the second half of 1964 measures were taken to accelerate drastically the stagnant land-reform program, may indicate that the "unilateral action movement" took on considerable import. This would indicate how effectively the BTI and PKI had organized the peasants. Militancy is generally not considered a characteristic of the Javanese peasants, and the traditional approach at the village level has always been the search for compromise and harmony.

The fact that in a good many instances this pattern was abolished seems to show how far the process of "de-traditionalization" had gone in Java. On the whole, it seems that local people took the new course of events for granted, and about half-a-million peasants could benefit from land reform in a relatively short time (the second half of 1964). It seems that during the rapid land distribution in the second half of 1964, little violence occurred. A ferociously violent reaction came after October, 1965, when, following an abortive coup by leftist officers, a military regime came to power. Sectors of the army, together with the youth of the mainly Islamic rural elite, assassinated over half-a-million peasants and peasant leaders. After this massacre, the BTI virtually ceased to exist (Wertheim 1966: 7).[4]

OVERALL CONDITIONS FAVORABLE TO THE RISE OF PEASANT MOVEMENTS

In comparing the different agricultural areas where important regional or nationwide movements began, it appears that they were not the poorest, most "marginal" agricultural areas. This was true of the sugar plantation area in the State of Morelos where the Zapata movement started and of the Department of Cochabamba, one of the richest agricultural areas of Bolivia. Also, Convención Valley in Peru; the sugarcane area in northeast Brazil; Pampanga in central Luzon; Java in Indonesia; and other regions, where at one time or another important peasant organizations came into being, have this in common. Another characteristic that these areas appear to share is that they are not isolated — most of them having easy access to major cities — and that they are less rigidly traditional and feudal than other areas. They are also densely populated.

In such areas, it seems to be the weakening, generally through economic developments, of the status quo that causes the peasants to organize. The situations where organizations have sprung up tend to have in common what could be called an "erosion of the status quo," which may occur in many ways. A CHANGE FOR THE WORSE in the peasants' living conditions can awaken them to defend the little they have. This happened, for instance, in the area where the *Ligas Camponesas* were started in Pernambuco, Brazil. The desire of the landowner to introduce sugarcane production on lands which for years had been cultivated on a tenancy basis for subsistence and commercial crops, and the efforts to effect this change through violent means, provoked the peasants to organize and defend their interests.

In Java the process of "agricultural involution" implied slowly worsening conditions for the rural population. In Japan, the economic diffi-

---

[4]   For an amply documented description of BTI history, see Huizer (1974).

culties that occurred in industry and agriculture at the end of World War I caused rural tension. In central Luzon, the concentration of land in the hands of a few owners and the "proletarization" of peasants, transforming small farmers into wage laborers, set the stage for agrarian unrest. Also in Morelos in Mexico at the beginning of this century, it was not the balance between *latifundios* and indigenous communities, but the usurpation of those communities by the land-hungry, sugar-estate owners and despoliation of indigenous peasants which set off what may have been one of the bloodiest revolutions in modern history.

The increasing demands of the *hacendados* versus their *arrendires* set off the peasant movement in La Convención, Cuzco. The wish to turn back the clock in land-tenure conditions in Ucureña, Bolivia, provoked a small peasant organization to become a radical, large-scale movement. It thus appears to be either the increasing exigency of economic power-holders or the "resistance to change" of the traditional landed elite against the "revolution of rising expectations" of peasants which finally creates the ideal conditions for the rise of militant movements.

A highly important side effect of the trend toward concentration of land in the hands of a few, mainly absentee, landowners, was that the traditional bond between landlords and peasants underwent a change. The exploitative aspects of the traditional system became more clearly visible.

THE PATRONAGE SYSTEM AND OTHER OBSTACLES

One of the results of increasing absentee landownership or other modern economic forces, was a decline in the paternalistic type of control (often called PATRONAGE) that the landlords traditionally had over the peasantry. Patronage is based to a large extent on continuous personal contact and mutual obligations sanctioned by tradition and by social control of the village society as a whole. The relationship of landowners not living in the villages with their tenants could more easily become blatantly exploitative. This enhanced the chance of class conflict in the rural areas. Originally, the patronage system may have had some benevolent implications for the peasants, but these were limited. Peasants were born into this system and more or less doomed to live under it all their lives, unless they were willing to take considerable risks. The patronage system and the resultant psychological coercion on the peasant to conform appeared to be main obstacles to the organization of peasant-interest and pressure groups.

In countries where landlords themselves lived in the villages and had only a small number of tenants with whom they were in almost daily contact, the patron-client relationship was particularly strong, and the tenants hesitated to be disloyal to their "patron" by joining a union or organization dedicated to the defense of their rights. The "patron" could indulge in illegal practices, e.g. asking a sixty-forty share of the harvest while the law allowed fifty-fifty, forty-sixty, or even a twenty-five–seventy-five division. But for emotional reasons, as well as to ensure minimum economic security, peasants often did not take steps to demand that their legal rights be respected. Economic changes that caused deterioration of the status quo could rouse the peasants to action, especially when the "patron" clearly showed his true face.

In addition to mere absentee ownership, other modernizing influences, particularly among the younger generation of the elite, contributed to a loosening of the emotional, paternalistic ties by which the poor peasants were bound to the upper classes. In some cases, the change in attitude was merely a more businesslike approach and neglect by the wealthy of feudalistic patronage obligations.

In some cases, it was under emergency conditions that the patrons showed that they were "protective" towards the peasants only as long as it was highly beneficial. Thus a great deal of more or less organized peasant protest in Japan occurred during the periods of bad harvests, when landlords refused to reduce either the rents or their share in the harvest in order to give the tenants a chance to survive. Such occurrences enhanced, at least temporarily, the peasants' awareness of merciless exploitation at the hands of their patrons.

One of the factors, however, which in some countries complicated the picture, was the entrance of party politics and election campaigns. Traditionally, the rural elite was divided among itself, and in most villages there were factions. It often happened that party affiliations among the electorate followed the factional divisions of the elite rather than class interest lines. Particularly in the Philippines, but also to some extent in Indonesia, the parties tended to make possible a strengthening of the patronage system. Political functions for which the election campaigns were held generally implied that the local elite influenced or directly controlled certain government resources such as funds for roads, schools, medical and health services. These modern resources could be utilized in addition to the more traditional ones of land and power to keep the peasants in a state of dependency. Promises of official help were used to make the peasants conform.

Because the large landowners in most developing countries had almost absolute control of economic, social, and political life in the rural areas, there were many ways in which they could prevent peasant organizations from arising. The most common means used to effect this were economic and other sanctions against the founders of peasant associations. Agricultural wage workers who began such activities were easily thrown out of their jobs, unless they found ways to organize a group of colleagues in secrecy or in a simulated way under the cover of a literacy club or mutual aid society. Tenants could, for the same reason, easily be evicted from their land. Generally by agreement among the landowners in a certain area, peasants who had been discharged or evicted found it very difficult to get a job or a parcel of land elsewhere in the same region. It was also found that because most agricultural workers and tenants had incomes at a mere subsistence level, there was little chance that they would take the risk of losing their jobs or plots, as this would practically mean starvation. The severe underemployment and indebtedness that existed in the rural areas made the risk of losing their means of survival even greater.

When economic sanctions were not enough to block the emergence of a peasant organization, other means were tried. One was to buy off a leader of a strong organization by offering him money, land, or access to higher social status. This was tried several times with Emiliano Zapata and many other leaders.

Frequently, when all other means failed to undermine a growing movement, its leader was assassinated. Countless cases of assassination of peasant leaders have taken place in Latin America, as well as in Southeast Asia. Violence in the rural areas under discussion was not introduced there recently by insurgents or revolutionaries, but has existed for many decades. With few exceptions, the formation of organizations that attempted a legal defense of the rights of the peasants was blocked by the traditional holders of power.

GROWTH OF "CLASS-CONSCIOUSNESS"

No matter where conditions for the creation of a peasant movement exist, little will occur if there is not among the peasants themselves an awareness of their conditions, including a belief that something can be done about them. In cases where peasants have an ideologically clear understanding of their conditions, one could speak of "class-consciousness." A clear consciousness of being a class, in the Marxian sense, is rarely present among peasants. This does not mean, however, that there is necessarily complete confusion about such issues.

In Marxian terms, the key issue was how certain categories of peasants could turn from being a "class-in-themselves" to becoming a "class-for-themselves." It was in this process of "becoming conscious," "conscientization," or "politicization," that a number of sociopsychological factors played an important role, often neglected by those interested in mass or class organizations. In some way or other, most of the peasant organizations described have utilized, more or less purposely, these sociopsychological factors:

1.   Stimulating in the peasants an awareness of being exploited.
2.   The role of strong or even charismatic leadership and a vanguard to counteract the residual influence of traditional patronage, which kept the peasant in psychological dependency.
3.   The utilization of the "conflict model" to bring peasants together in cohesive and militant groups.

Stimulating Awareness of Being Exploited: Use of "Counterpoints"

A better understanding of exploitative conditions and the possibilities of changing them could be stimulated among the peasants. This happened partly through the influence of outsiders, such as the fieldworkers of the Brazilian program of *concientizaçao* (according to the method of Paolo Freire), or the Communist Party cadres, as in Indonesia. Such outsiders generally utilized certain elements in the peasants' lives and culture considered to be "counterpoints" to the prevailing "culture of repression" in which the peasants lived.[5]

It was crucial to find "counterpoint" elements in the peasants' submissive attitudes and value system in order to be able to show them that they were already involved in some kind of resistance against the repressive system, and that the fatherly authority of the landlord was basically fiction. Such elements could be found in folktales and in the history of the village, particularly in the means through which the elite — by taking over more and more land — came to power. Thus, explaining to the peasants that their distrust was justified was a means of bringing greater awareness and some amount of self-confidence to them. The BTI activists in Indonesia did this in a more or less systematic way. The campaigns of the Communist Party leader, Aidit, to study local folklore and culture (which always contain a great deal of "resistance" elements and "counterpoints"), as well as the present and past land-tenure situation, were highly

[5]   The "counterpoint" concept is elaborated in Wertheim (unpublished manuscript). For the situation in Indonesia, see Huizer (1971: 104 ff).

important. Knowing the background of the peasants' grievances and the forms of expression of those grievances tolerated by the establishment as a safety valve (jokes and tales, for example), could help the organizers to rally the peasantry, in a more conscious way, to the defense of their interests. This approach had certain similarities to the campaign of "conscientization" initiated by the basic education movement toward radical social change in northeastern Brazil from 1963 to 1964 and to the use of rebel folk songs by the peasant league organizers there.

Some additional factors that made the trend toward "conscientization" in the rural areas feasible were:

1. The increasingly important role of primary education and other forms of contact and acquaintance with the world that differed considerably from the traditional peasant frame of reference.

2. Better communications with urban areas through roads and modern means of transportation. In particular, such densely populated areas as Pernambuco in northeastern Brazil; Cochabamba, Bolivia; Java; central Luzon; and, in Japan, the prefectures close to the big cities, showed the influence of this trend. Also, in some cases, the introduction of transistor radios had an impact.

3. The process of industrialization in some countries, particularly in Japan during World War I, gave many peasants a chance to participate in urban life and in new forms of organization. After a recess in the industrialization process, these persons had to go back to their villages and, as a result, the potential for new forms of organization and solidarity there increased. Some combination of the three above-mentioned factors, or their separate appearance, became more and more frequent. These are the reasons why, in Japan, the first large-scale, union-oriented peasant organizations were created exctly in those areas where urban influences were strong and growing — such as the regions around the industrial cities of Nagoya and Osaka, and later, Fukuoka and Tokyo. The urban experience factor played a particularly important role in the case of Zapata and of the peasant syndicates in Bolivia, which came up after peasants returned from the Chaco War. In other cases, the presence of a mining industry was a catalyst to the growth of a peasant movement.

Community development and similar programs can have a stimulating effect on the growth of peasants' critical awareness and readiness for action and organization, but the contrary may also be true. When community development was channeled merely through established traditional leadership, such as most of the *lurahs* in Indonesia, or the *barrio* notables in the Philippines, it could well strengthen the hold of these traditional leaders over the poor peasantry. Existing patronage relationships, which were an impediment to the creation of peasant protest against the traditionally dominant powers, were reinforced, and peasants were made more dependent. Such programs existed in most countries but were generally rather ineffective.

In evaluating the reasons why community development programs in so many countries have stagnated, the United Nations has emphasized the difficulty of bringing change to rural societies controlled by a traditional elite. In a document regarding the future evolution of community development, it was noted that in such cases "... conflict and disagreement rather than cohesiveness is a more true and realistic measure of development of communities, and in that way of the success of community development programs" (United Nations 1971: 6ff.). The United Nations document recommended that efforts be undertaken to stimulate new and more dynamic leadership representing the interests of the majority, rather than working through the traditional leaders who generally belonged to a small elite. A confrontation of the new with the old leadership was seen as unavoidable, and to be introduced gradually.

The Role of Leadership and Vanguard

It seems that the availability of charismatic, or at least solidarity-inspiring, leadership among the peasants is highly important in getting an organization to the point where it may confront the elite. A principal characteristic of such a leader is that he is able to express clearly what his peasant-followers feel more or less vaguely about their repressed condition. On the one hand, this capacity of the leader helps the peasants in their process of "conscientization." On the other hand, it facilitates a strong identification with the leader. This identification has to grow in such a way that the peasants feel through it a kind of horizontal solidarity among themselves.

Initially, vertical ties of admiration with the leader may be important. The leader has, to some extent, to replace in his followers the sense of security that was formerly inspired by the landlords, i.e. the PATRON, who played the role of a kind of father figure to the peasants. When the father image cannot be maintained any longer and takes on the characteristics of a tyrant, the possibility for replacement arises. Strong personalities among the peasants may take on this role. Sometimes they inspired respect for their skill and experience — a result of working for some time in the towns. They helped the peasants to break through the traditional patronage system and the hold the landlord had over them, not only economically but psychologically as well. Thus, several peasant organizations that occurred locally were the result of the almost accidental presence of such a special leader among the peasants themselves. Taruc, Zapata, and José Rojas are cases in point. It seems, however, that it is not necessary "to wait" until such a leader happens to appear.

Under certain conditions, other figures could fulfill the same function. Both the Japanese and the Indonesian peasant movements were built up mainly by organizers who came from an urban background and "went down to the villages." At the beginning such organizers generally encountered resistance and distrust, but if they managed to overcome this distrust through their personal qualities and the methods they employed, they could, relatively easily, become respected leaders. Villagers often (and with considerable justification) passively rejected an outsider. Once he had proved himself trustworthy, however, his nonpeasant background and dedication to the peasant cause could command for him more respect than if he had been a peasant. This explains the considerable success of persons like Hugo Blanco in Peru, Aoki in Japan, and the organizers of the BTI in Indonesia — many of whom were former students who gave themselves to the peasant struggle and won the people's hearts by going "down" to the villages under something like the rule of the "three togethers." But simply identifying himself with the peasants was not enough. For an organizer to become a leader, he had also to prove himself able to deal with and stand up against the powerholders to whom the grievances or demands of the peasants were directed. The leaders should not be easily intimidated, and at times had to take the risk of going to jail or facing threats from the landlords or local authorities.

When the leader of a peasant organization, because of his personal qualities, took over the landlord's "father" role, the danger existed that the strength of the organization might remain too long dependent on that specific leader. It has happened frequently with large-scale or small-scale organizations that, when a strong and dynamic leader disappeared or was eliminated, the organization, as such, collapsed, largely because there was no person or group of persons to replace him. This happened to Zapata's movement after his assassination in 1919. In some ways this was also true of the Huk movement in the Philippines when, in 1954, Luis Taruc surrendered. The continuation of an organization in the face of "decapitation," imprisonment, or elimination of its main leaders can be guaranteed only when a core of replacement leaders is available.

In the process of creating a peasant organization, it is, therefore, an essential strategy that initial leaders stimulate leadership qualities in potential successors. It is also essential to stimulate in the membership enough self-confidence to replace that confidence in charismatic leadership, so crucial to the initial process.

To guarantee the continuity of the organization in Japan, as well as Indonesia, one of the first activities of the initiators was to look for aides and give them a kind of in-service training. Once acquainted with the local situation and sure of the confidence of the people, it was generally not too difficult to find peasants with special qualities who could fulfill leadership functions in a militant organization. Especially after demands for action or protests about grievances had been made, potential leaders could make themselves known and go through a process of winning respect and adherence, similar to that of the original leader.

From almost all the cases known, it seems that the peasants who were relatively better off were most apt to participate as leaders or vanguard in the initiation of a movement. They were a little less dependent on the landlords or rich farmers and could thus afford to take more risks. For this reason, the Peasant Leagues in Brazil purposely bet on the relatively independent small landholders, only attempting to attract the mass of landless peasants after a start had been made and some strength gained. Alavi noted a similar trend in China from the twenties onward and in some of the peasant movements in India (1965: 241-277; Wolf 1969). The leadership of the newly created organizations generally came from a group of peasants who were somewhat better off.

It should be noted, however, that it was probably not the "middle-class" peasants, as such, who were in the vanguard of peasant protest movements, but rather those among the "middle class," who for some reason felt their relative security threatened or who were clearly frustrated by the power of the economic and political elite or by other forces.

The fact that leaders of peasant organizations have to fulfill a certain type of patronage role in order to compete effectively and replace the traditional "patron" explains why, not infrequently, leaders came from dissident sections of the traditional elite itself. Even in the communist-oriented BTI, a number of local leaders were landlords. This was the situation in the Philippines, most outstandingly in the case of the founder of the socialist peasant organization, Pedro Abad Santos. Similar situations obtained in Japan, in northeastern Brazil, where Juliao was originally a landlord, and in Peru, where Hugo Blanco came from a well-to-do family. One of the dangers of this situation was that leaders who had all the capacity to compete with the traditional patronage system were not consistently dissident in their own class but became themselves a traditional type of "patron." They then had a moderating, rather than a radicalizing, influence on their followers. Some of the leaders of the BTI may have been examples of elitist revolutionaries, and certainly many of the local leaders of the Petani (Nationalist Party Peasant Organization) and Islamic peasant organizations in Indonesia were from the elites.

Such moderate peasant organizations are sometimes formed by members of the rural elite in order to compete with the more radical leftist organizations. The Federation of Free Farmers created in the Philippines during the 1950's was such an organization; its leaders were moderate dissidents of the rural elite. In northeastern Brazil, the Church created such an alternative movement that was radicalized and integrated with the Leagues, however, at a later stage.

The Role of the Conflict Model: Utilizing Concrete Grievances

Once new leadership was solidly established, a confrontation with the old order might be initiated more openly by utilizing the CONFLICT MODEL as opposed to the HARMONY MODEL, frequently used in rural and community organization. The harmony model took as a point of departure the belief that basically all different interests at the community or regional level could be developed simultaneously and harmoniously. But because many concrete cases where this approach was tried were failures, the conviction grew that conflict, instead, might prove to be a rallying force in creating effective groups.[6]

After the peasants had been made aware of being exploited, and while their organization was still in the process of creation and growth, it could benefit from the existence of an "enemy" or a "negative reference group" (Coser 1956). Having an "enemy" helped to foster cohesiveness in the group because the peasant's great resentment toward the traditional landlords made of this class a natural enemy. Through the formation of representative interest groups of their own, the peasants brought into the open their resentment and channeled it in an effective way. Counterforces, provoked by utilizing the conflict-model, could awaken the peasants even more strongly to their best interests.

Efforts by the landed elite to halt the rise of the new peasant interest groups had a double effect. On the one hand, it could hinder considerably the process of forming the representative peasant organizations. On the other hand, however, it could accelerate the process through which the traditional form of dominance through patronage loosens its hold. As a

---

[6] For a case study where the conflict model was applied in a community development project in Chile, see Huizer (1972a).

result of repressive measures, peasants were brought to see increasingly that the traditional system was basically not benevolent and did not give the kind of "protection" and security they needed. The "true face" of the landlord was seen to be not that of a father but of a tyrant.

It was particularly when clearer forms of repression entered the scene that such concepts as "village devils" (a term applied in Indonesia to landlords, merchants, and money lenders during the land-reform campaign) began to express what the peasants felt about their "patrons." It was essential that great care be taken to distinguish between the "devils" and those landlords and merchants who fulfilled their traditional role without great excesses or abuses.

Going too far in this approach could easily lead to a reaction on the part of those rural people who were not directly involved in the conflict, such as small landholders and artisans who feared that an unjust struggle on the part of the peasants might disrupt all their values. It may well be that the massacre of members of the BTI in Indonesia in 1965 was, in places such as Bali, a reaction to overzealousness on the part of the BTI in not taking traditional factors sufficiently into account and disrupting village harmony beyond the limits felt to be just and bearable by those not directly involved. Through the years, similar factors have played a role in the serious setbacks suffered by the Huk movement in the Philippines. The overly doctrinaire approach of some of the leaders alienated them from important sectors of their followers, and when one of the more charismatic leaders, Luis Taruc, surrendered, partly for this reason, the movement lost strength very rapidly.

From almost all experiences cited, it can be seen that peasant movements generally develop only when there is a concrete event or acute conflict about which people become excited. It seems that, even if conditions are bad and growing worse, peasants will be mobilized only when there is some kind of clear-cut conflict. Moderate demands, however, can sometimes lead to such a conflict because of the intransigence of the elite. Peasant organizers generally look for sensitive points in the local setup if a clear, rallying issue is not too readily available. In Java, particularly, this strategy was utilized consistently, thus successfully introducing the conflict-model in a society in which *rukun* [harmony] was highly appreciated.

In applying the conflict-model, it was important to determine the kind of peasants on which the organization would base its strength. In countries where there existed a clear polarization between rich landlords and poor tenants, organizations simply represented the tenants' interests. They rallied the peasants in the villages or on the *haciendas* around such issues as security of tenancy, better tenancy legislation, sharecropping arrangements more favorable to tenants (e.g. forty-sixty instead of fifty-fifty), or even land reform, as a final or principal demand. The latter possibility came up particularly when landlords insistently rejected the other demands or indulged in illegal practices.

Where the land-tenure pattern was more complicated, it was more difficult to determine what kind of organization to create. There were often sharecroppers who tilled land not belonging to large landholders but to slightly better-off neighbors and relatives, who themselves had only a small plot and let part of that to the sharecropper, more to help him than from a desire for systematic exploitation. To organize such share-croppers in their own exclusive interest would be extremely difficult; many peasants who leased a part of their plot would be opposed. When-ever the differences between tenants and the lesser landlords were minor, both could be united into one organization that benefited the small owners in such a way as to enable them to give more favorable sharecropping or tenancy conditions to the tenants.

There are always problems, such as exploitation by money lenders and merchants, common to both tenants and small owners. The peasant organization can concentrate its struggle on these problems, trying to bargain for more favorable credit or marketing terms. Particularly where there was a tendency for money lenders, through loans and mortgages on the land of small owners, to try and gain possession of larger tracts of land (a situation that occurred in Indonesia and several other countries), organization of peasants appeared highly feasible.

In some areas of Java new types of landlords have emerged who, by clever manipulation of indebtednesses, have acquired much land formerly held by small landholders. The *hadjis* in Indonesia can probably be considered such a group of new landlords, often much less considerate of the peasants' interests than the traditional landowners.

The degree to which certain tenure patterns, or changes in such patterns, occur in a particular area or village (even more than in a clear-cut, landlord-tenant division) should be investigated carefully. It appears that the BTI in Indonesia was successful in preceding organization and action by such research into the "class contradictions" in the villages. Such research has been nonexistent or rare in most other cases. Particularly in countries where a complicated land-tenure structure exists, it seems to be crucial that any organizing effort evaluate those contradictions so that the conflict-model can be applied effectively.

THE STRATEGY OF PEASANT ORGANIZATION: ESCALATION AS A REACTION TO ELITE RESISTANCE

Once a peasant organization has come into existence, a process of consolidation and of gaining strength will generally follow. It has been recognized by many leaders and organizers that to obtain concrete benefits through struggle is the best way to consolidate and strengthen an organization. Cases of abuse are presented to the courts, and mass demonstrations and public meeting are held to support petitions for justice or land. Initially, the only steps undertaken are those to obtain justice, as indicated by the existing laws. This has happened in all the cases described above. Meetings were held and a petition, with or without direct support from a sympathetic or paid lawyer, was presented to competent authorities. Often, however, the authorities stood aloof or openly chose the side of the large landholders, despite the fact that the peasants had the law on their side, Continuous frustration, leading nowhere, encountered in following the slow course of legal procedure, prepared the ground for more radical peasant action to the limit of the legal possibilities.

It was not only the existence of an organization with a large membership, as such, that was the crucial factor in getting things changed, but also the way in which such an organization presented its demands and demonstrated the bargaining power to back them up. Generally some form of direct action from the peasants made it clear to the authorities, as well as to the vested interests and landholding groups, that the demands were serious. Among these forms of direct action, the peaceful or symbolic occupation or invasion of the lands considered to be expropriable was probably the most effective, and the most generally practiced.

Land reforms generally occurred only after such direct, usually nonviolent, action by peasant organizations had taken place. The "unilateral actions" in Java or the occupations of estates by the Bolivian peasants in 1953 are two examples. Some such actions were merely symbolic, designed to draw public attention or exercise pressure. In other cases, they effected immediate changes in the cultivation system or property relations. In most cases, such activities have been purposely nonviolent, a form of civil disobedience strategy. In several cases, the peasants even had the law on their side, and it was the authorities who failed to maintain or implement it. Effective or symbolic occupation of land, bringing it into cultivation or just organizing a "sit-in" on it, could not possibly be seen as violence, if violence is understood to be intentional damage to lives or goods.[7]

[7]   For a discussion of some examples of land invasions, see Huizer (1972b).

Similar nonviolent forms of direct action are the strike and the demonstration. An instance of a strike was the refusal of the peasants, organized by Hugo Blanco in La Convención, to observe the obligatory period of unpaid work days for the landowner; or as happened at times in Japan, to give the landlord the part of the yield he claimed. One of the many forms demonstrations can take is the sit-in or mass rally in front of courts, government offices, or landlords' houses, as has happened in northeastern Brazil, Peru, and Japan.

Peasant organizations and their leaders gain experience by organizing a strike, by symbolically occupying land, or by a mass demonstration. Such undertakings are risky in the sense that they may fail and lead to disillusionment. The many cases where errors were made without much damage being done, and needed experience for an effective movement was gained, appear to justify the risks involved.

It seems that a tolerant and benevolent attitude on the part of the authorities regarding the peasants' efforts to gain strength is helpful and important. This happened in the Bolivian revolution of 1952, when political groups at the national level needed the support of the peasant movement in order to overthrow the old regime and establish and consolidate a more liberal one. Also, the Sukarno government in Indonesia depended on peasant support as a counterbalance to the increasing influence of the army.

Frequently, however, nonviolent or civil-disobedience actions by peasants are not tolerated by the authorities. They may give the rural elite complete freedom to react violently, or even give them active support by using the army to repress the peasant movement. Despite the fact that peasant activities are generally not violent, the local and national press, the authorities, or the landlords themselves have interpreted such actions as violent and have retaliated with violence. It cannot be emphasized enough that in almost all cases where real violence occurred, it was introduced either by the authorities or by the landlords as a reaction to increased pressure from the peasants. It is this escalation of repression that then gives the peasants a clearer consciousness of the need for overthrowing the system under which they live. The cases of Zapata in Mexico, Hugo Blanco in Peru, and Luis Taruc in the Philippines demonstrate that the ruthless repression of moderate peasant action makes the peasants potential revolutionaries, willing to use violent means to defend themselves and change the social system radically. A great deal depends, at this stage, on the kind of guidance the peasants get from their leaders or allies.

One factor contributing to the escalation of the actions of peasants against the overall system was the increased knowledge peasants gained of their rights. Particularly in the stage where the landed elite began to repress, combat, or corrupt efforts by the peasants to exercise pressure, the latter learned to see clearly the illegal, not to say criminal, nature of the landlords', or of the government's, approach. Traditionally, the peasants' high respect for law and order is a guarantee of security. As can be seen from the cases in Peru, northeastern Brazil, and Mexico, whenever landlords used illegal means to terrorize peasants, the latter initially tried to find a solution by appealing to the appropriate authorities. Only after insistent demands to qualified authorities that they enforce the laws failed to produce results, did the peasants start to see the landlords as a class, as their main "enemy."

It has frequently been documented that legal authorities in the rural areas of most countries interpret the laws generally in favor of the landlords, even if this means circumvention or violation of the law. Peasants will sometimes resign and give up, in a resentful or embittered way, efforts to improve their lot. But whenever the legitimacy and acceptance of the prevailing system is seriously undermined by the way this system attempts to maintain itself, it requires only a relatively small effort to transform the new awareness of repression among the peasants into a stronger revolutionary consciousness.

At this stage, the need usually arises among the peasants to gain weapons to defend themselves against injustice and repression. In cases where peasants did acquire weapons, such as in Bolivia in 1953, they could prevent the elite from further escalation of their violent actions. The land reform process in Bolivia was carried out without any violence because the peasants could check the power of the landlords. When, in the Convención Valley, the first steps were made by the peasantry to acquire weapons, the government decided that lands would be distributed to appease them, thus essentially preventing the movement from becoming a threat to the national political system.

When peasants, as a result of the repression by landlords and army, gain a clearer understanding of the need for overall radical change and the weapons to struggle for it, they can become outright revolutionaries, as was shown by Zapata's movement and by that of the Huks in the Philippines. One important question in this context is how consciously revolutionary the peasants become. If by this term it is understood that peasants accepted a Marxist interpretation of society or Communist Party doctrines, it would seem that most of them were not consciously revolutionary. Research undertaken among peasants imprisoned for political reasons after the Arbenz government in Guatemela was overthrown (with support of the anti-land-reform forces, including the United

Fruit Company) in 1954, showed that the peasants were on the whole not ideologically indoctrinated by communism but rather were awakened to ideas of democracy and social justice (Newbold 1957: 338–361). Also, the peasants who had participated in an uprising stimulated by the Indonesian Communist Party in 1926 and who were imprisoned in the penal colony in the swamp lands of Boven-Digul, could hardly be considered sophisticated communists, as was noted by one strongly anticommunist author (Brackman 1963: 19,34). However, imprisonment of peasants in the Boven-Digul swamps or in the jungle, such as Ichilo in Bolivia (where between 1946 and 1953, 250 peasant leaders were kept), does not make peasants less radical or less politically conscious, but just the opposite.

In the Philippines, Indonesia, and Japan, guidance was given to the peasantry by socialist and communist political groups who took up the land-reform issue and organized the peasantry around it. In other cases, a leftist political group took up the peasants' cause once the latter had shown itself to be a strongly organized body. They tried to become allies of the peasants. This happened in Mexico and Bolivia, in particular.

There was, in such cases, considerable variation in the control exercised by the political parties over peasant organizations. Some, such as the movement created by Zapata, were almost completely independent and followed rather closely their own purposes. The movements in La Convención and in the Cochabamba area, although supported by political groups, had a dynamic of their own, the membership at times pushing the leadership beyond the goals set. The organizations created after 1952 in areas other than Cochabamba in Bolivia, mainly through the MNR party, were relatively more controlled. The *Ligas Camponesas* had their own representatives in the National Parliament of Brazil and appeared to be controlled by no specific party, although strife among groups to gain influence within the movement was noted.

A dilemma faced by most growing peasant movements has been whether or not to relate the conflict-model strategy clearly to a positive ideological purpose. Although all were socialist-oriented, Rojas in Bolivia and Juliao in Brazil were less clearly defined than Abad Santos, Aidit, or Hugo Blanco. Ideological obscurity may sometimes have the tactical advantage of being slower to arouse the repressive forces of the elite. On the other hand, not having a clear ideology behind its activities may leave a movement in the air, once it has gained enough strength to bargain effectively with the "enemy" or even to eliminate his influence. Then the organization may be without a clear purpose and might easily lose its strength or deteriorate.

In order to utilize to the full the potential for organized efforts, it seems crucial to orient the initial struggle not only against the "enemy" but also in favor of objectives having a wider scope, so that the organization may be kept on the move after it has gained strength in overcoming the main obstacles. Examples of places where this did not happen were Japan, Bolivia, and Mexico. The peasant organizations in Japan had as their main purpose the struggle with the landlords, first, to get better tenancy conditions and, later, to get an effective redistribution of land. Once this purpose was achieved, the peasant organizations, which could possibly have played a role in mobilizing the peasants for further efforts related to the solution of basic problems or the building of a socialist society, deteriorated. The possibility, which came to the surface later, of coopera- tive farming to overcome the disadvantages of small holdings, had to be tackled completely anew. In Bolivia the "feudal" class structure was broken in 1954, but after that the peasant movement became a willing instrument of the government to maintain a new status quo and check the struggle of miners and other workers.

It seems particularly important to anticipate the difficulties and prob- lems that may arise once the main demands, around which the peasants had rallied, are being fulfilled. It is important to orient the struggle in favor of the demand for land in such a way that the implications of the reform process itself, and any that may arise after its completion, are al- ready within focus before they actually come up. In this way the peasant organization will not immediately collapse after its main goal has been achieved, but will remain active and mobilized. Also the fact that post- reform measures and needs are being discussed before the reform has actually taken place gives perspective to the struggle and may boost the morale of the organization. Also, the peasants understand exactly what they are heading for, thus lending realism to the activities in favor of reform. Destructive elements in the old structure become clear in the light of the new aims, giving a greater justification to the struggle. Although at times motivated by a great deal of resentment against the traditional and repressive system, peasants are, on the whole, very respectful of law and order, and radical measures will be more easily endorsed if seen as leading toward a new and just order.

CONCLUSION

The Philippine, Indonesian, Bolivian, and Peruvian movements have demonstrated clearly how peasant movements reacted to intolerance or resistance from the elite by becoming a class-conscious, revolutionary force at the national level. This happened not because the peasantry was by nature revolutionary, but rather in spite of their prudent, traditional, and revolutionary approach. All these movements gained considerable success because they were not violent explosions of peasant discontent, repressed as quickly as they came up (as has happened with many movements in the past). Rather, they all started with a careful grass-roots organization that took up the most strongly felt grievances of the peasants — the counterpoints within the dominant traditional system — and tried to build up slowly around those grievances. Only by going carefully, and remaining well within the rules of the game, could the first step be made toward creating representative interest groups against the heavy weight of traditional patronage and economic repression. Only after the rural elite reacted to minor peasant demands and organizational success in ways clearly counter to the prevailing laws, and often including violence, did the peasant organizations become more radical. It is quite probable that at any stage of the movement toward radicalization and escalation of demands the organizations would have accepted a compromise if the rural elite had been willing to give them a fair chance. The elite generally did not do this. The intransigence of the elite, more than anything else, was the reason that peasant organizations finally took a revolutionary stand, demanding the radical overthrow of the system as a whole and acting accordingly. It is surprising that in view of so much historical evidence the elite has continued to follow the same fatal course.

REFERENCES

ALAVI, HAMZA
   1965   Peasants and revolution. *The Socialist Register*: 241–277.
BRACKMAN, ARNOLD C.
   1963   *Indonesian communism: a history*. New York: Praeger.
COSER, LEWIS
   1956   *The functions of social conflict*. Glencoe: Free Press.
DORE, R. P.
   1959   *Land reform in Japan*. Oxford: Oxford University Press.
HINDLEY, DONALD
   1964   *The Communist Party of Indonesia, 1951–1963*. Berkeley and Los Angeles: University of California Press.
HUIZER, GERRIT
   1971   *The role of peasant organizations in the Japanese land reform*. Occasional Papers 12. The Hague: Institute of Social Studies.
   1972a The utilization of conflict in community development and peasant

organization: a case from Chile. *International Review of Community Development* 16.

1972b   Land invasions as a non-violent strategy of peasant rebellion. *Journal of Peace Research* 2.

1972c   *The revolutionary potential of peasants in Latin America.* Lexington: Heath Lexington Books.

1974   Peasant mobilisation in Indonesia. *Review of Indonesian and Malayan Affairs* 8(1):81–138.

LANDSBERGER, HENRY A., *editor*
1969   *Latin American peasant movements.* Ithaca: Cornell University Press.

MARX, KARL
1963   *The eighteenth Brumaire of Louis Bonaparte.* New York: International Publishers.

NEWBOLD, STOKES
1957   Receptivity of Communist-fomented agitation in rural Guatemala. *Economic Development and Cultural Change* 5:338–361.

STAVENHAGEN, RODOLFO, *editor*
1970   *Agrarian problems and peasant movements in Latin America.* New York: Anchor Doubleday.

TARUC, LOUIS
1953   *Born of the people: an autobiography.* New York: International Publishers.

TOTTEN, G. O.
1960   Labor and agrarian disputes in Japan following World War I. *Economic Development and Cultural Change* 9: 194–204.

UNITED NATIONS
1971   *Popular participation in development: emerging trends in community development.* New York: United Nations.

WERTHEIM, W. F.
1966   Indonesia before and after the Untung Coup. *Pacific Affairs* 39:1.

WOLF, ERIC R.
1969   *Peasant wars of the twentieth century.* New York: Harper and Row.

Peasant Sindicatos *and the Process of* Cooptation in Bolivian Politics

JORGE DANDLER

Bolivia is one of the countries of the Third World which has experienced large-scale peasant mobilization and political participation since the 1952 Revolution. Peasants had an active role in the realization of agrarian reform itself and became an important base of support for the Nationalist Revolutionary Movement (MNR), the party that assumed power. In this process, the agrarian *sindicato* became a major social and political innovation in Bolivia and an instrument of local and class solidarity. But the development of the agrarian *sindicato* in Bolivia goes back for some time prior to the 1952 Revolution; it is interwoven with the history of peasant rebellions during the thirties and forties, as well as with the political and social struggles of the miners and urban proletarians.

Although during the early years of the revolution ideological factors played an important role in the mobilization and organization of peasants, during later years the *sindicato* and its affiliates at higher levels frequently became increasingly segmented into vertical political clienteles under a regional peasant leader, loyal to a prominent MNR figure or (in later years) to one of several contenders within the armed forces. Therefore, while including peasants in the political arena through suffrage and with the agrarian *sindicatos* as an important base of political support, the MNR and later governments reinforced dependence relationships by rewarding and supporting loyal peasant leaders and offering small projects to the villages. In this process, the possibilities for *sindicato* organizations at regional or national levels to mobilize people for collective efforts toward long-term economic development were limited. Several examples will be examined in order to illustrate the continued failure of several governments to connect agrarian reform with development. In this connection, recent tendencies to "depoliticize" *sindicatos* and further accentuate peasant marginality and dependence relationships will be analyzed, as will failures to implement cooperatives and community development programs.

The MNR was a broad populist party or movement (Malloy 1970), as the name implies, an alliance of various forces broadly committed to change but ideologically vague; it emerged victorious as a result of the critical participation of miners, workers, and some urban forces in the armed uprising of April 1952, against the army (the MNR had won the 1951 presidential elections but had been prevented from assuming power by a military junta). Having defeated and dismantled the armed forces, a civilian militia of miners, workers, and lower middle-class sectors soon became the bulwark of the new regime.

Although peasants did not directly participate during the uprising, it was only a matter of time until they joined in the general mobilization and enthusiasm about the new order which was being ushered in. Certain ruarl areas soon became critical focuses of agitation and mobilization which influenced the scope and impact of agrarian reform. Thus *campesinos* emerged as significant new actors and a power capability on the political scene. In this context the *sindicato* played a strategic role in mass mobilization. Peasants rapidly organized themselves into *sindicatos*, with the result that by 1955 there were about 20,000 registered *sindicatos*. Peasants quite distinctly created the *sindicatos* as their local organizations to govern themselves, affirm their land rights, and convey their new sense of identity. *Sindicatos*, horizontally and vertically through their provincial, regional, and departmental federations, formed an intricate web that became a new phenomenon in the countryside. These peasant organizations, in turn, interacted with governmental and party organizations at different levels.

As peasants became organized and some leaders amassed powerful followings in such areas as the Cochabamba valleys, they were armed and stood defiantly against traditional provincial authorities and hacienda administrators. In this threatening atmosphere, landlords fled the countryside and left a power vacuum that enabled peasants to assume *de facto* possession of the land. This was a precedent that took place even before the agrarian reform law was signed in August 1953, with the result that the government later legitimated such distribution of land. In other areas the *sindicato* became the legal instrument for initiating expropriation demands and getting titles, frequently under the guidance and influence of a regional peasant leader.

As agrarian reform was implemented, the government did not have the authority, the administrative infrastructure, the funds, or the personnel to establish production or marketing cooperatives, extend credit, and provide other means to transcend a mere distribution of individual plots.

The ideological element of mass mobilization was a crucial aspect, especially in certain areas, such as the Cochabamba valleys, where there was a large leadership pool among peasants, many of whom had previous organizing experience or affiliation with parties or the mining union movement (Dandler i.p.). Some proved most effective organizers and spokesmen because they did not merely transmit the revolution's message but instead developed their own culturally relevant ideology and formulated explicit goals that appealed most directly to peasants. The power of these leaders and their ideological message with broad mass appeal was evidenced in many ways, such as armed demonstrations to support the government, threats and attacks on provincial capitals, etc.

At the same time there was an important clientelist dimension during the early mobilization period (Dandler i.p.). There was strong competition among leaders to organize *sindicatos* and develop personal followings. These leaders projected themselves to their supporters as critical intermediaries and representatives, able to carry the peasant message and having resources and influence to reach higher levels of political decision making. These leaders also projected themselves to higher authorities as having a "power capability" (for the use of this term, see Anderson 1967). Armed militia units frequently were named after and identified with a particular prominent regional of national MNR leader. Because there were many authorities within the party and government at various levels, there were multiple legitimating sources, with the result that there was a differential distribution of resources and legitimacy. In this process some leaders were displaced, while others were favored.

The tendency toward the structuring of political relationships along clientelist lines was further reinforced by economic dependency relations. For example, peasant organizations at the provincial, departmental, or national levels, were greatly dependent on financial assistance from the party and government; the leaders of these organizations became increasingly dependent on higher authorities for salaries, fringe benefits, travel expenses and other privileges.

During the early years after the revolution, the MNR established many organizations — including the Ministry of Peasant Affairs and departmental agrarian reform offices — specifically to cultivate peasant support, to assist in agrarian reform, or to channel various resources and services to peasants. The National Workers Central (COB) and other labor organizations also had informal and formal ties with peasant organizations.

These institutional developments created an opportunity structure for numerous peasant leaders to occupy new positions. For example, several ministers of peasant affairs were prominent peasant leaders. Many peasant leaders also reached provincial, subprovincial, and municipal posts, as well as national electoral offices (after 1956), such as positions in the legislature. Some leaders rose very rapidly to higher positions. While there was greater turnover of leadership positions at lower levels, such as the local *sindicato* or a subprovincial organization (*sub-central*), competition was most intense around certain high or strategic positions, i.e. within the National Confederation of Peasants, the Ministry of Peasant Affairs, a departmental federation or provincial *central*, and, in the past, the legislature. Around these organizational nodes clustered a variety of coalitions among leaders and subordinates, in efforts to control coveted positions of prestige, power, and income. These loosely structured coalitions are referred to as *argollas* [rings] and *maquinitas* [little machines]. (For other instances of noncorporate elite positioning, see Leeds 1964; Schneider, et al. 1972.)

During interviews with many leaders, I found that a persistent theme was their concern with demonstrating their effectiveness by means of some concrete delivery of resources or services to their home communities and their followers in other villages. For instance, when X became minister of peasant affairs, one of his main goals was to build a secondary school in his home village to serve as an example to other localities and as a testimony of his effectiveness. During his first trips back to the village after he became minister, he personally delivered the construction materials to begin the work. Concern for the school construction, among other tasks, brought the leader back to the village most weekends for several months. Later the school was inaugurated during the national Day of the Indian, with considerable ceremony and the attendance of the vice-president and other authorities. Quite properly, the school was named after X, according to a plaque. On behalf of other communities that supported him, X brought construction materials and educational texts and personally intervened to obtain approval of road construction, change provincial authorities, and dismiss schoolteachers. This tendency to concentrate on the concrete and public prestation was also common among mining leaders, urban labor leaders, and political figures in general, in order to gain legitimacy and develop a loyal following.

In effect, a vast system of patronage developed in Bolivia after 1952, encouraged by the MNR and later governments in an attempt to win popular support. In this process, thousands of villages became involved in small-scale irrigation projects and in road and school construction; thus resources were channeled to the local *sindicato*, stimulated by the collective task it demanded.

As political participation was vastly expanded through universal suffrage, electoral politics accentuated internal dependency relationships and the vertical structuring of clienteles around particular leaders. The MNR had three presidential elections (1956, 1960, 1964) and two regular legislative elections (1958 and 1962). Because elections were also held for municipal, party, and *sindicato* posts on other election dates, there was an intense competition for positions and appointments. A peasant leader who had a strong following in an area was highly prized for votes he might deliver to a candidate.

The MNR was in power for twelve years, a constitutional period unusually long in Bolivia's history. But the MNR was not able to sustain itself; the transmission of party and governmental leadership generated major crises that threatened the stability of the party and eventually led to a gradual fragmentation of forces or party splits.

To better understand the MNR's internal problems and the process of *sindicato* cooptation, we should focus at least briefly on some external pressures to resolve national economic problems. During the early 1950's, Bolivia was faced with galloping inflation, a fall in tin production and prices, lack of foreign credit, and decapitalization of the mines and other sectors. In a favorable stance toward the Bolivian Revolution, the United States offered to the MNR advice and certain opportunities for credit, as well as preconditions, in order to solve some of these problems. The outcome was a compromise on the course of the revolution, reinforcing dependency relationships with the United States and exacerbating internal conflicts over policies. One major program that brought the MNR considerable political and social costs was the monetary stabilization plan (1956–1962). Pressed by the United States and the International Monetary Fund, the plan involved a wage freeze, control of labor demands, displacement of workers, especially in the mines, and other measures ostensibly recommended as "economically" sound. In effect, the stabilization plan was presented as a precondition for credit, development grants, deficit budget support, food surplus aid, and recapitalization of the mines.

Even before the plan was adopted, the MNR's programmatic "center" and the president were pitted against the left wing of the MNR, especially the labor and mining organizations, with the result that the government had to rely increasingly on peasant support to implement the economic stabilization measures. Another consequence of the plan was the rebuilding of the armed forces to guarantee stability and control strikes and other protests against unpopular economic measures. In general, the stabilization plan favored the centralization of power over the diffusion of forces represented by the civilian militia, many of whom were in open defiance of governmental policies by the latter 1950's.

The repercussions of the stabilization plan and the policy differences and leadership conflicts within the MNR were all reflected in the politics of labor, mining, and peasant organizations. There was a high incidence of leadership struggles, organizational cleavages, coups and counter-coups at various levels, even political homicides. To implement mone-tary stabilization, the president embarked on a collision course with the left-wing leader Juan Lechín, Vice-President Chavez Ortíz, the Bolivian Workers Central (COB), and the Mining Union Federation. President Siles proceeded to undermine their influence and establish alternative or parallel organizations with a leadership that was favorable to the sta-bilization plan. These organizations were aptly called *bloques re-estructu-radores* (restructuring teams or blocks).

The government relied on these new leaders and organizations for political support, while it also strongly cultivated loyal peasant political backing, thus further eroding working-class and peasant solidarity. In this connection, José Rojas, a powerful regional leader from the upper valley of Cochabamba (Ucureña), was appointed minister of peasant affairs by the president, a political strategy at a crucial juncture in order to win political support from peasants. Significantly, one of the first actions of Rojas as minister was to mobilize personally an armed regi-ment of peasants to confront striking miners opposed to stabilization and the wage freeze.

An extreme example of political dependency and a process of coop-tation was the protracted conflict that occurred between Ucureña and the town of Cliza in the upper valley of Cochabamba over a period of five years (1959–1964). During this period, peasant leaders became in-volved in a struggle for the political hegemony of the valley and neigh-boring areas, a rivalry that was intimately related to the internecine strife and institutional crisis within the MNR. Each of these two localities was a center of a competing "domain," controlled by a powerful regional leader and a core of lieutenants and involving a wide-ranging coalition with leaders of other provincial and local organizations. In certain contexts, *sindicatos* operated as an armed following loyal to the regional leader in Cliza or Ucureña. In turn, each of the two leaders was connected to a national figure seeking the presidency.

As violence erupted between rival groups and hundreds of people died, the army was sent to control the area. But sporadic fighting continued to occur over several years, because the armed forces themselves did not play a neutral role but instead favored Ucureña. By 1962–1963, a general (René Barrientos) promoted himself as mediator and brought peace to the region by forging an alliance between the two centers. Several leaders from the valley were banned and a broad leadership coalition that supported Lechín was destroyed. Barrientos won considerable peasant support in the Cochabamba valleys because, in the eyes of many, he had brought peace. This was an important factor in his election to the vice presidency and, four months later (November 1964), his rise to the presidency through a coup d'état which ushered in a new period of military governments in Bolivia. The rise of Barrientos symbolized the MNR's splintering forces and ideological crisis. Barrientos had developed a powerful political capability and had amassed considerable popularity at a time when there was no longer a civilian contender in the MNR to contest him or the armed forces.

AGRARIAN REFORM WITHOUT DEVELOPMENT

The most important means for the MNR to win and maintain the political support of peasants was land distribution. In the rhetoric of the party, peasants were constantly reminded that they had been liberated, that they now owned land, that they could now have schools for their children, and that they must solidly support the government because there were landowners and *falangistas* who threatened to overthrow the government and take away the peasants' land. The distribution of land titles was in general very slow, except in areas where peasants were more militantly organized, a factor that contributed to the sense of land insecurity and dependency relationships as a basis of support for the MNR.

In spite of the importance of peasants as a base of political support, the MNR and the various military governments that followed all failed to bring about long-term economic development in the rural areas where agrarian reform had occurred. This major limitation was intimately related to the internal political dependency mentioned earlier, as well as to Bolivia's deepening economic dependency on the United States in many areas.

Existing state agencies, such as the Agricultural Extension Service or the Agricultural Credit Bank, continued to operate along traditional lines. Once they obtained United States and other financial assistance in the late 1950's, their policies favored mechanization and low man/land ratios; consequently, they did not have a significant impact on the areas where land was expropriated for peasants. Not surprisingly, these and other agencies turned to the development of newly colonized areas and large-scale commercial agriculture and cattle raising in tropical eastern Bolivia as a more promising effort.

In general, there was a tendency to underestimate the economic changes that peasants themselves were undergoing. Some changes resulted directly from agrarian reform, not particularly from other direct government measures. For instance, there was a widespread belief that agricultural production had fallen sharply because of rural political mobilization and agrarian reform. The impression was reinforced by the lack of certain products in cities and the mines during the early years after the agrarian reform; but according to a study by Clark (1967), the main problem was marketing and transportation. The large-scale marketing network, which had been controlled and run by landlords and their administrators, particularly in the northern highlands, had broken down as a result of agrarian reform and the flight of landlords from the countryside. But within several years, there was a proliferation of new rural markets, peasant middlemen, and trucks and road networks to fill the demand. In this context, efforts to stimulate marketing and production cooperatives probably would have succeeded.

An extreme example of economic dependency that was reinforced after 1952 through United States surplus agricultural commodities was the failure to stimulate wheat production. Until 1952, Boliva imported considerable wheat from Argentina, a policy that benefited Bolivian mill owners with differential exchange rates. After 1952, as budgetary deficits and inflation mounted, Bolivia could turn to surplus flour from the United States, with the result that even the flour mills closed down. It was easier for Bolivia to obtain the necessary flour from the United States through soft loans in national currency (Public Law 480), than to promote domestic wheat production. As one official of the Corporación Minera de Bolivia [COMIBOL, the state mining corporation] told me:

We don't know how to even start buying the wheat from peasants, nor are there long-term incentives for them to produce. We have an easier way of doing things: we can call the U.S. embassy, cry for help to feed the miners, sign up for a speedy delivery within the next several months, and for this service we don't even have to pay cash.

The tropical region of Santa Cruz was one of the few areas where the MNR applied a long-term development policy, but ironically this led to the entrenchment of an entrepreneurial and newly landowning elite that eventually became the mainstay of Banzer's counterrevolution of 1971 (Whitehead 1974).

General Barrientos essentially continued (1964–1969) with the economic policies of the MNR and did not implement long-term or large-scale development in the densely populated highland or valley areas. Ironically, he drew significant popular support from peasants, particularly from those of the Cochabamba valleys. Barrientos carefully cultivated an intricate patronage network with loyal peasant leaders, and using an undisclosed palace budget, he himself delivered small tangible services and resources to thousands of villages and leaders, frequently presenting himself personally as proof of his dedication.

Barrientos uncritically accepted and stimulated the community development program begun by the MNR in the early 1960's. Financed and proposed by the United States Agency for International Development within the Ministry of Agriculture, the plan was attractive to many technical experts who tended to regard negatively the agrarian reform, particularly the accompanying politicization, the creation of an armed militia in the countryside, and the general attitude of self-assertiveness among peasants and leaders, which of course sharply conflicted with traditional stereotypes of the treatment accorded to peasants. These agricultural experts thought that the highland and valley areas had limited development possibilities, and they looked toward the settlement and economic development of tropical eastern Bolivia as a greater priority.

Like many other community development plans, the Bolivian program took little cognizance of the specific national or regional sociocultural milieu. The three most important goals were to change traditional values, to promote local organizations, and to develop a local leadership. The program established a scheme whereby *sindicatos* were to be replaced in the long run by *juntas comunales*, which in turn were to be the building blocks of future cooperatives. Leaders were correspondingly categorized as "natural or informal" and "formal"; the latter were *sindicato* leaders to be generally avoided or replaced at the local level by more representative ("natural") leaders. Characteristically, the program was to a great extent aimed at resolving "local" problems and establishing alternative local leadership and organizations; supralocal problems and the articulation of peasant interests at the national or regional levels were to be channeled through specialized bureaucratic agencies which, by implication, would be staffed mostly by nonpeasant specialists. Yet, paradoxically, the program ignored the significant transformation that had occurred in the Bolivian countryside with respect to each of the three goals mentioned above. It was at the local level that peasants most strongly identified with the *sindicato*, that the leadership most frequently circulated within the community, and that local projects (schools, roads, etc.) were accomplished.

Not surprisingly, because the program was viewed as an imposition, efforts to implement it met considerable opposition by *sindicato* leaders and peasants in general. Most seriously, the community development program, by creating a hierarchy of specialized bureaucratic agencies, tried to weaken the role of "supralocal" peasant organizations and their leaders. This was hardly a substitute to serve and represent peasant interests.

Throughout the last two decades, the governments of Bolivia have been unable to transcend immediate political demands and strategies in order to develop the Andean countryside beyond a mere distribution of land or localized public works projects. Highland and valley peasants themselves have on various occasions expressed dissatisfaction with such static policies. For example, in Ucureña, where the first rural *sindicato* was established in 1936, where the agrarian reform decree, symbolizing the peasant's struggle for ownership of a private plot, was signed in 1953, a group of peasants (neighbors with contiguous land) took the initiative in 1969 to discuss with me and others their interest in consolidating part of their land as an experimental production cooperative (for dairy, vegetables, and fruit). As one of them said, "the *minifundio* for us and our children no longer holds a future; it's a dead end." Their idea was to maximize land use by irrigation and land consolidation, which consequently would greatly raise productivity and year-round employment in agriculture.

Concurrently, several prominent leaders of Ucureña and the valleys (a senator and former minister of peasant affairs, a house legislator, a head of the departmental federation, and others) expressed their despair about the prospects of *minifundia* agriculture and the displacement of peasants. They questioned the impact of local projects and searched for policies and programs that could contribute in the long run to the development and well-being of peasant families. They emphasized the need to implement a regional development plan (encompassing an area of about 100,000 hectares), with irrigation and soil improvement as the main immediate target, to complement already existing factors. This idea was pursued with agronomists and others for several months. Later, the leaders formally presented the proposal to President Barrientos. They urged him to break away from small projects and to concentrate on an ambitious regional plan to transform the Cochabamba valleys and establish a precedent for other areas. This was presented to the president as a politically significant act that could win him many votes and ensure his popularity among peasants. Although the president at first expressed considerable enthusiasm for the plan, several months later he told me that such an idea was

...too visonary, too much into the future, whereas I have to work very fast, I need to show concrete results to the people tomorrow, in a week, in a month, in part because they want to see tangible accomplishments and also because I may not be around as president in five years.

Nor did the next four presidents (including the current one) follow up the suggestions of the peasant leaders.

This leads us inevitably to a reevaluation of the subject of social change, "modernization," development, the nature of internal and external dependency relationships, and bureaucratic models versus indigenous social movements.

REFERENCES

ANDERSON, CHARLES W.
   1967   *Politics and economic change in Latin America.* Princeton: D. Van
          Nostrand.
CLARK, RONALD J.
   1967   *Land reform and peasant market participation on the north highlands
          of Bolivia.* Land Tenure Center Reprint 42. Madison: University of
          Wisconsin Press.
DANDLER, JORGE
   i.p.   "'Low classness' or wavering populism? A peasant movement in
          Bolivia (1952–1953)," in *Ideology and social change in Latin America.*
          Edited by June Nash and Juan Corradi. New York: Gordon Breach.
LEEDS, ANTHONY
   1964   Brazilian careers and social structure: a case history and model.
          American Anthropologist 66:1321–1347.
MALLOY, JAMES M.
   1970   *Bolivia: the uncompleted revolution.* Pittsburgh: University of Pittsburgh Press.
NASH, JUNE
   1975   "Dependency and the failure of feedback: the case of Bolivian mining
          communities," in *Atti del XL Congresso Internazionale degli Americanisti.*

SCHNEIDER, PETER, JANE SCHNEIDER, EDWARD HANSEN
  1972   Modernization and development: the role of regional elites and non-corporate groups in the European Mediterranean. *Comparative Studies in Society and History* 14 (3): 328–350.
WHITEHEAD, LAURENCE
  1974   "Santa Cruz politics and the Bolivian revolution," in *Latin American Urban Research*. Russel Sage Publications.

The Peasants and the Bureaucracy in Chilean Agrarian Reform

JACQUES CHONCHOL

The following is the text of the keynote address delivered to the seminar by Dr. Jacques Chonchol. His talk was delivered in French; the text was then transcribed and translated into English. But Chonchol has not been able to approve the text at any stage. Shortly after he returned to Chile from the ICAES, a bloody military coup overthrew the regime whose accomplishments he describes with such objectivity in this paper. He was able to take refuge in the Embassy of Venezuela in Santiago, and as of June 1974, nine months after the coup, he was still there. Perhaps by the time these words are printed he will have been able to leave his refuge to continue his productive career. In the meantime, this text has a certain historical value, being an appraisal of the achievements and problems of the Allende government on the eve of its demise.

As Minister of Agriculture during the two initial years of the Popular Unity Government in Chile (1970–1972), Chonchol directed the massive agrarian reform program which liquidated the latifundia in Chile, liberating peasants from the landowning class that had dominated rural Chile for centuries. In 1972 he left the government for a teaching post and to found the Centro de Estudios sobre la Realidad Nacional (CEREN), an outstanding social science center in Chile which, among other activities, published the journal *Estudios sobre la Realidad Nacional*, well known for its theoretical discussions on the problem of socialist transformation. This institute is now closed and the journal has ceased publication.

I have been asked to describe the problem of land reform in Chile, and especially to point out a few aspects connected with the relationship between the farmers and the state bureaucracy.

I am going to try to give you as briefly as possible a few details on the land reform procedures in Chile, which I think offer some interesting lessons. First, I will discuss the relationships which occur between political factors, the peasantry, and the other state institutions (which sometimes work at cross-purposes to one another) in the process of the transformation of society.

I think that a second interesting aspect of the Chilean experience for other countries, although it may only apply to Chile because every country has its own history and its own experience, is perhaps the case of a country little developed economically and overdeveloped institutionally, politically, and culturally. And indeed, this contradiction adds a rather interesting complication to efforts to transform the society because we are trying to do something which is perhaps impossible: we are trying to establish a socialist system based on a bourgeois democracy in an underdeveloped country, and we are trying to do all this by transforming the institutions as quickly as possible, at the same time avoiding a violent explosion or a fratricidal conflict within Chilean society.

I do not know if finally we will be successful, but in any case we are trying to move in that direction. I would say that the land reform problem has been around in Chile as in many Latin American countries for a very long time. I think that Latin America is perhaps one of the regions in the world where you have the greatest concentration of land in the hands of a small group of people — those that are generally called latifundists. Some of them are traditional farmers, others are industrialists or merchants or very wealthy people who in any case belong to the small dominant group. And there is a peasant mass of quite a considerable size representing a very big part of the population which has no land at all or else absolutely insufficient plots of land where they cannot make ends meet or where they vegetate in deplorable conditions. So there is a very unequal distribution of land and for a very long time this has made land reform an essential problem in terms of society, of the perfection of the political system and also of economics.

A second reason why Chilean land reform has been an important problem for a long time is that traditional agriculture does not produce enough to meet the country's needs. Our population is not increasing as rapidly as in other Latin American countries; there are some Latin American countries where the population is increasing by 3 and 4 percent. In Chile, the population is only increasing at a rate of about 2 percent per annum. But in any case this considerable population increase is related to the process of industrialization which went on between the two World Wars and which, especially after the crisis of the 1930's, increased the population's income. All of this increased domestic demand for foodstuffs, and traditional farming could not respond adequately. In addition to the social and political factors, there is the economic factor of traditional farming's inability to develop at the same rate as the country's requirements.

But it is strange that, even though it is a real problem and a problem which has existed for a long time, land reform was only carried out very recently. Why? I think that basically the problems were political and connected with social organization. The political reasons are related to the power of the landowner groups who were represented by the conservative parties which had a relatively large majority in the parliament. The Chilean political system is a presidential system with a President of the Republic who is the Chief Executive and a Parliament that is the legislative power. There is also a jural power. But all laws have to be approved by Parliament. As a land reform law must be submitted to Parliament in an institutionalized system like ours, the power which these political groups representing the right wing and the latifundists had, always prevented Parliament from approving laws authorizing the government to carry out a land reform program.

This power held by the right-wing groups in Parliament was due to one thing which also exists in many other countries; this is unequal parliamentary representation. The cities generally elect a certain number of members of Parliament but the small rural constituencies elect a proportionally larger number of senators or members of Parliament. This means that fewer votes are needed to elect a political representative in the rural districts. The traditional structure of the domination of great landowners caused the peasants to be dependents and to support the traditional political system. Thus, the landowners had sufficient political power in Parliament to prevent the approval of the land reform laws.

The second weak point which prevented land reform was the lack of organization among the peasants. There were no unions, very few cooperatives, and very few forms of organization having sufficient social or political power to fight for a land reform that would serve their interests.

For instance, in the peasants' trade union organization, our system was very common in Latin America — to make laws in order not to make changes — that is to say, we had a trade union law that made a trade union organization possible, but it caused so many operational difficulties in setting up trade unions that we had the law but not the trade union. This is a procedure that conservative groups use quite often in undeveloped political systems to prevent social development and to prevent the organization and progress of the people.

The third important political point was that the left-wing forces, and especially the great Marxist parties (of which there are two in Chile, the Communist and the Socialist parties) were parties which, through their own Marxist formation, were closely linked with the world of industrial workers or miners; indeed, in their conception of the proletariat, in their proletarian basis, in their relations, they had always developed this social sector, but they had not worked in the rural areas. It was a sector without any industrialization or proletariat. Rather it was a semifeudal system.

On the other hand, the parties of the center or the left center representing the interests of the middle class, and which, during the twentieth century, had done a great deal to improve the population's standard of living, were also fundamentally urban parties; through their political struggles they had obtained a number of social benefits, such as allowance systems, housing systems, pay systems, and work-safety systems for the urban population, but they did not offer support to, nor had they been able to resolve the problems of the rural population. I should also mention in this connection that Chile, while being a very undeveloped country economically, is very urbanized. Seventy-five percent of the population is urban and 25 percent rural. This means that Chile's population structure is more similar to that of the far more developed countries of Europe or other parts of the world than to a population distribution structure that corresponds to the country's economic development level.

In the last ten years the land reform problem has at least been approached. I think this was due to several reasons. One of the main reasons was that the political struggle also started to penetrate into the countryside. That is to say, the land reform was not the consequence of a PRESSURE by the peasants and of a peasants' organization able to achieve it, but of the political struggle of the urban parties which, to conquer the peasants' votes, joined the traditional forces of the right wing; both the left-wing and center parties presented the peasants with the land reform problem as a problem to be resolved, in order to win both their support and their votes in the general political struggle taking place in the country.

There has been another fairly important point, not only in Chile but also, I think, elsewhere in Latin America. I do not know how important it has been in other regions like Africa and Asia. This has been the influence, I would call it intellectual, of the United Nations organizations. For a number of years a number of organizations such as the FAO (Food and Agricultural Organization) and the regional economic commissions, particularly the Economic Commission for Latin America, have posed the problem of development. And in their analysis of the development problem they have pointed out that it is impossible to accelerate the economic development of these underdeveloped countries if the farming problem is not resolved; that is, the problem of the economic and social integration of the peasant masses in the national system. Thus there was a good deal of intellectual preparation which also helped to change the traditional views and the ideas people had about the importance of the agrarian reform, which, for many people, a few years ago was something terrible. It was considered something which international communism was advocating to end democracy and liberty. Among the rather intellectual middle classes this intellecutal work, this demonstration of the relationship between agrarian reform and economic development, was a very important factor in approaching this problem of agrarian reform.

I think there were other political elements such as the Cuban Revolution in the early sixties and the new policy of the United States government in Kennedy's day. The Alliance for Progress also proposed the reform of the structures as a desirable goal and oriented somewhat the help given by the United States. These two factors were also essential to give more force to the possibilities of achieving agrarian reform in many of the Latin American countries.

All this meant that in the Christian Democratic government, under President Frei, which lasted from 1964 to 1970, the agrarian reform problem was tackled. It was tackled by the combination of center and left-wing forces which formed a majority in parliament. They proposed the approval of a new trade union law, an agrarian reform law, and the beginning of a policy of transforming the traditional rural society. The main idea of the Christian Democratic government was to limit the amount of land a person or a family could have to eighty irrigated hectares or its equivalent in inferior land. That is to say any properties exceeding eighty irrigated hectares could be expropriated. The idea was to end the great latifundial properties and create, rather, a medium-sized capitalist or intensive property structure, where an efficient agriculture could develop. At the same time the expropriated land would be given to the farmers, organized in cooperatives or in family properties, but with the families organized in cooperatives. The purpose was to create, along with the modern capitalist sector, a sector of small peasant farmers organized in cooperatives utilizing all those services which would help develop a more modern and more intensive agriculture.

But this experiment by the Christian Democrats had its limitations. The main one was that they tried to carry out a capitalist transformation and modernization of the traditional farming society with some vaguely socialist elements, without altering fundamentally the structures of the rest of society. That is to say, the government wanted to eliminate the large landowners, but it also wanted to turn some of them into modern capitalists; it wanted to develop the peasant organizations while keeping a modern intensive capitalist pattern in the industrial sector. So, gradually a number of contradictions emerged. At a certain moment, the government succeeded in separating the interests of the large landowners from those of the urban capitalist sector. But gradually, as the experiment developed, the conjunction of these rural interests and these urban interests slowed down the land reform process. Finally, the government did much less than it really wanted to do, according to its plans.

During this period a situation important in terms of its subsequent consequences arose; this was the trade union organization of the peasants. The Frei government modified the trade union law and established a new law offering numerous facilities for the organization of peasant associations. These associations, organized with state and government support, worked against the interests of the estate owners. Trade union activities were initiated. These trade union struggles were not only struggles for salaries and social benefits, but also increasingly became struggles FOR land, to obtain for the peasants, through the land reform law, the land which was held by the large landowners. So there was during this period a social organization of peasants which had not existed before, which with some support from the government became an important driving factor and which created pressure for land reform.

Finally, in 1970, at the end of that government, there were 1,400 properties which had been expropriated, covering 3,500,000 hectares, but there was a sizable peasants' trade union organization applying pressure for more land. At the same time there was a certain amount of frustration among the peasants because they felt that the government was not making sufficiently rapid progress in terms of their aspirations which reflected the organization of power in society.

In 1970 there were new presidential elections, and the left-wing candidate, President Allende, was elected with a relative majority, through a political coalition which included the two great Marxist parties, certain minor left-wing Christian groups, and the radical party which was a center left party. He found himself with a program which included several essential elements. One of these elements was the nationalization of all the great copper mines as well as the other mining resources which were in the hands of foreign companies. A second was the nationalization of the whole banking system. A third was the creation of what is called a sector of social property in which the state would hold the largest industrial monopolies. A fourth was the acceleration of the land reform to end, finally, the great latifundial properties of the country.

Now this government was in a very special situation. It had executive power, that is, it had the President of the Republic and the whole state apparatus which depends on the President of the Republic, i.e. the whole executive sector. But it was a minority party in Parliament where there were on one side the basically centrist forces of the Christian Democrats and on the other side those of the right wing. In terms of traditional political structure, this is perhaps the kind of thing you find in the United States, where you can have executive power and still be a minority in the Senate and the House; this creates many limitations. Socially speaking, the base of this government was chiefly the more class-conscious urban working classes and part of the peasantry, of the subproletariat and the lower middle-class groups. The remainder of these sectors and the dominant groups, were represented either by the center group, the Christian Democrats, or else the right-wing parties.

The government's action concentrated especially, in the first two years, on nationalizing all the mines. The nationalization of all the large mines through a constitutional reform created many problems with the companies, and especially the American companies. The government also nationalized most of the banks, using the law which had been approved under the Christian Democrat government; it accelerated land reform and expropriated about 3,500 large properties with about 6,000,000 hectares, which meant that after two years, 40 percent of the usable land was in the reformed sector.

In this transformation of the landed society, which was a part of a more general transformation of society, there were three types of contradiction — the contradictions we are currently experiencing. One was the lack of balance between demand and the increase in production; the second was the contradiction between different peasant sectors, a separate contradiction from that with the large landowners; a third was the contradiction between peasants and the bureaucracy.

Perhaps the most visible contradiction at the moment, and the toughest one, is the contradiction between demand and increase in production. This government, when it came to power, found itself in a very disastrous position: that is to say, there was a flight of capital and a crisis in the industrial sector. Many factories were running at half of their capacity. There were all the economic or political factors which can exist in an underdeveloped country governed by the standards of the capitalist system in which, suddenly, a government comes up and says: "Were going to set up a socialist system." So there was a stampede of capital, both intermediate and large capital, and all this created an economic crisis and much unemployment.

Then, faced with this economic situation, the government took, not socialist measures, but I would say Keynesian measures. They had to reestablish offer. They increased wages and redistributed wages. To give the people work, they introduced plans for housing and public works. All this allowed the government to control the economic crisis, but at the same time it created an enormous increase in the demand for foodstuffs.

This demand increased in the first year of the government, by 14 percent. And domestic agricultural production, even though it increased that first year, increased by only 6 percent. This was a much bigger rate of increase than the traditional growth of agriculture which had been progressing at a rate of 3 to 4 percent. But in any case there was a gap between the increased demand and the increased national production, which had to be compensated for by increased imports.

The same problem arose the year after. There were the social forces pressing for an improvement of living standards, workers who wanted full employment, and a 12 percent increase in demand for food. Production continued to increase but at a lower rate; that is to say, there were problems of maladjustment and climate, and production increased by only 2 percent. Again, the difference was made up for by increased imports.

This led us to an increase in foodstuff imports from $200,000,000, to between $400,000,000 and $500,000,000. In the international market, the prices were rising due to a lack of foodstuffs and this created additional pressure on the country's balance of payments.

At the same time, and in addition to this impact, copper, which was the country's main export, was dropping in price in the international market, and the big companies, to counter the nationalization measures, were causing difficulties. In Europe especially, where Chilean copper was sold, they were making all sorts of attempts to obstruct Chilean exports.

At the same time the country had, like many underdeveloped countries, a staggering foreign trade debt. The total debt of the country was $4,000,000,000 and every year it had to pay about $400,000,000 to $500,000,000 depreciation and interest on its debts for a total exports figure of little more than $1,000,000,000. The combined effects of the national debt to be paid, the lower prices for copper, difficulties in exporting it, and the increased food imports created a very acute and very serious problem of balance of payments.

These balance of payment difficulties had a negative effect on the increase of domestic production because the industrial and farming sectors were very dependent on certain items which were imported from abroad. For example, agriculture, in order to develop, needed fertilizers, especially phosphates, which the country could not produce, as well as agricultural machinery, and many items which had to be paid for in foreign currency. Similarly, industries, like many of those set up in the underdeveloped countries, depend on big international consortiums. These industries have to import raw materials; in fact, they are processing industries which, to increase their production, have to absorb more foreign currency. This is especially true of industry that produces for the middle classes rather than the people, for instance, the automotive industry and the consumer goods industry which depend on importing foreign licences and which, to increase their domestic production, must increase their foreign currency requirements.

This situation had much more serious consequences at the end of last year and this year, and we are now in a position where the nation's production has not increased. In some sectors, there is even a small reduction; in agriculture there was a decrease of 5 to 6 percent which makes the whole general economic situation worse.

So the first problem that has to be faced, and I think Chile is a good example for other countries, is the relationship between structural change and the redistribution of income to those members of the population who need to increase their consumption, and the dependence of the economy on outside forces through the balance of payments. Up till now we have not been able to adjust to this situation, and this is one of the serious economic crises which has led us to an inflation that at the moment has reached about 200 percent per annum.

In any case, I should like to point out this problem especially because in many of the reports that we have heard we have had a very interesting analysis from within the cooperatives, or the peasant groups, but always everything that happens in the country depends very much on what happens on the world market outside in the political conflicts. I think it is very difficult to analyze and understand if you do not put the situation in the more general national or international context where this particular analysis is made.

The second problem we should like to deal with is that of the contradictions between different groups of peasants. In the reformed sector, i.e. in the big latifundia, most productivity was lower than in the rest of the economy, since very few people operated with a relatively high level of capitalization. Eighty to ninety thousand peasant families live on the 40 percent of the land which has been expropriated and which is in the reformed sector. On the remaining 60 percent, where we find medium and small landholding, we have nearly 250,000 to 300,000 peasant families. The difference between the distribution of the land and the distribution of the population is a result of a historical system in which only part of the labor in the large latifundia was used, while a large portion of the labor serving the latifundia did not live inside them but was concentrated in the small estates and was eventually taken over by the big estates.

In the traditional system which is not peculiar to Chile but is characteristic of a number of countries in the latifundial sector, there were three types of estates. There were the highly capitalized enterprises using very little labor. There were more traditional enterprises where there was a little more labor that was paid in cash and had the right to have a house, the right to cultivate a piece of land, and the right to have a certain number of animals. There were others who had a lot of land but did not have any capital; they used sharecropping as a way of saving capital. Such people had little to do with the land; their only capital was the land. And the capital and the work were invested by the others, so they shared the expense. Whether there was an agricultural or proletarian worker or a sharecropper, the procedure was the same. On the whole, there was a much lower population-land ratio than in the small estates on the other side where there was a very dense population.

The final result is that we are in a situation where we ought to transfer a certain number of people from the small-estate sector to the big latifundia. But there we come up against two difficulties: one is the traditional concept of the peasants who lived in these great latifundia, who felt that once the boss had left, the land was for them and for their children, and not for the other peasants. They had the social consciousness of a group living inside the estate, but they did not have a national consciousness of the whole of the peasant problem. So they opposed the entry of more peasants because they thought that if more people came in they themselves would get less. The second problem is that in order to bring more peasants into the estates from the outside, a very large additional capital investment would be needed, which the country is not in a position to provide rapidly.

So we are in a situation where certain very poor peasants, who are very exploited, today are slightly opposed to the land reform because they consider it to be a benefit which served others but not them. They are politically encouraged by the latifundial sectors to oppose the government.

Thus we have a contradiction between different classes of peasants which is made worse by the political contradictions. In the peasant world there is a political struggle between the government and the opposition parties. Each party appeals to certain groups, and this doubles the property conflicts and organizational conflicts, creating one of the big problems which has arisen as a result of land reform.

The third contradiction, and it is a very important one, is that between peasants and officialdom. Generally one thinks that the problem of bureaucracy is a problem specific to the socialist countries. I think it is a much more characteristic and much more serious problem in the underdeveloped countries trying to transform themselves because the members of the existing officialdom, which is fragmented into many ministries and independent organizations, are basically urban middle-class people, who, through their political struggle, have obtained promotions through the state officialdom. They feel they are superior to the peasants; they are not in the oligarchy but they want to keep their advantages.

This officialdom, especially in Chile, where there is a civil service in which even with a traditional change of government, the major part of the bureaucracy stays in its place (ministers and department heads are changed but the bureaucrats continue in their positions), poses various problems for the transformation of society. First, there is a problem of class. They are middle-class people; the peasants are poor. They feel they are superior, even those who belong to the left-wing parties and work for the peasants. They have a kind of paternalism that is sometimes beneficial and sometimes harmful. There is an attitude toward the peasant that does not permit an adequate development of the peasant community organization.

Second, the officialdom is spread out in a very large number of different organizations. The underdeveloped countries, little by little, as new problems have been posed, have set up new organizations without eliminating the previous ones. So they all work side by side, each body wanting to keep its independence, and the political contradictions also exist within officialdom. This means that the government cannot take unified action, easily, but that there are a number of contradictory actions by different organizations, sometimes working along the same lines, sometimes opposing each other with different policies.

Furthermore, in a democratic system when there is a coalition government, with different political parties, each political party wants to use the bureaucratic structure for its own benefit. So the contradictions between political parties are also reflected within the officialdom.

Finally, there's a very important problem in that the officialdom lives in the towns, because in the underdeveloped countries, the living conditions are much more agreeable in towns than in the countryside; housing facilities, schools for the children, material goods, and distractions are found in the towns and are scarce in the country. So these are people who are separated from the countryside and to get there, to work, they need jeeps, they need cars, and very often they do not have enough of them. They spend a lot of time inside offices in the towns and have very few contacts with the peasants.

Now there is a problem which I should especially like to mention because I think it is a very important one. I think it exists in other countries as well. This officialdom generally has no direct responsibility in the production system and I am going to mention a comparison which I think will illustrate what I mean. If you find a factory in a town, there are the workers who live in the popular quarter. There are the engineers who live in a more elegant, middle-class quater. They all leave their homes in the morning and are together at the factory. Whether the factory works eight hours, sixteen hours, of twenty-four hours, there are always the technicians the staff, and the workers working together. If you eliminate the board of directors through nationalization, the factory does not suffer — it continues to operate. That is to say if you nationalize, if you transfer property, the internal structure of the economic enterprise is not changed very much; it can work very well.

But if you take a large country estate of the traditional or semitraditional type, you have the peasants who cultivate the land. You have the owner or the administrator who manages the estate and governs the workers; but at the same time he is the element which relates the farm to the rest of the economic system, for buying, for selling, for sales relations, etc. If you do away, by nationalization, with the owner or the director, you suddenly cut someone who has to be eliminated, the exploiter; but at the same time you have to replace him in his role in order to connect the farm or the big estate with the rest of the economic system. And this role, which had to be taken over by bureaucrats both for production and marketing, cannot be carried out adequately because the bureaucrats are not prepared to play their part; in fact, they are in the towns and not in the countryside where they are permanently needed.

So, for many peasants there is another contradiction: not with the owner who is no longer there, or with the exploiter, but with the state civil servant who is not ready to give the services which are essential in the new situation which he must assume today as in an economic enterprise.

So I think that we have a very difficult problem here, one not at all easy to resolve, but an essential problem, which we must find a way of resolving so that we can advance economically, in a positive manner, in the new enterprises arising as a consequence of the land reform.

Cooperatives, Participation, and Development: Three Failures

GABRIEL GAGNON

For a number of years the cooperative system has been offered by most international bodies as a panacea for the economic difficulties of the Third World peasant, as the most favorable pathway to his becoming a modern citizen in a modern state, and especially as an irreplaceable instrument allowing him to participate in development projects.

This optimistic ideology is beginning to be reexamined (Fals-Borda 1970), while the habitual theoretical perspective of development ideologists is being attacked by theorists of neo-imperialism (Amin 1971, 1973; Gunder Frank 1972; Emmanuel 1969) as well as by critics of the continued growth of capitalist countries.

In the course of the last ten years, my students and I have had the opportunity to observe on location the evolution of the cooperative system in three countries, which, even though they differ in culture, are on a quite similar level of development. These field studies were carried out in Senegal (1962–1963, 1967, 1971–1972), in Cuba (1966, 1967, 1972), and in Tunisia (1969–1970, 1971, 1973),[1] where we were able to follow rather closely the development and then the relative failure of the cooperative movement. While in the field in 1962–1963, we witnessed the political crisis over the orientation of Senegalese economic development which set Prime Minister Mamadou Dia in opposition to President Leopold Senghor (Gagnon 1965). In Cuba, our principal studies were carried out in 1966 and 1967, just before the "battle of the ten million tons" which ended in

Appeared originally as "Coopératives, participation et développement: trois échecs."
[1] I thank Alfred Sicotte and Jules Savaria, both doctoral students in sociology at the University of Montreal, for their important contribution to the empirical and theoretical content of this article.

putting a damper on the diverse forms of peasant organization that had been encouraged by the socialist revolution up to that point. In Tunisia, a project intended to study the implementation of cooperatives in agriculture, inspired by the minister Ben Salah in 1969, soon was transformed into a study of the elimination of cooperatives following a conflict between President Bourguiba and his minister concerning the role of cooperatives.

We have before us, then, three instances in which the highly sought-after coordination between cooperatives and the political system provokes either an overt or a latent crisis; each terminates to the detriment of the cooperatives even though the official ideology, if one studies the speeches of Bourguiba, Senghor and Castro, placed high value on the cooperative system.

Another characteristic that is common to the three cases studied and which is interesting from a comparative point of view, rests in the fact that a charismatic type of political leadership prevails in the three areas and has remained the same since the independence of Tunisia in 1956, of Senegal in 1960, and since the revolution of 1959 in Cuba.

Let us attempt then to analyze briefly each of these cases before arriving at a certain number of conclusions about the nature of the cooperative system and about its insertion into a social formation or a global society, whichever term one prefers.

SENEGAL

At the time of its independence in 1960, Senegal, the earliest colonized of the African francophone countries, decided to adopt its own policy of development based upon both national economic planning, wherein the cooperative system would play a dominant role, and an ideology newly defined as "African socialism" by the leaders of the time, President Leopold Sedar Senghor and Prime Minister Mamadou Dia (Senghor 1961; Dia 1960).

This new policy was realized through a number of administrative reforms concerning the rural sector, in particular the growing of peanuts. Since the end of the last century, the cultivation of peanuts had been imposed upon the Senegalese peasants by the French colonizers. The production of peanuts in shells thus increased from 200,000 tons around 1914, to 600,000 in 1936–1937, and reached the production record of one million tons in 1965. The importance of the peanut in Senegal has never decreased; it contributes three quarters of the money income from agriculture, makes up about 25 percent of the gross national product, and constitutes more than 70 percent of the country's exports (Van Haeverbeke 1970).

While forecasting a gradual diversification of the Senegalese economy, the new government, in particular Mamadou Dia who was primarily responsible for economic administration, wanted to improve first of all the lot of the peasants who produced peanuts. The first thing to be done was to supplant the network of traders by taking away its interior and exterior monopoly of the commercialization of peanuts and of rice and millet, the essential food products of Senegal.

This new policy was initiated by the creation of an Office of Agricultural Commercialization. Dia promoted the creation of cooperatives as the local agents of this governmental body; the cooperatives would also constitute a favorable way of assuring peasant participation in the country's development. Beginning with the first plan (1961–1964), Dia sought to cover the entire country with a network of purchasing cooperatives which were assured that they alone could participate in the peanut commerce. Though they were restricted at first to this operation, the cooperatives were to gradually become multifunctional. They would take charge of credit and consumption and eventually evolve into "development cooperatives," a new form of autonomous commune inspired by the Yugoslav model. Moreover, though in its early stages the cooperative movement was to be strictly controlled and guided by the state, it was subsequently to become, little by little, an autonomous and valid partner whose structure would cover the entire country. This evolution would be brought about by "rural animation," a "veritable People's Revolution," the method par excellence of setting up a politically and economically democratic African socialism. However, rural animation quickly became more than a method of development. Because it included peasants at the local level, centers and officials in the districts, and a central office in the commissariat of the Plan, it became, in effect, an autonomous institution within the state whose hierarchy was parallel to that of the political party in the Senegalese countryside.

In December of 1962, a political crisis brought about the fall and the imprisonment of Prime Minister Dia and his partisans. In spite of certain superficial explanations about rivalry between the party and the National Assembly, the crisis appears to have been the fruit of the resistance of certain local people of influence to the efforts of Dia to put his African socialism into effect. Local deputies in particular were in favor of economic liberalism and thus opposed Dia. At the time when the rural animators were attacking the leadership of the deputies and the *marabouts*, when the planned-for autonomy of the cooperative movement and its extension into the consumption sector were menacing both the large import-export firms and the small African merchants which had already been excluded from the peanut industry, President Senghor put a halt to the structural reforms which would have rapidly placed the power of the traditional elite, allied with the local representatives of capitalism, into question (Gagnon 1965).

Institutions such as the cooperatives and rural animation remained limited to a strictly technical role and were held in close check by the state and by the party. Moreover, from 1966 on, in spite of great efforts in the area of productivity, a considerable drop in the tonnage of peanuts harvested and in the area of land used for peanut cultivation (583,000 tons from 983,000 hectares in 1970–1971) indicates the great effects the reduced purchase price had on the producer. France was no longer supporting the peanut market. In spite of a recovery in 1971–1972 (960,000 tons), due in particular to a special sowing premium, it appears that the Senegalese peasant is gradually abandoning the peanut economy in order to devote himself to the cultivation of millet and sorghum which he can consume himself.

Of course, the cooperative system continued to develop. Made up of 1,750 basic units in 1972, it has controlled the commercialization of the peanut harvest since 1968. It is, however, subject to a double limitation which, in addition to the economic difficulties explained above, considerably reduces its role as an instrument of peasant participation.

First it is subject to the strict guardianship of the National Bank of Development of Senegal (*la Banque Nationale de Développement du Sénégal* – BNDS) and of the National Office of Cooperatives and Development Assistance (*l'Office National de Coopération et d'Assistance au Développement* – ONCAD). The organization of the latter was the condition on which two billion C.F.A. francs were loaned to the government by the European Development Fund (*le Fonds Européen de Développement* – FED) to overcome the peanut crisis in 1971. This control of credit and of materials distributed to cooperative participants and of prices, places the peasants in total dependence upon the state. The calculations made by Samir Amin (Amin 1971) clearly show how it is the peasants who, by their labor, furnish part of the surplus necessary for the maintenance of civil servants and for investments in other sectors.

Furthermore, new cooperatives, which almost always corresponded to not yet transformed traditional structures, have very often contributed to the reinforcement of these traditional structures. This applies particularly to the Islamic brotherhood of Mourides (O'Brien 1971) which, with its 500,000 adherents, includes a good number of the peasants in the peanut belt. It is a type of agricultural feudal system where the *marabouts* take care of the economic and religious needs of the faithful who, organized in *daara*, or [communal farming villages], work for many years without pay while the profits go to the *marabouts*.

The introduction of fertilizer and plowing teams, in the absence of reform of traditional property, also favored certain prominent individuals and thus contributed to the growth of inequality in the countryside, to a sort of "kulakization," obviously contrary to the spirit of the cooperative system.

Just recently a number of attacks against the state-controlled system of agricultural production have taken place. They come from private African businessmen who, in light of their present weak role, would like very much to participate in the distribution of the surplus which is now cornered by the governmental sector. This offensive, colored by a certain nationalism opposed to the "francophilism" of Senghor, has not yet developed in a manner significant to Senegal's future.

After this brief exposé, it is easy to see how a cooperative system first conceived for the liberation of the peasant has rapidly become a means to better link him to the world capitalist system by the intermediary of a dominant political class which, in the process, reaps a part of the surplus produced by the workers.

CUBA

The principal stages of the Cuban revolution and of its fundamental element, agrarian reform, are fairly well known and statistically established for the period from 1959 to 1967 (Dumont 1970; Karol 1970; Gutelman 1967; Huberman and Sweezy 1970). Even if certain data and especially precise figures are missing, except for those in one recent work (Alphandery 1972), it is possible all the same to trace the major steps of Cuban rural evolution since then.

The first law of agrarian reform, that of May 17, 1959, restricted the maximum surface area of farms to thirty *caballerias* [405.6 hectares] except in exceptional cases. After the law was applied, the state sector comprised 44 percent (3,903,000 hectares) of the total agricultural land surface and the private sector, 56 percent (5,173,800 hectares). Of this 56 percent, 36 percent was in farms with a land surface of less than five *caballerias* and 20 percent had a land surface between five and thirty *caballerias*.

For technical reasons having to do with the great dispersion of nationalized lands, and especially for political reasons having to do with the growing opposition of middle-level rural property owners to the policies of Castro, it was necessary to move rapidly on to a second law of agrarian reform. This law gave the state sector all farms larger than five *caballerias*. The state was thus owner of 5,513,700 hectares (60.1 percent of the total land surface), while the private sector only held 3,563,100 ha. (39.3 percent) (Gutelman 1967).

We will pass over the transformations of the governmental sector in order to concern ourselves exclusively with the private sector. Since 1961 the 200,000 peasants of the private sector have composed a single agricultural union, the ANAP, which groups them into three basic types of organizations: Peasant Associations, Credit and Services Cooperatives, and Agriculture and Animal Husbandry Societies (*Agropecuarial*).

The Peasant Associations, simple groups of farmers hoping to facilitate their procurement of credit and fertilizer, were especially popular at the beginning of the revolutionary process; they numbered 2,600 in 1963.

The Agriculture and Animal Husbandry Societies constituted, in the eyes of the government, the only truly socialist production unit, as the peasants pooled their land and tools; numbering 265 in 1964, there were no more than 136 in 1967 with a total of 1,707 members.

The most widespread organization was, in fact, that of the Cooperatives of Credit and Services; these cooperatives were the better structured Peasant Associations in which members were organized only to receive credit and materials in a centralized fashion. Three hundred cooperatives of this type were counted in 1961; they numbered 1,119 in 1967 and contained 77,933 members.

Two lines of force of Fidel Castro's agricultural policy seem to have been the refusal to create small farms and the slow and voluntary collectivization of the private sector.

At the time of our study of communities in the regions of Pinar del Rio and of Oriente in 1966–1967, the members of the units we studied retained ownership and management of their land. Already, however, one sensed the relatively strong pressure of the state through local representatives of the party and of the ANAP. They urged the Agropecuary Society to participate in the national sugar plan and wanted certain members of the Credit and Services Cooperative to give up their land to the state in return for new housing and monetary compensation. In this last instance, it was generally a question of contiguous lands situated in the least fertile areas of the community being studied (Sicotte 1968; Rochon 1970).

The progressive integration of the private sector had thus already begun at this time without provoking any great upheavals. This leads us to doubt the severe statement of Dumont (1970) about a so-called third agrarian reform which supposedly would eliminate the peasantry as such and thus force them to become opponents of the regime.

In fact, the new system, adopted since 1967, is that of the "micro-plan":

An agreement is made between the small farmer and the State; the latter agrees to construct for him, free of charge, a new house lavished with modern comforts, a stable, a pigsty, and a barnyard; in exchange, the peasant agrees to grow the product proposed to him by the government. Moreover, he gets beneficial aid in the form of agricultural materials and man power from the nearest state farm. Until the first harvest of his new crop, he will receive a monthly indemnity of 150 dollars, and of course, when the land begins to produce, he will receive the results of his sales. Finally, he has the right to maintain several hectares of the crop of his choice for his own consumption (Alphandery, 1972:49).

This idyllic, theoretical description of the micro-plan does not yet seem to correspond to Cuban reality. In fact, in 1970 the great battle of the ten million tons of sugar caused the private sector to be relatively abandoned, for private manpower was called up to join the population as a whole in the common effort. After the failure of the campaign and the self-criticism of the leaders, the situation of the private sector had not changed much in 1972, if one believes the documentation we gathered in Havana as we were not able to return to the communities already studied (ANAP 1972).

There are still 202,000 private farmers who, with their families, make up about a million in number, and who still occupy 25 percent of the agricultural land surface of the country; the private sector still retains its importance. The 6,000 basic organisms of the ANAP seem to be mostly Peasant Associations and Credit and Services Cooperatives because Agriculture and Animal Husbandry Societies are almost never mentioned anymore.

In his speech to the fourth congress of the ANAP, December 31, 1971, Fidel Castro leaves no doubt as to the place reserved for the private sector. Its future role will be determined by its participation in a number of plans (specialized, directed, integrated) conceived by the National Institute of Agrarian Reform (*l'Institut National de la Réforme Agraire* – INRA), the superministry of agriculture. Within this general framework, established first of all for strict reasons of productivity, the basic peasant organisms retain their traditional structure, and the peasants maintain ownership of their land. They are, therefore, free to participate or not to participate in the plans. This is partially due, as Castro admits, to the lack of the technical resources which would permit them to participate fully. Moreover, outside of what they need for their own consumption, the peasants can no longer sell part of their products on the open market as before. They must sell everything to the state at state-fixed prices.

One sees how, without directly limiting the property rights of the private sector, the state has almost completely substituted itself for the private sector in matters of agricultural planning and of management. At this point in time, the cooperative or noncooperative form of the basic unit no longer has any real importance, because the distribution of surplus whether for the benefit of the peasants themselves or for the benefit of any other class of society, is determined by the prices paid for agricultural products. The cooperative system is thus caught in the wake of the state's power. The state theoretically remains sensitive to the desires of the peasant who is represented by the ANAP at various administrative levels.

TUNISIA

In Senegal and in Cuba the cooperative system was more or less taken over by the state and the dominant political class during latent crises which put the system into question. In Tunisia, it was the cooperative system itself which was at the center of a serious political crisis.

Tunisia can also be considered as an underdeveloped agricultural country because agriculture represents almost one fourth of the gross national product and occupies 51 percent of the active population. At the time of its independence in 1956, Tunisia opted for a liberal economic policy in collaboration with France, in spite of the criticisms of the General Union of Tunisian Workers (*l'Union Générale des Travailleurs Tunisiens* – UGTT) which was already advocating an authentic socialism based upon the cooperative system.[2]

It was not until 1962 that Tunisia finally decided in favor of "Destourian socialism" in which state intervention would be much more pronounced. One of the first manifestations of this change of tack was the 1964 nationalization of all of the colonization lands, about 800,000 hectares. First entrusted to the Office of State Lands (*l'Office des Terres Domaniales* – OTD), these lands gradually served as nuclei for the establishment of cooperatives. Added on to them were tracts of peasant land from the traditional sector. Tunisian researchers have studied this period of cooperative building quite thoroughly (Makhlouf 1968; Zghal 1967).

In spite of this first stride forward, in 1968 only 38 percent of the cultivated lands were within the state-controlled sector, then dominated by

---

[2] Ahmed Ben Salah was then secretary general of the UGTT. He was soon to be replaced by someone more submissive to the dominant party.

cooperatives. In order to spread planned agriculture, it was necessary to attack the Tunisian agrarian bourgeoisie which still had possession of 700,000 hectares.

Ben Salah, holder of the portfolios of Planning and Finance in addition to several other ministries, decided to devote himself to this task. In January of 1969, entirely supported by President Bourguiba who was ill and trusted him completely. Ben Salah announced a veritable agrarian reform which was to bring about quickly the total collectivization of Tunisian agriculture with the aid of the newly created National Union of Cooperatives (*l'Union Nationale de la Coopération* – UNC). whereas in six years, only 1,700,000 hectares had been organized into cooperatives, by June 30, 1969, 1,592 cooperative units of production had already integrated 295,414 peasants on 3,800,000 hectares. At the end of August, 4,700,000 hectares were included in 1,994 cooperative units. Then came the crisis which, once settled, left only 358 units on 700,000 hectares intact at the beginning of 1971. What had happened in the meantime?

The policy of Ben Salah had as its special goal the expropriation of large and average property owners, who were at that time involved in disputes with the new state bourgeoisie for control of the dominant party. Ben Salah's policy also implied an attack on the well-integrated agrarian communities of the Sahel and of the Cap Bon, where smallholders remained strongly attached to their parcels of land, to their livestock, and to their olive groves.[3] An operation which, thanks to technical and organizational modernization of agriculture, should have established a permanent alliance among the smallholders, the farm workers, and the new political class, had the opposite effect. Because of its hurried and technocratic nature, the smallholders rose up against the government; President Bourguiba had to back down, fire Ben Salah, and reaffirm the importance of the position of the private sector in agriculture. The only ones to benefit from the operation were the large Tunisian property owners, who thereby escaped elimination without having to intervene directly. The intervention of the IBRD, which was financing a good part of the cooperative system, had a large but little-known influence on the government's decision.

Several observers have analyzed the "Ben Salah operation," insisting upon its weakness (Cherel 1971; Dumont 1972; Godart 1970). As for our team, arrived in the field in September 1969, we were only able to witness the dismantling of the cooperative movement while attempting to observe the surviving units (Savaria 1971; Sicotte 1973).

---

[3]   This policy was accompanied by a similar operation directed toward the merchants, whom they were also trying to group together in collective units.

As I have stated, the principal beneficiary of the halt in agrarian reform was the landed Tunisian bourgeoisie. This social stratum, thanks to state technical and financial aid, is in the process of consolidating and modernizing its enterprises; it has, moreover, a symbiotic relationship with the political class which itself is investing more and more in commerce, industry, tourism, and land. A sort of homogeneous national bourgeoisie of the capitalist type has been reinstated and is directly integrated in the world system.

The state and cooperative sectors have become a jumble where multiple formulas of property and organization,[4] ranging from the former cooperative to the agro-combine, coexist. At Khanguet-El-Hadjadj, near Grombalia, the four wine-producing cooperatives that we chose to study in 1969 still exist; they have all had operational surpluses in the course of their last annual programs. They are essentially composed of former properties of French and Italian colonists and have never had to absorb the lands of Tunisian property owners, large or small. Here again, however, the establishment of cooperative structures is often copied directly from the former social structure; thus, the distribution of positions in the administrative councils usually takes into account the distribution of the large traditional families in the interior of the cooperative unit. Even stronger than this is the role played in the organizational structure by those formerly employed by private landowners: those who had positions of power tend to get them back within the cooperative unit, and a certain inequality tends to be perpetuated.

Moreover, the study of these production units clearly points out the determining role played by the state first in the establishment of cooperative units and then in their financial control and technical management. The only liberty left to the cooperative members is the daily technical organization of their work; even here, they must respect the rigid norms imposed by agricultural technicians or suggested by the local party cell. Since the arrival, in the summer of 1970, of two agricultural technicians appointed by the OTD, in place of the four former directors, with instructions to intervene directly in the management of the production units, one wonders if the units have anything in common with cooperatives other than the name and the formal structure. It even appears that the tendency is toward establishing two or perhaps a single state farm in the valley. If this example means anything, then it appears that the little which remains of the Tunisian cooperative system may be swallowed up by the

[4] E. Makhlouf of CERES (*Centre d'Etudes et de Recherches Economiques et Sociales* [The Center for Economic and Social Studies and Research] of Tunis is presently working to untangle this confusion.

state sector, which is itself threatened by the increasingly voracious appetite of the landed bourgeoisie which has already gained control of some of the state land.

The small peasant, with or without land, finds it impossible to participate in modern agriculture in Tunisia; there is no place for him in the private, public, or cooperative sectors. Farming is concentrated in the hands of those who possess machinery and capital; they are the only ones to receive state aid. The peasant is reduced to choose among underemployment in the rural areas, urban employment, or emigration to France or Germany. Since 1969, large numbers of peasants have chosen to emigrate.

According to Dumont, Tunisian agriculture remains far from being able to furnish a surplus to distribute to the rest of the society, and is even incapable of assuring its own financing. The present policies which accentuate mechanization and one-crop (cereal) cultivation contribute to soil depletion and may lead to the eventual creation of deserts (Dumont 1972: 164–171).

Having blocked agrarian reform, the Tunisian political class is trying its hardest to integrate itself in the world-wide capitalist system by developing mineral resources, industry, and tourism; it thereby only accentuates the controlled and extroverted character of present-day Tunisian economy.

COOPERATIVES, POLITICS, AND SOCIAL CLASSES

The analyses summarized here[5] show what happens when the cooperative system, loyal to its ideology, surpasses the simple level of technical improvement and of economic well-being and tries to enter into politics and to question the agrarian structures and the class organization which it supports. The cooperative system thus quickly runs into obstacles which help to destroy it or to check its development.

1.   In the agricultural sector, the cooperative system is first of all a means of technical organization of resources and of manpower whose goal is better production. In the majority of cases where agricultural cooperatives succeed, they lead to a concentration and modernization of agriculture and accelerate the disappearance of the individual peasant. Strictly from this point of view, the agricultural cooperatives in the three cases studied constitute a relative economic success for the peasants that they managed to incorporate. Members of Tunisian cooperatives have an admittedly modest income, but it is clearly superior to that of the other peasants.

[5]   This work in its entirety is the subject of a book which is now in press.

Some Senegalese peasants have succeeded, thanks to peanuts and to cooperatives, in maintaining their income or in improving it despite a deterioration of the rural situation. As for the Cuban peasants, everyone agrees that they were the first and primary beneficiaries of the revolution. In a country in which there is so much insistence upon the creation of a "new man," state control of cooperatives seems especially to have had in mind the prevention of their becoming a separate class with its own individualistic mentality.

It is evident that the consequence of this relative economic success often is the creation of new divisions in village communities which were previously rather egalitarian. This phenomenon is well analyzed by Meillassoux (1964). It is a characteristic of the Senegalese experience, is less evident in Tunisia, where it reinforced already existing divisions, and has not yet made its appearance in Cuba.

2.   But the cooperative system is not only a form of techno-economic organization; it also constitutes a potential social movement. This double vocation was quite apparent at the moment of its birth in the last century, when both cooperative and trade union movements sought to struggle against the growing ascendancy of the capitalist mode of production. In the course of their later development, cooperatives have constantly oscillated between their desire for a global transformation of society and their desire to become a reality in some of the weakest links of the sociopolitical chain. It is known how, in capitalist societies, cooperatives finally renounced their role as a social movement in order to integrate themselves better into the dominant system. In most industrialized socialist countries they are one of the means by which state policy is transmitted to the people. But their introduction into underdeveloped countries since the end of the last world war gives rise to a series of new problems which allows their true nature to be better grasped. In the three cases which interest us, the cooperative system was not a grassroots creation of the peasants as is usually the case in capitalist countries. As in most underdeveloped countries, it was set up directly by the state and by the party in power which made it an essential element of their agricultural policy and ideology.

We hope to have demonstrated that when the cooperatives in Senegal, Cuba, and Tunisia had the opportunity to become social movements, to enter the political arena, and to threaten the dominant classes, they were rapidly curtailed by the ruling powers and obliged to fulfill only their techno-economic functions.

Before independence in Senegal, there was neither modern agriculture nor large farms, nor, consequently, an agrarian bourgeoisie; the cooperative system easily took control of the local peanut commerce and displaced a thin stratum of local intermediaries who were mostly foreigners. When, thanks to rural animation, the cooperative movement presented itself as a new means of rural political organization which could threaten the nascent political class (deputies, civil servants, African merchants, etc.), it was quickly made to understand its limitations at the time of the political crisis which brought about the fall of President Dia.

On the contrary, Tunisia had a modern, concentrated agricultural system. It was of course dominated by foreign colonists, but there were many influential Tunisians as well. This social class, allied to the commercial bourgeoisie of Tunis, played a relatively small role in the independence movement and subsequently had little influence on the course of the single political party which was chiefly composed of professionals, civil servants, and union members. The technocratic faction of the dominant political class, represented by Ben Salah, seems to have wanted to liquidate definitely, not only the foreign colonists, but also the rest of the indigenous commercial or landed bourgoisie, by extending the cooperatives through the entire commercial and agricultural system. The operation seems to have failed because it simultaneously attacked the middle peasant and because some members of the political class had begun to acquire economic interests in land and commerce. Far from bringing about a new alliance between the political class and the peasantry at the expense of the capitalist bourgeoisie, the rapid extension of cooperatives had the opposite effect: an accelerated fusion of the political class and of the traditional bourgeoisie, to the detriment of the peasant majority which was abandoned to its fate.

The case of Cuba is much more ambiguous. The agrarian bourgeoisie, Cuban or foreign, which practiced a modern type of agriculture, was quickly expropriated by the revolution which was thereby able to rapidly count upon an integrated state sector. The standard of living of agricultural workers, permanent or temporary, rose considerably. The 200,000 peasants who remained or became property owners after the revolution were urged in many ways to join cooperatives which, while improving their standard of living, would bring them closer to the socialist scheme applied by the other classes of the country.

During the "battle of the ten million tons," the process accelerated so as to integrate, permanently and painlessly, the remainder of the peasant class into the ensemble of Cuban workers. Here again, starting with micro-plans and state economic control, the role first intended for the cooperatives was reduced to its simplest form without, however, economically affecting a single section of the peasant population.

3. From our three examples it can be stated that there is a manifest con-

tradiction between an ideology which gives cooperation a key role in channeling peasant participation in the development process and the daily operation of the production units. The three countries studied illustrate the role of reality-masking played by cooperative ideology. The "African socialism" of Senghor, like the "Destourian socialism" of Bourguiba, which both deny the existence of social classes on African soil, envisioned cooperatives as the most suitable way of uniting the nation in a single economic development plan. The political crises which affected each of these countries indicate, however, how different social classes, or factions of a class, follow their own divergent interests. The cooperative system then appeared as the best means for the dominant social class to move the peasant masses into the capitalist mode of production in order to extract from them the surplus necessary for the maintenance of increasingly costly administration; the relative failure of this idea caused the governments to have quick recourse to increasingly extensive foreign economic aid.

In Cuba, the surplus demanded from agriculture was not obtained solely from the peasants; it seems to have been obtained from the totality of rural and urban workers through their permanent or temporary participation in farm labor. Here again the cooperative system was the means used to incite members of a potentially reticent level of society to join in the socialist mode of production.

In none of these cases does the cooperative system appear to be an instrument truly favorable to increasing peasant participation nor to transmitting the desires of workers to higher governmental levels. Viewed in this light, the three experiments seem to be total failures.

In conclusion, it can be stated that the cooperative system, even when it develops in a favorable context, does not preside over the birth of a new society, but rather serves to facilitate the passage of marginal classes into the dominant mode of production, whether it is capitalist or socialist. In spite of the cooperative ideology expounded by government leaders, interests of the political class in power prevail over popular participation.

REFERENCES

ALPHANDERY, J. J.
  1972   *Cuba: l'autre révolution.* Paris: Editions Sociales.
AMIN, SAMIR
  1970   *L'accumulation à l'échelle mondiale.* Dakar: IFAN; and Paris: Anthropos.
  1971   *L'Afrique de l'Ouest bloquée.* Paris: Editions de Minuit.

1973   *Le développement inégal.* Paris: Editions de Minuit.
ANAP
1972   *Discursos, Acuerdos, Reglamento, Communicado.* Proceedings of IVth Congreso Campesino, Havana.
CHEREL, JEAN
1971   Les unités coopératives de production du Nord tunisien. *Tiers-Monde* 46.
O'BRIEN, DONALD CRUISE
1971   *The Mourides of Senegal.* Oxford: Clarendon.
DIA, MAMADOU
1960   *Nations africaines et solidarité mondiale.* Paris: P.U.F.
DUMONT, RENÉ
1970   *Cuba est-il socialiste?* Paris: Editions du Seuil.
1972   *Paysanneries aux abois.* Paris: Editions du Seuil.
EMMANUEL, ARRIGHI
1969   *L'échange inégal.* Paris: François Maspéro.
FALS-BORDA, ORLANDO
1970   Formation et déformation de la politique coopérative en Amérique latine. *Bulletin de l'Institut International d'Etudes Sociales* 7:130–160.
GAGNON, GABRIEL
1965   "Associations économiques modernes et socialisme africain: l'expérience Sénégalaise." Unpublished doctoral dissertation, Paris: E.P.H.E.
GODART, A.
1970   "Les unités de production agricole en Tunisie," in *Rural cooperatives and planned change in Africa: case materials.* Edited by R. Apthorpe, 235–286. Geneva: UNRISD.
GUNDER FRANK, ANDRÉ
1972   *Le développement du sous-développement: l'Amérique latine.* Paris: François Maspéro.
GUTELMAN, MICHEL
1967   *L'agriculture socialisée à Cuba.* Paris: François Maspéro.
HUBERMAN, LEO, PAUL M. SWEEZY
1970   *Le socialisme cubain.* Paris: Anthropos.
KAROL, K. S.
1970   *Les guérilleros au pouvoir.* Paris: Robert Laffont.
MAKHLOUF, EZZEDINE
1968   *Structures agraires et modernisation de l'agriculture dans les plaines du Kef.* Cahiers du C.E.R.E.S., série géographique, 1:1–262.
MEILLASSOUX, CLAUDE
1964   *Anthropologie économique des Gouro de Côte d'Ivoire.* The Hague: Mouton.
ROCHON, LISE
1970   "Une coopérative de production à Cuba." Unpublished Master's thesis, Department of Anthropology, University of Montreal.
SAVARIA, JULES
1971   "Le mouvement coopératif, au Khanguet-El-Hadjadj (Tunisie)." Unpublished Master's thesis, Department of Anthropology, University of Montreal.

SENGHOR, LEOPOLD SEDAR
    1961   *Nation et voie africaine du socialisme*. Paris: Présence africaine.
SICOTTE, ALFRED
    1968   "Une coopérative de crédit et de services à Cuba." Unpublished Master's thesis, Department of Anthropology, University of Montreal.
    1973   "Le système coopératif tunisien." Unpublished doctoral dissertation, Department of Sociology, University of Montreal.
VAN HAEVERBEKE, ANDRE
    1970   *Rémunération du travail et commerce extérieur*. University of Louvain.
ZGHAL, ABDELKADER
    1967   *Modernisation de l'agriculture et populations semi-nomades*. The Hague: Mouton.

Political and Technical Factors
in Agricultural Collectivization in Tunisia

EZZEDDINE MAKHLOUF

At the time of the adoption of the Decennial Perspectives of Development in 1962, it would have been difficult to predict that only seven years later the decision would be made to put all of Tunisian agriculture and a large part of its economy in the cooperative system without having a change of political power.

This attempt at general collectivization did not succeed. A combination of factors (three consecutive years of drought and the difficulties of financing agriculture were not the least of them) weakened the cooperative structures established in 1962. This permitted those who were opposed to the cooperative experiment in particular and to the attempts to reform the structures of production in general to exacerbate the crisis and to obtain not only a stop to collectivization operations but also the rapid and general decollectivization of the country, including the commercial circuits which in the opinion of most observers were successful.

In this report I will try to analyze the process that brought about general collectivization of the agricultural sector under a political regime which had not explicitly condemned the principle of private property, limited the size of private property holdings, or programed agrarian reform. The Tunisian experience is unique in this sense, and it raises two series of problems which have become classic in the Third World:

1. In the search for, or gradual adoption of, a socialist method of development, are the motives essentially ideological and do the proponents of this method always refer back to Marxism? This problem may appear unimportant. But in underdeveloped countries more and more young people who daily confront these problems of development, modernization, and progress are sincerely, and with revealing naiveté, astonished

to hear the solutions they propose categorized as absurd references to an "imported ideology." Their proposals are immediately discarded although these youths have no Marxist training and have never given or sought a theoretical basis for their models or plans. These young technicians are educated in French or Tunisian schools where the teaching of Marxist theories has always been nonexistent or marginal. Yet they are accused by conservatives of being nourished on "illusions of imported ideology," while certain Marxists say they are pragmatic technocrats who know nothing about scientific socialism and its implications.

Certainly this is the entire problem of pragmatic socialism versus scientific socialism, but it is not my purpose to deal with this issue here. The point which seems important to understand and to analyze in the Tunisian experiment is the capacity and the limitations of young technicians from poor or middle peasantry, who are generally untrained ideologically and politically to define a policy of development and rural promotion, to make it acceptable to the political leaders, and to achieve the structural reforms necessary for its application in daily life.

2.   The second series of problems is likewise classic: reform or revolution? The debate is ancient and ever present. Do widespread reforms, which might go as far as overthrowing the structures of production, have any chance of success? Can they be successful as long as the bourgeoisie, even if it does not have all the economic power, remains capable of profiting from crises and forming alliances in order to throw everything into question?

Tunisia from this point of view has been a very interesting case during the last decade. This peculiarity stems from the strong personality of the chief of state, President Habib Bourguiba, and from his profound belief in the perfectibility of the human being. He has often repeated this conviction and recently proclaimed it from the rostrum of the *Organisation internationale du travail* (O.I.T.):

I think that it is desirable and possible to bring about dynamic arbitration between current forces. It is important, in fact, to reconcile the factor of individual gain, of legitimate profit, of the egoism basic to human nature, with the values of pure unselfishness: devotion, the need to struggle for one's own country, the desire to take one's part in collective work where the individual is fulfilled through fellowship which transfigures him.

National unity, which arose and was maintained throughout the political struggle for the country's independence, is something that President Bourguiba wished to maintain during the "struggle for economic development."

During the past decade the planners and technicians have worked toward modernization and innovation in the economic and social domains even though the peasants are not able presently to assimilate these changes technically, or to master them politically. The technico-economic model required structures to change whenever they opposed or restrained its application. But it did not take long to see that the reforms necessary for the application of the model were becoming more and more profound.

These reforms were not rejected by the political leaders; President Bourguiba worked to get them accepted by those whose interests ran the risk of being affected and by those who were ideologically opposed to them. The reforms were set up, not simply to appeal for support as is frequently done in numerous regimes, but because there was firm belief in their necessity for the development of the country. These reforms were immediately brought into question when they clashed with true capitalist interests, and they were easily abolished because the masses neither participated in their conception nor in their application and sometimes even suffered from numerous errors in their application.

However, this ten-year dialectic between the demands of the development plan and the political factors has permitted Tunisia, without adopting an ideological, scientific, socialist model, to greatly develop its production forces. No model of a capitalist type would have been able to accomplish this in so short a period of time. Due to this fact, the country finds itself in a new situation of contradictions and of conflict between the state of productive forces and the structures of production. This situation could be called classic.

THE ORIGINS OF THE PLAN AND THE COOPERATIVE EXPERIMENT IN TUNISIA

The first ideas of cooperation in credit, agriculture, and commerce were introduced into Tunisia in the 1920's by the syndicalists M'hamed Ali and Tahar Haddad. The Neo-Destour Party (founded in 1934), essentially oriented toward the political struggle for the independence of the country, scarcely supported the great syndicalist themes: socialist method of development, cooperatives and ties with the international workers' movement (Hermassi 1966:172). Once again in 1956 the central union, *Union Générale des travailleurs tunisiens* (U.G.T.T.) put into its program the themes of socialism and of cooperation. The Neo-Destourian party did not follow the union either and from independence to 1962, the liberal economic route was pursued. But not for long. In 1962 a ten-year development plan was launched. The socialist method was not adopted, but the structural contradictions and the inability of the liberal system to pull the economy out of the stagnation which had brought on the adoption of a planned economy led to a radicalization of planning which continued throughout the sixties.

As in many colonial countries, the economic and social situation of Tunisia was neither stable nor strong at the time of independence. There were also economic difficulties which arose at the time of the physical rupture with France: disturbances of commercial circuits, the departure of key personnel, etc.

In spite of the good grain harvests from 1957 to 1960, the average production was still inferior to that of the 1952 to 1956 period. Agricultural production in its totality continued to undergo the hazards of rainfall; the hard wheat harvest was equal to that of 1956, and inferior to that of 1911 (2,350,000 quintals).

Stagnation of hard wheat production, a 50 percent reduction in the soft wheat production, and a 64 percent reduction in that of legumes, made the first years of Tunisia's independence very difficult. There was a great increase (80 percent) in the importation of food commodities, in spite of a very low level of individual consumption and a monotonous diet (See Table 1).

Table 1.   *Level of consumption: kilogram/head/year (F.A.O.)*

	France	Bulgaria	Algeria	Tunisia
Grains	100	202	156	119
Meat	86	23	8	9
Eggs	11	4	1.6	0.5
Fish	11	2	2	2.6
Milk	195	83	68	45
Fat matter	19	12	6	5

The situation of the other economic sectors was scarcely better, especially that of industry.

In the social domain, the infrastructure was too small for the needs. There were only twenty-one hospital beds available per 10,000 inhabitants; some governments, Jendouba, Kasserine, Medenine, and even Nabeul, which is only sixty kilometers from the capital, had only one to three hospital bed(s) for 10,000 inhabitants. Life expectancy was forty-eight years. The rate of school attendance was only 23 percent, and out of 135,000 children ready to enter school each year only 12,000 to 13,000 could be educated per year.

On the economic level, as well as on the social level, Tunisia was starting from a relatively low point.

In the economic domain, important divergences impeded any fundamental choice between options. There was not even any economic program for five years. The program suggested by the U.G.T.T. was rejected, as we have mentioned, by the Party and the regime.

On the contrary, the cultural Malthusianism, which predominated among the colonial authorities and a part of the Tunisian bourgeoisie even during the phase of internal autonomy (and still today), was rapidly replaced by an option for total literacy.

It was a matter of two fundamentally opposed policies which will always be in conflict in the country. It seems important to elaborate upon them since the process of development could depend upon them.

In 1955, Vibert wrote:

What risks being sterile — and even more important sterilizing — is education which has no use, which fabricates uprooted or maladapted citizens, which produces year after year large classes of diploma-holders without work, which creates premature needs that the collective could not satisfy and which could create a mortal imbalance between intellectual progress and economic progress. It is instead indispensable that these two sustain one another, each one being the condition and justification of the other.

This policy subordinating the degree of education on all levels to the rate of economic growth was quickly opposed by another policy which favored generalized teaching and instruction as objectives in themselves and which saw them as preliminary and necessary conditions to all economic development.

A U.G.T.T. report stated in 1956 that:

For all countries, and especially for all underdeveloped countries, human beings are the most precious capital. What good is economic expansion if the people do not have the means to appreciate and profit from it.... An economic revival can only be valuable and profitable for our people if the leaders of the country's activity are Tunisians. But this cannot be the case without universal education....

Finally, if one believes in the equality of all citizens, we must work for the disappearance of the essential inequality which exists between illiterate citizens and others. Everybody must be given the same opportunities in life in order to assure to the mass of second-class citizens a simply human advancement.

This option and demand of the U.G.T.T. responded to a significant, long-standing popular aspiration. As one director of higher education said to some foreign visitors who were surprised at the importance of the influence given to schools: "One can do nothing about it; a Tunisian accepts the fact that he cannot find work, but he will not accept the fact that his children are refused schooling." The Tunisian's aspiration for education was very quickly and clearly perceived by the chief of state who made it the subject of numerous speeches. President Bourguiba, in a speech on September 15, 1968, said that:

The development of education makes demands which should be met in spite of the fact that the economists give priority to other options. Let me tell you that often, in work sessions and even in front of the Council of the Republic, I have had to intervene to tip the balance in favor of education.... I have not ceased to repeat that development of education, though its profitability cannot be counted, has repercussions on all economic activities because it improves men and this is the goal of all our work.

Some sociologists have tried to conceptualize this option. Fougeyrollas (1970) even speaks of a psycho-sociological accumulation:

Just as economists since Marx speak of an accumulation of national capital as an essential condition for the subsequent development of the society, we can consider the appearance of new behaviour patterns in labor and the emergence of new attitudes and new images in diverse sectors of collective life as a kind of psycho-sociological accumulation which, added to the former, should one day start the process of free development all over the world.

In Tunisia, this phase of psycho-sociological accumulation began much sooner than that of the accumulation of capital. The position taken by the Chief of State brought about the adoption in 1958 of a ten-year education plan whose objective was total literacy and the training of personnel necessary for the development of the economy; this also silenced, for a while, the voices raised in opposition to the democratization of education.

This option was important. The psycho-sociological accumulation, which developed rapidly thanks to massive education in the entire country, not only permitted an accumulation of capital, BUT DEMANDED IT. A new process quickly started taking place in Tunisia: people were educated, not according to what the economy could provide, but rather the economy developed in response to the needs of more educated and more demanding new generations.

This new process and its requirements were quickly perceived. One might wonder if the first economic difficulties and the first contradictions between the rhythm of economic development and the new demands of the psycho-sociological accumulation were largely responsible for the adoption of the principle of planned economy in 1960. Until then only the central union and the Marxists had demanded economic planning.

The option for "the promotion of the human being" required capital and especially reforms. After laws concerning the status of women and universal education, came economic planning which would also have its requirements.

THE AGRARIAN PROBLEM AND AGRICULTURE IN THE DEVELOPMENT PLAN

It is often affirmed that the Decennial Perspectives adopted in 1962 only put into the form of a plan the economic report of the Sixth Congress of the U.G.T.T. in 1956. Mr. Ahmed Ben Salah was the promoter of the Perspectives as secretary of the state of the plan and author of the report as general secretary of the central union. The affiliation is certain and very clear, and we find in both documents the same analyses of the economic and social situation, the same philosophic inspiration, the same approaches to a socialist method of development. Likewise, one would search in vain in either document for any Marxist analysis or approach to development, even though Marxist terminology was adopted for the economic "report" of 1956. This is particulary clear concerning the agrarian problem. The importance of the problem is emphasized in both documents, but agrarian reform or revolution is not explicitly recommended in either, as it had been in Algeria since the Charter of Tripoli. However, the Decennial Plan of 1962 marks a certain step backwards from the position taken in 1956.

In fact, the earlier program did not recommend agrarian reform, but in its conception of the structural reorganization of the rural world, large private property was to be implicitly controlled and limited: "Moreover, the U.G.T.T. believes that truly democratic economic development ought to base itself on the application of cooperation and the generalization of cooperatives in all forms, infinitely varied, as we all know" (U.G.T.T. 1956:41).

In the cooperative villages, which the authors of the report recommended creating in the rural areas (the institution of kibbutzim and their results seemed satisfactory), the problem of private property was raised. The answers were always ambiguous, as these few quotes indicate, but the authors seemed to favor the disappearance of private ownership of land:

However it may be, even if one goes as far as the ownership of land, it seems necessary in Tunisia, taking into account the concrete sociological situation in which we find ourselves, to safeguard private ownership of the home and even of a small individual plot of land (0.5 hectares, for example).... Even if one conserves private property for a while (reduced to a ceiling, etc.), we must not forget that there will be an important part of the village people who will not own anything and who ought to be assured a useful task. (U.G.T.T. 1956:45).

The U.G.T.T. report stated further (1956:47):

Thus, little by little, we proceed toward the projected form of our cooperative village. During the transition period (whose duration has not been set), we can have three types of land in the village.
1.   We will have, first, landowners individually cultivating their own plots.
2.   Next, we will have groups of landowners who will voluntarily work their lands in common, in their own interest, as production cooperatives.
3.   Finally, we will have an area of land belonging to the village as a whole.

The report does not indicate the source of these lands belonging to the village. Is it a question of lands coming from a limitation on property size? An allusion is made to this. Or, on the contrary, is it a matter of nationalizing colonial lands?

Realizing the idealistic character of this project, and also taking into account the ancient sociological framework of the country, the U.G.T.T. report did not want to precipitate matters and run the risk of raising many misunderstandings. It recommended a long period of explanations of the program and implementation through stages.

The stages are foreseen and accepted, but the risks are very clearly stressed.

In the chapter on agriculture, we also find this notice which now has the character of a prediction:

If it is acceptable to maintain a capitalist sector in Tunisia, we should not ignore the dangers of this situation. The capitalist system has never tolerated, to the present day and in any country of the world, significant development of the cooperative system. It knows quite well the risks it runs and it would prefer to crush any nascent attempts before they gain momentum.
We know too well, through long and sorrowful experience, that capitalism is the same everywhere and we do not want the same thing to happen to us. Therefore, it is necessary to establish, at the very beginning, a system of cooperatives which is powerful, organized and coordinated enough not to succumb to the attacks of capitalism.... In particular, it will be necessary to establish a link with the credit system in order not to see our villages deliberately isolated by this all-power hold-out of capitalism (U.G.T.T. 1956:47).

Such was the general format of the agrarian model of the Sixth U.G.T.T. Congress in 1956. The Decennial Perspectives and the Triennial Plan of 1962–64 only partially followed it, even if we consider them as a step forward.

The introduction of the first document refers to the Sfax Congress of the Neo-Destour Party in 1955, whose economic plank stated, "after a courageous analysis of the situation, that there was no other way but planning," and not to the U.G.T.T. Congress of 1956, where the plan was considered not only a necessity from the narrow point of view of economic efficacy but likewise an instrument leading to socialism.

The plan set up social and economic objectives (minimum individual income of 50 D.T. per year); the agricultural cooperative was presented as one of the measures "which corresponds best to the enumerated imperatives," one of which was a "size of exploitation allowing the full use of the selected technical means." In the northern grain-growing areas, the standard was to be one caterpillar tractor and two tractors with wheels, corresponding to an area of 500 hectares used for the cultivation, in rotation, of grains. This plan did not reiterate or it deliberately ignored, the emphasis on cooperatives as a socialist form of reorganizing the society, on its result (the cooperative village), and on its implications. There was no allusion made to limiting the size of private land-ownership or to its disappearance. It was no longer a question of generalizing the cooperative system, even though several types of them were recommended and the creation of a National Federation of Cooperatives was mentioned.

In the National Plan, which clearly appears as a compromise in the framework of national unity, economic and technical arguments were doubtless the only ones possible. Another argument also arose undoubtedly to make the cooperative formula, which was being timidly launched, acceptable to those who were opposed to it. In fact, one can read in an article in the review of the Ministry of Agriculture:

The first question which can logically be asked is "How did the necessity of creating production cooperatives in Tunisia make itself apparent?..."
   The Tunisian Government found itself faced with a dilemma. It could refrain from undertaking reforms of the land structure and let things go along naturally. In that case, the phenomenon of concentration of property and of exploitation would continue to develop and small property owners would swell the ranks of the unemployed workers. We would also witness an evolution which would one day create an explosive situation which could be remedied, as has been done in a large number of countries, by a series of agrarian reforms.
   The Tunisian Government prefers to anticipate agrarian reform and will take measures now to change the structure of exploitation (Secrétariat de l'Etat à l'Agriculture [S.E.A.] 1963).

The Ten-Year Development Plan was a global model of economic and technical actions resulting from the growing awareness of the underdeveloped state of the country following colonialization and several years of inaction in the economic domain. This model is a compromise between a socialist, fourrierist conception of society, a political reality in which the petit bourgeois and the bourgeois held power, and President

Bourguiba's profound and fundamental belief in the promotion of man and progress in all domains, but within the framework of national unity, not class struggle. The Ten-Year Development Plan was an essentially technical and modernist program. In the agricultural domain which interests us, for want of an agrarian revolution, the plan proposed in fact an agricultural revolution. Without going into statistical detail, some data permit us to grasp the progress projected in several technical domains:

1. To double the capacity of available water by creating four large dams (240,000,000 cubic meters), four medium-sized dams, and three small ones.

2. Planting of 90,000 hectares of forests, fixation of 13,000 hectares of coastal dunes, creation of a forested strip in the south of 8,000 hectares.

3. To fight soil erosion, 200,000 hectares of grazing land to be treated as C.E.S. Moreover, 400,000 hectares of agricultural land to be treated as tabias, 234,000 in semi-cultivable work, 670,000 in C.E.S., and the improvement of pastures, 1,300,000 hectares in bands of rotating crops. In Tunisia the cultivation of a single grain, for practical or speculative reasons, has become more and more widespread during the last half-century, and now has spread into all types of natural milieu. It accounts for over 80 percent of the arable land in most regions. The Plan wished to apply a vast program of diversification, intensification, and scientific rationalization of cultivation.

4. To plant 560,000 hectares of fruit orchards.

5. To increase the area of irrigated market gardens from 26,400 to 50,000 hectares and the production from 315,000 to 777,000 tons.

6. Areas which receive more than 400 millimeters of rainfall a year now employ biennial crop rotation (wheat-fallow-wheat). This would be changed to more intensive triennial or quadrennial rotation with fodder, leguminous plants, a manure crop, and industrial and grain cultivation, in order to put the area to the best use and respond to the national need for foodstuffs and exportation.

The planners wanted to reduce the area sown with wheat by 180,000 hectares in the north and 280,000 hectares in the central south (a total reduction on the order of 20 percent), to try to double, during the same period, cereal production, to increase, at the expense of fallow land, the area set aside for leguminous crops by 250 percent, that for fodder by 230 percent, and that for manure crops by 830 percent. All this seemed not only indispensable for the needs of the country, but possible given the potentialities of the milieu.

The Plan was sufficient to satisfy those who wanted to see the country become developed and who wanted to assure its self-sufficiency in food-stuffs. Thus, no one in Tunisia could oppose its objectives. It was put into operation and in October 1962, fifteen production cooperatives were created in the north. A process was begun. It would have its own dynamics.

THE REALIZATION OF THE PLAN, ITS DYNAMICS AND ITS IMPLICATIONS

The Decennial Perspectives foresaw the constitution of production cooperatives. They would be formed from exclusively private lands, or by the grouping of private lands around a central nucleus, a small parcel of nationalized land about a hundred hectares in size. Around 60,000 hectares of state land, acquired through the nationalization of colonial estates, would thus become integrated into the mixed co-operatives. The rest of the state land (600,000 hectares by 1964) would come under state management to maintain its productivity. Nowhere did the Plan explicitly envision the generalization of cooperatives. This method was simply seen as a way to help small farms catch up with technical progress.

The first triennial Plan of 1962–1964 initiated the grouping of an area of 100,000 hectares from the traditional sector into Cooperative Units of 500 hectares. But very soon it became apparent that peasants could own very small plots. One could only establish a 500-hectare unit by adding to peasant-owned land a large core of state land and renting the enclaved fields from large and small absentee landlords, either residing in the region or elsewhere. The cooperative units were supposed to be formed by peasants who owned at least five hectares, but it was necessary to open up the cooperatives to people owning less than 0.5 hectares. The agrarian reality was more complex than the Plan foresaw. The first difficulties appeared.

At the end of the Triennial the successes, the failures, and the problems were analyzed closely.

In October 1965, 146 cooperatives were established in the north on 117,000 hectares with 8,735 cooperators. But it was necessary to add to the 46,500 hectares of peasant land an equally large area of state land (46,900 hectares) and 24,000 hectares of rented land. From this came a series of problems.

TECHNICAL PROBLEMS   Lands belonging to the peasants were often marginal, mediocre, eroded, and exhausted by the cultivation of the same crop for many consecutive years. It was often necessary to convert them into pastures, orchards of various types, and sometimes into forests, which the peasants rarely liked. These lands necessitated large investments and the day when they would pay off was remote and for many doubtful.

The crop rotation chosen was new for the cooperators and the technicians; neither managed to master it. Conflicts were already arising between technicians and peasants. The former wished to apply a plan which was entirely foreign to the peasants and which necessitated long-term and medium-term investments. That meant credit, refunds, and depreciation. The peasant was used to only grains and livestock; he wished to have his reserve of wheat, and he could only balk at the complex system of production and the incomprehensible bookkeeping which meant only a small salary for him and five to twenty years of debt for the cooperative.

SOCIAL PROBLEMS   The "rightful owners" of the land were so numerous that choices had to be made among them. In spite of all the precautions taken, the choices were difficult and often necessarily arbitrary. The number of jobs in the cooperative was determined in advance according to the needs of the unit once in full production. This number was always lower than the number of "rightful owners." When there were five co-owners on one parcel of five, or even of one hectare, it was difficult to incorporate them all into the unit. Of course they did not all live on revenue from the micro-parcel of land used for grain cultivation. Some had already emigrated, others were too young or too old to work, but often a large number were there in the prime of life, continually looking for jobs in agricultural labor, peddling, etc., on a day to day basis. The cooperators received only a small income, but it at least had the advantage of being stable and guaranteed. In fact, the small landowners were applying pressure to enter into the Unités Coopératives de Production (U.C.P.) of the north (contrary to those of Sahel and those who lived in regions of truck farming and arboriculture). The administration and the technicians had to choose the members of the U.C.P. Great conflicts arose between technicians and peasants, but no less important were those which came up between members of the same family group.

The local officials and the peasants put pressure on the technicians to try to make them take on as many cooperators as possible. This gave the cooperative a demographic burden which often exceeded its labor needs. These needs themselves were limited by the difficulties of starting new systems of cultivation and by the decision to use mechanized labor as much as possible.

POLITICAL PROBLEMS   Before cooperatives were set up, the cores of state land and a large part of the peasant land were rented by the big local landowners or by city people, who owned tractors and threshing machines. These same machines were rented for high fees by the peasants who farmed their own land but did not want to keep farm animals.

The establishment of cooperatives took away from farmers with large or medium-sized farms the hope of one day acquiring the former colonial estates. It likewise eliminated a good part of the land which they rented; this land was often more than they owned. Moreover it absorbed a good part of the people who used to rent their farming equipment.

There was no agrarian reform in the north, but the establishment of cooperatives resulted immediately in a great decrease in the size of large farms based on rented land. The discontent began with this group of farmers who had always shared the domination of the countryside with the colonists. The strongest active hostility against the cooperative movement developed in this class of people.

FINANCIAL PROBLEMS   Peasant lands were, as we have seen, mediocre and needed a great deal of work. They had to be protected against erosion, their soil needed restoration, rocks had to be removed, and trees planted. Credit through long-term investments proved indispensable and more important than predicted.

These colonial lands, bought back or nationalized, were worn out through many phases of overfarming and bad farming before they were integrated into cooperatives. After independence, the colonists no longer invested money in their lands since they knew they would have to abandon them. The large farmers who took their place by renting the land used the land as intensively as possible. They hardly used any fertilizer and they did not even practice biennial crop rotation which lets the soil "rest."

The cooperatives inherited farms which were damaged, exhausted, and without any equipment. Farm buildings were often dilapidated. The French offices which drew up the technical plans of the cooperative units did not hesitate to present their plans in the form of model farms equipped with complete and complex inventory. The price was high. Credit was given at the start, but it soon became evident that the volume of credit necessary risked becoming too large. Credit for the construction of village cooperatives and for the acquisition of income-producing livestock was considerably limited. That could not be the best solution since animal husbandry should occupy an important place in the production systems of all the U.C.P. in the north. But, as there were not enough jobs on the cooperatives and the fodder was accumulating, it was absolutely necessary to instigate the amount of animal husbandry which had been recommended in the Plan. The most unfortunate operation, which should have been absolutely avoided, was set up: the collectivization or even semi-collectivization of the cooperators' livestock.

Was the first balance sheet after the triennial plan positive? It is necessary to look at nuances because everything depends on the objectives to which one is referring.

After a fair analysis of the situation, the U.G.T.T. economic report placed the blame on a very widespread idea that man, the "peasant mentality," was the most serious obstacle to the recovery and development of the country. The new approach accords, on the contrary, an important place to human promotion. The peasant, working within the framework of the new structures, was supposed to be the principal force in the development of the country. For the U.G.T.T., the plan was not a simple question of technique. "The technicians often want to deal only with mathematical equations ... this points out the vanity of technical projects when they are not conceived to fit human needs or thought of as a function of those needs."

The realization of the Triennial Plan was in fact considerably removed from the objective of human improvement through participation. The cooperative programs responded to real national needs. The technicians were tempted to apply it in the name of economic rationality and were also obliged to apply it in the name of the national imperatives of the Plan.

The peasant did not understand it and was not enthusiastic about it; some peasants even opposed it because the plan of crop rotation was opposed to their interests as small stock raisers. They were opposed to the disappearance of fallow lands because the soil normally used for pasturing their cattle was used for growing legumes and fodder.

Thus, from the start the program became a technical affair: men were not able to be closely associated with the elaboration or the function of the Plan (cf. Ben Salem, this volume).

Moreover, the degree of innovation involved in these programs was great in comparison to that tried by small landowners and even by colonists. The cooperatives almost became experimental farms which always entail certain risks. Furthermore, the programs were not financed by subsidies but by credit which the cooperators had to reimburse. They also had to be content with low salaries. Thus, a double contradiction began to make its appearance.

1.   The cooperative workers, i.e. the most deprived class of the rural

population (agricultural workers and property owners with less than five hectares), had the financial burden of the vast national plan of modernization, innovation, intensification, and diversification of agriculture in the country. The upper- and middle-class property owners did not make any such investments; they accumulated the revenues which cereal cultivation on a large scale easily provides and did not participate at all in the realization of national objectives. Many of the peasants were conscious of this and spoke out against it.

2. The U.G.T.T. program distrusted, as we have seen, the banking system, which it called the omnipotent lair of capitalism, and advocated the creation of an investment cooperative. The large number of investments which modernization necessitated brought on a massive recourse to the banking system. A special bank, the National Agriculture Bank, was created. It borrowed foreign money from the U.S.A.I.D. first, and then from IBRD. The latter ended up creating a bureau of control over the cooperatives (B.C.U.P.) in Tunis. The cooperative system was thus subjected to credit.

But in spite of increasing difficulties and hostility from the social environment of the upper- and middle-class property owners and from the economic environment (creditors and suppliers), the modernization plan was being realized and began to affect the landscape and the society.

All the projects of the Triennial Plan were not realized, but the important steps were made in the domains of water and soil conservation, of reforesting, and of the hydraulic system. Agriculture was beginning to be better equipped and more diversified. In September 1965, 117,000 hectares (90,000 hectares of arable land only) were being worked by cooperatives in the north. There was an incontestable evolution towards agricultural diversification (see Table 2).

Table 2.   Diversification of agriculture

Hard wheat	26,000 hectares
Soft wheat	13,000 hectares
Barley	4,000 hectares
Legumes	8,000 hectares
Fodder	5,400 hectares
Truck farming and industrials	1,000 hectares
Arboriculture	12,000 hectares

But modernization and diversification was left to the State and the cooperatives. Overall, the diversification of Tunisian agriculture was progressing very slowly, slower than the Plan had foreseen and slower than the exigencies of the country's needs. The planners and the technicians could not ignore this.

Treating the problems which this lag posed, the Quadrennial Plan of 1965–1968 noted:

It is necessary to emphasize that the lag is not the fault of the cooperative sector. Out of 180,000 hectares of total surface incorporated into the cooperative sector, the surface used for grain cultivation is 107,000 hectares. This statement clearly proves that, for the execution of the objectives of the plan, structural reform must be pushed to the maximum, so that the whole sector is controlled by the organization of the Plan."

The Plan stated further:

In conclusion, the Pre-Plan period has shown the difficulties in developing and controlling the sector of extensive cultivation when its structures have not undergone reform. The fundamental objectives have only been partially achieved:

The application of rational crop rotation, with the diminishing of fallow areas and the extension of fodder and edible legume cultivation, is very slow and slows down the general evolution of agriculture.

The extension of modern culture has also been slow; without the help of Office des Terres Domaniales (O.T.D.) and Unités de Production (U.P.) there would have been regression in this area.

The rise in yield caused by mechanization and the use of fertilizer is hardly noticeable. The new equipment which has been put into use really only replaces old equipment, instead of being added to it. The use of fertilizer has increased, thanks largely to the O.T.D. and the U.P.

The importance of such a statement can hardly be overemphasized.

The U.G.T.T. economic report of 1956 only timidly and indirectly approached the problem of large private farming. Neither the Decennial Perspectives nor the Triennial Plan had expressed doubts about the ability or the will of large private farmers to cooperate in agricultural development through the intensification of their production systems. It was the modern sector and it was necessary to let it be.

For the first time the traditional peasant sector was not officially considered as being uniquely responsible for the stagnation of the agricultural economy; the "traditional" modern sector, based on the colonial patterns, was no longer considered the model. The large private farming was held partly responsible because it did not participate in the realization of national objectives even though it had good land and financial means.

Numerous factors contributed, directly or indirectly, to this change in attitude toward the large private farmers who had been warned not to let this happen.

In 1959, a law threatening to take over poorly or inadequately farmed property was adopted and promulgated. It was not solely meant for the colonists who had more or less abandoned their lands. The census of 1962 (published later) revealed an agrarian and agricultural situation which some had suspected but which had not been documented before.

In the north of the country, where it makes sense to speak of the size of farms, small farmers with less than five hectares made up 45 percent of the farming population, but only had 6 percent of the land at their disposal. Large farmers, with over a hundred hectares, only made up 3 percent of the farmers, but used 47 percent of the land. Agrarian reserach showed that the smallholders' land was largely mediocre. Their low production was not the result of a "retrograde peasant mentality" but the result of bad soil which did not permit the implementation of modern farming techniques. The census and research clearly demonstrated that the use of innovations (fertilizer, hybrid seeds, weed killers) and of farming techniques (deep plowing, numerous recrossings, and respect for crop rotation, even a rudimentary one) were not as frequent as one had believed them to be on the large estates. The only factors of progress that were generally used were the tractor and the threshing machine. Cattle-raising occupied a very small place on the large farms, and it was conducted in as extensive a fashion as on small farms.

The myth of the large private farm which was modern, which generated progress, and which was a technical model for the peasant was destroyed. Moverover, since the beginning of the plan a great deal of money had been spent for studies and research on the potentialities of the natural milieu and its rational use. Precise pedological maps of vast areas, a phyto-ecological map, and studies of bioclimatology rapidly led to the creation of maps at 1/20,000 which, taking into account all the data of the physical sphere, listed all the possible crops with their expected yields according to the farming techniques which were adopted. These different scientific works could not be doubted because they were done at the request of the planners and had been supervised by the highest French scientific institutes (C.N.R.S., ORSTOM, I.S.E.A.). They confirmed what the planners and technicians had known for a long time: the natural potentialities of the area are great; much progress could be made. Planners, technicians, and researchers came to realize more and more that there was under-utilization and irrational use of the potentialities of the land. This was due in many regions to the structures of production on both the small farms and the large estates, although the reasons for poor utilization of natural potentials differed according to the size of the farm.

Numerous experiments in the areas of animal husbandry, of plant varieties, and of different types of crop rotation were carried out by the

Institute of Agronomic Research and the experimental farms, functioning within the framework of PNUD/FAO, UNESCO, and bilateral cooperation. These experiments showed after many years that the proposed systems of production were possible and profitable for farming.

A new type of analysis imposed itself scientifically. A new school of technicians and of researchers, well-trained in the problems of Tunisia, was born. Its scientific and technical arguments had much weight since they were in accordance with the great national plan. They had all the more weight because President Bourguiba believed that technical innovations and science could lead agriculture out of its stagnation and the resultant low productivity.

Several times President Bourguiba spoke on the theme of the "social and economic function" of property. Property should not satisfy only the objective needs and, for stronger reasons, the subjective needs of the owner. It should also satisfy national needs. Private property should bend to the production imperatives set up by the National Development Plan, especially if the agronomic potentials of the property were scientifically known and if state aid was being given.

This theme was the subject of hot debate at the Seventh Congress of the Neo-Destour Party (Bizerte, 1964), which here changed its name to Parti Socialiste Destourien (P.S.D.)

In his opening speech, President Bourguiba declared again:

> The problem of land in Tunisia is of prime importance; it is evident that our first job is to make the land produce as much as possible....
>
> The Destour Party itself has evolved and has adopted socialism. It is ready to deal severely with and to render harmless those who wish to gain personal profits at the expense of the community. It affirms that it will allow the private sector to subsist, that it will not bother the industrials or the bourgeois as long as their activity is compatible and in full harmony with the general interest. Their activity must fit into the framework of the plan and conform in every way to national objectives (P.S.D. 1965a:41–42).

These very points are taken up again in the motion of the congress on agriculture.

Private farmers were not condemned by the P.S.D. but were given a choice: either comply with the national objectives or disappear.

THE RADICALIZATION OF DOCTRINE AND THE PLAN

The debates of the 1964 Congress were continued by the economic and social committees of the Party. A national seminar on the coordination of economic sectors, held in Tunis on the tenth and eleventh of September, 1965, took the discussion further and ended with more radical conclusions. The quotations are long but important:

Without ambiguity, we say that private enterprise now plays a large role in Tunisia and will continue to do so in the future....

However, this large role which we recognize is not guaranteed to all private enterprises whatever they may be. Destourian socialism encourages and sustains only those which go beyond egoistic and individual interests and work for the general good and for social cohesion.... (P.S.D. 1965b: 34).

In the current phase of the evolution of our developmental structures, we assign the private sector a choice position for the realization of our objectives. This presupposes, of course, a renovated private sector which is free from the methods it formerly used, which resolutely follows the path outlined by our socialism and our plans of development, and which is in strict collaboration with other sectors. These are the only conditions under which a private sector can subsist in Tunisia, under the solicitous umbrella of the State and of the Party.... One of the conditions of this socialist rehabilitation of the private sector is the obligation each enterprise has to go beyond its own individual interests.

Private initiative must be forced to leave sterile individualism and to get involved in the union of forces, i.e., as cooperatives or societal units (of limited or anonymous responsibility, for example) (P.S.D. 1965b: 35).

While changing its objectives, the private sector is also called upon to improve and modernize its methods of management. In effect, it has remained almost totally subject to archaic modes of organization (poor labor division, confusion in financial or administrative areas, lack of book-keeping, etc.). Private enterprise continues to ignore the elementary rules of good management and production and generally draws its profit from infractions of economic and social legislation (salary, social benefits, fiscal policy). We are certain that modern management of private enterprises would permit them to find new opportunities for expansion and profit without having to use fraudulent methods. However, we do not consider all profit the same. Let us define the concept of profit. The prime concern of capitalism, that is the remuneration of its capital, is legitimate as long as it remains within the limits of the law on one hand, and follows the national objectives of economic and social development on the other hand. Moreover, profit does not constitute a total mass which is only subject to the discretion of its possessor (P.S.D. 1965b: 36).

If this adhesion (to national objectives) is lacking, the private sector will create the causes of its own ultimate failure and disfavor (P.S.D. 1965b: 37).

In no document of P.S.D. or of the Plan was there mention of the total disappearance of private farming or of the generalization of cooperatives. But implicitly, this possibility was not rejected. It was necessary to bring private farming into the increasingly urgent process of development by persuasion and encouragement.

In fact, psycho-sociological accumulation, of which we spoke in the beginning of this article, was happening faster than the accumulation of capital. The number of students in school increased considerably (see Table 3).

Table 3.   Increase in school enrollment

	1954–1956	1961	1968
Primary	188,000	465,000	845,000
Secondary	20,000	43,000	133,000
Higher education	695	2,200	10,350

The students were not all doing literary studies and preparing for the rapidly expanding educational system. Out of the 10,350 university-level students, the Faculty of Letters had only 1,775. Jobs were necessary for these young people who were trained in science and in technology. Only a modern and developing economy could provide them. The private sector in its present form could scarcely use people with an advanced education.

The population likewise increased. In 1956 it was 3,601,000; in 1966 it had grown to 4,530,000. For 1971, 5,223,000 persons were predicted. The unemployment rate was high and from 45,000 to 50,000 young people entered the job market each year.

The annual per capita consumption of different agricultural products had been so low that all improvements in income, in cultural level, in growth rate of urbanization, and all contact with any modernism (even something as rudimentary as sending children to school) only increased consumption, both quantitatively and qualitatively.

All this in fact contributed to a TRUE EXPLOSION OF NEEDS OF ALL KINDS. It became apparent on all levels that it was indispensable to respond, and to prepare to respond, to the needs which, given the changing mentality of the younger generation, became veritable requirements.

At the same time research, studies, and projects were accumulating. They all indicated that a high rate of economic growth was possible. Capital and structural reforms were necessary. Those with political power openly accepted this principle. The task could be begun. But how far would it lead?

Until 1965, attempts were made to reorganize part of the traditional peasant sector. The creation of agricultural cooperatives, following the same model, was continued, and the rhythm increased (see Table 4).

The area organized into production cooperatives in August 1968, reached 900,000 hectares at the end of the second Four-Year Plan. However, collectivization in the strictest sense of the term was hardly

Table 4. Evolution of agricultural cooperatives during the second Quadriennial Plan, 1965–68

	Number of cooperatives	Surface area (hectares)	Number of cooperators
August 31, 1965	177	205,000	14,346
August 31, 1966	246	279,000	17,745
August 31, 1967	372* +310	500,400 +114,200	29,535 + 7,960
	682	614,600	37,495
August 31, 1968	422* +266	642,500 +245,000	31,364 +14,182
	688	887,500	45,546

* The upper figure shows the production and mixed cultivation cooperatives, the lower one shows livestock cooperatives and especially precooperatives formed from state lands; their number diminished, as some were transformed into production cooperatives.

that widespread. The land from which cooperatives were formed was usually from the public domain. Public domain land was the nucleus for the Unités Coopératives de Production (U.C.P.) or was made into precooperatives in the north and polycultivation cooperatives in the center and in the south, where the land in general came from large ex-colonial olive plantations and from areas developed by the public services on collective lands which had formerly belonged to tribes and to public *habous*. (See Table 5.)

Table 5. Source of lands made into cooperatives (August 31, 1968)

	State land (public domain) (hectares)	Land owned by the cooperative members (hectares)	Rented land (hectares)	Total (hectares)
Production cooperatives	256,900	277,500	30,400	564,800
Precooperatives	201,800	10,900	0	212,700
Cooperatives: polyculture & developmental	99,600	13,500	0	113,100
Total	559,300	301,900	30,400	890,600

Moverover, the collectivization of private lands up to August 1968 only included peasant lands belonging to the small landowners generally possessing less than five hectares. The upper- and middle-class landowners had hardly been touched, although, as we have noted, large farming based on rents had considerably diminished in area and in clientele.

Up to this date, the central and regional administration and the technicians dominated the situation in spite of the accumulation of all kinds of difficulties (climatic, technical, financial, and, of course, political).

New modern agriculture was diversified and conformed to potentialities. The Plan wished to establish it, and it was beginning to become a reality.

The end of the agricultural campaign of 1967–1968 gave the results for soil utilization shown in Table 6.

Table 6. Results of soil utilization for 1967–1968. Surface in hectares (cooperative sector)

	North	Central	South	Total
Grains	170,508	9,507	4,822	184,837
Fodder cultivation	33,752	5,390	113	39,258
Edible legumes	32,500	147	6	32,653
Truck farming	2,978	251	79	3,308
Industrial farming	2,761	0	3	2,764
Arboriculture*	68,194	10,954	57,526	136,674
Fallow land	104,500	23,200	33,000	160,700
Prairie and pasture	44,400	21,800	27,800	94,000
Runs and forests	91,300	15,000	15,400	121,700
Non-agricultural land	27,800	22,900	12,000	62,700
	598,800	130,400	162,400	891,600

* A large part of the tree planting in the north, excluding vineyards and citrus groves, was done by cooperatives.

Great effort was put into the extension of fodder cultivation, of edible legumes, and of orchards in the north. The use of fertilizer and the improvement of cultivation methods was also stressed.

The Four-Year Plan of 1969–1972 took stock of the results and the difficulties in a realistic manner concerning the economic and technical plans, but it was much less realistic about the social and political plans.

The agriculture and fishing section of the Plan of Economic and Social Development, 1969–1972, stated:

From these principal observations, one can conclude that the cooperatives have done what was expected of them in the technical and economic areas; they can still be perfected but the system established has proven its capacity to absorb and utilize progress which is of prime importance in the end.

The social and human aspect, which is no less important, also boasts many accomplishments: employment has practically doubled, the intellectual level has improved at all stages, including both the cooperative workers' realization of the importance of group work and the cultural and technical assistance given by technical and social organisms.

And nevertheless the active population of production cooperatives is the same as it was when productivity was so low; these elements should encourage us to accelerate our efforts in the same direction; certainly, for the production cooperatives already established it is a matter of going beyond the semi-intensive system which exists at this time, to a totally intensive system which would be the proof of the technical autonomy of these enterprises; likewise, the imperatives of production demand that the traditional sector change to the semi-intensive methods. One can say, taking into account the experience acquired, that the transformation of the traditional system to the intensive system requires about ten years. In countries with highly developed agriculture, this change sometimes took several centuries.

All of this demonstrates that the direction we have chosen is the best one and that it is necessary to continue along the same path and to simultaneously raise the traditional enterprises to the semi-intensive level, and the semi-intensive ones to the intensive level.

This is the language of the modernist and progressive technician; but there were other men and politics.

Three consecutive years of drought had, as usual, seriously reduced production, especially of cereals. The cooperative sector was not to blame for the reduction. Its production was scarcely lower than that of the best private farms. The area used for grain cultivation by all the cooperatives in the country in 1968 was only 178,000 hectares, although the total area used for grain cultivation was 1,562,000 hectares. But for the 45,000 cooperative workers the low level of production of legumes and of grains in the north, of olives in the center and the south, and the great number of investments and reimbursements meant only lower income. This gave them no enthusiasm for the system; they did not defend their cooperatives or the system since they still considered themselves as salaried workers. And in fact they were.

An objective analysis of the situation of the majority of the 45,000 persons who were incorporated into the cooperatives before the end of August 1968 (former landowners with less than five hectares, former salaried agricultural workers, or former unemployed workers) would allow one to think that the workers' income, in kind or in cash taken from the cooperatives (around 100 D.T. per year), was hardly inferior to their previous income. And in fact, before August 1968, there were no serious incidents in the cooperatives in the north. However, crop "thefts" were becoming frequent.

But the plan was supposed to be total, and after the Congress of Bizerte attempts were made to get private farmers to follow the movement. Three years later, the Plan stated again, as it had in 1965, that only the collective and state sectors had really begun modernizing agriculture. Climatic difficulties could not threaten the acceptance of the projected model. Threats and persuasion turned to often sizeable encouragement offered to cooperatives emphasizing service rather than production.

Service cooperatives had been started very early in the Sahel where they were to rejunevate old olive orchards, but after great difficulties at the start, the operation was practically suspended (see Sethom, this volume).

After 1965 the new service cooperatives were supposed to work essentially on the large and middle-sized grain farms in the north of the country. In some administrative areas a developmental plan was proposed, after summary study, for each large or middle-sized farm. These plans were much less intensive than those of the cooperatives. The necessary investments were to be financed simultaneously by a loan and by a subsidy which was always higher than, sometimes double, the credit. The sum was attractive, the cultivation system was not too complex. Was there a lack of available capital at a time when the cooperatives were themselves insufficiently financed?

Did the farmers refuse to engage in a process which risked becoming more exacting and more imperative? It is difficult to take one side or the other. At any rate, in its report in 1968, the Plan of 1968–1972 only points out the attempt. In fact it had failed; people did not hesitate to base whole theories on that. The large property owners had been treated gently, while the small ones were, voluntarily or by force, incorporated into the cooperatives and involved in a complex and costly production system.

In September 1968, the process of collectivization was accelerated but still only on the land of small landowners and of the state.

Three months later, a million more hectares had been made into cooperatives; the land came mostly from tribal collective land in the

Table 7. Land made into cooperatives

	Production cooperatives (hectares)	Poly-cultural cooperatives (hectares)	Livestock cooperatives (hectares)	Pre-cooperatives (hectares)	Service cooperatives (pilot projects)	Public organisms	Total (hectares)
North	360,948	53,644	2026	201,766	5,511	34,500	658,395
Central	0	444,636	0	30,173	0	201,864	676,673
South	0	219,369	60	294,628	18	29,505	543,580
Total	360,948	717,649	2086	526,567	5,529	265,869	1,878,648

center and from the entire ex-colonial plantations in the Sfax region and from Zarzis. (See Table 7.)

As we have already noted, overall area is important, but the amount of collectivized private lands remained limited to about 400,000 hectares which were mostly from the traditional sector. Were the large private farms going to sidestep the plan for modernization once again?

The doctrine adopted by the Congress of Bizerte is once again affirmed in the Four-Year Plan, 1969–1972:

The problem is in the identification of the most appropriate structure for each case and for each given country. In Tunisia, after several experiments and tentative efforts which illustrate the essentially pragmatic character of our action in this domain, it seems that a clear plan of action is taking form.

In the domain of production, we have reached the conviction that the three sectors (state, cooperative and private) can and should coexist.

Thus, for example, in agriculture the cooperative structure seems to us the most evident way to resolve problems of fragmentation of landholdings, of the diffusion of technical progress, of the diversification of crops, and of the implementation of modern farming methods. The production units already set up should consequently be consolidated and this experiment should be progressively extended through the creation of new units. In the case where the surface area of an individual farm does not necessitate additions of land to make it profitable, it is nevertheless necessary to make sure that these farms follow the movement toward modernization. This could be facilitated by the creation of service cooperatives which these farms would join.

And so, starting from September 1968, the service cooperative formula for large farms, tried in vain since 1966, became obligatory. On January 31, 1969, 873,000 hectares were in service cooperatives. They were rapidly transformed into production cooperatives. The operation was identical to that used for the constitution of the old production cooperatives: one production unit was made from a large estate and the surrounding small farms. General collectivization began at a rapid rate. Data in Table 8 furnished by the monthly bulletin, *Informations Rapides*, from the Secretary of State for the Plan, allow us to follow the development in the country as a whole.

Table 8.   Development of collectivization

	Product cooperatives (hectares)	Service cooperatives (hectares)	State land (hectares)	Total (hectares)
February 1969	1,995,000	675,407	277,188	2,947,646
April 1969	2,981,100	287,000	257,300	3,525,400
May 1969	3,533,300	108,400	257,300	3,899,000
July 1969	4,668,700	43,400	57,300	4,769,000
August 1969	4,738,400	43,400	57,300	4,838,100

It is not necessary to describe the technical, financial, psychological, and political conditions of this collectivization. Collectivization until 1968 was a technical question which technicians were, in spite of many difficulties, able to control. In 1968 it took on a new aspect. They were no longer able to control it because it was happening so rapidly. In August 1969, general collectivization was achieved, but the only real production cooperative, firmly established and structured, were those in the north, Unités Coopératives de Production du Nord (U.C.P.N.), the precooperatives, and the polycultural cooperatives which had been established through the work of the Four-Year Plan, 1965–1968, that is 650,000 hectares.

The peasantry of the Sahel, of the Cap Bon, of the Sahel of Bizerte, and of the oases, where arboriculture and truck farming were practiced, had been accustomed for millennia to familial structures of production and small properties. They could only refuse the new hastily established structures for which they were not prepared. This movement of discontent was really a movement of the people in these regions which are small but important because of their population and their political position. The middle- and upper-class property owners of the grain regions of the north and of the oil plantations of the center and the south quickly took advantage of their discontent.

In the beginning of September 1969, a Council of the Republic stopped the movement; a new process began: decollectivization. It would be more rapid than the texts which organized it predicted.

The law of September 22, 1969, relative to the new reform of agricultural structures reaffirms in article two the coexistence of three sectors: state, cooperative, and private. However, it limits production cooperatives to regions of extensive cultivation. It also insists again on the idea which pervaded the Plan from the beginning: the necessity for private farming to conform to the fundamental objectives of the national plans of development. "The farming of agricultural land by individuals must conform to the fundamental objectives of national plans of development. It will be principally carried out on fruit orchards and truck-farms. A decree will set up the obligations of each farmer in an instruction book" (Law 69–56 of September 22, 1969).

The instructions given to technicians and administrators were precise. The production cooperatives constituted before January 1969 would be maintained. Those constituted after that date would likewise be maintained if their technical, financial, and psychological conditions permitted their success. Otherwise they would be dissolved and the lands farmed privately if conditions were not good. In this case the plans for crop rotation and modernization were to be respected, however. The law of 1969 and the first instructions which came out of it tried to put order into the structures rapidly set up since September 1968. It announced decollectivization, of course, but it tried to safeguard all collectives which had solidly established themselves since the beginning of the cooperative movement, especially the production units of the north. This law was very quickly made obsolete by the facts, however.

By December 31, 1969, no more than 1,494,000 hectares remained in cooperatives. Starting from January 1970, decollectivization became more rapid. In fact, in the euphoria which followed, meetings were hastily organized in the cooperatives: the private lands left the collectives. During 1970 the whole system was dismantled. Nothing was left of the old production cooperatives of the north and of the polycultural cooperatives but the state-owned nuclei. This accounted for an area of 208,000 hectares in the north and approximately 130,000 hectares in the center and the south. A great part of the income-producing livestock and of the material used for farming of the dissolved cooperatives was sold at public auctions. A law establishing modalities of transfer (sale) of public lands was promulgated on May 19, 1970. State lands which were not set up as production or polycutural cooperatives or which the administration did not wish to reserve for public use, could be sold. The law distinguishes between:

1. Dispersed lands or lands of a very small area which can be sold to the present occupant, to coparcenaries of the state, to bordering property owners, and if none of these existed, at public auction.

2. Lands of large area were to be divided up and sold first to current occupants employed on the land and not having other resources, to technicians coming out of teaching establishments and agricultural training schools, and finally to young people from civil service centers.

A national commission of property transfer and regional commissions were created for the evaluation of applications. This law obviously aroused great unrest among the socialists in the country who saw it as the liquidation of the real estate heritage of the state after that of the cooperative system. At first hope was aroused among the middle- and upper-class property owners: later, they felt deceived when they saw themselves theoretically brushed aside by the law. The unrest of one group and the hope of the other were at a high point in the summer of 1970 when large public notices announcing the sale of state land from former cooperatives began to appear in the newspapers.

The sale which was hoped to be rapid and massive did not take place. However, it is difficult to know exactly how much land was sold at this time.

Seventy thousand hectares of state land and 26,000 hectares belonging to the Office of the Medjerdah had been sold well before 1969. By 1972 these sales had not yet been finalized for many reasons. But, of the land hastily put up for sale in June 1970, the Office des Terres Domaniales (O.T.D.) had only sold 35,300 hectares within the following three years, including 10,000 hectares which had already been sold, the sales being finalized during this period. In total conformity with the spirit of the law of May 1970, the only people to benefit from the sales were the former workers and cooperators of the subdivided farms, and to a lesser extent small farmers and some technicians. To these figures one must also add 25,000 hectares which was divided up and sold by the Office of the Medjerah. The social category of the new owners of these lots, which were close to the capital and usually planted in trees, is not known.

The phase of general decollectivization was a success. It was generally of a political nature and went far beyond the law of September 1969, through its generalized and blind application of the principle of free choice between the cooperative and the private farm. Not a single hectare of private land was in cooperatives. On the other hand, the sale of state land raised a number of problems and presented many difficulties.

The technicians, and one can add technical and scientific rationale, had been subordinated to the politicians since 1969. They were getting back a voice in these matters and a part of their influence, but with difficulty.

The year 1972 saw in effect the State Land Office which was in charge of government land create regional technical commissions for the regularization of the status of these lands.

For ten years technicians had been accustomed to a fundamental idea accepted by everyone and reconfirmed by the law of September 1969: the grouping of lands into large areas of cultivation is an indispensable operation for all technical progress, including diversification and intensification of crop rotations and improvements in productivity. It was difficult for them to understand that even cooperatives which were well established before the general collectivization of 1969 had to be broken up. Working in the field, they saw the private lands which had formerly been collectivized FALL BACK INTO THE SYSTEM OF RENTAL to middle- and upper-class property owners. Triennial or quadriennial crop rotation which had taken place for several years was stopped and the OLD BIENNIAL WHEAT-FALLOW LAND SYSTEM was usually reestablished.

Likewise it was difficult for them to see the orchards, planted by the cooperatives on the private land of its members, not maintained, invaded by weeds or by grains, and often even uprooted. It was also painful for them to see innovations such as fodder crops (fescue-grass, truffles, etc.) gain thousands of hectares on more or less swampy land only to be abandoned and the land returned to the cultivation of wheat with yields of only three to five quintals per hectare.

Was it also necessary to take apart the large state properties? Were there not great risks of seeing realizations, carried out a long time ago on those farms, undergo the same reversal? The lots sold before and after 1969 were most often restored to traditional cultivation. Some were already rented out, others were given out to sharecroppers by the allottee, and others were still simply rented out as *achaba* [pasture] instead of being intensively cultivated. The public irrigation zones installed at great expense had long been underfarmed because of the fragmentation of landholding.

The technicians were clearly aware of these dangers and risks. Their arguments, technical and not political, halted the splitting up of state property three years after the beginning of decollectivization. This would have had serious consequences for the modernization and the diversification of agriculture.

The state's landholdings, an area of 727,000 hectares (without taking into account some 70,000 hectares sold before 1969), was administered by two offices: the State Land Office (O.T.D.) (637,000 hectares) and the office of the Medjerdah (89,000 hectares). The consolidation of the U.C.P. in 1970–1971 maintained about 208,000 hectares in cooperative farms. These lands hardly posed any problems. The reduction by about two-thirds in the number of cooperatives as compared to the previous situation where private lands were incorporated into these units, the favorable climatic conditions of three successive years, and better farming technique brought a very clear improvement in production and in the income of the cooperators, in spite of the reimbursement of big, accumulated debts. Out of 218 cooperatives, only twelve had financial difficulties in 1972. This improvement of the situation undoubtedly explains the current pressure from excooperators who want to return to the cooperatives.

From the beginning of decollectivization some large state farms were rapidly made into agro-combinations directly managed by the O.T.D. They totaled about 116,000 hectares.

The rest of the state lands under the direction of the office, about 330,000 hectares, were to be "regularized." These lands are currently farmed as best as possible, either as polycultural cooperatives (138,000 hectares) or as pilot and state farms. This is being done to save orchards and other improvements which have already been achieved. Other farms have been provisionally assigned to establishments doing agriculture research or instruction, or to state or para-state societies and organisms. Some are also rented to private farmers.

Many of these lands, in general large nationalized farms, would be underfarmed and their production would diminish if they were divided up. Polycultural cooperatives, management by public organisms, or any other form of collective farming which would allow the potential and the investments already made to be conserved and the system of production to be intensified, seem to the technician to be the best methods of "regularization." Twenty-five thousand hectares of land dispersed in small plots could be sold, while there are 90,000 hectares which can be divided up because they cannot constitute true production units. It will be necessary to set up technical programs to assure that this land is well farmed so as to avoid the underfarming which is common on the lots already sold.

The problem, so well known, is controversial and not only so in Tunisia. To distribute the land to the peasant is an old and tenacious idea, even among certain socialists who consider this operation as necessity before collectivization can take place.

To give the lands to middle- and upper-class farmers capable of modernizing and intensifying agriculture, and not to small farmers without means or technical know-how, is also a widespread and clearly formulated idea in Tunisia.

One knows what the small peasantry of the grain and steppe regions can do. The peasants themselves are conscious of their capacities and especially of the dangers which the large private farmer, always greedy for land, would bring upon it. Therefore they have not demanded this land. This may be surprising, but history and the disorganization which the peasants have undergone for almost a century explain this situation.

One also knows what the upper- and middle-class property owners of the region can do on a rational level, such as the intensification of production systems, the diversification of cultivation, and the realization of national production objectives considered essential.

To have agricultural structures capable of bringing rapid progress and of using optimally the natural, scientifically determined potentialities of the environment, in a country where resources are limited and needs are great: this is the basic argument of the technician when confronted by the politician and the producer. In Tunisia, this position has often been convincing for the politician, but rarely so for the producer, whether he owns a small or large farm and for different reasons. This position permitted the politicians in power to accept certain kinds of reform of agrarian structures leading to modernization and progress but upsetting neither productivity nor social structures.

This type of reform was stopped as soon as it began to threaten the social structures which coincided with the first important economic difficulties. This was its limit. Was it possible to rapidly transform a reform which until 1968 conceived of itself as being modern and technical? The example of Tunisia has shown the difficulties and, indeed, the impossibility of such an operation.

But for ten years this reform brought on great modernization at all levels, an understanding of the true problems of underdevelopment, and especially an important development of the productive forces. It is certainly possible to reconsider a large part of the reforms carried out in the economic domain, but it is difficult, if not impossible, to negate the gains brought about by these reforms because these achievements will have their own demands and their own, new dynamics.

REFERENCES

BOURGUIBA, HABIB
1968   "Discours du Kef du 15 Septembre 1968." Tunis: S.E.A.C.I.

FOUGEYROLLAS, P.
1970   *Les conditions sociologiques préalables au développement.* Colloque d'Accra, 20–29 July, 1970. Dakar: Institut de développement économique et de planification (Mimeographed.)

HERMASSI, ABDELBAKI
1966   *Mouvement ouvrier en société coloniale.* Paris: Ecole pratique des hautes études. (Mimeographed.)

PARTI SOCIALISTE DESTOURIEN
1965a   *7ème Congrès, Bizerte 19–22, Octobre 1964.* Tunis: Société l'Action d'Edition et de Presse.
1965b   *Proceedings* of the National Seminar on the Coordination of Economic Sectors, September 10–11. Tunis.

SECRETARIAT DE L'ETAT A L'AGRICULTURE
1963   L'expérience tunisienne en matière de coopération agricole. *Terre de Tunisie.*

UNION GENERALE DES TRAVAILLEURS TUNISIENS
1956   *Rapport économique du 6ème Congrès.* Tunis: U.G.T.T.

VIBERT, J.
1955   Tableau de l'économie tunisienne. *Bulletin économique et social de Tunisie* 105:48.

Cooperatives in the Republic of Guinea: Problems of Revolutionary Transformation

WILLIAM DERMAN

Guinea has considered herself, and has been considered by many out-siders, as a socialist and revolutionary state. Sekou Touré, the leader of both the party and the state, has generated a changing but consistent view of the revolutionary transformation needed to establish a socialist state. In Guinea, as in most African nations, the rural agricultural sector predominates. This rural sector thus plays a critical, if not decisive, role in the proposed socialist revolution. Few studies have assessed local conse-quences of Guinea's national policies. This paper attempts to integrate local, regional, and national arenas in order to portray the uneven, shifting, and halting effort to develop cooperatives as the means to fun-damentally alter the countryside of Guinea. The paper, then, moves beyond the limits of my own fieldwork to link what I observed in the Fouta-Djallon to larger questions involved in the revolutionary transfor-mation of the lives of the Guinean peasants.

GUINEA: THE BACKGROUND

Guinea won her independence in 1958, the sole French colony to vote "no" on Charles De Gaulle's referendum establishing the Fifth Republic.

I was in the Republic of Guinea from December 1965 through August 1967. During most of that time I lived in a former serf village in the Fouta-Djallon. The village is called Hollaande-Popodara, which is also the committee name. The area is entirely Fulbe and all speak Fulfulde or Pular. My research was made possible by grants from the National Institute of Mental Health and a dissertation grant from the National Science Foundation.

All of France's colonies voted "yes" or "no" on whether or not to accept the constitution of the newly created Fifth Republic following the demise of the Fourth, largely caused by the Algerian War. In reaction to the Guinean "no" vote the French attempted by economic and political means to overthrow the new government of Guinea and to depose her new leader, Sekou Touré. De Gaulle ordered all French workers, teachers, and professionals to leave Guinea, all French assistance was stopped, and the French exerted diplomatic pressure to prevent any other nation from coming to Guinea's aid.

The French strategy failed, at least in part, due to the assistance of East Bloc countries. The French strategy also forced Guinea to employ her own nationals in all areas of the economy and society, which the French thought would destroy Guinea, but which actually led to a very early and full Africanization (a decade or more ahead of Africanization programs of other nations). The external threat of the French also increased internal solidarity and internal support for Sekou Touré and the *Parti Démocratique de Guinée.*

The *Parti Démocratique de Guinée* (PDG) was originally organized as part of the old *Rassemblement Démocratique de l'Afrique* which led the early struggles for national independence. Since that time the PDG has remained the only party of Guinea, and its national control has never been seriously threatened. Since its inception, the PDG has been a mass party. All Guineans are eligible for membership in the PDG, with full political mobilization of the populace as a high priority of the party. Mobilization necessitates changes in the lives of all Guineans, including changes in the values held by them. It also demands an increasing commitment of Guinea to the liberation of the rest of Africa from colonial and imperial control.

Since the fall of Nkrumah in Ghana, Guinea has become isolated from other African nations. Looking back, Guinea, with Ghana, Mali, and Algeria (before their military coups) appeared in the forefront of African struggles for independence and development. Over time, the situation has reversed and Guinea is the sole remaining representative of that bloc of African nations. However, recent developments (such as visits to Guinea by leaders of Algeria, Ivory Coast, Liberia, Sierre Leone, Cameroon, Zaire, and Cuba) suggest a breakdown of that isolation. In addition, the Portuguese attempt to invade Guinea (November 22, 1970) along with many other internal and external efforts to unseat the regime, has placed severe pressure on Guinea. In these conflict situations the support and involvement of the people as a whole have contributed decisively to the continuing stability of the PDG in Guinea. Despite the apparent stability of the regime, there remain contradictions in trying to be a socialist state while depending on external capital for development.

One of the contradictions concerns the relationship between the national party leadership and the countryside. National decisions and programs may not be adopted in the countryside or the ultimate form of village actions may be quite different from the intentions of the national party. Although there has been a constant interplay between the mass of the people and the PDG, national decisions often bear little resemblance to local understanding and action.

Much of the initial international interest and enthusiasm for the regime of Sekou Touré and the PDG stemmed from their belief that ideas and experiences, and therefore programs, were to originate from the masses. Despite early attempts to encourage this, over the past seven years decisions and programs have been formulated at national levels, dependent upon national priorities. Villagers have been forced to comply whether or not a specific decision or program made sense to them. This paper focuses on the analysis of how this occurs despite the formal local-level committee structure and mass party. But first a brief discussion of the Fulbe and the Fouta-Djallon.

THE FOUTA-DJALLON AND THE FULBE

The Fouta-Djallon forms the most densely populated area of the Republic of Guinea. From these rich and varied highlands originate many of the major river systems of West Africa — the Senegal, the Niger, the Konkouré, and others. Not only is the human population both dense and high, but the bovine population surpasses the human one. For many centuries, the Fouta-Djallon has provided a relatively secure and bountiful life for the succession of peoples living there. Ever since the Holy War (*jihad*) of 1726, the Fulbe people (also known as the Fulani or Peul) have dominated the area. The Fulbe entered as pastoralists during the sixteenth and seventeenth centuries. As they became transhumant and then sedentary in the Fouta-Djallon, conflicts developed with the Soussou and Diallonke peoples who, after many wars, ultimately left the Fouta-Djallon to escape from Fulbe hegemony.

After the *jihad* of 1726, the Fulbe created an Islamic confederacy which lasted until the French subjugation of the Fouta-Djallon in 1896. Prior to French domination, the Fouta-Djallon had come to refer to a confederation of nine provinces under the aegis of the *almamy* (from the Arabic *imam*) of Timbo, one of the nine provinces. In precolonial times, the Fulbe spoke a common language (Fulfulde or Pular), were all members of the Islamic faith, recognized common political leaders, and felt their own unity.

Before colonialism, the basis of the economy of the Fouta-Djallon underwent a gradual transition from pastoralism to sedentarism based on a mixed economy, to an increased dependence upon serf labor. Through trade and warfare, wealthier Fulbe acquired serfs whom they placed in separate villages and who worked the land owned by the Fulbe. Thus, despite social and ritual emphasis upon cattle, agricultural wealth increased in both relative and absolute importance. To the Fulbe, land ownership was essential, while the serfs (who comprised forty to fifty percent of the population of some parts of the Fouta by the end of the nineteenth century) owned no land at all. We will return to the question of land later in discussing the successes and failures of the cooperatives.

We can visualize the sociopolitical organization of the Fouta-Djallon as having been in a state of tension between a territorial organization based upon an Islamic model, and a kin organization based upon maximal, major, and minimal patrilineages.[1] Territorially, the Fouta-Djallon consisted of nine relatively autonomous provinces. The leaders of the various provinces were the direct patrilineal descendants of the *jihad* leaders in that area.

Each province was divided into clusters of villages with every cluster having one village which contained a mosque as its religious and political center. The cluster of villages around a mosque and the village itself were known as *missides*. *Missides* could be satellites of other *missides*. The two other kinds of villages present were the *fulasso*, Fulbe villages, and the *runde*, serf villages. The three kinds of villages could not be distinguished from each other in physical form but Fulbe villages tended to be on higher ground than serf villages. *Missides* were invariably on strategically important high ground overlooking large areas. Villages were and are permanent.

The kin organization consisted of patrilineages, which were named, agamous, dispersed groups. There are Fulbe equivalents for what we have termed maximal (*leenyol*), major (*gorol*), and minor (*suudu*) lineages. Four major social strata cut across the territorial and kin organizations: the chiefs and their patrilineal kinsfolk, the free Fulbe, the Fulbe of the bush, and the serfs. One's membership in a maximal patrilineage also determined one's membership in one of the four social strata. This is a very abbreviated

---

[1] For more details on Fulbe social and political organization, see Derman (1973) and Dupire (1970).

version of the complex sociopolitical organization of the Fulbe. However, it serves to indicate the dimensions and complexity of the system.

The economy of the precolonial Fouta-Djallon depended primarily on agriculture and secondarily on cattle. Agricultural production consisted of the slash-and-burn fields where rice and fonio were the most important crops and of the annually cultivated women's gardens. Taro, manioc, corn, yams, and peanuts were grown there by the women. Cattle, goats, sheep, and chickens were kept. In the most densely populated areas of the Fouta, cattle remained somewhat less important than in the outlying areas. Nevertheless, until recently cattle played a critical role in the ritual and social life throughout the Fouta-Djallon.

In my view, colonial rule greatly altered the economic and social foundations of Fulbe culture.[2] In understanding the contemporary situation, we need to understand the impact of colonialism upon the peoples of Guinea. The French greatly overestimated the potential contribution of the Fouta-Djallon to their colonial enterprise. Early French explorers and administrators predicted a flow of riches out of the Fouta-Djallon to the coffers of France. Yet, the Fouta never fulfilled the dreams of the French, nor has it yet contributed significantly to the agricultural needs of the nation of Guinea. This is largely because the ecology of the Fouta-Djallon has, at least until the present, mitigated against large-scale cash cropping, inhibited the formation of plantations, and provided few mineral resources of significance. The Fouta-Djallon, while providing a rich and diversified diet for its own inhabitants, contributed little either to the colony or independent nation of Guinea. In consequence, no sources of large-scale employment have existed or exist now within the Fouta-Djallon. Instead, the Fouta exports large amounts of labor. In the cities, much of this labor force is underemployed or even unemployed, while simultaneously much of the Guinean countryside lacks agricultural labor.

However, it is not only the ecology which hampers agricultural expansion. In addition, problems arise from social divisions stemming from the earlier system of Fulbe-serf stratification. At this point, let us digress slightly to outline the pattern of Fulbe-serf relations, essential in understanding Guinean efforts to fundamentally alter the social and economic order of the Fouta-Djallon.

During colonial times, the distinctions between the Fulbe strata declined

2 This argument is greatly elaborated in Derman (1973).

in importance while the distinctions between Fulbe and serf did not.[3] The serfs, while they all spoke Fulfulde and their village organization came to resemble that of their masters, lived in separate and subordinate villages. Individual Fulbe (as opposed to kin groups) owned the serfs. Typically, the serfs of many different masters (who came from different villages) would be found within one serf village. Serfs owned no land, but cultivated and lived on land borrowed from the Fulbe. Although subject to certain customary restraints, the master of the serfs, as well as the land owner (the two were not necessarily the same individual) retained the final right to remove a serf from his borrowed land.

Land for the fields had to be obtained each year from the owner of that land, typically from the serf's master. Since the master desired the fields of his serf to be next to his own, the owner of the fields and the serf's Fulbe master were most often, but not always, the same individual. This arrangement provided for a more efficient exploitation of labor since little of the serf's time would be lost in traveling. The land for the compound of a serf was granted in perpetuity by the Fulbe. Due to the Fulbe mode of inheritance of serfs (the owner of a female serf inherited her children) the owner of the compound land and the owner of the serfs were not likely to be the same individual. This is because a serf's male children would live on or near the compound of their father, while daughters would live in the compounds of their husbands.

Each serf had to give 10 percent of his crops to his master, and all serfs provided labor to their masters. Men, women, and children worked five days a week for their masters from early morning until early afternoon at the various key economic tasks. Serfs were also the major craftsmen: blacksmiths, leather workers, cloth weavers, and basket weavers. None of these groups of artisans was endogamous and they all lived and participated in the life of the serf villages.

Ownership and labor of serfs constituted a key part of Fulbe wealth. French colonialism dramatically, if unintentionally, altered the status of serfs. Due to the introduction of money, taxes, and markets, and to French needs for forced labor, reciprocal obligations between masters and serfs broke down. The labor obligations of serfs gradually declined as the Fulbe lost political hegemony to the French, as masters stopped providing taxes for their serfs, and as there was competition among the chiefs, French, and masters for the labor of the serfs. Meanwhile, the divisions among the Fulbe lessened so that one found a merging of strata:

[3]   Serfdom came to an end with independence in 1958. After 1958 I refer to former serfs, and prior to 1958, to serfs.

the divisions between the chiefly, free, and bush maximal lineages became of less and less importance. However, at the time of independence the separation between serf and Fulbe remained strong.

INDEPENDENCE: INTEGRATION OF THE FOUTA-DJALLON INTO GUINEA

In my discussions with former serfs two events stood out during the movement toward independence. The first was the ending of forced labor announced in the Fouta-Djallon by Diallo Yacine, a Fulbe member of the French National Assembly. The second was the abolishment of the *chefs de canton*. The ending of this chieftainship marked the success of the PDG in mobilizing the countryside and in achieving much needed relief for the peasants from the exactions, seizures, and extortions of the *chefs de canton*.[4] Serfs, though, were not the only ones who supported the PDG and the abolishment of the *chefs de canton*. Many of the strongest members and supporters of the PDG were Fulbe. These Fulbe came primarily from the nonchiefly lineages. Under colonial rule they had lost land, cattle, and freedom. And, in a less direct but nonetheless important way, they were concerned over the general deterioration of the Fulbe way of life. The political organization of the Fouta-Djallon was drastically altered by colonial rule. French-appointed chiefs replaced the councils, elders, and religious leaders and "chiefs." These French-appointed *chefs de canton* were the most hated component of the colonial system. The PDG gained widespread support through their efforts to end chieftainship.

At the instigation of the PDG, the *chefs de canton* were at first replaced by *maires* for each village. This very decentralized structure was then replaced by a dual organization — an administrative one and a political one at the national, provincial, and regional levels — which merged into one form at the local level — the committee. In the Fouta-Djallon, groups of villages formed committees in which both former serfs and Fulbe became members of the same committees and competed for positions within them. Committees served as the key local political arena. Thus, shortly after independence the committee supplanted the appointed French agents as the local arm of national leadership in the countryside.

In the transition from colonial rule to independent rule the question of land arose in the countryside. Following independence there were meetings

---

4   For a summary of the changes leading up to the abolishment of the *chefs de canton* see Suret-Canale's excellent article "La fin de la chefferie en Guinée."

held throughout Guinea to deal with the problem of the seizure of lands and animals by the former *chefs de canton*. These meetings, led by PDG officials, proposed the following solutions: If the land had been seized from a Fulbe and was still held by the seizer or his descendant, it was to be returned to the rightful owners or his descendants. If the land was seized but then sold to a third party, the original owner could return to or use his land only if the original purchase price was paid to the purchaser. And if the land had been bought during the colonial period from land not seized, it was to remain in the hands of the present owner. Elders of different villages in consultation with party members drew up land claims and the claims were resolved.

At the same time that illegal properties accumulated by the *chefs de canton* were being returned to their proper owners, the national leadership decreed all land in Guinea to be the property of the state. Thus, it is of particular significance that the question of land for the landless, i.e. the serfs, never became an important issue in the Fouta-Djallon. For, according to the new decree of October 20, 1959, land belongs to those who work it, with all customary rights being lost on land not in cultivation. In the area where I worked the peasants did know of the law and its principles. Yet the question of giving land to the serfs never arose. And I could find no former serfs who had asked the PDG for land. Instead, most former serfs continued to borrow or rent land from Fulbe land owners. Those former serfs who did own land had bought it during the colonial era. In short, the national program of changes in land tenure had no effect upon the former serfs of the Fouta-Djallon.

COOPERATIVES IN THE COUNTRYSIDE OF GUINEA

Sekou Touré has said:

Nous avons choisi la coopération simple de travail qui nous apparait comme le moyen le plus efficace pour assurer une évolution au niveau de chaque unité de production. La coopération permet en effet la mise en commun des forces de travail au niveau d'une même cellule sociale et dans le cadre de cette unité de force de travail, d'apporter les instruments de production qui permettront une augmentation de la production (1960: V, 394).

Cooperatives, Franz Schurmann has observed, work best in peasant countries where shared labor impedes exploitation and increases the wealth of members.[5] In Guinea, particularly in the Fouta-Djallon, but

[5] In *Ideology and organization in Communist China*. For a discussion of peasantries in Africa, see Derman (1972), and Woods and Saul (1971).

also in Upper Guinea (where the Malinke sociopolitical organization resembled that of the Fulbe), the wealth of Fulbe and Malinke nobles depended on their utilization of the agricultural labor of others. Gradually the Fulbe depended less and less on their cattle as they relied more on serf labor.

In my view, this Fulbe-serf division has in the past, and does now, largely determine local responses to national programs of cooperatives. In short, then, the preconditions necessary for success of cooperatives according to Schurmann were not present in Guinea while social and economic divisions in the countryside were underestimated. And, as the Guinean government now acknowledges, the cooperatives formed during 1961–1971 have failed. We will explore the reasons for their failure; but first let us examine the cooperative structures the Guinean government tried to set up.

Following Guinean independence, the PDG adopted a socialist policy founded on economic independence, political neutralism, and support for African liberation movements. Guinea's agricultural policy base lay in the formation of cooperatives and the use of voluntary collective labor to overcome the problems of the rapid withdrawal of the French. The PDG formed four different institutions to develop the rural sectors: (1) the National Centers of Agricultural Production, essentially state farms meant to serve as models for other sectors of the rural economy; (2) Centers for Rural Modernization, diffusion centers for techniques, seeds, and organization; (3) Agricultural Production Cooperatives; and (4) "Human Investment" (*les investissements humains*), mobilization of villagers for collective labor projects — schools, hospitals, dispensaries, mosques, party buildings, roads, etc.

Despite much enthusiasm for these projects, the limited state resources committed to these different institutions meant that they all failed outright or fell into disuse. In the case of *investissement humain*, collective labor was successfully utilized for some short term maintenance or building projects, but for more extensive projects such as the prevention of erosion, collective fields, reforestation, drainage canals, or irrigation voluntary collective labor simply did not work. The Agricultural Production Cooperatives failed, and after their failure formerly collectively owned tractors, plows, seeds, and land fell into the hands of private individuals.

Initial attempts at cooperatives did not succeed. In response, a conference was called in 1965 to discuss the rural sector, and the PDG proposed the formation of Agricultural and Consumption Cooperatives (*Coopératives de production agricole et de consommation*). Although each region according to this scheme was to form one pilot cooperative, many regions in fact formed none. The consumption aspect never worked at all, because during this time period much difficulty was encountered in providing a steady flow of imports which in turn made equitable distribution through state stores impossible. The black market thrived and illegal trade undermined most efforts to provide goods for the newly functioning Agricultural and Consumption Cooperatives.

As it became clear that the Agricultural and Consumption Cooperatives had neither resolved nor pointed a way to the resolution of Guinea's rural production and organization problems, education came to be viewed as a new and fruitful direction. The *collèges d'enseignement rural* (CER) were formed. These schools, to follow primary level education, were to provide basic economic and agricultural information and techniques and also to act as cooperative units of production. And so, for example, in the area where I worked what had been the cooperative state farm was turned into a *collège d'enseignement rural*, spelling the temporary end of the state farm.

Currently (in 1972) all rural cooperative efforts are assessed as failures, as Guinea and the PDG undertake the most serious and dramatic overturning of rural production to date. But before I turn to this point let me cite some of my own field observations on cooperatives in the villages where I worked.

When I initially observed attempts to develop cooperatives in the Fouta-Djallon, I felt that they must be atypical within Guinea as a whole. But upon reading Jean Suret-Canale's descriptions of the cooperatives he visited,[6] my observations appeared typical of conditions throughout the country. My own observations concerned attempts to grow cotton and to market tomatoes, mangoes, and oranges. I learned of other earlier local attempts to grow rice and to sell cattle. As mentioned earlier, land reforms had little effect on Fulbe-serf land relationships.

The two most ambitious attempts at forming cooperatives in the area of Popodara consisted of a rice- and a cotton-growing cooperative. In 1961, the Agricultural Production Cooperative stimulated the initial rice-growing effort. Members of the cooperative (usually members of the same committee) each contributed 1,500 Guinean francs (around $6.00) to buy rice seed and to rent the use of oxen and plow. The first year the rice seed was left outside before it was to be planted and consequently spoiled. The second year the seed was stored properly, cultivated, and harvested.

---

[6]   Suret-Canale has written the best work to appear so far on Guinea, *La République de Guinée* (1970). For another account of the formation of cooperatives in Guinea during the early years of independence see De Decker (1967).

However, the time and effort required to grow the rice produced only minimal returns, and the cooperative ended after that second year.

One of the more humorous incidents associated with this failure concerned an elderly religious man. He refused to buy or sell any of the harvest maintaining that it was ritually impure because the *farilla* had not been paid on the rice. The *farilla*, giving away ten percent of the harvest of any grain crop, is an obligatory ritual for all Muslims in the Fouta.

Rice which had formerly been grown in abundance in the area of Popodara, had not been grown there for many years prior to the establishment of the cooperative. The decline in fertility of the soil and problems of erosion, due to the decline in number of years that the fields are left fallow, led to the cessation of rice cultivation. Neither of the two major techniques for growing rice — slash-and-burn on the hillsides and paddy rice in lowland valleys — are possible now around Popodara. The method which can be utilized is called *mukti*. The land employed is called *hollaande* in Fulfulde, meaning a depression where water gathers during the rainy season.

In the *mukti* technique the area is cleared of grass and brush, which are formed into little mounds where manure is put. Then the whole field is burned and the rice is placed in the mounds. The burned manure and brush serve as fertilizer, while the lowness and nature of the soil of the *hollaande* make possible retention of enough water to permit the successful growth of rice. The success of *mukti* depends on intensive labor. Those who work must be willing to give up their other fields (principally fonio) and rely on the production of rice. Yet the purpose was to try to sell rice to other Guineans. The project failed and rice has not been grown since in the area of Popodara.

Another major effort at forming a cooperative in the area stemmed from Guinea's efforts to increase internal production of cotton in order to decrease dependence on foreign cotton imported for the new textile mill in Guinea. My knowledge of this project is greater since I personally observed most facets of the attempted cotton cooperative. I think a detailed description is worthwhile here since it illuminates many of the problems involved in breaking down older patterns of Fulbe — former serf relationships, committee and higher level party interaction, and the lack of consciousness on the part of the local population.

The committee of Hollaande-Popodara, like most other committees in the area, was told by the national government that it must grow cotton. The government would provide the seeds, but the labor involved would be considered as *investissement humain*, that is, voluntary unpaid labor. In sum, villages would receive no remuneration other than their own sense of contribution to the self-sufficiency of Guinea and perhaps an eventual reduction in the price of textiles. The government was to purchase and to distribute the seeds to the various areas of Guinea where cotton could be grown.

In the Fouta-Djallon, villagers have grown cotton for a long time. Yet since the French colonial era, the Fulbe have grown less cotton and instead have purchased more and more imported cloth. However, many individuals (former serfs) have continued to grow their own cotton and make some of their own clothing. The cotton is grown in the women's gardens, on land which is annually cultivated and fertilized. Successful production requires much work and care.

The local committees did not participate in the decision making that led to the cotton program; thus, they had no opportunity or possibility of raising objections to the plan designed at the national level and implemented at the regional level. The villagers acquiesced in the orders. The tasks faced by the local committee were several: it had to acquire suitable land, to organize the labor necessary to build and repair the fences and clear the land, to provide fertilizer, to plant the seeds, to weed the garden several times, and then to harvest the cotton. All of this was to be accomplished with no extra resources other than the cotton seeds themselves.

Land was obtained from a deserted compound in a former serf village. A compound provided several advantages over field land; it was already fenced, limited in area, and had been fertilized for many years. A day was set aside for the committee members to come and do the work. I talked with many of the villagers who indicated that they felt little connection with the purpose of the work and thought that the project would fail. They were correct in no small measure because of the separation of the villagers from the national goals.

The villagers did the minimal work necessary. Although they did it on time, the seeds arrived very late, in fact long after they should have been planted and long after those peasants who grew their own cotton had planted their seeds. Nevertheless, the seeds were planted and began to grow. However, the fence surrounding the compound fell into disrepair; goats and sheep penetrated the garden and ate the very young cotton shoots, putting an end to that project. The experience of these villages must not have been so different from the experiences of other villages, for the following year the government made no similar effort to develop self-sufficiency in cotton.

In concluding this discussion three aspects of the nature of the peasants' participation can be observed: (1) Earlier social distinctions between Fulbe and former serfs continued to be observed. The former serfs did far more of the actual physical labor of hoeing, weeding, fence-building. So, despite years of efforts to break down this distinction and despite Fulbe and former serfs belonging to the same committees, the earlier social divisions continue to play a significant role in the allocation and accomplishment of work. (2) Manure provides an essential component in the cultivation of cotton. Manure is very scarce and very valuable in the area of Popodara because of the high human population and the relatively lower bovine population (for the Fouta). A small amount of manure is sold to the only French-owned plantation in the area. (This plantation produces essence of orange for French perfumes.) Besides that, manure — the collection of which is women's work — is essential for the success of the women's gardens. The villagers did not see the advantages nor did the regional party leaders convince them as to why they should give up precious manure to be used for the cotton rather than for their own gardens. (3) The peasants did not conceive of cotton production as their own cooperative and/or collective effort. They saw the planting of cotton as a government order issued without their consultation. The resentment they felt was ultimately expressed by permitting the cotton to be eaten, something which rarely happened to individual compound gardens. Cooperative may have been the term employed by the PDG but it had no applicability to the experience of Hollaande.

In its results the cotton experience resembled the buying cooperatives presumably established for tomatoes, mangoes, and oranges. That is, they were not really local cooperatives at all; instead the government actually bought, at less than market prices, items produced by individual peasant households for market sale. Governmental attempts to get the Fulbe to provide more meat for the cities were organized similarly. For example, where I lived, the government demanded forty cattle from the committee but paid much less than market prices. Just prior to that the government had, at a national level, tried to make cattle the property of the committee as a whole. This early effort at collectivizing cattle failed and to the best of my knowledge has not been repeated.

In examining the peasants' reactions to cooperative efforts one cannot avoid discussing the political aspects. In my view, it takes much time for peasants to see the collective needs of a committee and a region. But it is even more distant and therefore more abstract and difficult for them to see national goals. When peasants neither understand nor accept these goals the result is the reversion to almost forced labor by local political and administrative officials. These officials, whose success or failure in political performance is judged according to the implementation and success of these national programs, have resorted to forced labor, and many have also used it for their own private gain. At the same time no concrete specific results or advantages accrue to the peasants, making their participation still less likely in other programs. Suret-Canale's analysis of the operations of several cooperatives in other parts of Guinea suggests that similar problems occur throughout the nation — at least until 1970.

In the Fouta-Djallon these problems cannot be solved without resolving underlying questions of land and land tenure. While Guinea has declared that land belongs to those who work it, the reality is increasing land scarcity, which results from the continuation of traditional forms of cultivation while soil fertility is declining and population density is increasing. At the same time there is an increase in the rental of land (something which did not take place in the past) while most former serfs and an increasing number of Fulbe suffer from a lack of field land. Thus, while Guinea has declared the local committee to have been the root and base of politics, the peasants join the party in the same accepting but reluctant way they pay taxes. Many peasants felt forced to buy party cards as they were forced to pay taxes. At the same time, the government has not provided any large investment for the rural areas. In short, demands and requests made of the peasants evidence little return to them. Returns which do accrue to the countryside at all add to the wealth of many of the cadres in the rural areas, further discrediting government efforts.

What I have written thus far deals with my own experiences through 1967 and some more up-to-date material footnoted in Suret-Canale's book. However, Guinea has since dramatically shifted her course toward socialism. 1973 has been named *Echéance '73*, the year of the collective. The proposed major financial investment in collectives and altered basis of their formation mark a fundamental shift toward the whole rural sector. This shift also marks a major reanalysis of the failures of all earlier cooperatives (not admitted, at least not publicly until very recently). With the emphasis of the Guinean revolution shifted to rural socialist cooperatives, the government and party have been reorganized. Indeed, the basic political units are no longer the committees, but *les pouvoirs révolutionnaires locaux* (PRL). And all of these changes are placed in the context of a new stage of the Guinean Revolution:

La Révolution est entrée dans une phase nouvelle et exige des cadres des qualités qui appellent une rupture radicale avec les habitudes du passé. Cette phase nouvelle est en effet essentiellement caractérisée par la volonté ferme et inéluctable du Peuple de passer vigoureusement du stade de la formation de l'Homme, stade accompli avec bonheur et efficacité, au stade du développement, de la production intense en quantité et en qualité (*Horoya* 1972b).[7]

[7] *Horoya* is the national newspaper of the *Parti Démocratique de Guinée*, appearing almost daily.

The government has now revamped the education system and based the success of the Guinean Revolution upon youth, especially upon the example which youth can set for the rest of Guinea society. As Touré has said:

Disons que ces jeunes sont plus accessibles au progrès parce qu'ils n'ont pas la même mentalité mercantile, bourgeoise et capitaliste. Ils constituent une force productive puissante qui ne doit pas échapper à la révolution. N'oublions pas la réalité que sont les villages (*Horoya*, 1972a).

When young people graduate from school they are to form *les cités socialistes*, socialist cooperatives which will be embedded in the PRL. But the youth, because they are freer of bourgeois and capitalist mentalities, will develop further and faster, thus serving as models for the other villagers.

Admitting the failure of the other efforts to change the countryside, the PDG has attempted to develop new institutions and strategies to continue the Guinea revolution. A reporter in *Horoya* put the analysis this way:

Analysant les causes du mauvais fonctionnement, et de l'extinction des coopératives agricoles, le camarade stratège Ahmed Sekou Touré a dit que leur défaut permanent c'est de refléter des conceptions capitalistes, par la seule recherche du profit individuel. La coopérative n'est pas considérée comme le bien de l'ensemble de la collectivité sur lequel chacun, à titre égal, possède un droit de regard (*Horoya*, 1972c).

Thus, the PDG judges past attempts at the formation of rural cooperatives as failures because they were based not on socialist conceptions, but capitalist ones. I searched for more detailed and specific criticisms of earlier cooperative efforts. I assume they exist even though I did not find them. Nevertheless to explain the failure of the past on the incorrect ideas of the population without asking where they got them, why they maintained them, and what will now lead them to change those ideas, is inadequate. Not to examine how national cooperative policies were carried out in the countryside leads one to wonder what the actual form of the new socialist cities and socialist cooperatives will actually be and how the peasantry will understand them.

My own experiences lead me to also wonder about the roles projected for Guinean youth. When I was there, many rural youth had developed deep suspicions of the motives and actions of the local PDG leaders. While they are opposed to many Fulbe traditions they do not see how the PDG had resolved their more basic and immediate concerns: being able to earn enough money to make marriage possible, to buy good clothes, to find rural lands or jobs in the cities, to obtain better medical care.

They did not participate in real decision making when I was there. Virtually all of the youths' activities were responses to regional or national programs, demands, or requests; little was done from local initiative. This is not necessarily of great import, except that the youth did not identify with the programs they were involved in. For example, youth often provided much of the entertainment for visiting dignitaries who included during my stay: the board of directors of FRIA, Deputy Attorney General Katzenbach, King Faisal, and Kwame Nkrumah.

CONCLUSION

Cooperatives in Guinea have failed up to the present. I have tried to indicate the reasons for the failure in the Fouta-Djallon in terms of the unresolved questions of land, continuing social divisions in the population which affect participation in such national efforts as cooperatives, and the relationship of the national and regional levels of the PDG to the committees in the countryside. Guinea has faced many grave problems, not the least of which is outside intervention exemplified by the Portuguese attack of November 22, 1970. However, despite many accomplishments of Guinea since her independence, the latest attempts to revolutionize the countryside must be looked at very critically, given the history of collectives and cooperatives in Guinea.

REFERENCES

DE DECKER, HENRY
    1967   *Nation et développement communautaire en Guinée et au Sénégal*. The Hague: Mouton.
DERMAN, WILLIAM
    1972   Peasants: the African exception? *American Anthropologist* 74: 779–82.
    1973   *Serfs, peasants and socialists: a former serf village in the Republic of Guinea*. Berkeley: University of California Press.
DUPIRE, MARGUERITE
    1970   *Organisation sociale des Peul*. Paris: Plon.
Horoya
    1972a *Horoya*. March 23.
    1972b *Horoya*. April 24.
    1972c *Horoya*. August 12.
SCHURMANN, FRANZ
    1966   *Ideology and organization of Communist China* (second edition). Berkeley: University of California Press.

SURET-CANALE, JEAN

1966 La fin de la chefferie en Guinée. *Journal of African History* 7: 459–493.

1970 *La République de Guinée.* Paris: Editions Sociales.

TOURÉ, SEKOU

1960 *L'action politique du Parti Démocratique de Guinée. La planification économique,* volume 5. Conakry, Guinea: Imprimerie Nationale.

WOODS, R., J. SAUL

1971 "African peasantries," in *Peasants and peasant societies.* Edited by A. Shanin. Harmondsworth: Penguin.

The Practicalities of Participation: Some Problems Facing the Advisor Employed by an Integrated System of Cooperatives in Peru

CHARLES DE WECK

In discussions of the difficulties involved in getting cooperative members involved in the decision-making process, we have often made the technical advisor or administrator a scapegoat. It is his single-minded attention to efficiency or his past experience in strictly hierarchical administrative forms of the "old system," which we often blame for early setbacks.

After the devastating earthquake in Peru in 1970, hundreds of square miles of the rural landscape were destroyed. Tragic though this was, it nonetheless provided an impetus, aided by large inputs of foreign loans and aid, for quite radical experiments in integrated cooperative building over entire ecological zones. A number of young agronomists, strongly sympathetic from the start with the concept of peasant participation, became involved in these schemes. While they were especially sensitive to their position as "educated specialists," they nonetheless faced other hindrances to development.

This article, written by one such "*técnico*," provides an important balance for our understanding of the daily problems faced in the field. While acknowledging that there are extremely delicate problems to be faced at the base, Mr. de Weck suggests that no really long-term gains can be made unless the entire apparatus of the government is prepared to provide the cooperatives with the kind of economic environment essential to their advancement.

In this short article I wish to outline the kind of integrated system of cooperatives which we are developing in Peru, and also to point out some of the difficulties which we have faced in the first two years of operation. To do this I will concentrate on such a system located in the Santa Valley of the northern coast. The difficulty of creating viable production cooperatives in isolation from one another has been recognized in Peru and has led to plans to form extensive series of what are referred to as PIARs (Integrated Projects of Rural Development or *Proyectos Integrales de Asentamiento Rural*). One such PIAR is located in the Santa Valley.

The Santa Valley was seriously affected by the 1970 earthquake in

Peru. Virtually all the equipment and homes of the area were destroyed and extensive areas of well-cultivated land were seriously flooded. There was, however, at least one advantage to the situation: the zone became a privileged area for the receipt of credit from national and international sources. The government initiated an Integrated Development Plan (PID or *Proyecto de Desarrollo Integral*) to embrace three neighboring valleys: Santa, Lacramarca, and Nepeña. This was to be the first operational PID in Peru, and as such provided a pilot scheme for later projects elsewhere.

This Integrated Development Plan involves the participation of various state agencies such as the Ministry of Agriculture, the Ministry of Education, the special government agency set up to deal with earthquake relief (CRYRZA), and the National System for the Support of Social Mobilization (SINAMOS). All these organizations are involved in short-, medium-, and long-term plans but with the acknowledged participation of the region's *campesinos*. Between these two groups are the *promotores de capacitación*, more familiarly referred to as the *técnicos*. We live in peasant communities and spend each day working with the peasants. Through this daily interaction we obtain the kind of information needed for the functioning of the Plan, detect what most vitally commands interest among the people, and what they most need.

The extent of this Integrated Plan can best be indicated by saying that despite the fact that it has only been in existence for eight months so far, it has begun six development programs, undertaken a thorough socioeconomic analysis of the area, and is entertaining more than 130 separate projects which, needless to say, will await the availability of sufficient capital.

My experience has been with the PIAR of Santa. This has included work on both its initial organization (sometime before the set-up of the Integrated Development Plan) and subsequent development. Essentially a PIAR involves a specific and relatively homogeneous area which has been the subject of the agrarian reform program, in an attempt to integrate the various economic units on the basis of cooperative arrangements.

The PIAR Santa comprises the lower, coastal part of a long valley running inland and includes roughly 12,000 hectares (29,640 acres) of cultivated land. Production consists of maize, cotton, rice, sugar cane, and market gardening. Under the PIAR, all the former *haciendas* have been transformed into separate agricultural production cooperatives. Some of the *haciendas* had been subdivided prior to the Agrarian Reform by their owners and rented out to tenants (*arrendatarios*) in order to assure landlords a stable income. The agrarian reform has forced these tenants and the owners to turn over the land to peasants. Moreover, there are some newly irrigated sections in the valley which had previously been desert and which had been bought by *hacienda* workers prior to the agrarian reform. As such, they have not been affected by the agrarian reform but have been organized into a service cooperative. Finally, there are small properties of less than 15 hectares which have largely remained unaffected by the agrarian reform, except where there was evidence of failure to comply with various laws.

This then was the situation which we faced as the PIAR was to be organized. Eight production cooperatives were set up, with a Central Cooperative (*Central de Cooperativas*) designed to integrate them. In addition to these eight cooperatives, a SAIS (Agricultural Society for Social Interest) was also set up in order to include all the SERVICE cooperatives in the area. Finally, within the actual PIAR area itself there is a peasant village recognized by the government as a *comunidad campesina*.[1]

The problem for the technical advisor is that each of these many cooperatives is really a world of its own. There are differences among the various production cooperatives, as well as between these and the service cooperatives, not to mention the *comunidad campesina*, since there are different types of peasants involved and a variety of tenure situations, settlement patterns, and socioeconomic forms of organization. Our goal is that eventually there will be only production cooperatives in the valley and that all these will be integrated into the *Central de Cooperativas*. This will include the SAIS as well, which we hope to convert eventually into a series of production cooperatives.

Our concentration is largely focused on the *Central*, which will eventually become the most important unit for all Peruvian agriculture. Although the *Central* is presently the most vital unit, the eventual aim will be to form a *Central de Centrales*, articulating at the national level the various regional *Centrales*.

The *Central* does not claim to be an organization apart from the cooperatives of which it is comprised, but rather concentrates on the political, economic, and social integration of the various units at the base. Nor is it simply a services headquarters from which the cooperatives can draw. Through the *Central* the entire planning of the valley takes place with the participation of all the different units at the base level. Also it integrates all the economic activities of the cooperatives, such as marketing, the purchase of inputs and machinery, credit arrangements, and so forth.

The *Central* also acts as a balancing mechanism between the rich and

---

[1] A legally recognized administrative unit, usually possessing some communal property.

the poorer base units and will coordinate any transformation into increased industrialization. Seventy percent of net sales from each cooperative is transferred to the *Central* and the decision as to what to do with the income from this is also taken at the *Central* level. For its part, the *Central* must guarantee to all workers the same level of income in accordance with their specialization or type of work, whether they are in fact cooperative members or not.

Much has been written about the kind of power which the technical advisor in an organization like the PIAR is able to use to the detriment of the peasants themselves. To avoid this in Santa there are Management Committees formed by the peasants, but also including the *técnicos*. The latter must consult the Committee concerning any work they may be doing. The overall administrative Council of the *Central* decides at a more general level what is to be done and then the Management Committee supervises the work of the technical staff or hired personnel. In the case of very important issues, the General Assembly of the *Central* sees to it that the technicians do not get control of the *Central*, and particularly of its political network, by obliging them to work within its framework of participation.

For our own part, as technical advisors, the main problem we have faced at this level has been one of communication. There are many *técnicos*, myself included, who have previously worked within the pre-agrarian reform structure. In my case, for example, I worked for a firm of sheep farmers in the Sierra as a subadministrator taking a position entirely from the viewpoint of the landlord, and yet now I work for an entity comprising no less than eight production cooperatives and a *Central*, and my point of view has changed 180 degrees to seeing everything from the point of view of the peasant.[2] The process has been such an education for me that I now take a position which is exclusively cooperativist and opposed to the old system. Nonetheless, it should be recognized that for those *técnicos* with less experience than I have had it is far more difficult to understand the new system of work, now entirely reversed, so that those who gave the orders now find themselves receiving them.

Our jobs are entirely dependent now on the confidence which the peasant has in us, because at any time he can decide that our presence is no longer required. To give some idea of the context of the position which we find ourselves in, I would like now to turn attention to the kind of problems which we are having to deal with.

[2]   Mr. Charles de Weck is a Peruvian agricultural specialist now associated with the *Centro de Estudios y Promoción del Desarrollo* (DESCO), Lima, Peru.

It must be remembered that the *Central* is a group of cooperatives united into one organization in order to defend themselves against the surrounding capitalist system. Despite the government's declared enthusiasm for the formation of cooperatives, the present capitalist system still threatens to drown them. The cooperatives are entirely dependent on the capitalist system for the purchase of goods such as fertilizer, seed, and insecticide. Sales are also made on a competitive basis. One such example would be the marketing of maize which is sold exclusively to large mills for conversion into flour. In Peru there is a monopoly in the milling industry so that it is this sector which sets the prices; thus the agricultural sector remains dependent upon that sector of the economy which has not yet seen any transformation away from capitalism. The only way in which we can hope to modify this is by having the *Central* purchase all inputs on the wholesale market and thus give its members a savings. In the past year I personally have seen the price of these inputs go up three times. Thus, by controlling both the sale of inputs as well as the marketing of the produce of the cooperatives, the capitalist system effectively strangles the cooperatives.

Another of the problems which we face is similarly the result of forces outside our immediate control as *técnicos*. Adjudication of land in the valley has been piecemeal. In one cooperative, for instance, a thousand hectares were adjudicated but only half were actually handed over and the rest stayed for another four or five months in the hands of the tenants and the landowners. Obviously, the tenants (*arrendatarios*) disagree with the revolutionary changes; and as they control the wages and social benefits due to the workers, they can succeed in raising opposition to the cooperative system, an alternative or counter-policy based on economic power alone. In many instances they manage to break what was once a single *sindicato* into two groups — those who are for and those who are against the cooperative system. Even though the tenants or landowners know that they are going to lose the land, they go against the PIAR by offering, for example, to divide it into individual plots.

The PIAR Santa does not allow division into individual plots because there are too many *campesinos* for so little land. The only viable approach is to create cooperatives, to try to stop secondary produce from leaving the valley, and to have it manufactured into something which absorbs more labor in the valley itself. Thus an effort is being made to close the gap in the economic circle and to keep everything within the self-managed system.

We have direct contact with about 1,500 peasants who are members of the production cooperatives and we have indirect contact with approxi-

mately 15,000 people in all. Sixty percent of these agree with cooperativization and 40 percent do not, believing that individual plots and effort are
better for them. Instruction is the way in which we challenge this belief, and
for this, first of all, we have to become involved in their daily lives and
make ourselves known. Personally, I suffered the handicap of having a
foreign name, being white and a "*gringo*," although I am in fact Peruvian.
At first I could not even reveal my name. Later on, through my work, they
began to appreciate my position and what my ideas and commitments
were, and they came to accept me. At times they take decisions contrary
to our advice and we have found ourselves obliged to lend a hand, for
instance, in two important protest movements in the valley. One was a
strike in one of the production cooperatives for higher wages.

In practical terms, the peasant is unaware of any change in his daily
life because the nature of his work has not changed much. He who previously was a manual laborer (*lampero*) continues as such and those whose
jobs were to irrigate or to cut crops keep doing the same. They do not feel
any real change in their work. They feel members of the cooperative only
after 5 P.M., when they receive their training and have their meetings and
assemblies in which they make decisions together and get a feeling of
change.

There are problems in work which stem from old *sindicato* or labor
union successes. At the moment there are cooperatives where members
work only four hours — a four-hour work day being an old labor union
victory won through strikes and peasant movements in the valley. It
remains simply because the wage was, and is, very low. In some cooperatives the peasant earns an equivalent of U.S. $1.00. In others where
wages are higher, they obtain U.S. $1.50 and even U.S. $2.00. In the
Santa Valley, the reduction in labor hours was instituted in order to
provide work for more people. Another achievement of the *sindicato*
was obtaining access to small plots ($1^1/_2$ hectares on the average) on the
borders of the *haciendas* to make up for the low wages, while at the same
time protecting the owners' lands from the encroachment of the desert.
These plots have persisted because there have not been significant wage
increases. There has been a tendency for wages to rise throughout this
present year (1973), but unfortunately, high production costs, the decapitalization of *haciendas* by landowners who took machinery, tools, etc.,
are forcing the cooperatives to wait if they do not want to see their economies thrown into jeopardy. Besides, many cooperatives have started off
with debts predating their organization.

Therefore credit is another major problem; the cooperatives are unable
to finance themselves and thus depend exclusively on credit given by the

Banco Agropecuario [Agricultural and Livestock Bank]. Consequently, the cooperatives are perennially in debt; they always feel dependent and thus *campesinos* believe that the land does not belong to them. As far as they can see, the land belongs to the government. It is very hard for us to explain to them that the land is theirs when they know that they are burdened with the agrarian or land debt (*deuda agraria*) to the Ministry of Agriculture and the Bank for twenty years. How do you convince someone who is going to be tied in debt for twenty years that the land is his own? It is very difficult indeed.

Basic instruction is carried out in study groups (*círculos de estudio*), in which we do not attempt to train all four hundred members at once, since this would be almost impossible. Instead, we divide them into small groups of about thirty to thirty-five persons. At the beginning we introduced the various topics to be discussed and covered, so that people would gain more confidence and become more articulate since the groups were relatively small. Before this, we had been going along to the cooperatives where there was no participation and no one said anything. Issues were brought up to give people a chance for discussion and for drawing their own conclusions. Now, after two years' work, the topics for study and discussion are chosen by the peasants themselves.

With the study groups we succeeded in bringing on new leaders or new people who are really beginning to understand and be interested in the issues. The result was that in six cooperatives the managers were obliged to resign and to call for new elections, since most of them had continued to behave like the landowners. We think that the study groups are the best system of giving instruction to peasants.

Another way is to use bulletins in which we spread information about what is happening in the valley or offer certain instruction and information in simplified form for those who cannot read. The bulletins are illustrated with drawings to depict what is being described.

To extend working in partnership, we set up small produce gardens, the responsibility for each of which was taken on by one of the cooperatives. Whatever is produced is sold to all the members at cost price.

Another medium of instruction to encourage cooperative work is the formation of a new work plan in which we are considering the organization of work brigades. The aim is that the responsibility for a task should not be assumed by a single person but should be shared between seven or eight members of a group, the oldest being helped by the youngest. This accomplishes the daily work and furthers the changeover from individual labor to work of a more social nature.

In this brief article, I have tried to give some idea of the specific problems which we have faced in the first two years of operation and the ways in which we are going about solving them. Ideally, of course, the *técnico* to some extent should be working himself out of a job in these cooperatives. As the extent and scope of the new PIARs expand, so will he move on to new projects and bring with him ever richer experiences.

The Crisis of Rural Cooperatives: Problems in Africa, Asia, and Latin America

ORLANDO FALS-BORDA, RAYMOND APTHORPE, and
INAYATULLAH

During 1969 and 1970 research teams of the United Nations Research Institute for Social Development studied thirty-seven rural cooperatives in developing countries – fourteen in Asia (Sri Lanka, Iran, and Pakistan), twelve in Africa (Ghana, Kenya, Tanzania, Tunisia, Uganda, and Zambia), and eleven in Latin America (Colombia, Ecuador, and Venezuela), within a common frame of reference and using comparable research tools and techniques. The results of these case studies, published by the institute in seven volumes (Apthorpe 1970, 1972; Carroll et al. 1969; Fals-Borda 1970, 1971; Inayatullah 1970, 1972), illustrate the richness of the cooperative experience and the depth of information obtained on the mechanisms of social reform in the selected countries. This article is an overview of these research reports.

The discussion and reflection that follow do not represent a résumé of our findings, for which reference should be made to the regional studies themselves. For comparative purposes, however, it is useful to single out three issues of basic importance for future cooperatives on national and international levels: (1) factors concerning the adoption and diffusion of rural cooperatives; (2) the impact of the performance of cooperatives; and (3) policy implications of cooperative work.

DIFFUSION AND ADOPTION OF RURAL COOPERATIVES

Initiation and Sponsorship

In Latin America, cooperatives have been sponsored by three agencies:

(1) government, (2) church, and (3) private individuals and organizations. The forms of sponsorship provided by these agencies have conditioned and shaped the scope and purpose of cooperatives. The state-sponsored cooperatives (as in Venezuela and Ecuador) are generally multipurpose, undertaking various types of activities, including marketing, credit, and distribution of consumer goods. They are part of larger development programs and are particularly related to land reforms. The church-sponsored cooperatives (especially in Colombia) have generally been single-purpose: those sponsored by the Catholic church specializing in credit and those sponsored by the Protestant church specializing primarily in production. Most of the individual-sponsored cooperatives have been initiated by concerned intellectuals.

In the three Latin American countries studied, primary cooperatives developed first and were then federated into larger units, sometimes organized on a territorial basis, other times on a sectoral basis. In general, then, federations did not initiate the first cooperatives, although later they did assume responsibility for promoting others.

Political parties have played almost no role in sponsoring and organizing cooperatives. The governing party in Venezuela, however, has attempted to control the primary cooperatives in order to extend its political influence.

In northern, western, and eastern Africa, rural cooperatives have been sponsored by numerous groups, including the World Bank, the United States Agency for International Development, national governments, churches, political parties, and private individuals and organizations. However, the task of organizing cooperatives has now been taken on almost exclusively by the national governments, depending on their commitments to development planning and on their administrative capacities to carry out development at local levels. Governments committed to a socialist ideology are most prominent of all. The capacity of governments to organize cooperatives is greater in those countries that have programs of local development, such as community development and *animation rurale*.

In general, religious groups in Africa (especially in socialist states) do not have the direct or immediate access to local communities that would enable them to organize independent cooperatives. The contribution of the churches tends to be channeled through state projects. In single-party states, the tendency is for the party explicitly to articulate the sponsorship of cooperatives but not actually to organize them. As in Latin America, however, political parties tend to interrelate with the cooperatives in order to extend their political influence and diffuse their ideology. In some cases membership in the societies and benefit from the facilities available to the cooperative from various sources are believed necessarily to be one and the same thing.

In the three Asian countries in which cooperatives were studied, the governments are the exclusive sponsors of cooperatives. In Pakistan and Sri Lanka, cooperatives were introduced by colonial regimes. The successor governments in general have followed the patterns of sponsorship and organization set by those regimes. In Sri Lanka, however, increased emphasis has been placed on the organization of cooperatives since the governments embarked on several programs of planned change in rural areas to relieve pressure on land, to improve food distribution, and to increase rice production.

In Pakistan, because the cooperative approach to problems of rural development has not been emphasized, the state's activity in organizing cooperatives is considerably restricted. During the 1960's, when agricultural development was given high priority, a number of service cooperatives were organized to supply fertilizer and improved seeds. The Comilla experimental project in cooperatives, organized by the Pakistan Academy for Rural Development, is supported by the government.

In Iran, cooperatives are organized by the state. Their organization has been stepped up since the second phase of land reform. Cooperatives are multipurpose in form but in fact serve primarily to funnel government funds to raise food production. The political purpose of organizing peasants and securing their support for the existing regimes seems to be much more evident in Iran than in Pakistan and Sri Lanka, where economic considerations outweigh political ones.

In general, political parties in Asia play almost no role in organizing cooperatives. However, in Sri Lanka, the political sympathies and affiliations of cooperative members sometimes lead to internal dissension in the cooperatives, and in Iran, the ruling party has attempted, but without great success, to reach the peasants through state-organized cooperatives.

Religious organizations in these three Asian countries have not organized cooperatives, probably because the religious groups (especially in Iran and Pakistan) limit their village activities to dealing with religious problems and are neither inclined nor in a position to organize groups oriented toward change and development. Islamic prohibitions on interest as interpreted by religious functionaries may also dispose them to avoid an organization engaged in apparently extrareligious practices. In Sri Lanka, where religious groups are better organized and more involved in secular affairs and have extended their influence down to the village, local Buddhist monks in general have supported the cooperatives.

As in Latin America and Africa, national federations of cooperatives in the three Asian countries have not attempted to organize cooperatives on their own initiative, although they tend to help cooperatives to survive once they have been formed. In Sri Lanka, federations are comparatively more active in serving the cooperatives than are federations in Iran and Pakistan. In Bangladesh, however, the Central Association, under the Comilla program, plays a considerable role in organizing new cooperatives and providing them with diverse services, including credit.

Compulsion to Join

Pressure can be brought to bear on people to join the cooperatives principally through three means: (1) direct compulsion and coercion, (2) the creation of a monopolistic situation in which the individual is deprived of certain economic benefits if he decides to stay out, and (3) the offering of inducements in the shape of prospective benefits.

Coercion is employed considerably more often in state-sponsored cooperatives in Latin America than in cooperatives organized by churches or private individuals. In church-sponsored cooperatives, the fear of being stigmatized as someone indifferent to religion, a heretic, or a subversive, frequently compels people to join the cooperative. In privately organized cooperatives, faith in the organizer and economic and social benefits more frequently attract the potential members.

A similar situation prevails in Africa, where considerable coercion is employed to force individuals to join. The legitimacy of this coercion rests on the idea that if the power of the state were not applied to organize new groups capable of transforming the traditional order, groups such as cooperatives would not emerge. The cooperative is therefore to be responsible for the rise of a welfare socialism, and tendencies toward an economic class formation can be checked or reviewed.

In the three Asian countries studied, coercion is not employed in the organization of cooperatives except to a limited extent in Iran. In all three countries, inducement through provision of certain needed services and supplies is one of the important means of securing support for organizing cooperatives.

Diffusion

Knowledge about cooperatives in Africa diffuses through several means or combinations thereof: (1) mass-media dissemination of national and international policies, (2) personal local contacts, (3) personal official contacts, and (4) demonstration effects. In Latin America, although government officials are a source of initial information about cooperatives, seeing personally a nearby functioning cooperative or learning about it through personal contacts, often motivates the individual to join the cooperative, where he has such a choice. But these cases are still rather rare.

The situation differs in Asia. In Sri Lanka, individuals come to know about cooperatives from diverse sources (newspaper, radio, personal contact, etc.). In the Comilla program, members usually learn about cooperatives from personal contact. In Iran and Pakistan, radio and personal contact are more frequently cited as sources of information about cooperatives.

Training

While all the countries officially recognize the need for training the local cooperative officers and members, training is seldom well organized and its methods are often defective. The cooperatives in the Comilla program in Pakistan are exceptions to this generalization. Under their more effective system, the chairman and manager of the cooperative and some "model farmers" attend training sessions at the headquarters of the Central Association once a week; they in turn transmit this information to the cooperative members at their weekly meetings.

Class Control

In all the countries studied, the multipurpose cooperatives and the credit cooperatives generally serve best the farmers with medium-sized holdings, for these individuals can make the most use of the services provided by the cooperatives. The landless classes, though not excluded from cooperatives by policy or legislation, often find these cooperatives less useful and therefore do not join them. It seems that the more heterogeneous the membership, the less class-conscious the cooperative becomes, and hence the less effective as a real agent of social change.

Generally, no legislation has provisions to prevent the vested interest groups inimical to cooperatives from joining them or controlling them from the inside. One exception, however, is in Sri Lanka, where local contractors cannot become members of the executive committees of the cooperatives, as cooperatives sometimes compete against these contractors in undertaking contract work.

Social Organization

In the three Latin American countries, the primary cooperatives are generally based on some social-ecological group — a hamlet, neighborhood, or village group. In the African regions studied, the cooperatives are organized less directly on the basis of local social or administrative entities and more commonly on the basis of an economic interest. In the three Asian countries, most of the multipurpose cooperatives include more than one village community, while credit cooperatives (including those in the Comilla program) are based on one-village communities.

Leadership

Leadership of cooperatives in Latin America is in the hands of "pivotal men," persons in contact with the outside government and other agencies who interpret the cooperatives and other innovations to the members. Independent at first, these leaders generally later come under the influence of government officials, carrying out their instructions and communicating them to the members. They cease to act as spokesmen of the members. Sometimes they are a part of the local administrative or political hierarchy, and often they end up being assimilated by it. There are many cases of pilfering of funds and of personal social advancement coming before the interests of the local group. The leaders are formally elected and can be changed, but in reality certain leaders tend to be reelected indefinitely or elections are held only rarely. There are many similarities with Africa in this regard, although the bases of cooperative leadership in Africa are more diverse. Nonetheless, the real decision-making powers concerning the general policies and the functioning of the cooperatives lie with government officials rather than with the formal leaders of the cooperative. The "intercalary man" enjoys considerable personal advantage. There are severe problems of financial abuse and mismanagement in which local social participation is often minimal.

The leadership of Sri Lankan cooperatives rests with relatively more educated men who have worked outside the villages in some capacity, frequently in government service as clerks or schoolteachers. Often they are not the largest landowners in the village and are not former village headmen. Generally they belong to the dominant castes and kinship groups in the village.

The leadership of cooperatives under the Comilla program in Pakistan has similar characteristics, except that leaders are less frequently in contact with the outside world and are relatively less educated than their Sri Lankan counterparts. In contrast, the leaders of cooperatives in West Pakistan own more land than those in Sri Lanka and Bangladesh, although they are not necessarily the largest landowners in the villages. Leaders in Iran are less literate than are leaders in other countries, and they are not generally chosen from among the landlords. Finally, as parts of their village communities, leaders frequently act as spokesmen *vis-á-vis* the government bureaucracy. However, this is less true for Iranian leaders, whose role is considerably eclipsed by government officials.

Resistance

Resistance to cooperatives comes from different sources for different types of cooperatives. The strategy of opposition generally changes with the development of the cooperative.

In Latin America, there is practically no resistance at the introductory stage, when the cooperative exists as a "cultural enclave" relatively independent of its milieu. Later, however, the vested interests in the political, religious, and economic structures tend to assert themselves and the vitality of the cooperative is sapped. The cooperative contradicts its own principles and becomes a business enterprise like any other, that is, if it survives at all.

In Asia, the Sri Lankan consumer cooperatives face limited but overt opposition from local shopkeepers. If a cooperative survives this resistance, the shopkeepers then try to control it covertly. In cooperatives under the Comilla program, limited resistance has come from religious functionaries and from various factions. In Iran, there is little resistance to cooperatives, though in certain cases groups loyal to absentee landlords have tried to control them.

For the regions studied in Africa, resistance is not systematic and is mixed with indifference. The spontaneous and voluntary movements built on grass-roots enterprise have diminished in importance, but the pattern of use of the cooperatives may vary or agree in different districts.

THE PERFORMANCE OF RURAL COOPERATIVES

As many official government inquiries in Africa and as independent appraisals have shown, rural cooperatives have seldom achieved the goals set for them by economic and social planners and others, especially where these goals have included structural change. Indeed, especially in Asia, if governments were now to withdraw the legislation that established the cooperatives, popular support probably would not be strong enough to enable them to continue on their own.

Cooperatives have been introduced, but the scope of their activities bears little relation to the dominant economic patterns — their performance is simply irrelevant in the wider context of social and economic change. In the Third World, only a very small proportion of the total number of farmers are even touched by cooperatives, let alone effectively dependent on them.

Complicating any assessment of this situation on all three continents is the problem of other events and forces that have paralleled the development "from above" of the cooperative movement. For instance, in the Pakistani communities studied, the influence of moneylenders has waned, primarily because after independence, professional moneylenders migrated to India.

Another difficulty besets the appraisal of the performance of cooperatives. Their impact *in toto* may bear little relation to their stated goals. Indeed, conceptions of the official sponsoring agency concerning the aims and objectives of a cooperative may differ considerably from the views of the local farmers.

For these and other reasons, assessing the performance of cooperatives is a highly complex task. Even where positive results are obtained, they are difficult to evaluate satisfactorily. This section therefore will simply discuss some of the themes that any comparative appraisal of cooperatives must take into account, in light of the aims to which cooperative policies are commonly directed. These include: (1) self-reliance, (2) agricultural innovation, (3) social and economic equalization, and (4) structural change.

Self-reliance

Liberal ideology, under the influence of which the cooperative movement developed, aimed at self-reliance for villages and local communities, which would be served by voluntary organizations showing "a healthy independence from government." Contemporary socialist planning in Asia and Africa started from the assumption that the rural areas were, first and foremost, in need of animation, political education, and further economic development before they could fulfill their potential. Where the old emphasis on community self-sufficiency continued, it was in a somewhat different context.

While cooperative policies were proposed from both liberal and so- cialist points of view, with similar reformist aims in some circumstances, the differences between them should not be forgotten. In Latin America, the liberal point of view has been the more relevant of the two. Coopera- tives there aimed less at the stimulation of local movements than at their control, in the interest of national integration. The situation reported for Asia, where the landlord dominates local institutions, is similar. Self-reliance has been especially prominent as an objective of African policies.

The introduction of cooperatives into local social systems that are al- ready strongly structured along hierarchical lines often has not brought about much reform. These systems are not characterized by "communal- ism," as so many cooperative policies suppose. Far from having restruc- tured those social systems, overall the cooperatives have mounted to little more than minor irritations. New leaders, like the "pivotal men," are quickly co-opted. In some cases, cooperatives, whether as mechanisms for the control or the release of local initiative (or for the admin- istration and rationing of scarce resources), are established only by means of that same local patronage that both social reformism and more comprehensive approaches aim to overthrow. Here the sway of the latter has, if anything, been strengthened rather than weakened, and the net performance of cooperativism has been to prevent, rather than to foster, new local initiative or power groups.

One assumption about rural areas that argued the need for coopera- tives was that the rural areas were underdeveloped because they were underproductive. This unfortunate state of affairs was said to be due to inappropriate social values, attitudes of dependency on the outside, and so on. As often as not, however, the net effect of the external linkages with these remote areas that the cooperative superstructure represents has been the creation of such conditions of dependence where they did not exist before: the state becomes a new "patron." Organizational blockages between the local level and the outside world have been introduced. Then countervailing social forces meet head-on the objectives of coop- eratives.

Of course, despite many setbacks, the performance of cooperatives in promoting local initiative and self-reliance has not been entirely negative. The cotton and coffee cooperatives in Africa, for instance, have at least brought in new forms of social organization at the local level; often there is significant local social participation when these organizations are small in scale, despite the high degree of identification they have with central governments.

If self-reliance were significantly stimulated, however, the central governments might consider the resulting situation to come dangerously close to subversion. Under these circumstances, the cooperatives with less social content (those mainly concerned with economic ends) may, in the end, have more social impact than those that explicitly aim to reform "the human factor."

Finally, through cooperatives labor-intensive methods might foster self-reliant enterprises while they cut capital costs, but even these methods require some recurrent expenditures that central governments and other "external" donors cannot meet.

Agricultural Innovation

Often what is meant by "agricultural innovation" is simply the diffusion of known agricultural practices, including credit to finance them. We have not found rural cooperatives to be particularly significant, either positively or negatively, in their effects on this diffusion process. Both failures and successes are known, but nothing suggests that any general policy could be formulated here.

At issue in agricultural diffusion is, essentially, a function of extension and administration literally down to the grass-roots level. Where cooperatives have meaning at this level, and where the methods of agricultural demonstration have meaning to individual farmers in the context of their own farms, a new practice may well be propagated successfully. But ALL the circumstances, especially those concerning prices and transportation, must be suitable. This points to an overall happy combination of circumstances for which there is no single organizational formula in the cooperative or any other sector.

Farming plans or budgets drawn up for the cooperative or its constituent units are just as subject to technical error as are other agricultural development plans drawn up for land that either has not been settled before or has been farmed only extensively. For such areas, adequate physical or social statistics, for example, are seldom available to allow better planning. There is no evidence that rural cooperatives are especially well suited to provide basic information for planning authorities.

Here a special word on credit is necessary, because in all regions studied, credit intended for agricultural use is one of the services made available through the cooperatives. Where, as in Latin America and Africa, credit thus supplied provides people with an alternative to the big commercial banks (which may be far distant), cooperatives may fulfill an important function in rural development. Where cooperatives have brought new organizational facilites to the local level, agricultural credit can be channeled through them directly to those who wish to use it. In many countries, however, credit through cooperatives has not been used for productive purposes, but rather has been restricted to secondary functions tied to local control groups, while the head office of the organization may be in another country.

Social and Economic Equalization

As means to greater economic opportunity, more social participation to achieve this, and more equitable distribution of income and wealth, the activities of the cooperatives must touch significantly on the main resources involved. They do not always do so. Few cooperatives in Asia, for instance, are concerned with land redistribution. In Pakistan, with its emphasis on private enterprise, the implications of the "green revolution" are entirely outside the cooperative sector. Any equalization that could be achieved, therefore, could affect only a highly selective category of people in the rural areas.

Furthermore, as regards the distribution of credit, an improved system may produce only an apparent equality because in the long run, all credit has to be repaid.

In all the regions studied, where credit cooperatives have been extended, the net effect of issuing credit through them has been to increase rather than decrease existing inequalities. What starts as a cooperative venture may not develop as such when other organizations and forces in the community are, if not anticooperative, then noncooperative.

Moreover, the introduction of cooperatives can further harden the lines of bureaucratic communication. Where a local community is firmly structured in terms of a local power elite, and where the cooperative committees have been captured by inimical vested-interest groups, democratization of local institutions by the cooperative is not to be expected.

A key factor in social participation is the level of aspirations on the part of local farmers. In Africa and Latin America, these levels vary widely, being high in some regions but low and nonrevolutionary in others. In Sri Lanka, despite high literacy, they are low. In Iran and Bangladesh, the levels are higher. Where economic aspriations are high and the cooperatives are unable to help to meet them, as in Latin America, all that may be achieved is to raise the level of frustration and to sow new seeds of discontent.

Again, actual achievements in equalization through rural cooperatives fall far short of the goals envisaged by the policy makers. In Sri Lanka, for example, probably only one-third of the members of credit cooperatives are eligible for new loans because the other two-thirds have not repaid the old ones or bought the requisite number of shares. Few multifunctional cooperatives in Sri Lanka, Latin America, or Africa are effectively implemented. In those societies where several functions are performed in the same structure, it has not been proved that losses suffered on the roundabouts are made up by profits gained on the swings. Some African studies suggest that most benefits of the marketing cooperatives may be confined to those farmers who are not in greatest need of them within the district. Where neither the smallest farmers nor the most efficient benefit most, those who do gain are, in effect, unjustly subsidized by the less underprivileged or the more competitive.

Structural Change

Structural change may include an institutional recombination of circumstances and/or resources. When this is done by central governmental planning, the state plays an entrepreneurial role in the reallocation of human resources. Toward this end, the state may adopt a strongly coercive or interventionist position, holding that the development problems are too pressing and too intransient to be left to voluntary action and chance. As in Latin America and Africa, the outbreak of violence, or the threat of it, may help to shape this approach to a development policy.

In theory, cooperative policies epitomize structural change, both in spontaneous "explosions" of cooperative ethics at the grass-roots level and in "planning with socialism" at the center for the benefit of the periphery. They aim to help in the transfer of resources, authority, and influence from one social group to another, and to bring about a closer relation between reward and effort. The results achieved, however, might be precisely the reverse of the goals. The use of violence and coercion to implant cooperatives in an unwilling area does not alter the fact that the aims of the interested groups are different. Indeed, the incidence of violence may be an index of such differences and their importance. Furthermore, where "social obstacles to economic growth" are found, grass-roots ideas about structural change may differ from those of central government planners. The pioneers of Rochdale, for instance, saw the main social obstacles in the social values, relations, and aspirations of the middle and upper social classes. Similar points of view are evident at the grass-roots level in Africa, Asia, and Latin America today. Central planning, on the other hand, in Europe and elsewhere, tends to blame the economic backwardness of rural areas on the "traditional" social and cultural features of peasant or tribal society, i.e. on the social relations of the working classes.

We have found no satisfactory way of generalizing about the effects of tradition on the performance of cooperatives in changing the social structure, where departures from social continuity are the most strongly marked. While some traditions in the religious and cultural spheres do significantly influence economic behavior, as in Asia, the opposite may be equally true, especially in Africa and Latin America. This is but one of the difficulties.

For such factors as levels of literacy or education, African studies, for instance, have not yet established cross-cultural correlations with levels of performance of cooperatives (although it is obviously self-defeating to have nonnumerate bookkeepers and nonliterate secretaries). Even as regards health and nutrition, little is known with certainty. Many of the activities involved occur in a context known to social science and planning as "the subsistence sector." Though this sector covers perhaps the greater part of the world's population, unfortunately there are still more preconceptions about it than hard facts at the disposal of social planning.

In this connection especially, the subject of women's work is of crucial importance. While women are often the chief agricultural producers and distributors within the subsistence sector (as well as the mainstays of cash-crop production), cooperatives are neither specifically concerned with "subsistence" crops nor especially open to women's membership. In some circumstances the introduction of cooperatives has come between women's work and its returns, resulting in adverse effects on agricultural output.

In practice, there is much evidence of the marginality of rural cooperatives in implementing structural change, in spite of their goals. Sometimes this is related to a conservative political context in which the new organizations have reinforced rather than reformed the existing social structures and values. Sometimes more important is the ambivalent nature of the ideology behind these development models in the countries of origin; in the process of transplanting the models, this ambivalence may have been left unresolved.

GENERAL POLICY IMPLICATIONS

That the cooperative ideas we have examined and criticized have been imported from Europe to Latin America since the middle of the nineteenth century and to Asia and Africa since the beginning of the twentieth century poses the usual problems of transfer, diffusion, and adoption of an alien cultural complex, one that was supposed to help to overcome "social obstacles" impeding fuller Westernization. Local elites, politicians, missionaries, and international experts were among those who played determining roles in furthering Westernizing efforts in the name of "modernization." In Africa and Asia, the introduction of cooperative policies became part of the colonialist policy of social change after, and alongside, some spontaneous developments "from below" and in different forms. In Latin America in particular, another aspect was the part played by an intelligentsia closely linked with local political power groups.

The intensity of imposition of this Western model varied. In Asia, for example, the intensity was low where British policy aimed to maintain existing forms of local institutions intact, and cooperatives were introduced mainly to tackle the problem of rural indebtedness. In Africa, a welfare function of cooperatives was particularly prominent. In Latin America, commercial and capitalist dimensions were quickly grasped locally without need for much coercion by the state. In all three areas, the predominant ideology related to the liberal revolution with its democratic and educational tenets, to which utopians and revivalists had added some semireligious trappings.

After several decades of trial and error in effecting this cultural transfer, and after the addition of models from the United States, Scandinavia, and Israel, on the whole the results achieved at the local level, especially from the social standpoint, are not convincing, as the above broad review of present performance of rural cooperatives illustrates. The question arises, then, about the wisdom of continuing along this dubious way, with its low probability of success and its waste of expectations, talents, resources, and funds. More promising solutions to the problems of social change must lie elsewhere. Given the levels of organization and resources already invested in the cooperative sector, however, the possibility of creating new forms of rural cooperatives should be explored before beginning to search for other solutions. Where the aims and spirit of existing cooperative policies are genuinely intended to benefit the rural populations to which they are directed, but where the institutions and inputs are ineffective or even counterproductive of the original intentions, a more radical reorientation of social-planning policy would now seem to be a crucial and urgent necessity.

Administrative Reforms

The focus of the studies we have considered here is further social and economic development at the local level. Where, as in some African countries, a cooperative sector has become an integral part of a central planning system concerned, NOT with marginal economics, but with crops and environments that are of major economic importance locally, any generalizations that can be made on the basis of inquiries largely focused on the local level are obviously greatly limited in their application. Furthermore, while cooperatives in the three regions exhibit many similarities, they differ in the scope of institutionalization, as, for example, between religiously motivated, small credit societies and government-sponsored, national cooperative organizations covering credit and production of major items. The following reflections on administrative change within the existing order, where other than marginal change of this kind is for some reason precluded, are to be interpreted accordingly.

Where membership in the cooperatives is confined to a minority of the population affected, or is on a basis where productive and other activities eventually are structured on other grounds, reform is needed to bring about wider representation and participation. The existing priorities of the policies of many cooperatives should be revised. Tutelary control "from above" should not be so inflexible as to stifle local initiative. Moreover, if cooperativism precludes the rewards and sanctions that development in other sectors demands, it will foster a specious form of social welfare. Real rural development is diverse, not unitary, in its forms, because rural communities, like others, are and will continue to be socially, politically, and economically differentiated. Categories of cultural homogeneity, useful though they may be for positivist scientific description and analysis, are misleading when applied to individual cases. Average man is no man in particular; this is as true of peasants as of anyone else. Degrees of uniformity are convenient and necessary for administrative purposes, but where flexibility disappears altogether from the local bureaucratic component, the original administrative purpose of making social and economic savings is defeated.

Rural Action Units

A more creative alternative to self-defeating, minor administrative re-forms of existing institutions would be a policy that aids new social organizations that could stimulate the dynamic potential of a peasantry, helping it to break out of both new and old forms of exploitation and disadvantage and to gain a just measure of social and economic participation. To provide farmers in developing countries with all the services essential for their work and well-being would require profound social and structural transformations. The liberal, pragmatic cooperative models exported from Europe during the last century, which were designed and functioned mostly to accommodate social change in capitalist systems or to promote only partial forms of social welfare, as a whole have proven to be inadequate for more demanding tasks. Given the speed with which social and political pressures mount in the Third World, a strong effort appears to be necessary in order to combat imitative practices and to encourage local formulas and local creativity. This may imply the perfecting of an essentially economic model with social components rather than a social model with economic components, as well as a new political idealism. It does not mean that old controversies concerning the feasibility of the socialist and capitalist models of cooperation, for instance, left unresolved in Europe, should simply be transferred to the Third World.

There are at least two structural factors that may limit the actual evolution of new approaches in developing countries. One is the weight, in rural traditions, of vested interests in unjust patterns of land exploitation and trade practices, and of certain features of caste and class impeding full participation of subordinate groups. In this context, however, it would be incorrect to conceptualize peasants as always (or necessarily) passive or fatalistic, incapable of reasoning and creating. Such passivity, ignorance, and individualism as do exist must be seen at least partly as a result of generations of cultural and other conditioning to poverty and insecurity.

A potential for change and progress in peasant populations has been demonstrated in numerous sporadic uprisings and revolutions (especially in Latin America and Africa), in readiness to accept technical innovations that are clearly beneficial, and in willingness to undertake genuinely collective projects or communal tasks. The main problem faced here by social policy is how best to stimulate this dynamic and gregarious portion without giving impulse to the other, more autistic parts of peasant society that profit from the status quo. Tagore, Gandhi, and Allende attempted to bring about change at the local level through peaceful means and failed; the results of the Arusha Declaration are yet to be seen; the Mexican and Bolivian revolutions have spent their initial force and, for rural development, are now in need of recommencing.

The second structural factor limiting the development of new rural action models, on the one hand, and administrative reform, on the other, is excessive control and coercion by central political and religious authorities. Granted the need to survey national efforts to achieve economic goals or to promote the common good, such control and coercion frequently appear as a new form of alien domination when they are not truly responsive to local conditions and needs.

This is especialy clear in those countries where independence has been achieved but where the governing elites (mostly foreign-educated or foreign-oriented) still live mentally in the colonial world or profit from imperialist connections. New reform ideologies may make their appearance there, some under the guise of socialism, others as coups against feudalism, yet at the local level little of the peasantry's social participation is effective. Central control should reflect the dynamic contribution that local culture could make. It should not mean merely that central elites maintain the same commercial, credit, and marketing cooperative models developed either *in situ* during the colonial period or in dominant countries outside.

Cooperatives have usually been introduced in response to economic and social cycles of increased poverty, violence, or crises of various kinds. They represent a liberal choice to promote "democracy." For them to succeed in the task, as recognized by the International Co-operative Alliance and other international bodies (e.g. the International Labour Organisation and the Food and Agriculture Organization) the philosophical bases of the cooperative movement must be modified to respond to those conflicts and contradictions encountered in developing countries. Their proposed modifications, however, have not gone far enough. Students of cooperatives face today a grave dilemma: either to sanction and support "cooperatives" that have little, if any, chance of realizing their aims or to promote active peasant organizations that would indeed challenge the status quo.

REFERENCES

APTHORPE, RAYMOND
   1972   *Rural cooperatives and planned change in Africa: an analytical overview*. Rural Institutions and Planned Change, volume five. Geneva: United Nations Research Institute for Social Development.

APTHORPE, RAYMOND, *editor*
   1970   *Rural cooperatives and planned change in Africa*: *case materials*. Rural Institutions and Planned Change, volume four. Geneva: United Nations Research Institute for Social Development.

CARROLL, THOMAS, G. ETIENNE, X. A. FLORES, V. VON MURALT
   1969   *A review of rural cooperation in developing areas*. Rural Institutions and Planned Change, volume one. Geneva: United Nations Research Institute for Social Development.

FALS-BORDA, ORLANDO
   1971   *Cooperatives and rural development in Latin America: an analytical report*. Rural Institutions and Planned Change, volume three. Geneva: United Nations Research Institute for Social Development.

FALS-BORDA, ORLANDO, *editor*
   1970   *Estudios de la realidad campesina: cooperación y cambio*. Rural Institutions and Planned Change, volume two. Geneva: United Nations Research Institute for Social Development.

INAYATULLAH
   1972   *Cooperatives and development in Asia: a study of cooperatives in fourteen rural communities of Iran, Pakistan and Ceylon*. Rural Institutions and Planned Change, volume seven. Geneva: United Nations Research Institute for Social Development.

INAYATULLAH, *editor*
   1970   *Cooperatives and planned change in Asian rural communities: case studies and diaries*. Rural Institutions and Planned Change, volume six. Geneva: United Nations Research Institute for Social Development.

Cooperatives, Collectives, and Self-Management in Commerce and Industry

The Reform of Marketing Structures in Tunisia: State Capitalism or Collectivization of the Means of Exchange

KHALIL ZAMITI

For several years in the late 1960's all of the shopkeepers (grocers and dry goods merchants) in Tunisia were organized into marketing coopera- tives. This structure of marketing cooperatives was to complement the agricultural cooperative structure in the farming areas. Using the market- ing cooperative of Menzel Bou Zelfa in 1968 as an example, this paper explores the structures and implications of the process of integrating shopkeepers into cooperatives. The major theme will be the contradiction between state capitalism and the collectivization of the means of exchange.

The State, in order to divert part of the marketing revenue formerly allocated to family consumption and home savings towards industrial development, appropriated administratively the means of exchange. It also weeded out a number of retailers and conferred the status of wage- earners on those it retained.

These two fundamental characteristics of the new system (i.e. state appropriation of the means of exchange and the placing of workers on a wage basis) thus define the emergence of state capitalism.

However, this fact could not constitute the final goal of the analysis, inasmuch as the question of "state capitalism" raises the problem of the political nature of state power.

It is true that the central power grappled with a real contradiction which existed between the collective aspect of marketing service and the individual aspect of the appropriation of the means of exchange. How- ever, a new contradiction was to arise between the social character of the latter and their appropriation by the State.

Trade activity was orginally deployed for the satisfaction of needs; however, these were individual and not collective needs. With state appropriation this activity was to become supraindividual, but separated from the needs of the individuals who practiced it directly.

This severance of the results of work from the conditions of workers' existence means that the nature of the State excluded a socialist planning policy.

This does not mean that the return of the value of goods and services to direct producers cannot be delayed. But it is nonetheless necessary for the political composition of the factions participating in state power to be such that the State acts on the inegalitarian structure of society by instituting the objective conditions for the immediate and delayed return of the products of labor to the workers.

This is the real reason why the builders of state capitalism are going to enslave those they pretend to serve; to estrange the popular masses; and to be incapable of mobilizing and organizing them within a revolutionary movement capable of resisting the impending reaction of the privileged classes.

GOALS OF MARKETING COOPERATIVES IN TUNISIA

The "General Guidance Memorandum" concerning "The Reform of Marketing Structures" circulated by the Secretary of State for Planning and the National Economy, following the meeting of Governors held on 2 November 1967, clearly defined the strategy adopted in the "Ten-Year Development Plans" and repeated in the "Four-Year Plan" for trade. It consists essentially of a "utilisation of marketing channels to release the maximum of savings capital destined for the financing of investments." Thus, according to the memorandum:

...since 1962 reform had been directed towards the improvement of allocation of resources through a redeployment into industry of capital badly employed in trade. This involves a using of the marketing apparatus to tap capital which, through this channel, can be directed towards investment in priority sectors. The marketing enterprises which have arisen in the first stage of the structural reform have already proven their ability to play this role.... The management structure of consumers' cooperatives must also be so organized as to make these marketing organisations an effective network for collecting savings.

The memorandum insists on the need to collect "a substantial saving" and on "the mission with which the cooperatives are entrusted, i.e. to participate in the general development of the country and, first and foremost, in the formation of savings through taxation." This is why "a significant proportion of profits will be assigned to the formation of savings." Thus a new goal is assigned to the marketing sector, since the latter must now become "a focus for the spread of progress in all its forms." After having stated "that the real problem of the cooperative system in Tunisia is the scarcity of capital," the Secretary of State for Planning asserts in the memorandum quoted that "the distribution channels, reorganised in this manner, with an adequate system of organisation, will be supplemented and consolidated gradually before the end of the four-year plan and will serve as support for actions to be undertaken within the framework of the third plan."

But how in practice can one manage to subordinate the old forms of individual marketing activity to the demands of the new economic rationality and to the imperatives of planning? In other words, what are the specific means of intervention advocated by the planner to attain these ends? Now the "General Guidance Memorandum" is explicit on this subject. It sets forth the actions to be undertaken to transform individual marketing enterprises into "an effective network for the collection of savings capable of attaining the double objective: self-financing of the marketing sector and the participation of business in the formation of capital in industry." In fact, the planner envisages "retaining of shopkeepers accompanied by a reorientation of men and capital towards productive sectors." In clear language it is a question of reducing the number of individuals devoted to marketing activity. The shopkeepers retained are increasingly going to be amalgamated into a certain number of sale points, for "a marketing enterprise must no longer be an individual business; it must become collective." The new organizations thus established will then be readily amenable to the regulations necessary to allow them to release a monetary surplus. In fact:

...the distribution of profits after the payment of tax must be carried out as a matter of obligation and in accordance with the statutes (so that the rule on equal votes cannot endanger the system), according to a plan reserving a percentage (to be defined) of these profits to the owners of the capital (and which is to be shared among them in proportion to their share in the capital); a percentage to the customers (a refund to be shared in proportion to purchases made); a percentage to the workers (to be shared among employees according to their output); and finally, a last percentage to a savings fund destined for the financing of investments inside or outside the enterprise.

The process used to release the supplementary saving desired is still more clearly explained in the two "Memoranda for the application of marketing reform in the general grocery sector and in the textile sector."

These two documents, distributed by the Under-Secretary of State for Trade and Industry, mention "the supplying of the State budget through taxation" and "the creation of savings" among the "principal requirements" for the setting up of the cooperative. It is clearly specified that "results may be noticeably improved... by a reduction of expenses through better productivity by staff." It is a question of releasing a substantial savings from the distribution sector, particularly by a "selective reduction of the number of operators," in order to increase "productivity."

Finally, by way of an annex to the memorandum drawn up by the Secretariat of State for Planning and the National Economy "and devoted to marketing reform," a text is included which explains that "some studies are being pursued with a view to determining practical procedures... for the collecting of savings from marketing enterprises."

ORGANIZATION OF THE INQUIRY

In order to understand better the impact of the new changes introduced with regard to marketing activity, it is necessary to determine relationships which have arisen between the carrying out of official objectives and the emergent attitudes towards the setting up of the cooperative and modernization.

Now, the reactions of shopkeepers to state planning depend on the manner of the establishing of the modern marketing system and its immediate effects on the personnel weeded out and on the level of income. Thus, it is important to consider the problem of the cutting of jobs through the application of the "Reform of Marketing Structures" before analyzing new economic trends and tensions which have arisen in the customary milieu.

The sector studied presents a unity of general features not found everywhere in the country, and the changes which have occurred proceed from an overall plan or, more accurately, have a common orientation which has been clearly stated. Insofar as this is true, certain results (which may be established by direct survey) concerning the essential problems relating to the process of setting up the modern system are capable of being obtained regardless of the geographic area demarcated and chosen by the investigator. In fact, wherever marketing reform has been applied, there has been a reduction in the number of operators instigated for the purpose of realizing an additional saving. There are several factors which are evident to anyone undertaking to carry out a succession of surveys for purposes of demarcating a geographic area for research. These permit one to generalize, without great risk of error, certain results worked out in a specified place to the whole of the marketing sector. It thus saves work which more extended investigations dealing with a representative sample of urban and rural units and subunits would have entailed.

These restricting factors in favor of justifying a choice relating to any area of research thus depend on two kinds of facts. Some of these proceed from the environment to which the reforms are applied, and others from the general orientation common to the reforms. Let us examine these two points in order.

The common characteristic which the reformers tend to attack and which confers a certain homogeneity on the usual marketing sector is that the latter is consistently "over-equipped" with small businesses "in excess." This general characteristic of the branch, made by actual observation, is probably linked on the one hand to the limitation of jobs available in productive sectors. The overexploitation of the marketing sector thus refers to a phenomenon often observed in the so-called "underdeveloped" countries, i.e. a proliferation of service activities. It appears that the number of marketing enterprises existing at a given moment is such that if a new unit were to be set up, all conditions being otherwise equal, there would not be sufficient customers to permit it to achieve the minimum turnover allowing it to attain the break-even point of viability. The result is that in spite of regional variations, the saturation of the retail trade and the extremely scattered condition of small individual operators are permanent features of the sector which are revealed whatever the geographic area chosen by the investigator.

The second factor justifying an "arbitrary" choice of the place for the survey is that the new measures applied to the marketing sector engender similar effects, because they obey a common orientation and attack precisely the unchanging feature of marketing, that is, its "excessive overcrowding." In fact, it is known that one of the principal goals of the reform was to realize a savings by a surplus growth of productivity due to a maximum reduction in the number of operators for a given turnover. Finally, we preclude any claim here to too much strictness, since we are dealing with dynamic processes which made it unfeasible to construct a representative sample at a national level before the reform was completely finished.

MENZEL BOU ZELFA MARKETING COOPERATIVE

These considerations have led to the arbitrary choice of the site for the

enquiry, Menzel Bou Zelfa. This is a Cap Bon village of average importance, grouping 14,500 persons (municipal area and sheikdom) where
marketing reform (for general groceries and the textile sector) was begun
on 13 April 1966 and was completely carried out. This is in the sense that
there were no longer any individual businesses existing which functioned
privately. To study the repercussions of the marketing structure reform
we proceeded with a month-long survey. We questioned local authorities (Delegation, Municipality, Office of Financial Administration),
the manager of the cooperative, and also some members and employees
of the latter. Finally, we approached some former shopkeepers still living
in the village as representatives of those who were eliminated from the
modern circuit.

The survey was conducted in the form of semidirect interviews. After
having supplied the quantitative information requested, the subject was
invited to elaborate on the questions dealt with.

To appraise the impact of structural reform on the staff formerly
mobilized (i.e. before 1966) by marketing activity, we had to examine
the "Licence File" deposited at the Office of Financial Administration
in Grombalia. We thus established the number of grocers, dry-goods
dealers, and booksellers (the activities affected by the setting up of the
cooperative) existing before the amalgamation. One hundred and two
persons were surveyed, among which were 62 shopkeepers exercising their
trade on their own, 4 having three employees each at work, 4 others
employing two persons, and 6 employing one person.

In addition, the persons amalgamated in the cooperative were counted,
i.e. 53 persons, of whom 44 were shareholders and 9 nonshareholding
employees. Among the 44 shareholders were 2 farmers who had not
engaged in marketing before the setting up of the cooperative and 7
members of the family of one of the shareholders, an old tradesman-
farmer (4 daughters, 2 sons, and the wife). They also had never previously been engaged in marketing. These 9 persons form part of the total of
20 out of 44 shareholders who are not employed in any work in the cooperative and who participate only through their shares.

Thus, 58 jobs were abolished for the village of Menzel Bou Zelfa
(102 persons in the old system, but 53 amalgamated in the cooperative,
from which one must subtract 9 persons amalgamated without having
previously engaged in marketing) out of a total of 102; that is, 57 percent of the total manpower formerly mobilized by the normal marketing
sector.

It may be observed that no census of the number of jobs abolished was
carried out when the reform was applied. The significance of this "over-

sight" becomes clear when one inquires about the future of the people whose jobs were abolished. As nothing had been provided for them, their only way out was to leave for Jerba (15), Tunis (7), Libya (3), and France (2) in search of work, once their shops were closed by the authorities after a minimum time period. Some others were about to depart or were staying while attempting to change their employment and continuing to sell those few products not yet affected by the cooperative, such as charcoal and kerosene.

This limitation of manpower employed in marketing is in keeping with the general choice adopted by those responsible for planning. In fact, whereas "in 1964 there were about 85,000 persons employed in marketing activities" in Tunisia, the action taken by those responsible for the economy "has reduced this figure by about 15,000 persons in 1966."[1]

In addition to this abolition of "supernumerary" small shopkeepers, the second important effect of the setting up of the cooperative was to create a specialization of jobs and a new employment structure according to qualifications in place of the old and simple distinction between bosses and multipurpose employees.

In the modern system, out of a total of 37 active persons, 32 are employed directly in selling. Of these, 6 heads of shops receive a monthly salary of 26 dinars and 26 sales clerks draw a salary of 22 dinars. There are five administrative staff members, distributed as follows:

Job description	Monthly salary
1 Manager	60 dinars
1 Cashier	45 dinars
1 Invoice clerk	25 dinars
1 File clerk	25 dinars
1 Warehouseman	25 dinars

This job specialization is clearly linked to the increasing complexity and multiplication of operations being carried out within the framework of new marketing units which are very much larger than the old shops and have more customers.

The amalgamation of shopkeepers resulted in an initial contribution of capital of 17,379,430 millimes, at the start of the fiscal year; the capital at the end of the fiscal year (31/12/67) reached 31,250,905 millimes. The breakdown by shareholders is shown in Table 1. The essential mod-

[1] See the *Sectorial and overall prospects for the level of employment in 1980* (1968: 127).

ification caused by this pooling of money, capital, and goods is the increase of productivity and the realization of savings.

Table 1.   Menzel Bou Zelfa consumers' cooperative: capital on 31 December 1967

Shareholder	Number of shares	Capital	Income per share	Total income	Present total capital
1	200	1,000,000	2,929	585,800	1,585,800
2	130	650,000	,,	380,770	1,030,770
3	103	515,000	,,	301,687	816,687
4	83	415,000	,,	243,107	658,107
5	80	400,000	,,	234,320	634,320
6	80	400,000	,,	234,320	634,320
7	80	400,000	,,	234,320	634,320
8	57	285,000	,,	166,953	453,953
9	47	235,000	,,	137,663	372,663
10	44	220,000	,,	128,876	348,876
11	41	205,000	,,	120,089	325,089
12	40	200,000	,,	117,160	316,160
13	40	200,000	,,	117,160	317,160
14	36	180,000	,,	105,444	285,444
15	30	150,000	,,	87,870	237,870
16	28	140,000	,,	82,012	222,012
17	27	135,000	,,	79,083	214,083
18	24	120,000	,,	70,296	190,296
19	21	105,000	,,	61,509	166,509
20	20	100,000	,,	58,580	158,580
21	20	100,000	,,	58,580	158,580
22	20	100,000	,,	58,580	158,580
23	20	100,000	,,	58,580	158,580
24	20	100,000	,,	58,580	158,580
25	20	100,000	,,	58,580	158,580
26	20	100,000	,,	58,580	158,580
27	20	100,000	,,	58,580	158,580
28	20	100,000	,,	58,580	158,580
29	20	100,000	,,	58,580	158,580
30	20	100,000	,,	58,580	158,580
31	13	65,000	,,	38,077	103,077
32	11	55,000	,,	32,219	87,219
33	10	50,000	,,	29,290	79,290
34	10	50,000	,,	29,290	79,290
35	10	50,000	,,	29,290	79,290
36	8	40,000	,,	23,432	63,432
37	6	30,000	,,	17,574	47,574
38	5	25,000	,,	14,645	39,645
39	5	25,000	,,	14,645	39,645
40	4	20,000	,,	11,716	31,716
41	4	20,000	,,	11,716	31,716
42	1	5,000	,,	2,929	7,929
43	1	5,000	,,	2,929	7,929
44	1	5,000	,,	2,929	7,929
Total	1,500	7,500,000	–	4,393,500	11,893,500

Given this turnover, these new results can be established. One may assess that the turnover corresponding to the heading "Sale of merchandise" realized by the old marketing system and the present one, at a given time, does not vary to any great extent. This is because the habits of consumption represented by this figure cannot vary appreciably in the course of the short period covered.

The average turnover per person, which is the measure of employees' productivity, rose from 4,089,400 d. to 11,273,481 d. for the six months of the fiscal year ending on 31/12/67. In fact, the overall turnover during this period was 417,118,823 millimes. This was realized by 37 persons (32 employed by the 6 sale points, plus an administrative staff of 5). One may allow that this was realized by the 102 former shopkeepers in the course of a similar six-month period. The average turnover per person during this period increased by:

$$11,273,481 \text{ d.} - 4,089,400 \text{ d.} = 7,184,081 \text{ d.}$$

which is a remarkable figure.

This increase of productivity permitted the realization of 6,583,034 d. under the heading "Trading results." Of this amount, 42.38 percent, or 2,538,594 d., was levied by the State under the heading of profit taxes, and the remaining 4,044,440 d. was set aside and intended essentially for the supplying of savings (Table 3).

Table 2. Generation operations as of 31 December 1967

Debit	Amount	Credit	Amount
Stock at beginning of 1967 fiscal year	34,734,862	Stock at end of 1967 fiscal year	45,871,754
Purchase of merchandise	390,818,726	Sale of merchandise	417,118,823
Staff costs	18,147,788		
Duties and taxes	425,790		
Works, supplies, external service	6,541,618		
Transport and ships	2,051,544		
General management expenses	1,571,751		
Financial expenses	1,090,122		
Dating of 1967 fiscal year in accounts	1,025,342		
Amortizations			
Trading results	6,583,034		
Total	462,990,577		462,990,577

Thus, the fundamental economic objectives fixed by the planners were attained, since at the same time there was the realization of savings, a funding of the State budget through taxation, and an increase of productivity, thanks to the reduction of the number of operators.

However, these accounting figures are only one aspect of marketing concentration, the application of which has had multiple consequences on the lives of the former shopkeepers. Thus it is necessary to consider the reactions caused by the State's strategy.

Table 3.   Profits and losses as of 31 December 1967

Debit	Amount	Credit	Amount
Taxes on profits (42.3%)	2,538,594	Trading Results	6,583,034
Results set aside	4,044,440		
Total	6,583,034		6,583,034

THE RESISTANCE OF THE TRADITIONAL MILIEU

The reform of marketing structures is in keeping with the many actions undertaken by the State aimed at industrialization and modernization. So it is that the essential economic machinery unleashed in the marketing sector consists of a creation of savings intended, in theory, to provide funds for investments directed towards productive sectors.

However, while the State pursues its method of industrialization in this manner, the actual social processes engendered by the State's intervention stir up tensions among shopkeepers. These will strengthen any concrete attempt to challenge all actions directed towards modernization. A second group will thus join rural elements to constitute a potential social force ready to appear or to be manipulated, according to the circumstances.

Thus, to understand the general outline of attitudes adopted towards the modernization program instituted by the State, it is essential to examine the objective conditions in terms of which the shopkeepers react. According to the replies obtained, these conditions may be grouped around three principal themes: the reduction of the standard of living, the added effort required, and the diversion of actual processes from their proclaimed objectives.

With regard to the reduction of the standard of living, all the amalgamated shopkeepers, including the manager, reckon that their income and consumption have clearly diminished since the setting up of the cooperative. Only one employee (not a shareholder), who is in charge of a shop where oil is sold, regards his situation as unchanged.

However, experience teaches us to distrust this type of answer. In fact, the unanimous assertion of the lowering of the standard of living is usually accompanied (21 replies) by a demand for an increase in wages from the first contact with the person questioned. Later on, on numerous return visits to the village, those concerned hasten to ask for "news from Tunis" with regard to a "possible increase in wages."

Thus, in spite of the precautions taken to arrive at objective appraisals, it could be that an excessive belittling of the present with regard to an idealized past takes place to support claims for increased benefits.

However, in spite of this probable distortion, the agreement of the details supplied concerning restrictions on consumption with one of the essential objectives of the reform, the realization of a substantial saving, makes the idea of an actual lowering of the standard of living more realistic.

By way of illustration, we quote three typical replies: that of the manager, that of an important shareholder, and that of an employee who is not a shareholder.

The manager declares:

I can't tell you exactly how much I earned before the amalgamation and how much I earn today. Before, I had ample means and I spent for my family without restriction. I had a business worth 9,000 dinars divided between three stores.

I deposited 200 dinars each year in the Central Bank and realized a net profit, after all our expenses, of 700 to 800 dinars per annum. All expenses for food, clothing, school, and all living requirements were drawn directly from the till, without counting.

Now I have 60 dinars per month. After having liquidated most of my stock before being taken into the snare of the cooperative, I joined with a capital of 400 dinars and earned a profit of 40 dinars on my shares for the 6 months of the fiscal year. Everything I earn no longer suffices for my family expenses; I have difficulties at the end of each month and I no longer put a penny aside. When I was free, my oldest son from time to time used to take 500 millimes from the till, even without telling me in advance, to go to the cinema or enjoy himself. Now, seeing the financial situation, he no longer dares to ask me for anything. I do not like to discuss these details, but we all know each other here and they will all tell you the same thing.

This answer is the prototype of all those given by the 9 cooperators of the privileged category, as defined by the size of their initial capital contribution. Thus, one important shareholder, while confirming the lowering of the standard of living, attempts to explain this by the disappearance of free private enterprise:

I had a business worth 600 dinars and realized a profit of 800 to 1,000 dinars, in spite of the State tax, which was 45 percent. Fifty-five percent remained to me and that was enough. The cooperative system introduces too many obligations. What I earn now is very little in comparison with before. Now we only buy necessary things and we have become badly off. I earn much less because I no longer work for myself. For example, previously when I was here, someone might come to tell me that there is an excellent deal on a nearby farm. I would accompany him at once to buy and resell hay or something else. Now I no longer stir from the café. That period is finished.

With the less-favored class of cooperators, questions about the comparative standard of living raise vehement emotive outbursts:

I haven't eaten any meat for two months. Before the cooperative I used to eat meat twice a week, or at least once. Before, the boss gave me food, paid for my shaving, bath, clothing, and lodging and 6 to 15 dinars were left to me each month. They have promised us many improvements, but everything is a lie.

Now I have to make 8 persons of my family live with 22 dinars. They take part of this amount from me and I am only left with 20 dinars 334 millimes; I am ashamed to walk in the street, among the people, with holes in my smock. It is the only one given to me since the beginning. What do they expect me to do with 20 dinars? I pay 7 dinars for rent, whereas previously, with the boss, I did not pay any rent. I was able to buy on credit and I paid every Wednesday. They no longer give credit. We no longer eat our fill.

Before we were able to buy 10 millemes worth of tomato paste. Now, either one buys a whole can or else, if we don't have enough to buy the whole can, they don't sell us anything. What can a poor person do? Money has diminished because the large shopkeepers have hidden away their money before the State could take it away from them.

Furthermore, the management makes deductions from our wages, by force, before paying us: one time 150 millimes for the "Destour party cell," another time 500 millimes for the "National Guard," another time one dinar for the festival. If I do not want to pay for these things, well, one has only to leave me alone. But if I say that I do not agree, they tell me that I have gone against the government. I used to live better before, but I had no choice. It is planning, and the government, which decide. No one has asked me for my opinion.

The attempt to make comparative assessments of individual incomes before the forming of the cooperative and after comes up against a difficulty that was pointed out in the replies. That is, how to provide specific accounting information on the old activity, which was basically centered on consumption.

Nevertheless, the replies obtained permit one to assert, with a high level of probability, that there has been an actual reduction in the standard of living.

Out of 31 persons who supplied comparative figures, 17 reckon that the level of their income has diminished by half, 9 think they earn three times less than before, while 5 others, important shareholders, earn (according to them) four to ten times less than before.

Questioned on possible solutions they could imagine for this problem of the decrease in income, the shopkeepers envisage only one way out, i.e. an increase in wages and a reduction in the share deducted for the State.

Even among those who regard the failure of the cooperative movement in marketing matters (as conceived at the present time) as inescapable, no one hopes for a return to the previous state of free private enterprise.

This attitude seems to reflect an assurance by the Secretary of State for Planning and the National Economy who, inaugurating the week of cooperation held from 23 to 27 April 1968, called the setting up of the cooperative an "irreversible movement."

In fact, the real attitude of the shopkeepers questioned with regard to the reforms is far from being identified with the "enthusiasm" claimed by the official ideology or the revolt ready to be organized which is desired by socialist opponents of the regime of state capitalism. Indeed, curiously, this has something in common with the attitude which those principally concerned would have adopted towards a disaster of a new type, but one just as fatal as the old natural calamities whose obscure power renders any attempt at reaction as illusory. Everyone allows himself to be carried away passively by a unanimously deplored movement.

The remainder of this paper will seek, among other things, to explain the possible conditions of this phenomenon, insofar as the marketing system is able to operate while dispensing with the "participation" of individuals.

However, in addition to the lowering of the standard of living, there is a second objective condition causing shopkeepers to adopt a hostile attitude to the setting up of the cooperative. This is the extra effort required at work.

The problem raised here first appears in a confusing and paradoxical form. While the shopkeepers regard the 12 statutory hours of daily work as excessive, if one questions them on the amount of time they used to work in the old days, the majority give replies such as: "all the time"; "even at night"; "I sometimes used to open the shop at 4 A.M."; "I opened the shop at the time of the first prayers"; "we never closed"; "the whole day"; "from the crowing of the cock"; "even during mealtimes"; "I used to open the shop while people were still sleeping and I closed it after they had all gone to sleep, after the last person had passed in the street."

Thus, with the present 12 prescribed hours it seems difficult to explain and justify the demands for a reduction of working hours, especially with regard to the almost uninterrupted nature of the old activity. However, the reality is quite another thing and the problem raised here seems to require immediate analysis.

For instance, 26 out of 32 of those employed in the new shops complain of pains in their legs and of having swollen feet. They even show these off and claim to have gone for medical advice on the subject.

One seller, surrounded by his fellow-workers and customers, claims he has spent 40 days in hospital, showing documents to support this. He says that as a consequence he lost his post as "head of the shop" when he came out, two days before our meeting, because of the "swelling of his 'lower' feet and 'his' pains in his legs from being forced to remain standing."

The other employees working with him confirmed his words by complaining likewise of aching legs, and with an amazing virulence. "To be standing up" has become an almost obsessional subject with sales clerks. Thus, it was a question of finding out why the limitation to only 12 hours of work from the former uninterrupted activity should lead to a greater exhaustion at work, in spite of having a day off each week. Two explanatory factors are then called to mind.

First, the 32 sellers assert that in the course of the 12 hours they provide considerably more effort than during an old working day. This is because of the larger number of customers with whom they have to deal as a result of the reduction in the number of shops. The extreme case is represented by a shop maintained by three employees and which now serves customers formerly served by twelve shops. This shows that the geographic redistribution of the new shops has taken place in an anarchical manner and that better deployment must be sought.

In fact, the old activity, spread out over a long but discontinuous time, has been replaced by 12 hours of actual work, since 32 sales clerks have replaced 102 former shopkeepers and serve the same number of customers who, in addition, now concentrate their purchases within the limits of a shorter working period.

The shopkeepers describe the intermittent aspect and slow rhythm of the trade as it was practiced before:

It is no longer the same thing. Before I used to work all the time and I even opened my shop at 4 A.M. But I closed it any time I wished, and I was able to stretch out inside or go do something else while leaving a friend or someone else in charge. Between one client and another some time would go by.

Now one has to stay 12 hours standing at the counter to serve people who constantly fill the shop. This shop, which we staff with only 4 persons, replaces nine shops which were done away with in this street and the one alongside.

On top of this the head of the shop keeps an eye on us. I am standing all the time. To run my errands I am forced to ask relatives to go instead of me. Before I used to go alone. As a result of remaining standing here like a nail, I end up wanting to go for a walk without any reason.

I can no longer even say my prayers on the hour. We all have painful feet and health is undermined because of keeping on our feet. Twelve hours of work are too much. At times I fall asleep at work from fatigue. We wish to work for the country but this is abnormal. There is more exhaustion and less money. Furthermore the management is always asking us to come to work on our statutory days off and during holidays. The government says that "cooperation is the *joie de vivre*."[2] This is a lie.

The actual working time at the counter in the old activity, for one day, has been estimated at three and four times less than at the present time, according to shopkeepers. This represents the counterpart deductible from the increase of productivity and decrease in the number of operators.

Although the excessive aspect of the work period seems clear because of actual physical difficulties, the solution to the problem posed depends on how much the 12 hours of activity represent an "excessive" effort, insofar as it relates to a defined standard of profitability or tiredness, and how much this same effort was only felt in comparison with the former norm, in the old trade. This would bring in the concept of adaptation and the notion of time for adaptation to new requirements.

This consideration leads us to consider the second factor explaining the tiredness of shopkeepers, and which is of a more subjective nature than the preceding one.

Seventeen sellers out of 32 mix criteria which are more of a psychological nature among the objective causes of their excessive fatigue. They declare that they tire more because they are not motivated by an adequate salary; or that they do not work for themselves; or else that they feel a strong dissatisfaction because of the supervision exercised by the "Head of the Centre" and the injustices of the administrative hierarchy (delay in payment of salaries, denial of statutory days off, and favoritism towards Jerbans against the natives of the village, because of the regionalist sympathies of the manager, who is Jerban in origin).

Finally, one last point raised by the shopkeepers explains their suspicion with regard to the amalgamation: the diversion of the actual course from the objectives proclaimed.

In addition to the various views of the persons interviewed concerning, on the one hand, the loss of freedom of initiative, the elimination of individuals, the reduction in the standard of income and consumption,

---

[2] Slogan of an official notice-board distributed during "The Week of Cooperation."

and the supplementary effort imposed, and on the other hand, the reorganization and modernization of the marketing network, the stability and security of employment, the application of hygiene measures, the increase of productivity, the setting up of social security and family allocation, and the introduction of bookkeeping, a basic problem emerges. All the attitudes and present worries of the cooperators revolve around this problem. This central fact, raised by 41 cooperators questioned, may be summed up in the following manner: the gap noted between the objectives proclaimed by local and national leaders and the actual development of events questions the legitimacy of the methods used. It engenders a resentment which is all the stronger because marketing reform was carried out at the cost of heavy sacrifices and draconian measures.

This attitude is based on the conviction that the profits realized through the elimination of a large number of shopkeepers, the lowering of the standard of living, and an increased expenditure of energy for those integrated into the new network have been diverted from their proclaimed goal, i.e. the local and national collective good, to the benefit of an administrative and political minority, which, under the pretense of a bountiful ideology, indulges in the traditional forms of speculation. Dissatisfaction has crystallized around this deviation even more than against the fact of the initial despoiling.

Before searching for its objective basis, let us examine some of the replies obtained on this subject. One of the most important shareholders declares:

It isn't us who reform profits; we have given our money, but we no longer have any possibility either of recovering it or of using it or of controlling what becomes of it. The manager acts as a private trader. There are two categories of people. Those who work, that is, us, and those who profit from it, the manager and those further up in the administration and politics. The only thing cooperative here is the name. The manager has placed a notice in the accounting office addressed to the cooperators where it is written that it is forbidden to sit down and to speak. We see nothing; we know nothing. That is what cooperation is!

A second shopkeeper, while asserting he is a member of the Destour party, says:

I am 200 percent with the government and have always been on the side of the legislators. What they do is always right. But what is bad comes from the fact that politics has sought to influence trade, while at the same time knowing nothing about it and remaining far from it. When the government and the Plan send a directive to the governor or to the delegate, and which the latter two wish to apply, they remain in their offices, calling people together to tell them what must happen, and then, as they are outside the marketing world, they no longer know how people are going to behave. Then many injustices take place.

Now everything gets mixed up. One no longer knows what comes from commerce and what comes from politics, and the more wicked abuse this fact.

The majority of the shopkeepers are fully aware that marketing activity in the village is bringing in substantial profits, which they regard as coming to them by right but which are pinched by the State for its own purposes:

I have more than 13 years experience of retailing and I know how much business in the village brings in. What accrues to the shopkeepers is a very small part of the gross profits which the cooperative is able to realize. It isn't that we are not patriots. On the contrary, we would like them to take away from the rich so that everyone can live well; but we are no longer in agreement when this money taken from us serves to pay for beer in the Café de Paris,[3] to enrich the politicians and administrators. Where does the money come from which finances these receptions they show us on television, all those receptions? We aren't stupid. I am familiar with the houses built in Tunis with loans which the "big men" will never repay. On television they show us dinners, the moon, drinks, magnificent services. The country is poor, so where does that money come from? The leaders travel abroad all the time. It is with our sweat that they pay for these things. What good is it to take the money away from us which we need to eat and live normally, in order to throw it out the window. But a day will come. Here in Menzel Bou Zelfa none of the shopkeepers have come out ahead. It is the people in the administration and politics who command everything, control everything, and reap the profits.

We have all become like civil servants who are badly paid each month.

The majority of the replies to the question of who profits from the setting up of the cooperatives name "the people in Tunis," "the ministers," "the big people in politics," "the Party," and "the State."

The true implications of these assertions can only be made clear if one is able to evaluate the proportion of national savings going to productive investments and the part which is in fact allocated to the ostentatious expenses of the political-bureaucratic minority. As this task exceeds the limits of this enquiry, let us simply ask two questions which explain the cooperators' attitude: on what facts do they base their assertion, and how is it that their productivity improves in spite of their protest?

With regard to the first problem, it appeared that the role of what one might call "subversive propaganda" only appeared to a small degree as a factor explaining the interpretations gathered from the cooperators.

Besides the ostentation revealed by the mass media (basically public

---

[3] A fashionable and very visible café in Tunis.

television), it is the perpetuation of old speculative behavior in the new marketing networks which is the source of cooperators' suspicions as to how savings "realized at their expense" are finally used.

In fact, besides the reasons already indicated, all the shopkeepers complain of the manager's behavior. The latter is regarded as being bound up with the administrative and political leaders (the delegation and the Destour cell, at the local level) who had him appointed.

The manager, a former shopkeeper, clever, possessing a basic knowledge of accounting, knowing how to draw up a balance-sheet, continued to manage the "cooperative" according to old marketing procedures, i.e. in the manner of a private speculator, motivated to maximize profits. He has been determined to act and "to get along alone," as he puts it, rejecting the principles of cooperation and the right of inspection of members, since "he cannot explain anything to illiterates who do not know how to read a balance-sheet."

Whereas one of the purposes of the cooperative is to provide regular supplies to the consumer, the latter from time to time has had to bear a shortage of goods (flour, tea) for quite long periods (one shortage of tea at the time of our research lasted 7 days), while the goods in question were stocked in normal quantities in the cooperative's stockroom. The general hostility focused on the person of the manager finally led the local authorities to ask the latter to give an account of his behavior. Summoned to explain his conduct by the delegate and the board of directors, the manager demonstrated at the meeting that by the method he uses he manages to obtain a larger profit. For "from the time of the reappearance of goods removed from consumers for a certain period, the latter hasten to buy amounts three to four times above their normal purchases and at the maximum price fixed by law." "A person who used to buy 100 grams of tea now takes 300 grams." Similarly, the desire for speculation made the management adopt the maximum price fixed by law, though according to the cooperative's statutes prices should normally fluctuate between two extreme limits according to profits earned and variations in economic conditions.

So it is that a villager, passing through Soliman or other neighboring localities, declares that in Menzel Bou Zelfa a "one-kilo box of tomato paste costs five and even ten millimes more," according to one of the cooperators.

This situation has incalculable psychological consequences. In fact, distrust starting here has generalized to the whole cooperative movement.

While in the former free competition situation the buyer expected the seller to seek to gain the largest profit possible at his expense, at least he was still entitled to buy elsewhere if he felt he had been wronged.

But once his defense mechanisms were lowered in the face of the presumed legality of the new network and he suddenly became aware that under the apparent legality the old tricks were still being played, he felt he had been betrayed. He lost confidence and went on the defensive. In order to shorten the necessarily inquisitive aspect of this part of the enquiry, we have deliberately omitted a number of details obtained concerning the phenomenon analyzed here.

This comment is inserted so the occasionally formal or abstract appearance of subjects raised should be attributed not to a deficiency in the collecting of concrete data but to a deliberate desire to disguise, and thus to try to keep the investigation within the limits of pure research.

Besides, the manager's behavior is quite normal when viewed within the context of former methods. But it is the advent of a new context which confers the nature of abnormality on his acts. Now he tries to reconcile his old speculative reflexes with the requirements of the new legality. But according to cooperators' replies, it seems that this reconciliation is often only apparent. This gives rise to accusations such as:

Provided that the officials sent by the authorities see that the cooperative is bringing money to the State, they do not look for anything else.

The manager buys and sells. No one controls him since he can contrive the balance-sheet as he wishes. We have never had any meeting with him, nor a chairman's report or financial report, not since the beginning.

He alone decides, fixes the prices of products for which no prices have been authorized. We have asked him to meet us on several occasions, but each time he refuses.

We do not know the price he pays or the price at which he sells. He acts as if I did not exist, whereas I am the foundation of this cooperative, because of the importance of my capital share.

They have amalgamated us on one basis and we have ended up on another. He leaves everything in the dark and enriches himself by acting as if the capital of all the cooperators belonged to him. He buys land. The day before yesterday I happened to be in the office passage and an agent working on behalf of a Tunis wholesaler was in the process of handing 25 dinars to the accountant, saying, 5 for you and 20 for the manager. This wholesaler had sold 100 pairs of shoes directly to the manager without invoices. The manager had brought them to the cooperative, but the warehouseman refused to accept them because there weren't any invoices. Previously the manager had acted as he wished, but now we are all against him. We have complained to the delegate and the warehouseman has received an order not to accept anything any longer without invoices.

The manager had explained to the warehouseman that the owner of the shoes was a poor blind man whom it was necessary to assist. But the warehouseman was determined not to listen to anything. Then the manager took the shoes directly to a shop where his brother is the head.

With our money the manager is working for himself. He does not wish to pay the workers; he makes them work on their free days and the last time we had a fight before he would pay the workers. Furthermore, because he is Jerban, he favors Jerbans and replaces the local people with Jerbans. The cooperative has only served to take our money and it is the manager who profits from this, along with the State.

Before everyone worked for himself; now we all work for others who get rich while our situation gets worse.

The old shopkeepers are clearly aware that they have been used, that they have become means after having been their own end.

However (and here we are tackling the question of professional activity), in good conditions of productivity, in spite of the opposition of the cooperators, the latter's reticent attitude in no way alters the cooperative's good progress and financial situation.

The following question was asked: "If you judge the work load as excessive, why not work less during the 12 hours?" The answer, which was easy to predict, ran as follows in the majority of cases: "Whether I like it or not, if a customer asks me for a kilo of sugar, what can I do but give it to him; if I do not, I can be dismissed." This reply shows that, regardless of the degree of the sales clerks' "participation," the present productivity of the staff and the turnover realized are determined by the consumers' level of needs and purchasing power.

The sales clerks' increased productivity is in no way a result of their participation. On the contrary, it results from the limits imposed by the volume and rhythm of the demand for foodstuffs, which are here the determining factors.

So it is that insofar as the satisfaction of food needs is imperative and demand is effected at its own rhythm, marketing activity develops independently of sales clerks' "participation." This relationship to inelastic needs is the basic factor permitting marketing reform to "succeed" independently of the mood of cooperators who are, to a certain degree, obliged to adjust their actions automatically to the rhythm of demand.

CONCLUSION

The reduction of the number of shopkeepers and the restrictions imposed on consumption have been the predictable consequences of a choice: the accumulation of additional savings. A proportion of the expenses which have been allocated in the normal marketing system to household consumption and home savings has been released, and thus becomes available for possible reinvestment in priority sectors.

This elementary economic process was carried out through "structural reform," which tended towards an elimination of forms of personal dependence governing relationships which had been established between "bosses" and "employees," as well as towards a collectivization of the former individual exploitation. Thus, it seems to respond not merely to classical economic imperatives of rationalization, but also to the innovating of ethical norms which challenge contradiction between the collective aspect of marketing service and the individual aspect of private appropriation of the means of exchange.

Nevertheless, the political-economic choice retained with regard to marketing reforms has (a) brought about a transformation of latent unemployment into explicit unemployment, (b) required extra effort from those employed, and (c) imposed limitations on consumption.

Still, despite the seriousness of these actual problems which became obvious when we supplemented the overall outlook (which was necessarily abstruse) by the direct survey, it is clear that it is the deviation of the cooperative movement (from the time of its emergence) from its proclaimed collective goal which is the decisive risk.

In fact, the case analyzed reveals even the manner in which "structural reforms" were carried out.

Drawing attention to this deflection of the cooperative movement towards individual goals, the Secretary of State for Planning and the National Economy (M. Ahmed Ben Saleh) at the inaugural meeting of "the Week of Cooperation," raised the fact of "bringing together naïve people and 'dragons' who know how to manipulate a balance-sheet" as a basic obstacle to the success of structural reform.

Imposed authoritatively by the central government, rather than arising from a voluntary adhesion of individuals, cooperative behavior remains superficial because it is not supported by the corresponding attitudes. Quite to the contrary, the traditional motivation of maximum individual profit is reflected in the newly instituted behavior.

One finds oneself in the classic situation of a time lag between attitudes and behavior.

The persistence of traditional attitudes under new legalist guises disturbs the free play of abstract mechanisms conceived and anticipated by the planner.

But from the more synthetic point of view, which consists of putting the case envisaged back into its overall context, it is a question of asking if forms of organization of activity can acquire the collectivist content implied by the concept of "cooperation," insofar as these forms, far from being rooted among broad classes of the population, and desired as such, appear instead to be an authoritarian state's attempt to confiscate former property and centralize additional savings whose ultimate uses, rightly or wrongly, give rise to popular suspicion.

The breakdown that occurred between the leaders of the structural reform and the shopkeepers explains the readiness manifested by the latter to return to old forms of individual enterprise in September 1969, as soon as the failure of the agrarian reform policy brought about the removal of the government faction which had been involved in the setting up of the cooperative.[4] Although the leaders still asserted their support of marketing cooperatives even while agrarian reform was attacked by the government, the "reprivatization" of marketing, which occurred through a series of successive measures, was general from the month of March 1970 on.

REFERENCES

SECTORIAL AND OVERALL PROSPECTS
  1968 *Sectorial and overall prospects for the level of employment in 1980*, part one: *Overall study*. Tunis: I.S.E.A.-A.N., Secretariat of State for Planning and the National Economy.

---

[4] Cf. the paper by Makhlouf in this volume.

The Tunisian Experiment with Service Cooperatives

HAFEDH SETHOM

It is not our intention to make an exhaustive study of service cooperatives in Tunisia; the subject would be too broad and we would not have enough documentation to deal with it. We will present an experiment with farm-service cooperatives on the Cap Bon peninsula, a more limited geographical area, but one which provides us with a number of object lessons. Study of such a case will allow us to outline some conclusions as to the attitude of different strata of the peasantry regarding a form of cooperative which basically respects private property.

In contrast with production cooperatives, which have been tested only since Tunisia gained its independence, service cooperatives were introduced as early as the colonial period. They were even promoted, encouraged, and financed by the government of the Protectorate.

SERVICE COOPERATIVES IN THE COLONIAL PERIOD

The government of the Protectorate favored the establishment of service cooperatives in two areas which were of particular interest to colonial farmers: (1) wine growing and wine making and (2) the growing and marketing of citrus fruits. This was done by promoting wine cooperatives and cooperative processing stations for fruits and vegetables.

Wine Cooperatives for Small-Scale or Medium-Scale European Vinegrowers

The creation of wine cooperatives was a step taken by the government to help solve the problem of the colonial vineyards, whose numbers had been greatly reduced by phylloxera, and to help return them to full operation. The wine cooperatives were to serve the small- and medium-sized French vinegrowers who did not have the means; to help them restore their vineyards while maintaining scientific standards; and especially to help them make wine from their grapes under very advantageous financial conditions and at a very high technical level.

The wine cooperatives were thus originally a means of rescuing an endangered economic sector and of supporting the colonial settlement which was to insure the colonial state a solid foothold in the Tunisian countryside. To the degree that vinegrowing was the major type of speculation engaged in by the Cap Bon colonists, the wine cooperatives were intended to support colonists of small or modest resources, in the face of competition from the big, commercial wine producers. The number of colonists in the area, which was even then very limited (700 persons or so) had to be kept from falling to 100 or 200, through the elimination of small- and medium-income farmers who were in difficulties.

Since the colonists were not numerous, the five wine cooperatives never included more than a few dozen members each, and at the most around a hundred. On the whole, the large vinegrowers continued to do their own wine making and, with a few exceptions, did not join the cooperatives. Only the small European vinegrowers banded together in large groups around these new institutions.

The Tunisian peasants were largely outside of this movement, for wine grapes are a rare crop among Tunisians; moreover, most of the Tunisian vinegrowers owned small plots of ground and had very limited crops. European members of cooperatives always put forward this sort of argument to avoid being overwhelmed by a flood of Tunisian vinegrowers who, while having only small areas under cultivation, were more numerous than the colonists, for the very reason that they had very tiny holdings. Only a few large Tunisian vinegrowers were able, in certain cases, to gain admittance; the vast majority of peasants growing wine grapes were kept out. Most Tunisians sold their crops to the large private European wine makers at the going price and were unable to take advantage of the rebates which the cooperatives paid their members.

Thanks to the subsidies paid by the colonial state, the wine cooperatives were able to outfit themselves with ultramodern equipment which they would have had much difficulty acquiring with the money from assessments or from deductions on produce delivered by their members. The cooperatives provided members with advance credit on their crops, which enabled them to stock up on fertilizers, pesticides, etc.

The experiment with these wine cooperatives was, on the whole, a success. The vineyards were fully restored and even expanded, according to the new technical standards required by specialization, and the small- and medium-sized colonial holdings were not only saved but consolidated as well. The prosperity of the European wine-producing community in Tunisia in 1956 was in large measure the work of the wine cooperatives. The peasant vinegrowers, while they remained outside these cooperatives, benefitted from them indirectly by following the example of the colonists and by taking advantage of the supplementary payments on wine made by France to the colonists in North Africa.

The success of the wine cooperative formula accounts for the various attempts by the peasants to become members.

The Cooperative Stations for Processing Fruits and Vegetables, Serving the French Markets

The promotion of processing stations is a result of the development of Tunisian production of citrus fruits in order to assure a sufficient supply for the French market which was suffering a shortage about 1936 (on account of the war in Spain and of the economic sanctions against Fascist Italy, after Italy's aggression against Ethiopia). The Protectorate government tried to induce the colonists to take part in this new venture, but it had little success, since the colonists did not have enough land suitable for growing citrus fruits.

The development of citrus fruit production could succeed only with the cooperation of the Tunisian peasants. A whole series of incentive measures — such as the granting of plantation contracts, or *mgharsa*, by the Société des Habous Publics[1] to the poorer peasants for planting citrus crops — were introduced and began to show results as early as 1945.

But exporting was still in a state of confusion, and the processing of fruit was not always carried out properly. The private exporters of Tunis and Cap Bon took care of the gathering and marketing of the produce, at prices which were too low for the producers and not always attractive to the dealers in Marseilles.

This was the situation when, at the instigation of the public authorities,

[1] *Habous* are inalienable possessions, belonging to private individuals, groups, or the state. They have achieved this status through a procedure provided for in Moslem law. A *mgharsa* contract provides that one party supplies the capital for planting an orchard on land belonging to another; at the expiry of the contract period, when all the fruit trees are producing, the improved land is divided equally between the two parties.

two service cooperatives were set up for processing and marketing fruits and vegetables, one at Soliman (the SOCOMAF) and the other at Mensel-Bou-Zelfa (the SCAAM). They were to serve the farmers, fight against price speculation, promote the importation of quality fruit, and give farmers credit to enable them to stock up on fertilizers, pesticides, etc.

Thanks to a precise knowledge of prices at Marseilles, the major destination of Tunisian citrus products, the cooperatives were able to regularize prices, reduce speculation, and pay their members rebates, which were calculated in proportion to the profits earned.

These cooperatives took in all the citrus growers and the market-gardening peasants, with both large and small holdings, who wished to join them. The success of this enterprise can be seen in the increase in membership: starting out with a few dozen persons, the SCAAM at Menzel-Bou-Zelfa included 350 members in 1963.

The success of the enterprise caused the movement to mushroom: after Tunisian independence, a new cooperative — the CEPA — was created at Beni-Khalled.

At Soliman, the size of the vegetable crop caused SOCOMAF to take in peasants as well. The accessibility of the Tunis market, only 30 kilometers away, was a powerful impetus for these new patterns of production and consumption.

The cooperative stations thus played a great role in the expansion of citrus growing, especially in the region of Soliman/Menzel-Bou-Zelfa/Beni-Khalled.

The cooperatives, however, did not come to include all the peasants whose interests were at stake. In 1963 the cooperatives' members represented around one-third of the citrus growers in Menzel-Bou-Zelfa. The cooperatives did not manage to replace and eliminate the private exporters of Tunis and Cap Bon. The latter, indeed, continued to prosper and expand by taking advantage of the enlarged production of citrus fruits.

This state of affairs may be explained by the type of cooperatives created. Certainly, these took in peasants of different economic levels, those with small-, medium-, and large-sized holdings. But they were dominated and directed by the big farmers. At Menzel-Bou-Zelfa the cooperative's president is the richest landholder in the *cheikhat*[2] and the director is also a large farm owner. The citrus growers, large and small, who sell their produce to private exporters, recognize the "theoretical" advantages of the service cooperative but accuse the present management of serving

[2] The *cheikhat* is an administrative unit taking in a rural and urban territory, the subdivision of a *délégation*, which is itself a subdivision of a *gouvernorat*.

its own interests first. Certain peasants who are members of the cooperative, deliver part of their produce to the private exporters and part to the cooperative, which shows that, under present circumstances, the advantages and disadvantages of the two alternatives — service cooperatives versus private exporters — seem equivalent to the farmers.

Nevertheless, all the peasants admit that the service cooperatives have brought about a stabilization of prices and a major reduction of speculation. The private exporters have had to bring their prices closer to those set by the cooperative stations. The exporters still have the advantage of paying in cash for all merchandise delivered, whereas the cooperatives only give advances, with the final reckoning occurring only after the actual sale at Marseilles; even if the sum of the cooperative's two payments is higher than the price paid in cash by the private exporter, the latter solution is preferred, because the farmer has all his money right away.

In sum, these farm-service cooperatives were created at the direct instigation of the authorities, with their moral and, especially, financial support. They were made up almost exclusively of colonists, in the case of the wine cooperatives, and of large Tunisian farmers, in the case of the cooperative processing stations. They were mainly concerned with commercial crops intended principally for export, i.e. wine and citrus fruits, and only secondarily with market gardening and olive growing. A small experiment with cooperative production of olive oil was conducted by the colonists of Bou-Argoub in order to make it possible for the colonist, with their small production of olives, not to be dependent upon the large private Tunisian olive growers.

The cooperatives played a major role in the rebuilding of the vineyards after the phylloxera outbreak and in the expansion of citrus production in the plain of Grombalia, in order to supply the French market. They were created at the instigation of the public authorities, but no force of any kind was used to make farmers join them. Membership was always voluntary. That is why they were careful to attract members through concrete advantages and to come out with a positive balance, so as not to risk bankruptcy and dissolution for lack of viability.

From a social point of view, the cooperatives affected only a few hundred colonists and between one and two thousand Tunisian farmers, especially citrus growers. The bulk of the peasants on the Cap Bon peninsula remained outside the movement, even after independence. Indeed, until 1956 no new service cooperatives were created in areas other than those of vinegrowing and production of citrus fruits. However, there were announcements, in the ten-year forecast for 1962-1971, of the creation of service cooperatives in every village.

THE ENROLLMENT OF PRACTICALLY ALL THE CAP BON PEASANTS IN TERRITORIALLY-BASED SERVICE COOPERATIVES

Starting in 1965, forty service cooperatives, one per *cheikhat* on the average, were set up. Here again we have a case of an enterprise carried out by the government with great enthusiasm to bring together all farmers — those on the plains, on the coast, and even on the hillsides and the uplands; nurserymen, citrus growers, winegrowers, or olive growers, but also market gardeners, wheat and barley farmers, etc.

The goal was to gain the membership of all landholders, whether their lands were large or small, though not that of landless farmers. The minimum assessment was set at 5 dinars, regardless of the amount of land owned. The price-scale was a follows: owners having more than 5 hectares in dry crops, more than 2.5 hectares in garden produce or olives, or more than 1 hectare in citrus fruits had to pay a supplementary fee of 1 dinar per hectare of annual dry crops, 2 dinars per hectare of olives or garden produce, and 5 dinars per hectare of citrus fruits.

These cooperatives has as their purpose to provide farmers with indispensable products — fertilizers, pesticides, seed, plant cuts, etc. — at lower prices than did the private dealers. Moreover, it was necessary to do as much as possible to make modern mechanical equipment available to the peasants, to diffuse new techniques and cultivation practices, and to open up the doors of credit to most of the peasants. This general recruitment of peasants for the service cooperatives was to lead to more modern and more intensive farming.

Initial Euphoria, Despite the Authoritarian Nature of the Enterprise

The creation of one service cooperative per *cheikhat* and of one local branch of the Crédit Mutuel in each *délégation* was supposed to bring all farmers into the cooperatives. As matters developed, the inclusion of all farmers, however large their holdings, was brought about in a semiauthoritarian fashion, for many peasant farmers did not see the advantage of joining a cooperative.

In point of fact, most of the large farmers did not need the cooperative's services. They had trucks, tractors, harvesters, and threshing machines. They went to the large towns of Cap Bon or even Tunis to stock up on fertilizers and pesticides for their own needs and, sometimes, for resale to the small peasant farmers nearby. Some of them were also merchants, buyers of tomatoes or peppers, or else exporters of citrus fruits, and it was not in their interest to have cooperatives set up in competition with them.

The conflicts of interest became very acute when the service cooperatives began to take an active role in the marketing of certain key products, such as tomatoes and peppers for canning. The elimination of private intermediaries for the two products in question led to hostility and then to sabotage on the part of the merchants, who were often farmers as well.

At first, the large private citrus exporters were kept going, but the government authorities subsidized the service cooperatives, enlarging their scope of action at the expense of the private merchants. The authorities even set up a large processing station, the Union Régionale des Coopératives (URC) at Hammamet. Then, beginning in 1967–1968, policy favored the service cooperatives; the private exporters were obliged to cease operations in 1968–1969.

Wine making and the sale of wine, which after nationalization of colonial lands had been put in the hands of the wine cooperatives, reorganized under the control of the Union Centrale des Coopératives Viticoles of Tunisia (UCCV), presented no special problem, inasmuch as almost all the large wine producers were European and were eliminated in 1964 as part of the nationalization of colonial lands.

This policy of centralizing services and of marketing major farm products by authoritarian means had many different effects. Its consequences for the development of citrus growing were rather minor; this reorganization, as a matter of fact, coincided with a dry decade, marked by a steady fall in water levels. Credit funds for rural areas, provided by the Caisses de Crédit Mutuel, did not bring about the anticipated results because of this continual drought.

The wine cooperatives took over the wine production for the whole Tunisian vinegrowing area and replaced the large European wine makers. Tunisian wine thus continued to be produced, but the service cooperatives did not manage to solve the serious problem of low sales of wine and low prices following the breaking off of the trade agreement with France. Indeed, the problem was more than they could deal with.

The development of service cooperatives and of the Caisses de Crédit Mutuel had very noticeable effects upon the progress of irrigation of market-gardens in the pioneer areas of the back country in Korba-Menzel-Horr and El-Haouaria-Dar-Allouche. Tomato farming received the most benefit from this policy: the area of land under cultivation was greatly extended and production increased spectacularly. Fertilizers and pesticides were sold in the most remote parts of the peninsula by centers which the service cooperatives created; the farmers bought them largely with the aid of credits given most peasants by the Caisses de Crédit Mutuel. Widespread use of fertilizers and pesticides brought about a considerable rise in crop yields.

Tomato growing became virtually a mystique. Thanks to the cooperatives and the Caisses de Crédit, this type of farming caused many areas to move into a completely money-based, commercial economy. The use of checks became common for all payments made by the cooperatives and the Caisses de Crédit. To a large extent, the peasantry gave a favorable reception to this new policy, the tangible results of which were quickly felt, especially from 1965 to 1967. Only the large farmers who had all the necessary resources, had no need for the cooperatives' services and saw them as competitors who were beginning to replace private enterprise, which was often carried on by these same large farmers. The majority of the peasant farmers, with small- or medium-sized holdings, profited at first from the boom in tomato growing.

Advance Signs of the Failure of an Ill-Begun Experiment

Beginning in 1967, however, signs of discontent began to appear among most of the peasants working market gardens in the pioneer areas, and who at first had looked favorably upon the new forms of organization. The use of larger and larger areas for planting tomatoes had in fact led to overproduction. The factory owners, who had only grudgingly accepted the new regulations introduced by the service cooperatives, sabotaged the gathering of tomatoes by not providing packing crates in sufficient quantities and at the proper times. This serious shortage of crates accounted for the long waits by crowds of farmers in front of cooperative locals, the quarrels over crates, and the rotting of part of the tomato crop. In 1967–1968, one-fourth of the crop was lost in this way.

The factory managers were thus unwilling to come and collect the yield of fresh tomatoes. They took more and more time to pay the cooperatives, claiming that they lacked liquid assets because sales of tomato paste were down and because the banks were reluctant to give them credit. The cooperatives could no longer pay the peasants in cash. Payments were a few weeks late at first, then began to require several months, and eventually more than six months. The peasants were in a helpless position. They could not repay loans from the Caisses de Crédit Mutuel on time, and they were forced to pay interest because of these delays, which were not their fault.

In addition, the fact that all farmers needed to market their tomatoes through the intermediary of the service cooperatives allowed the state, i.e. the legal guardian which exercised sovereign authority over the entire movement, to "tax" the peasantry as it saw fit. Thus a whole series of withholdings were made on behalf of the state or of bodies under state control. In 1966, 1 dinar out of the 18 dinar price per ton of tomatoes was deducted for "Regional Development." Theoretically this money was a means of participating in the development of the region by buying shares of stock. The URC, however, paid 49,000 dinars for as many tons of tomatoes, collectively, on behalf of all the farmers. No peasant knows what his share is. These shares of stock bring no dividends; they were collected from all the farmers like taxes.

In 1967, additional deductions were put into effect: 5 millimes for every 25-kilogram box of tomatoes, in the name of "Social Solidarity" and 50 millimes per 100 kilograms of tomatoes, for the "Final Statement." Furthermore, the peasants who are well off, or presumed to be so, are required to purchase shares in the tourist union of their *délégation*, for the sum of 12.5 to 50 dinars, according to their means.

These various withholdings were made at the most basic level by the local Caisses de Crédit, which paid the farmers on behalf of the cooperatives: the Caisses kept the deductions, calculated the repayment of debts, and paid the farmers the rest.

These automatic deductions, of ever greater frequency and quantity, affected all the peasants but worried the small farmers more than those with larger holdings.

The lack of packing crates and the rotting of part of the tomato crop, as well as the serious delays in payments and the withholdings, at first aroused quite a general feeling of discontent, which from 1968 on became a wave of resentment. Since 1967 the service cooperatives had taken on the appearance of a state bureaucracy, taking the place of private businessmen and replacing their excessive profits with other excesses. The reorganization of sales and production and the modernization of farming were taken more and more as hollow slogans, intended to disguise a government policy of taking over the sale of certain key products as a way of increasing its revenues considerably.

It became more and more obvious to all the peasants that the spread of service cooperatives and the incorporation of about 20,000 farmers into the movement had no other purpose than that of making the state taxation system more effective and of keeping the managers of cooperatives prosperous. Discontent gradually turned to hostility directed toward the cooperative system and its representatives. Peasant anger was pushed to its limits when, in 1969, they saw the service cooperatives giving way to production cooperatives and collectivization of farm labor.

Indeed, the experiment with service cooperatives had had very different effects on peasants in different parts of Cap Bon. The service cooperatives set up in the inner, grain-producing zone, a remote area where modernization of farming is difficult, had almost no impact. The peasants were too impoverished to buy fertilizers, etc., and the crops were too undependable to allow them to make regular payments on the loans they had contracted at the Caisses. After a one-year experiment, the organization found its efforts at a total standstill.

In the vinegrowing regions, the effects of the service cooperatives and Caisses de Crédit were likewise very slight, given the situation — falling off of sales and a decrease in wine values.

The service cooperatives and Caisses de Crédit Mutuel had a very noticeable effect in the pioneer market-gardening areas and in the citrus-growing region because they were able to gain control over the sale of two key products, tomatoes and citrus fruits, and to collect an appreciable amount in taxes from the farmers by the method described above.

All in all, just before the decision was made to collective farm labor, the small- and medium-sized farmers of Cap Bon had moved from willing membership in the service cooperatives and Caisses de Crédit Mutuel to a sense of distrust which gradually turned to hostility. The large property owners, opposed to the experiment from its beginning because it was contrary to their interests, could only rejoice at the spread of discontent and opposition to this policy.

When the government announced in 1969 that it was time to proceed from service cooperatives to production cooperatives on every piece of farm land, the peasants felt that the cooperative experiment, begun on Cap Bon in 1965 had been designed to deprive them of their freedom of action, of their goods, and of their wealth. The production cooperatives were going to turn them into "salaried farm laborers," waiting for hypothetical end-of-the-year bonuses, as shown by the experiments with production cooperatives on reclaimed land at Cap Bon.

The general opposition of farmers to the spread of production cooperatives quickly became an opposition to the entire cooperative policy, including that with regard to service cooperatives, with whose abuses the Cap Bon peasants were well acquainted. Following the government's decision in September 1969 to halt the collectivization policy, the whole cooperative system set up since 1965 was to be progressively dismantled.

THE COLLAPSE OF THE COOPERATIVE STRUCTURES
ESTABLISHED BETWEEN 1965 AND 1969

The service cooperatives which began to be created in 1965 were set up in a semi-authoritarian fashion. They included the majority of farm owners and imposed on them a new system of regulations and "taxes," which seemed intolerable to those involved. This was why the entire structure put together since 1965 was to be dismantled, going far beyond the wishes of the authorities who in September 1969 began with the elimination of cooperatives.

Elimination of Cooperatives

The first measure decided upon was that of giving up the commercial monopolies which had been granted to the service cooperatives: trading in tomatoes, citrus fruits, etc., was made once again open to all. These measures, together with the withdrawal of the government's moral and financial support of the service cooperatives, caused the activities of each unit to diminish considerably. This is why the cooperatives in each *cheikhat* were closed, with a few exceptions, and were reorganized on the level of the *délégation*. There were to be around ten cooperatives in the whole government territory, instead of about forty.

Moreover, the cooperatives had progressively lost their meaning, inasmuch as they had been deserted by almost all the peasants. The slump in the revenues of the cooperatives and of the Union Régionale des Coopératives (URC), established at Nabeul, meant that it was no longer possible to pay the majority of the officials and clerks hired by the new institutions. Dismissal of URC personnel and of workers in the cooperative offices began at the end of 1969 and went on until 1970–1971, when the URC disappeared entirely.

The service cooperatives vanished completely from the grain-producing zone, where they had never operated at normal capacity. In the market-gardening areas, a large number of cooperatives closed their doors. Even those which survived underwent a considerable reduction in operations. Certain units were kept going if they had been well administered and had not had problems with their members between 1965 and 1969. At Maamoura, for example, the output of canning tomatoes is not large. The cooperative there was not affected by the problems of a crate shortage, delays in payment, and withholdings outside the normal tax structure. In addition, the village had no big businessmen who were organized to ship vegetables to Tunis. That is why the service cooperative there survived and continued to be quite active.

But this sort of continuity has for the most part been quite rare. At Dar Chaabane, the presence of a large number of businessmen — vegetable shippers with a great deal of experience — has, for all practical purposes, put an end to the service cooperative there. The cooperative at El-Haouaria is only a center for selling fertilizers and pesticides on the same terms as those offered by private merchants.

The peasants have thus deserted most of the service cooperatives and have not even sought to regain their dues or the money withheld on their behalf from their shipments of tomatoes or citrus fruits, deductions which were supposed to represent shares of stock. The collapse of the URC was such that it was unable to make any refunds at all. In addition, all the money paid by the peasants had been collected in exactly the same way, as taxes. The peasants' reaction after September 1969 was, in this respect, typical: so long as there was no more talk of cooperatives and so long as the existing cooperatives, service cooperatives included, were eliminated, the peasants were ready to sacrifice all the money which had been paid or withheld.

The cooperative experiment has been completely broken off, and little now remains of the structures set up between 1965 and 1969. The peasants have aided in the discontinuation of a movement whose serious abuses overshadowed its initial virtues. They considered these abuses so intolerable that they were prepared to accept others on the part of private traders and they did not have to wait long before discovering what these abuses were.

The liberalizing of tomato sales quickly led to a decrease in price from 18 dinars per ton for fresh tomatoes to 16 dinars, in spite of the steady rise in costs. The Caisses de Crédit Mutuel no longer granted credit as easily as before. This new situation caused a decline in tomato growing, which was compensated for by the production of other, less perishable and more dependable crops, like peppers, peanuts, etc.

Retention of Service Cooperatives Established Before 1965

The dissolution of the cooperative movement affected only the cooperatives created between 1965 and 1969. Older cooperatives have been retained. The cooperative stations for processing fruits and vegetables at Soliman, Menzel-Bou-Zelfa, and Beni-Khalled resumed their activities on the same basis as before. Only the URC station, established after 1965 at Hammamet, was eliminated, because the citrus growers at Hammamet had no tradition of service cooperatives and the management of the station between 1965 and 1969 had been entirely bureaucratic and had in no way involved the local peasant farmers in its enterprise.

As was the case during the previous phase of the cooperative movement, the cooperative processing stations once again exist side by side with private stations.

The cooperatives' wine cellars have likewise been kept in operation. Private wine makers, however, are allowed to reopen their own cellars, if they so choose. Insofar as most private wine producers were formerly Europeans, this liberalization has had limited effects. Only a few Italian vinegrowers who are naturalized Tunisians, or a few rare Tunisian farmers, are starting to produce wine again. In all, nine-tenths of the wine continues to be produced in the cooperative cellars of the UCCV. But these are cooperative bodies only to a slight extent. Their previous members were primarily European colonists. After the latter left the country, the cooperatives had only a few scattered members remaining, including some of the large Tunisian wine producers. Low volume of wine sales made it impossible for the cooperatives to go on paying rebates to their members. During the difficult period from 1964 to 1969, they provided a genuine public service, taking charge of processing the nation's entire crop of wine grapes. Almost all the vinegrowers are considered by the cooperative cellars not as members but as clients.

Since 1970, the UCCV has decided to open a membership campaign. In addition, each wine cooperative grants its clients, as well as its members, annual credits in the form of fertilizers, pesticides, etc.

The wine cooperatives, like the cooperative processing stations, have shown that they are solidly constructed and are continuing to develop. But they affect only a few thousand members and clients.

The service cooperatives which were created in each *cheikhat* beginning in 1965 and which included tens of thousands of farmers, have turned out to be short-lived. The Caisses de Crédit Mutuel, established during the cooperative period, have not of course disappeared, but their activity has diminished considerably and in practice they have now become mere branches of the Banque Nationale de Tunisie (BNT). In 1970, the local Caisse at Nabeul gave only about 10 loans to the peasants of Tazerka, as opposed to around 100 in 1968. This is because the farmers had large unpaid debts.

The experiment of extending service cooperatives to all the *cheikhats* of Cap Bon was, on the whole, a failure. This failure may be explained by the absence of public participation. The experiment was begun by the government authorities, who used every means, including force, to make all the peasant farmers join. When farmers were free to leave the cooperatives, they abandoned them in droves.

The goal sought by the government was not simply that of providing services for the farmers, as was claimed, but also that of collecting taxes on farm incomes, which were difficult to tax directly. The fiscal purpose of the operation was obvious. The service cooperatives were intended to be a device for modernizing agriculture, a means of developing a commercial economy in the place of subsistence agriculture. Government control over the nation's major form of production, agriculture, would have allowed the state to deduct surpluses which were necessary for financing the developing social services, education, health, etc., as well as for industrialization.

Basically, the failure of the 1965–1969 experiment with cooperatives is a response on the part of the peasantry to the policy of forced withholdings carried out by the state in rural areas. To the extent that these withholdings had a real effect on everyone, whether they farmed on a large, small, or medium scale, opposition increased rapidly and became widespread, especially when the country started on the path toward collectivization, which would give the state absolute control over all farm production.

But now that force has ceased to be used and state intervention has been appreciably diminished, it is difficult to understand why small- and medium-income farmers do not re-establish viable service cooperatives, which are more advantageous to them than the networks of private trade. The government authorities, moreover, are seeking to induce the peasants to organize new service cooperatives which would increase the use of fertilizers and pesticides and would combat the current anarchy on the commercial scene.

The passivity of the peasants can be explained by their disappointment following the 1965–1969 experiment. The peasants prefer the inconveniences of a liberal economy, fearing a return of the abuses of the cooperative period. In addition, the big farmers are the fiercest enemies of service cooperatives, especially in cases where they themselves are merchants and are not at all anxious to create major competition for themselves.

Thus the 1965–1969 experiment has left a huge negative balance: it has discredited the very idea of cooperatives, regardless of type, including even the service cooperatives, which are not at all opposed to the notion of private property. In the future it will be difficult to undertake new experiments with cooperatives. It will probably be necessary first to gain the membership of the masses and to provide them with tangible and un-deniable advantages. Particularly unrealistic would be the desire to bring together in a single body large and small peasant farmers who have divergent, and indeed contradictory, interests. One cannot claim to bring about a social revolution which does not bring perceptible advantages to at least one layer of society.

French Farmers' Cooperatives in Crisis

MICHÈLE BROGNETTI

I.   Cooperatives play an important role in French agriculture.[1] Although cooperative organization developed in other fields as well, in the first half of this century (through the efforts of country notables) and later, paralleling the growing strength of agricultural syndicalism, agricultural cooperatives organized the production and marketing of farm products that was original because it preserved the role of the independent farmer.

At present, cooperative farming is a controversial issue opposing government, farm authorities, and peasant protestors. Because of its origin and the ideology which developed in it, it is the ideal focal point for the struggle between the different tendencies, which have appeared in politics and trade unions in recent years, in relation to changes affecting agriculture. Rural society was long kept isolated from the ideological currents of the wider society by those — landowners, country notables, politicians,

---

[1]   Cooperatives market 75 percent of the wheat, 42 percent of the milk, 37 percent of the wine, 25 percent of the fruit and vegetables, and 10 percent of the meats.

Thirteen cooperative groups have gross sales of more than 100 million francs, against 69 private firms in the line of agriculture and nutrition. Cooperative organizations handle 17 percent of the gross sales of the agro-alimentary industry. Yet, not many cooperatives compare favorably with the most important private French firms. Only four cooperative groups were ranked among the top twenty French concerns in the agro-alimentary line in 1971:

  1:   Gervais-Danone (private), 2.07 billion francs.
  2:   U.L.N. (cooperative), 1.98 billion francs.
 11:   Landerneau (cooperative), 0.92 billion francs.
 14:   UNICOPA (cooperative), 0.69 billion francs.
 20:   Ancenis (cooperative), 0.55 billion francs. These cooperative groups have large memberschips: 52,000 in U.L.N., 20,000 in Landerneau, UNICOPA (the two main cooperative groups in Brittany), and Ancenis.

etc. — whose interests lay in keeping the peasant electorate ignorant and submissive, a factor of political stability. Rural people traditionally conceived of cooperatives as the ideal meeting place for all agricultural workers (peasants, laborers, cooperative officials) and all independent farmers. The cooperative reflects all the farmers who belong, whether they are small or large, modern or backward. The farmer or the sharecropper is on an equal footing with the landlord, thus neutralizing the class struggle.

For several years, cooperative agriculture has been going through a crisis. Its value is once more challenged violently in some regions (Brittany, Loire Valley, Vosges), where the farm population is large and the size of farms is small.[2] The most violent struggle broke out in Brittany (May-June 1972).[3] Cooperative farming developed late — only after World War II — in this region, which was lagging behind only a short time ago. But its growth was rapid. Today Brittany occupies an important position as a producer of livestock, the only commodity that can still be produced profitably on small farms.

Cooperative farming was the answer which the trade unionists of western France (Brittany and the Loire Valley) proposed around 1960 as a solution for the problems of farmers who had modernized. Ten years later, cooperation was challenged by these same union men, with whom younger farmers, all designating themselves as peasant-workers, have aligned themselves.

What has happened in the meantime? Agro-alimentary concerns are being set up in Brittany, either directly or by acquiring local concerns which are on the verge of bankruptcy. Craftsmen are losing control of the

---

[2] For example, in Brittany, the average tillable acreage (S.A.U. — surface agricole utile) of farms having more than one hectare is 14 hectares. Half of the farms have an acreage of less than 11 hectares and utilize 19.3 percent of the S.A.U.; 7 percent of the farms (that is, 1,080) have an acreage greater than or equal to 50 hectares (64 hectares on the average) and make use of 3.6 percent of the S.A.U. (*Recensement Général de l'Agriculture* 1970–71).

A family farm rarely owns more than 40 cows. The average herd in Brittany is 16.9 head of cattle, of which 8.7 are cows. The average yield per year is under 3,000 liters of milk per cow.

[3] The milk strike or war: during two weeks (from May 18 to June 5, 1972) in Brittany and in several other regions of France, farmers refused to deliver milk to cooperatives or private concerns in order to force an increase in the price of milk, which is the same regardless of the type of concern because price is established by agreement among all the dairy farmers. The strike, the initiative for which came from the peasant-workers, developed outside the union structures. This was the first time that a movement of this size had taken place in rural France. It shows that the time has passed for demonstrating before public authorities at the instigation of the F.N.S.E.A. or C.N.J.A. to demand governmental measures favorable to farmers (price supports, subsidies, etc.). Farmers do as laborers do and attack the businesses upon which their incomes depend.

processing and marketing of farm produce. A new kind of relationship between cooperatives and farmers is emerging, making traditional cooperative ideology obsolete and giving rise to a different analysis of cooperative farming.

Cooperative farming is considered to be a characteristic agricultural institution, which farm organizations and labor unions have always supported. It is one expression of the view that agricultural society is a privileged world all by itself, different from society as a whole. This special quality is based on the continued presence to this day of a farm enterprise in which family and work coincide: the family farm. The vast majority of French agricultural enterprises are small trade concerns which employ few, if any, hired hands, and in which the manager of the farm owns the means of production.

The ideology which has developed around farmers' cooperatives is opposed to capitalism. In the eyes of farmers, the position of the peasant, sole master over his farm, seems infinitely preferable to that of the worker who is subjected to the demands of capitalistic industry. The farmer fears proletarianization and sees in cooperative organization a means of protection against this degradation. Indeed, cooperative farming seeks first of all the betterment of mankind. The end is Man, not profit. If cooperative organization is civilized, capitalism is savage. Farmers should be pleased that cooperatives keep them marginal to the economic system. In fact, the cooperative is a peculiar society, in which the farmer, however small and impoverished, is like every other member, coowner of all the property and equipment of the cooperative of which he is a member, thanks to shares levied on his contributions in farm produce. He is a boss. But unfortunately, not many farmers have this feeling, since only a few of them feel they are participating in decisions. Nevertheless, that is the magical affirmation which, when workers of a cooperative are on strike, can make a strikebreaker of a farmer.

Each farmer who is a member of a cooperative has the right to vote. He expresses his opinion once a year in the Assemblée Générale by selecting his delegates (the directors), according to the principle, "one man, one vote." During all the rest of the year, directors meet once a month with their president (elected from among themselves) and the salaried director of the cooperative. They decide on absolutely everything from investments to short-term loans, which are made by the cooperative to one of their number. Each director, in a completely informal manner at random meetings, channels decisions back to the lower echelons. One frequently finds cooperative members who are unaware of major decisions taken several months previously by the board of directors, and who do not try to find out about them. Certain clues would lead one to suspect that the director of a cooperative also has the role of sounding out possible reactions of the membership when a reputedly unpopular measure must be passed.

It is verifiable that the terms of office of directors and president are remarkably stable, especially in older cooperatives. The terms of salaried directors are also notably stable. It is not easy to dismiss these officers legally, but the reason for the long terms is to be found in the elected directors long-standing custom of relying upon their cooperative director to make decisions which they deem themselves incapable of judging. Democracy, as it is exercised in cooperatives, is the result of a long history of ignorance and deference to authority.

Cooperative ideology has been assimilated only by key agricultural personnel (officers of cooperatives, administrative personnel of unions, public authorities) and by the most progressive of the farmers. Most farmers believe "*la coopération, c'est bien à condition qu'elle paye autant que le privé*" [cooperatives are fine as long as they pay as much as private enterprise]. In expressing this opinion, they have the reputation of selling to the cooperative what they are unable to sell elsewhere (except when the contractual basis of production prevents them from doing so). In large, polyvalent cooperatives, farmers are encouraged to deliver all their produce to the cooperative, but they do so only if they see in it private gain.

II.   French peasants, who are reputed individualists, persons of habit, and traditionalists, adopted cooperative organization from the end of the nineteenth century on. But if the promoters of cooperatives were idealists, adepts of the utopian socialists, the farmers themselves accepted the institution and rejected the ideology. Cooperatives were never conceived of as providing a collective structure to farming. They were conceived of as a confederation of little producers, with each individual entrepreneur cut off from the others.

The development of cooperatives in the milieu of agriculture has not seemingly changed the isolation of farmers. Members of the same cooperative are not necessarily neighbors. In the same commune, milk producers may deliver to four or five different concerns; it never happens that all the producers of one commune are members of the same concern. Having membership in the same cooperative does not necessarily create ties. Accordingly, the cooperative has hardly challenged peasant individualism. Farmers see each other once a year in the general assembly and at the banquet which follows. There are winter regional news meetings in large cooperatives, but these are not attended by all. The farmer goes to the cooperative to get his fertilizer and feed — but he can have these items delivered as well. He is visited by technicians for compulsory inspection; he receives the truck which delivers young animals and which returns for them once they are fattened (the truck comes every day for milk pick-up). The member of a cooperative remains isolated on his farm, as much so as the client of private enterprise. The latter has neither the instructional meeting, nor for the most part the general assembly, but in some cases there exists a group of producers who meet. The dissatisfied member, who believes himself wronged in the appraisal of his produce or by a delay in services due him, can go to see the director of the cooperative; this is fairly easy in small coops, but is rather difficult in large ones.

Relationships between farmers are exterior to the cooperative. Farmers who are part of C.N.J.A.[4] are acquainted and continue to meet, even if they reside in different *départments*, whereas they do not know and may even scorn many members of the cooperative to which they belong. Cooperatives have only perpetuated the isolation of the farmer, and no doubt the cooperative concern turns that to advantage. The farmer is alone when he receives receipt of payment for his produce; he can go to complain to his neighbor who, not selling to the same cooperative, gets the same total price, but with differences in the details of the components. Thus a genuine comparison is impossible. (Let us disregard the case of those who do not tell their neighbors what they earn.) The isolation of the farmer, despite some improvement, has not permitted him to see his problems on the level of total society. Not being able to project beyond the limits of his *canton* or neighborhood relationships, he did not suspect that his problems had any causes other than human incompetence and dishonesty.

Farm cooperatives which were created directly before or after the war of 1939–1945 continued to follow established routines for a long time. For want of having renewed their board of directors and other personnel, they became sclerotic; continuing well into the sixties they remained blind to market research, rationalization of production, and marketing

---

4   The Jeunesse Agricole Catholique (J.A.C.) was founded in 1929 by young peasants at the instigation of priests. About 1955, some J.A.C. militants who had reached the age of 25–28 (at which time they were supposed to leave the J.A.C.), refused to drop their concern for the peasant problems they had spent ten years studying, neither in favor of the younger generation of farmers, nor of the F.N.S.E.A. members who were older than they were and who did not share their views. They persuaded the F.N.S.E.A. (Fédération Nationale des Syndicats d'Exploitants Agricoles, i.e. National Federation of Unions of Independent Farmers) to found a union, the Centre Nationale des Jeunes Agriculteurs (C.N.J.A.), independent of the F.N.S.E.A., in which militants of the J.A.C. assumed key positions. The modernist and reformist ideas of the C.N.J.A. of the time contributed to the development of the law on orientation of farming in 1962.

problems. Advantages accruing to cooperatives, such as government aid, subsidies, tax exemptions, low interest loans from Crédit Agricole (Farm Credit), allowed them to survive without effort. Cooperatives in this case shielded the small farm from the outside world, but also from progress. In spite of a strong trend toward modernization in the days after the war — mechanization spread and production increased — French agriculture, long protected from foreign competition, had remained traditional. General farming with livestock production was still in 1945 the principal type of farming, except in areas of extensive cultivation (Beauce, Soissonais). Consequently, production was unpredictable, because it was subjected to climatic variation and to seasonal rhythms of animal life; it was sporadic, because each peasant sold only a small quantity at a time; it was not very uniform because the herd lacked standardization (little or no selection). To that production corresponded a marketing network equally scattered and not very effective (a large number of middlemen), consisting of wholesale merchants working locally, alone or with their families, who were only the first of numerous go-betweens from production to consumption. As to processing, it was not very well developed, and produce was generally marketed without processing.

To a farm operated without knowledge of bookkeeping corresponded a small cooperative which was managed without concern for profit making, and where turnover was stagnant. The sudden interest in farm production, which was shown by large financial houses, jolted farm society and launched it into an evolution which transformed the lives of farmers, and which alarmed them.

III.   About 1960, concerns arose which encouraged farmers to develop new crops. Farm production also began to attract concerns of national importance (for example, the Périer group, with financial backing from the Lazard bank, has bought interests in a large number of agro-alimentary industries). At that time farmers were solicited endlessly by canvassers who came to offer them the services of the interested firms. Thus, intensive stock farming developed in France, especially in Brittany, with considerable lag behind the other countries of Europe. Dairy farming experienced a notable increase. Farming became the direct supplier of raw materials for the growing agro-alimentary industry.

Farmers with a high degree of consciousness, such as militants of the C.N.J.A., would like to see cooperatives concern themselves with these crops because they fear domination by capitalist enterprises. They are afraid of losing their position as independent producers, since in the ideology which developed around cooperation, they associate family farming with cooperatives while equating capitalism with wage-earning. They are brought to this understanding of the problem by the development of "integration"[5] in the line of intensive stock farming, which seems to them to be a definite threat. Indeed, in integrated production producers are tied to the integrating enterprise by a complex of obligations. They lose all independence in the choice of techniques of production because these are imposed by the firm and are controlled by a technician from the firm. They lose all independence in marketing, inasmuch as they are obliged to sell to the firm to which they are tied. Deprived of all initiative, they merely follow instructions; some say they have become little better than manual laborers.

Most of the shrewdest farmers have been shaped by the Jeunesse Agricole Catholique. They acquired from it practical instruction and a humane orientation which distinguish them from other farmers, and from the older ones in particular. In order to become heads of enterprises, they accepted the necessity of hard work and of going heavily into debt. They made a powerful union of the group of young farmers, the C.N.J.A. In a few years they persuaded the government to pass measures which would aid young farmers in making a profitable business out of the family-operated farm. The result was the *Loi d'orientation* of 1962, which established subsidies, low interest loans, and land companies. Because of their personal qualities, these farmers were led to assume positions of authority (such as directorships) in unions and cooperatives, as well as in groups devoted to popularization.

These farmers hoped for the founding of cooperatives which would engage in intensive livestock farming. Dairy cooperatives united and made pooled investments. They were interested not only in marketing produce, but in processing it as well. The resulting concentration and modernization created cooperatives of a size previously unheard of, which assumed

[5] The contract of integration defined relations between farmer and concern. The conditions of contract are the same, whether the integrating concern is cooperative or private. If it involves rearing young animals, the concern supplies to the grazier, generally, the young animals and feed which, according to previous studies, should insure maximum growth. The firm supplies technical assistants: technicians from the firm watch over the growth of the animals, which should follow a definite curve. Sometimes the integrating enterprise has a staff veterinarian, but his services are not gratis to the grower. The enterprise decides the time when the animals must be marketed. The price paid to the grazier is generally the average price for the week or month (in general there is no guaranteed price). One might observe that it is less a question of exchange than of an operation subjected to a series of instructions which the farmer must follow. The firm, on the other hand, has no obligation apart from marketing the finished product when it chooses.

regional, and not only local importance. Corresponding to these dynamic cooperatives are farmers who do not hesitate to update their methods of farming or to invest. Both bring about changes which affect the structure of farming and the mentality of the farmer.

Faced with the threat of bankruptcy, the farmer began to calculate his income, to learn bookkeeping, and to improve his farming techniques in order to reduce his production costs. He was plunged headlong into acquiring technical know-how from specialists who were strangers in the rural world. As opposed to traditional knowledge, which is handed down from father to son and is relatively unchangeable, this knowledge is perpetually changing, though once it is acquired it is retained. This is the break from rural society by the most dynamic farmers, the most educated (self-taught), who have adopted the culture and life of townsmen, thus putting an end to the artificial unity of farm society. Neighborhood relationships disintegrate while relationships emerge among men with common problems and activities. Farmers who have brought about this revolution in their farming and in their lives would like to see the profession of farming become a profession like all others; to be specific, a profession which supports a decent living. Modernization of farming and cooperative organization have not been successful in overcoming the increasing gulf between farm income and the generally increasing incomes and salaries in France. The family-operated farm lost its independence with post-war mechanization. It definitely entered into the world economy when it was able to invest and then borrow very large sums of money.[6]

Between 1960 and 1970, competition among agro-alimentary corporations was fierce. Cooperatives in search of market openings had to peddle their products in order to corner the markets. This made it necessary to lower their production costs and, in consequence, to reduce as much as possible the amount paid to producers. The latter were paid in proportion to their production and not in proportion to the labor supplied. The value of farm produce is generally determined by market prices. Cooperatives and concerns deduct their charges (for collection of produce and transportation to the factory) from this. The items which cooperatives supply to the producer (feed, fertilizer, medicines, young livestock) have fixed prices (with a tendency to increase). The producer receives the balance remaining after they have deducted from the selling price of his produce

---

[6]   A study which was made of a small region of Morbihan, a Breton administrative district, showed that the capital still owed by integrated farmers varied between 2,000 and 3,000 francs per hectare, that is to say, half of the book value of the land in this region (Lamarche 1971).

the cost of items which were sold him at fixed prices. In case of a slump, it may be that the payment to the producer covers only the production costs and his labor is underpaid or is not paid at all. For other commodities (milk, for example), the government fixes a regional price index at the beginning of the season. Cooperatives and private enterprises determine among themselves the price to be paid locally, in accordance with the price scale of the region.

Compelled to struggle against private firms, cooperatives adopted their methods. The many agreements of market sharing and pooling of investments occurring between cooperatives and private firms demonstrate this point. Cooperatives were required to make large investments to insure processing of produce, but in spite of that, they were not capable of doing the necessary market research in time to design a trademark and to set up a network of sales outlets. They were rivaled in their own territory by cooperatives from outside Brittany. Processing of farm produce by the cooperative had to allow the farmer to realize the value of his produce and to profit from the increase in value. But processing calls for large investments, which must be amortized with increasing rapidity (in five to six months for fresh produce) and which are immediately replaced by others. And payment on capital is made before payment to the producer.

The *Loi d'orientation* of 1962 stipulated that cooperatives must acquire the efficiency of private firms. The Fifth and Sixth Development Plans have written into their programs that the food industry, still scattered and craft-like in some areas, must concentrate and industrialize in order to meet European competition. Acting in conjunction with these projects, the minister of agriculture set up appropriate measures to sharpen the struggle between private enterprise and cooperatives.

The minister of agriculture is able to impose his policy through cooperatives and groups of producers, since he has complete authority over Crédit Agricole, the licensed banker of farmers and cooperatives. On this issue, a bill which was being debated in the National Assembly in 1973 is very clear. It calls for development of agro-alimentary industries, private and cooperative, thanks to Crédit Agricole, which will finance not only those organizations which group the farmers, but also industrialists who are interested in food products. The main duty which falls to the cooperative is forwarding directives from the Ministry of Agriculture, as well as the financial grants which reinforce them. This tends to orient production and to give direction to the farms.

Changes in rules of procedure of Crédit Agricole determined that cooperatives will be financed the same as other agro-alimentary concerns, that farmers will no longer be the sole recipients of this credit, and thus that farm society will no longer have privileges which protect it from competition. It is obvious that the private manufacturer has no reason to deal gently with the small farm. In any case, for a long time the cooperative has not protected the small farmers. Numerous cooperatives have rid themselves of members who are not very profitable by enforcing a modernization of farming which small producers found beyond their reach, and by demanding from others an increase in productive capacity. Cooperatives desiring to be competitive were obliged to reorganize production and to obtain a reduction in the production costs for farming. Such cooperatives have rather remarkable growth rates.[7] On the other hand, most of the farmers who accepted the challenge of becoming "true entrepreneurs" have not been able to escape the vicious circle of ever-increasing loans and exhausting work that never ends. Although the owner of his means of production, the farmer is bureaucratized and advised by the cooperative which imposes on him the same methods and the same prices that private concerns would do.

Power, while lost on the farm, should theoretically be exercised by the farmer within the cooperative; but the cooperative, under the effects of competition, obeys economic imperatives which are those of private enterprise and inconsistent with the exercise of democracy by producers. Cooperatives increased in size, those of local influence growing to regional importance, and the already feeble contacts between the farmer and those in positions of authority in the cooperative disappeared along with the last links which allowed a member of a cooperative to consider himself to be different from the client of a private firm.

IV.   Some disappointed farmers are beginning to think that the success of the farmer on his own farm and the growth of the cooperative are antagonistic. Farmers who have regrouped under the name of "peasant-workers" developed their thinking along these lines. The movement originated among union members in western France who, in their region in the past two years were also instigators of short, violent actions directed not against public authorities, as is usually the case, but against the private industries upon whom they depended. The violence was in direct propor-

[7]   As an example, one can mention the two foremost French alimentary groups, one private and the other cooperative: the rate of growth of the gross sales for Gervais-Danone (private) from 1970 to 1971 was 18.5 percent; that of Union Laitière Normande (U.L.N., cooperative) was 23.5 percent. In Brittany, the gross sales for the cooperative group UNICOPA was increased 7.5 times from 1965 to 1971, an average growth of more than 40 percent.

tion to the degree that the political consciousness of the farmers was aroused against the cooperatives.

These farmers, to be sure, were conscious of their defeat. All realized that they were doomed, not only to work without respite in order to pay off their loans but also to invest endlessly. They did not become "true entrepreneurs" but instead became peasant-workers. The peasant-worker defines himself as one who works alone or with his wife, with or without familial help and without hired hands, on a small farm (25 to 30 hectares at the most). He is owner of the means of production, which he can buy through loans from Crédit Agricole. When an investment is paid off, it generally must be replaced. The peasant-worker is perpetually in debt. Individual appropriation of the means of production, far from making the peasant-worker a capitalist, is a liability rather than an asset. The peasant-worker and his family live from their labor. The payment for this labor is insufficient, often lower than S.M.I.C.,[8] and it cannot pay him or any members of his family to work on his farm. The price which he is paid for his produce does not cover his production costs. A farmer fitting this description is not head of the enterprise, contrary to the myth which is spread by the C.N.J.A. in its talk. He lives from his labor alone. His position is the same, whether he is a member of a cooperative or a client of a private firm. In either case, he must get along like all other workers in order to maintain his standard of living and to try to improve it. As a worker facing an employer, he demands from agro-alimentary industries a price, which covers his cost of production and guarantees a wage equal to the S.M.I.C. He considers the position of the salaried employee, which he had dreaded several years earlier, preferable to his own.

In revolt against a traditional analysis of cooperatives, the peasant-workers have questioned their place in society. They no longer see themselves as an essential part of rural society, but as workers allied with all other laborers. They want most the backing of the employees of the cooperatives: they want farmers to support the cooperative employees when they go on strike; they want the employees to support the farmer, when the latter refuses to deliver his produce. This alliance between peasants and laborers of cooperatives is a noteworthy event: in the traditional ideology, the farmer is a boss of his cooperative, and in the case of a strike he is encouraged to be a strikebreaker, while contradictorily it is maintained that coop members, staff, and workers all have a common interest in the smooth operation of the cooperative. Cooperatives are unassailable

---

[8] S.M.I.C., *Salaire minimum interprofessionnel de croissance* [progressive interprofessional minimum wage], which up to 31 December ,1972 was about 700 francs per month based on a forty-hour work week.

then from all sides. But nevertheless, the peasant-workers attack them: they want to ally themselves with other workers (those of industry, in particular) against employers (who correspond to the staff and director of the cooperative). And thus they depart from the agrarian milieu where agrarian institutions (mutuals, etc.) and cooperatives have shut them in — an isolation which their unions have sustained.

REFERENCES

CANEVET, CORENTIN
   1971   *La coopération agricole en Bretagne.* Etude géographique. Thèse de troisième cycle. Rennes.
GARNIER, P., D. LEY, A. PLAUD
   1971   *L'organisation contractuelle des productions animales en Bretagne.* Essai de description. Rennes: ENSA.
LAMARCHE, HUGUES
   1971   *La région centrale du Morbihan.* Paris: C. N. R. S.
LAMBERT, BERNARD
   1970   *Les paysans dans la lutte des classes.* (Collection "Politique.") Paris: Editions du Seuil.
   n.d.   "Une agriculture au service des travailleurs." *Frères du Monde* 54–55:1–96. Bordeaux.
Recensement Général de l'Agriculture
1970–71 *General Census of Agriculture*, France.

The Political Role of Cooperatives in Maharashtra, India

B. S. BAVISKAR

BACKGROUND

Maharashtra is one of the larger states of India in terms of both its area and its population. The political leaders and political parties in the state played an important role in the freedom movement before Independence, and they continue to play an important part in national politics today. During the struggle for independence, Maharashtra produced eminent national leaders, among them Tilak, Ranade, and Gokhale. Most of the founders of the various political parties, including the Communist party of India, the Socialist party, and the Hindu Maha Sabha, have come from Maharashtra. The state suffered a political decline after the death of Tilak and during the Gandhi era in Indian politics. However, after the 1930's the Congress party emerged as the strongest party, with a mass following, when it attracted the leading men from the dominant peasant caste of Marathas and the other non-Brahmin castes.

Since Independence the state has been dominated by the Congress party. Although the top leaders of the several opposition parties came from Maharashtra, they have not successfully challenged the overwhelming position of the Congress except for a short period following the second general election in 1957, when the opposition parties seriously jolted the position of the Congress party through the popular movement for the creation of a separate state of Maharashtra. The Congress rule in Maharashtra, unlike its rule in many other states, has been fairly stable, without any serious dissensions within it ranks.

Apart from some historical reasons (which I shall not discuss here), two major factors have contributed to the dominant position of the Congress party. First, most members of the dominant caste have been with the Congress all this time. They constitute a solid block of about 40 percent of the total population in the state. The next largest single caste group consists of the neo-Buddhists, the former untouchables, who comprise about 9 percent of the population. These people were known as Mahars before their conversion to Buddhism in 1956, following a call by their leader, Dr. B. R. Ambedkar. Although the Mahars are numerically a fairly large group, because of various disabilities they are not in a position to challenge the power of the Marathas. Second, the Congress party derives its strength mainly from the network of local power structures such as the *panchayat raj* institutions and the cooperatives. In fact, the party derives its strength primarily from its control over the cooperatives at various levels.

Maharashtra is a leading state in the field of cooperatives. (Again, I shall not go into the historical factors responsible for the relatively significant growth of cooperatives in Maharashtra.) After Independence the cooperatives received a great impetus from government policy and various programs for economic development.

Although cooperation was introduced as far back as 1904 in the Cooperative Societies Act, for a long time it was confined mainly to agricultural credit. Even in this limited sphere, it did not make much progress except in the former provinces of Bombay and Madras. Its extension into other spheres was slow and limited. The picture has changed significantly during the last twenty-five years. The number of cooperatives and their membership and capital have grown several times. Cooperative activity has also been extended significantly into such spheres as marketing, processing, farming, banking, and housing. Cooperatives now deal with the intersets of millions of people, handle vast amounts of money, and command numerous resources. As a result, the politicians and political parties find it politically advantageous to work in them.

To give an idea about the spread of cooperatives in Maharashtra, let me give some details about Ahmednagar District,[1] one of the twenty-six districts in the state. This district has an extensive network of about 1,400 primary cooperatives, covering almost every village. The district has ten cooperative sugar factories. These factories together provide regular employment for more than 13,000 workers and crush more than 2,500,000 tons of sugarcane annually. The annual turnover of each factory is about 100,000,000 rupees. The District Central Cooperative Bank of Ahmednagar annually distributes loans of more than 100,000,000 rupees. The district has about a dozen marketing societies, some of which handle huge

---

[1]   For a social, economic, and political background of the region, see Baviskar (1969).

amounts in their transactions every year. The position is more or less similar in several other districts.

The above description will give some idea about the extent of the growth of cooperatives in the state and the vital role they play in the lives of many people. Thus the cooperatives in Maharashtra have many achievements to their credit. More important, these cooperatives are run on the initiative of local leaders who have emerged from among the members, whose interests are safeguarded by the cooperatives. Unlike many other areas, the management of cooperatives is subjected to little official interference. This has helped the emergence and growth of a genuine cooperative leadership.

COOPERATIVES AND POLITICS BEFORE INDEPENDENCE

The association between cooperatives, on the one hand, and politicians and political parties, on the other, has increased significantly since Independence. Broadly speaking, the following factors seem to have contributed to this development: the policy of alien rulers to discourage emergence of spontaneous leadership in the cooperative field, the reluctance of politicians to actively participate in the cooperative movement before Independence, the increase in the scope and scale of the movement, and the demands of democratic politics since Independence.

Under colonial rule, as Gadgil (1963:69–70) pointed out, initiative in cooperative work was almost invariably taken by the government and its officials. The alien rulers tended to discourage spontaneous leadership in the potentially powerful cooperative organizations. Such a leadership, they feared, would pose a challenge to their own rule. Leaders with nationalist leanings and associations with political activities were therefore "looked down upon by the alien government in entrusting any such work." The nonofficial leadership in cooperatives consisted largely of loyalists or those who were not opposed, at least not militantly opposed, to colonial rule. Any work in the cooperatives required a degree of collaboration with the government. In the days of the anti-British struggle, politicians in general did not favor such a "collaborationist" role. They also found cooperative work to be highly limited in political effectiveness. For example, there was no place for cooperatives in Gandhi's constructive program. It was only after Independence that the cooperative movement received full popular support. Thus the slow and limited growth of the cooperatives was associated with the lack of interest on the part of the political leaders in the pre-Independence period. There was a separation between the leaders of cooperatives and the leaders in the political sphere.

COOPERATIVES AND POLITICS AFTER INDEPENDENCE

As described above, cooperative activities have increased in the state as a result of both the government's policy and the initiative of the local leaders. No cooperative can function successfully on the basis of governmental support alone. It needs the initiative and drive of the members and their leaders. Such a leadership can emerge only if the cooperatives perform certain important economic functions vital to the interests of the people. Cooperatives in Maharashtra seem to perform these functions very effectively and they have generated a great deal of popular interest and enthusiasm among the people. The encouragement and support from the government as well as its policy of noninterference in the management of the cooperatives have further strengthened these institutions.

If the cooperatives have changed qualitatively and quantitatively since Independence, so has politics in the state. After Independence, India's adoption of a democratic political system based on adult franchise resulted in competition among various political groups and parties to capture and retain power at the various levels. The demands of democratic politics since Independence have induced politicians and political parties to take an active part in the management of cooperatives. The adoption of a democratic constitution based on adult suffrage and the program of *panchayat raj* have significantly changed the style of politics, at least in the rural areas. To get elected a politician has to build a following for himself. For this purpose he tries to strengthen the traditional networks of relationships based on caste, kinship, and village loyalties, as well as to establish new networks of relationships based on distribution of loans, jobs, and other forms of patronage. This is done through his control over local cooperatives and *panchayat raj* institutions. Post-Independence politics thus induces politicians to take an active interest in the work of cooperatives.

To understand politics from the village to the district level in Maharashtra, one must take into account the three most crucial political structures: (1) the *panchayat raj* institutions, consisting of village *panchayats* [councils], *taluka panchayat samities,* and a *zilla parishad* [district council]; (2) the various cooperative institutions, including the primary village cooperative societies, marketing societies, processing industries such as the cooperative sugar factories, and district central cooperative banks; and (3) in district politics, the organization of political parties, mainly the dominant Congress party. Thus the *panchayat raj* institutions, the cooperatives, and the Congress party organization together constitute the real stuff of district politics in Maharashtra and several other states.

As we shall see later, these three structures are interrelated. The politicians try to control these, and controlling one structure helps them to control the others as well. Thus, at the village level, the village *panchayat* and the village cooperative society are the most important structures. Control over these structures in the villages helps the political leaders to control the politics of the district through the district-level *panchayat* bodies, cooperatives, and party organization.

Links Between Cooperatives and Politics

Cooperative institutions and politics have a symbiotic relationship. To describe the nature of political involvement of cooperatives, the following questions must be examined: (1) Why is there an intense struggle for power over the control of some of the cooperatives? (2) How do politicians come to occupy important positions in many of them? (3) Why do political parties or factions take keen interest in the affairs of cooperatives?

The affairs of many cooperatives in Maharashtra are characterized by competition between rival personalities and factions for control over their management. This is true not only of the bigger and more important cooperatives, such as the district central banks, sugar factories, and sale and purchase unions but also of smaller cooperatives at the village level. In villages this leads to the establishment of more than one cooperative performing the same functions.

The struggle for control over a cooperative becomes particularly intense during the election of its management committee. The rival contenders for power resort to various means to win over the voters. Various pressures are used to induce voters; much money is spent and other resources are exploited to capture a cooperative. Greater efforts are made in the case of bigger cooperatives. In parts of Maharashtra candidates for directorships of cooperative sugar factories and banks spend from 5,000 to 10,000 rupees each. Sometimes the technique of "kidnapping" the "key" voters is employed to ensure the election of a particular candidate as director or chairman. In the areas where there are many cooperatives, people always appear to be preparing for one election or another, making the rivalry between contenders for power perpetual and all-pervading.

A certain degree of competition and rivalry seems to be inherent in the structure of cooperatives organized along democratic lines. The cooperative movement, almost from its beginning, has functioned democratically. Because all members are equals as voters and are equally entitled to seek an office, the competition for power seems to be normal, if not inevitable.

The keenness shown by members in the elections is generally a reflection of their interest in the cooperative and its affairs and of their willingness to participate in its working. It indicates at least that they are not indifferent toward it. This is of special significance for the growth of the movement. Ostergaard and Halsey (1965:73) have reported that many cooperatives in England face "a problem of apathy" on the part of their members. This is indicated by poor attendance (0.5 percent) at the business meetings and poor voting (1.65 percent) in the elections to the managing committees. In contrast, in Maharashtra more than 50 percent of the members attend the general meetings and more than 95 percent vote in the elections of cooperative sugar factories, sale and purchase unions, banks, and other cooperatives. This is evidence of greater awareness and desire for participation on the part of the members. Of course, the various regions of the state and the various types of cooperatives exhibit some differences in this regard. Generally speaking, those cooperatives that are vital to the economic life of the members are characterized by a greater degree of participation and consequently by a greater competition for control over them.

The leaders invest considerable money, time, and energy to get elected to important positions in the cooperatives. The control over a cooperative ensures the economic interests of the leaders and provides for other material gains. But it also confers prestige and provides access to patronage and power. It is no surprise that some of the political leaders find chairmanship of a sugar factory or a cooperative bank more attractive than membership in a legislature. The cooperatives, along with the *panchayat raj* institutions, have emerged as new centers of power. The control of these centers provides ambitious individuals with an opportunity for advancement. In a sense, leadership of cooperatives provides a new avenue to mobility. This is particularly significant in a society in which other avenues to mobility are limited. As a result of all these factors, the new centers of power have become arenas of political rivalry.

Politicians occupy key positions in many cooperatives. The majority of members of the legislative Assembly and Members of Parliament in the state have played prominent parts in the cooperative field. Most of the politicians in rural Maharashtra, particularly those belonging to the Congress party, are intimately associated with cooperatives in their areas. Several party bosses and ministers in the state cabinet have occupied top positions in cooperative sugar factories, banks, and other institutions.

The important question is, How did politicians come to occupy major positions in the cooperatives and how do they continue to do so? With the extension of the cooperative sector and the vital role assigned to it in the government's planning for economic development, politicians realized the importance of controlling these new centers of power. The new centers provide them with reliable and durable bases for building up their followings in the area through the distribution of favors and patronage. Moreover, control over cooperatives helps them to secure control over *panchayat* bodies, educational institutions, and the party organization, and facilitates entry in the legislatures. Thus, controlling cooperatives means dominating the political system in general, at least at the local level. In Maharashtra, one cannot understand local politics without understanding the local cooperatives, and vice versa.

A politician, in order to acquire power, needs both resources and skills. Participating in cooperatives and the constant efforts required to retain control over them helps him to improve his political skills. More important, cooperatives provide the necessary scarce resources, both human and material, for his political activities. This is particularly evident during elections. In every general election there are reports in local papers about the use of vehicles and other resources of cooperatives in the campaigns of many candidates in various parts of Maharashtra. Not only do the candidates for the Legislative Assembly and Parliament use the resources, including the vehicles and employees, of the cooperatives under their control, but many cooperative societies contribute indirectly, if not directly, a substantial part of the election funds of these candidates. During the last assembly elections, held in 1972, some of the candidates who controlled important cooperatives were reported to have spent 300,000 to 500,000 rupees on their election campaigns, and most of this amount came not from their own pockets, but from the coffers of the cooperatives under their control.

In Maharashtra many congressmen occupy key positions in various cooperatives. The role of a congressman often overlaps with that of a cooperator. But the party is involved in cooperatives in other ways as well. It uses them as its political instruments. They often contribute, directly or indirectly, to party funds. There are several instances of party meetings, party workers' conferences, and party volunteer camps being held on the premises of cooperatives. In some cases, cooperatives acted as hosts to these gatherings and provided all the necessary facilities. It is quite common for leaders to use the vehicles of cooperatives for transportation to party conferences at distant places. The association with cooperatives and its resources proves most useful to the party, particularly during elections. It is therefore not surprising that congressmen in Maharasthra are often encouraged to be active in cooperatives by their top leaders.

Although, before Independence, the Congress party was not opposed to the ideology and program of the cooperative movement, it did not participate actively in it for reasons discussed above. After Independence, it started to take an active interest in the cooperative movement. This has been necesssitated largely by the transformation of the Congress itself from a movement to a party. As a movement, it was dependent on a mass following and was inspired by nationalistic ideology and sentiments. As a party, it has to compete with rival parties and to build bases of support to acquire and retain power. It can no longer do this on the basis of ideology and sentiments alone. It has had to create a following based on networks of patronage. The cooperatives and *panchayats* have provided a fertile soil for developing these networks. It is important that the cooperative movement has received a great impetus from the Congress government since Independence. It has become one of the basic programs of rural reconstruction. As a result, members of the ruling party have come to be associated increasingly with the cooperatives.

The control over cooperatives makes a significant difference in the relative strengths of political parties, particularly in the rural areas. The Congress party is by far the most powerful party in Maharashtra because of its historical role in the freedom movement and the relative weakness of other parties. What are the sources of its strength? The Congress in Maharashtra is identified with the interests of the dominant peasant caste of Marathas, as are the cooperatives and *panchayat* bodies. The leaders of the party at the national level attribute the strength of the party in Maharashtra mainly to its "constructive activities" in the cooperative field.

Political Functions of Cooperatives

The political involvement of cooperatives has implications for the wider political system. Economic objectives are the manifest functions of cooperatives, but certain political functions that are latent in nature are also performed.

The early leaders of the cooperative movement in the West emphasized the economic functions of the movement, but in adopting democratic principles in managing the cooperatives, they were aiming to achieve something more. They hoped that by participating in cooperatives the members would learn the lessons of self-government. Past experience justified their hopes. Through cooperatives, members learn the rules of the democratic game. Participation in cooperatives also promotes the development of new values and attitudes toward political institutions and toward the individual's role as a member of the democratic society. Cooperatives thus perform the function of political socialization in relation to the wider political system.

Cooperatives in Maharashtra are also performing the function of political recruitment. Several observers have noted the change in the character of political leadership since Independence. The old upper-caste, Western-educated, middle-class, and urban-based leadership is being replaced by a new peasant-caste, vernacular-educated, and village-based leadership. While there are several other factors contributing to this change, it cannot be denied that cooperatives, along with *panchayats*, provide a new source for the recruitment to the political elite. The cooperatives contribute to the training of aspiring politicians and provide them approved means of acquiring a political base. Cooperatives also provide a training ground for acquiring and developing political skills and building support that is useful in the wider political arena. It is not surprising, therefore, that a large majority of political leaders in Maharashtra, from the village to the state level, have emerged from work in the cooperatives of various kinds and at various levels.

Cooperatives also provide an effective link of communication between politicians and voters. This is particularly important in a country where specialized communications media have not adequately developed and penetrated in the rural areas. Cooperatives have made it easier for politicians and political parties to convey their messages and programs to a larger number of people. Cooperatives have also contributed to greater political awareness among the people. This has helped to bring out greater political participation by the citizens. For instance, constituencies with a network of important cooperatives have generally shown a higher rate of voting in the elections. Thus cooperatives help in popular participation not only in the programs of economic development but also in the political field.

In some situations, cooperatives act as interest groups and articulate the interests of their members. Wherever strong cooperatives have emerged, their leaders have been more articulate and effective in pressing for various local demands. They have been pressing for better irrigation facilities, more fertilizers, new processing industries, and even ambitious projects like a paper mill or a fertilizer factory in the cooperative sector. The leaders of sugar factories have been acting as a pressure group at both the state and national levels by trying to secure better terms and higher prices for their produce. Their close links with ministers and legislators (some of them are legislators themselves) generate in them a remarkable sense of confidence. In a sense, cooperatives have helped to create, to some extent, a kind of "infrastructure" in the rural areas that is essential for an ongoing democratic polity.

CONCLUDING OBSERVATIONS

In the foregoing discussion, I have listed several successes and achievements of the cooperative movement in Maharashtra. I should also note the limitations of this movement. In Maharashtra, cooperatives have achieved greater success in the areas where cash or commercial crops are grown. They have been particularly successful in the sugarcane-growing areas in the field of the cooperative sugar industry. To a lesser extent, they have also shown good results in the processing of groundnuts and cotton.

Cooperatives have not shown similar achievements in the areas where subsistence crops are grown. Similarly, cooperatives have flourished more where there are adequate irrigation facilities, either through river canals or through well irrigation. Consequently, cooperatives have benefited the farmers and landowners cultivating cash crops on irrigated lands rather than the other sections of the population. This means economic benefits and political power are being enjoyed by and large by the well-to-do members of the peasant castes such as the Marathas, Malis, and Dhangers.[2] The consumer cooperatives and worker cooperatives have on the whole shown poor results. One should keep in mind, therefore, that the material and other benefits from cooperatives have accrued only to a section of the people and not to the people in general.

Cooperative leadership has also been characterized by some inherent limitations. It has been observed that the progress of cooperatives has contributed to the emergence of a new "economic class" which has a vested interest in the perpetuation of certain institutional structures from which they have derived benefit. The leaders of cooperatives have also tried their best to perpetuate their control over cooperatives and thus to perpetuate their political power. The top political leaders often appeal to the leaders of cooperatives to share their prosperity with their less fortunate brothers in the dry and subsistence crop areas, as well as with other sections of the population that are not covered by the present complex of cooperatives.

Although cooperatives play a significant role in politics at various levels, this role is mainly characterized by patronage and manipulation. Political leadership associated with the cooperatives is not inspired by any ideology or program of mobilization of the people for higher goals in the interests of the weaker sections of the population, nor is it interested in bringing about basic changes in the existing social structure. There is no doubt that the Congress party, as discussed above, derives its strength

---

[2]   I have analyzed the relationship between caste and cooperatives elsewhere (Baviskar 1971b).

from its control over the cooperatives, but this very advantage also restricts its capacity to bring about any radical or far-reaching changes in the society at large.

Control over cooperatives is not always an unmixed blessing for the Congress party. While the cooperatives provide strength and certain advantages to the party, they often lead to divisions within it. The struggle over the control of sugar factories and banks is one of the main causes of factionalism within the party in most districts of Maharashtra. Many party workers believe that the top leaders tend to support the stronger factions and that the strength of rival factions is generally measured on the basis of the number of important cooperatives under their control. Rival factions use the control of cooperatives to strengthen their position within the party. At times the rivalry between factions becomes so intense that they are unable to work together in support of the official party candidates in the elections of the legislatures and *zilla parishads*. The dissident faction frequently works against these candidates, which often leads to the defeat of the party even in constituencies known to be traditional Congress strongholds.[3]

Certain recent developments have dramatically revealed the inherent weaknesses in the cooperative leadership in Maharashtra. Some individuals have preserved their power over the cooperatives for long periods, often using unfair means. They have also acquired enormous wealth as a result of their positions in these institutions. Some of these leaders have indulged in conspicuous consumption and thus have attracted the attention of people even from outside the state. The style of life and style of politics of these leaders have led some critics and other observers to call them "cooperative kings" and to name them as members of the "sugar syndicate." Some of the cooperative leaders have openly opposed radical land reforms on the ground that such measures would adversely affect production. Such perpetuation by fair or foul means of some leaders in positions of power has blocked the circulation of leadership that is essential for the healthy development of both cooperatives and politics.

The government and the political leaders at the higher levels have been aware of some of these weaknesses in the movement. They have tried to check these by certain legislative and political policy measures. For instance, it has now been decided that an individual cannot hold more than one or two major positions in the larger and more important cooperatives, and a person would be legally prohibited from continuing in one office for more than six years. This has been vehemently opposed by those who have

[3] This is described in detail in Baviskar (1971a).

controlled the cooperatives for a long period. The Congress party has also recently tried to reduce the influence of powerful cooperative leaders in the party and in the legislature. For example, during the last assembly elections, in 1972, a deliberate attempt was made to bypass some of the powerful cooperative leaders while distributing the party tickets for the elections. However, both these measures have not yet effectively solved the problem of concentration of power in the hands of a few powerful individuals both in the cooperative field and in the wider political arena.

The cooperatives in Maharashtra have undoubtedly served an important and historical function in both the economic and the political fields during the last twenty-five years. However, they seem to have reached a stage where their limitations are becoming increasingly exposed. They also appear to be incapable of bringing about more basic changes in the socioeconomic field which would spread the benefits of cooperatives to the wider sections of the population that have so far remained outside the spell of the cooperative system. To distribute the benefits from cooperatives to these sections would require a new orientation in the objectives and methods of cooperative organization and a new political orientation based less on patronage and manipulation and more on commitment to an ideology and a program. Whether the cooperatives and the political leaders in Maharashtra will be able to achieve this in the near future is still an open question.

REFERENCES

BAVISKAR, B. S.
  1969   "A sociological study of a cooperative sugar factory in rural Maharashtra." Unpublished doctoral dissertation, University of Delhi.
  1971a Factions and party politics: general elections in an assembly constituency in Maharashtra. *Sociological Bulletin* 20:54–77.
  1971b "Cooperatives and caste in Maharashtra," in *Two blades of grass: rural cooperatives in agricultural modernization*. Edited by P. M. Worsley, 275–292. Manchester: Manchester University Press.
GADGIL, D. R.
  1963   "Socio-economic factors underlying patterns of leadership in South-East Asia," in *Patterns of cooperative leadership in South-East Asia*. Bombay: Asia Publishing House.
OSTERGAARD, G. N., A. H. HALSEY
  1965   *Power in cooperatives*. Oxford: Basil Blackwell.

The Process of Industrialization in the Israeli Kibbutzim

URI LEVIATAN

PRESENT STATUS OF THE KIBBUTZ INDUSTRIALIZATION PROCESS

During the last few years, there has been a revolutionary change in the economic structure of the kibbutz movement in Israel.[1] Until several years ago, farming was the sole, or at least the main, source of income for most kibbutzim, while industry as a source of income was insignificant. Now many kibbutzim have established industries, and the number of new plants is growing at an ever faster rate. This trend is illustrated in Tables 1 through 3.

Table 1 shows the growth trend of kibbutz industrialization over the last decade. It is evident that the kibbutz is undergoing an industrial revolution. This impression is strengthened when one recalls that during that same period, the kibbutz population increased by only 37.2 percent (from 39,421 in 1960 to 54,093 in 1970).

Table 2 illustrates that dramatic shift even more strongly by comparing labor investments in farming, in industry and workshops combined,[2] and in industry alone.

Table 3 represents the shift in emphasis from farming to industry in the Kibbutz Ha'artzi movement, one of the three large kibbutz move-

[1] It would be impossible in this short review to describe a kibbutz. It is therefore assumed that the reader has a general knowledge of the kibbutz way of life. The interested reader is referred to such general books as Darin (1962) or Leon (1969).
[2] Many of the kibbutz industries started as small workshops that specialized in a particular product and were initiated by a member who had a special interest in the technology. Later these small workshops expanded into industries. For many years the accounting books of the kibbutzim did not differentiate between the two.

Table 1.   Indicators of industrial growth in the kibbutz movement over the last decade

Year	Number of workers	Percent compared with 1960	Number of plants	Percent compared with 1960	Output in millions of Israeli pounds	Percent compared with 1966	Investment in millions of Israeli pounds	Percent compared with 1969
1960	4,860	100	108	100	fixed prices of 1966			
1966	6,980	144	148	137	248	100	fixed prices of 1966	
1969	8,434	174	157	145	380	153	53.3	100
1970	8,868	183	170	157	428	173	63.3	118
1971	9,125	188	185	171	475	192	60.3	113
1972	9,944	205	197	182			73[1]	136

[1]   Estimate.

Sources: Stanger (1971); Association of Kibbutz Industry (1972).

Table 2.   Investment of labor in farming, in industry and workshops combined, and in industry alone, in the kibbutz movement (as percentage of 1958 = 100)

Year	Total	Farming	Industry and workshops	Industry alone
1936	69	59	72	
1954	83	81	77	
1958	100	100	100	100
1965	113	90	240	358
1969	125	95	290	461

Source: Barkai (1972).

Table 3.   Output and labor in farming and industry as percentage of all production jobs in the kibbutz ha'artzi movement

Year	Percent of output in production		Percent of labor in production	
	Farming	Industry	Farming	Industry
1960	73	20	66	18
1966	64	29	60	22
1969	58	35	55	24
1970	50	40	54	25
1971			51	28
1972			49	30

Source: Kibbutz Ha'artzi statistical summaries for the years 1960–1973.

ments. Its members comprise one-third of the total kibbutz population, and it is responsible for about 40 percent of the total industrial production of the kibbutzim. The numbers in the table represent percentages of all production jobs (excluding services).[3]

Table 3 reveals that about 30 percent of the total work force of the Kibbutz Artzi is engaged in industry. That percentage holds for all other movements (Stanger 1971). This overall percentage conceals the fact that in 7 out of 70 kibbutzim, industrial workers already constitute more than 50 percent of all production workers while in another 29 kibbutzim they constitute between 25 and 50 percent of all production workers. Furthermore, the percentage of industrial output in a few kibbutzim has reached 80 percent of the total output. Of the 242 established kibbutzim, 154 have at least one industrial plant, and some have two or even three plants.

It also should be emphasized that the shift toward industry was not accompanied by a reduction in the labor force in farming (Table 2). While the labor force in industry increased fourfold, the labor force in farming remained about constant.

All the data shown above clearly indicate that industrialization has been increasing in the kibbutzim.

REASONS FOR THE SHIFT TOWARD MORE EMPHASIS ON INDUSTRY

Several conditions in various combinations have been responsible for the growing emphasis on industry in the kibbutzim, particularly in the larger and older ones.

1. A surplus of workers has developed. Technical and genetic agricultural developments in their various farm products have enabled the kibbutzim to increase their production without increasing their labor requirements. Farm production in the last ten years has increased by an annual average of 3.7 percent, while the number of workers has remained more or less constant. In the Kibbutz Ha'artzi movement, for example, 1,087 million workdays were put into farming in 1961 and 1,098 million workdays in 1970, while production increased by 120

[3] The internal accounting systems of the kibbutzim differentiate between "production jobs" and "service jobs." Production jobs are those that produce for the market or maintain jobs that do so. Service jobs serve the individual members and children. Service jobs are put on the liability side of the accounting sheet, while production jobs are put on the credit side.

percent during the same period. Because of restrictions imposed by the scarcity of land and water, the technical agricultural improvements could be translated, not into more jobs, but into savings in the number of workdays. At the same time, the kibbutz population kept growing, and new jobs had to be created.

Industry that did not demand more of the scarce resources of land and water was one solution. Yet these industrial plants could employ relatively few workers, because the number of workers released from farming could not exceed a certain percentage of the total production labor force. This number is in the range of 50 to 400 workers in each kibbutz.

2. Farm work, even with its technological advancements, still calls for physical fitness and is not appropriate for most older persons. However, the kibbutz population, on the average, is getting older every year. This is because the kibbutz movement was established by young pioneers, but it has now become a three-generation society with a population of aging founders. For example, in 1961, 17.9 percent of the total population of the kibbutzim was over forty-five years old. By 1969, this percentage had increased to 27.2 percent (Zarchi 1969). Thus, jobs more appropriate for physically disabled or elderly members are needed, and again industry is one solution.

3. Women, in particular, are a disadvantaged group with respect to work in a society, like the kibbutz, that values production work more than services (Rosner 1967). While few farm jobs at the present technological stage are appropriate for women because of their physical demands, industry may offer a larger choice of jobs for them.

4. Because of governmental policies in Israel, farming has become a much less profitable enterprise than industry. For the last twelve years, the average income of self-employed farmers has been smaller than that of workers in general, and in the last seven years that gap has grown at an increasing rate (Nachtomi 1971). In 1970 the income of self-employed farmers, on the average, was only 68 percent of the income of Israelis in general. The kibbutz, which has to cope efficiently in the economic market of the state, has had to adapt itself to these conditions and to seek more promising alternatives, such as industrialization.

5. Second-generation kibbutz males are technologically oriented and desire technologically sophisticated jobs. At its present stage of development, farming is less sophisticated technologically than some industries. Indeed, one study of the second generation showed that, while 59 percent of the second-generation men work as farmers, 31 percent work in industry or workshops, and 10 percent work in various services, the distribution of desired jobs is different: 38 percent in farm-

ing, 36 percent in industry and workshops, and 26 percent in various services.[4]

Young kibbutz males also aspire to jobs that demand more education and training. While only 8 percent of them need formal education above the high school level in their present jobs, more of their desired jobs demand high formal education.[5] In our second-generation sample, 56.4 percent stated that they wished to study more than one year, while in our first-generation sample, only 24.6 percent gave this response.

VARIOUS REQUIREMENTS OF IDEAL INDUSTRY

The conditions that made the kibbutzim turn to intensive industrialization also restricted severely the characteristics of the appropriate industries. These industries had to be small yet economically profitable, had to provide jobs for the physically disabled and for women, and had to use well the human intellectual potential. These criteria did not exhaust all the relevant conditions that the ideal kibbutz industry had to fulfill. Two additional sets of requirements became relevant once a kibbutz decided upon industrialization.

The first group of requirements reflected adherence to the ideological and normative principles of kibbutz society:

1. Minimum use of outside hired laborers. This meant, if the principle were kept, that a plant could require no more than 50 to 100 workers (because of the relatively small size of the individual kibbutz).

2. Managerial practices based upon values and principles of democracy and participation of workers in decision making, and not upon principles of coercion or reinforcement by material incentives.

3. Rotation of offices, including the highest offices in the managerial hierarchy, among workers.

4. Vesting of the final authority relating to major decisions in the industry in the general assembly of the kibbutz.

The second set of requirements concerned the individual members who were the proposed workers. Because the goal of kibbutz society is

---

[4] These data come from a study conducted in 1969 by the Center for Social Research on the Kibbutz, Givat Haviva, Israel. The study dealt with intergenerational differences and similarities with respect to various aspects of kibbutz life and values. The sample included about 1,600 respondents of various subpopulations of the kibbutz.

[5] This trend toward jobs that require higher formal education is also true of young kibbutz women: 27 percent of the women need formal education beyond the high school level in their present jobs, while 47 percent would need that level of education in their desired jobs.

the welfare of its members, not just their possible contributions to its economic viability, the industrial solution had to ensure that the needs of the workers were satisfied to at least an acceptable level and that attention was paid to such possible negative effects of industrial work on the well-being of the worker, as feelings of alienation, loss of self-esteem, and other negative symptoms of mental or physical illness. Such negative effects of work in industry upon the individual worker have been found in many studies conducted in the United States, Europe, and the developing countries (e.g. Kornhauser 1965; Blauer 1964; Inkeles 1960). The kibbutzim, therefore, had to find ways and types of organization and technology that would avoid these ill effects.

Two questions now arise:

1. How successful were the kibbutzim in achieving, simultaneously, all the goals imposed by the above criteria and requirements?

2. What were the relationships among the variables that came into play in dealing with these goals?

REALIZATION OF GOALS

The present situation of the kibbutz industries will be examined to determine their degree of success in accomplishing their various objectives. Most of the data and the findings reported below are from a series of studies conducted by the Center for Social Research on the Kibbutz at Givat Haviva. Of particular relevance here is the kibbutz industrialization research program which was begun in 1969. Two phases of that research program have been completed.

The first phase was part of an international study that compared industries in three European countries, the United States, and Israeli kibbutzim.[6] The major dimensions of comparison were managerial and organizational practices and values, and workers' behavior and attitudes.

The second phase of the research program focused upon a representative sample of kibbutz industries (twenty-seven plants), examining their managerial and organizational practices, their structures and technologies, and the ways in which these variables affect workers' behavior and attitudes, and the organizational and economic efficiency of the indus-

---

[6]   This study was directed by Arnold S. Tannenbaum of the Institute for Social Research, Ann Arbor, Michigan, United States. The responsibility for the collection and analysis of the Israeli kibbutz data was undertaken by Menachem Rosner of the Center for Social Research on the Kibbutz. The sample comprised about 300 respondents from ten plants.

tries.[7] Another focal point of the study was the comparison along relevant dimensions of industrial plants and their workers with farm branches and their workers.

Several aspects of the study of the second generation are also relevant to the topics discussed here.

The various goals are discussed below.

Economic Viability

Kibbutz industry clearly has proven its success economically. Although the kibbutz population is only about 3 percent of the total population of Israel, its industrial output comprises between 6 and 7 percent of the national industrial output.[8]

The growth rate in sales, as compared with Israeli industry in general, is illustrated by the following figures. If 1969 is taken as a base of 100 percent, then sales in kibbutz industry grew to 119 percent in 1970 and 149 percent in 1971 (current prices). For Israeli industry in general, the figures are 115 percent in 1970 and 141 percent in 1971 (Association of Kibbutz Industry 1972). In terms of efficiency, kibbutz industry had an average yearly increase of 6.8 percent between 1957 and 1965, compared with a rate of 5.5 percent for Israeli industry in general (Barkai 1972).

Another index of economic viability is the rate of growth of industrial exports. This rate has been 28 percent per year for the last four years and about 35 percent for the last two years (Association of Kibbutz Industry 1972). It was 25 percent in 1970, compared with 13 percent for Israeli industry at large (excluding diamonds) (Stanger 1971). In a comparative study of kibbutz and nonkibbutz industrial enterprises, Melman (1971) showed that kibbutz plants were more efficient and profitable in economic terms.

Small Size

Kibbutz industry is composed of relatively small plants; 92 percent of them employ fewer than 100 workers and 75 percent employ fewer than 50 workers.

---

[7] This phase was directed by Uri Leviatan of the Center for Social Research on the Kibbutz. The data were collected in 1970. The research was sponsored by the Kibbutz Federation, the American Council for the Behavioral Sciences in the Kibbutz, and the Fritz Naphtali Foundation. A total of about 700 respondents from twenty-seven plants and thirty-four farm branches were included in the study.

[8] At the same time, the kibbutz movements produce more than 30 percent of the agricultural output in Israel.

Avoiding Hired Labor

In this sphere are the fewest successes. The kibbutz movement has failed to adhere to the value of using its own labor. This principle was important in kibbutz ideology, and abandoning it has been very painful to many members. In the farm branches the percentage of hired workers (wage-earning nonmembers employed by the kibbutz) has been kept relatively low, ranging (in 1970) from a minimum of 6 percent in one of the three large movements to a maximum of 20 percent in another of the large movements. In industry, the percentages were much higher, ranging from 21 percent to 76 percent.

In 1971, 52 percent of all industrial workers in the kibbutzim were hired from outside the kibbutz. However, the above summary numbers are a bit misleading. In 1971, 79 percent of all the hired workers were concentrated in only 15 percent of the plants (thus, 85 percent of the plants had only 21 percent of the hired labor), and about 26 percent of all plants had not even one paid worker. Moreover, the trend is toward reducing the percentage of paid workers employed in the kibbutz industry. From 1969 to 1972, there was a recorded increase of 8.7 percent in the number of paid workers, while the number of kibbutz members working in industry increased by 28.3 percent during the same period.

Employment for Older People

Our study comparing farm workers and industrial workers revealed that the industrial workers were, on the average, five years older than the farm workers (forty-two years old compared with thirty-seven). Our intergenerational study showed that the ratio between the number of young kibbutz members in farm jobs and those in industrial jobs was about 2.1 to 1.0 (36 percent to 17 percent). The ratio for the first-generation sample was one to one (17 percent to 17 percent). These numbers are for males and females together. When analyzed according to sex, the differences remain very much the same.

Employment for Women

This goal has been achieved only partially. According to our industrialization study, about 30 percent of the workers in the industrial plants are women. This equals the percentage of women working in farm branches in our sample. (It is very possible that the percentage of women working in farm branches in our sample is an overestimation because, for various reasons, the poultry branches were oversampled among the farm branches. The poultry branch is known to offer more jobs for women than do other farm branches.) In any case, the fact that only one-third of the workers in industry are females means that more should be done to find industrial jobs appropriate for women.

Opportunities for Training Relevant to the Job

Our studies consistently showed that people who worked in industrial plants had greater chances for relatively long training periods. Of the workers in industry who had worked at least five years, 6.7 percent had three months or more of job-related training during that period. The percentage among farm workers with the same seniority was less than 2 percent. Of the industrial workers who were employed during the year of the study (1970), more than 6 percent had three months or more of training during that year; among the farm workers the respective percentage was less than 1 percent. Moverover, the average length of time for job-related training was two months for industrial workers, but three to four months for farm workers. Together these data suggest that training is more differentiated in industry than in farming. Because of several measurement problems,[9] the above numbers underestimate the training time accorded to workers in industry and in agriculture, but the relative positions of the groups probably represent the real situation.

Findings from our study of the second generation lead to the same conclusion. About 59 percent of the young kibbutz men work in farming, but this group provides only 7 percent of the young men currently studying in academic institutions. The industrial workers, who comprise about 31 percent of the young men, provide about 40 percent of the total number of young men studying at the present. This last finding means that industrial jobs are, on the average, more sophisticated than farm jobs and call for more training.

---

[9] We suspect that many individuals who received extended training in the form of formal studies in academic institutions did not enter that fact as a response to the question about job-related training but rather added those years to the acount of their formal education. Furthermore, some workers may have received their job-related training more than five years before the time of the study — they were asked to give an account of only the last five years.

We shall now inspect some of the goals related to kibbutz ideological values and principles in management practices.

Rotation in Managerial Offices

Our studies revealed that officeholders in industry were replaced periodically, although this practice was somewhat less frequent and prevalent in industry than in the farm branches.

A plant manager held his position, on the average, between three and four years. The term was about the same among managers of farm branches. Another indication of rotation in industry was that about 20 percent of those who worked in their plants at least three years and who served during that period in any managerial position were, at the time of study, regular workers without any office title. Furthermore, about 31 percent of all workers who were employed at least three years in industry held an office at the time of study, but 46 percent of them did have an office during at least one of those three years.

Among farm branch workers the probability of having an office was higher. Some 36 percent of all those who worked at least three years in their farm branch held an office during the year of the study, and 55 percent of them had an office for at least one year during that three-year period.

These summary numbers do not describe the whole picture. Plants varied greatly in the extent to which they adhered to the rotation principle. This variance will be examined more closely below. It can be safely stated, however, that the principle of rotation has been followed, although not to its fullest potential.

Worker Participation in Decision Making

Compared with industrial workers in other countries, including those in plants managed by workers' councils in Yugoslavia, the workers in the kibbutz plants participate to the highest degree in making decisions related to their own work and to general plant policies. In response to questions about this aspect of participation, the mean score of kibbutz members from ten plants was 2.8; in the Yugoslavian sample the score was 2.6; in the United States sample, 2.0; and in the Italian sample, 1.7 (all scores are based on a 4-point scale).[10]

[10] These data were made available to me by Menachem Rosner from a preliminary draft of a summary of the study cited in Note 6.

We see, then, that the style of management in kibbutz industries allows more participation than do outside industries. For example, very few industrial plants would have general meetings with the authority to decide nomination of officers, investment policies, production policies, and the like — yet this is very common among kibbutz industries.

However, industrial plants in the kibbutzim allow much less participation than do farm branches. In a measurement of a factor of participation which could have scores ranging from 1.00 (lowest participation) to 5.00 (highest participation), the mean score for industry was 2.76 (standard deviation 0.58; number $= 24$), while the mean score for farm branches was 3.39 (SD $= 0.96$; N $= 25$).

On another index of personal influence over what happened in the workplace, industrial workers again had less influence. The median frequency of formal general meetings was somewhat higher among the plants in our sample than among the farm branches, but the latter more than compensated for this deficiency by providing other opportunities to discuss, plan, and decide matters relevant to the work and the workers. The median frequency for such opportunities in the farm branches was daily, while in the plants the frequency was twice a month.

Together these two measures make clear that the industrial plants still lag in the opportunities that they offer for meetings geared toward decision making. (It should be emphasized that no difference was found between farm workers and industrial workers with regard to the desired frequency of such meetings — both groups wanted them once a month.) Furthermore, workers in industrial plants saw their general meetings as less useful than did workers in farm branches.

Managerial Styles

We constructed an index to measure the degree to which superiors displayed a people-oriented approach and consideration for their subordinates as human beings. The data show that although superiors in industrial plants are very high on this dimension (a mean score of 3.54 from a maximum of 5.00), they are still significantly lower than supervisors of all levels in farm branches (a mean score of 3.91). Industrial supervisors also differ somewhat from farm supervisors in their use of bases of power (French and Raven 1959) to make subordinates comply with their demands. Although both groups are very high on the use of the legitimate (highest) and the expert bases, and very low on the use of the coercive (lowest) and the reward bases, the industrial supervisors are less so.

Job Satisfaction and Mental Health

We turn now to the last type of requirement that ideal industrial plants should fulfill. Here again, our frame of reference is the farm branches, because they seem to have upheld these objectives until now.

The extent to which industrial organizations offer opportunities for the satisfaction of the needs and aspirations of the individual workers is relatively high, compared with industrial organizations outside the kibbutzim. Four surveys conducted in the kibbutzim in the last three years have indicated that the general level of job satisfaction among kibbutz members is very high. Between 57 and 70 percent of the workers said that they were very satisfied with their jobs; 9 to 14 percent said that they were dissatisfied with their jobs; the rest were slightly satisfied. On this global job satisfaction measure, no differences were found between farm and industrial workers. Among the farm workers, 58 percent were very satisfied and 14 percent were dissatisfied; among the industrial workers, the corresponding figures were 57 percent and 11 percent. The level of "satisfaction from the job" is, by the way, more positive than that found for any occupational group in surveys of employed American workers (Morse and Weiss 1955) and of workers in other countries (Inkeles 1960).

Table 4.   Comparison of farm workers and industrial workers on indexes of alienation

Alienation Components	Farm workers			Industrial workers		
	X^1	SD	N	X	SD	N
Social Isolation[2]	3.8	1.0	164	3.8	1.0	460
Powerlessness	3.7	1.0	163	3.6	1.2	454
Meaninglessness	4 0	1.0	163	3.9	1.0	451
Self-estrangement	3.8	1.1	160	3.9	1.1	455
Normlessness	4.1	1.0	165	4.0	1.1	452

[1]   The scores had a potential range from 1 to 5.
[2]   None of the differences between farm workers and industrial workers reached a statistical significance of $p < 0.10$.

No differences were found between industrial and farm workers in measures of mental health (such as feelings of depression, resentment, self-esteem) either. Table 4 illustrates this with variables designed to measure five aspects of alienation (Seeman 1959): social isolation, powerlessness, meaninglessness, self-estrangement, and normlessness.

Although no differences were found between farm workers and industrial workers with regard to satisfaction and mental health in their strictest senses, we did find differences in some related variables that some writers (French and Kahn 1962; French 1963) might put under a broader definition of mental health. Specifically, farm workers were consistently higher on opportunities for self-actualization, for autonomy, for influence, and for social relationships. Farm teams and farm workers were more adaptive in their behavior in that they exercised more "initiative-taking" behavior (solving problems, suggesting new methods, and the like) with regard to their work and showed higher motivation (by being more involved psychologically) to contribute to the success of the organizations of which they were members.

In summary, the kibbutzim have done quite well in achieving some of the goals that they had set concerning the process of industrialization. They have done very well economically. They have solved the problem of size restriction. They have achieved the demographic goals of providing jobs for elder members, for women, and for technologically oriented and training-oriented youth. They have done relatively less well, compared with the farm branches, on aspects that relate to kibbutz values, such as hired labor, rotation of officeholders, worker participation in decision making, supervisory styles of management, and opportunities to satisfy the needs of workers.

Why is there a discrepancy between industries and farm branches on these variables? We can only speculate on this at the moment, because we have no valid research data on it.

Our current analyses do not support the notion that size has significant explanatory power for this phenomenon, although this line of research (the effect of structural variables) should be pursued further.

Another plausible explanation for the discrepancy rests on the differences between the way industry was introduced into the kibbutzim and the way farming was introduced. Farming has been with the kibbutzim since the very beginning, and the kibbutzim have always been the pioneers in Israel with regard to the introduction of new techniques and products. There were thus no outside models from which to learn ways of organization and administration; hence, there were no constraints on the freedom to adapt and adjust the organizational methods and principles to the social values of the kibbutz. With industry, however, many of the plants were imported into the kibbutz framework from outside. Their technology, know-how, and market were bought intact. In many cases, package-deal type importation has carried with it the belief that the organizational principles used with a particular technology outside the kibbutz were inseparable from the successful operation of the industry within the kibbutz. These imported organizational principles were, of course, alien to the social values of the kibbutz and led to relatively poorer results in terms of adherence to kibbutz principles and to satsifaction of individual needs.

The achievement of the normative goals dealt with in this section was in no case a matter of all or nothing; rather, it was a matter of where on a continuum a kibbutz found itself with regard to each goal. These goals can be considered, therefore, as variables. The next section will consider the interrelationships among these variables. How do organizational principles and management methods affect individual behavior, motivation, satisfaction, and health? How does job satisfaction relate to behavior that is associated with economic success? How important are worker behavior and worker motivation in determining economic efficiency, and what is the role of organizational practices? Are the relationships among the variables mentioned here in the kibbutz setting the same as these relationships in societies such as the United States, Europe, and other developed countries? Indeed, the basic question for many kibbutz members is whether the economic success of the kibbutz industries has come BECAUSE of the adherence to kibbutz values or IN SPITE of the restrictions imposed by these values.

RELATIONSHIPS AMONG DEGREES OF ACHIEVEMENT OF VARIOUS GOALS

Hired Labor and Economic Efficiency

The important question here is whether or not the employment of hired workers affects profitability and productivity of the industries in the kibbutzim. We do not have a conclusive answer to that question, but in several analyses a negative relationship between the employment of hired labor and indexes of profitability and productivity has been indicated.

In our own industrialization study, we sampled plants where hired workers accounted for 30 percent or less of the total number of workers. We therefore had a very restricted range on the variable "percentage of hired workers employed in the plant." Nevertheless, we found that the plants with no hired labor at all were more profitable on the average than were those with even some hired labor.

Carmon (1972) reported, on the basis of 1971 data, a positive relationship between percentage of kibbutz (member) labor and the volume of sales per worker (Table 5).

Another study compared the industrial plants of two movements. The one with the lower percentage of hired labor was more profitable.

Table 5. Percentage of self-labor (labor by members of the kibbutz) and sales per worker in two kibbutzim

Percentage of self-labor	80	26
Number of workers 1971	2,590	4,550
Total sales in millions of Israeli pounds	232	292
Sales per worker in thousands of Israeli pounds	89	64

Source: Carmon (1972).

Several hypotheses might explain these relationships (two of these even have some empirical support):

1. The use of hired labor diminishes the immediate motivation and pressure to invest in improving technology and increasing its efficiency. Therefore, it reduces the productivity per worker. Zamir (1972) has analyzed some data pertaining to this problem (Table 6).

Table 6. Differences among the main branches of kibbutz industry in percent of hired labor, size, and investment per worker in 1971

Industrial branch:	Wood	Food products	Metal	Rubber and plastics	Electricity and electronics	Total in kibbutz industry
Percent of hired workers	76	65	47	18	10	52
Investment per worker in 1969–1971 (in thousands of Israeli pounds)	12.9	17.0	21.9	42.0	26.0	23.2
Planned investment per worker in 1972 (in thousands of Israeli pounds)	5.2	8.4	7.6	13.8	16.0	9.2
Mean number of workers per plant (1971)	147	90	48	33	15	48

Source: Zamir (1972).

Table 6 shows that the higher the percentage of hired labor, the lower the investment per worker. Unfortunately, this relationship is equivocal because it is confounded by other variables — size and branch of industry.

2. Another hypothesis that gained some support in our data related the percentage of hired workers to managerial practices. It was found that supervisors tended to interact differently with workers (members) and to allow less participation when hired workers were employed. This attitude might have been responsible for the lower profitability of the plants.

3.   The motivation and contribution of paid workers would be expected to be lower than those of members. This, too, might produce a lower profitability.

4.   We also hypothesized, on the basis of open-ended interviews in several kibbutzim, that young members would be more reluctant to join plants with a high percentage of paid workers because they would view the situation there as far from kibbutz ideals and also because of cultural differences between them and the hired workers. The relative absence of young members would probably decrease profitability.

We are now testing these hypotheses.

Worker Behavior and Motivation as Causes of Organizational Performance

Our data show that the behavior and the motivation of the individual workers explain about 40 percent of the variance in the economic effectiveness of the industrial plants that comprised our sample (Leviatan 1972). For example, a measure of the rate of capital recovery (RCR) correlated 0.50 with an index of initiative-taking behavior, −0.39 with a measure of tardiness, 0.34 with a measure of motivation, and 0.35 with a measure of worker quality. The multiple correlation was $R^2=0.40$. This is impressive because the plants differed from one another along almost all relevant dimensions: branch of industry (food, textile, metal, electronics, plastics, paper), size (nine to sixty workers), number of years in business (three to thirty years), political affiliation, and geographic location.

Another way to express the relationship between worker behavior and economic outcomes for the plants is by a regression analysis. We found that a positive shift in one standard deviation score on the variable of initiative-taking behavior would produce, on the average, an increase of about 70 percent in the yearly net profits of a plant. Figure 1 displays the combined contribution, for predicting the RCR, of the index of initiative-taking behavior and the index of involvement with organizational goals.

The above findings and similar ones (Leviatan 1972) reveal that the human factor is of great importance in determining the economic outcomes of industrial plants in the kibbutzim. Indeed, this relationship has also been found outside the kibbutz (see, for example, Likert 1967; Kahn and Katz 1960; Bowers 1969). What is significant in the present findings is the magnitude of the relationship, which implies that investment in the development of the human resources of the workers in kibbutz plants is a wise economic choice for management. This very emphasis is in accord with kibbutz values, which consider the development of human resources as a goal in its own right. We may conclude, then, that in this instance kibbutz values were at least not in conflict

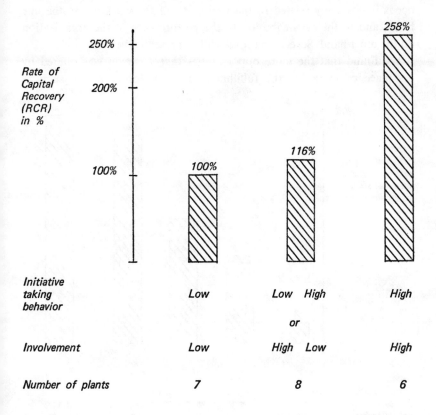

* $F = 3.53$ $p < .05$

Figure 1.   Combined contribution of initiative-taking behavior and personal involvement with organizational economic goals to rate of capital recovery, as expressed in percentage of lowest group

with purely economic values. We could even venture to claim that these values were in harmony with organizational effectiveness.

We shall now investigate the organizational variables that would determine the types of worker behavior and motivation presented above.

Opportunities for Fulfillment of Psychological Needs as Determinants of Individual Behavior and Motivation

A general finding in our studies is that the degree to which an organization offers opportunities for its workers to fulfill their psychological needs is positively related to the well-being of the workers, on the one hand, and to their contribution to the performance of the organization on the other hand. Several examples will be presented below.

We found that the more opportunities that a person was offered by his place of work for the fulfillment of higher-order needs, such as

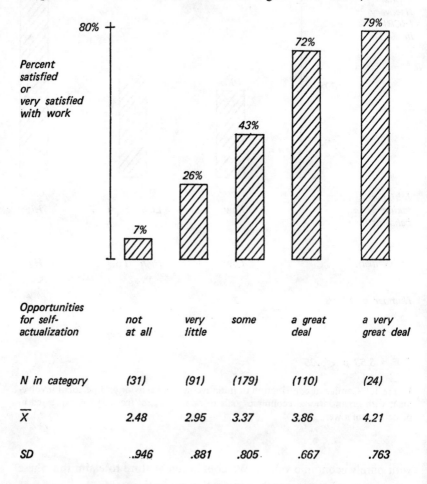

Opportunities for self-actualization	not at all	very little	some	a great deal	a very great deal
N in category	(31)	(91)	(179)	(110)	(24)
$\overline{X}$	2.48	2.95	3.37	3.86	4.21
SD	.946	.881	.805	.667	.763

* The Pearson Correlation Coefficient was $r = .49$, $p < .05$

Figure 2.   Satisfaction with work as a function of extent to which opportunities for self-actualization are offered

self-development and self-utilization, the more likely he was to behave
in a way conducive to the economic efficiency of his plant. We had combined these two needs into a single "self-actualization" index and found
that it was strongly related to psychological commitment to the plant's
goals, to initiative-taking behavior, and to satisfaction with the job. This
last variable was related to tardiness. Figure 2 displays the relationship
between the opportunities for self-actualization and satisfaction with
the job.

The opportunities for social interaction that the work offered to a
person were strongly related to his illness behavior as expressed by the
frequency of his visits to physicians. People with few opportunities

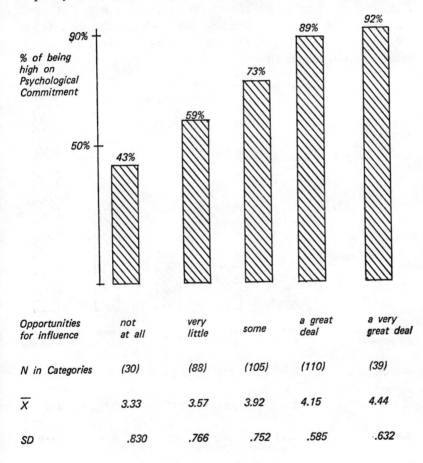

Opportunities for influence	not at all	very little	some	a great deal	a very great deal
N in Categories	(30)	(88)	(105)	(110)	(39)
$\overline{X}$	3.33	3.57	3.92	4.15	4.44
SD	.830	.766	.752	.585	.632

* *The Pearson Correlation Coefficient was r = 4.3, p < .05*

Figure 3. Psychological commitment to economic success of organization as a
function of opportunities for influence within it

for social interaction were about three times more likely to visit a physician than were those who had many such opportunities. Feelings of alienation were also negatively related to the extent to which a workplace offered opportunities for the satisfaction of the psychological needs of the workers. The same was true of other behaviors and symptoms of mental illness.

Workers who had no opportunities at all for influence in their work were three times more likely to be absent from work than were workers who had many opportunities for influence in their work (Leviatan 1970). Workers with more opportunities for influence were also more likely to feel psychologically committed to the success of their plants (as Figure 3 illustrates) and were more likely to behave in other ways that would contribute to the economic success of their work organizations, such as solving problems, putting more effort into work, and the like (initiative-taking behavior [Figure 4]).

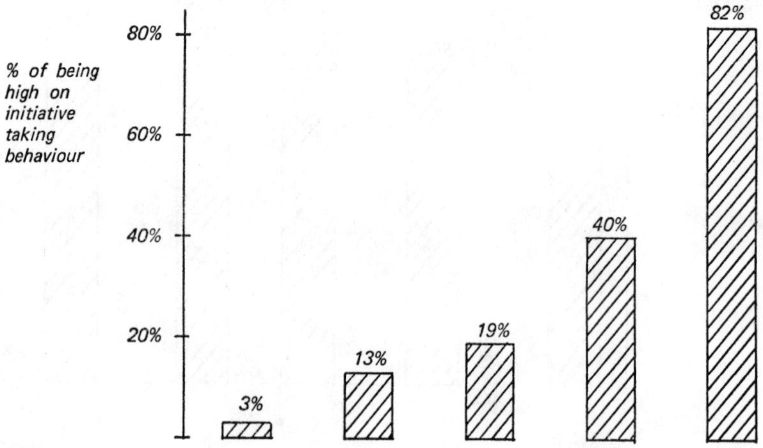

Opportunities for influence	not at all	very little	some	a great deal	a very great deal
N in categories	(39)	(98)	(129)	(125)	(44)
$\overline{X}$	2.23	2.52	2.77	3.29	4.09
SD	.794	.883	1.021	.978	.668

* The Pearson Correlation Coefficient was r = .50, p < .05

Figure 4. Initiative-taking behavior as a function of opportunities for influence offered to the individual

Worker Participation in the Decision-Making Process

The variables representing the opportunities for influence in the work-place indicated the degree of actual participation of workers in the decision-making process. We have seen that the greater the participation of all workers, the greater the effectiveness, in terms of organization, of the plant.

We also had a measure of the degree of formal worker participation in the decision-making process by way of the general assembly of all workers. This measure indicated the level of the formal authority of the general assembly with regard to decisions about various aspects of plant activities (e.g. election of officers, investment policies, production policies, training plans, etc.). Although the index was related to the index of the individual's perception of his influence, it did not relate positively to the effectiveness measures (with some of them, the relationship was even negative). This is contrary to our expectations and we do not yet have a satisfactory interpretation of it.

One hypothesis about this finding concerns the PROCESS of conducting general meetings, as opposed to their CONTENT. It is possible that although meetings have the formal authority to decide issues, these decisions are actually made elsewhere because of the poor conduct and preparation of the meetings. The participants are not supplied with all relevant information, alternatives are not presented, and people are not encouraged to explore the problem or to suggest solutions. Participants in these meetings may become more frustrated from such experience with participation in decision making than are workers who do not have legitimate authority through the general meeting. This frustation may express itself in negative reaction to management goals and thus may hinder effectiveness. We have some impressionistic indications that in many plants, the above description of the way the general meetings are conducted is fairly typical.

Rotation of Workers in Managerial Positions

Our data have shown a very clear relationship between the hierarchical level of the office that a person held and the degree to which he was offered opportunities to fulfill his psychological needs. The coefficients of correlation were $r=0.38$ with opportunities for self-actualization; $r=0.55$ with opportunities for influence; and $r=0.40$ with opportunities for social interaction. Figure 5 illustrates this relationship.

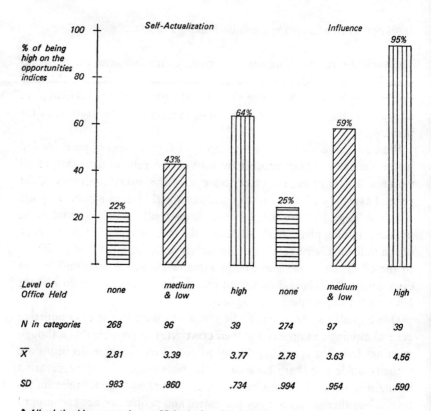

Figure 5. Opportunities for self-actualization and influence as a function of level of office held

Level of Office Held	none	medium & low	high	none	medium & low	high
N in categories	268	96	39	274	97	39
$\overline{X}$	2.81	3.39	3.77	2.78	3.63	4.56
SD	.983	.860	.734	.994	.954	.590

* All relationships are at the p<.05 level of statistical significance.

Another hypothesis was also confirmed: workers who had held offices in years past but who were not holding offices in the present had more opportunities for influence than did workers who had never held offices. This relationship was not true for individuals who had held offices four or five years earlier or who had not held any office during the last five years. Individuals who were designated to hold an office in the year following our study were also accorded more influence in the present than were those who had held no office in the last five years. Figure 6 illustrates this relationship

The relationship between hierarchical level and opportunities and the time-lag effect suggest two ways to increase the total amount of influence available in a given organization:
1. Increase the proportion of officeholders to a certain optimum.
2. Rotate as many (capable) individuals as possible in a given number

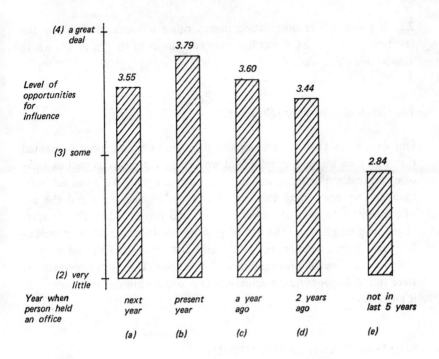

The Ns. are too small for a full analysis. Groups (a), (d), and (e) are different from group (b) at the p < .05 level.

Figure 6. Opportunities for influence at present as a function of length of time since holding an office

of offices, so that during a period of three years a maximum number of workers will have experience with holding managerial or other offices.

For a theoretical treatment of these problems, see Leviatan (1969, 1970).

Because the total amount of influence in an organization is supposed to determine its effectiveness (Tannenbaum 1968), and because the more influence a person has, the more he can contribute to his organization's goals, the implementation of the two suggestions offered above would be expected to lead to greater effectiveness. Our analyses in this direction are not yet completed, but the trend of the findings is in the direction hypothesized. For example:

1. In eight plants where 41 percent or more of the workers held any office in the last two years, the RCR (the economic efficiency index) was more than twice that of plants where the number of officeholders in the same period was 40 percent or less.

2. In plants where no rotation in any office was exercised during the last two years, the RCR was less than two-thirds of that in plants where at least one office was rotated.

The Effects of Supervisory Style

Our data show that supervisors and managers who are people-oriented (i.e. who care about the individual worker as a person) as well as task-oriented realized better results in organizational goals. This was achieved through the intervening variable of workers' cohesiveness and the use of the legitimate basis of power (French and Raven 1959). These supervisors also emphasized the use of positive reinforcements for contributions (as against negative reinforcements for wrong deeds) and emphasized the free flow of information in all directions. These last two variables were found to promote the achievement of organizational goals (economic efficiency).

SUMMARY AND CONCLUSIONS

Only a few of our findings have been reported, and only a brief and superficial theoretical treatment of the various relationships has been given. Further theoretical treatment is not possible here, but for the sake of clarity, Figure 7 diagrams the hypothesized causal flow among the variables treated above.

We may conclude confidently that kibbutz ideals and values by no means hinder the achievement of economic goals. On the contrary, they often promote them. The more successful kibbutz industrial plants are those that conform to the values of kibbutz (member) labor, rotation of officers, equality through distribution of responsibility among many workers, democracy and worker participation in the decision-making process, attention to individual needs, supervisory practices that emphasize the worker as a whole individual, and emphasis upon the group as a unit of organization.

The kibbutzim do in fact differ from one another in the practice of organizational principles and in the adherence to kibbutz values and norms. There is great variability among kibbutz industrial plants on various dimensions. This variability means that many kibbutz industrial plants could still improve their output by moving toward better use of kibbutz values and organizational norms.

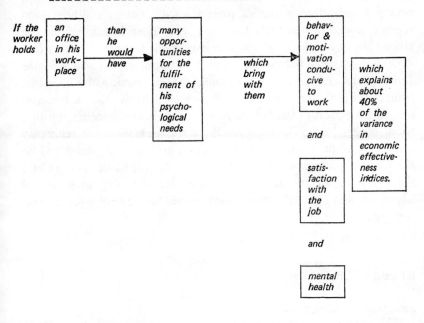

A. At the individual worker's level of analysis.

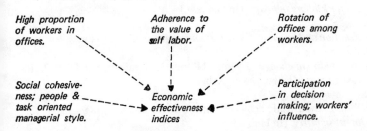

B. At the Plant Level of Analysis

Figure 7.   Causal flow models (the broken lines indicate that the relationships portrayed are mediated by other variables not shown here)

The third, and perhaps the most optimistic, conclusion is that the kibbutz society is aware of the various problems that the industrialization process brings. It is aware of the need for research and the application of research results in solving these problems. Putting resources into this research activity may allow the kibbutz to become one of the first societies where planning precedes action and the prevention of social ailments precludes the need for their cure.

Some of the principles of human behavior transcend cultural boundaries and are fairly general in the world we know. All the relationships among organizational variables, psychological variables, and behavioral variables found in our study have also been found in Europe and the United States, although the absolute level of the kibbutz on the various dimensions is very different from that of social organizations in the United States and Europe. (For example, the least participative industrial plant in the kibbtuz movement is still more participative than is the most participative plant in the United States.) This is very encouraging to a social scientist because it means two things: (1) the kibbutz researcher may consider sociopsychological and organizational theories developed in the Western world as valid tools within the kibbutz framework, and (2) the world outside the kibbutz may use kibbutz society as a natural laboratory and may gain from its experience ideas relevant for its own conduct.

REFERENCES

ASSOCIATION OF KIBBUTZ INDUSTRY
1972   *Annual report.* (In Hebrew.)
BARKAI, H.
1972   Is there an industrial revolution in the kibbutz? *Al Hamishmar supplement for kibbutz industry.* (In Hebrew.)
BLAUER, R.
1964   *Alienation and freedom.* Chicago: University of Chicago Press.
BOWERS, D. G.
1969   *Three studies in change.* Technical Report, Institute of Social Research, University of Michigan, Ann Arbor.
CARMON, D.
1972   Kibbutz industrial achievements. *Al Hamishmar supplement for kibbutz industry.* (In Hebrew.)
DARIN, H.
1962   *The other society.* London: Victor Golancz.
FRENCH, J. R. P, JR.
1963   The social environment and mental health. *Journal of Social Issues* 19:39–56.
FRENCH, J. R. P., JR., R. KAHN
1962   A programmatic approach to studying the industrial environment and mental health. *Journal of Social Issues* 18:1–47.
FRENCH, J. R. P., JR., B. RAVEN
1959   "The bases of power," in *Studies in social power.* Edited by D. Cartwright. Ann Arbor, Michigan: Institute for Social Research.
INKELES, A.
1960   Industrial man: the relation of status to experience. *American Journal of Sociology* 30:556.

KAHN, R., D. KATZ
 1960 "Leadership practices in relation to productivity and morale," in *Group dynamics research theory*. Edited by D. Cartwright and A. Zander. New York: Harper and Row.

KORNHAUSER, A. W.
 1965 *Mental health of the industrial worker: a Detroit study*. New York: John Wiley.

LEON, D.
 1969 *The kibbutz: a new way of life*. Oxford: Pergamon Press.

LEVIATAN, U.
 1969 "Status structure in social systems as a causal variable to individual mental health and performance and to the system' performance and effectiveness." Department of Psychology, University of Michigan, Ann Arbor, Michigan. Mimeographed manuscript.
 1970 "Status in human organization as a determinant of mental health and performance." Unpublished Ph.D. dissertation, University of Michigan, Ann Arbor, Michigan.
 1972 "The importance of the human factor in determining the effectiveness of economic organizations." Unpublished manuscript, Givat Haviva, Center for Social Research on the Kibbutz.

LIKERT, R.
 1967 *The human organization*. New York: McGraw-Hill.

MELMAN, S.
 1971 Managerial vs. cooperative decision making in Israel. *Studies in Comparative International Development* 6(3).

MORSE, N., R.S. WEISS
 1955 The function and meaning of work and job. *American Sociological Review*. 20:191–198.

NACHTOMI, Y.
 1971 Trends and developments in production branches. *Hedim* 96:70–84. (In Hebrew.)

ROSNER, M.
 1967 Women in the kibbutz: changing status and concepts. *Asian and African Studies* 3:35–68.

SEEMAN, M.
 1959 On the meaning of alienation. *American Sociological Review* 24: 783–791.

STANGER, S.
 1971 *The kibbutz industry*. Association of Kibbutz Industry. (In Hebrew.)

TANNENBAUM, A. S.
 1968 *Control in organization*. New York: McGraw-Hill.

ZAMIR, D.
 1972 Is hired labor related to structural changes in the kibbutz? *Al Hamishmar supplement for kibbutz industry*. (In Hebrew.)

ZARCHI, S.
 1969 *Economic and social changes in the kibbutz during the sixties*. Tel Aviv: Ministry of Housing. (In Hebrew.)

Structural Problems of Cooperation: The Case of an Israeli Transport Cooperative

RIVKA WEISS BAR-YOSEF and HANA ROSENMAN

Cooperative and communal forms of work organization were created in Israel as part of the general organization of the labor force into trade unions and the less specialized federation of labor. From its very beginning, the labor movement in Israel was an ideological movement, not a trade union or a federation of unions. It has defined itself as a class organization of workers (a worker was very broadly defined as any person who earned a wage or a salary). As a class organization, it tried to create and maintain a quasi "worker's society" with all the necessary institutions that existed within the larger society. Thus, the general federation of labor — the Histadrut — was running such welfare services as health insurance with its clinics and hospitals, pension schemes, recreation houses, and day-care centers. It had schools at all levels (including kindergartens), a daily newspaper, a publishing company, and other cultural activities. It also entered into large-scale production, banking, insurance, and retail businesses. The range of these activities is constantly changing. The schools, for example, were incorporated into the network of compulsory state education and lost their specific character.

The avowed aim of the federation is to penetrate all areas of society, whatever the variations or complexity, for two reasons:

1. A political reason. The Histadrut accepted democratic coexistence with nonsocialist, nonlabor social and political forms of societal organization. But it wanted to ensure its firm basis of power, which would be rooted not only in the power of withdrawal, as in strikes, but also in a strong economic and organizational position that would ensure its participation in the process of decision making at the highest levels of the political and economic hierarchy.

2. An ideological reason. The Histadrut intended to initiate, encourage, and develop a new focus of organization in which some of the basic values of the movement (equality, mutual help, democratic participation) would be realized. While these values were seen as binding norms, they were not constantly translated into organizational models. The cooperatives and communes, while an integral part of the labor movement, encompassed only a small number of its membership. They were relegated to specific areas and did not dominate the organizational structure of the Histadrut — either in its administration or in its production or service units. Nevertheless, some cooperatives and communes have achieved very important positions in the economic life of the Histadrut and of the larger society.

A simplified organizational model will illustrate the variety of values and principles embodied in various types of organizational structures coexisting within the framework of the Histadrut. We have chosen the economic and the political structures as our main parameters. We chose the economic and power rights as variables because we believe that they are best suited to illustrate the levels of attainment of the values of equality and participation.

We have defined three dimensions of economic powers:

1. Possession rights — the rights of controlling part or all of the capital. Possession rights should be distinguished from ownership, as the Histadrut is the formal "owner" of all these units and additional rights are always partial.
2. Profit — income from capital earning.
3. Wages and salaries — income paid in exchange for labor.

The power structure was defined as:

1. The opportunity structure for the attainment of power positions.
2. The locus of decision making.
3. The type of control through which decisions can be directed or restricted.

Obviously, such a scheme is very imprecise. The profile is thus one of the dominant trends and does not take into account the complexity of the system or the subtleties and the dynamic nature of each type.

We wanted to emphasize through Table 1 that the acceptance of non-capitalistic principles does not necessarily lead to the emergence of new organizational types. In the administrative units, we find conventional bureaucratic characteristics. In the industrial enterprises, profit sharing and some form of codetermination were introduced — fairly recently — in the same type of bureaucratic operation. These were imposed on the structure by the power center of the federation. Although profit sharing and codetermination are defined as formally binding decisions, they have not

Table 1. Model of various organizational types within the Histadrut

	Administrative units	Industrial corporations	Cooperatives	Communes
Economic structure				
Possession rights	Histadrut as owners	Histadrut as owners	Shareholding members	Commune as a unit
Profits	Respective unit firm	Respective enterprise; some sharing to workers	Incorporated in wages	Communal
Wages or salaries	Hierarchical, equity and seniority principle	Hierarchical, equity and seniority principle	Equality and seniority	No wages or salaries — consumption rights according to needs
Power structure				
Power position	Appointed	Appointed	Elected	Elected and rotated
Decision making	Centralized at top	Centralized at top; some representation of workers	Dispersed committees and general assembly	Dispersed committees and general assembly
Control	Formal bureaucratic	Formal bureaucratic	Formal and informal bureaucratic	Informal participation; democracy

been enthusiastically accepted by firm and plant management, nor have they been fully and uniformly implemented. Thus they do not represent, at this stage at least, a radical change of the bureaucratic model. At most, they can be considered as the initial steps toward industrial democracy.

There seems to be an intrinsic contradiction in the existence of conventional hierarchical bureaucracies within an organization with an equalitarian socialist ideology. The legitimation for this situation is provided by reasoning rooted in certain Marxist concepts.[1] The Histadrut has defined itself as a class organization of workers. By its entrepreneurial activity, the Histadrut has become the owner of instruments of production, thus eliminating the dissociation between labor and capital. It was assumed that "class-owned" factories were basically different from structurally similar "capitalistic" enterprises. For this reason, it was expected that the worker

[1] It must be remembered that the Histadrut as an organization does not have a Marxist ideology, although there are recognizable Marxist influences. Among the political factions operating within the Histadrut are some that define themselves as Marxist and others that proclaim their anti-Marxist conception.

would see the plant as his own. Profit sharing was rejected, as it provided profit for some workers — those working in "rich" places — while others went without. Profit was intended to be returned to the working class in the form of social services and investment in cultural and political activities. This consistent orientation toward the class as a whole was slowly relinquished, and the particularistic rights of occupational and working units were fully recognized as legitimate.

The cooperatives and the communes were spontaneous associations of people who affiliated themselves with the Histadrut. The most obvious result of this growth into, and not from, the organization was the recognition of a certain autonomy in these units, which were within the working class but represented special identities and ways of life. Accordingly, in the cooperatives and the communes there are two levels of ownership: the very amorphous class ownership through the Histadrut and the restricted, controlled ownership of the unit. But because of the strong solidarity and feeling of identy, the unit commitment usually has higher priority than the class or the Histadrut commitment.

THE TRANSPORT COOPERATIVES

Here we shall analyze one passenger transport cooperative and shall try to show the problems inherent in its structure and those resulting from its position in the Histadrut and the larger society.

There are two cooperative companies engaged in the bus transport of passengers: Egged and Dan. These are the largest cooperative enterprises in Israel. They provide the major part of the intercity and intracity commuter services. They have monopolistic rights on regular commuting routes all over the country, as well as a touring and sightseeing branch which competes in the tourist market. Our discussion will focus on Egged, as there are no significant structural differences between the two.

Egged in its present form is the result of a forty-year process of mergers between many small cooperatives. The process started in 1933 with the combination of four smaller cooperatives. Forces pushing toward additional mergers and those pushing against them accompanied the process throughout its relatively long history.

Nearly all the integrative forces, important for the continuous functioning of a cooperative work unit, oppose the enlargement of the unit through merger. The members of the cooperative are reluctant to accept new people; they do not want to renounce their former collective identity and particularistic status. Often, when one partner is economically or organizationally more successful than the other, it is also averse to sharing with a poorer partner and is possibly worried about the outcome of a merger.

On the other side appear more businesslike reasons: tendencies toward growth and expansion or toward consolidation in times of crisis, reduction of competition, more rational organization. But it seems that the strongest forces promoting mergers were outside the cooperative. The Histadrut consistently pressed for unification of competing units. The general economic policy of the Histadrut is to avoid the emergence of competition within its own framework. Consequently, it tends to enforce mergers among those Histadrut-owned or Histadrut-controlled production or service units that have identical or even similar products. This tendency is enhanced by economic and political considerations. Undoubtedly, one large and growing company has more economic power than do many small companies. It is also easier to acquire special monopolistic rights for one big company than to control a market in which many small forms are operating.

The Histadrut tries to maintain some modicum of organizational control over the cooperatives, and this seems to be less difficult when control is exercised at the central level than when the controlling power has to maintain its position in geographically and organizationally dispersed units.

After the establishment of the state in 1948, the labor government seems to have adopted the approach of the Histadrut. It also attempted to control the prices of important consumer items, among them public transportation. Commuter service is highly subsidized by the government to secure relatively low prices. Given the continuous inflationary trends, price control involves nearly constant transactions and readjustments. Here, too, centralized dealings were preferred.

THE ORGANIZATIONAL STRUCTURE

The organizational blueprint of Egged does not differ in its main aspects from the pattern of cooperative associations over the world. Some specific characteristics emerge as the result of its affiliation with the Histadrut through the Central Union of the Workers' Cooperative Productive Societies, or for short, the Cooperatives Center (*Merkaz Hakooperatia*).

The company has a democratic, egalitarian structure. The supreme authority is vested in the General Assembly of all members of the cooperative. The Cooperatives Center and the Histadrut have nonvoting representatives in the assembly. The representatives are the guardians of the values and principles of the Histadrut in general and of cooperation in particular. They have the right to demand that any questions on these matters be brought before a special arbitration committee.

The council is the legislative body which decides matters involving general principles. It ratifies changes in the statutes, and it is the forum that decides on the expulsion of a member.

The managerial board consists of sixteen managers, among them representatives of the Cooperatives Center. The daily routine management is in the hands of a seven-member committee comprising the heads of the functional units, such as finances, organization, traffic, planning, maintenance, etc.

There are also an auditing unit and a judicial body. The latter has jurisdictional legal power within the company in matters of discipline and is empowered to exact fines which are then used for cultural purposes.

This system of elected bureaucracy was intended to provide a democratic system of power management in which the only status differentiation is that linked with the functional requirements of the office and is limited to the term of office. The supreme authority remains vested in the General Assembly, which elects a more workable standing committee of 170 members. The members are thus the formal bearers of power, but democracy tends to degenerate and needs the constant interest of those involved and systematic reinforcing activities. The officeholders might develop vested interests in their offices and might try — as has sometimes happened — to manipulate the system to ensure their positions. Lack of member interest or lack of coordinated action reinforces these tendencies. A complicated, decentralizing procedure was created to counteract the functional pressure against democracy. There is a dynamic approach toward procedures, which are, from time to time, adapted to emerging exigencies. We do not yet have any reliable research data to show the levels of democracy achieved or the failures of the system.

The transport cooperative began outside the Histadrut as a special form of entrepreneurship. Egged first contacted the Histadrut as a trade union and only later became affiliated with it. At present the Histadrut control is institutionalized in the following ways: (1) the Histadrut has representatives in the managerial board and in the executive committee; (2) the Cooperatives Center is responsible for general policy and coordination; and (3) financial supervision is exercised by the central audit union.

MEMBERSHIP IN EGGED: THE *HAVER*

The Hebrew word for membership, *haver*, also means an associate or a peer — even a friend. The first transport cooperatives were indeed friendly associations of worker-entrepreneurs who had the same skills and brought to the associations their own "means of production." The very same principles, although in a more abstract and sophisticated form, are still the basis of membership. Egged is no longer "a friendly association" as there are too many members for face-to-face relationships; at the national level, members do not even know one another. But at the local level, the daily routine maintains much informality and — more important — these first principles are embodied in the formal requirement for membership. The common basis is occupational, and every member must have a bus driver's license, whether or not his actual job is driving.

Today the company has, necessarily, a differentiated division of labor, and many other functions besides driving must be fulfilled. Nevertheless, it is assumed that the central function of driving can be executed, at least theoretically, by any member. Thus the image of the driver is predominant in the company and has acquired a sort of ritual symbolic status. To the outside world, Egged means buses and drivers, not a complex business enterprise with managers and diverse functions.

The modern driver-member does not bring with him his own means of production; instead he has to buy a share that represents its equivalent value. Each member must have one and only one share, which gives him full "citizenship" rights. The value of the share has risen constantly over the years, and the determination of its price is a complicated procedure which depends only partly on accountancy.

High prices for shares are in the economic interests of the members, as a share can be sold at the defined value. But the higher the price, the lower the opportunity for would-be members to buy membership. Symbolically, share prices are expressed in monthly wages, which means that each increase in wages changes the price of the shares. Shares may be paid in monthly installments subtracted from the monthly wage.

The price of the shares has to be approved by the Histadrut, which generally tries to lower the price and ease the conditions for its payment to maintain the openness of the association. The Histadrut may also enter into negotiations about shares and eligibility for membership on behalf of nonmember employees.

The income of the members is paid in the form of wages based on the usual items of the Israeli wage structure. Dividends as such are not paid, but the wage level is higher than that of the labor market, taking into account the investment made by the members. The peculiar feature of the wage-dividend system is the lack of differentiation between the two. As a price-controlled public service, the cooperative very often works at a deficit, but the members are not expected to carry this. Low ticket prices are maintained with the help of a governmental subsidy. Thus the wages of the cooperative members include profits that do not exist in reality. Hence, the nearly structural conflict between the public interest as represented by the government and the members' interest.

In the Israeli inflationary economy, prices and wages are constantly rising and needing readjustment. Egged thus legitimately asks to be allowed higher fares to cover higher operating costs and higher wages. But to the public, these demands often appear as requests for the taxpayers' money in order to pay exceptionally high wages for members, who are seen as a privileged group. The public has not assimilated the idea of status equality of the entrepreneurial, managerial, and operational functions, while it has accepted the concept that entrepreneurs and managers should be better paid than operators. It resents the fact that Egged drivers, whom it meets in their roles as operators, enjoy the sort of average income of entrepreneurs, managers, and drivers. This public resentment in turn irritates the Egged people, who react in an aggressive-defensive way that is often expressed in driver-commuter interactions.

The cooperative succeeded in reducing the structural alienation resulting from the segregation of ownership, management, and operator roles. It did not solve the problems of full participation. Its organizational structure is well suited for participation, especially at the level of the local unit, but the size of the company and the complexity of its business operations bar the average member from full understanding of the proceedings. In this situation, specialized knowledge is more important than the common occupational basis, and the rise to power of small groups of technocrats is nearly inevitable. Thus, not only is the power structure the source of feelings of alienation, but it creates objective power differentiation which, when realized, stimulates feelings of frustration.

Besides these strains, which grow as side effects of an expanding, cooperatively organized business, there is a wholle different complex of problems arising because the cooperative principles are not fully enforced and many nonmembers are employed by the company. In the asymmetrical model thus created, all owners are operators, but not all operators are owners.

About 40 percent of all workers are not members of the cooperative. The nonmembers constitute another class, with lower income than the member class, fewer social benefits, less security. They are organized in trade union locals and have their own shop committee. On the formal level, their relations with the cooperative are like labor relations in any public or private enterprise. Industrial disputes and strikes occur, and the Histadrut acts in a rather peculiar double role as mediator and representative of both sides. On the informal level, forces specifically related to the nature of the cooperative pattern emerge to attenuate or aggravate labor relations. First, the day-to-day relationships do not distinguish between members and nonmembers. The work organization is democratic and there is much contact and common work group interest. Second, employees (we use this term for all categories of hired labor, wage, and salary earners) are candidates for membership, and one of the main points of contention concerns the extent of membership opportunity given to the tenured employees. The desirability of the membership status together with the rather slim chance of attainment acts as a forceful irritant against the company, but also as a partial reinforcement of loyalty and conformity.

The existence of a hired group contradicts the principles of cooperation, and on the ideological level it is not condoned by the Histadrut. Nevertheless, it is a reality fed by powerful interests. The company tends to grow and expand. The needs for passenger transportation are increasing in spite of the growing number of private cars. Buses are convenient means of transportation in a small country, and Egged provides one of the most efficient and cheapest forms of intercity transportation. Increasing the number of members raises the cost of transportation and reduces the fluidity of the manpower. Thus, neither the members nor the government have a real interest in radical change in the situation. The private income of the members is also threatened by a large influx of new members.

CONCLUSIONS

This article intended to point out some problems inherent in a cooperative pattern of organization. In this case, the strains result from the interaction of principles and interests of functionally different institutions. Each of these operates as a set of constraints which may be mutually contradictory.

In our case, the relevant factors were:

1. A cooperative organization assuming a set of directives such as mutual aid, equality, unity of the entrepreneurial and operative statuses, and democratic organization.
2. The Histadrut in its role as representative of class interests and social

values restricting the purely entrepreneurial tendencies of the association. At the same time, the Histadrut sees in the cooperatives a realization of some of its basic principles and an important power position, the strengthening of which is among the aims of the federation.

3. The association is a business organization in which, at both the company and the individual levels, the motivations and rationales of business are to be found.

4. The association may enlarge its entrepreneurial activity and enter into conventional labor relations with nonmembers. In this case the Histadrut necessarily appears as a trade union representing the workers versus the company.

5. The product of the company is a public service under government control. Each of the partners — the Histadrut, the company, and the government — is expected to serve the public, but obviously the legitimacy of particularistic interests is also recognized. The interests of the cooperative association clearly are not identical with the interests of the general public.

Finally, we should ask whether the technological and organizational characteristics of a transport organization are especially suited for cooperation. Although we are unable to prove such an assertion, our impression is that some of its features enhance tendencies toward cooperation. These include the relative homogeneity of manpower, the autonomy and responsibility vested in each driver, the dispersion of the workplace, and the decentralization of work group organization and control. To these were added, at least at the beginning, an egalitarian value orientation and a desire to control one's own fate. Later, the status achieved by the company and the economic success replaced the value commmitment. We feel that being part of such a cooperative gives a feeling of power and cuts across the limits of stratification imposed on blue-collar occupations.

Worker Participation in the Nationalized Mines of Bolivia, 1952–1972

JUNE NASH

Worker participation in industry has been, historically, a management innovation to gain worker cooperation in times of labor-management tension. One of the first experiments was promoted in Canada when, after the strike of 1913 in the Colorado Fuel and Iron Company, John D. Rockefeller and W. L. Mackenzie, the Minister of Work, signed the contract for a short-lived plan for worker participation in the management. During World War I, a few Italian industries introduced worker councils as a means of increasing productivity. After the war, Antonio Gramsci promoted the councils in Turin after the failure of a general strike in May 1920. Gramsci (1957:23) viewed worker councils as a kind of territorial base for promoting workers' self-government. He envisioned the role of the factory council as follows:

In the Factory Councils, the worker, because of his very nature, plays the role of producer as a result of his position and function in society, in the same way as the citizen plays a role in the democratic parliamentary state. In the party and trade unions, the worker plays his role "voluntarily" participating in a contract which he can tear up at any moment. The Party and the trade unions, because of this "voluntary" character, because of their "contractual" nature, are not to be confused with the councils which are representative institutions and do not develop mathematically but morphologically, and in their higher forms tend to give a proletarian meaning to the apparatus, created by the capitalist for the purpose of extracting profit, of production and exchange (1957: 25).

This was the first concerted attempt by the Left to transform factory councils, which were set up by managers to accelerate production, into a defense of workers' interests for the purpose of "preparing the working classes organizationally, politically, and culturally for the task of managing industrial enterprises" (Gramsci 1957:13).

The reality of worker participation in industry has been more closely approximated in Yugoslavia than in any other industrial nation. Vanek, using his knowledge of the movement in Yugoslavia and contrasting that movement with experiences in the Soviet Union and the United States, defines the ideal nature of a participatory democracy (1971):

1. Firms controlled and managed by workers with management by all on the basis of equality, to be carried out by a workers' council, an executive board and a director of the firm.
2. Income sharing based on an income-distribution schedule that is equitable.
3. Worker usufruct of capital assets.
4. Market economy with fully decentralized management, no direct interference from outside except in fixing of maximum and minimum prices.
5. Freedom of employment with firms free to hire and fire, and individuals free to come and go.

The judgment of the effectiveness of the new organizations, designed to increase worker participation, has to shift from a straight evaluation based on gross national product to an assessment of self-fulfillment of people. The motivation to work and the greater social aims of production are an immediate concern of firms organized under such a plan. The Marxist adage about capitalism — that it is designed to create more useful products for more useless people — might be reordered to consider a social design that will create more useful people concerned with producing for more socially gainful ends.

Vanek's model has been widely disseminated in Latin America, and the Peruvian edition of his book (1971) has influenced the formation of industrial communities there. I shall assess Bolivia's experience in worker participation in the tin mining industry from the point of view of the two conditions Vanek uses in his model of equilibrium analysis: degree of efficiency and degree of self-determination. I should point out several problems in data analysis that make such an analysis nearly impossible. First of all, efficiency in tin mining cannot be measured by simple productivity ratios either per capita, per man hours, or per enterprise because of the constantly dwindling resource base. The figures of fine tons produced are misleading because of the lowering levels of metal content — it takes continuously more work to get out the same amounts of mineral. Metric tons are a better index of sheer human productivity, but the comparative indices are hard to get because they do not enter into international trade.

The second condition of equilibrium proposed by Vanek, "self-determination," is hard to measure because it is contingent on the level of worker consciousness, not only of their exploitations as a class but of their potential to be prime movers in history. This consciousness is dependent on ideological inputs as well as concrete experiences that reinforce the willingness of workers to sacrifice themselves for an end. Bolivia's trade union movement has relied in the post-1952 period more on the former and less on the latter. The rhetoric of revolution was honed to a fine point in the annual succession of coups from September 26, 1969, when Ovando seized power from Barriento's Vice-President Siles, to October 8, 1970, when Torres caught the presidential ball as it was flipped from one to another military pretender in the "Week of the Generals," to the August 19 takeover by Colonel Hugo Banzer, who moved up through the American stronghold in Santa Cruz, where Gulf Oil had its holdings, to seize the presidency after only three days of sporadic fighting. Action on the part of the workers in these sorties into and out of power by various military representatives was limited to imploring the real power holders for guns. Technology had outmoded political persuasion. Without an active role in decision making in industry, the workers' ability to enter into decision making in politics was limited.

The first stage of worker participation in industry began with the nationalization of the tin mines on October 31, 1952. Anayo (1952) traces nationalization back to 1949 when the Left Revolutionary Party (PIR) called upon the legislature to nationalize mines without indemnization and with a strong worker control. Bedregal (1963), on the occasion of the tenth anniversary of the nationalization decree, claims that this act, along with the Agrarian Reform, formed the nucleus of the National Revolutionary Movement (MNR). Lora (1972) traces it to the Thesis of Pulacayo which he, as leader of the Revolutionary Party of Workers (POR), helped to draft in 1946. These claims to paternity prove one thing: the bastard form of nationalized mines was a popular creation, and all political parties that had a stake in labor claimed to have fathered it.

Those who moved toward nationalization of the mines pointed out that the mines under the tin barons were more exploitive of the labor force than during the colonial period (Anayo 1952). Certainly the production was more intense: during three centuries of colonial rule, 105,454 metric tons of minerals were extracted from the *Cerro Rico* of Potosi, while during the Republic, the same amount was exported in three years. In the period from 1935 to 1949 alone, over one million tons were extracted (Anayo 1952:42).

Assessing the damage of unrestricted mineral exploitation during the first half of the twentieth century, Canelas (1966:20) asserts that the tin barons succeeded in (1) maintaining a permanent national budget deficit such that the government lacked even the minimum impulse to economic growth, (2) extracting an extraordinary amount of natural resources with low taxes, (3) constantly increasing the external debts to cover deficits in costs for imports to care for public services that directly or indirectly serviced the mines, and (4) contributing to growing inefficiency in the recuperation of minerals by failing to invest in modern machinery for concentration work within the country. The profligate waste of human resources is summarized in Anayo's statement (1952:105) that "Capitalism... signifies the destruction of one man for each four that enters to work."

Despite severe exploitation and the high risk of their work, miners have always been poorly paid in Bolivia. The level of living in mining communities as described by Bloomfield, sanitary engineer of the Institute of Inter-American Affairs (cited in Anayo 1952:101 ff), was lower than that described by Marx for the Lancashire workers in the eighteenth century. Several families lived in a single habitation, with up to fifteen persons living in eight square meters. People took turns to cook, even to sleep in the few beds. He noted that:

Problems related to morals result in the dissolution of many marrigage ties.... The absolute impossibility of rest for workers is because those occupying the same quarters work in different shifts, and on returning from a hard day's works, find others engaged in activities.

The hope of nationalization was summarized by Anayo (1952:143) in the following litany:

To liquidate the fifty years of backwardness, of exploitation, of extermination imposed by the great mining companies, we must nationalize the mines.
To destroy the reactionary forces that block progress we must nationalize the mines.
To make possible the economic, social and cultural transformation of the welfare and of the liberty of the Bolivian people we must nationalize the mines.

Nationalization became a reality at a sunrise ceremony at Siglo XX-Catavi six months after the revolution — time enough for the former owners to return shiploads of capital goods destined for the mines to the country of origin and to cut off further explorations and to exploit to the maximum existing shafts. A worker relates the meaning of nationalization for underground workers:

On the 31st of October they signed the act of nationalization in Siglo XX in the Field of María Barzola. They declared a day of festivities. All the works were paralyzed, neither factories, nor masonries, nor those who worked in the constructions in the city of Oruro worked that day. We workers of all the mines gathered together for this act in Siglo XX where there was a huge concentration. They set off some dynamite as if they were in a ferocious combat, a war.

When we worked in the companies of the ex-barons of tin, there were no drilling machines nor automatic shovels for the majority of us in Santa Fé. They had compressed air only where there were no drills, and this was in only a very few areas. After nationalization they put in pipes in all parts, even into the most oppressive areas where the heat was so intense you could hardly stand it. Before a worker had to swing a wet burlap in all directions to drive out the heat into the tunnels or the shafts when they were driving a shaft down to another level. After the revolution they had pipes set up for ventilation.

Before the nationalization of the mines, many workers could not secure a contract. They had to work two years as a peon of the house at the behest of any *cuadrilla* [work group], earning no more than the base wage without a contract. For example, in my case, when the month of May came I should have been let on the job after I was fired serving as a peon for two years. Instead when I came back to work the engineer told me, "Listen, Rocha, you cannot continue as a *pirkin*; you have to work as a driller." I was afraid when he said this because never in my life had I worked with a machine, nor did I know anything about the sickness of the miners and how one contracted it. It just scared me to hear, "You are going to work with the drilling machine."

Nationalization of the mines was a grandstand play for the peasants and workers who had brought Paz Estenssero to power. Leaders of the labor movement tried to promote a greater participation by workers through the Control Obrero, or Worker Control. The revitalized Federation of Mine Workers Unions of Bolivia (FSTMB), along with the newly organized Bolivian Workers' Central (COB), drafted the decree for worker participation that was passed for the mines on December 15, 1953. This same worker summarizes the effect of the decree on workers from his perspective:

After the Central Obrero Boliviana (COB) was organized, the secretary general of the Federation declared that the administrators of the nationalized mines were taking advantage of their position in the cashier's office, the head office of personnel, the supply office, the heads of the encampment and of welfare. In the personnel office there was a list of workers called *maquipuras* [irregular, nonsupervised workers] who were not people who worked, but only appeared as names on the pay ledger and the chief received their pay.

As a result of these abnormalities, the secretary-generals in the nationalized mines asked that COMIBOL organize a directive which would serve as a base to control each company. They wanted to form a Worker Control with the right of veto. The government of Victor Paz Estenssero prevented the organization of this group. With great effort, the miners organized it but without the right to a veto. Without this, nothing had any worth. The workers of Siglo XX took a stronger position than the other mines. They wanted to enter into a strike, the first threat during the time of Victor Paz Estenssero. Paz Estenssero did not want any problem in this period of office and he gave in to their demand. After that they did not have these kinds of arbitrary acts that were happening in the nationalized mines. They had more earnings than ever because every receipt had the signature of the men in charge of Control Obrero. No one had the right to dispatch any drug, any work material in any part, no matter how urgent it was, without passing through the Control Obrero.

In Santa Fé we did not know what the Control Obrero was and for what it served since our company wasn't nationalized in the year 1953. We only knew that the Control Obrero had to interfere in all kinds of arbitrary acts that existed in the company. In the year 1954 our company was nationalized as well as Japo. Immediately we organized the Control Obrero with the right to veto. The first secretary general was Victor Carrasco who was secretary of the union organization in the Federation of Miners. He apprehended various employees who had taken advantage of the earnings of the company. For example, Señor Manuel Cano had made a good house in Oruro with materials from the company. He came in person to Oruro to collect materials for the shops in Santa Fé saying that he needed pipes, wood, all kinds of fixings for the construction of housing. They discovered it when the Control Obrero looked over a mountain of receipts from the year 1952. He was changed to another post. Also they discovered a Señor Minaya, chief of the offices. He was a Paraguayan who had taken advantage of $b30,000. Another chief of the offices, a Chilean, had taken $b25,000 to his country, but they couldn't get it back. The Control Obrero is the one which put a quota on everything and made things more rational.

The decree called for Worker Control to intervene in production planning, organization of work, decision making in investments, vigilance over expenditures, and disciplining of personnel (Ruiz Gonzalez 1965:279). However, the main concentration of Worker Control in fact was an attack on the administration which took for granted that the managers were the owners of the house and the workers were the outsiders. The very function of being a watchdog was at odds with the other administrative functions contained in the decree. The aggressive stance taken by miners in the Worker Control minimized one of the common weaknesses of the system: the assimilation of workers' outlook to that of administrators. But it severely limited their managerial functions.[1]

The limitation of functions exercised by Worker Control had a structural base in the failure to take a position independent of the union. Even after such councils are formed and operating smoothly, it is important to retain a strong union organization that operates in the capacity of watchdog over both managerial and worker representatives and that over-

---

[1]   Selsef (1970) has spelled out the major problems encountered in the Argentine experience as follows: (1) difficulties in the exchange of information with the base, (2) workers dedicate more energy to salary and welfare than to management of enterprise, and (3) workers assimilate to the point of view of managers. These problems point to the need for continued surveillance of trade unions independent of the Worker Control group operating outside of the particular enterprise.

sees the problems of salary and welfare in which worker control councils often get bogged down. In the case of Bolivian mine workers, there never developed a clear-cut separation of functions. The FSTMB controlled the selection of Worker Control representatives and dominated in the selection of issues. Frequently the secretary general of the union was the director of Worker Control. The ever-present fear of the rank and file that their representatives were becoming an elite corps as they entered into managerial functions was exacerbated.

Another structural weakness was the fact that there was only one worker representative in the Worker Control. As Ruiz Gonzales (1965:272ff) said, "Only one such representative who carries out functions of control and effective intervention in complex administrative tasks as required by the decree is in the same situation as the shipwrecked sailor hanging from a log on the high seas."

As a result of these functional ambiguities and structural inadequacies in defining lines of jurisdiction between Worker Control and the union, workers failed to gain a sense of participation and this increased their sense of frustration.

The experience with Worker Control was one part of a larger contradiction that existed in popular participation in the MNR government from 1952 to 1964. The working class held positions in the senate, in up to four ministries, and their foremost leader, Juan Lechín Oquenda, occupied at one time the post of Minister of Mines and Petroleum and the vice-presidency in Paz's final term, at the same time that he continued as president of the COB and of the FSTMB. The contradiction between these roles became particularly sharp as labor's discontent with the government, particularly over the issue of the economic stabilization that put a freeze on wages and prices in 1957, sharpened. The same replication of functions was found at lower levels of the union and political hierarchy.

As a result of the elite positions union leaders occupied in a nonlabor government, the rank and file workers felt more and more disinherited by the revolution they had made a reality in 1952. In a postmortem on the MNR period made by a rank-and-file worker at the San José mine in April 1970, this lack of confidence is underscored:

During cogovernment we had many workers as senators and congressmen, and what did they do for the workers' movement? Nothing. But we can indicate clearly that they had a great opportunity to traffic with syndicalism because they are the new rich. Many of the worker ministers live very comfortably; they have automobiles, houses not only in Coban, but in Cochabamba, and they don't even belong to the working class because they do not know the mineshaft while we, of the working class, continue living in the mine shafts.

He concluded his attack on the old leaders with a call for the independence of the working class. Of the many such attacks that I heard in the months following the regeneration of the labor movement in the April 1970 Congress of the FSTMB, the phrase that seemed to sum it up best was that of a rank-and-file member of the San José mines who said at a union meeting, "This kind of petty-bourgeoisie politics broke the skull (*descalabró*) of the working class." Lechín himself admitted in an address to union delegates to the COB meetings in May 1970:

We have to recognize that the experience of cogovernment caused the compromise to the working class and the entrance into power by governments of this period. This experience and the attitude assumed by different political parties undermines our union independence of political parties.

But he concludes with this ambiguous statement: "However, we must recognize that we cannot remain simply a spectator because that is a peril to the working class."

The reversal of nationalization began with vigor in the 1960's and was accelerated by the Triangular Plan signed in August 1961. The plan called for the recapitalization of the mines with a loan of U.S. $ 37,750,000 from the Bank for Inter-American Development (BID), West Germany, and the United States, to be used for exploration of new mineral deposits, metallurgical work to increase recovery rates, replacement of needed material, equipment to rehabilitate mines, and commissary supplies (Zondag 1966:232). The loan was contingent on the "rationalization" of the labor force. It was this provision that split the ranks of labor, and Worker Control was the scene on which the battle was fought. Federico Escobar, leader of the Siglo XX-Catavi mine union and head of Worker Control there attacked the plan as an imperialist design to gain control over the mines. Lechín defended it in the publication called *Control Obrero* (1961:4) stating:

Since when can something die before being born? The Triangular Plan has not yet been born in this country; perhaps it will be born today in accord with the information of the press. The comrades have begun blaming the Triangular Plan for all the evils of the working class and their social problems. But the means adopted are prior to and not a consequence of the plan but of other things (Quoted in Canelas 1966:1067.)

Because of the resistance of the workers, the plan did not bring about a reorganization of the work force until 1965. There was in fact an increase in the number of above-ground workers from 1962, when there were 16,813, to 18,819 in 1965. The increase in above-ground workers was due in part to an overinflated bureaucracy expanding in accordance with

Parkinson's law, but also to a policy of absorbing men too sick to work underground in supernumerary posts above ground. The "rationalization" of the work force did not begin until 1965 when General René Barrientos, who had seized power after the November 4, 1964, rebellion when Paz was unseated by the combined action of workers and students, sent troops into the mines in May.

The decade of the sixties was a time for the attack on the nationalized mines from managerial and government leaders as well as from workers. From the time of nationalization to 1965, the mines had lost $106,000,000, a figure partly inflated by fiscal manipulation but accurate enough to demoralize the operation of the mines (Arce 1965:17). Labor costs had gone up from U.S. $.70 a pound in 1952 to U.S. $1.29 in 1960. United States critics such as Stokes (1963) and Zondag (1966) blame worker inefficiency for the increase of costs. In defense of workers, Canelas (1966: 43) pointed to the Ford, Bacon, and Davis report made in 1957 which showed that, despite reduction in overall figures for refined exported tin, there was an increase of 30 percent of gross mineral extracted in the first five years of nationalization. He pointed out that men in Catavi, who had turned out 1.22 tons per *mita* [work shift] in 1950, were turning out 1.31 tons per *mita* in 1955, and there was an overall production increase of 1,052,405 tons of crude ore in 1950 to 1,459,389 tons in 1955. The declining production noted by Stokes, who used figures on refined mineral to prove his case, was due to the fact that it required ten meters of advance to extract a ton in 1960, in comparison with one meter in 1950. The failure to explore new tunnels and declining administrative efficiency were blamed for this.

Federico Escobar, the secretary general of Siglo XX-Catavi's union and head of Worker Control, attacked the administration for having benefited Patiño, one of the former owners, more than the workers in the course of nationalization. Bedregal, then president of COMIBOL, countered the attack by claiming that COMIBOL was crippled by world market prices which had dropped severely in the post-Korean war period. The United States had taken advantage of the nationalization of mines to break its contracts with the former companies which were pegged at the high war-time price of U.S. $1.83 per pound of refined tin and reset their price at U.S. $.90. He tried to enlist the support of labor with his statement that:

Nationalization of the mines does not have as an object only the betterment of the conditions of work and of the life of the miner, but also the entire transformation of the economic and social conditions of the Bolivian nation (1959:14).

His appeal to nationalism in an attempt to overcome the developing class antagonisms in the mine is summed up in the position that:

In the natural order of political priorities, first is the country and then unionism; first is the national liberation and then the liberation of the working classes. If one insists on altering this nationalist order of priorities, believing that the union can earn when the nation is losing, we have confronted the interest of the workers to the interests of the nation as a community weak and irresponsible; that is, we have added the new forces of the proletariat to the old forces of the counterrevolution.

Labor did not buy this position and advised the management of their discontent by calling a strike. Later, Bedregal tried a frontal attack on labor with the report of a national investigation commission's summary of the damage caused by the union. The report (Comisión Investigadora Nacional 1965) arrived at a sum of U.S. $45,076,718.29 with the following items included:

Cost of Control Obrero and directors $5,604,725.29
Loss of production by directors of unions failing to attend jobs. 8,333,063.40
Loss for excess workers on surface 15,813,723.19
Cost of strikes 13,187,942.32
Cost for activities during disputes 47,944.19
Debts of FSTMB 350,552.58
Debts of union leaders 295,113.38
Debts of workers 1,315,618.00
Debts of clubs 128,036.03

Assessing this balance sheet, one can see that labor was charged for all the damages caused by the failure of the industry to settle labor disputes. In addition, one can clearly see the dependency that trade unions had fallen into, relying on income from the administration to maintain them in power.

While both sides in the attack on COMIBOL used the Ford, Bacon, and Davis report to bolster their claims, the conclusions censure both low worker productivity and technicians' failure, but with the target being managerial inefficiency in overcoming these pitfalls. Arce, an engineer in Patiño mines, pointed to the nub of the technological problem in nationalized mines stating (1965:15) that "a fiscal administration cannot carry out risks of long range exploration" since they are constantly subjected to criticism and review, oftentimes by men who had little or no knowledge of mining. The resulting policy in the mines was one of intensive exploitation of existing reserves, a point most of the workers made to me on the basis of their immediate experience. Arce's recommendation was that there should be holding companies of *Sociedades Anonimas* which were decentralized, with directorates including workers to "create a spirit of belonging between workers and employers that would reinforce efficiency and production by both health and constructive competition."

Despite the attack from both management and labor on the policies of COMIBOL, both sides were dedicated to vindicating the process of nationalization and preventing the mines from falling back into private hands. In part this was due to self-interest. The union leadership had benefited in the 1952 populist period, when unions had a greater recognition and opportunity to benefit financially under nationalized restraints which were more subject to populist pressures and more willing to invest in cooptation funds. Management benefited in the very position they occupied in replacing previous foreign incumbents at technical and managerial levels. These vested interests made nationalization an irreversible process. Neither the government nor the military attacked COMIBOL because they were using it as their own private purse, as one miner said in the Congress at Siglo XX-Catavi in 1970.

The problem was to overcome the lack of confidence of the workers with nationalization. The thesis worked out by the political commission at Siglo XX-Catavi pointed to the fact that COMIBOL "as inheritor of the *rosca* [oligarchy of tin barons] has constituted a true superstate over the blood of the workers, limiting the role of the workers to produce and obey." But it attributed this failure to a false nationalization in which the middle class maintained control of the decision-making apparatus and continued as subservients of the international private capitalists. The union "line" became one of splitting the economic and political consequences of nationalization. This was expressed by an aspiring candidate for union office at the San José union meeting:

I believe that nationalization of mines and of Gulf is a positive step for the Bolivian people and for the liberation of Latin American countries, but it is a negative step economically because the world market is controlled now by imperialism.... Who fixes the prices? It is no more than the imperialists who are the great monopolists.... Nationalizations are positive from a political point of view, but from an economic point of view we do not control the world market.

One of the theoreticians from the Universidad Mayor de San Andrés who was called upon to give a course in the union of San José gave a Marxist class analysis of nationalization and its failure:

COMIBOL does not benefit the worker because it is not in the hands of the workers. The passage of property from private hands to the state only means that the same internal relations continue. State capitalism produces a bureaucracy in conformity with administrators, superintendents who belong to the bourgeois class. This bourgeoisie has a self-interest in the company. The bougeoisie is antinational.

He went on to point out that the bourgeoisie is not a great homogeneous block but has internal contradictions that the working class must learn to take advantage of. While nationalization benefits one sector of the bourgeoisie by giving them more possibilities of work and earning money, it disfavors another group, the commercial sector, because many *gringos* leave, and they lose many dollars in the sale of whisky, good clothing, and other luxuries.

In analyzing the failure of nationalization in the brief period of revitalization of the union movement from the XIVth Congress of Miners in April 1970 until the Ranzer coup of August 1971, union leaders pointed to the error of letting COMIBOL fall into the hands of "the politicians of turn, the bourgeois bureaucrats, and the military" and the necessity of regaining Worker Control to ensure the gains made by the revolution. During this period, the union started an all-out drive to reestablish wages at the pre-Barrientos level and cut down bureaucratic expenditures in order to finance labor's demands. They pointed out that COMIBOL personnel in the La Paz central office increased from 265 in 1954 to 475 in 1970, with administrative employees earning up to one hundred times as much as interior workers. Expenditures for the central office were U.S. $2,750,000 per year, without counting funds for purchases that never arrived in the mines. Lechín summarized the case in a report to the delegates on September 29, 1972: "There is no possibility for a worker to enter in the mine to produce and leave his lungs there, but there is to increase the bureaucracy. For this there is no limit. There we have to get rid of the parasites." (Tape recording.) He called for the workers to manage the funds they contributed to the Social Security and the reinstatement of Worker Control with the right of veto.

A week later, and only twelve days after the first anniversary of his September 26, 1969, coup, Ovando had to yield the presidency to Torres after Miranda made a bid for power that failed. One of his first moves to coalesce the waning labor support of his predecessor was to increase wages. Contract workers were still dissatisfied, but Torres promised to give more support to the unions, and so the miners rallied around him when Banzer made the first of his abortive moves to unseat him in January 1971.

In a move to gain greater worker contribution to production, Torres proposed a plan for coparticipation in nationalized industries. In theory, coparticipation was to mean a "substitution of exclusive authority of the employer by the collective authority of all those who take part in production." However, the degree of entry by workers was not explicitly stated (Andrade 1971). The Bolivian Petroleum Company (YPFB) and the National Housing Cooperative (CONAVI) accepted the proposal as presented immediately. The FSTMB made it a central point for discussion in the Popular Assembly that opened on May 1, 1971. The proposal was designed to gain greater cooperation from the workers in raising production; but since they lacked a veto power, the miners considered it a company ploy.

The Assembly included representatives of most of the organized segments of labor except for the peasants, whose representatives were considered either too much subject to government control or too far left,[2] Party representatives from the Workers' Party of Bolivia (POR), the Communist Party of Bolivia (PCB Moscow line), the Left National Revolutionary Party (PRIN), and the National Revolutionary Movement (MNR), as well as some student representatives of the Left Revolutionary Movement (MIR) and the Christian Revolutionary Democrats (DCR). In the discussions, the union representatives of the FSTMB dominated proceedings. They differentiated coparticipation from Worker Control in that they proposed to work "from below to above rather than the reverse," as had occurred in the early years of nationalization when only top leaders entered the councils. They demanded that a majority of the representation in the council of workers and managers should be labor, and they demanded that the president of COMIBOL should be chosen by the directors of COMIBOL from a list drawn up by the directorate. COMIBOL rejected these two proposals and called for the president to be named by the executive power in a council of ministers from a list presented by COMIBOL. The ultimate aim of coparticipation as envisioned in the Assembly was "the social property of the means of production" (Andrade 1971).

The duties drawn up by the FSTMB and presented to the Popular Assembly were more specific than those included in the 1953 decree for Worker Control:

1. Attend with voice and vote in the directors' meetings.
2. Inform themselves of all aspects relating to activities of the company, such as plans, projects for exploitation of minerals, reforms of administrative structures, costs, accounting, commercialization, financing, evaluation and control of growth of these plans and works without any limitation.

[2] The Union of Poor Campesinos (UCAPO) was refused a seat in the Popular Assembly along with some unions of *campesinos* considered to be dominated by the government.

3. To take into account contracts of purchases, local contracts, transportations and to prove to themselves that the prices, qualities and conditions are the most favorable that can be obtained.
4. Control the distribution of articles in the *pulperia* and shop with the interest of avoiding favoritism.
5. Interview for the hiring and firing of workers.
6. Control and intervene in the increases and modifications of day work of personnel and transfer of workers and employees.

The FSTMB combined its presentation of demands with an attack on the administration of COMIBOL by generals. They pointed out that before the Barrientos regime began, when the president of the company was civilian, the bureaucracy cost U.S. $40,000, and after that the costs rose to U.S. $400,000 as the presidency became occupied by the military. They asked that the administration seek a new market for minerals in the socialist countries. Lora (1972:84) summed up the contrast between Worker Control and coparticipation, stating that while the first was individual and bureaucratic, coparticipation was collective and exercised by the working class itself. The contradiction in function between that of vigilance over the operation of management and participation in the administration as coequals that I pointed to above remained implicit in the new plan.

The Left was divided on the importance of the assembly and its major proposal for coparticipation. While some called it "a symphony of the Left" (*Presencia* 1971) others accused it of being reformist in orientation and self-seeking (Lora 1972:16).

The Banzer coup makes any speculation as to how coparticipation would have worked out an academic issue. However, the reaction of the rank and file in the period when the plan was still being discussed in July of 1971 revealed a lack of confidence in the labor leadership and a fear of the resurgence of the elitism that characterized the labor movement in the cogovernment period. Rank-and-file leaders in San José mine broke up a meeting sheduled for a discussion of the plan when I visited that center in July 1971. They resented the fact that Juan Lechín, who was scheduled to appear and explain the new measure, had not come; and many expressed suspicion of both local and national leaders and their motivation for implementing the plan before many of the concrete problems of contract prices and incentives had been ironed out. The heritage of corruption from the period of cooptation had born its harvest of mistrust.

Bolivia's experience with worker participation reveals the contradictions implicit in any compromise form of entry into management short of a socialist reorganization of the aims and structures of industrial enterprises. However, this should not imply that such movements should not be undertaken. Many of the Worker Control representatives rose to the occasion and gained enough entry into the administrative process to thoroughly shake up the bureaucratic process and threaten its usurpation of control over the lives of thousands of workers. Worker Control succeeded in establishing some of the minimal conditions for living and working in mining encampments that had, under the old management, reduced workers to bestial levels. For the first time they questioned the premise of production geared to meeting external demands and lacking even minimal interest in the lives and welfare of the men and women who produced the wealth. In the early years of nationalization, miners did produce more ores, although these yielded less refined metal than before. Poor administration and ineffective technical control were probably as much, or more, responsible for declining productivity in later years as lack of discipline in labor.

As for the criterion of self-determination for judging Bolivia's experience with participation in the tin mining industry, I felt that, in the accounts miners gave and in the reports I have read on the experience in the fifties and sixties, there was a growing awareness of the need for further exploration and capitalization; but these demands never were channeled through the Worker Control representatives. Many workers have told me of the failure of the administration to open new shafts. They respected the ability of some of the old foreign technicians and felt that the demagoguery of nationalist leaders inhibited the efficient exploitation of the mines. Their growing alienation from the administration of COMIBOL caused them to resist yielding information about veins they knew existed. However, these demands for opening up new shafts and providing the equipment to work effectively were not publicly aired. Their watchdog function was simply a reversal of the Robin Hood role; the administration was still the owner, they were still the underdog, although they patrolled the streets of the managerial elite instead of stealing from them.

One could probably make a good case for decline in efficiency in the nationalized mines. In the old *pirkin* system of exploitation favored in the time of the *rosca*, the worker was paid for the mineral content of what he produced. He was highly motivated to use all his ingenuity and senses to work the veins. Miners develop an eye and a taste for where the veins are. Some even explore the face of a newly blasted area with their tongues to sense the location of the vein. Under the private companies, some could get fairly high returns, and they exploited their bodies and souls, which they sold to the devil,[3] in the desire to find the metal. After nationalization

---

[3]   I have summarized rituals and beliefs concerning the devil, or Supay, a pre-Conquest hill spirit, in "Devils, witches and sudden death" (Nash 1972).

they were paid in relation to brute loads, a fairer system from an overall perspective, but one that failed to mobilize the total involvement of the miners as the old system had done. In the *pirkin* system, self-exploitation was greater, but workers reported a greater sense of adventure. They followed the veins of metal without too much concern for organizing tunnels and channels of entry and exit, and they profited in terms of the value of the ore.

Worker participation cannot be conceived of as a solution for the class struggle or as the conquest of socialist aims. It is only a prelude to such victories that at best can provide an arena where workers can gain the experience necessary to gain full control over their destiny in the future. Trade-union movements too often bog down in bread-and-butter questions. Even worse, they generate alienation not only against the owners of industry but against the work itself. This serves to minimize the sense of social participation in productivity that would provide the basis for a socialist economy. With a division of labor between trade unions and worker councils, the former could retain the function of preventing the exploitation of workers and attending to their economic concerns, while the latter could enter into the transformation of administration into a concern with the wider interest of the community. The failure to maintain this division of functions minimized the effectiveness of both worker activities during the populist period of nationalization.

Vanek envisions a democratic form of socialist enterprise achieved through a modified market-controlled system to avoid the bureaucratic state apparatus of the Soviet state. He does not, however, go into the contradictions that still exist in a production system part free market and part planned. These contradictions are just now rising to the surface as inflation, unemployment, and inadequate incomes for most workers in Yugoslavia are stirring up worker resentment; and this is exacerbated by the high lifestyle of some management representatives who have profited from the enterprises (*New York Times* 1971). Latin American countries must work out their own model for worker participation in administration whether prior to or after a revolutionary transformation of structures.

Worker participation shifts the workers' perspectives from a concern with the class struggle to an interest in the division of labor. It makes postrevolutionary decisions a priority before the revolution. For the Bolivian rank and file during the revival of interest in the issue when the Popular Assembly was convening in June and July 1972, it seemed to indicate a concern with the division of spoils rather than a reconstruction of their role in industrial production. Without careful planning and preparation for this phase, the experience can end in the frustration that would defeat ultimate aims.

REFERENCES

ANAYO, RICARDO
1952 *Nacionalización de las minas de Bolivia.* Cochabamba: Inprenta Universal.

ANDRADE, CARLOS
1971 *Presencia* August 8, 1971.

ARCE, ROBERTO
1965 *Recomendaciónes para la rehabilitación de la industria minera.* La Paz.

BEDREGAL, GUILLERMO
1959 *Nacionalización y la responsibilidad del sindicato.* La Paz.
1963 *COMIBOL: Una Verdad.* Departamento de Relaciones Pública. La Paz.

CANELAS, AMADO
1963 *Nacionalización de las minas de Bolivia: historia de una frustración.* La Paz: Libreria Altiplano.
1966 *Mito y realidad de la Corporación Minera de Bolivia, COMIBOL.* La Paz: Edit. Los Amigos del Libro.

LA COMISIÓN INVESTIGADORA NACIONAL
1965 *Daño y costos del sindicalismo a COMIBOL.* Informe 4. La Paz.

Control Obrero
1961 *Control Obrero* August, number 8.

FORD, BACON AND DAVIS, INCORPORATED
1956 *Report on the mining industry of Bolivia,* nine volumes. Volume one: *Summary,* 14–15; Volume two: *Significant Aspects of the Bolivian Mining Industry.* La Paz: Ministry of Mines and Petroleum.

GRAMSCI, ANTONIO
1957 *The modern prince and other writings.* New York: International Publishers.

LORA, GUILLERMO
1972 *Bolivia: de la Asamblea Popular al Golpe del 21 de Agosto.* Santiago, Chile.

NASH, JUNE
1972 Devils, witches and sudden death. *Natural History Magazine* (March).

New York Times
1971 Article appearing August 8th.

Presencia
1972 Article appearing November 18th.

RUIZ GONZALES, RENÉ
1965 *La administración empirica de las minas naciónalizadas.* La Paz.

SELSEF, JORGE
1970 *Participación de los trabajadores en la gestión ecónomica.* Buenos Aires: Ediciones Librero.

STOKES, WM. S.
1963 "The *Contraproducente* consequences of the foreign aid program on Bolivia," in *The new argument in economics: the public vs. the private sector,* edited by H. Schoeck and J. Wiggin. New York: Van Nostrand.

VANEK, JAROSLAV
1971 *La economia de participación: hipótesis evolucionista y estrategia para el desarrollo.* Lima: Instituto de Estudos Peruanos. (Published 1974 as

The participatory economy: an evolutionary hypothesis and a strategy for development. Ithaca: Cornell University Press.)

ZONDAG, CORNELIUS
1966   *The Bolivian economy 1952–65. The revolution and its aftermath.* New York: Frederick A. Praeger.

Workers into Managers:
Worker Participation in the Chilean
Textile Industry

PETER WINN

THE CHILEAN CONTEXT

Worker self-management does not take place in a vacuum. There are always specific societal contexts, both local and national, that powerfully influence its character and success. The context within which Allende's Chile initiated its experiment in worker participation in the management of the nationalized textile industry in 1971 shaped the contours of the experience and presented mixed auguries for the future.

President Salvador Allende came to power in November 1970, with a commitment both to the nationalization of Chile's major industries and to some form of worker participation in their management. His Popular Unity government, however, was a heterogeneous coalition of Marxists, Social Democrats, and Christian Socialists — a diverse alliance of six parties, united only by adherence to the generalities of a common electoral platform. Moreover, Allende had received only a narrow plurality at the polls and a disputed mandate for change. He faced a hostile legislature, judiciary, and bureaucracy, and uncertain support from the armed forces.

Although the Allende government's power to enact and implement a coherent program of worker participation was questionable, there were important sources of strength upon which it could draw. One was the powers of the Chilean presidency, an executive so strong it was known as a "six-year elective monarchy." Another was Chile's long democratic tradition. A third was the existence of a powerful organized labor movement, led by Marxists and with a long history of authentic representation and militancy.

The textile industry, where the experiment in worker participation in factory management was initiated, was typical of much of the manufacturing sector in pre-Allende Chile. It was an import-substitution industry, protected against foreign competition but tied to foreign capital and dependent upon the importation of machinery, spare parts, and most raw materials. Although there were many textile mills in Chile in 1970, production was concentrated in a few highly capitalized, modern factories, which were controlled by four families of Arab origin and linked by interlocking directorates. Moreover, each factory specialized in different lines of production, so that competition among the mills was minimal. Concentration of ownership and production, division of the market, and monopoly pricing characterized the industry on the eve of its nationalization.

Yarur, the factory upon whose experience this paper is based, was the oldest of the large textile mills, with machinery dating from the founding of the factory in 1936. It dominated both the production of cheaper cotton textiles for mass consumption and cotton spinning. Technically a joint-stock company, Yarur was run as a family firm in patrimonial style. In 1970, power and decision making were concentrated in the hands of Amador Yarur; managerial and technical personnel were stripped of independent initiative and authority by the personalistic way in which the factory was run. Supervisory personnel frequently held their positions more through favoritism than through competence, and responded with sycophancy and informing, accepting their role as instruments of Yarur's will.

Social control of the workers in the industry was ensured by a combination of paternalism and repression. For the favored, there were special privileges, promotions, and loans, as well as personal praise and occasional gifts from the *patrón*[1] as rewards for their loyalty. "Deviance" from this norm of loyalty, on the other hand, was punished by harassment, transfer to undesirable sections, suspension, and dismissal. Discussion of national politics or the formation of an independent union was prohibited, and no criticism of the Yarurs or working conditions in the factory was tolerated. Any violation of these canons of behavior was reported to the Yarurs by informers and was severely punished. The system was sustained by the workers' internalization of an intense fear of

---

[1]   The word "*patrón*" is best translated as "boss," but it also carries the connotation of a preindustrial relationship of mutual obligations, at once personal and paternalistic, over and above the contractual relationship between worker and "boss." The Spanish word conserves many of the connotations of the English word "patron," and I have elected, therefore, to retain the former term in the text.

punishment and was maintained by a web of worker-informers, who competed in demonstrations of loyalty to the *patron* by the frequency and virulence of their reports. As a result, there were very low levels of social interaction and solidarity (*compañerismo*) among the workers and a high rate of turnover of labor.

At the point of production, the control of the labor force was assured by the Taylor system, in which every movement was regulated and each moment monitored, converting the worker into an optimally efficient extension of the machines he or she tended.[2] *Taylorismo* had been introduced into the factory during 1959–1961 and had been the prime cause of a long and bitter strike in 1962, during which 800 to 1,000 of the most militant workers had been fired, reducing the number of blue-collar workers in Yarur to some 2,000 — the number required for maximum efficiency under the Taylor system.

Another aim of the strike of 1962 had been the consolidation of an independent union. The struggle for an independent bargaining agent has been a recurring theme in the factory's thirty-five-year history and has led to periodic strikes. All of these conflicts ended in management victories, through a combination of bribery, threat, and repression, frequently with the complicity or open assistance of the state. As a consequence, although in other Chilean textile factories the workers had won the right to have independent unions, at Yarur there was only a company union, and both union elections and collective bargaining were rigged charades.

During the decade that preceded the election of Allende, however, the composition of the labor force at Yarur had changed. In 1960, the average age of the workers was over forty; most of them had been at the factory for many years, and many of them were women.[3] This group, which had learned the lessons of survival and the wisdom of passivity from successive labor defeats, still constituted a sizable portion of the 2,000 blue-collar workers in the factory in 1970. By then, however, they were outnumbered by a group of younger, male workers, who had entered the factory after the introduction of the Taylor system and the strike of 1962 and whose average age was under thirty. They had learned to live with the history of defeat and atmosphere of repression in the factory but were much less

---

[2] Under the factory's Taylor system, in addition to the disciplinary stick, machine operators were also offered the carrot of incentive pay, although the workers considered the incentives offered to be inadequate compensation for the additional labor, which in some cases amounted to a speed-up of 300 percent.

[3] Women workers had predominated among machine operators until the mid-1950's, when protective social legislation raised the cost of their labor and the Yarurs began to phase them out. By 1970, women workers constituted only some 10 percent of the labor force.

resigned to it than were the older workers. Moreover, they tended to be better educated and less receptive to paternalistic management. During 1969–1970, a small group of these younger workers began to organize clandestinely, but no sizable movement had been created before the election of Salvador Allende in September 1970.

Within three weeks of Allende's election victory, however, an independent union to represent the factory's 500 employees[4] was formed, while a slate of leftist independents swept the blue-collar union elections held less than a month after Allende's assumption of office in November 1970. By the end of 1970, therefore, a repressed group of workers at Yarur had cast aside their apparent passivity and crowned a generation of struggle for independent representatives with success — a local activism and triumph made possible by the national political victory of the Chilean Left. By early 1971, the new union leaders at Yarur were looking past this conquest and the historic demands of the Chilean labor movement for better working conditions; increasingly, they stood ready to carry out the structural transformation that Allende had promised the workers of Yarur during his campaign — the nationalization of the factory.

The Allende government had proclaimed its commitment to nationalizing all Chilean factories with a capital of more than U.S. $1,000,000, but it was without either the political power to legislate this transformation or the military strength to carry it out by force. As a consequence, the nationalization strategy of the new government was both gradualist and legalistic. Nationalization of domestic industry was to be delayed until politically and economically convenient, planned with care, and carried out in a manner controlled from above. Moreover, nationalization had to be both constitutional (to avoid the threat of a military coup) and extraparliamentary (to circumvent the opposition's majority in Congress).

Faced with these confining conditions, the Allende government decided to employ the considerable, but rarely used, emergency powers of the Chilean presidency to requisition a factory when the supply of an item of basic necessity was threatened by the policies of its management and to intervene in the management of a factory where a labor dispute had proved incapable of resolution through collective bargaining. In both

---

[4] The word "*empleado*", translated here as "employee", implies a legal distinction between "manual" and "intellectual" labor embodied in the Chilean labor code of 1924, which distinguishes the *empleado* from the *obrero* [blue-collar worker]. In fact, while most *empleados* at Yarur were white-collar workers, many skilled blue-collar workers (in addition to technical and supervisory personnel) had also secured the status of *empleado*, prized for its higher wage levels, more ample benefits, and implied middle-class social status. For a more complete discussion of the *empleado-obrero* distinction, its evolution, and its implications, see Angell (1972: 66–68).

cases, the Chilean president has the right to name a government manager (*interventor*), who takes over the running of the factory from the private owners for a temporary, but indefinite, time period and whose administrative decisions are binding.

Under Allende, however, once the government had assumed the management of a factory, made known its reluctance to return it to the owners and its readiness to purchase a controlling share from the stockholders at a reasonable price, the latter were expected to sell their stocks to the government, thus completing the process of nationalization. The factory, whether its nationalization was *de facto* or *de jure*, would be placed under the aegis of the preexisting state development corporation. This agency, the Corporación de Fomento (CORFO), was to be transformed into the central planning and management authority for the public sector of the emerging mixed economy, a sector composed of the large and strategic industries, which would permit the government to realize its expressed aim of controlling "the commanding heights of the economy" (Unidad Popular 1970).

In these early plans of the Allende government, the place of worker participation in the management of the newly nationalized factories was ambiguous. Allende's Popular Unity coalition had a public commitment to worker participation but was internally divided about its scope and nature — some favored a high degree of worker power and spontaneity through workers' councils, others a more controlled and structured participation through existing union channels. To the left of the governing coalition, the Movement of the Revolutionary Left (MIR) was demanding worker control through untrammeled participatory democracy; while to the right, the Christian Democratic opposition was formulating a proposal for a "workers' enterprise," in which the workers of a factory would become shareholders and run the industry along neocapitalist lines, dividing the profits among themselves, *à la* Vanek and the Yugoslav model.[5]

The problem for the Allende government was to evolve a scheme of worker participation that would satisfy the divergent views within the coalition yet would retain the allegiance of the workers in the face of competing alternatives to the left and the right. Moreover, for both economic and political reasons, the Popular Unity could not afford the

---

[5] For a recent exposition of Vanek's views, including his favorable discussion of the Yugoslav experience, see Vanek (1971). Although Vanek draws a distinction between the workers owning the factory as shareholders (which he opposes) and the workers dividing the profits as shareholders (which be favors), the profit motive remains the economic *raison d'être* of his model (Vanek 1971:27).

luxury of failure — falling production, political squabbles, or charges of irresponsibility — and was disposed to proceed with caution. The coalition had yet to resolve these issues when the Allende government was compelled by forces beyond its control both to accelerate its nationalization timetable and to agree to a scheme of worker participation. One stimulus was the sabotage of production and machinery by private owners attempting to torpedo the government through the creation of an economic crisis; the other was the pressure from below for rapid fulfillment of the nationalization plank of the Popular Unity program — pressure from workers and their local leaders, frequently encouraged by elements within the governing coalition, seeking a radicalization of the revolutionary process.

THE CHILEAN MODEL OF WORKER PARTICIPATION

On April 28, 1971, the Yarur cotton textile complex in Santiago was seized by its workers, setting off a wave of factory seizures which forced the Popular Unity coalition to resolve its differences and agree to a scheme of worker participation in the newly nationalized industries. The accord (Chile-Central Unica de Trabajadores 1972)[6] between the government and the national labor federation, the Central Unica de Trabajadores (CUT), that emerged from these political negotiations reflected the divisions within the Chilean Left and represented a compromise that all of its parties could accept but that satisfied no one.

In this agreement, the participation of the workers was defined in revolutionary terms — "the transfer of power from the minorities to the great majority." The list of new power holders, however, included not only the blue-collar workers, but also the professionals, technicians, and white-collar workers, an alliance that reflected the heterogeneous social base of the Popular Unity government. The working class would participate in the direction of the nation, but indirectly through their class representatives — the Marxist parties and the national union leaders of the CUT.[7]

At the level of the nationalized enterprise, worker participation in the management of the factory would have two aspects — advisory and decision making. Advice and consultation would be the functions of

---

[6] A revealing source for this analysis of the CUT-government agreement was the CUT poster summarizing the accord, which was displayed throughout Chile in factories, railway stations, and other public places.
[7] Beginning in 1972, however, the national leadership of the CUT was to be directly elected by its members, instead of indirectly as before.

production committees elected in secret and of direct balloting by the workers of each section, department, and division of the industry. Workers' power over decision making was to be embodied in their representatives on the council of administration, which would replace the old board of directors. Union officials were barred from simultaneous service as councilors, who were to be chosen by the workers in factory-wide balloting.

The role of the old labor union in the new participation scheme, however, was stressed in the agreement and in the publicity that followed. The union, all were assured, would remain an independent organ of working-class representation. It would retain all of its old functions as the defender of the interests of its members, including collective bargaining. In addition, the union would "oversee" the management of the factory and "orient" the process of worker participation, ensuring its effectiveness.

The ambiguities in this formulation reflected the tensions within the governing coalition on the nature, scope, and agencies of worker participation, while the creation of parallel structures of participation symbolized the political compromise that underlay the CUT-government agreement. Now the question was whether the workers could resolve in practice the conflicts that had proved so troublesome in leftist theory and government policy.

This Chilean model of worker participation was first put into practice (with great fanfare) in August 1971, at the already symbolic factory of Ex-Yarur. What was implemented at Ex-Yarur, however, was a modified form of the original structure agreed upon at the national level (see Figure 1). To both union and government representatives at the factory level, the full structure of participation — section, department, division, factory — each with its own committee and assembly, was far too cumbersome, complex, and demanding to permit either effective worker participation or efficient factory management. The elaborately indirect and tiered structure of the CUT-government agreement would act either as a complex screen against authentic worker participation or else as a mechanism for interminable discussion and delay in the name of industrial democracy, sapping the patience and enthusiasm of all involved, without accomplishing its presumed objective.

As a consequence, government and worker representatives at Ex-Yarur agreed to experiment with a simplified structure of participation in which the intermediate levels of department and division were eliminated.[8] The

---

[8] A formal commitment to the full structure of the CUT-government agreement was maintained, however, as was a formal commitment to its eventual implementation at Ex-Yarur (Poblete Zamorano 1972).

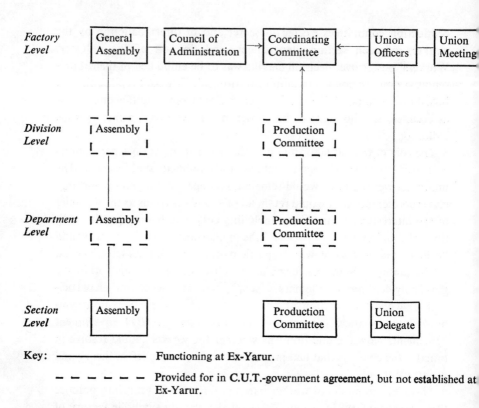

Key: ——————————— Functioning at Ex-Yarur.

‐ ‐ ‐ ‐ ‐ ‐ Provided for in C.U.T.-government agreement, but not established at Ex-Yarur.

Figure 1:   The structure of worker participation at Ex-Yarur

base of participation remained the production section, united in an assembly and electing a production committee and a delegate to the coordinating committee. The production committee would handle those questions relating to production and labor relations within the section that did not affect broader policy considerations, passing on more transcendent matters to the jurisdiction of the coordinating committee for action. In addition, the production committee was to act as a vital link in the chain of two-way communication between the rank-and-file worker and the upper levels of factory management: it would explain to the workers policy decisions taken by the coordinating committee and the council, while articulating to these higher bodies the complaints and concerns of the workers in its production section.

The coordinating committee, composed of one representative from each production section, the worker representatives on the administrative council, and the union officers, was the hub of the whole structure of participation (see Figure 1). Here problems and demands from all sections of the factory were articulated, discussed, and decided. Some might be sent back down to the production committee for decision, others dismissed or settled, while still others would be sent across to the administrative council or the union for resolution.

The supreme expression of worker participation in the management of the factory, however, was the council of administration, the new "board of directors," which was composed of five workers' councilors, elected annually in direct and secret balloting by the entire factory, and five government councilors, appointed by the CORFO.[9] In addition, the government manager of the industry doubled as chairman of the council, giving the government a theoretical majority of one. Voting on the council, however, never seemed to break down along these lines, and conflicts were more likely to be resolved by reaching a "sense of the meeting" than by a "division of the house." The council had broad powers to hire and fire, to allocate funds, and to make all the policy decisions within the purview of the factory administration.

In addition to electing representatives to the council, at the level of the factory the workers would participate in the direction of the industry through the general assembly, a town meeting of all the workers and employees of Ex-Yarur. In essence, this assembly replaced the old stockholders' meeting and its major function was the same — to receive and approve periodic reports from the council and the government managers on their administration of the factory. The three managers — a general manager plus associates in charge of labor relations and finances — were appointed by the CORFO, to whom they were responsible for their actions. In theory, however, the managers had to justify their administration to the General Assembly of the workers as well.

Parallel to this new structure of participation remained the old union structure, with delegates elected from each section, officers elected by the entire factory in annual secret balloting, and a monthly membership meeting. The CUT-government agreement guaranteed that the new structure of participation would not reduce the powers of the union. Moreover, the union officers had led the struggle against the Yarurs and were regarded by the workers as their natural leaders.

---

[9] Three of the worker councilors were to be elected from the production division, one from administration, and one from maintenance and other divisions. The workers of the entire factory, however, voted for all five, including the councilors chosen from other divisions. In mid-1972, the government councilors included the three managers of Ex-Yarur, two former managers who had become leading members of the Textile Committee of the CORFO, and a labor leader from the metallurgical industry, whose opinion was sought after and highly respected by the rest.

The result of this parallelism, however, was that THREE groups claimed a mandate to represent the workers of the factory: the delegates to the coordinating committee, the councilors, and the union officers. Moreover, two assemblies at the factory level — the union meeting and the general assembly — claimed to offer the workers of Ex-Yarur the direct power of participatory democracy. The demarcation between their roles and powers was sufficiently ambiguous to make tensions — both personal and structural — all but inevitable, to which were added the inexperience and confusion of the workers themselves.

THE FIRST YEAR OF WORKER PARTICIPATION AT EX-YARUR

During the three months between the seizure of the factory and the inauguration of the CUT-government scheme of worker participation in the management of Ex-Yarur, the factory was run by "parity committees," composed equally of government representatives and local union leaders, and the workers in the industry were given crash courses in political economy and worker participation. The necessary training and consciousness raising, however, were unlikely to be accomplished in this manner — particularly where no prior experience existed to serve as a guide.

Moreover, while some workers were psychologically (if not technically) prepared to take over the management of their factory, many (perhaps most) were not. The limitations of their world view were captured by one old worker at Ex-Yarur, who recalled his own attitude when the factory was nationalized:

That we should have an independent union, which the *patrón* had to listen to, had to respect — yes. That was something we had fought for all these years, something we all believed in, all knew was right. But, that there should be NO *patrón*! That WE, THE WORKERS, should be our own *patrón*! How was this possible? Who would run the factory? That was something which I could not understand at all.[10]

All this made it inevitable that the first year of worker participation at Ex-Yarur would be essentially a learning experience, one that revealed the problems inherent both in the new system of factory management and in the rapid transformation of workers into managers.

The success of the system depended upon the active and effective participation of the workers. Courses on worker participation notwith-

[10]   Luis Bascuñan, interview of April 28, 1972.

standing, their role in the management of Ex-Yarur was not clear to many workers, who continued in their accustomed passivity or limited their intervention in the affairs of the factory to electing delegates, councilors, and union officers and to funneling their complaints to one or all of these representatives for solution. As a consequence, the sectional assembly, the base of the new industrial democracy, tended to be stillborn, and the relations between the production committee and its mass base, atrophied.

A similar pattern of uncertainty and passivity was manifest in the initial meetings of the general assembly, which tended to become a vehicle of one-way communication from above, a report of managers and councilors to the workers in order to inform, educate, or exhort them, instead of the participatory town meeting of the theory. Only the union meeting, the one familiar form of direct participation, functioned as an active forum from the start, although the ambiguity in the minds of the workers with respect to the division of powers within the factory was reflected in their tendency to bring to the union meeting issues and demands that fell outside its competence and that should have been presented to representatives elsewhere in the participation structure.

Most of the representatives elected at the start of the first year of worker participation at Ex-Yarur were chosen because of their prominence in the struggle leading to the seizure of the factory, and some were less suited for their new roles. Most were young and almost all were male. Several proved inarticulate or impatient at the seemingly interminable meetings of the committees to which they had been elected; others neglected boring duties or resisted the responsibility to report back to their mass bases and be guided by their constituents.

In other cases, initial failings were more the result of inexperience than of unsuitability. Delegates' notions of their functions were frequently no more developed than those of the workers who had chosen them. The initial meetings of the coordinating committee were like gatherings of beginning swimmers, and its first president confessed to being paralyzed by stage fright in a role so unfamiliar.[11] The representatives with the clearest opportunity to exercise worker power in the management of the factory — the workers elected to the administrative council, the body charged with establishing general policy and making major administrative decisions — at first limited their interventions to registering minor complaints and demands more suitable to bodies lower down on the participatory totem pole.

[11] Hector Plazaola, interview of August 16, 1972. In the end, Plazaola did so well as president of the coordinating committee that he was elected to the administrative council the following year.

Where these difficulties stemmed from a lack of experience, inadequate preparation, or too narrow a world view, progress in overcoming them was marked by the second year of the experiment in worker participation at Ex-Yarur. The sectional assemblies and the production committees — less than half of which had functioned well during that first year — began to take on lives of their own. Workers' demands on their representatives for information and action multiplied, and production and coordinating committee delegates who had proved unsuitable or unwilling to act as democratic conduits were replaced in the annual elections by representatives who promised to be more responsible and more responsive to their constituents.

This awakening of the workers to their new powers and responsibilities was symbolized by the general assembly, which rejected the annual financial report of the government manager on the grounds that it was incomprehensibly technical in some parts, inappropriately political in others, and delivered orally. If they, the workers, were to have the responsibility of passing judgment on this important report, they argued, it would have to be drawn up in a form that they could understand and be handed to them in writing a fortnight before the general assembly, in order to give the workers the time to study it and discuss it among themselves. The assembly directed the manager to rewrite the report and distribute it to all the workers in the factory a fortnight before a special general assembly to be held within thirty days.

At the same time, the workers began to use the union meeting as a forum for launching initiatives relating to broad policy questions — such as the closing of the factory-outlet store as a measure against black marketeers and speculators — although they were aware that such issues were outside the union's jurisdiction and powers. Once the question had been raised from the floor of the union and approved by acclamation, however, the worker councilors were persuaded of its salience and were more willing to press the issue in the administrative council, where the power of decision lay.

The consequences of a year of experience were equally evident among worker representatives. Union officers, committee delegates, and administrative councilors had taken great strides in the comprehension and execution of their new functions and in the expansion of their vision — from their production section to the factory as a whole, and beyond to the factory's place within the textile industry, its relation to the Chilean economy, and the problems facing the Allende government. Competence increased with the degree of participation, and the greatest gains were made by those with the greatest responsibilities.

At all levels, however, an enormous amount had been learned both about worker participation and the factory in particular, and about the political process and political economy in general. Not all the workers had learned at the same rate (the greater the responsibility and the more intense the participation, the greater the growth in expertise and consciousness), but all the workers at Ex-Yarur had shared in the experiment and had learned something from the experience.

Not all the problems encountered during the first year of the experiment in worker participation were problems of learning and transition. Some were embedded in the structure of the new participation scheme and reflected the vagueness of the boundaries between the authority and functions of the various organs of worker participation and the representatives elected to them. This led to overlapping pretensions, competition, and tensions between councilors, coordinating committee delegates, and union officers. While these problems were typical of an era of transition, they also revealed the underlying tensions in the structure of worker participation established by the CUT-government accord.

Although the coordinating committee tended to usurp functions (and its section delegates to vote where only a consultative voice was formally stipulated), the new structure of participation — assemblies, production committees, coordinating committee, council of administration, general assembly — was essentially coherent, and the tensions within it had mostly been overcome by the end of the first year. The more intractable tensions lay between this new structure and the old — the union, whose officers were the proven leaders of the workers and the heroes of the struggle leading to the nationalization of the factory. However clear it may have been in theory, the actual or ideal new role of the union in Ex-Yarur was less clear in practice. Moreover, the existence of competitors for the mantle of "spokesman of the workers" even cast doubt upon the union's *vox populi* mandate. But by the second year, a *modus vivendi* that minimized damaging conflict was emerging at Ex-Yarur, while the rivalry that remained showed signs of producing a healthy competition in authenticity of representation which would help to keep all three groups of worker representatives conscientious.

In other ways, too, the first year of worker participation at Ex-Yarur was a learning experience, but one in which the central problems that the new form of industrial organization would have to face in Chile emerged to confront the unprepared workers-turned-managers of Ex-Yarur. The old system of discipline — authoritarian and repressive, but efficient at the point of production — had been decapitated, but no other positive basis for discipline had replaced it. During the first weeks following the nationalization of the factory, this problem was masked by the high élan produced by that triumph; but the seriousness of the problem became clear as the euphoria evaporated and an ethos of normality returned. Absenteeism, "bathroom breaks," and lower productivity became a serious concern in some shifts of some sections, even though in the factory at large the problem did not reach significant levels or was brought rapidly under control.

In part, this slacking off was a natural reaction of the workers to their liberation from the tyranny of the factory's Taylor system, in which every moment of the worker's time had been rigidly controlled; in part, it reflected the letdown predictable when the victory at the Apocalypse failed to lead to the immediate creation of the New Jerusalem. Whatever the cause or justification, the problem began to affect both the production and the morale of the factory and was treated with the seriousness it deserved. In the end, the workers themselves voted for the creation of a new disciplinary code, but one that would be drawn up by their own representatives and discussed and approved by their own assemblies. By the end of the first year, it was an article of faith at Ex-Yarur that the way to improved work discipline at the point of production led through more worker participation in the management of the factory.

The problem of discipline on the factory floor, however, reflected the new insecurity of foremen as much as it did the new assuredness or disappointment of the workers. Foremen who had previously ruled their sections with iron hands, certain of the support of the *patrón* and an authoritarian system, now hesitated to discipline workers upon whose benediction (so ran the fear) their jobs might now depend. This was particularly true of foremen whose positions under the old regime had resulted more from paternalistic ties of loyalty to the *patrón* than from personal qualifications. They tended to relate to their new bosses — the workers — in the same manner and for the same reasons. Bad foremen remained bad foremen — only now productivity, not the workers, suffered as a consequence.

The uncertainty of supervisory personnel about what the rules of the new game were and where power now lay was equally evident in their attitudes to those perceived as being higher in the hierarchy. Some foremen continued to bring informers' reports on workers to the new head of labor relations — an old Communist union leader who had been fired from Yarur some decades before as a "troublemaker" — until the latter made clear his opposition to such practices.[12]

[12] Oscar Ibañez, interview of June 21, 1972.

More serious was the passivity and reluctance to take initiatives that characterized too many of the old technical and supervisory personnel. In part, this was a continued effect of the discouragement of independent initiative under the old regime; in part, it was a result of fear of taking chances in a situation perceived as uncertain and filled with unknown dangers. Yet for a new and more efficient organization of production and decision making to emerge, the imaginative participation of technicians and supervisors is as important as that of the workers — particularly if new production and social relations are not to be purchased at the cost of human potential and productivity.

The progress and innovations made in several sections of the factory during the first year of Ex-Yarur, however, were encouraging, with the imaginative conversion of the maintenance department into a machine shop for the production of unobtainable spare parts being the most important. Moreover, it was striking that even technical personnel who were politically opposed to the Allende government spoke of the increased opportunities for innovation and professional satisfaction afforded them at Ex-Yarur. With all its errors, tensions, and problems, the first year of worker participation at Ex-Yarur was a positive experience, one in which production and productivity indexes remained at a high level but were less important than the new system of social relations that was struggling to be born.

THE IMPACT OF WORKER PARTICIPATION

In less than a year, the advent of worker participation in the management of Ex-Yarur had contributed to major changes in the life of the factory and its workers. Among the most obvious were the improvement in working conditions, the easing of the rigors of the Taylor system, the introduction of a full hour for lunch, and the establishment of a model day-care center for children of the workers. Increased expenditure on housing, medical care, education, and recreation reflected a similar pattern of increased material benefits that accrued to the workers collectively, rather than to favored individuals. Wages were increased, but only to the extent that they were augmented nationally, and wage differentials among the workers were decreased in the process.[13]

---

[13] The incentive pay for machine operators was maintained, although there was increasing talk in 1972 about the necessity of devising a new system in which the entire section, rather than individual machine operators, would benefit from production bonuses.

Even more important was the increasing equality of social relations in the factory — a change symbolized in the replacement of *"señor"* by *"compañero"* as a form of address, a verbal assertion of the new social equality in the plant, irrespective of position or work task, which also carried the notion of an organic relationship among the workers and employees of Ex-Yarur. Moreover, this shift in rhetoric was accompanied, in the everyday life of the factory, by an increase in *compañerismo* — in social interaction and solidarity. What had been merely a workplace — and one where the iron discipline of the machine and the boss ruled tyrannically — was being transformed into what might be called a "community."

The increase in social equality was also reflected in the erosion of the differences between "employee" and "worker." The separate unions were merged and the industry's recreation facilities opened to all, as was the new cafeteria constructed with the proceeds from the sale of the Yarurs' stock of imported champagne and whiskey. This leveling of social distinctions was not free from resentment, particularly among the white-collar office workers, who feared the erosion of their middle-class status and domination by the workers and did not have the technical skills upon which to base their crumbling sense of superiority. The tensions generated, however, themselves denoted significant social change, with the white-collar and supervisory personnel assuming an unaccustomed defensive posture before the blue-collar workers, who found themselves in an equally unfamiliar situation of power.

Equally clear was the replacement of the old patriarchal and authoritarian structure of work relations by a more democratic one that favored initiatives from below and compelled foremen and other supervisory personnel to treat workers with equity and respect. In general, the social hierarchy in the factory was weakened and had given way to a more open and fluid social order in which status was based upon consciousness, *compañerismo*, productivity, and role in the system of participation.

One might expect that the destruction of so authoritarian a system of work and social relations would carry with it severe economic costs. At Ex-Yarur, although problems of work discipline arose, no such economic collapse took place during 1971–1972. Productivity and efficiency remained at a high level. Production norms were surpassed and production during the first year of worker participation showed a 7 percent increase over the previous year (Chile, Corporación de Fomento n.d.; Ex-Yarur n.d.).[14]

---

[14]   The 7 percent increase in production was calculated after allowing for the loss of an hour and a half daily, from the extension of the meal break from thirty minutes to an hour for each of the three shifts.

Moreover, this economic performance was maintained in the face of problems of spare-parts replacement, an obstacle that was eventually overcome by the transformation of the factory's maintenance division into a machine shop capable of manufacturing 75 percent of the factory's requirements; spare parts had been imported previously at a cost of $3,000,000 annually.[15]

The factory did show a large financial loss on paper for its first year of operations as Ex-Yarur, but this was not due to mismanagement, featherbedding, or outsize wage increases. It was the result of an experiment in "socialist accounting." As part of the Allende government's redistribution of income, Ex-Yarur concentrated its production on cheaper textile lines and maintained price levels to the lower-class consumer, despite a rise in costs during that first year of more than 75 percent. The result was what were termed "capitalist losses" and "social profits."[16] The strategy was that the profits from the other nationalized textile factories, which produced more expensive cloth for the middle and upper classes, would finance these losses.

"Social profits" also accrued to individual workers at Ex-Yarur. The most inportant of these was the increase in personal social mobility, which took several forms. Within the factory, workers benefited from new opportunities for promotion within the job and participation structure and from special training to qualify for supervisory or technical posts.[17] In addition, the extension of adult education at the factory school gave workers without a secondary education the opportunity to obtain one and qualify for the special places and scholarships set aside for workers at the University of Chile and the State Technical University. Moreover, workers who demonstrated leadership capacity at Ex-Yarur could expect to encounter greatly expanded horizons outside the factory. Workers who proved themselves effective and responsible leaders and managers at Ex-Yarur were elected to the council of the national trade union federation, named to manage a newly nationalized textile factory, and chosen as their party's congressional candidate for Santiago.[18]

An equally important "social profit" was the transcendence by many

---

15 Luis Ogno, interview of June 26, 1972; *El Siglo* (1973a:6).
16 Vicente Poblete Zamorano, interview of August 30, 1972.
17 Initially, the union officers and other worker representatives insisted that workers in the factory be given preference in filling ALL technical and supervisory vacancies. Experience demonstrated, however, that some posts demanded special technical qualifications (Juan Carvajal, interview of August 20, 1972).
18 By mid-1972, the Textile Committee of the CORFO was evolving a policy of appointing workers to managerial vacancies wherever possible (Juan Francisco Sánchez, interview of September 6, 1972).

workers of certain types of alienation. When asked what they considered the most important changes in the factory since its nationalization, most replied: "Before I was working for the *patrón*, now I am working for Chile," and "Now I can work tranquilly." The meaning of these affirmations became clear with further questioning. The classic Marxist alienation "from the fruits of one's labor" had been overcome by the consciousness that with nationalization their labor was benefiting the national society with which the worker identified, instead of the capitalist whom he considered his exploiter.

"Tranquillity," however, was a code word for the overcoming of another kind of alienation — the alienation of powerlessness at one's place of work, of being transformed into a "thing" by the imposition of external controls and conditions that one cannot influence. "Tranquillity" resulted from the substitution of participation for authoritarian control, democracy for hierarchy, free speech for repression, and *compañerismo* for informing.

Not all workers at Ex-Yarur had shared in this internal evolution, and the extent of the transformation tended to reflect reciprocally the degree of the worker's participation. Moreover, a third form of alienation — the industrial alienation of the assembly line, the product of becoming an extension of a machine for eight hours a day, six days a week — proved more intractable. What was startling, however, was not the considerable distance that remained to be traveled before alienation could be declared a problem of the old order and not merely an inevitable aspect of the human condition, but the rapidity of the progress during the first year of worker participation at Ex-Yarur.

This transcendence of alienation, however, must be viewed within the broader context of a transformation of consciousness, itself inseparable from the major changes taking place in the surrounding nation. Only within a Chile whose government was committed to the redistribution of income and power and the nationalization of industry could that shift in workers' perceptions from "the government they" to "the government we" take place, which is the precondition for such a transcendence of alienation from the fruits of one's labor through an identification with the nation. Only where the political process encourages and sustains worker participation can the alienation derived from impotence at one's place of work be overcome.

Moreover, this national political context was essential for a further transformation of consciousness — the transcendence of trade union consciousness. At Ex-Yarur, this change could be seen in the moderation of wage demands and in the voluntary reduction in the traditional bonus of cotton cloth, in view of the national shortage of textiles. In its place was emerging what might be called a "socialist consciousness," symbolized by the workers' rejection, in the Council of Administration elections of August 1972, of candidates advocating the transformation of Ex-Yarur into a "worker's enterprise" in which the workers would become shareholders and receive the profits as dividends. "We are not managing our factory just for ourselves," one worker explained to me, "but for the people of Chile."[19]

Another aspect of this transformation of consciousness was the emergence of the transfer of power to the workers in both the factory and the nation as a salient concern. If worker power in the factory stemmed from the national political context, the precondition of the demand for worker power in the nation was the experience of the workers as managers of their own factories. Only this personal experience could explain the transformation of consciousness exemplified by the old worker who confessed that when they had seized the factory the previous year, he could not conceive of workers running Ex-Yarur without a *patron*, but that he now realized that workers could indeed manage factories — even ministries — and that the bosses would never return again.[20]

This experience and this transformation of consciousness were themselves the preconditions for the more active participation and more aggressive demands by the workers and their representatives in the factory, in the textile industry, and in the nation at large as the second year of worker participation began in Chile. At Ex-Yarur, this was evident in the attendance, discussion, and actions of the various committees and assemblies. Furthermore, the impact of worker participation began to reach beyond the factory gates into the surrounding society.

Although Ex-Yarur was in the vanguard of the experiment in worker participation, its experience was not atypical of the 80 percent of the Chilean textile industry that became part of the public sector through purchase, requisition, or intervention. The degree to which the other factories shared in the transformation observed at Ex-Yarur became clear during the *Encuentro Textil* held during July 1972 to assess the experience of the first year of the nationalized textile industry. At this three-day encounter of government and worker representatives from all the nationalized mills — in which the workers predominated, and "one man, one vote" was the rule — the worker representatives presented a series of criticisms and proposals for the future management of the industry.

---

[19] Juan Chavez, interview of August 30, 1972.
[20] Luis Bascuñan, interview of April 28, 1972.

Most of these critiques were leveled at the Textile Committee of the CORFO, which had run the nationalized textile industry from above through its bureaucrats and technicians, with minimal worker participation, thus circumscribing the reality of worker power, as well as the influence of both worker and government factory managers on policy making in the industry. Clearly, there had been too little unity of theory and practice. At the *encuentro*, the Textile Committee was criticized for being bureaucratic and "bourgeois" in its attitudes and procedures, incompetent, and undemocratic. The workers demanded the resignation of the head of the industry (a cousin of President Allende) and the restructuring of the Textile Committee, so that the industry would be run by committees with equal representation from the government and the workers, integrating worker participation into the uppermost levels of the industry's decision-making structure.

Expanded worker participation in the planning of the textile industry was another demand, and one that went beyond the joint committee that would draw up the annual plan at the Textile Committee. The worker representatives proposed that this tentative plan should then be carried to each factory for discussion, criticism, and suggestions from workers meeting in sectional assemblies and a special general assembly. Only then would a final plan, incorporating these criticisms and suggestions, be formulated by the joint committee and submitted for final approval to another industry-wide *encuentro*, which would become an annual "industrial legislature."

The workers also suggested major policy changes for the textile industry, the most important of which were intended to remedy weaknesses in financing and marketing. To minimize the negative consequences of bureaucracy at the center upon operations and planning in the factory, they proposed a new fiscal and pricing policy which would enable each factory to become essentially self-financing. To combat the black market in textiles, the creation of a national distribution agency which would have a monopoly on distributing the products of the nationalized factories was suggested.

More surprising than the informed and incisive critique and assertive demands of the workers at the *encuentro* was the substantial agreement with their criticisms and suggestions by the government factory managers present. The proposed changes in structure and policy were approved overwhelmingly and the Allende government, elements of which had viewed the *Encuentro Textil* with apprehension — fearful of political conflicts, "purely negative criticisms," and "irresponsible demands" — embraced both the results and the institution of worker participation that had produced them. *Encuentros* were projected for the other nationalized industries. [21]

More tentatively, one could begin to trace by 1973 the impact of the experience of worker participation in the factory upon politics at the level of community and nation. The most dramatic and important example was the formation of the *cordones industriales*, workers' councils composed of delegates chosen by all the factories within an industrial belt or region. Although originally formed as a means of mobilizing the workers during the "bourgeois strike" of shopkeepers, professionals, and truck owners in October 1972, the *cordon industrial* took on a life of its own and emerged as an autonomous instrument of worker power in local and national politics. By 1973, the *cordon industrial* had become one of the most important agencies of mass mobilization and direct political participation in Chile, a major source of support for the Allende Government, and a powerful force for the radicalization of the Chilean revolutionary process.

SOME REFLECTIONS

Within a year of the accession to power of a government committed to a "democratic road to socialism," the bulk of the Chilean textile industry was nationalized through a legal process accelerated by the pressure and actions of its workers. During the year that followed, the nationalized textile industry pioneered a system of worker participation that was a uniquely Chilean blend of workers' council and trade union, participatory and representative industrial democracy, worker power and worker advice. This participation system survived an initial period of experimentation and learning, emerging from the experience strengthened and dynamic. Although constricted by being forced to operate within the context of the old institutional order, worker participation in the Chilean textile industry was an important agency of diverse social change at the level of the factory, the industry, and the community, without exacting unacceptable economic costs in exchange.

Whether worker participation in Chile could also be an agency of revolutionary change during a national transition to socialism was less clear and remained to be seen. In the textile industry, at least, worker par-

---

[21] By mid-1973, the idea of worker participation in the formulation and discussion of economic planning in Chile had even been adopted for the national economic plan, through an agreement between the CUT and the CORFO of May 9, 1973 (*El Siglo* 1973b:5).

ticipation played an important role in the restructuring of planning and decision making, as did the *cordones industriales* in transforming political relations in the community and radicalizing the revolutionary process in the nation. Moreover, it is significant that worker participation in Allende's Chile increased over time and had consequences unintended by the political and governmental bureaucracies. The agencies and institutions of worker participation — at the level of the factory, the industry, and the region — tended to aggregate functions and power to an extent far beyond that originally conceived.

The danger of the limitation or cooptation of worker participation by party and union bureaucracies remained as the nature and scope of worker power were not resolved within the Popular Unity coalition, and powerful forces within the left distrusted spontaneity, direct democracy, and unguided participation. There were, however, both structural and political reasons why such cooptation would have been difficult.

Within the electoral systems of both union and political democracy in Chile, the competition for the allegiance of the workers within the left and between the Popular Unity and the Christian Democratic opposition to its right made bureaucratic cooptation more difficult and authentic representation more probable. Moreover, the creation of parallel systems of worker participation at the factory level, with rival claimants for the mantle of "representative of the workers," tended to create a competition among local leaders in the authenticity of their representation of the interests and concerns of the workers.

In addition, the logic of the revolutionary process in Chile — where the chief support of the government in a crisis was the power of mobilized workers and where crises were endemic because of the unresolved struggle for power — tended to convert worker participation into worker power, and consciousness and organization at the factory level into class consciousness and organization at the regional and national levels. The logic of the revolutionary process, therefore, pointed in the direction of increasing worker participation and worker power.

The other threat to the continued development of worker participation in Chile however, stemmed from the danger that the Allende government might be overthrown violently by a counterrevolution or defeated electorally, although many believed that the changes already introduced were irreversible. A thesis of this paper, however, has been the importance of the national context in defining the character and limits of worker participation at the level of the factory and the community. It was the advent of a government committed to structural change, nationalization of industry, and a democratic road to socialism that conditioned the evolution of worker participation in Chile and was responsible for its rapid development and diffusion — and it was the fall of this government and its replacement by a military dictatorship bent upon turning back the clock fifty years and reversing all those "irreversible changes" of the Allende years that were responsible for its even more rapid demise.

POSTSCRIPT 1974

This paper, written in early 1973, was based upon fieldwork completed in September 1972. The period I observed was one of progress through trial and error and struggle and I ended on a note of guarded optimism. It is this optimism which has been overtaken by events. My caveat at the time was that there should be no drastic change in the national political context which had created worker participation in Chile and fostered its development in the textile industry. Unfortunately, such a transformation of national politics is precisely what took place.

A month after my departure from Chile, the October strike of merchants, truckers, and professionals began a new and decisive phase of the revolutionary process. Although the crisis was responsible for an increase in working-class consciousness and the emergence of the *cordon industrial* as its expression, the October strike and the year of life-and-death political struggle which it inaugurated also had important negative implications for the development of worker participation in Chile, to which the textile industry was no exception.

Within this context of national crisis, most of the measures taken at the *Encuentro Textil* for the reform and extension of worker participation at the national level were shelved. At Ex-Yarur and other factories, the advance of worker participation was slowed, as factory concerns were subordinated to national necessities and local initiatives gave way to directives from above. Tensions among worker representatives and within the structure of participation reemerged, but were papered over rather than resolved.

The promise of the first year of worker participation in the Chilean textile industry and the proposals for its perfection and extension could not be fulfilled within the context of a struggle for survival of the revolutionary process which had spawned and nurtured it. When the end came on September 11, 1973, in the brutal military coup which overthrew the Allende Government and ended the Chilean experiment in worker participation, it found a participatory system at Ex-Yarur which had made little progress past the gains of the first year.

In the end, the workers of Ex-Yarur had only one year to carry out their social revolution through worker participation, before transcendent national political events intervened and changed the context and the issues. One year is a very short time, particularly for a revolutionary process attempting to transform both social relations and economic structures while struggling for political power. What the workers of Ex-Yarur were able to accomplish in a year was remarkable and demonstrated the promise of worker participation. That they were unable to pursue their experiment any further underscores not the failure of the experiment, but the critical role played by the national political context in determining its parameters, character, and destiny.

The events of September exploded the myth of "people's power" in Chile, in the face of a united armed forces willing to use their superior firepower ruthlessly against their own compatriots. The *cordones industriales* were liquidated, the nationalized factories were occupied by soldiers and returned to their old owners. The national and regional trade unions were proscribed, their leftist leadership killed, imprisoned, or driven underground. Both political and union democracy were destroyed. The political parties that had sponsored the Chilean experiment in worker participation were banned, the political activity of individuals or groups was made a penal offense and severely punished. At the textile committee of the CORFO, worker representatives were replaced by management spokesmen. All local union elections were prohibited, with gerontocracy replacing democracy as the principle of selection. Vacancies for union officers will now be filled by the oldest worker in the factory, while the unions themselves have been reduced to formal ciphers, barred from actively defending the interests of their members (*La Prensa* 1974:2).

At Ex-Yarur, a general assembly called on the day of the coup decided to surrender the factory without resistance, in view of the hopelessness of the military situation. It was the final act of worker participation. During the weeks that followed, soldiers occupied the factory, military intelligence purged the work force of "activists," and most of the union leaders and councilors were arrested, tortured, and imprisoned. The entire structure of worker participation vanished, as did many of its former representatives, democracy on the production floor, equality in social relations, and the sense of community. Hierarchy, alienation, repression, and fear returned, accompanied by mass firings and starvation wages.

Under the watchful eye and electric baton of the Chilean army, an industrial discipline even more authoritarian and repressive than the old order was imposed upon the factory by the time it was returned to the Yarurs in January 1974.

REFERENCES

ANGELL, ALAN
1972 *Politics and the labour movement in Chile.* London: Oxford University Press.

CHILE-CENTRAL UNICA DE TRABAJADORES
1972 *Las normas básicas de la participación de los trabajadores en la dirección de las empresas de la area social y mixta.* Santiago: CUT.

CHILE, CORPORACIÓN DE FOMENTO
n.d. "Estadísticas de producción: sector algodonero." Unpublished data. Corporación de Fomento, Comité de Industrias Textiles y del Vestuario.

El Siglo
1973a "4 millones y medio de dolares ahorran a Chile trabajadores de la maestranza de Ex-Yarur." August 2, 1973. Santiago.
1973b "Trabajadores estudian Plan Económico." August 14, 1973. Santiago.

EX-YARUR
n.d. Unpublished data. Ex-Yarur, Departamento de Ingenieria Industrial.

La Prensa
1974 "El estatuto sindical no satisfacen a trabajadores." January 9, 1974. Santiago.

POBLETE ZAMORANO, VICENTE
1972 Address of the general manager, Ex-Yarur, to the General Assembly of the Workers of Ex-Yarur, Santiago, June 25, 1972.

UNIDAD POPULAR
1970 *El programa basico del gobierno de la Unidad Popular.* Santiago: Unidad Popular.

VANEK, JAROSLAV
1971 *La economía de participación: hipótesis evolucionista y estrategia para el desarrollo.* Lima: Instituto de Estudos Peruanos.

Biographical Notes

HAMID AÏT AMARA (1935–   ) is a Lecturer at Algiers University where he teaches Rural Sociology and Rural Law. He holds diplomas in Sociology (*Doctorat 3ème cycle*) and in Law (*Licence*). From 1963 to 1970, he was responsible for cooperative development and self-management in the Ministry for Agriculture and Agrarian Reform in Algeria. His primary research interests are in the areas of self-management, cooperatives, and agrarian reform.

GIORGIO ALBERTI (1936–   ) was born in Bologna, Italy. He studied Political Science at the University of Florence, where he received his doctorate in 1963. He also studied at Cornell University, where he recieved an M.A. in Sociology in 1966 and a Ph.D. in Organizational Behavior in 1970. He resided in Peru between 1968 and 1975, where he worked first as Associate Director of a program of research between Cornell University and the Instituto de Estudios Peruanos (IEP) and later as member of the staff of the IEP. His most recent publications include a study on regional transformation and peasant movements (*Poder y cambio en el Valle del Mantaro*, 1974, Lima: Instituto de Estudio Peruanos) and an edited volume with Enrique Mayer on exchange and reciprocity in the Andes (*Reciprocidad e intercambio en los Andes*, 1975, Lima: Instituto de Estudios Peruanos). He is a member of the Instituto Peruanos and is now teaching the theory of complex organizations in the Department of Political Science at the University of Bologna.

GAVIN ALDERSON-SMITH.   No biographical data available.

RAYMOND APTHORPE is Professor of Development Studies at the University of East Anglia, Norwich, England. He previously worked for the UNRISD in Geneva and for the UNDP in Asia. From 1957 to 1968, he worked in Africa where he was Professor of Sociology and Dean of the Faculty of Social Studies, Makerere University College, Kampala. He has published widely on development and social change including: *People, planning and development studies* (1971, Frank Cass) and *Rural cooperatives and planned change* (1972, Frank Cass).

RIVKA WEISS BAR-YOSEF is a sociologist at the Hebrew University of Jerusalem. She studied at the Hebrew University, where she received her Ph.D. She served as Chairperson of the Department of Sociology and currently she is Director of the Work and Welfare Research Institute of the University. She is especially interested in policy-oriented research in the areas of sociology of work, social welfare, and the status of women, in which areas she has published a number of research studies.

BABURAO SHRAVAN BAVISKAR (1931–   ) is Reader in Sociology at the University of Delphi. He studied at Poona and at Delphi, receiving a Ph.D. in Sociology from the latter in 1970. He was Visiting Fellow at the Institute of Devlopment Studies, University of Sussex during 1975–1976. His special interests include political sociology and sociology of development. For the last several years he has been engaged in the study of cooperatives in the rural areas of Maharashtra in India. He has published several papers in professional journals and international symposia, and has recently completed a monograph on *Cooperatives, politics and development*.

LILIA BEN SALEM.   No biographical data available.

SANTIAGO BILBAO.   No biographical data available.

MICHÈLE BROGNETTI.   No biographical data available.

THOMAS F. CARROLL.   No biographical data available.

JACQUES CHONCHOL (1926–   ) was born in Santiago. He graduated as an Agricultural Engineer from the University of Chile and did postgraduate studies at the Institut Agronomique (Paris) and at the London School of Economics. He has worked for the Ministry of Agriculture of Chile and on several missions on agrarian reform problems for the FAO and ECLA (UN) in Mexico, Cuba, and other Latin American countries. He was Professor at the Catholic University of Santiago, Head of the Agriculture Development Institute under the Frei government in Chile (1964–1968) and Minister of Agriculture under the Allende government (1970–1972). He is presently Associate Professor at the Institut des Hautes Études de l'Amérique Latine, University of Paris III.

JORGE E. DANDLER (1940–   ) was born in La Paz, Bolivia. He received his B.A. in Political Science from Dartmouth College in 1963, an M.A. (1967), and Ph.D. (1971) in Anthropology from the University of Wisconsin (Madison). He has been teaching since 1972 at the Programa de Ciencias Sociales, Universidad Católica del Perú, Lima and is author of *El sindicalismo campesino en Bolivia: estructurales en Ucureña (1935–1951)*, Instituto Indigenista Interamericano, 1969 (Mexico) and other works on Boliva and Peru. His special interests include agrarian reform in Latin America, Andean society peasant movements and political and economic anthropology.

WILLIAM DERMAN (1940–   ) is Associate Professor of Anthropology and African Studies at Michigan State University. He received his B.A. from Brooklyn College and his Ph.D. from the University of Michigan in 1969. His fieldwork has been with the Fulbe of the Fouta-Djallon, the results of which have been published in *Serfs, peasants and socialists: a study of a former serf village in the Republic of Guinea* (1973). His current research interests include the consequences of the drought and famine in the Sahel agrarian change in souther Africa and race (racism) and ethnicity (ethnicism).

CHARLES DE WECK.   No biographical data avai able.

SHLOMO ECKSTEIN (1929–   ) studied Economics at the National Autonomous University of Mexico (Lic. Ec. 1975) and at Harvard (Ph.D., 1964). He is Professor of Economics at Bar-Ilan University in Israel. He has served as advisor to the Government of Mexico on Agrarian Programs and policy. During 1972–1973 he conducted research on land reform in Latin America, working for the World Bank in Washington D.C. He wrote or coauthored the following books: *El ejido colectivo en México* (1966), *Intervillage cooperation in agricultural production services* (1974), *Estructaur agraria y desarrollo agrícola en México* (1974), *La agricultura colectiva en México: la experiencia de la Laguna* (1975).

ORLANDO FALS-BORDA (1925–   ), author of *Peasant society in the Colombian Andes, Subversion and social change, history of the agrarian question in Colombia*, and other books, was born in Barranquilla, Colombia. He received graduate degrees in Sociology at the Universities of Minnesota (1952) and Florida (1955), returned to Colombia where he became Director of the Ministry of Agriculture and Founder-Dean of the Faculty of Sociology at the National University (1959–1967). After a period as Visiting Professor at the University of London and Director of Research at the United Nations in Geneva, he and other colleagues founded the experimental action-research instute Rosca (1970–1975). He is now Director of Cerco (Centro de Estudios de la Realidad Colombiana) in Bogotá, where he concentrates on studies of social and economic history and applied research in rural areas.

GABRIEL GAGNON (1935–   ) was born in Mont-Joli, Quebec. He received his M.A. from Laval University in 1960 and his Doctorat de troisième cycle (Paris) in 1965. He has been teaching anthropology (1963–1970) and sociology (1970–   ) at the University of Montreal, where he is presently Associate Professor. His fieldwork has been in Senegal, Cuba, Tunisia, and Quebec; his main interests are epistemology and sociology of development. He is a member of the Executive Bureau of the Association Internationale des Sociologues de langue française.

GABRIEL GOSSELIN (1938–   ) is Professor of Sociology at the Université des Sciences et Techniques de Lille. After his studies at the Sorbonne which led hem to a Doctorat de Recherche (Sociologie du travail en pays GBEY, Centrafrique), he defended his thesis "Formations et stratégie de transition en Afrique Tropicale" in 1973 .While serving as an expert for the Ministère de la Coopération, he took charge of lectures at the École des Hautes Études (Paris). He belonged to ORSTOM from 1964 until 1966 and between 1966 and 1970 was Consultant for the BIT and the UN. In 1967 he became Professor at the University of Lille. He is also presently Professor at the Institut du Développement Économique et Social (Paris), Director of the Institut de Sociologie of the University of Lille, and President of the Société de Sociologie du Nord de la France. His last works to appear were: *Modèles et moyens de la réflexion politique au 18 siècle* (editor, 1976); *L'Afrique désenchantée* (1976); and *La question du progrès* (editor, i.p.). He is presently carrying out research on the sociology of science.

THOMAS C. GREAVES (1941–) attended the University of Washington in Seatlle and completed graduate studies at Cornell University, earning his Ph.D. in Anthropology. His fieldwork has been conducted in Peru, Colombia, and the urban United States. His recent professional writing focuses on the identity and behavioral changes accompanying the transition from peasant to rural-dwelling postpeasant. He served on the faculty of the University of Pennsylvania prior to being appointed Professor and Director of the Division of Social Sciences of the newly established University of Texas at San Antonio.

NICHOLAS S. HOPKINS (1939–) is Associate Professor of Anthropology at the American University in Cairo, Egypt. He received a B.A. from Harvard in 1960 and a Ph.D. from the University of Chicago in 1967. He taught at New York University from 1967 to 1975. He carried out research in Mali (1964–1965) and in Tunisia (1971–1973). Between 1969 and 1970 he held a Fulbright-Hays research fellowship in Tunisia, and between 1973 and 1974 he was acting Executive Secretary of the Middle East Studies Association of North America. His publications include *Popular government in an African town: Kita, Mali* (1972) and articles on Mali and Tunisia. His interests are social change, economic, and political anthropology.

GERRIT HUIZER (1929–) studies social psychology at Amsterdam University and has been active in community development and peasant organization since 1955. He worked as a volunteer in a village in Central America and later with Danilo Dolci in Sicily. From 1962 to 1971 he worked with different agencies of the United Nations (particularly ILO) in Latin America and Southeast Asia in field projects and action research. He has written numerous articles in literary and professional journals and readers and a book, *The revolutionary potential of peasants in Latin America* (1972, Lexington, Mass.: Heath Lexington Books) which came out also in Spanish and a Dutch version and in an abridged edition (*Peasant rebellion in Latin America*, 1973, Harmondsworth: Penguin). He has been Visiting Professor at the Institute of Social Studies, The Hague, and Fellow of the Institute of Development Research in Copenhagen and has been Director of the Third World Centre, University of Nijmegen, Netherlands, since 1973.

INAYATULLAH (1931–) was educated both in Pakistan and the United States. He received his M.A. degrees in Economics from Punjab University (1956) and in Sociology from Michigan State University (1960). His

Ph.D. in Political Science came from the Indiana University in 1968. He is an Associate Professor in International Relations at the University of Islamabad, Pakistan, and is currently on leave from the University. At present he is an Expert in Development Administration at the Asian Centre for Development Administration, Kuala Lumpur. Included in his more recent publications of articles and books are "The Transfer of the Western development model to Asia and itsimpact," (1975); "The emergence of the contemporary world order and strategies for changing its economic aspect," (1976); "The role of internal and extrenal factors in the failure of the national integration of Pakistan," (1975); Cooperatives and development in Asia (1972); and (editor) *Management training for development: the Asian experience* (1975).

URI LEVIATAN (1940–   ) is a member of kibbutz Ein Hamifratz in Israel. He studied psychology and sociology at the Hebrew University, Jerusalem, where he received his B.A. (1967). He received his Ph.D. in Organizational Psychology from the University of Michigan, Ann Arbor (1970). He served as Director of the Center for Social Research on the kibbutz at Givat Haviva, Israel (1971–1975), and currently he is Senior Researcher at that center and a teacher at the Kibbutz Management College at Ruppin Institute. His current research interest are in the kibbutz society with emphasis on the spheres of work, structure, the mental health of its members, the aged, organizational effectiveness, and organizational development and change.

EZZEDDINE MAKHLOUF. No biographical data available.

JUNE NASH (1927–   ) is Professor of Anthropology and chairs the Department of Anthropology, City College of the City University of New York. She received her Ph.D. from the University of Chicago. She has done fieldwork in Guatemala and Mexico with the Maya, and in Bolivia with Quechua- and Aymara-speaking Indians. She has written two monographs on the Maya, *Social structure in Amatenango del Valle*, and *In the eyes of the ancestors*, has coedited *Sex and class in Latin America* with Helen Safa, *Ideology and social change* with Juan Corradi, and has just finished a book on the Bolivian mining community.

JUAN-VICENTE PALERM VIQUEIRA. No biographical data available.

S. A. RAHIM. No biographical data available.

HENRI RAULIN (1918–   ) studied at the University of Paris-Sorbonne. Since 1956, his fieldwork has in been West Africa and his special interests have been agricultural activities: land, tenure, agrarian structure, implements and tools, work organization. His main study and thesis, *La dynamique des techniques agraires en Afrique tropicale du Nord* (1967, Paris CNRS) was put together from many articles. Among them are: "Le champ d'application et les modalités de l'aide extérieure dans le secteur agricole" (1968, Paris: UNESCO), "Communautés d'entraide et développement agricole au Niger "(1969, Études rurales 33), "Partie Niger du World Atlas of Agriculture "(1972, Verone), and "Diffusion et blocage de cultures matérielles. Rôle du Sahara dans ce processus" (1973, Paris: Cujas).

HANA ROSENMAN is a graduate in Sociology and Political Science of the Hebrew University. She specialized in rural cooperation and regional planning. She served as consultat for the OECD and is currently involved in a comparative research study on regional planning and development in Ceylon, Spain, Holland, and Israel.

WARREN J. ROTH (1931–   ) was born in Jersey City, New Jersey. He received his B.A. in Philosophy from Maryknoll College, Glen Ellyn, Illinois, in 1954 and his Ph.D. in Anthropology from the Catholic University of America, Washington, D.C., in 1966. He has done fieldwork in Tanzania, Peru, and Guatemala. Currently, he is Associate Professor of Anthropology at Chicago State University, Chicago, Illinois.

JANE SCHNEIDER (1938–   ) received a Ph.D. in Political Science, with a specialization in political theory, from the University of Michigan. In the two years which followed the award of the degree (1965–1967) she conducted anthropological fieldwork in Sicily. She now teaches anthropology at York College and the Graduate Center of the City University of New York. With Peter Schneider she coauthored a book, *Culture and political economy in western Sicily*, which Academic Press (in the Studies in Social Discontinuity Series) will bring out this year.

PETER SCHNEIDER (1933–   ) is Associate Professor of Sociology and Social Pshychology at the Liberal Arts College of Fordham University in New York City. He received the B.A. from Antioch College in 1956 and the Ph.D. from the University of Michigan in 1965. He has done field research in western Sicily (in collaboration with Jane Schneider) and is now preparing to return to that area to study the relationships between political economy and population dynamics.

HAFEDH SETHOM (1932–   ) was born in Tunisia. He studied at the Institut des Hautes Études de Tunis (1953–1954), at the Faculté des Lettres de Grenoble in France (1954–1957), and at the Faculté des Lettres de Paris-Sorbonne (1947–1961). From 1964 to 1975, he was Assistant Professor of Human and Economic Geography at the Faculté des Lettres de Tunis and is presently Maître de Conférences at the same university as well as Head of the Geography Department. He published several articles in the *Revue Tunisienne des Sciences Sociales* about agrarian geography in Tunisia and Algeria. His Doctorat d'État, "Les fellahs de la presqu'île du Cap Bon (Tunisie), is now being published by the Service des Publications de la Faculté des Lettres de l'Université de Tunis.

HEBE M. C. VESSURI.   No biographical data available.

JOAN VINCENT is Professor of Anthropology at Barnard College, Columbia University in the City of New York. She studied at the London School of Economics and Political Science (B.Sc. Econ), the University of Chicago (M.A.), and Columbia University (Ph.D.). Her fieldwork was carried out in Teso, eastern Uganda, in 1966–1967 as a Research Fellow of the East African Institute of Social and Economic Research at Makerere University College, Kampala. A return visit was made possible by Barnard College in 1970. She is currently doing fieldwork in Northern Ireland, where she began as a Guggenheim Research Fellow in 1974. Among her publications are *African elite: the Big Men of a small town* (1971), "Anthropology and political development" in Colin Leys (editor), *Politics and change in developing countries* (1969) and "Room for manoeuvre: the political role of small towns in East Africa" in Maxwell Owusu (editor), *Colonialism and change* (1975). She is at present a Visiting Research Fellow at the Institute of Development Studies, University of Sussex.

PETER WINN (1942–   ) was born in New York City. He studied at Columbia College (B.A., 1962), St. John's College, Cambridge, Cornell, and Harvard, receiving his doctorate in History from Cambridge in 1972. Since 1969, he has been Assistant Professor of Latin American History at Princeton University. His central research interests are imperialism and revolution and his publications include *El imperio informal britanico en el Uruguay en el Siglo XIX* (1975 and numerous articles on the Chilean revolutionary process of 1970 to 1973 and its aftermath.

KHALIL ZAMITI.   No biographical data available.

Index of Names

Index of Subjects

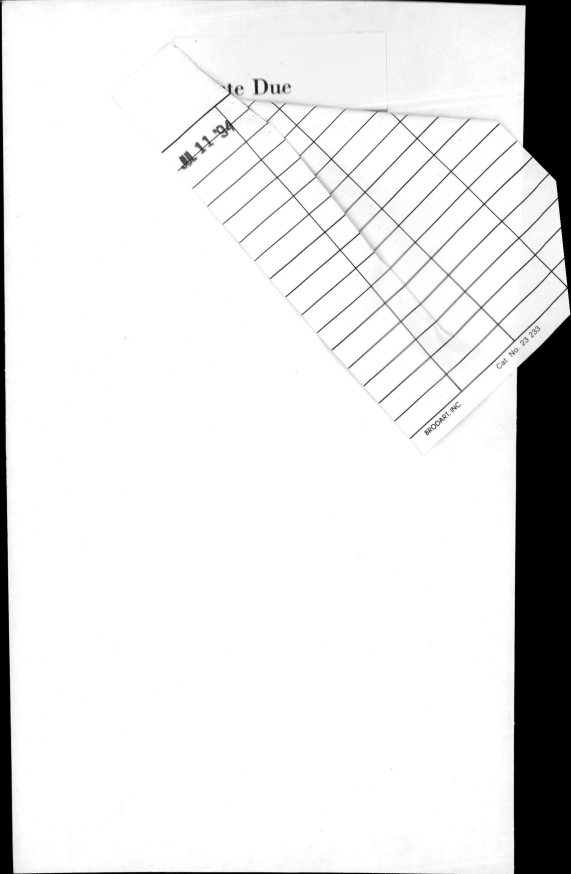